5-

Principles of Security Management

BRIAN R. JOHNSON

Grand Valley State University

PEARSON

Prentice
Hall

Upper Saddle River, New Jersey 07458

Library of Congress Cataloging-in-Publication Data

Johnson, Brian R.
  Principles of security management / Brian R. Johnson.
    p. cm.
  ISBN 0-13-028438-6
  1. Industries—Security measures—Management. 2. Private security services—
Management. 3. Security systems—Management. I. Title.
  HV8290.J62 2004
  658.4'7--dc22

                              2004002071

Executive Editor: Frank Mortimer, Jr.
Assistant Editor: Korrine Dorsey
Production Editor: Tempe Goodhue, nSight, Inc.
Production Liaison: Barbara Marttine Cappuccio
Director of Manufacturing and Production: Bruce Johnson
Managing Editor: Mary Carnis
Manufacturing Buyer: Cathleen Petersen
Creative Director: Cheryl Asherman
Cover Design Coordinator: Miguel Ortiz
Cover Designer: Robin Hoffman, Brand X Studios
Cover Image: Anna Goldberg, Brand X Pictures
Editorial Assistant: Barbara Rosenberg
Marketing Manager: Tim Peyton
Formatting and Interior Design: Laserwords

Pearson Prentice Hall™ is a trademark of Pearson Eduction, Inc.
Pearson® is a registered trademark of Pearson plc
Prentice® **Hall** is a registered trademark of Pearson Education, Inc.

Pearson Education LTD
Pearson Education Singapore, Pte. Ltd
Pearson Education, Canada, Ltd
Pearson Education–Japan
Pearson Education Australia PTY, Limited
Pearson Education North Asia Ltd
Pearson Educaçion de Mexico, S.A. de C.V.
Pearson Education Malaysia, Pte. Ltd

10 9 8 7 6
ISBN 0-13-028438-6

Dedicated to the two people who taught me
the value and importance of an education

—*Dick and Jane*—

My parents

May your adventures in life continue...
(thanks for not naming Lisa Sally and the dog Spot)

Contents

Preface

A recurring theme often heard from leaders in the field of private security is that although managers typically possess the technical skills needed to excel in the workplace, they often lack the fundamental "people" skills that are equally important to ensuring that an organization runs smoothly. In my experience teaching at the university level, many of the major discussion points and questions from my students are not related to security systems, technology, or hardware. Instead, they deal with the interpersonal aspects of managing people and with the daily activities a security manager is expected to perform. My own employment and other practical experiences with security organizations has validated these concerns and prompted me to address these issues in this book.

I wrote *Principles of Security Management* with an orientation aimed at providing the reader with a comprehensive understanding of what it takes to be an effective security manager. This book is premised on the fact that security operations and practices do not operate in isolation. Regardless of whether the security organization is proprietary or contractual, it operates in a broad context and interacts with other departments, organizations, or systems.

This implies that students and security practitioners need to apply cutting-edge business practices and principles in their organizations if they are to ensure personal and organizational success. In order to help readers achieve this goal, this book incorporates contemporary research and information drawn from the social science and business literature. It provides the reader with a comprehensive and balanced understanding of the role and functions of security in the twenty-first century.

The organization of this book reflects the knowledge, skills, and abilities that are needed to be a successful security manager and maximize an employee's potential. The focus is on the management of the greatest asset any company can possess—its employees.

The first three chapters provide the basic framework for the remainder of the text. Chapter 1, the introduction, provides the reader with a general discussion of the current state of security and management principles. A historical review of the industry is also presented to help the reader gain an understanding of the current state of security. Chapter 2, meanwhile, provides the reader with an understanding of the need for leaders in security organizations and reviews principles and theories related to effective leadership. Chapter 3 summarizes the major points of being an effective supervisor, including the diverse roles and responsibilities of the supervisor. The fundamental managerial activity of planning and decision making is discussed in detail in Chapter 4.

The next five chapters focus on the progression of managerial activities related to supervising employees. Chapter 5 examines the recruitment and selection process as well as legal issues that must be considered when hiring new employees. Chapter 6 provides a general overview of issues related to training employees. Once these employees are properly trained, another managerial responsibility is motivating them to maximize their potential and contribution to the organization. Motivation is addressed in Chapter 7. The need for monitoring the performance of individuals is also a fundamental managerial activity. Chapter 8 discusses contemporary approaches to properly managing and designing an appraisal system that is acceptable to employees and managers in the organization. Chapter 9 deals with issues related to the discipline and discharge processes in organizations. It includes a discussion on the need for the creation and maintenance of a disciplinary program as well as procedures for discharging employees in an ethical, fair, and legal manner.

The next three chapters examine specific issues in private security. Chapter 10 exposes the reader to a greater understanding of the history of unions and collective bargaining in the United States, the grievance administration process, and security's role during strikes. One activity that all managers will need to engage in over the course of their careers is conducting security surveys. Chapter 11 provides the reader with a general understanding of the need for security surveys, including various approaches when conducting security audits. It includes a discussion of the minimum requirements for what should be included or analyzed. Organizational planning also requires the creation of budgets. Chapter 12 provides an analysis of the budgeting process in organizations by examining the various purposes behind budgeting and the roles of managers in the budgeting process.

Another regular managerial responsibility is scheduling employees. Chapter 13 examines the process of putting together a schedule and various types of models that can be used to effectively schedule employees in an organization. The last chapter is an overview of issues that the security industry will be expected to address during the next three decades, such as defining security as a profession, changes in the legal environment, and expansion into new markets.

ACKNOWLEDGMENTS

There are many individuals who played a part in the completion of this book. Friends and colleagues at Grand Valley State University contributed to this text through their thoughtful suggestions and comments. I greatly appreciate the support of the late Professor Clifford VanMeter, Ph.D., who was always helpful and encouraging. I would like to thank my good friend, mentor, and colleague Dave Kalinich, Ph.D., for assisting me in my intellectual development throughout the years and for writing the chapter on motivation. I would also like to thank Phil Bridgman, Ph.D., for his valuable contribution and assistance in the writing of the chapter on budgeting. Another big thank you goes out to Frank Horvath, Ph.D., Tom Ackerman, Dan Carncross, Steven Dyke, and Shannon Sosnowski as well as the security firms, managers, and employees who provided me with a great deal of information for this book.

My thanks also to reviewers Holly Dershem-Bruce of Dawson Community College in Glendive, Montana; Jim Reynolds of the Melbourne Police Department in Melbourne, Florida; and David Streater of Catawba Valley Community College in Hickory, North Carolina.

Other individuals were involved in the production of this book. Perhaps my greatest critics were my students, who were my test subjects and a sounding board for draft chapters that I used in my security management course. I would like to recognize Jennifer Loeks, James Harmsman, Laura LeRoy, Paul McCatty, Matt Redmond, Jeanne Heidtke, and many other former students who are now putting their security education into practice. Their comments, insights, and encouragement were quite valuable and are reflected in this book. The future of security is in good hands. I would also like to recognize my graduate assistants, Andrew Brown and Amanda Tweedale, for their editorial work.

ABOUT THE AUTHOR

Brian R. Johnson is an associate professor in the School of Criminal Justice at Grand Valley State University in Grand Rapids, Michigan. He received his Ph.D. in the social sciences from Michigan State University in 1998. He also holds an MLIR in industrial relations and human resource management and an MS in criminal justice from Michigan State University. He received his BA from the University of

Wisconsin—Eau Claire. His primary areas of interest are organizational and legal issues in private security and law enforcement. Johnson has served as a trainer and consultant to a number of private security organizations, has worked in proprietary and contract security organizations, and is the author of several articles and publications in the field of private security and law enforcement. He is also a member of the American Society for Industrial Security.

chapter one

Introduction to Security Management

The term "security" has various definitions. According to *Merriam-Websters Collegiate Dictionary*, 10th ed., security is "freedom from fear or anxiety . . . something that secures . . . measures taken to guard against espionage or sabotage, crime, attack, or escape . . . an organization or department whose task is security." "Security" has also been defined as a relatively predictable environment in which individuals or groups of people can pursue their ends without harm or disruption or the fear of injury or disturbances in pursuing their ends (Green and Fisher 1987). Post (1970) says that security attempts to provide protection from man-made, natural, and environmental hazards. Ursic and Pagano (1974, 24) define "security" as "a readily recognizable condition but its definitions tend to be vague and difficult to formulate in a comprehensive and inclusive manner."

The Task Force on Private Security (1976, 3) defines "private security" as simply "business enterprises that provide services and products to achieve this protection" and offers the following composite working definition:

> Private security includes those self employed individuals and privately funded business entities and organizations providing security-related services to specific clientele for a fee, for the individual or entity that retains or employs them, or for themselves, in order to protect their persons, private property, or interests from various hazards (p. 4).

Green and Fisher (1987) eliminate the notion of profit motive in their definition, arguing that many private entities, such as hospitals and schools, employ private

1

security forces but do not exist to generate a profit. Green and Fisher propose that private security be defined as nonpublic services that provide for the protection of specific individuals or organizations.

Other definitions are far narrower in scope, considering security in the context of private policing. For example, Shearing and Kempa (2001, 206) define "private policing" as "non-state agencies that consciously participate in the process of bringing about and guaranteeing security." In his analysis of the emergence of private security services and companies in the former Soviet Union, Volkov (2000, 484) defines "private security organizations" as "commercial entities whose business consists in the management of organized force and information" that operate in the pursuit of profits.

Based on the preceding definitions, the term "private security" lacks a precise definition. As pointed out by the Task Force on Private Security (1976), defining that term is difficult because it can be identified based on the performance of certain functions and activities of a public nature. Of course, the term also includes activities in the private sector. The Hallcreast Report II (Cunningham, et al. 1990) also found disagreement over, and lack of, a generally accepted definition of private security.

■ THE SCOPE OF PRIVATE SECURITY

In a very simple perspective, private security deals with protection of assets. The Hallcreast Report I states that security programs are designed to prevent and control losses and to protect the organization's assets, which can be divided into three main areas: personnel, property or physical security, and proprietary information (Cunningham and Taylor 1985). Others propose that private security attempts to prevent unlawful events from occurring to nations, states, municipalities, and individuals. In this perspective, the scope of security is placed on two levels. The first level is proprietary in nature and includes measures that individuals and organizations take to protect their private property or interests. The second level extends to governmental security issues, including national security and the administration of governmental services carried out by law enforcement agencies (Post 1970).

The scope of private security can also be analyzed by comparing it to its public-sector counterparts. In this context, private security differs from public services in three areas. First, the goal of private services is profits. Second, the two fields have different statutory powers; the public sector, for example, has greater arrest powers. Third, the two entities have different functions. For example, private security is concerned with loss reduction and prevention, the detection of crime against property, and deterrence, whereas the public sector is more concerned with the detection, investigation, prevention, apprehension, and investigation of criminal activities. Although they both may perform these functions, the two entities differ in the degree of emphasis placed on those activities. Private security is concerned with the prevention and reduction of crime on private property, whereas public law enforcement is concerned with enforcing laws, apprehending criminals, and maintaining order (Task Force on Private Security 1976).

The Task Force on Private Security (1976) also differentiates private and public security according to funding sources. Today, as in the mid-1970s, private security organizations are contracting with public entities, such as municipalities, to perform work traditionally delegated to public-sector employees. In other situations, the private/public distinction has been defined according to police powers, with the private sector not empowered with the same degree of power and authority as the public sector. Some of the other differences are shown in Table 1-1.

Another way to understand the nature and scope of private security is to categorize the field by line. The security industry can be divided into three distinct lines: alarm, armored car, and guard services, which includes private investigative services (McCrie 1988). According to Forst (2000), private security personnel are estimated to be three times as numerous as public-sector law enforcement personnel. U.S. Department of Labor (2001) statistics estimate that the United States has approximately 995,000 security guards, 31,000 private detectives, and 9,000 gaming surveillance and investigation personnel.

However, the true nature and extent of the field of private security is difficult to ascertain, and these numbers probably do not adequately reflect the true number of security-related employees in the United States. This difficulty can be attributed to the multifaceted roles that security has in modern-day society and organizations. Although some positions can be clearly defined as performing a security function as indicated by Department of Labor statistics, other positions are not classified as or considered to be security positions. For example, individuals employed in the area of information security could be classified as information technology specialists or as security specialists, depending on their overall job descriptions, as well as the philosophy and attitude the company has toward the security function. Hence, a

TABLE 1–1 ■ Differences Between the Private and Public Sectors

	Private Security	*Public Services*
Primary users of services provided:	Clients and guests of organization	General public
Traditional roles or functions:	Crime prevention	Responding to/reacting to criminal activities
Services directed toward:	Specific clients	General public
Goals of services provided:	Protection of assets and loss reduction	Enforcement of laws and apprehension of offenders
Delivery of services provided by:	Private entities	Government
Primary motive for delivery of services:	Profit	Social good
Statutory powers:	Narrow and limited	Broad (U.S. and state constitutions)

multitude of individuals whose numbers escape official recognition as being a part of the security profession are performing security-related functions.

A general conclusion that can be reached is this: The scope of the field of private security is broad and is continually expanding to meet the needs of clientele and to exploit new opportunities. This continuum includes activities traditionally associated with the early origins of law enforcement, such as watching for fires, to the relatively new market niche of providing consulting and training activities for countries in need (Spicer 1999).

■ GOALS OF SECURITY

Unlike the definition and scope of security, the fundamental goals of security are simple. Dalton (1995) argues that the goal of security departments is to reduce property losses, injuries, and conflicts. Another way to look at the goals of security is to examine them in the context of basic human need. All human beings and their organizations have a fundamental need and goal: security.

To gain a better understanding of this basic human need and desire for security, one can examine this concept in a theoretical manner by applying Abraham Maslow's notion of a hierarchy of needs. In Maslow's view, human motivation comprises a hierarchy of five needs ranging from the most basic, or physiological, needs to the highest need, that of self-actualization. The theory proposes that an individual's lower-level needs must be met or achieved to some satisfactory level before higher-level needs can be met. For example, individuals have some basic physiological drives for shelter, food, and warmth. If these needs are adequately met, a set of new, higher needs for safety and security emerges. Once these safety and security needs are met, individuals can progress up the hierarchy to social and love needs (belongingness), then to esteem needs (stable high evaluations of themselves, confidence, self-esteem, and recognition from others) then to the last stage, self-actualization (things that make one ultimately happy) (Maslow 1998; Crainer 2000).

The hierarchy of needs serves as a rational basis for security. In this context, safety and security include shelter, clothing, and *ways of defending oneself*. The nexus between Maslow and security is the concept of defending one's self. Although individuals still have the capacity to defend themselves, they have, in many situations, abdicated their personal responsibilities of doing so to the authority of the state and other official institutions. For example, individuals have delegated to law enforcement officials the activity of patroling the streets and providing a modicum of safety in public. In other situations, individuals have taken control of their own safety and security by protecting their homes and property and altering their environment through CPTED (crime prevention through environmental design) and target-hardening activities.

Maslow's hierarchy of needs also applies to security in organizations. Employees must have some degree of safety and security in the workplace and other settings. If employees, for example, perceive that their workplace is safe and secure, they will seek higher-order needs: those associated with social interactions and esteem issues that affect their level or productivity in the workplace. If a violent episode occurs in the workplace, productivity decreases and stress levels increase because the lower-order need for safety and security is not being met and has therefore become more important. Other organizations also experience a ripple effect from a violent event. Discussions about the episode serve to further increase tension, and fear of such activities leads to safety and security becoming the primary need for employees. After September 11, 2001, this ripple effect could be seen in the public's fears about flying and working and living in high-rise buildings and in large urban areas.

This theoretical position for security subsequently applies to all entities. Individuals need to be free from safety and security issues at home, in public, while shopping in malls, eating in restaurants, and being in public institutions, such as hospitals and airport terminals. People's need to perceive that they are safe and secure in the workplace is recognized in the legal system. Regulatory agencies, such as OSHA (Occupational Safety and Health Administration) are a good example of legal protection that holds employers and merchants liable for those activities (or "inactivities") that occur in their organizations.

■ THE HISTORY OF PRIVATE SECURITY IN THE UNITED STATES

Private security is by no means is new concept in the United States or other societies in the world. A simple review of prehistoric peoples and where they lived also shows these early concerns for security, as people banded together for protection and built their homes on the sides of cliffs or in caves to protect themselves from natural and environmental hazards.

Sklansky (1999) writes that the growth of private policing can be understood as the natural product of three private functions: self-defense, the free market and economic exchange, and the enjoyment of property, including the right of owners to place conditions on people who are invited onto their property. Other functions of private security are based on individualistic and communistic grounds. On an individualistic level, private security appeals to the notion that all citizens should take responsibility for their own protection to some degree and that it is enfeebling for people to rely on the government for protection. On a communistic level, having individuals and business unite for mutual aid and protection, or joint security, builds what is known as social capital, which serves to reduce crime.

Early forms of private security existed in the 1700s in colonial America. As early as 1636, every able-bodied citizen was required to participate in the City of Boston's night watch to maintain order and to watch for fires (Lane 1967). Although the watch was sufficient at the time, the rapid growth of cities and crime required the establishment of formalized public police forces.

In the rural southern colonies, law enforcement consisted of slave patrols and vigilantes. Composed of armed civilians, slave patrols existed in the South before and during the Civil War. They worked with the local county courts and the militia to enforce slave laws, watching over and patrolling the slave and free-black populations (Hadden 2001). The first vigilante movement was in 1767, when prominent citizens known as the Regulators (Vila and Morris 1999) took the law into their own hands after the South Carolina government failed to provide protection from outlaw activities.

Pre–Civil War Security

Police agencies were created in the mid-1800s and even earlier in some eastern cities but were ill-equipped to deal with many issues associated with urbanization and the growing crime problem. One such issue was the increase in property crime and the detection and recovery of stolen goods. In response, public policemen in several cities created their own private detective agencies in the 1840s: New York (1845), St. Louis (1846), Baltimore (1847), and Philadelphia (1848). In the 1850s, individuals with minimal or no police experience set up private detective agencies; private police emerged as well. In Chicago, for example, the city had public police in 1856, but the demand for protection was more than what the police could provide. Private watchmen formed the Merchant's Police, which protected only those stores that subscribed to its services. The stores paid $0.50 a week for this service (Johnson 1979).

In 1850, Henry Wells formed the American Express company with Walter Fargo, who transported bank documents from Buffalo, New York, to New York City. In 1852, they expanded into California to transport valuables, including gold, under their own names: Wells, Fargo & Company. By the end of the 1850s, the company was using the railroads to transport valuables (Lipson 1988). Later, the company had all the business west of the Missouri River, and American Express had the territory east of the Missouri River. Because they carried valuables, these companies needed of guards to protect their cargo and detectives to investigate criminal activities (Lipson 1975).

The public police were not equipped to deal with the increase in crime in the mid-nineteenth century. In many situations, they lacked jurisdictional authority to address other crimes that were occurring. Criminals and crimes were no longer confined to a particular city but instead were becoming regional in nature. Because the public police lacked the authority to intervene in these types of crimes, Allan Pinkerton founded the Northwest Police Agency in 1855 to deal with transregional crimes, including criminal activities against the railroad industry. Pinkerton received $10,000 from six Midwestern railroads to provide guard, patrol, and investigative services (McCrie 1988). According to Voss and Barber (1981,7), Pinkerton's success can be attributed to the circumstances of the times:

> In an age when local police forces were small, often corrupt, and frequently disinclined to pursue the fleeing criminal into other jurisdictions, it was soon apparent that Pinkerton's Detective Agency was filling a crucial need. For, while constables and sheriffs tended to call off the chase once the wrongdoer had escaped to other climes, Pinkerton was ready, willing, and determined to stalk his prey.

In 1857, Pinkerton formed the Pinkerton Protection Patrol to provide watchmen services. For approximately 50 years, this force was the only national police force in the United States (Task Force on Private Security 1967).

Post–Civil War Security

After the Civil War, the United States continued its westward geographical expansion. Here too the theme of lawlessness and the need for the protection of assets were evident. As early as 1860, when gold was discovered in Idaho, the arrival of many undesirables in the area created a sense of lawlessness. As a result, citizens formed vigilante groups to rid their territory of such individuals. This led to struggles between the outlaw gangs and vigilantes, with both groups wanting to eliminate the other (Hart 1999).

Another major problem was the theft of cattle. The Wyoming Cattle Growers Association created a force of approximately 20 private detectives known as Association detectives, that operated on the open range in the 1880s to fight this cattle rustling (Morriss 2001). Individuals too banded together to fight rustlers. John Chisolm, a cattleman in New Mexico, armed 100 men in 1877 to protect his cattle herd from Native American rustlers. Because the army could not give him any protection, in this conflict, known as the Lincoln County War, Chisolm's employees killed 175 Native Americans suspected of stealing cattle (Frink, Jackson, and Spring 1956). In another case, 50 cattlemen who were concerned that laws were not being enforced against rustlers set out in 1892 to capture or kill about 25 rustlers on their "black list." Eventually, army cavalry troops intervened and rescued some suspected rustlers who had banded together to defend themselves from the cattlemen (Frink, Jackson, and Spring 1956).

Elsewhere, government officials recognized their inability to provide protection from criminal activities. To deal with the rustling problem in Texas, the governor gave cattlemen permission to hire "Home Rangers," who were paid by local ranchers and had official status to shoot on sight any unauthorized stranger on ranch property (Morriss 2001).

As industrialization increased after the Civil War, new opportunities arose in the field of private security. But the growth of private security was also related to labor unrest, with companies using both in-house and contractual private security forces to protect company assets and to perform strike-breaking activities. These incidents were often quite violent. During this same period, railroads began establishing their own security forces to deal with the growing crimes attributed to unemployed Civil War veterans (Norfolk Southern Police Department). The railroads also lobbied states for greater police powers, and many states passed such legislation. Other large companies in the shipping, iron, and steel sectors established private security forces to maintain order in their company towns and factories (Lipson 1975).

Until 1924, when the FBI was created, police services could be provided only on a local basis. This restriction created vast opportunities for private security companies. Private forces, such as Pinkerton, Brinks, and the Burns Detective Agency, which conducted all investigations for the American Banking Association, provided law enforcement and investigations beyond these local political boundaries. But as public forces began to improve their services and gained the technical ability to conduct investigations beyond their local boundaries, the role of private security shifted from investigative to guard services (Kakalik and Wildhorn 1971). Indeed, the public and private police can be said to have evolved together.

Private Security in the Twentieth Century

In the context of private security, the twentieth century saw the creation of industrial security programs. Such programs, however, were not new to countries that had experienced industrialization before the United States and recognized the need to protect their new and emerging industries. For example, one of the oldest industrial security organizations is associated with Krupp Steel in Germany. In 1838, after touring England under a fictitious name, Alfred Krupp stole industrial secrets related to the production of steel. To ensure that his secrets would not be stolen in turn, he created an industrial security unit for the House of Krupp. Krupp even required his employees and his industrial spies to take an oath of loyalty and faithfulness to him. He also established a code of security:

> Whatever the cost, workers at all times must be watched by energetic and thoroughly experienced men, who will receive a bonus whenever they arrest anyone guilty of sabotage, laziness, or spying. (Bergier 1975, 19)

Modern industrial security in the United States has its origins in the two world wars. During World War I, all railroad and express companies were nationalized to protect them from acts of sabotage. Their guard forces were subsequently nationalized, whereupon security guards became employees of the federal government (Lipson 1975). On December 12, 1941, President Franklin Roosevelt enacted Executive Order 8972 (1941) giving the Secretary of War and Navy the authority to establish military guards and patrols and other appropriate measures to protect national defense–related industries and premises from injury, destruction, or sabotage. Approximately 200,000 guards were incorporated into the military police as civilian auxiliaries and were sworn in by the Internal Security Division of the War Department. These guards were responsible for protecting material and approximately 10,000 factories (Ursic and Pagano 1974; Jensen 1985/1986). Later, the increased need for security in defense-related industries in the Korean War and the cold war led to the establishment of the industrial defense program in 1952 (Lipson 1975). This program, now known as the National Industrial Security Program (NISP), is administered by the Defense Security Service (DSS). Employees of DSS oversee, advise, and assist approximately 11,000 facilities involved in defense-related activities (Defense Security Service).

Security Since 9/11

The terrorist attacks on September 11, 2001, redefined the importance of private security in the United States. One of the factors contributing to the successful terrorist attacks against the World Trade Center and the Pentagon was the lack of airport security. The attacks also revealed that the U.S. government and industries worldwide are vulnerable to such attacks and that security is a critical aspect of business life, regardless of industry sector.

Immediately following the attacks, some security companies, such as Guardsmark, reported a 15 percent increase in demand for their services (Beman 2001). A survey of approximately 6,000 employees in companies throughout the United States found that 59 percent of the respondents reported being more anxious about security. Corporate responses to 9/11 were also found to be limited: 29 percent had changed some aspect of physical security whereas only 21 percent had considerably tightened up security in their company. The researchers concluded that companies were underprepared for large-scale crises and that "American corporations had been lulled into a false sense of security" (Mainiero 2002, 3). To date, the ramifications of the attack are still present. Construction of the new World Trade Building #7 has been planned with security in mind: blast-resistant glazing, in addition to increased fire suppression and other life-saving features (Sonnenberg 2003).

Other authors discussing the events of September 11 have raised issues that have faced the security field since its inception. These authors have commented that the true value of security often escapes convincing and defensible numbers, whereas security measures often lag behind threats and vulnerabilities in creating a security program that can safeguard the entire system (Raval 2003). To combat these problems, security professionals need to look behind the history, work more proactively, and anticipate rather than react (Raval 2003, 44). An article in *Security Management* best sums up the role of modern security:

> In addition to coordinating with government whenever appropriate, private security can continue to do what it has always done: work to convince management that attending to the basics by putting good access controls, contingency programs, and evacuation plans into effect is critical to protecting corporate staff and assets against both minor disruptions and major catastrophes. And perhaps most importantly, security professionals can ensure that even when the memories fade—and they will—the safeguards remain. (Horowitz 2001, 8)

This quote and the diverse functions of security suggest that any successful security program requires the proper administration and management of the organization.

The review of the security industry from a historical perspective shows that security programs have been undertaken for three basic reasons: moral/humanistic, legal, and economic.

1. In a moral or humanistic perspective, safety and security programs were created to ensure the safety of employees and visitors, as well as to prevent and reduce accidents and criminal events.
2. Regulations imposed by federal and state agencies have also required some organizations to establish security programs. Case law resulting from civil liability has also resulted in many organizations' reevaluating or creating security programs.

3. Economic factors have contributed to the growth of security. The monetary losses associated with injuries to workers, turnover, and lost productivity as the result of a violent episode in the workplace, for example, have increased security programs. In addition, the loss and theft of property, interruptions in production, and the legal costs associated with a civil suit, not to mention paying out claims from these suits, put a large economic or financial burden on organizations.

■ WHAT IS MANAGEMENT?

Stoner and Freeman (1989, 4) write that management can be defined as the "process of planning, organizing, leading, and controlling the efforts of organizational members, and using all other organizational resources to achieve stated organizational goals." Management is a process in that all managers must engage in certain interrelated activities while using all the resources of the organization to meet their goals. Mintzberg (1989) defines a manager as someone who is in charge of the organization or one of its subunits. Managers are vested with formal authority and a degree of status, have interpersonal relationships, and have access to information that allows them to make decisions. Writing that management is the specific tool, function, and instrument that makes institutions capable of producing results, Peter Drucker (1999, 40) defines the concern and responsibility of management as "everything that affects the performance of the institution and its results—whether inside or outside, whether under the institution's control or totally beyond it."

Although some authors may think that management is an organized and systematic process, others propose that it is not. Henry Mintzberg (1989) presents some folklore and facts about management. One bit of folklore is that managers are reflective and systematic planners who have no regular duties to perform. Mintzberg's research, however, concluded that managers often work at an unrelenting pace; that their activities are characterized by brevity, variety, and discontinuity; and that they are strongly oriented to action activities. At the same time, managerial work can be characterized as handling exceptions—the brush fires that need to be addressed and put out—as well as performing a variety of regular duties that align the organization with its environment. Mintzberg also dispels the motion of management as a science. He argues that science involves the enaction of systematic and analytically determined procedures and programs. In reality, however, a manager's work is often quite complicated, involving brevity and fragmentation, which are unscientific and have defeated scientific attempts to change them.

Some authors propose that organizations and hence managers do not operate in stable, forseeable environments but rather operate under chaotic conditions. According to Overman (1996, 489):

> The modern administrator probably knows chaos best from first-hand experience. Chaos is too much happening too quickly all at once, and seemingly out

of control and incomprehensible. Chaos is when everything seems on the verge of collapse today, yet somehow emerges tomorrow or next month in a new form with new structures and new relationships.

This perspective is known as chaos theory. A key component of chaos theory is that all systems—be they natural or created—operate in environments in which behaviors are unforeseeable (Dolan, Garcia, and Auerbach 2003). This perspective tries to gain an understanding of the relationship between chaos and order and asserts that organizations move through cycles of uniformity and order to turbulence and chaos.

This new perspective of chaos has its origins in math and the natural sciences and is the study of how collective or mass units have the ability to evolve over time. Chaos theory is based on three assumptions. The first is that nonlinear events affect the natural or created system; a small change at one level in a system can produce large effects at that level or other levels of a system. The second assumption is that a chaos system exhibits structural and behavioral forms of instability. For example, structural forms of chaos could include legislative changes in the environment or incidents that could change the growth path of the organization. The third assumption, known as emergent order, is that systems can self-organize to accommodate the chaos and to maintain stability (Doherty and Delener 2001). Essentially, a new order emerges as the organization restructures itself.

Doherty and Delener (2001) propose that chaos systems exhibit structural and behavioral instabilities that are interrelated. Structural forms of chaos could include legislative changes in the environment and incidents that somehow change the growth path of the organization. Perhaps the best example of chaos theory is the "chaos" the airline industry experienced following September 11, 2001. Because of the creation of the Department of Homeland Security and the Transportation Security Administration and related legislation, airport security and screening procedures have changed. Many airlines have had to change their security procedures, lay off employees because of lost revenue, and file for bankruptcy protection. This affected many employees, including pilots and flight attendants, and spread up the organizational hierarchy, changing the growth patterns and operations of various airlines. These "small" changes led to behavioral changes and a different evolutionary path for the airlines, and companies reduced fares and restructured their routes to increase market share and become more financially solvent (Velocci 2002).

Of course, managements differ among organizations. Peter Drucker (1999) writes that although organizations do differ in their mission, size, and scope, the fundamental principles of management do not vary; what varies is how they are applied. Drucker even suggests that managers' tasks and challenges do not differ greatly across various types of organizations.

Organizations need managers for five fundamental reasons (Mintzberg 1973): to ensure that the organization serves its basic purpose, which is the efficient production of services or goods; to maintain the stability of the firm's operations; to take charge of the firm's strategy-making system and adapt the organization to its changing environment; to make sure that employees' values are integrated with organizational preferences or the focus of top management; and to provide an information link between the organization and its environment by interpreting incoming information, transferring it within the organization, and managing the dissemination of outgoing information.

Managers have key responsibilities to perform. Early in the twentieth century, Henri Fayol, a French mining engineer, developed some ideas that are still applicable today. Fayol believed that, when it comes to organizational success, an individual's managerial abilities are more important than technical abilities. Fayol suggested that management involves five elements: planning, organizing, coordinating, commanding, and controlling (Wren 1994). In 1930, Luther Gulick adapted Fayol's functional analysis of management and created the acronym POSDCORB to describe managerial functions or activities. These composite functions of managers are listed in Box 1-1.

BOX 1–1 ■ Composite Functions of Managerial Work

Planning   A key managerial function that involves choosing a course of action and outlining what needs to be done. Planning also requires establishing standards and setting evaluation measures to make sure the organization's goals and objectives are achieved.

Organizing   Involves establishing a formal structure of authority and arranging, coordinating, and defining work subdivisions necessary to get the job done.

Staffing   Encompasses the entire human resource management process, including recruitment, selection, and training. It involves finding and assigning the right person for the right job.

Directing   Is related to the manager's leadership style and how he or she provides guidance to employees. Directing is related to making correct decisions and ensuring that all resources, including personnel, are used properly to achieve organizational goals.

Coordinating   Consists of interrelating various components to ensure that personnel and resources work together toward specific goals and objectives.

Reporting   Involves keeping superiors and subordinates informed as to what is going on by making sure that the information keeps flowing through the organization. Reporting includes both verbal and written forms of communication.

Budgeting   Includes all aspects of the budgeting process, including fiscal planning, accounting, and expense controls.

Adapted from Mintzberg (1973, 9).

Although the writings of the classical managerial perspectives are almost 100 years old, these early functions of management still apply today and provide a degree of conceptualization of what management is. However, managerial thought has extended beyond these principles and is much more complex, reflecting the environment in which modern-day mangers must operate.

Managerial Roles

According to Mintzberg (1973; 1989), managers perform 10 roles that can be categorized as either interpersonal, informational, or decisional. One of the most significant interpersonal roles is that of a leader. The leadership role pervades all managerial roles and activities. As leaders, managers guide and motivate employees. Their primary purpose is to integrate the needs of the employee and the organization, which in turn will create what Mintzberg calls a cooperative enterprise. Another interpersonal role is that of figurehead, which includes performing ceremonial duties such as taking customers to lunch, attending employee weddings, and providing tours for dignitaries. Managers also serve in a liaison role that deals with establishing relationships outside the organization. These external relationships serve to link the organization with the environment. When necessary, the manager can use these relationships to further the interests of the organization.

The manager's informational roles deal with receiving and transmitting information. Mintzberg proposes that in this role, managers are often the organization's nerve center. Because of their position, they have access to and receive a great deal of unofficial information from internal and external sources on which they base their activities. It is the manager's role to use this information in an appropriate manner to further organizational success. One informational role is that of a monitor. As monitors, managers receive information on events related to the internal operations of the organization. In other situations, the manager collects information from external sources that keep him informed of events and trends that could impact the organization. Other information comes from a combination of internal and external sources. These include solicited and unsolicited reports and briefings from employees or trade organizations, comments from clients or customers, customer information, and conferences. In the role of monitor, the manager collects information from all of these sources.

In their informational role, managers must also be disseminators and spokespersons. As disseminators, managers are responsible for passing along factual and value-based information. Factual information is information that is objective and valid. It includes such things as financial data and meeting times. Value-based information consists of value statements that are not necessarily wrong or right. Instead, they are statements of preference on what the manager perceives the company "ought" to do. They come from multiple sources, including clients, subordinates, employees, and other "pressures" that are attempting to somehow change or control the organization. It is the manager's role to consider these statements of preference in the context of what the organization prefers or wants. In their role as the spokesperson, they transmit these statements as the organization's value preferences. In this role they must meet the needs of two groups: key individuals in the company, including their superiors and the chief executive, and members of the external environment such as customers, various governmental agencies, and suppliers.

The third primary managerial role is the decisional role. One decisional role is that of entrepreneur, where the manager makes changes freely, seeking to improve the organizational unit while adapting to the changing conditions in the organization's environment. These entrepreneurial activities are voluntary, with the manager always looking for new opportunities and ideas. Another decisional role is that of disturbance handler. In this role the manager must respond to a variety of pressures or events that are outside the manager's direct control. These include disagreements among employees (conflicts), the loss of a client (resource losses), or conflict between units in the organization (exposure difficulties). The common denominator among all of these events is that employees or the organization look to the manager to immediately resolve the situation. Another decisional role deals with resource allocation. As a resource allocator, the manager is responsible for scheduling and prioritizing how time will be spent at work, based on what the organization deems most important. As allocators, managers also program the work of others and make all significant decisions regarding the allocation of organizational resources, including personnel and funds. The last decisional role is that of a negotiator. As a negotiator, the manager is responsible for representing and intervening on behalf of the organization in nonroutine situations with individuals and groups that come into contact with the organization.

Managerial Levels

Managers can practice at various levels in the organization and have various ranges of responsibilities. First-line managers, or supervisors, are at the lowest level of management in an organization and do not supervise other managers. In the security industry, a first-line manager might be the shift supervisor, who is responsible for monitoring and directing the work of line-level employees. At the next level of management, middle managers oversee, or direct, the activities of lower-level managers and, in some instances, the operations of employees. The principal responsibility of middle managers is to ensure that organizational policies are carried out. Top-level managers, or top executives, are responsible for establishing operating policies and procedures. The CEO, vice-presidents, or presidents of the organization are all top-level managers (Stoner and Freeman 1989).

Managers can also be classified according to their scope of activities. Functional managers are responsible only for a collection of similar activities in the organization. For example, managers may be grouped according to the types of services they provide, such as uniform operations, investigations, and sales. General managers, by contrast, oversee a complex unit that might include a company or a subsidiary of that company and might be responsible for all activities of that unit. In a large proprietary security company, for example, general managers are responsible for a certain geographical area and all the security operations in that specific territory.

Managerial Skills

Managers have some basic skills they perform, regardless of the organization they work for or at what level. A traditional typology of skills created by Robert L. Katz proposed that managers need at least three skill areas: technical, human, and conceptual (Box 1-2).

BOX 1–2 ■ Managerial Skills

Technical skills The ability to use one's knowledge, methods, techniques, and equipment necessary for the performance of specific tasks; acquired from experience, education, and training.

Human skills One's ability and judgment in working with and through people. This area includes an understanding of motivation, an application of effective leadership, and the ability to motivate individuals and groups.

Conceptual skills One's ability to understand the complexities of the overall organization and where one's own operation fits into it. This knowledge permits one to act according to the objective of the total organization rather than only on the basis of the goals and needs of one's own immediate group. These skills address one's ability to coordinate and integrate the organization's interests and activities.

Adapted from Hersey, Blanchard, and Johnson (2001, 14).

All three skill areas are necessary for effective management. However, the mix of these skills varies according to the level of management. Because they interact daily with workers performing specific tasks that may require assistance from them, line-level managers, for example, need more technical skills than do top executives. Top executives, by contrast, do not necessarily need to know how to perform specific tasks but instead, require the conceptual skills needed for integrating the organization's activities. Because they are interacting with both first-line managers and the top executives, middle managers may require more human skills than either of the other skill areas. As a general rule of thumb, the higher the managerial level, the lower the level of technical skills needed and the higher the level of conceptual skills needed (Hersey, Blanchard, and Johnson, 2001; Stoner and Freeman 1989).

■ THE EVOLUTION OF MANAGERIAL THOUGHT

Management in organizations was practiced or performed in ancient cultures, including China, Rome, and Mesopotamia. However, the concept was not examined or formalized until the late 1800s, when the work of managers was examined and identified because of the complexities associated with the growth of industries and the subsequent issues and problems that business leaders had to deal with (Allen 1958). The term "manager" was first used not in the business community but in the public sector, when cities created the position of city manager. Management principles were first used to reorganize the U.S. Army in 1901. The concept of management can be traced to the late nineteenth century, when large organizations began to emerge in the United States. Before this time, companies were small and had no organizational structure. Companies were operated simply by the owners and their helpers (Drucker 1999).

Managerial thought in the United States and in other countries evolved along with the rise of industrialization. Two early stages of managerial thought were scientific management and the human relations movement. Table 1-2 presents the similarities and differences of these two schools of thought.

Scientific Management

Frederick Taylor was a central figure in the development of early managerial thought. Taylor and other theorists at the time comprised the so-called classical approach to management. The classical school is associated with the concept of scientific management, also known as "Taylorism," which can be considered the systematic management of activities in the organization. Taylor defined scientific management as "a system devised by industrial engineers for the purpose of subserving the common interests of employers, workmen and society at large through the elimination of avoidable wastes, the general improvement of the processes and methods of production, and the just and scientific distribution of the product" (Nyland 1996, 985).

Taylor began his career in 1878 as a machine shop supervisor at Midvale Steel in Philadelphia and found that workers engaged both in natural and systemic soldiering. Natural soldiering was the tendency for workers to "take it easy." This tendency, Taylor believed, was easy to overcome by simply having managers to inspire or force employees to work harder. Systemic soldiering, by contrast, came from relationships with other workers; the workers tended to conform to

TABLE 1–2 ■ Comparison of Scientific Management and the Human Relations Movement

	Scientific Management	Human Relations Movement
Time period	1890s to 1930s and beyond	1930s to present
Primary focus	Production	People
Methodologies	Scientific analysis/Time studies	Scientific analysis/Behavioral science research

group norms of not working faster, based on the belief that working faster would lead to an increase in production, which would put employees out of work. Further, group norms about work methods were handed down from generation to generation (Wren 1994).

To overcome the effects of soldiering, Taylor proposed that organizations carefully investigate work activities and then set appropriate performance standards. He believed that once workers saw that the rate of production was properly set and based on facts, their motivation to soldier would be reduced. Thus, soldiering was the fault of management, not the worker, and it was management's responsibility to design jobs properly and to offer appropriate incentives to overcome soldiering. Taylor recommended the use of scientific fact finding to determine what workers ought to be able to perform, based on their equipment and materials and the correct way to perform tasks.

Taylor's work was the origin of scientific management. Taylor believed that management, not the worker, had the responsibility of setting standards and that it was the worker's responsibility to be motivated to meet those expectations set forth by management. Task management required managers to develop performance standards and to select workers who could meet those standards when motivated to do so. Having a wage rate for meeting the standards and a piecework rate for exceeding the standards would be a motivator for workers to work harder. Taylor also believed that improved productivity was mutually beneficial for the organization and the workers. Improved productivity would lead to more profit for the organization and gains for the workers, too (Wren 1994).

Time studies were one of the main components of Taylor's system of scientific management. These time studies consisted of analytical and constructive phases. In the analytical phase, jobs were broken down into their simplest tasks, and the investigator recorded the time it took to complete each task. The best methods for completing that particular task were then identified and recorded, and those specific movements were timed and averages calculated, based on the rest periods, unavoidable delays, and the competency level of the worker. The competency level of the worker was based on what Taylor called the "first class man," or those workers who could perform that particular task at a pace they could keep up for years without injury to their health. In the constructive phase, all the basic movements or components were built, the movements tested, and the job reconstructed. This phase also was concerned with standardization of all the elements of the job and considered the tools, machinery, and other elements needed to improve production capabilities (Wren 1994).

Taylor's work at the Bethlehem Steel Company of South Bethlehem, Pennsylvania, in 1899 applied the principles of scientific management. Bethlehem Steel was selling 10,000 tons of pig iron at a time, and Taylor wanted to study worker fatigue related to loading 10,000 tons of pig iron, with each "pig" weighing 92 pounds. Ten of the best workers were selected to load the pig iron at maximum speed; each worker loaded 75 tons on the first day. The researchers then deducted 40 percent of the workday to rest periods and delays and established a new standard: 45 tons a day. A piecework rate was then established, based on 45 tons a day; if they exceeded this amount, the workers would receive a bonus for their hard work (Wren 1994).

The key to Taylor and scientific management was work measurement, whereby managers could establish appropriate production rates, using scientific principles, and an incentive payment for increased output. With this differential rate system, workers who exceeded the first-class worker rate could make more money, based on their performance.

Scientific management has been criticized for making jobs dehumanizing and unchallenging. Based on the true nature of Taylorism, or scientific management, the goal was to increase productivity and employees' pay (Flynn 1998). In fact, Taylor's use of time-and-motion studies was aimed at developing the workers' full capabilities and increasing their skill levels in the process. Taylor believed that a modern approach to management was friendly cooperation between the workers and managers through the scientific analysis of work.

In short, Taylor and the true principles of scientific management called for planning, which began by looking at the nature of the work, finding the right employees for the work to be performed, and making sure that the workers had the right tools, machinery, and equipment. Taylorism was a systematic analysis of the production process (Nyland 1996). Scientific management was compatible with the views of the workers, who now knew that production rates were established through scientific studies and that by following the established procedures, they could meet and exceed those standards (Wren 1994).

As pointed out by Flynn (1998), Henry Ford, who introduced the assembly line to produce automobiles efficiently (on a unit-per-hour basis), was also responsible for creating dehumanizing work, as under true scientific management principles, workers would be motivated to work harder and hence would take pride in their accomplishments. However, in assembly line positions, with each worker reliant on other workers, piecework pay would not be an incentive, as workers were tied to a rigid production rate, with no benefit to finishing the job early (Flynn 1998). Despite the criticism for its often dehumanizing approach, principles of scientific management are still heavily used in organizations to ensure efficiency in their production processes.

The Human Relations Movement

This concept of scientific management prevailed in the United States until the 1930s. One factor that was omitted from the scientific management movement was the worker's personal needs. As pointed out by Crainer (2000), Taylor discovered work, whereas industrialists, such as Henry Ford, discovered work on a massive scale and regarded workers as instruments of production, with managers concerned only with production and organization rather than with the human side of management. In many organizations, managers concentrated on the tasks and work performed and failed to recognize the personal needs of the workers.

The Hawthorne studies led to the recognition of workers' personal needs. In 1927, researchers, led by Elton Mayo from Harvard University, were studying how improved lighting could improve productivity and morale at the Western Electric Hawthorne Plant. The theory was that improved lighting would increase worker morale and productivity. The key was to find that level of lighting that would increase productivity and still be cost-effective for Western Electric. Workers were divided into two groups; lighting was increased in one group and remained at the same level in the second group. The researchers found that productivity increased in both groups. Further research led to the conclusion that the researchers had missed the people involved—particularly their feelings, attitudes, and relationships.

Later experiments concluded that successful management requires an understanding of the structures and relationships of informal work groups. By having managers recognize the human side of the organization and understand that workers form relationships, output would increase and employees would subsequently be happy and more motivated in the workplace. This belief that people would work harder if they believed that management was concerned about them was labeled the Hawthorne effect (Crainer 2000).

This research and subsequent findings and recommendations triggered a movement that shifted the management of organizations toward a concern for the worker and participative management. This movement became widespread during World War II to ensure that production of vital war materials would not be interrupted. The basic premise is that the workplace is not simply a production system but rather a social system involved in the production of goods or services. This concern for the worker and the subsequent theories and practices have been collectively named the human relations movement in management. From the early works on the Hawthorne studies, other researchers have used the behavioral sciences—psychology and sociology—to study human behavior in relation to management and organizations. Motivation, workers' needs, leadership, worker empowerment, team building, and decision making are but a few of the areas that behavioral scientists have examined in the context of managerial practices to design jobs that meet workers' needs (Crainer 2000).

■ KEY TERMS

Chaos theory
Executive order 8972
Functional managers
General managers
Hallcreast Reports I and II
Hawthorne effect
Human relations movement
Industrial Security Programs
Management
Managerial roles
Maslow's hierarchy of needs

Pinkerton
POSDCORB
Private security
Private Security Task Force
Scientific management
Security
Slave patrols
Supervision
Taylorism
Time-and-motion studies

■ DISCUSSION QUESTIONS

1. What are some of the primary differences between the private and public sectors in the context of security?
2. What are the origins of private security? How have the role and function of private security changed?
3. What is management? What are some primary responsibilities of a manager?
4. What are the two major schools of thought on how to manage people?
5. What are the key elements or components of scientific management?
6. What are the key components of the human relations movement?
7. What is chaos theory? How does it apply to the field of security?
8. What was the impact of September 11, 2001, on security?
9. Define "private security." Can "private security" be easily defined? Why or why not?
10. What are the broad categories of managerial roles? Which is most important and why?

■ REFERENCES

ALLEN, L. A. 1958. *Management and organization.* New York: McGraw-Hill.

BEMAN, D. K. 2001. Aftermath: Economic impact: Security companies to tighten standards to meet post-attack needs. *Wall Street Journal.* October 2.

BERGIER, J. 1975. *Secret armies.* New York: Bobbs-Merrill.

CRAINER, S. 2000. *The management century: A critical review of 20th century thought and practice.* New York: Booz-Allen & Hamilton.

CUNNINGHAM, W. C., and T. H. TAYLOR. 1985. *The Hallcreast report I: Private security and police in America.* Boston: Butterworth-Heinemann.

CUNNINGHAM, W. C., J. J. STRAUCHS, and C. W. VAN METER. 1990. *The Hallcreast report II: Private security trends 1970–2000.* Boston: Butterworth-Heinemann.

DALTON, D. R. 1995. *Security management: Business strategies for success.* Boston: Butterworth-Heinemann.

Defense Security Services. Who we are. www.dss.mil/aboutdss.

DOHERTY, N., and N. DELENER. 2001. Chaos theory: Marketing and management implications. *Journal of Marketing Theory and Practice* 9 (4): 66–75.

DOLAN, S. L., S. GARCIA, and A. AUERBACH, 2003. Understanding and managing chaos in organizations. *International Journal of Management* 20 (1): 23–44.

DRUCKER, P. 1999. *Management challenges for the 21st century.* New York: Harper Business.

Executive Order no. 8972. (1941). *Federal Register* 6, 6240.

FLYNN, J. 1998. Taylor to TQM—Part 1: 100 years of production management. *IIE Solution* 30 (10): 22–28.

FORST, B. 2000. *Boundary changes in criminal justice organization (vol. 2).* Washington, D.C.: National Institute of Justice.

FRINK, M., W. T. JACKSON, and A. G. SPRING. 1956. *When grass was king.* Boulder: University of Colorado Press.

GREEN, G., and R. J. FISHER. 1987. *Introduction to security*. 4th ed. Boston: Butter-worth-Heinemann.

HADDEN, S. E. 2001. *Slave patrols: Law and violence in Virginia and the Carolinas*. Cambridge, MA: Harvard University Press.

HART, J. W. 1999. Vigilantes. *Advocate*, (June): 442–445.

HERSEY, P., K. H. BLANCHARD, and D. E. JOHNSON. 2001. *Management of organizational behavior*. 8th ed. Englewood Cliffs, NJ: Prentice Hall.

HOROWITZ, S. 2001. A different order of magnitude. *Security management* 45 (10): 8–10.

JENSEN, E. M. 1985/1986. The NLRA's "guard exclusion": An analysis of section 9(B)(3)'s legislative intent and modern-day applicability. *Indiana Law Journal* 61: 457–494.

JOHNSON, D. R. 1979. *Policing the urban underworld*. Philadelphia: Temple University Press.

KAKALIK, J. S., and S. WILDHORN. 1971. *The private police industry: Its nature and extent*, vol. 2. Santa Monica, CA: Rand.

LANE, R. L. 1967. *Policing the city*. Boston: Cambridge Press.

LIPSON, M. 1975. *On guard: The business of private security*. New York: Times Books.

LIPSON, M. 1988. Private security: A retrospective. *Annals of the American Academy of Police and Social Sciences* 498 (July): 11–22.

MAINIERO, L. A. 2002. Action or reaction? Handling businesses in crisis after September 11. *Business Horizons* 45 (5): 2–10.

MASLOW, A. 1998. *Maslow on Management*. New York: Wiley.

McCRIE, R. D. 1988. The development of the U.S. security industry. *Annals of the American Academy of Police and Social Sciences* 498 (July): 23–33.

MINTZBERG, H. 1973. *The nature of managerial work*. New York: Harper & Row.

MINTZBERG, H. 1989. *Mintzberg on management*. New York: Free Press.

MORRISS, A. P. 2001. Returning justice to its private roots. *University of Chicago Law Review* 68: 551–575.

Norfolk Southern Police Department. History of railway police. http://nspolice.com/history2.htm.

NYLAND, C. 1996. Taylorism, John R. Commons, and the Hoxie report. *Journal of Economic Issues* 30 (December): 985–1016.

OVERMAN, E. S. 1996. The new sciences of administration: Chaos and quantum theory. *Public Administration Review* 56 (5): 487–491.

POST, R. S. 1970. *Security administration: An introduction*. Cincinnati: Anderson.

Private security: Report of the task force on private security (1976). Washington, DC: National Advisory Committee on Criminal Justice Standards and Goals.

RAVAL, V. 2003. Security, society and skepticism. *Information Strategy* 19 (3): 43–48.

SHEARING, C. D., and M. KEMPA. 2001. The role of "private security" in transitional democracies. *Report on the proceedings of the conference Crime and Policing in Transitional Societies with the South African Institute for International Affairs, 30 August to 1 September, 2000*.

SKLANSKY, D. A. 1999. The private police. *UCLA Law Review* 46: 1165–1283.

SONNENBERG, J. 2003. Built to last. *Crain's Chicago Business* 17 (April 28): SR1–SR3.

SPICER, T. 1999. *An unorthodox soldier*. London: Mainsteam.

STONER, J. A. F., and R. A. FREEMAN. 1989. *Management*. 4th ed. Englewood Cliffs, NJ: Prentice Hall.

URSIC, H. S. and L. E. PAGANO. 1974. *Security management systems*. Illinois: Charles C. Thomas.

U.S. Department of Labor. Bureau of Labor Statistics. 2001 national occupational employment and wage estimates. Protective service occupations. http://www.bls.gov/oes/2001/oes_33Pr.htm.

VELOCCI, A. L. 2002. Can majors shift focus fast enough to survive? Question haunts industry as low fare carriers grab market share, and high costs, low productivity begin to strain some airlines. *Aviation Week and Space Technology* 57 (21): 52-53.

VILA, V. and C. MORRIS 1999. *The role of the police in American society*. Westport, CT: Greenwood Press.

VOLKOV, V. 2000. Between economy and the state: private security and rule enforcement in Russia. *Politics and society* 28 (4): 483-501.

VOSS, F., and J. BARBER. 1981. *We never sleep: The first fifty years of the Pinkertons*. Washington, DC: Smithsonian Institution Press.

WREN, D. A. 1994. *The evolution of management thought*. 4th ed. New York: John Wiley.

chapter two

Leadership

Bennis and Nanus (1985, 22) cite a *Wall Street Journal* article that made a dramatic appeal for more leadership and less management. Among the more pointed excerpts from the article, entitled "Let's Get Rid of Management," are the following:

- "People don't want to be managed, they want to be led."
- "Have you heard of a world manager? world leader yes?"
- "We have educational leaders, political leaders, religious leaders, and community leaders that lead instead of manage."
- "Ask your horse. You can lead your horse to water but you cannot manage it to drink."
- "If you want somebody to manage, manage yourself. Do that well, and you'll be ready to stop managing and start leading."

The theme is still relevant today. The same concerns exist in many security firms. Firms may have good managers, but leadership is apparently lacking.

In order to succeed in a climate in which opportunities are growing and challenges come as surprises, an agency needs leadership. Leaders keep a close watch on the external environment in which the organization functions, looking for changes in demands and expectations as well as opportunities for the organization. Leaders must also keep an eye on the internal mechanisms and culture to ensure that the organization is adapting appropriately to the external environment. In short, a leader sees change coming on the business horizon and creates change within the organization to enable the organization to successfully meet new challenges.

■ WHAT IS LEADERSHIP?

Leadership is a multifaceted concept. It is a process that accomplishes organizational goals (Tosi, Rizzo, and Carroll 1986). It is a reciprocal relationship between those who lead and those who follow, creating a leader-constituent relationship (Kouzes and Posner 2003). It is the process of persuasion whereby one person induces and influences others to pursue certain objectives. Kotter (1990, 3), argues that "leadership refers to a process that helps direct and mobilize people and/or their ideas." Leaders see new challenges and enable their organizations to take advantage of the opportunities ahead. Through the efforts of leadership, an agency's purpose, structure, and routines are shaken up and realigned to take advantage of new conditions.

Inherent in the process of leadership is challenging existing ways and finding new ways of thinking and doing. Leaders create change by working to alter the atmosphere and culture of a system, creating options and opportunities in the face of problems. Leadership helps clarify problems and choices and provides a vision of better possibilities. Leaders establish direction by creating a vision of the future and align people by creating teams and coalitions that share and understand the vision. Leaders also motivate, inspire, and energize people to overcome political, bureaucratic, and resource barriers to change.

Leaders look for strength in themselves and others, as well as inspire and motivate those around them. Leaders inspire others, give them confidence, and thereby enlist individuals in the process of change. However, leadership does not belong only to top executives of an agency. Leadership exists throughout healthy agencies poised to change direction to meet new opportunities.

Leadership is also an important ingredient in getting the most out of an organization. Leaders are coaches (Bennis 1994) who set expectations, give workers the skills and the latitude to carry out their tasks, and recognize and reward good work. Leaders create high morale by giving workers responsibility and the opportunity to get the job done. Leaders are also change agents and remove obstacles to productivity by challenging and changing unworkable systems, policies, and routines. Leadership, almost tribal in nature, focuses on the symbols, rituals, and the most basic values and beliefs of an organization's culture (Dupree 1989).

■ LEADERS VERSUS MANAGERS

Some people are leaders, and others are managers. However, the two roles are not totally independent but often overlap. The importance of leadership does not minimize the importance of management. Leadership and management are both important to the health of an agency. An individual with properly balanced experience and training can perform both roles in response to changing needs and conditions, although most likely will be stronger in one skill than in the other. However, leadership and management have certain clear differences.

Management has been defined as the "process by which the elements of a group are integrated, coordinated and/or utilized so as to effectively and efficiently achieve organizational objectives" (Carlisle 1976). To reach the objectives of an agency, managers promote certainty, stability, and perpetuate routines that staff can follow easily. Managers are also classic good soldiers, promoting, protecting and following policies and procedures. Managers focus on planning and budgeting, set short-term goals and procedures to reach their goals, and monitor the progress of employees. The manager's role is to control and to ask how and when, not to ask why or create change (Nanus 1992).

One of the major differences between managers and leaders is that managers can be appointed and be given management authority. Whether they are excellent or poor as managers, they have their role by virtue of an official appointment. Their official authority gives managers a degree of power over their subordinates. For example, managers can parcel out official rewards or reprimands and even terminate workers for poor performance. Managers are primarily responsible for such administrative functions as budgeting and monitoring employee activities (Maccoby 2000). Managers are responsible for task issues and getting the job done.

Leadership is very different. It cannot be granted by official agency decree, and appointment to an executive position does not in and of itself make the executive a leader. Rather, followers identify leaders. In many organizations, unfortunately, members are forced to follow the "leader's" directions out of fear of retribution. True leaders are selected by groups looking for someone to lead them. Although agencies may try to promote individuals who have the potential to be good leaders, the power of leadership comes primarily from the values, traits, and skills of the individuals who are recognized as leaders. Agency top executives are typically expected to play a leadership role and are in a position to affect the organization to a much greater extent than are middle management or line staff. Conversely, organization members who have no official power may be good leaders and can and often do play a leadership role. Leaders do not rely solely on official power and authority or policies and procedures. Leaders see organizations being driven by people, not rules, and rely on intrinsic values and rewards to direct workers.

Leaders motivate and inspire followers to achieve higher levels of performance in the organization (Buhler 1995). Weiss (2000) provides additional insight into some fundamental differences between managers and leaders. These differences are listed in Table 2–1.

■ LEADERSHIP THEORIES

Some theorists have suggested that a person's traits impact leadership effectiveness. Other theorists argue that leaders possess certain behavioral attributes that make them effective. Contingency-based theories focus on the situation as dictating what

TABLE 2–1 ■ Leaders versus Managers

Feature	The Typical Manager . . .	The True Leader . . .
Responsibility	Accepts it	Looks for it
Status	Demands respect	Gains respect through achievement
Goals	Follows company objectives	Adds to company objectives
Rules	Follows the company line	Exceeds the rules when necessary for results
Getting Results	Meets requirements	Betters requirements
Dealing with Subordinates	Protects self at all costs	Fights for subordinates, even at a personal cost
Dealing with Superiors	Accommodates superiors' requests	Suggests ways to improve operations

type of leadership skills will be used. Other theories have categorized leadership as extraordinary, or transformational; ordinary, or transactional; and laissez-faire.

The Trait Approaches

Trait approaches originated in the late nineteenth and early twentieth centuries, when "great-man" leadership theories were popular. These theories asserted that leadership traits are inherited and that leaders are born, not made. These theories were met with some skepticism then and now. As pointed out by Bennis and Nanus (1985, 222) "biographies of some great leaders read as if they entered the world with an extraordinary genetic endowment. . . . Don't believe it. The truth is that major competencies of leadership can be learned. . . . whatever natural endowments we bring to the role of leadership, they can be enhanced; nurture is far more important than nature in determining who becomes a successful leader."

Early in the twentieth century, these great-man perspectives evolved into trait theories. Trait theories do not make the assumption that leadership characteristics are inherited but instead assert that leaders have characteristics that are different from those of followers (Kirkpatrick and Locke 1991). Trait theories assume that leaders possess certain personality traits, intelligence levels, and skills that separate them from followers. These theories assume that leaders are the "right people," not that they were in the right place at the right time to become leaders. Trait approaches look at the personal qualities of the leader and ask, What traits distinguish leaders from followers? Are some universal traits associated with effective leadership? For example, research that incorporated personological and nonsituational variables concluded that IQ, height, attractiveness, tidiness, and achievement were personality traits associated with "great" presidents (McCann 1992).

In the mid-twentieth century, the validity of trait theories was brought into question. Stogdill (1974) reviewed 30 years' worth of trait studies and concluded that no individual or clusters of leadership traits apply across all situations. Instead, he found that situational factors are influential in effective leadership.

More recent authors have agreed with Stogdill's conclusions, positing however, that having appropriate traits increases effectiveness in leadership roles (Kirkpatrick and Locke 1991). The research conclusion is that a number of traits differentiate leaders from followers. These traits are enhanced by the situations in which leaders function, whereas traits have a stronger influence when the situation permits leaders to express their individual dispositions or behaviors (House and Adita 1997).

Trait theories have fallen out of favor among leadership researchers, primarily because the research has failed to find consistent proof that good leadership starts with one's traits. Nevertheless, some contemporary authors have suggested that certain core values and traits make one an effective leader. Self-reported surveys of more than 2,000 lieutenant colonels and colonels in the U.S. Army found that sensing-thinking-judging behaviors—analytical logical decisiveness traits—were the most preferred behaviors (Gailbreath et al. 1997). Yukl's (1998) comprehensive review of trait research, meanwhile, found that effective leaders have high energy and high stress tolerance, are self-confident, believe that their life events are caused by their own actions—an internal locus of control, have high levels of emotional maturity, and enjoy influencing people and events—power motivation. Other effective traits are personal integrity, a low need for affiliation—are more task than relationship oriented—and a high need for achievement.

Leadership Styles and Behaviors

Besides investigating the traits of effective leaders, researchers have investigated and attempted to isolate those behavioral aspects or styles of leadership. Leadership style can be defined as "those relatively stable patterns of behavior displayed by leaders" (Eagly, Johannesen-Schmidt, and vanEngen 2003, 569). These theories, instead of attempting to determine what makes leaders effective, based on their personalities, look at what leaders do to make them effective.

The Managerial Grid

One of the most popular and well-known behavioral approaches to leadership is Blake and Mouton's Managerial Grid, which assumes that leadership is multidimensional. As proposed by Blake and Mouton (1964), the two primary behavioral dimensions of leaders are concern for production and concern for people. Concern for production includes issues related to quality, results, and profits. Concern for people deals with getting the results done, based on trust and respect of the follower.

Blake and Mouton suggest that all organizations have three interrelated universals: a purpose, people, and a hierarchy. The behaviors of leaders can be identified on how these three universals are connected or related to one another. For example, a leader's behavior could be a concern for production—what the leader wants people to accomplish—over a concern for people—the productive unit of the organization. What is significant in this model is how leaders combine these two concerns in the workplace. The way these two concerns are linked defines how people manage and lead situations in the workplace. For example, the leadership style of a leader who tends toward a high concern for production over people will differ from that of a leader who has a high concern for people over production.

Based on these two concerns, the model contends that leadership styles are not fixed and not totally based on one's personality. The model assumes that a leader's behavior is changing and flexible, with a range of possible interactions. These leadership alternatives are affected by pressures acting on the individual and include external situations and organizational issues, as well as tradition, policies and procedures, and the management/leadership style the person has adopted. As Blake and Mouton (1964, 223) point out, the goal of a manager is to learn to "apply the principle of human behavior in the context of production in such a manner that individual goals and organizational needs are geared to one another."

A leader can take a total of 81 grid positions. Figure 2–1 shows the five primary interactions, or orientations, and subsequent behaviors that Blake and Mouton identify leaders as using.

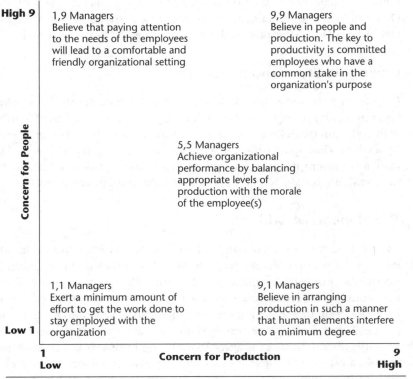

Adapted from Blake and Morton, 1964.

FIGURE 2–1 ■ The Managerial Grid

- **1,1** A leader in the 1,1 position has little concern for production and people and does as little as possible to get by. The 1,1 leader avoids conflict and does not take responsibility for mistakes, leaving employees to fend for themselves and handle their problems any way they see fit. With organizational survival as their only goal, this leader is not concerned for the organization or employees and tries to maintain isolation from supervisors and subordinates. This approach is considered to be unnatural and is reserved for those who have accepted defeat in the organization.

- **1,9** A 1,9 manager has great concern for people and little concern for production. Followers are encouraged rather than being driven to work. This type of leader avoids conflict and concentrates on being liked, producing a country club atmosphere in an effort to create good working conditions, high morale among followers, and a sense of togetherness and group harmony among employees, while taking a hands-off approach to directing work. Because of the great concern for people, production, or output, subsequently suffers.

- **5,5** Management occurs when the leader has a moderate concern for both production and people. The 5,5 leader is not committed to either and tries to balance production and concern for people while emphasizing relevant aspects of work. People are considered as important as production. Furthermore, employees' feelings, attitudes, and morale are important. Conflict is managed by considering tradition, common sense, or past practice. A basic assumption is that people will work willingly when they are given reasons for doing the work. The 5,5 leader relies on norms and tradition to solve problems, is not creative, and seeks to maintain or preserve the status quo rather than change things. This type of leadership is considered to be entrenched in many organizations and is considered to be superior to both the 9,1 and 1,9 approaches to management.

- **9,1** This type of manager has a high concern for production and a low concern for people. The success of this type of management and leadership is measured in profits, not people. The 9,1 leader accepts and demonstrates being in a position of authority. The primary responsibilities of this type of leader are to plan, control, and direct the work of subordinates to meet the production needs of the organization, with employees turning out tasks and contributing to the thinking aspects of the task(s). The 9,1 leader expects employees to follow the lines of authority and obedience. The goals of subordinates are ignored, and employee conflicts are controlled through an authority/obedience framework.

- **9,9** The 9,9 manager has a high concern for both people and production, which is considered the optimal form of leadership and management. An underlying assumption is that meeting the needs of people and of production do not conflict. The primary goal of this type of management is to integrate creativity with high productivity through team action. Employees in this framework are aware of organizational purposes and their own stake in the organization, including their responsibilities for organizational success. The role of the leader is to build organizational commitment under conditions of cooperation while encouraging employees to experiment and to be creative. The role of the leader is to challenge employees to excel and to solve problems while giving the organization a competitive advantage in the marketplace.

Contingency Theories

In the 1960s, another point of view about leadership emerged. These theories, or perspectives, looked at leadership in the context of how the situation dictates the type of leadership that will be used. Contingency-based theories take the perspective that a leader, by influencing the behaviors of followers, will affect organizational outcomes (Butler and Reese 1991).

One popular contingency-based theory is the Situational Leadership Model (SLM). Known originally as the life-cycle theory of leadership, this theory posits that effective leadership depends on the leader's ability to adapt their leadership styles to the particular situation (Hersey and Blanchard 1996). Essentially, leaders diagnose situations and respond to them with certain behaviors. The SLM assumes that no one leadership style fits all situations and that leadership depends on the maturity level of the follower(s). The model is shown in Figure 2–2.

The SLM focuses on two types of leadership behavior—task behaviors and relationship behaviors—and how they interact with the follower's level of maturity. Task behaviors are associated with the amount of guidance and direction a follower needs to accomplish organizational goals. The more a leader gives detailed rules, monitors, and instructs an employee, the higher the task behavior.

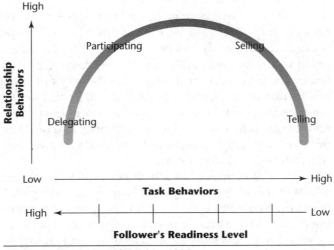

Adapted from Norris and Vecchio, 1992.

FIGURE 2–2 ■ The SLM Model

Relationship behaviors, by contrast, are associated with the level of socioemotional support the leader provides (Goodson, McGee, and Cashman 1989). These behaviors include communicating, listening to, recognizing, and encouraging followers.

The model is also divided into four quadrants, or leadership styles, that provide behavioral guidelines for leaders. These quadrants, listed in Table 2-2, entail telling, selling, participating, and delegating (Norris and Vecchio 1992). Low-readiness followers, according to the model, require a higher level of task-related behaviors combined with a low relationship style, or telling. Followers having a moderately low maturity level require a high task structure combined with a high relationship on the part of the leader, requiring the leader to use selling behaviors. The participative style of leadership is associated with a person who has a high relationship with the follower and low task behaviors. A delegating behavior style is associated with a follower who has a moderately high level of maturity. The leader's behavior in this setting consists of behaviors that include a low task structure combined with a low relationship style (Norris and Vecchio 1992; Goodson, McGee, and Cashman 1989).

The leader's task and relationship behaviors interact with the follower's level of maturity. Maturity, or "readiness," can be defined as "the ability that the follower has to take responsibility for his/her actions" (Silverthorne 2000, 68). Hersey and Blanchard (1996) simplified this concept even more and referred to "maturity" as being ready, willing, and able. Readiness is a combination of willingness and ability the person demonstrates while doing a specific task. Willingness is a combination of the follower's self-confidence, motivation, and commitment. Willingness is also referred to as "psychological maturity." Ability is the person's knowledge, experience, and demonstrated skills. Ability also known as "job maturity." This maturity is considered to be the key situational variable in the model that moderates the leader's behavior and effectiveness.

The SLM implies that leaders need to be adaptive and flexible in how they treat subordinates and to treat followers differently, depending on their maturity and the situation, as shown in Table 2-2. For followers who have the highest level of maturity, the best leadership style is delegating, and telling would be the worst. For followers who have the lowest level of maturity, the best style is telling, and delegating is worst (Goodson, McGee, and Cashman 1989).

TABLE 2–2 ■ **Leadership Styles Relative to Readiness Levels**

Maturity Level	Best Style	Worst Style
Low	Telling	Delegating
Low/Moderate	Selling	Delegating
Moderate/High	Participating	Telling
High	Delegating	Telling

Adapted from Goodson, McGee, and Cashman, 1989.

According to Hersey and Blanchard (1996, 44), the SLM "isn't as much about leadership as it is about meeting followers' (employees') needs. Getting people to focus on followers can improve leadership skills more than trying to teach a particular leadership style." The SLM has been used by corporations and the military and has become one of the most widely accepted managerial philosophies in the United States (Butler and Reese 1991). The model has also been intuitively appealing and popular with managers. However, it has received some mixed and weak support: The theory lacks a clear explanation of the relationship between subordinate performance and leader behaviors, and it addresses only one situational variable—subordinate maturity—that affects leader behaviors (Yukl 1998).

Path/Goal Theory

One of the first theories to focus on a leader's effectiveness and the moderating effects of the situation was path/goal theory, developed by Robert House. The premise of this theory is that the leader's responsibility is to assist followers in reaching their goals while ensuring that the goals are compatible with those of the organization. The theory also holds that a leader's behaviors are influenced by situational variables. House (1971, 234) states that "the motivational function of the leader consists of increasing personal pay-offs to subordinates for work-goal attainment, and making the path to these pay-offs much easier to travel by clarifying it, reducing road blocks and pitfalls, and increasing the opportunities for personal satisfaction en route." This theory is illustrated in Figure 2–3.

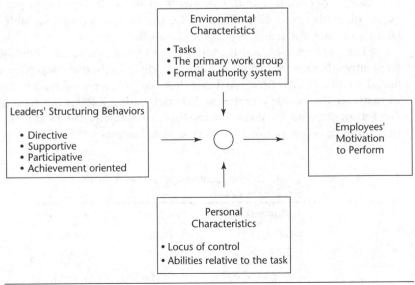

Adapted from House, 1971.

FIGURE 2–3 ■ **Path/Goal Theory**

Path/goal theory has two propositions. First, a leader's behavior is acceptable to followers when they see it as immediately satisfying or as an instrument to future satisfaction. Second, a leader is motivational by providing the appropriate rewards, coaching, guidance, and support needed for effective performance.

The theory tries to explain the effects of four specific kinds of leadership behaviors, which in turn are based on three attitudes and expectations shown by followers. The four types of leader behaviors are

1. Directive leadership, characterized by having followers adhere to specific rules and regulations and specific standards of performance, while also providing specific guidance on what is expected of employees
2. Supportive leadership, characterized by an approachable and friendly leader who shows concern for the well-being and status of followers
3. Participative leadership, with the leader consulting with followers and taking their suggestions seriously before making a decision
4. Achievement orientation, with leaders continually seeking improvement in performance, emphasizing excellence, and expecting followers to perform at their highest level

These leader behaviors are affected by (1) the satisfaction of the followers, (2) their acceptance of the leader, and (3) their expectations that their efforts will result in effective performance and that this performance is the path toward rewards (House and Mitchell 1974).

In addition, two situational, or contingency, variables impact leadership behaviors and outcomes: (1) environmental pressures that followers need to deal with to satisfy their needs and (2) followers' work goals and personal characteristics. The contingency factors in the environment include the subordinates' tasks, the primary work group, and the formal authority system of the organization. Although these variables are not within the follower's control, they have an impact on motivation, and the leader can help the subordinate deal with environmental uncertainty, threats from others, and other sources of frustration. The environment provides stimuli to motivate and direct the follower to perform certain tasks. It also constrains variability in behavior and helps people learn from the primary work group what they can and cannot do, providing cues on rewards and how to do the job.

The acceptability and leadership style that followers prefer is determined in part by their personal characteristics. A person's personality determines whether the leader's behavior is an immediate source of satisfaction or will be instrumental for future satisfaction. These perceptions are based on one's locus of control, or the degree to which one sees the environment as responding to one's behavior. People who believe that what happens to them results from their personality prefer participatory leadership, whereas those who believe that what happens to them results from luck or chance prefer an authoritarian leadership style. Other characteristics of subordinates are their perceptions of their own abilities relative to the tasks they perform. In these cases, the higher the perceived ability of the follower, the less effective a directive or coaching leadership style would be.

Transformational, Transactional, and Laissez-Faire Leadership

Contemporary research on leadership has focused on factors that differentiate extraordinary from ordinary leadership styles, or transformational/transactional styles of leadership and their relative subscales. With both types of leadership, the leaders actively intervene to prevent problems (DenHartog, VanMuijen, and Koopman 1997). Although transformational/transactional leadership styles possess different dimensions, leaders can possess both types of behavioral dimensions (Eagly, Johannesen-Schmidt, and vanEngen 2003). A third leadership category, laissez-faire leadership, is a failure in leadership. Table 2–3 provides an overview of these types of leadership.

Transformational Leadership Transformational, or extraordinary, leadership suggests that effective leaders are role models who gain the respect, trust, and confidence of their followers (Kuhnert and Lewis 1987). This type of leader is proactive, seeing the present state of the organization and its people as a springboard to achieve future aims (Micha and Eliav 1994). The main premise is that a transformational leader can change the followers' awareness of organizational outcomes by encouraging them to pass up their own self-interests for those of the organization (Bycio, Hackett, and Allen 1995). Transformational leadership is group and individual based; the leader's behaviors are directed at

TABLE 2–3 ◾ Leadership Styles

Type of Leadership	Description
Transformational	
• Idealized Influence	Exhibits and/or displays attributes that make employees proud to associate with the leader
• Inspirational Motivation	Shows optimism and excitement about the goals and future state of the organization
• Intellectual Stimulation	Investigates alternate approaches and viewpoints for solving problems and completing tasks
• Individualized Consideration	Concentrates on mentoring followers and attending to their needs
Transactional	
• Contingent Reward	Provides rewards for the satisfactory completion of responsibilities
• Management by Exception: Active	Addresses failures and mistakes so followers meet standards
• Management by Exception: Passive	Waits until problems become severe before taking action
Laissez-faire	Lacks involvement and is frequently absent during critical turning points in the organization

Adapted from Eagly, Johannesen-Schmidt, and vanEngen, 2003.

the group and influence the group as whole but also influence individuals in the group (Kark, Shamir, and Chen 2003). A transformational leader shifts the needs, beliefs, and values of followers and does not demand compliance (Kuhnert and Lewis 1987). Research has found that leaders who exhibit transformational behaviors are judged by their followers as more effective (Judge and Bono 2000).

The transformational leader facilitates the growth of followers by empowering them. As pointed out by Kark, Shamir, and Chen (2003, 246), this type of leadership is "likely to result in growth, independence and empowerment of followers" and looks at how a leader can motivate and transform the values and priorities of followers, namely, by delegating responsibilities and encouraging followers to be creative and think on their own. The transformational leader inspires followers by setting challenging goals and creating a shared vision (Bradley et al. 2002). The leader inspires and encourages followers to excel, as well as nurtures their abilities to contribute to the organization (Eagly, Johannesen-Schmidt, and vanEngen 2003). Followers' confidence levels are raised and their needs broadened by the leader to support development to higher potential. Such total engagement—emotional, intellectual, and moral—encourages followers to develop and perform beyond expectations (Burns 1978; Bass 1985; Sergiovanni 1990).

Transformational leaders' belief systems include such values as justice and integrity. These are referred to as end values and cannot be negotiated or exchanged between individuals (Kuhnert and Lewis 1987). The nature of this leadership style involves heightened emotional levels on the part of the leaders and follower(s), requiring leaders to monitor and manage emotions within both themselves and others. This type of leadership subsequently requires leaders to have a higher level of emotional intelligence: a set of abilities on how effectively one manages, monitors, and deals with emotions in oneself and others (Palmer et al. 2001).

According to Bass (1985), transformational leadership has four dimensions, through which followers personally identify with the leader. The result is role modeling, whereby the followers mold their beliefs, feelings, and behaviors around those of the leader. Research by Kark, Shamir, and Chen (2003) shows that these dimensions include idealized influence, inspirational motivation, intellectual stimulation, and individual consideration.

- *Idealized influence* Idealized influence can be defined as the leader's charismatic dimensions that cause followers to identify with the leader. The charismatic leader gains the respect and trust of followers, instills pride, and excites and inspires them (DenHartog 1997). These leaders are in control of their emotions and have a positive sense of self-determination (Sarros and Santora 2001).
- *Inspirational motivation* Although inspirational motivation too deals with charisma, the concept of inspiration does not require identification with the leader. The leader acts as a role model for subordinates (DenHartog, VanMuijen, and Koopman 1997). A leader who has a clear, appealing vision for people

to follow is inspiring. Such a leader uses symbols, emotional arguments, optimism, and enthusiasm to encourage and challenge workers and may lead by example, have high ethical standards, and demonstrate and show self-sacrifice for the group (Kark, Shamir, and Chen 2003).

- *Intellectual stimulation* This involves questioning assumptions and challenging the status quo. According to Bass (1985, 99), this means "the arousal and change in followers of problem awareness and problem solving, of thought and imagination, and belief and values." Followers are challenged to increase their awareness of problems and to look at issues from a new perspective (Kark, Shamir, and Chen 2003). According to Sarros and Santora (2001, 392), "leaders who intellectually stimulate workers encourage creativity and accept challenges as part of their job. They keep their cool, working out ways of dealing with problems in a rational manner. These leaders cultivate the same skills in their workers. They work through difficulties with their staff in a calm, calculated fashion, and use problem solving techniques for reaching decisions that reflect a mutual consensus between leaders and employees."
- *Individual consideration* Individual consideration focuses on developing the employee. The leader treats the follower as an important, valued contributor to the workplace. This dimension involves encouraging, attending to, coaching, and supporting the individual needs of the follower (Kark, Shamir, and Chen 2003). It also involves mentoring the employee through continuous feedback that links the needs of the employee to the organization's mission (DenHartog, VanMuijen, and Koopman 1997).

Although transformational leadership empowers people, meaning that they become more independent and autonomous in their actions, one of the concerns with this type of leadership is that followers may become dependent on the leader. Thus, empowerment is a double-edged sword. This type of leadership may be associated with both empowerment and dependence. Although empowerment is good, dependence in many cases is not. In transactional-leadership settings, followers may perceive the leader as an exceptional, or extraordinary, person with whom they identify. As a consequence, a follower's main motivation may be recognition and approval from the leader. In addition, if the follower's self-esteem becomes tied to the leader's evaluation, the follower may become too dependent on the leader for inspiration and guidance (Kark, Shamir, and Chen 2003).

Transactional Leadership Transactional, or ordinary, leadership is based on an exchange relationship whereby follower compliance—effort, productivity, loyalty—is exchanged for expected rewards, such as wages and prestige. This give-and-take-based relationship is reactive in nature; the leader reacts to the actions of the subordinate (Micha and Eliav 1994).

Transactional leadership looks at the influence process of the leader, based on the premise of exchanging rewards for compliance or implicit bargains between the leader and follower(s) (DenHartog, VanMuijen, and Koopman

1997). These types of behaviors do not empower followers but simply influence their behavior by reducing resistance to organizational goals, implementing decisions, and substituting goals. In this relationship of mutual dependence, the leader gives something the follower wants in exchange for getting something in return.

These transactions can be low order or high order. Low-order transactions are related to the leader's control of resources, such as special benefits and pay. High-order transactions are nonconcrete, or intangible rewards or values, and include issues related to respect and trust. Generally, leaders have greater control over these higher-order transactions than over pay, a low-order transaction that may not be under their direct control (Kuhnert and Lewis 1987).

Following are three dimensions of transactional leadership (see DenHartog, VanMuijen, and Koopman 1997, Judge and Bono 2000).

- *Contingent reward* This is the most active form of transactional leadership. It deals with providing an adequate exchange of valued resources for follower support. The leader rewards followers for reaching certain performance levels, and the employee's reward—pay, promotion, recognition, prestige—is contingent on his or her expending effort(s) and level of performance.
- *Active management by exception* This dimension involves the leader's actively monitoring performance and taking corrective actions when needed. The leader actively looks for problems or deviations. For example, a security supervisor may commonly interact with line-level employees and assist them in improving their quality of work. Through these simple daily actions, this supervisor can be considered to be engaging in transactive leadership, as employees at a minimum receive recognition for their work. This process requires subordinates to participate in decision making, and respect is shown for opinions and suggestions. Good leaders encourage the subordinate's participation by carefully listening and giving positive feedback.
- *Passive management by exception* This dimension involves the leader's passively monitoring the follower's performance and taking corrective action only when a problem becomes serious. For example, this type of leader may recognize that two employees do not get along and have lower productivity levels but do nothing until two employees get into a physical fight.

Laissez-Faire Leadership Laissez-faire behavior is not really leadership at all. In fact, it can be thought of as nonleadership, or avoiding leadership duties and responsibilities. The major indicator of laissez-faire behavior is the manager's or leader's incapacity to get involved. The laissez-faire leader is not motivated or skilled enough to perform the responsibilities associated with leadership, avoids decision-making and supervisory responsibilities (DenHartog, VanMuijen, and Koopman 1997), and avoids involvement or confrontation, keeping personal interactions to a minimum. According to Sarros and Santora (2001), leaders with this style are fast losing their power base, are out of touch with their workers, and are a daily reminder to the organization of old-fashioned work practices.

■ THE ESSENCE OF GOOD LEADERSHIP

Becoming a successful leader does not simply mean having a grasp of leadership theory. Although the theoretical perspectives provide a framework for gaining a better understanding of the concept of leadership, they also raise more questions on what it takes to be a leader and what traits, skills, and abilities a leader needs to be successful in today's organization.

Leavy (2003) writes that three main elements affect leadership effectiveness: conviction, or a strong belief in issues; credibility; and the context of leadership. Leaders must believe in their visions. Otherwise, followers may soon realize that such a leader is not truly "sold" on the issue, and support for the leader and the vision will weaken. The term "credibility" means having influence or power that originates from followers' having confidence in the leader's abilities. A follower who does not believe the messenger will not believe in the message.

"Context" deals with the conditions under which leadership occurs. Individuals often do not have control of this realm. Leavy asserts that great leaders make history but not always in circumstances of their own choosing. Rather, the context of time is a factor to consider. Great leaders are often forced into situations that make them great. These contexts may include organizational crises, ranging from the loss of market share to natural or other disasters. The context of military operations is one of the best examples of how a situation can make a great leader. Consider, for example, what would have happened to Norman Schwartzkopf or Dwight Eisenhower if there was no war to be fought and won.

Ethics and Leadership

Understanding leadership theory is only one aspect of becoming good leader. Leaders also need to understand themselves, especially in the context of how their core beliefs influence and determine their ethical behaviors. "Ethics" describes and prescribes moral behaviors and requirements; it is the study of standards for determining what behaviors are right or wrong and good or bad. "Morality" is concerned with the effects of one's actions on other people (Aronson 2001).

A leader's success can often be tied to ethical behaviors. The success of the organization is subsequently tied to the leader's ethical behaviors. Organizations that have ethical leaders have an increased employee effort and a lower turnover rate and so are more effective. Leadership integrity has also been found to have a positive relationship with employee satisfaction levels and higher ratings of leader effectiveness (Parry and Proctor-Thomson 2002). According to Sims and Brinkmann (2002, 328), nothing is more important to an ethical corporate atmosphere than the role of the leader: "The personal values of top leaders, powered by their authority, set the ethical tone of an organization. Failure by top leaders to identify key organizational values, to convey those values by personal example, and to reinforce them by establishing appropriate organizational policies demonstrates a lack of ethical leadership on their part that fosters an unethical organizational culture."

The ethical leader also has integrity, or a commitment to action in morally justified values and principles (Parry and Proctor-Thomson 2002). Other theorists propose that the concept of integrity includes a moral commitment to both personal morals and company standards (Morrison 2001). This moral self-governance occurs at the individual and collective levels in organizations. At the individual level, a leader needs to have what is known as integrity capacity: one's capability to align moral awareness of situation, character, and conduct to demonstrate balanced judgment, enhance moral development, and promote supportive systems for moral decision making. Individuals who possess these characteristics are said to have a coherent unity of purpose and a high integrity capacity. People who are irresponsible in their moral decision-making capabilities or show poor or distorted judgment and succumb to administrative evils—or are not morally mature—are considered to have a low integrity capacity.

Integrity capacity is considered to be a key strategic intangible asset that can improve the competitive advantage of firms. Those organizations that have a high integrity capacity will be more successful in the marketplace, based on their moral positions. A high integrity capacity also increases the reputation of those organizations, and reduces distorted business judgments, and educates employees on moral awareness (Petrick and Quinn 2001).

Creating an Ethical Culture Organizational culture is a "pattern of basic assumptions, invented, discovered or developed by a given group as it learns to cope with problems of external adaptation and internal integration that has worked well enough to be considered valid, and therefore is taught to new members as the correct way to perceive, think, and feel in relation to those problems" (Schein 1990, 111). One of a leader's roles is to make sure that ethical behaviors and attitudes are followed on a daily basis in the organization. Accordingly, leaders must be responsible for developing an organizational climate or culture, that not only fosters ethical conduct that justifies ethical principles but also clarifies the ethical dimensions of their decisions (Minkes, Smal, and Chatterjee 1999). Through these actions, leaders will have a profound and positive impact on organizational culture, as they can change, maintain, and reinforce the ethical behaviors of organizational members. These actions will ultimately impact how individuals behave and shape the organization's culture.

According to Schein (1992), a leader has six primary embedding mechanisms that shape organizational culture.

1. *What leaders pay attention to, measure, and control* The values on which the leader focuses attention influence what employees concentrate on in the organization. What the leader systematically and consistently pays attention to, rewards, and controls communicates to followers what is important. These

areas of attention could include casual questions, agendas at meetings, and emotional reactions to issues. For example, if an employee is rewarded and praised for getting a new client at "all costs," that is what employees will strive for. Conversely, employees who are criticized for not being open and honest with clients about the installation of new security technologies that would not be appropriate yet would make money for the company would avoid this issue later and seek other alternatives. For example, Sims and Brinkman's (2002) analysis of unethical behaviors by Solomon Brothers president John Gutfreund led to the firm's losing its reputation among many of its clients. Gutfreund forced employees to produce profits immediately. This short-term focus made individuals ignore long-term ramifications of their actions, which was one reason for the company's being implicated in insider trading of U.S. Treasury bonds.

2. *Reaction to crises and critical incidents* The way leaders deal with a crisis reveals underlying assumptions, values, and norms. Shein (1992) states that survival issues are the most potent in revealing the deep assumptions and therefore the most likely to become the basis of shared learning. This shared learning then becomes embedded in the organization. Leaders who lie, cheat, and try to cover up ethical issues reveal their true values to followers. Conversely, leaders who are honest, open, and fully admit wrongdoing send a different message about their ethical framework.

3. *Observed criteria for resource allocation* Observing how leaders allocate funding in the organization gives followers an understanding of what is important to the leader. The leader's budget behaviors reveal how much they trust the competence of followers and their level of risk taking. A leader who takes a great degree of control over the budget may signal to followers that they have little decision making and trust. But a leader who allows managers to allocate funding to certain projects and ideas sends a message of faith in the followers.

4. *Deliberate role modeling, teaching, and coaching* A leader's actions communicate assumptions and values to followers. These visible behaviors communicate the leader's value system, and, in turn, become part of the organization's value system and culture. But a leader who preaches one virtue and does not exercise it will be regarded as a hypocrite.

5. *Observed criteria for allocation of rewards and status* The reward system created by the leader tells employees what is expected and prized in the organization. These criteria may differ from what the leader publishes or preaches. When performance standards are ambiguous, people are not sure what they should do. As a consequence, aggressive individuals pursue what they believe to be acceptable, which may include unethical activities (Sims and Brinkmann 2002).

6. *Observed criteria for recruitment, selection, promotion, retirement, and excommunication* A leader's decisions about who will be hired, fired, and promoted let other employees in the organization know what a leader's values are. Schein (1992) writes that leaders become culture reproducers or

changers. Thus, cultural assumptions get embedded because they operate below the surface. Leaders hire people with certain traits, values, and beliefs, and it is difficult to see this unless someone outside the organization detects a particular pattern, as leaders may be unaware of their actions.

Although these six values are not mutually exclusive, the key point is that leaders shape organizational cultures. Schein (1992, 245) further writes that "it is not necessary for newcomers to attend special training or indoctrination sessions to learn important cultural assumptions. They become quite evident through the behavior of leaders." Through these six primary executive functions, one can have a tremendous impact on creating and maintaining an ethical organizational culture.

Defective Ethics and Leadership

What causes leaders to engage in unethical activities? One failure of leadership is known as the "violational explanation" for ethical failures in leadership. This explanation assumes that the leader knew that the action was immoral. Such actions may be based on ego or self-interest; they occur because leaders have privileged access to information, people, and objects, as well as unrestrained control of organizational resources. The leader may believe that those actions and their subsequent effects can be concealed. All these factors contribute to the leader's motivation to commit unethical acts. In short, the leader thinks that position and power will provide immunity (Price 2000).

Some theorists suggest that leadership, by its very essence, creates cognitive challenges that can lead to ethical failures. According to Price (2000), cognitive mistakes are of two varieties. The first variety—mistakes about morality's content—deals with what actions are morally permissible. An example of this type is that lying is a morally permissible way of achieving follower compliance. The second variety—mistakes about morality's scope—deals with beliefs about the moral status of individuals: what individuals are part of one's moral community, or to whom they owe a moral obligation. For example, a contract security agency owes a moral duty to its client but may also degrade the moral status of nonemployees of the company to the point of treating them with disrespect or contempt.

For Price (2000), failures of moral leadership are attributed to mistaken beliefs about morality's scope. Leadership brings with it justifications for doing things that others are not permitted to do. Leaders are often removed from normal moral requirements that apply to followers, based on their positions of power whereby they justify their behaviors. However, ethical failure occurs when "leaders pay no heed to the fact that their behavior is well within the scope of a requirement that applies to the rest of us" (p. 182). Price asserts a leader is exempt from the scope of normally permitted moral action only when another moral requirement legitimates the exception.

deVries, Marvin, and Doyle (1994) state that in some instances, leaders fail to recognize the potential destructiveness of their actions because of their personalities. According to the psychoanalytical approach, defective leaders have poor interpersonal skills, the result of uncontrolled or compulsive narcissism, which he calls reactive narcissism. Narcissism is a stage of infant development that all individuals go through, whereby one's core patterns of personality are shaped. The dynamics that occur during one's narcissistic stage of development shape one's later view of the world, leading one to become either a constructive or a reactive narcissist.

Examining leadership in a psychoanalytical perspective, deVries and his coauthors argue that reactive narcissists have an inner drive to get even or to come to grips with their past. They have a grandiose sense of self-importance and entitlement; they feel that they deserve special treatment and perceive that rules are not made for them. They also are addicted to compliments, lack empathy, and habitually take advantage of others to achieve their own ends. According to deVries (1994, 86), "constructive narcissists have the capacity for introspection; they radiate a sense of positive vitality and are capable of empathetic feelings. . . . This contrasts with the reactive narcissists who are continually trying to boost a defective sense of self esteem and are preoccupied with emotions such as envy, spite, revenge, or vindictive triumph over others." He states that one's past experiences influence current and future behaviors whereby some personality traits, especially interpersonal skills, lead to destructive leadership. According to deVries, leaders need to come to terms with their past or their inner forces in order to gain an understanding of their narcissistic behaviors. If not, they will never be effective leaders.

Charisma and Leadership

Charisma is charm or appeal. In the context of leadership, charisma refers to the leader's actions to build loyalty and to inspire and motivate followers to accomplish organizational goals. Charisma is considered by some theorists to be an observable behavioral process that leaders possess. Instead of relying on other forms of solution-related power, a leader becomes charismatic by successfully changing the follower's attitudes to accept the leader's advocated position. Conger and Kanungo (1987, 640) say that the behavioral components of charismatic leadership are interrelated and form a "constellation of components." Following are some of these specific behavioral components.

- Charismatic leaders have a vision that is different from the status quo but still within an acceptable latitude of acceptance for their followers. These leaders portray the status quo as intolerable and their vision as the most attractive and obtainable alternative.
- Charismatic leaders take high personal risk in such areas as finance, status, career success, or employment and engage in self-sacrifice to achieve a shared vision. The greater the leader's personal risk for the common good, the more the leader is charismatic and worthy of follower's complete trust.
- Charismatic leaders have expertise in their areas of influence, show the inadequacies in the status quo, and have the ability to transcend the existing order through the use of unconventional means to achieve their vision.

- Charismatic leaders are active innovators whose behaviors often run counter to the established norms of the organization; they are unconventional and counternormative, take personal risks, and have a high probability of harming their own self-interests.
- Charismatic leaders' unconventional actions are based on realistic appraisals of environmental conditions. Such leaders realistically assess environmental resources and constraints in order to achieve objectives and to avoid ineffectiveness.
- Charismatic leaders lead through assertive behaviors and expressions of self-confidence, expertise, unconventionality, and concern for followers' needs.
- Charismatic leaders' influence comes from idiosyncratic power—expert and referent—rather than from the legal, coercive, and reward power associated with the position.
- Charismatic leaders act as reformers or agents of radical change. Their charismatic leadership fades when they act as managers or administrators.

■ FUNDAMENTAL LEADERSHIP PRACTICES

Other issues also need to be considered regarding effective leadership. Kouzes and Posner (2000) found that successful leaders follow five fundamental and exemplary practices: *challenge the process, inspire a shared vision, enable others to act, model the way,* and *encourage the heart.* Each practice is discussed below.

Challenging the Process

Leaders have the energy and courage to look for challenges. "Leaders are pioneers—people who are willing to step out into the unknown" (Kouzes and Posner 2000, 9). Leaders take risks by presenting or supporting radical ideas. "We have always done it that way" is not part of their lexicon. The risk such individuals take are calculated but contain several degrees of uncertainty. These leaders are eager to experiment and expect and accept failure. To these leaders, mistakes are common occurrences and are useful in learning about the organization and themselves. The most significant mistake for a leader is the common belief that in rigid hierarchical organizations the existing structure and assumptions of the agency are infallible. For example, in rigid paramilitary organizations, such as many private security firms, people get blamed for system errors and problems and tinkering with procedures; worse, new policies and procedures are created and routines begin to "stack up." Leaders, on the other hand, look for fundamental problems in the system and challenge the process. Also, rigid organizations view changing business conditions as a threat, whereas leaders find opportunity in change. Thus, for example, private security organizations that retain their paramilitary philosophy are in need of leadership and leaders to keep systems from becoming more rigid and to prepare for the future turbulent and unpredictable business environment.

Inspiring a Vision

Leaders inspire a vision that is shared by members of the organization. A vision is not the same as a mission. In an organizational sense, a vision is a realistic but imaginative and highly attractive future for the organization (Nanus 1992).

The most significant contribution a leader makes is to craft a vision that guides the agency into the future. Change is inevitable over time. Organizations without direction react to change, typically after new conditions are perceived as threats. Organizations blessed with forward-looking leaders participate in change. These organizations are proactive and seek opportunities in the changing environment. Forward-looking leaders craft visions for their organizations and make proactive thinking and acting part of the organization's culture.

Crafting a vision is not witchcraft or a mystical process but rather one based on knowledge of one's organization, future trends, and articulated preferences for the improvement of the organization in the future. Burt Nanus (1992) describes a step-by-step process for creating a vision for an agency. The six steps can be summarized as follows.

1. An agency's mission may remain stable over time, whereas a vision prescribes a way to meet the mission more effectively than competitors to the benefit of both consumers and organizational members. Achieving the mission typically requires change in the culture, structure, and ways of doing business. A vision is not a planning document. Creating a vision must proceed planning. Visionary leaders create mental pictures that attract and inspire others. Without visionary leadership, sophisticated planning documents often gather dust. One sign that an organization needs visionary leadership is confusion about purpose, manifested as a decline in pride among the staff, accompanied by complaints of boredom and lack of challenges. Other indicators are a hyperactive rumor mill, a passive staff concerned with its own survival, and a sense that the organization is losing legitimacy in its field. The clearest sign is the realization that the organization is not in step with current trends.

2. A well-formulated vision shared by the members of an organization can become a driving force. If most members of an agency share the picture of a better future for them and the agency, they will get behind it and put their efforts into proposed changes. Visionary leadership attracts commitment and energizes followership. In effect, a vision gets people involved and adds new meaning to their work. A vision also implies a belief in improvement and sets standards of excellence. Visionary leaders empower organizational members by sharing the future with them.

3. Visions are developed by intuition and an instinct to look for opportunities. Asking the right questions and seeking information and facts about the organization, its environment, and future trends and possibilities are crucial components in crafting visions. Visions must also address the needs of the entire organization and be shared by a critical mass of its members.

4. A good vision should have the following qualities:

   - Future oriented
   - Utopian (ideal perfection)
   - Appropriate
   - Reflect high ideals
   - Clarify purpose
   - Inspire enthusiasm
   - Reflect uniqueness
   - Ambitious

5. Creating a working vision begins with creative imagination. A visionary leader pulls bits and pieces of information together, mixes them with a few ideas, and creates mental models of a number of attractive future states for the organization. The next step is to determine to whether the visions are credible or can be made a reality in the future. This requires having a clear view of the organization's present state in the context of its mission, contribution to society, and the general characteristics of the industry; what is unique about the organization; and what it takes for the organization to succeed. It is also important to define the boundaries of the organization, which requires identifying the realistic boundaries in which change can be made. It also requires identifying significant stakeholders, whether individuals or groups, what they require, and the threats and opportunities they present. For example, unions have a stake in the success and profitability of their companies. Unions can also be threats to a company's profitability and erode management authority through contract negotiations.

6. Implementing a vision is the real test of leadership. Implementation is about pulling people in a new direction, keeping them excited, and getting them to adopt new attitudes and routines. This requires getting and keeping a commitment for change from a critical mass of organizational members. To pull this off, leaders need to be visible, positive, encouraging, and continually communicating the benefits of the new direction to organizational members. Well-written vision statements, like planning documents, will gather dust without the human energy, desire, and commitment to make them a reality.

Enabling Others to Act

Leaders enable others to act. Achieving agency goals requires activity and effective participation by workers. Leaders understand that success is the product of group effort and that individuals must have the skills, knowledge, and desire to act out their roles. Exemplary leaders "enlist the support and assistance of all those who must make the project work.... Leaders know that no one does their best when feeling weak, incompetent, or alienated; they know that those who are expected to produce must have a sense of ownership." Kouzes and Posner (2000, 5) found that leaders who were particularly skilled at enabling workers didn't use the word "I" in discussions but instead always used the word "we," meaning all members of the organization, not just a select group. This simple change in dialogue gives workers the message of inclusion.

Leaders encourage staff to work in teams and to create coordination efforts on their own. Teams and cooperation can be facilitated by establishing discussion groups, eliminating artificial barriers among workers, creating common meeting spaces for staff, receiving group consultation from employees, and keeping department sizes small enough for members to know one another personally.

Leaders also enable others by sharing power and information with workers. In classic paramilitary organizations, power is theoretically rationed by rank and information is parceled out on a need-to-know basis. Under conditions of rationed power, workers feel relatively powerless, tend to follow orders just far enough to project themselves, "pass the buck" when things go wrong, and may be skilled at passing blame upward. Leaders distribute power by giving workers responsibility, decision-making power, and visibly offering them support for their decisions.

These steps may seem impossible for agencies that are run like bureaucracies, and the steps require the reduction of rules and regulations and supervisory layers in the chain of command. To be enabled, workers must also be made competent by ensuring that they understand agency goals and values and be well trained to carry out their responsibilities.

Modeling the Way

Leaders are identified as the people who always model the way. Leaders walk the talk. They do what they inspire others to do. "There are always moments when the commander's place is not back with his staff but up with his troops. . . . The men tend to feel no kind of contact with the commander who, they know, is sitting somewhere in headquarters. What they want is what might be termed a physical contact with him. In moments of panic, fatigue or disorganization, or when something out of the ordinary has to be demanded from them, the personal example of the commander works wonders." So wrote Field Marshal Erwin Rommel during his North African desert campaign against the British in 1942 (Liddell-Hart 1953, 241).

The first principle of modeling the way is visibility. One cannot act as a role model from behind a desk. Individuals who are given the status of leadership are active people who need to move around almost randomly but without being intrusive or a threat to employees. The second condition for modeling the way is to "walk the walk." Managers often say, "I will not ask my people to do anything I wouldn't do." This is the language of leadership. But true leaders do more. They often "take the lead" by doing and saying things others are reluctant to say or do. Leaders believe in addressing problems openly and hence will make explicit what is implicit in the group. Leaders will bring simmering issues, criticism, and radical ideas to the table for everyone to view in an effort to encourage everyone to speak out.

Through their visible behaviors, leaders set the example. They are role models. Workers may or may not listen to what bosses have to say but will watch their behaviors carefully. Workers will learn by what is done, not by what is said, what is expected from them, and what the real values and rules of the organization are. Everyone has or will work for a boss, for example, who will announce an "open-door policy" and that the workers' views are important but in practice is inaccessible and a poor listener. In this case, the boss has talked one policy but walked another. Individuals who are granted leadership status by followers are conscious of this and use their actions to make their views, beliefs, and practices known to followers. Leaders search for opportunities and visibly act out the behaviors, values, and ideas that they think are important to the success of the group.

Research on the degree of contact with followers has concluded that the more personal contact there is between them, the more a follower's perception of a leader will be based on fact. According to Micha and Eliav (1997), "the shorter the distance between the leader and the led, and the closer and more personal the contact, the more the leader will be seen, judged and evaluated by his/her people on what they are, their way of thinking, behaviour, professionalism, diagnostic ability, interpersonal sensitivity and so forth. Conversely, the more distant the leader from the led, the greater the tendency to see, judge and evaluate him or her not on what he or she is but on what he or she is supposed to be in their fantasy, projection or schema."

Encouraging the Heart

Leaders encourage the heart of those around them. Workers are more productive when work is fun and rewarding. When work is not fun and rewarding, workers are creative at finding alternative and unproductive activities to bring fun to the workplace. For example, managers have observed security officers having fun talking to one another while ignoring customers and other work-related responsibilities. If the assigned tasks are not fun for security staff, they may read, extend their breaks and lunch hours, or devise other creative and unproductive ways to put fun into their jobs. Kouzes and Posner (2000) discovered that successful leaders find ways to recognize workers' contributions.

First, successful leaders are creative about developing rewards, especially intrinsic rewards. Intrinsic rewards include spontaneous strokes and celebrations, letters of appreciation, or simply paying attention to workers' activities. Leaders search for intrinsic rewards and apply them generously but appropriately, as rewards need to attach to accomplishments and productive behavior. Individuals with "great personalities" who are always giving strokes do not make good leaders, as they do not successfully attach rewards to productive and positive activity. Recognition needs to be made public to provide feedback for all employees. Effective reward and recognition systems are typically made with feedback and consultation with workers.

Second, leaders celebrate accomplishments on a regular basis. Leaders act as cheerleaders and help people bring fun and spirit to the work and the workplace. Herb Kelleher, the CEO of Southwest Airlines, has recreated the airline business. He requires staff to entertain and have fun with passengers. Southwest evaluates staff on how much fun they have contributed. Herb spends much of his time working with ticket agents, luggage handlers, stewards, and other employees. He has fun with them and is their cheerleader. It is reported that he often shows up for a flight wearing comical costumes. He is exemplary in the process of encouraging the heart.

Private security agencies that are managed by rules, a strict chain of command, and a distance between management and labor are probably weak at encouraging the heart and often don't actively develop a system of intrinsic rewards. Agencies that don't make a substantial effort at making work fun and rewarding will suffer low morale and productivity and have a high turnover rate. It is easy to understand the need to encourage the heart.

■ LEADERSHIP FOR PRIVATE SECURITY

Law enforcement agencies, prisons, and private security organizations are often referred to as paramilitary organizations. These bureaucratic organizations rely on a chain of command and have clear superior/subordinate relationships. Military titles, such as sergeant, lieutenant, and captain, are assigned to supervisors. In addition, the staff members wear uniforms, sometimes carry firearms, and are authorized to apply coercive force under certain circumstances to carry out the mission. Managing the organization relies heavily on rank and chain of command, orders, and rules and regulations, or policies and procedures. Change comes from the top through changes in new policies and procedures. What is being described is an organization that relies heavily on management but does not promote, sanction, or purposefully seek leadership. To the extent that leadership is used, it is likely an artifact of leadership personalities that belong to particular executives. Trying to infuse a greater element of leadership into a paramilitary organization may be considered counterculture or just another fad. It would be difficult, but it can be done.

To foster leadership in any organization, a number of myths and traditional management beliefs must be cast out. "Good" organizations are assumed to be orderly and to run like clockwork. Organizations simply don't work that way, however. An organization that is innovative—ready to make changes to improve or to meet anticipated shifts customer or market demands—simply will not run like a clock.

An example of creative chaos is the development of the Polaris submarine. The people who created this submarine in the 1960s were pulled out of the Department of the Navy and the Department of Defense, freed from their huge agencies, and formed a new small group composed of engineers, scientists, and technicians. The group was thought to be well organized as it developed and appeared to rely on the sophisticated management tools of Program Performance Budgeting and PERT (Program Evaluation and Review Technique) charts. The truth, however, is that the suborganization that created these sophisticated techniques functioned in pure chaos. The energetic people involved argued, screamed, and kicked, but they got the job done.

Another traditional belief is that leaders should be cool, aloof, and analytical. This is not always the case, however. As we have seen, leaders live by their feelings. Leaders are often part inspirational and share the passion they feel. They are proud to say that they are caring and kind and often express love to the people around them. They are often quite charismatic too. But the energy, dynamism, and enthusiasm come from a strong belief in purpose. Management seeks control. Leaders believe, as stated earlier, that the more people are controlled, the less they will excel and that the more they are controlled, the less they will trust the leadership. Despite the belief that managers should be detached from the day-to-day operations, leaders must be visible and part of the day-to-day operations. The purpose is not to micromanage but to seek opportunities to communicate and to reinforce their basic beliefs, "model the way," inspire people, pass out intrinsic rewards, and celebrate and enjoy successes. The essence of leadership is commitment, and that is something leaders come by through their beliefs.

Leaders need to be concerned with morale. Often, however, the concern for morale is based on the faulty belief that when morale goes down, productivity goes down. The opposite is true. When people can't get their jobs done, productivity and morale go down. Under conditions of diminishing morale, the right question to ask is, Why can't people get their jobs done? Often, the reason is that the organization is overmanaged and that people are overwhelmed with rules, regulations, and routines that keep workers from meeting what they believe to be the purpose of their work. Because the organization is so entrenched in its present way of doing things, it cannot change to meet new demands. The leader looks at low morale and knows that a change must be made to enable people to get the job done. Enabling them to do so may mean restructuring the rules and regulations and retraining the people. It always involves empowering people and knowing that they do the job. Rules, regulations, and training do not get the job done. The emphasis must be on the people, as the leader knows.

Leaders in private security need to be concerned about accountability, a contemporary management philosophy that, in practice, is often counterproductive. In theory, accountability means that individuals should be responsible for their own actions. In practice, however, accountability systems are created when the organization fears the loss of control. Based on this fear, agency resources are expended to add more systems to get control back. In turn, workers expend some of their resources to create methods to minimize accountability. If this cycle continues, resources continue to be allocated to control and countercontrol, which subsequently results in resources' being taken away from the means of production. Consider, for example, how much time is often allocated to the investigation of employee conduct or performance rather than to production issues. In addition, the organization becomes more rigid as new rules and procedures begin to stack up (Downs 1967). The effect is to ignore the good work of the good group of people by focusing energy and resources searching for mistakes.

Leaders are concerned with building trusting relationships. Such relationships are not created simply by saying, "Trust me," and certainly not by getting angry with people when they do not trust their leader. Leaders cannot assume to be trusted because they have been given a management position. They are trusted because they have earned trust, just as they are respected because they have earned respect. Being trusted sounds easy but may require overcoming some old habits. To be trusted, one must always act in a trustworthy manner; thus, leaders seek to understand people and in turn strive to be understood. This means that leaders must listen carefully to people, let them finish what they are trying to tell them, and not debate with them during a discussion. Leaders may think that they are the most trustworthy people in the world, but they will not be trusted if they insist on having their opinions accepted. Likewise, if they "know everything" or don't listen, provide inconsistent information, gossip, and talk about people behind their backs, trust will erode. In short, such so-called leaders will lose in the spiritual battle of leadership.

■ CONCLUSION

An agency that is highly structured and well managed but lacks leadership will be watching in wonderment as other firms grow and prosper and as new firms enter the field and have immediate success. This chapter has shown that leadership is a dynamic, challenging process. Leaders are inspirational, have charisma, and promote a vision.

Several theories explain what makes a leader. Trait approaches assume that leaders possess or have inherited certain characteristics. Behavioral-based theories, including the Managerial Grid, suggest that leaders use certain behaviors that make them effective. Other theories argue that the situation determines the appropriate style of leadership. One popular contingency theory is the Situational Leadership Model, which looks at the amount of guidance a follower needs relative to the leader's relationship behaviors. Another contingency theory, path/goal theory, takes the position that leaders use four behaviors that are affected by the environment and characteristics of the follower. Leaders can also engage in transformational, or exceptional, styles of leadership, which are superior to ordinary, or transactional, styles of leadership.

Leadership theories provide insight into effective leadership, but this chapter has also revealed that industry leaders have a vision of the future; they see opportunities in changing conditions where others see threats and problems. Leaders are the individuals who will encourage others to take risks, overcome obstacles, and create new systems that will meet future challenges. Leaders must monitor their leadership ability and adjust their actions accordingly. Effective leaders transform employees to excel in the workplace, are charismatic, and have a strong conviction in what they do. They have integrity and adhere to ethical principles while creating and maintaining an ethical culture. Leaders also inspire a vision and challenge existing practices and processes. They model the way through their visible activities and make work fun and rewarding for their followers. True leaders are those individuals who are willing to confront tough issues and changes that are needed for the success of the organization.

■ KEY TERMS

Accountability

Charisma

Contingency theories

Integrity

Integrity capacity

Laissez-faire leadership

Leadership

Management

Managerial Grid

Narcissism

Organizational culture

Path/goal theory

Situational Leadership Model

Trait theories

Transformational leadership

Transactional leadership

Vision

■ DISCUSSION QUESTIONS

1. According to Kouzes and Posner, what makes a leader successful?
2. What are the fundamental differences between trait and behavioral explanations of leadership?
3. What are the benefits for a leader who has a high integrity capacity?
4. What is tranformational leadership? How does it compare to transactional forms of leadership?
5. What are the primary embedding mechanisms that shape organizational culture?
6. What makes a leader charismatic?
7. What are some explanations for unethical acts committed by leaders?
8. What is a vision? How can leaders craft one?
9. What is the difference between leadership and management?
10. Review the Managerial Grid. What is the best leadership behavior? What is the worst leadership behavior?

■ REFERENCES

ARONSON, E. 2001. Integrating leadership styles and ethical perspectives. *Revue Canadienne des sciences de l'administration* 18 (4): 244–256.

BASS, B. M. 1985. *Leadership and performance beyond expectation*. New York: Free Press.

BENNIS, W. G. 1994. *On becoming a leader*. Reading, MA: Perseus Books.

BENNIS, W. T., and B. NANUS. 1985. *Leaders*. New York: HarperCollins.

BLAKE, R. R. and J. S. MORTON. 1964. *The managerial grid*. Houston, TX: Gulf Publishing.

BOLMAN, L. G. and T. E. DEAL. 2001. Leading with soul: An uncommon journey of spirit. San Francisco: Jossey-Bass.

BRADLEY, J. P., A. M. ADELHEID, D. CHARBONNEAU, and J. P. MEYER. 2002. Personality correlates of leadership development in Canadian forces officer candidates. *Canadian Journal of Behavioral Science 34* (2): 92–103.

BUHLER, P. 1995. Leaders v. managers. *Supervision* 56 (5): 24–26.

BURNS, J. M. 1978. *Leadership*. New York: Harper & Row.

BUTLER, J. K., and R. M. REESE. 1991. Leadership style and sales performance: A test of the situational leadership model. *Journal of Personal Selling and Sales Management* 11 (3) 37–46.

BYCIO, P., R. D. HACKETT, and J. S. ALLEN. 1995. Further assessment of Bass' [1985] conceptualization of transactional and transformational leadership. *Journal of Applied Psychology* 80 (4): 468–478.

CARLISLE, H. M. 1976. *Management: Concept and situations*. Chicago: SRA.

CONGER, J. A., and R. N. KANUNGO. 1987. Toward a behavioral theory of charismatic leadership in organizational settings. *Academy of Management Review* 12 (4): 637–647.

DEVRIES, M. F. R., L. MARVIN, and J. DOYLE. (1994). The leadership mystique: executive commentary. *The Academy of Management Executive* 8 (3): 73–93.

DENHARTOG, D. N., J. J. VANMUIJEN, and P. L. KOOPMAN. 1997. Transactional versus transformational leadership. *Journal of Occupational and Organizational Psychology* 70 (1): 19–34.

DOWNS, A. 1967. *Inside bureaucracy*. Glenview, IL: Scott Foresman.

DUPREE, M. 1989. *Leadership is an art*. New York: Brill.

EAGLY, A. H., M. C. JOHANNESEN-SCHMIDT, and M. L. VANENGEN. 2003. Transformational, transactional, and laissez-faire leadership styles: A meta-analysis comparing women and men. *Psychological Bulletin* 129 (4): 569–591.

GAILBREATH, R. D., S. L. WAGNER, R. G. MOFFETT III, and M. B. HEIN. 1997. Homogeneity in behavioral preference among U.S. Army leaders. *Group Dynamics, Theory, Research, and Practice* 1 (3): 222–230.

GOODSON, J. R., G. W. MCGEE, and J. F. CASHMAN. 1989. Situational leadership theory: A test of leadership prescriptions. *Group and Organizational Management* 14 (4): 446–461.

HERSEY, P., and K. BLANCHARD. 1996. Great ideas revisited: Revisiting the life cycle theory of leadership. *Training and Development* 50: 42–47.

HOUSE, R. J. 1971. A path goal theory of leader effectiveness. *Administrative Science Quarterly* 16: 321–338.

HOUSE, R. J., and R. N. ADITA. 1997. The social scientific study of leadership: Quo vadis? *Journal of Management* 23 (3): 409–473.

HOUSE, R. J., and T. R. MITCHELL. 1974. Path-goal theory of leadership. *Journal of Contemporary Business* 3: 81–97.

JUDGE, T. A., and J. E. BONO. 2000. Five-factor model of personality and transformational leadership. *Journal of Applied Psychology* 85 (5): 751–765.

KARK, R., B. SHAMIR, and G. CHEN. 2003. Two faces of transformational leadership: Empowerment and dependency. *Journal of Applied Psychology* 88 (2): 246–255.

KIRKPATRICK, S. A., and E. A. LOCKE. 1991. Leadership: Do traits matter? *The Academy of Management Executive* 5 (2): 48–60.

KOTTER, J. P. 1990. *A force for change : How leadership differs from management*. New York: Free Press.

KOUZES, J. M., and B. Z. POSNER. 2000. *Five practices of exemplary leadership: When leaders are at their best*. San Francisco: Jossey-Bass.

_____ 2003. *Credibility*. San Francisco: Jossey-Bass.

KUHNERT, K. W., and P. LEWIS. 1987. Transactional and transformational leadership: A constructive/developmental analysis. *Academy of Management Review* 12 (4): 648–657.

LEAVY, B. 2003. Understanding the triad of great leadership—context, conviction and credibility. *Strategy and Leadership* 31 (1): 56–60.

LIDDELL-HART, B. H. 1953. *The Rommel papers*. London: Collins.

MACCOBY, M. 2000. Understanding the difference between management and leadership. *Research Technology Management* 43 (1): 57–59.

McCANN, S. J. H. 1992. Alternative formulas to predict the greatness of U.S. presidents: Personological, situational, and zeitgeist factors. *Journal of Personality and Social Psychology* 62 (3): 469–479.

MICHA, P., and Z. ELIAV. 1994. Transactional, charismatic and transformational leadership. *Leadership and Organizational Development Journal* 15 (6): 3–7.

MINKES, A. L., M. W. SMALL, and S. R. CHATTERJEE. 1999. Leadership and business ethics: Does it matter? Implications for management. *Journal of Business Ethics* 20 (4): 327–335.

MORRISON, A. 2001. Integrity and global leadership. *Journal of Business Ethics* 31: 65–76.

NANUS, B. 1992. *Visionary leadership: Creating a compelling sense of direction for your organization*. San Francisco: Jossey-Bass.

NORRIS, W. R. and R. P. VECCHIO. 1992. Situational leadership theory: A replication. *Group and Organizational Management* 17 (3): 331–342.

PALMER, B., M. WALLS, Z. BURGESS, and C. STOUGH. 2001. Emotional intelligence and effective leadership. *Leadership and Organizational Development Journal* 22 (1): 5–10.

PARRY, K. W., and S. B. PROCTOR-THOMSON. 2002. Perceived integrity of transformational leaders in organisational setting. *Journal of Business Ethics* 35 (2): 75–97.

PETRICK, J. A., and J. F. QUINN. 2001. The challenge of leadership accountability for integrity capacity as a strategic asset. *Journal of Business Ethics* 34 (3/4): 331–344.

PRICE, T. L. 2000. Explaining ethical failures of leadership. *Leadership and Organizational Development Journal* 21 (4): 177–181.

SARROS, J. C., and J. C. SANTORA. 2001. Leaders and values: A cross-cultural study. *Leadership and Organizational Development Journal* 22(7/8), 383–393.

SCHEIN, E. H. 1990. Organizational culture. *American Psychologist* 45 (2): 109–119.

SCHEIN, E. H. 1992. *Organizational culture and leadership*. 2d ed. San-Francisco: Jossey-Bass.

SERGIOVANNI, T. J. 1990. Adding value to leadership gets extraordinary results. *Educational Leadership* 47 (8), 23–27.

SILVERTHORNE, C. 2000. Situational leadership theory in Taiwan: A different cultural perspective. *Leadership and Organizational Development Journal* 21 (1/2): 68–74.

SIMS, R. R., and J. Brinkmann. 2002. Leaders as role models: The case of John Gutfreund at Solomon Brothers. *Journal of Business Ethics* 35 (4): 327–340.

STOGDILL, R. M., 1974. *Handbook of leadership: A survey of theory and research*. New York: Free Press.

TOSI, H. L., J. R. RIZZO, and S. J. CARROLL, 1986. *Managing organizational behavior*. Marshfield, MA: Pitman.

WEISS, W. H. 2000. Effective leadership: What are the requisites? *Supervision* 61 (8): 3–6.

YUKL, G. 1998. *Leadership in organizations*. 4th ed. Upper Saddle River, NJ: Prentice Hall.

chapter three
Supervision

In a field survey on skills needed to effectively supervise in the twenty-first century, the Association for Quality and Participation found that a supervisor needs knowledge, skills, and abilities (KSAs) in the following areas (McManus 1995):

- Inspiring change
- Facilitating teams
- Training
- Process planning and improvement
- Satisfying customers
- Problem solving in groups
- Promoting quality and participation
- Designing employee involvement systems
- Using statistics to improve productivity
- Involving unions

In addition, a supervisor must be able to troubleshoot issues, be the resident expert in production processes, and have the ability and tact to monitor and discipline employees. Supervisors must have these abilities while also meeting the diverse needs of their superiors, subordinates, and customers. Supervisors need to be effective communicators and coaches and be able to motivate employees while adapting their leadership style to match the employees' work styles. Supportive or considerate supervisors who can accomplish this myriad of skills and responsibilities in the workplace cause employees to put greater effort into safety in the workplace (Parker, Turner, and Turner 2000). In short, effective supervision is not a simple task and should not be taken for granted.

■ THE SUPERVISOR AND THE ORGANIZATION

The origins of supervision, or overseeing workers, can be traced back to the practice of indentured servitude, whereby a person signed a contract with a master to serve a certain period of time—usually in years—in exchange for passage to America, for example. The origins of supervision can also be traced back to slavery, under which a master oversaw and directed the activities of these individuals. A contemporary understanding of supervision is not as harsh and does not necessarily carry the negative perspective of these earlier forms of supervision. A modern and simple definition of supervision is to work through others to accomplish organizational goals (Lee and Cayer 1994).

Anshel (1992, 11) offers a more comprehensive definition of supervision as "the process of establishing accountability, developing personal and professional skills, evaluating job performance, and promoting job satisfaction through the interaction between two parties, the supervisor (manager) and supervisee (subordinate or worker)." Some theorists consider supervision to be a science in that it is a process and requires cooperation and information (Anshel 1992). Other definitions have included the supervisor's role in being a coach, facilitator, and motivator of workers. Supervisors have also been described as individuals who, in order to achieve organizational goals, have to remove barriers, provide resources, and make sure that employees possess positive attitudes and skills (Lee and Cayer 1994).

The designation of supervision also covers a variety of positions. In one company, a supervisor might be responsible for a group of employees and be called a foreman; in a similar company, the supervisor might be called a supervisor, coordinator, or team leader. Regardless of the name given to the practice of supervision, a supervisor can be considered the official manager of the work group. Supervisors are part of the management team, based on the activities they perform. But unlike other managers in the organization, supervisors' subordinates are not managers but operatives. Supervisors are given authority for the work of their groups and can be considered a link between the workforce and other managers in the company (Evans 2003). The roles and functions of a supervisor are critical to organizational success.

Often, organizations neglect the significance of effective supervision and its importance to the success of the company. Supervisors themselves may fail to realize their importance. For example, employees often follow, or align with, supervisors rather than with the organization itself. Because of their responsibilities and activities, supervisors are psychologically and physically closer to employees than to the interpersonal system of the organization itself. Hence, an employee's attitude will have a stronger impact on a supervisor's performance than the supervisor's attitude toward the organization. Further, the organization is not "human." It cannot interact with employees and respond to employee behaviors and needs. That is the role of the supervisor. People interact with one another. The supervisor is the "agent" of the organization, interacting with employees on a daily basis, enacting formal and informal procedures for organized activities, and administering rewards to employees (Chen, Tsui, and Farh 2002).

Supervisors are often considered to be leaders. This may not always be the case, however, as there are distinct differences between a leader, a supervisor, or, in some cases, someone who is both. As discussed in Chapter 2, leaders are often role models; they teach by example, inspire, and motivate individuals to higher levels of performance in the organization. Many leaders are also creative and proactive in nature. Supervisors, meanwhile, rely on their legitimate power or authority to get the job done instead of on their charisma or expertise, as is the case with many leaders. Supervisors, unlike leaders, are also less inspirational and less proactive than leaders are. In an ideal situation, and in the interest of organizational effectiveness, these roles should overlap; a supervisor should have leadership skills, and a leader should have effective supervisory skills. Progressive firms need to recognize that these roles are not mutually exclusive and to promote and develop those individuals who possess these overlapping traits (Buhler 1995).

■ LEADER-MEMBER EXCHANGE THEORY

Leader-member exchange (LMX) refers to the quality of the relationship between a supervisor and an employee. As a model of supervisory behavior, LMX explains how the supervisor and the employee develop behavioral role interdependencies: Each party in an LMX must offer something the other sees as valuable, and each must see the exchange as reasonably equitable and fair (Graen and Scandura 1987). LMX describes how supervisors develop various exchange relationships that affect the development of employee roles in the workplace. Accordingly, LMX does not concentrate on the characteristics of the supervisor or a specific situation. Instead, LMX looks at the quality of the supervisor/employee relationship in the context of a vertical dyad whereby the quality of exchange between the two can range from low to high (Gerstner and Day 1997).

LMX also assumes that relationships will vary, with each employee having a unique relationship with the supervisor. Thus, supervisors may act differently toward each employee in the same work group, depending on the quality of the relationship that evolves. Hence, employees with the same job titles may receive different responsibilities, based on the development of interpersonal trust within the supervisory relationship (Bauer and Green 1996). For example, an individual in a supervisor/employee relationship based on mutual respect and common interests may be given more challenging responsibilities than an employee who does not have this same level or quality of relationship with the supervisor.

In high-LMX dyads, supervisors become leaders, and the employee's role expands beyond the formal job description to include more management responsibilities. In this relationship, marked by increased levels of trust, the supervisor delegates tasks. In return for such positive treatment, the employee works hard to please the supervisor. Some outcomes of a high-LMX relationship include the employee's having greater decision-making authority, higher performance evaluations, fewer work-related problems, greater supervisory attention, and more opportunities for career development, more organizational citizenship activities, and greater work effort (Townsend, Phillips, and Elkins 2000).

Low-LMX employees, by contrast, are characterized by negative reciprocal relationships. Employees receive less supervisory attention, support, consideration, and communication. Low-LMX employees perceive that they have less autonomy in their decision-making scope, and supervisors treat them less favorably than they do high-LMX employees. Low-LMX employees receive less challenging tasks and are not promoted as rapidly as high-LMX employees are. In low-LMX situations, supervisors may limit the subordinates' opportunities for career development and advancement. In response to their perceived injustices, low-LMX employees may engage in such retaliation activities as calling in sick, damaging equipment, working less, and engaging in avoidance activities to get even with supervisors. Employees may also violate organizational rules and publicly criticize the supervisor (Townsend, Phillips, and Elkins 2000).

The LMX has received a great deal of research attention. Research has found that an employee's perceptions of fairness of even a singular event becomes part of the history of experiences that influences that person's attitudes and behaviors toward the other party (Masterson, Lewis, and Taylor 2000). Other research has found that supervisors distinguish among subordinates in the extent of delegation (Leana 1987). Likewise, similarity in supervisors' and subordinates' personalities was found to be related to a more positive LMX (Bauer and Green 1996). In the context of supervisory communication practices, higher-quality dyads were found to have communication patterns whereby the supervisor provided a high quality of information and permitted participation by the employee. In lower-LMX dyads, employees reported receiving adequate information but were not allowed to participate in communication (Yrie, Hartman, and Galle 2002). In the context of in- or out-group status, the LMX relationship has been found to occur early in the supervisor/employee relationship and may be resistant to change. Demographic variables, such as age and gender, have also been found to affect the LMX dyad (Settoon, Bennett, and Liden 1996; Yukl 1998).

One issue that this model fails to address is the balance of high- and low-quality LMX relationships a supervisor should have to be effective. Although a low LMX has negative consequences for supervision and the organization, this model fails to determine what balance is needed for effective supervision. The model does not prescribe whether supervisors should spend a great deal of time fostering high-quality relationships with a few employees or whether supervisors should spend time with lower-LMX employees to form higher-quality LMX relationships (Sherony and Green 2002). Other researchers have suggested that the exchange between supervisors and employees will also affect coworker exchange relationships. Research has found that employees who have high levels of LMX have higher-quality relationships with one another. At the same time, employees with low-LMX relationships also bond together, implying that both in- and out-group members form strong relationships with one another. The mix of the two, however, could lead to increased conflict among employees, leading to an increase in supervisory- and performance-related issues in the workplace (Sherony and Green 2002). The LMX model also does not fully consider the impact of team activities in the workplace. This issue suggests that individual employees at times may not be the primary cause of outcomes that lead to a high or a low LMX (Sparrowe and Liden 1997).

■ EFFECTIVE SUPERVISION

The literature on organizational behavior and industrial-organizational psychology is full of perspectives on what it takes to be a good supervisor. Regardless of the theory or model used, a common denominator is that supervisors are committed to the organization's objectives and goals and to their employees. In turn, employees need to develop commitment to the organization. This commitment, which can be understood as a psychological mindset, increases the likelihood that employees will stay with an organization (Herscovitch and Meyer 2002) and that they accept and are willing to dedicate themselves to the goals and values of the organization (Ellemers, deGuilder, and van den Heuvel 1998).

Contemporary research suggests that employees have various foci of commitment to particular entities: coworkers, teams of workers, superiors, subordinates, customers, or any other individuals who make up an organization (Becker 1992). Employees also have bases of commitment: the motives that engender attachment. Three bases of organizational commitment identified by the research are listed in Box 3–1.

BOX 3–1 ■ Bases of Commitment

Bases of Commitment	Description
Affective	Refers to the employee's emotional attachment to, identification with, and involvement in the organization and its goals. This type of commitment results in the employee's wanting to remain in the relationship.
Continuance	Is an exchange-based type of commitment referring to the costs associated with leaving the organization. Continuance commitment results in individuals' feeling that they have a say in the relationship because leaving would cost too much—loss of pension or status, for example—or because employment alternatives may not exist elsewhere.
Normative	The employee's desire to stay with the organization, based on duty, loyalty, or obligation, because it is the right thing to do.

Adapted from Clugston, Howell, and Dorfman (2000).

These categories of commitment are not mutually exclusive. Employees can possess a variety of foci and bases of commitment, and these may change and vary in intensity over time. Although all three bases of commitment reduce the likelihood that a person will leave the organization, they have different implications for job-related activities. Those employees who have affective commitment, as presented by Meyer and Allen (1991), perform tasks to the best of their ability, attend work regularly, and do extra activities to help out. Employees who remain with the organization primarily to avoid costs may do only what is required of them to remain employed. Those who are normatively committed have a sense of duty, or a sense of reciprocation for the benefits they receive for doing their jobs. These employees do what they need to do to remain employed with the company (Herscovitch and Meyer 2002).

Supervisors have a unique role in improving all three bases of commitment. Research has confirmed that measures of supervisory support are positively correlated with one's level of commitment, regardless of what base of commitment was measured (Ko, Price, and Mueller 1997) and that feelings of commitment are important to implement changes in the organization (Herscovitch and Meyer 2002). Employees' foci commitment to proximal and immediate supervisors were found to be the strongest (Gregersen 1993).

It is proposed that commitment to the supervisor occurs at two levels: identification with the supervisor and internalization of the supervisor's values. Identification occurs when the employee admires the supervisor's attitudes and behavior, personality, or accomplishments. The employee is proud to be associated with the supervisor and is loyal to this person. However, the employee may not adopt these attributes. Internalization occurs when the subordinate adopts the supervisor's attitudes and behaviors because they are congruent with the employee's value systems. In other words, the values of the subordinate and supervisor are similar (Chen, Tsui, and Farh 2002).

In short, supervisors, because they are often physically and psychologically the closest to employees, are integral to their level of organizational commitment. Of all the necessary traits to build employee commitment, the three most important elements are trust, honesty, and self-respect.

Trust

An effective supervisor must nurture and build levels of trust among subordinates. Trust comes slowly and goes quickly. It is recognized as a positive element in any working relationship and can be considered the lubricant that makes relationships work. Trust leads to cooperative behaviors, reduces conflict, and promotes adaptive organizational forms in the workplace, as people who trust one another, regardless of position or responsibility in the company, will work together more readily.

Trust has two components: objective credibility and benevolence. Objective credibility is the extent to which the person can be relied on, whereas benevolence is the extent to which the supervisor is concerned about the well-being of the employee (Doney and Cannon 1997). Some supervisory characteristics that build trust are listed in Box 3–2.

> **BOX 3–2 ■ Trust-Building Characteristics of Supervisors**
>
> - Keep promises that you make to your employees.
> - Always tell the truth, regardless of whether it is painful for you or for them.
> - Be quick to apologize when you have done something wrong.
> - Be fair to everyone.
> - Cooperate with coworkers willingly.
> - Strive to understand how others feel about issues.
> - When making decisions or actions, seek input from those employees who will be affected.
>
> _____
> Adapted from Afholderbach (1998).

Honesty

Supervisors need to be honest. They need to report honestly so that others may use their observations in coming to valid beliefs. Supervisors need to admit errors when they occur and make all possible efforts to correct them. If supervisors are not honest, especially when they know that they've made a mistake and won't own up to even though the employees know it, the employees may focus on this issue instead of what they are paid to do. Supervisors' lack of honesty may also create a ripple effect, leading to a decrease in morale and productivity and an increase in employee dishonesty.

Self-Respect

Respecting oneself or one's position leads to greater levels of self-esteem, or having confidence and satisfaction in what one does professionally and in one's personal life. Self-esteem is of several types. Global self-esteem is the degree to which individuals believe that they are capable and worthy of performing various activities, based on prior experiences. Task-based self-esteem is the degree to which individuals perceive that they can perform tasks that they undertake frequently or that are important to them. Individuals with high levels of task-based self-esteem have greater levels of job satisfaction and perceive themselves as important and having high levels of ability and confidence (Gardner and Pierce 1998). For example, a security manager may review incidents on a daily basis but not regard this task as important in the context of self-esteem. This person may consider this task as having little or no impact on the safety and security of the factory. Instead, the major duty of making sure that employees in a large manufacturing firm are protected against safety violations may be more important to this security manager, adding meaning to the job and increasing self-esteem.

Effective supervisors need to recognize how they can contribute to maintaining and improving the employee's level of self-esteem in the workplace. General activities include reaffirming the employees' worth to the company, empowering and trusting them to perform their jobs well, giving them meaningful tasks that challenge their intellectual and creative abilities, and making sure that they are successful in completing their tasks (Newstrom, Gardner, and Peirce 1999). The key to self-esteem is to never ignore, undermine, or demean the employee's worth as a human being.

■ SUPERVISORY ROLES

As pointed out in the beginning of this chapter, supervisors accomplish work through others to accomplish organizational goals. This means that supervisors do not perform the work themselves. However, continuing on with the work they used to perform is often a common error with new supervisors. New supervisors may have been promoted because of their good work and technical expertise. However, the role of the supervisor is not to perform good work but rather to achieve organizational goals through others. As pointed out by Lee and Cayer (1994, 6), "a supervisor's tools are no longer his or her own hands but the hands of others." Supervisors also need to recognize the needs of their subordinates, while also cultivating their allegiance to the company and its mission and values (Lee and Cayer 1994).

Depending on job design and the organization, a supervisor may have several diverse responsibilities in an organization. Research has shown that one of the most common job responsibilities of a supervisor is setting and monitoring subordinates' job tasks. Another common responsibility is having responsibility over subordinates' pay and promotions (Rothstein 2001). Some other activities supervisors perform can be broadly categorized as controlling, establishing and regulating worker autonomy, defining responsibilities, managing performance, monitoring behaviors, delegating, communicating, influencing, and maintaining an ethical climate.

Control

Regardless of the industry sector a supervisor is in, a key responsibility is to ensure productivity by maintaining a degree of control over production processes and subsequently the employees themselves. Although the concept of control is often interpreted as simply monitoring the actions of employees, it can be examined in a different and more comprehensive context. For instance, control over information and resources to get the job done provides a broader context for the supervisor's knowledge over operations and production processes to ensure that subordinates are given the opportunity to excel. These production processes include knowledge of the organization and faith in subordinates to get the job done. Supervisors are also in control of many managerial activities to ensure organizational success. Within these two broad categories, the supervisor needs to be able to "read" and orchestrate movements and know what is needed, when it is needed, and where it is needed. The supervisor needs to understand the organization and its products, customers, and employees. When one has a comprehensive understanding of these variables, one can be said to have control.

Take, for example, a supervisor's role in a security agency. Employees show up for work, check out their equipment, and maintain their daily logs. In a basic perspective, they are doing their jobs. Some of their work is done perfectly, some is done satisfactorily, and some is forgotten or ignored. It appears that everything is going well because superiors, customers, and clients have no complaints. However, the supervisor does not fully know whether the work is being done effectively and efficiently. Does the supervisor really know what the employees are doing? Does the supervisor have a good understanding of the quality of work the employees are performing? Is work being done effectively and efficiently? Perhaps not. Lacking control over the work processes, the supervisor has an incomplete understanding of what employees were doing, and perhaps employees lacked direction and accountability. Maintaining control would fix these situations.

Span of Control or Span of Support?

Another issue related to the control of work processes is the number of individuals a supervisor should control. Span of control refers to the number of subordinates who report to a single superior (Sheehan and Coriander 1989). The span of control refers to how relationships are structured between superiors and subordinates in the organization. A wide span of control exists when a supervisor oversees many subordinates. A narrow span of control exists when a supervisor has only a few subordinates (Meier and Bohte 2003).

A supervisor's span of control is an important organizational variable because it often impacts how well the company functions. Although a rule of thumb is that an effective supervisor can supervise only 10 people, based on a military structure, for example, span of control is not uniform among organizations. Companies may have some unique qualities that make their span of control irrelevant for similar organizations. Span of control also varies hierarchically within organizations. The span of control may be narrower at the line level and broader at the managerial level (Meier and Bohte 2003).

The traditional perspective on the span of control has identified the following key variables: diversification of function, time and stability, and size and space (Meier and Bohte 2003).

Diversification of Function

One theory is that organizations that combine diverse functions have a narrower span of control because a supervisor has to interact with many types of individuals. On the other hand, if employees are all performing the same tasks, the jobs can be routinized, which will result in a supervisor's being able to oversee more people. This variable assumes that the diversity of functions employees perform, the diversity of occupations, and the diversity of inputs—customers—will require more supervision. For example, an alarm company may have salespeople, repair technicians in the field, and employees who monitor alarms at a central monitoring station. Because these functions are diverse more supervisors may be needed to monitor them.

Time and Stability

Time deals with the issue of stability. In stable organizations, supervisors may not have to spend as much time training and overseeing new employees. Stability includes not only workers but also the organization's external environment. In security organizations that experience a high turnover rate, the supervisor will need to train new employees on a regular basis. External environments that may be experiencing a lot of technological changes, for example, may also require more supervisory oversight than more stable environments in which traditional, or stable, activities remain relatively constant in terms of employee responsibilities and tasks. In the alarm and guard sectors, for example, the alarm sector has experienced a great deal of change, owing to technological advancements, whereas in the guard sector, technological advancements have had less impact on the activities of asset protection.

Size and Space

Space, an element of size, includes the number of buildings that house the organization. For example, the more numerous the buildings, the less face-to face interaction supervisors can have with their employees, and the more supervision is required. In both proprietary and contractual settings, for example, multiple geographically dispersed locations will require a change in supervision activities. A multinational company that has factory locations in the United States and abroad will require more supervisors at various plant locations than does a smaller contractual security company that services its clients in a specific city or region.

The span of control is also affected by other factors. Increasing the span of control can reduce the number of supervisory personnel in an organization, which in turn will reduce costs associated with supervisors' salaries and related expenses. Span of control also varies with management styles and the philosophy of the organization. Some organizations that are less "dictatorial" about quality and performance have shifted the supervisory role toward monitoring rather than control, focusing on individual performance issues and making employees more accountable and responsible for their work.

One example of how the organization's underlying philosophy affects the supervisory span of control can be seen in comparing supervisory activities at American Airlines and Southwest Airlines (Gittell 2000). At Southwest, supervisors were responsible for only eight or nine employees. At American Airlines, by contrast, supervisors had between 30 and 40 subordinates. This wide span of control at American was attributed to its emphasis on accountability, with supervisors responsible for locating the origin of a problem and then dealing with the problem area.

Southwest, on the other hand, was not concerned about identifying the sole cause of the problem. Instead, Southwest's team approach diffused blame for issues while encouraging learning from mistakes. Employees were also considered to be internal customers, and the role of the supervisor in this context was to help them do their jobs better by facilitating learning among the employees. As they were now responsible for educating individuals, Southwest supervisors needed a narrower span of control than did American's, where the personal intervention of supervisors was often limited to problem situations.

At American, performance was based on objective criteria, and supervisors monitored employees through impersonal forms of measurement. This type of monitoring could be carried out from a distance and supervisory functions were minimized. At Southwest, supervisors played more of a coaching role, and a narrower span of control was needed because supervisors relied on active feedback from the employees and monitored them through personal intervention. This smaller span of control led to a fine-tuned interaction between employees and supervisors. Instead of supervising to control the activities of employees, Southwest's model of supervision was a support mechanism for employees; supervisors were not controlling but took on a more supportive role and considered the employee as an internal customer. This comparative analysis concluded that "greater cross-functional accountability, smaller supervisory spans of control, greater selection for teamwork, and more active cross-functional conflict resolution are associated with more frequent communication, stronger shared goals, greater shared knowledge, and higher levels of mutual respect among employees in different functions" (Gittell 2000, 109).

Regulating Autonomy

Supervisors can also regulate the degree of autonomy, or freedom, an employee has. In some cases, supervisors may need to give their employees autonomy, especially when the organization and the supervisor want to empower them, allowing them to learn and explore. McGrath (2001) found that the degree of supervisory autonomy impacts the degree of exploration that employees will exhibit and use in the workplace. In these situations, the old adage that one learns from one's mistakes is an appropriate concept to consider. In situations characterized by standardized behaviors and formal job roles and definitions, the desired result is reliability, replicable performance, and safety, rather than novelty, although clear goals and less supervisory autonomy might be appropriate. In these types of settings, which are quite common in the security industry, employees have specific shift responsibilities and goals.

Contemporary firms also require adaptation and innovation. One way to ensure adaptation and innovation is to allow employees to explore where there are supervisory-oversight processes that influence exploratory learning, for example, where the supervisor encourages creativity, investigation, and novel solutions to various problems and issues that arise. McGrath (2001) reported that greater autonomy allows for innovation in problem solving while also minimizing the strain on the organization's information-processing capacity by loosening the coupling between those involved in the exploratory projects and the balance of the company.

Surprisingly, this factor may require supervisors to not set clear goals for their employees. In some cases, supervisory autonomy is associated with increases in learning effectiveness. According to McGrath (2001), setting clear goals may impede creativity because these specific and measurable goals truncate discovery processes that are critical to creating knowledge bases among individuals, as learning processes that include feedback seeking, experimentation, and discussion of errors may be suppressed. If clear goals are set with little room for deviation, deviation from set goals may be personally threatening. Although this point may fly in the face of conventional wisdom—that when group members share specific goals and targets, learning will improve—research has shown the opposite, namely, that learning effectiveness through exploration increased with increased supervisory autonomy (McGrath 2001).

The preceding points suggest that supervisors need to create and regulate levels of employee autonomy through supervisory oversight. Supervisors can set performance goals or can control operational decisions and activities. These two concepts exist on a continuum. For example, one supervisor may grant subordinates a great deal of goal autonomy, allowing them to focus on opportunities and possibilities. Another supervisor, by contrast, may be very directive, giving employees little or no autonomy in terms of organizational goals. Although clear goals "help to absorb uncertainty and create focus" (McGrath 2001, 122), they can be detrimental to creativity in certain situations. In these types of projects, mistakes will happen as employees explore opportunities. Through these mistakes, subordinates will learn and be able to apply what they have learned in successful ventures or applications.

While engaging in oversight activities, supervisors also need to respect employees' privacy rights. This could be a delicate balance at times, however. Part of the supervisor's job, of course, is to monitor employee behavior on the job, which can require a valid intrusion on the worker's privacy. In some instances, surveillance of employee activities serves a legitimate business need. Legitimate forms of surveillance activities are important for safety; surveillance of activities improves productivity, reduces theft and other illegal activities, and is a quality check for customer service. But surveillance issues become illegitimate and may expose a company to civil actions by employees when supervisors violate employees' right to privacy by, for example, controlling employees' personal lives off the job, blackmailing employees, or prying into their personal lives (Ramsey 1999).

Defining Responsibilities

Job descriptions and policies and procedures define the nature of the job, but it is often the role of the supervisor to assist in identifying job breadth. Job breath is one's personal definition of prescribed work behavior. In one case, for example, the official job description of a corporate hotel security force was narrow in the responsibilities assigned to the role of security and dealt specifically with safety and security issues in the complex. Supervisors expanded security's role and, as a result, increased the employees' job breadth, which employees did not object to because of the team culture that existed in the organization. Some of these activities that extended the official job descriptions included assisting setting up banquets, "plating" meals, and helping room service deliver items to rooms when not enough staff employees were available.

Job breadth is also framed by employees' cognitive perceptions of the supervisor. The cognitive evaluation of supervisory contact is how employees may shape their job breadth. For example, an employee who perceives the supervisor's role as controlling will have a narrower job breadth. An employee who feels that the supervisor's role is informational will have a wider perception of job breadth. Of interest, however, is the research finding that employees and supervisors often do not agree on what the employee's roles are in the organization (Klieman, Quinn, and Harris 2000).

Managing Performance

Another key responsibility of any supervisor is performance management, the process through which companies ensure that employees are working toward organizational goals. It encompasses a variety of performance-based objectives and employee behaviors and is therefore part of, and also known as, performance appraisal. Because the performance management system encompasses all employee activities and behaviors, its success or failure lies with the supervisor, who is ultimately accountable for, and is the linchpin of the program with the employees of the organization (Glendinning 2002).

The taxonomy of supervisory behaviors by Komaki, Desselles, and Bowman (1989) looks at performance management and is called the Operant Supervisory Team Taxonomy and Index (OSTTI). It suggests that three supervisory behaviors are related to employee performance: antecedents, monitors, and consequences. Performance antecedents deal with instructing, directing, and conveying expectations of performance. Performance monitors deal with collecting performance information by talking with and observing an employee's activities. Performance consequences deal with the supervisor's acknowledging the employee's performance in a variety of formal and informal methods. Monitoring and consequences are the key components of the model.

To ensure that consequences are contingent on performance, performance monitoring is necessary. An effective manager should regularly evaluate performance and then, on the basis of the individual's performance, provide consequences. An ineffective manager, on the other hand, is thought to assess performance sporadically, if at all, and to provide infrequent consequences. As Komaki (1994, 30) points out:

> What distinguished [effective managers] is the amount of time they spend seeking out information about subordinates' work. The effective manager finds out how employees are doing. They do not leave this fact-finding to chance. They ask employees how they are doing. They examine the work. They observe workers in action. In other words, they monitor. Based on what they learn, they then feed this information back to workers. They point out what they like and dislike. They also drop casual comments into conversations indicating that they know what is happening. That is, they provide consequences.

Monitoring Behaviors

Monitoring is a form of contact between supervisors and employees and manifests itself in a variety of ways. Monitoring may include reviewing activity logs, and having formal and informal discussions with employees. Although monitoring serves a positive function by communicating information about particular tasks and employee responsibilities and clarifying work expectations and roles among employees, supervisors need to be conscious of the problem of overmonitoring the actions of their employees. Overmonitoring could cause employees to exhibit poor attitudes and decreased performance, as they may perceive that they are not trusted by the supervisor to get their work done on their own (Klieman, Quinn, and Harris 2000). This is often a delicate balance, as each employee's level of monitoring varies, based on the competency of the employee and the tasks being performed.

The supervisory role conveys the legitimate right to prescribe and monitor behaviors. Employees are expected to comply with these supervisory perceptions and responsibilities. As a consequence, supervisors need to set expectations about performance, and employees must agree with these performance standards. Disagreement over the performance standards will lead to conflict. This point reveals that supervisors must win the cooperation of employees (Balser and Stern 1999). This can be accomplished through the effective monitoring of employees, which will help them define their roles in the organization. Assisting employees in defining their roles, or organizational role development, is a gradual and dynamic process whereby employees reach mutual consensus with other organizational members and the supervisor on what their work roles and appropriate behaviors are (Klieman, Quinn, and Harris 2000).

Delegating Responsibilities

Delegating tasks and responsibilities, or getting things done through other people, is another supervisory responsibility. Delegation appears to be a simple task but, in many situations, supervisors are reluctant to assign individuals various tasks. This reluctance could be out of concern that the subordinate may not thoroughly complete the task and that the employee's performance might reflect poorly on the supervisor's ability. Reluctance could stem from the supervisor's fear that others will think they are shirking their responsibilities. Further, the supervisor may fear losing some degree of supervisory power and authority.

One of the most important ways to foster trust is through the delegation of work (Anshel 1992). Effective delegation empowers and motivates employees. Delegation of activities will also keep employees interested and give them the opportunity to learn and grow. Delegation is a form of job enrichment for employees. At the same time, delegation allows supervisors to concentrate on their core responsibilities that require their personal authority and levels of expertise that others may not possess. Delegation requires that supervisors trust their employees to get the job done (McConnell 1995). This element of trust also requires that supervisors give employees the latitude to do the job without excessive control (Painter 1995).

Delegating is a long-term, future-oriented employee-development process (McConnell 1995). It does not simply entail giving someone the responsibility to do something or handing off tasks when time is short or the organization is exerting time pressures. Delegating requires careful preparation, and the supervisor needs to consider a variety of issues. Some of the actions to consider prior to delegating tasks include:

- making sure employees completely understand the task and the related performance standards
- completely informing the employees about all aspects of the task
- telling the employees why they were selected
- communicating deadlines for the task's completion
- providing employees with information about where they can go for assistance and what degree and type of assistance is available
- telling the employee what results are expected.

Supervisors should delegate whole tasks. By delegating a complete task and not just pieces of a task, employees will be more motivated to complete their responsibilities, as they can see the importance of the task. Supervisors also need to make sure that the tasks are meaningful and important for employees. Supervisors may need to match the task with the employee (McConnell 1995).

Not all tasks should be delegated, regardless of the skill level or expertise of the employee. Managerial or supervisory tasks, such as hiring, performance appraisal, pay issues, promotion recommendations, and employee discipline issues should not be delegated. Technical tasks related to the job at hand, such as a specific project to improve security, is an appropriate task to delegate (McConnell 1995).

The failure to effectively delegate impacts both employees and supervisors. In a holistic perspective, supervisors who fail to delegate responsibilities limit subordinate development and job enrichment. The failure to delegate also limits the level of ownership an employee has in tasks. An employee who is not given a sense of ownership when delegated responsibilities will not be fully motivated to complete the task. At the same time, an employee who is made responsible for the tasks must also have the authority to make major decisions. For example, a security officer who is given the responsibility of designing a new public relations brochure should be given a great degree of latitude in doing so. Yet the ultimate responsibility for the task still remains with the supervisor. If mistakes are made or the employee does not complete the task, the supervisor will be held accountable, not the employee. Transferring complete blame would deter the employee from willingly taking on additional responsibilities and erode trust.

Besides impacting their subordinates, supervisors who do not delegate enough will soon find that they are unable to keep up with their assigned duties and so attend only superficially to their responsibilities. The failure to delegate may also be evident in those supervisors who are unable to get all their work done, leading to longer workdays, working beyond their shifts, and taking work home. The result might be supervisory performance problems, impacting the image of the supervisor and the department (McConnell 1995). As a consequence of these performance issues, higher-level managers may soon question the supervisor's competence.

The failure to delegate will also reveal that supervisors do not know how to do the job. As a component of effective supervision is achieving organizational goals through workers, a supervisor who does not delegate and instead performs the work is violating the fundamental tenet of supervision and may lead to micromanaging the employee. In such a situation, the employees may stop caring about the quality of their work, knowing that the supervisor will eventually do the work instead (Lee and Cayer 1994).

Taking credit for employees' work and punishing them for making mistakes when delegated tasks are also delegation failures. In some situations, supervisors may take credit for the employee's work, failing to have this person recognized by upper management and their coworkers for a job well done. Such failures may be attributed to fear of losing credibility with peers, forgetting to give credit to their subordinates, or failing to recognize that their employees' successful performance represents their success in getting the job done (McConnell 1995).

The supervisor must remember that subordinates will make some mistakes when challenged with new tasks (McConnell 1995). One purpose of delegation is to encourage employees to excel in the workplace while enriching their jobs; subordinates who are punished for mistakes will become adverse to delegated tasks, perhaps perceiving that they are being "set up for another failure." Other employees too will become averse to increased or delegated responsibilities. Experimentation as the result of delegation will inevitably lead to errors. These mistakes will serve as a learning tool for the entire organization.

In some situations, supervisors overdelegate. Delegating responsibilities to employees who lack the knowledge, skills, and abilities or delegating too much work to some employees who cannot complete it in a timely manner is destructive. These delegation failures could lead to poor performance evaluations, increased levels of frustration, and perhaps an increased turnover rate in the company. In short, supervisors need to ensure a proper match between delegated responsibilities and the employee.

Communicating

Have you ever had a supervisor ask how you are doing and keep walking by, failing to acknowledge you? Have you ever received a written memo or verbal request that you did not understand? Supervision is a people profession, and communication is the most professional tool one can have. Effective communication skills are the lifeblood of an effective supervisor. Employees want to be informed, listened to, and valued. They also want clear expectations and guidance. In one study that asked students to rate the most important competency skills for safety managers, the highest-rated competency was communicating effectively, followed by active listening (Blair 1999).

Supervisors have a variety of communication mediums at their disposal: written forms of communication, such as memos and formal letters; electronic methods, such as e-mail; and other technological-based forms of communication, such as cellular phones and radio communication devices. Regardless of the medium, supervisors need to ensure that their communications are sent and acknowledged correctly by the receivers of the messages.

As the role of supervisor implies direct contact with employees, one of the most common and essential means of communication is a verbal exchange. Effective verbal communication is complex and can be considered an art involving a series of steps and actors. Figure 3–1 shows an effective communication model.

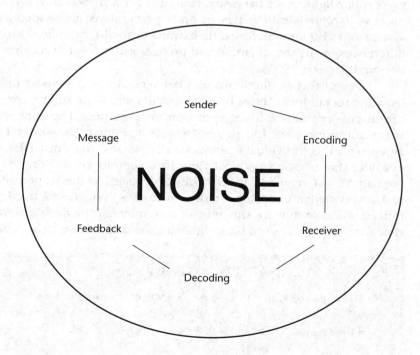

Sender

Message   Encoding

NOISE

Feedback   Receiver

Decoding

FIGURE 3–1 ■ **Effective Communication Model**

The communication process begins with a message that is communicated by a sender to a receiver. This sender must encode the message by selecting the right words to make sure that the receiver understands the message. The message receiver must then decode the message. The sender must then verify through feedback that the message was received and was the same one that was sent (Buhler 1992).

Effective communications is a two-way street; the sender needs to make sure that the receiver understands what has been communicated. As Figure 3–1 shows, communicating well with subordinates comes down to an interaction between what the supervisor thinks was said and what the subordinate heard. However, this is often a missed or overlooked step in the communication process. One way to correct this issue is to ensure that a feedback loop is used. This feedback loop includes paraphrasing what is said, asking clarifying questions, and having the receiver repeat the message. Supervisors should also avoid asking close-ended questions, such as "Is your project done?" The person may acknowledge understanding but may not want to admit not understanding the message. Instead, open-ended questions, such as "Can you tell me about how your project is coming along?" are more appropriate, because they require the receiver to provide a detailed response to the question.

Barriers to effective communication, or noise, can be thought of as anything that interferes in the communications process (Buhler 1992). These barriers may be physical, psychological, or semantic. Physical barriers, such as background noise, poor lighting, or excessive heat, distract a person in the communication process. Psychological barriers, or one's perceptions, are shaped by one's value system and assumptions. Semantic barriers deal with meanings, such as language differences or the use of jargon and professional terms the receiver may not understand (Umiker 1993).

Many of these communication barriers can be overcome by using active-listening techniques. Active listening occurs when the supervisor is engaged in the discussion. Active listening begins with respect. The supervisor must respect and appreciate the person who is speaking. The supervisor need not agree with this individual's points or perspective but must take the time and consider that person's point of view. If the employee is taking the time to discuss a point of view or concern, the supervisor has the responsibility to listen and acknowledge understanding the speaker's concerns. Active listening takes time. It will take time for the individual to transmit the message, and it will take time for the supervisor to thoroughly understand what is being communicated.

KEY ASPECTS OF ACTIVE LISTENING

- **Listen for Feelings**   Because the majority of information sent is nonverbal, the real message can be understood only if the underlying feelings are brought out in the open.

- **Respond to Feelings** Instead of acting defensively toward a person's feelings of frustration or anger, give that person permission to express those feelings. Instead of an act of confrontation, this is an act of support.

- **Engage in Paraphrasing** Restating in another form what the person just said will give the person additional encouragement to express feelings and let the person know that you have received the message. Paraphrasing elicits more information from the person.

- **Ask Questions** Asking open-ended and exploratory questions helps speakers get in touch with their thoughts and feelings and provides more information to the listener.

- **Give Your Undivided Attention** The speaker needs to feel that the listener cares about what is being said and cares about the speaker as a person. Supervisors should remove distractions or ignore ones that cannot be removed.

Adapted from Cousins (1996).

Supervisors need to consider their body language in the communication process. The encoding process is not limited to words alone. The majority of face-to-face communication is nonverbal and may comprise up to 70 percent of what is said (Birdwhistell 1970). Body language is the external expression of one's internal thoughts and feelings. For example, facial expressions and other forms of body language may be a more honest assessment of what the person is truly thinking. Body language also includes one's physical posture, hand gestures, and eye movements. It can either enhance or confuse an intended meaning of the verbal message (Chambers 1996). Suppose, for example, that when an employee makes a comment, the supervisor steps back with his or her arms crossed. The employee could interpret this "language" as a defensive or uninterested response. Some of the ways to address this concern are by using nonverbal attending microskills, as discussed in Chapter 8.

Effective communication also occurs through meetings. Supervision meetings should be used and scheduled regularly, in advance. These meetings, depending on their content and purpose, can be group or individual oriented. The meeting schedule should be mutually comfortable for both parties, not just the supervisor. For example, if subordinates are given a deadline to a get specific task done and a supervisor schedules a meeting just before the deadline, subordinates may perceive that the supervisor is not being considerate of their needs and time. The agenda, or content, of the meeting must be prepared in advance. The agenda will serve to make sure that no issues are neglected, will ensure a more productive task-oriented meeting, and will improve time management during the meeting by inhibiting numerous single-item discussions on topics that can wait until after the meeting. The content of the meeting can incorporate some banter or ice breaking, but the content must be productive and beneficial for all the parties (Anshel 1992). This means that the supervisor must come prepared for the meeting and have those skills necessary to conduct it.

Influencing

Another determinant of a supervisor's effectiveness is the ability to influence others to achieve organizational objectives. Supervisors can influence three groups of individuals: subordinates, peers, and supervisors. Although this chapter has addressed the supervisor's downward influence, supervisors also have upward influence in the organization. Upward influence is the supervisor's behavior directed at maintaining good rapport with the manager so that the latter will act favorably on behalf of the members of the work unit (Fulk and Wendler 1982). Horizontal influence, by contrast, deals with a supervisor's ability to get along with and influence other supervisors in the organization to achieve organizational goals and outcomes.

Research by Yukl and Tracey (1992) has found that supervisors can use nine influence tactics. These tactics are shown in Box 3–3.

The most effective influence tactics were found to be consultation, inspirational appeal, and rational persuasion. These tactics were also found to be socially acceptable for trying to influence groups. Socially undesirable and ineffective influence tactics could make the target become resentful or angry with the supervisor. These include efforts to coerce or manipulate through pressure, coalition, and legitimating, regardless of the target group.

BOX 3–3 ■ Influence Tactics

Tactic	Definition
Coalition	The person seeks the assistance of others to persuade you to do something. The person may also use the support of others as a reason for you to agree.
Consultation	The person requests your participation in planning a strategy, activity, or change for which your support and assistance are desired. The person may also be willing to modify a proposal to address your concerns and suggestions.
Exchange	The person offers an exchange of favors, indicates a willingness to reciprocate at a later time, or promises you a share of the benefits if you help accomplish the task.
Ingratiation	The person seeks to gain your favor before asking you to do something.

Inspirational appeal	The person makes a request or a proposal that arouses enthusiasm by appealing to your values, ideals, and aspirations or by increasing your confidence that you can do it.
Legitimating	The person seeks to establish the legitimacy of a request by claiming the authority or right to make it or by verifying that it is consistent with organizational policies, rules, practices, or traditions.
Personal appeal	The person appeals to your feelings of loyalty before asking you to do something
Pressure	The person uses demands, threats, or persistent reminders to influence you to do something.
Rational persuasion	The person uses logical arguments and factual evidence to persuade you that a proposal or request is viable and likely to result in the attainment of task objectives.

Adapted from Yukl and Tracey (1992).

The effectiveness of some tactics was also found to vary among groups. Ingratiation and exchange were found to be moderately effective for influencing subordinates and peers but not effective for influencing superiors. Inspirational appeal, ingratiation, and pressure were used most often in a downward direction, whereas personal appeal, exchange, and legitimating were used laterally, or among peers. Coalitions and rational persuasion were also found to be used in upward directions to influence superiors.

Maintaining an Ethical Climate

Supervisors have a significant impact on organizational climate and behavior, including its ethical climate. An ethical climate exists when organization members have stable, psychologically meaningful perceptions about ethical policies and procedures in the organization. A theoretical basis for an ethical climate is based on the premise that a supervisor's behaviors provide a foundation for and shape how employees will act in the organization (Wimbush, Shepard, and Markham 1997).

Workers and supervisors engage in shared perceptions of defining, learning, and evaluating each other's behaviors through shared events in their daily actions. The supervisor's verbal and nonverbal interactions then determine what is acceptable and unacceptable in the workplace (Wimbush and Shepard 1994). For example, a supervisor who is late but logs in for an earlier time and jokes that "it won't hurt anyone" has probably committed a violation of policy and procedure and definitely committed an unethical act. This act, unfortunately, could then be modeled by subordinates as an appropriate and acceptable but nevertheless unethical behavior.

The preceding example shows that supervisors give meaning to what is acceptable or unacceptable conduct in the workplace. Supervisors give meaning to the policies and practices of the organization by enforcing those policies in their own departments. Supervisors subsequently moderate the relationship between policies and procedures and the ethical climate in the workplace.

This process can be quite complicated. Each supervisor in an organization could have a different interpretation about what is important, which could lead to problems. When the supervisors have shared perceptions, the organization is said to have a collective ethical climate (Wimbush and Shepard 1994). What could make this situation even more complicated, however, is that each level in the organization may have a different ethical climate. Regardless of this point, some characteristics of ethical supervision are universal (see Box 3–4).

BOX 3–4 ■ Characteristics of Ethical Supervisors

- Looks out for the interests of employees and customers and considers the needs and rights of as many employees as possible when making a decision
- Commits to the ideals of honesty, quality work, and fair play
- Focuses on the ultimate objective or mission (the ends) more than rules and regulations (the means)
- Respects the "whole" person, not just the worker, including their religion, personal life, and out-of-work responsibilities
- Demands the same fair, objective standards from everyone
- Sticks with the major mission of the organization—quality, service, meeting the needs of the clients/customers—as a guide to decision making
- Considers employees' personal and professional needs, the needs of the minority and majority of workers, and the service side of the business, balanced with the profits side

Adapted from VanAuken (1992).

SUPERVISORY DEVELOPMENT

Employees are often promoted to supervisory positions because of their demonstrated competency related to the knowledge, skills, and abilities for specific activities they performed as line-level employees. Promotion based on merit, not seniority, is preferred; merit alone will not ensure supervisory success. This individual's new responsibility as a supervisor requires a different set of skills. Unfortunately, new supervisors are often underprepared for their new roles and responsibilities and may experience some confusion and frustration, leading to performance-related issues and a downward spiral of activities. For example, being uncomfortable with their work, new supervisors may revert to their former, comfortable, and secure roles performing the basic functions of a line-level production employee, which could lead to further role conflict and confusion among employees.

This raises the issue of whether the organization is properly developing its personnel for supervisory roles. Organizations need to recognize that the transition from employee to supervisor is not immediate. It is fraught with new challenges for the new supervisor and the organization alike. This will require effort from two directions. First, new supervisors must be willing to learn. Second, the organization must nurture and invest in supervisory-development activities. These activities could include mentoring in administrative responsibilities and requiring additional in-service training programs and external developmental training programs. For example, a company wanted to promote an individual, based on his performance. This individual was told in advance that he was being considered for promotion. A social contract was agreed on, and the employee was given the option of attending supervisory-development training programs at the company's expense. Based on this individual's development, he would then be considered for future promotional opportunities within the company.

■ SUPERVISORY PROBLEMS

Abusive Supervision

Often considered to be subjective and perhaps situation specific, abusive supervision "refers to subordinates' perceptions of the extent to which supervisors engage in the sustained display of hostile and verbal behaviors, excluding physical contact" (Tepper 2000, 178). Abusive supervision can also be characterized as sustained, or enduring, in the sense that it will continue until the employee terminates the relationship, the supervisor terminates the relationship, or the supervisor modifies his or her behavior.

Enduring abusive relationships have certain characteristics. Employees often feel powerless to take corrective action because they are economically dependent on the abuser. Further, the abuse is not constant but mixed in or interspersed with normal behaviors, reinforcing the employee's belief that it will end; in some cases, the employee will fear the unknown associated with separation more than the abuse (Tepper 2000). Another problem with abusive supervision is that employees may perceive and subsequently react differently to that abuse.

Abusive supervision can also be thought of as petty tyranny. Research by Ashforth (1994) narrowed petty tyranny at work into six dimensional categories. The behaviors are:

- self-aggrandizing (administering company policies and rules in an arbitrary manner and "playing favorites" among employees)
- belittling subordinates

- demonstrating a lack of consideration for employees
- forcing and demanding others to take the manager's point of view
- discouraging subordinates from taking initiative on decision-making and work activities
- reprimanding and punishing employees for no apparent reason, even when they are performing well

Petty tyranny exists for several reasons. In some organizations, these behaviors, although not actively promoted, may reflect institutionalized values and norms that facilitate the emergence of such actions. This may be the case if the organization has an overriding concern for compliance. For example, in basic military training, recruits, under the control of drill sergeants, were traditionally subjected to verbal and physical abuse to seek their total compliance. Abusive supervision may also exist in organizations concerned with standardized and formalized operating tasks and emphasizing compliance with centralized conditions. In addition, Ashforth (1994) found that individuals who perceive themselves as relatively powerless often "lord" what power they do have over their subordinates to enhance their own self-perceptions of superiority and to affirm the legitimacy of their hierarchical control.

The impact of petty tyranny can be serious on an organization, leading to a vicious circle in which supervisors attribute subordinates' successes to themselves rather than to the subordinates, develop an inflated sense of self-worth, prefer more psychological distance from subordinates, and view the employees as objects to be manipulated. Petty tyranny may undermine employees' self-esteem, increase their sense of helplessness, and alienate them at work. In addition, petty tyranny may undermine social solidarity in the workplace and increase individuals' frustration and stress levels. The end result of these problems will be lower productivity in the workplace (Ashforth).

Research by Zellars, Tepper, and Duffy (2002) has shown that abused subordinates perform fewer organizational citizenship behaviors (OCBs): being courteous to other employees, not complaining about the company to outsiders, and not complaining about trivial problems or concerns that arise. OCBs are discretionary actions that promote organizational effectiveness. They are also behaviors or actions that, if not used by employees, are often not punishable. Actions that run counter to OCBs can be thought of as low-intensity forms of revenge against the company or its representatives.

Research by Tepper, Duffy, and Shaw (2001) found that employees respond in two distinct ways—constructive and dysfunctional—to the abusive supervisor. Constructive responses are employee activities that attempt to open a dialogue with the supervisor in an effort to resolve a misunderstanding or to clarify responsibilities. These constructive and genuine responses may include asking a supervisor for clarification on an issue or negotiating with the supervisor. Such responses are nonconflictive messages of nonconformity. Dysfunctional resistance strategies, on the other hand, are passive-aggressive responses that satisfy the employee's need for redress. With these types of activities, it cannot be proved that employee is retaliating against the supervisor. But the employee may purposefully "forget" to do a task, procrastinate, or perhaps act as if they did not hear the supervisor's requests. Because these dysfunctional resistance techniques question and threaten a supervisor's authority, they can lead to further conflict between supervisor and employee and among other employees, who may be called on to complete or perform the work.

Problem Employees

For the purpose of this chapter, problem employees are those having work-related or personal problems that impact their productivity and effectiveness in the workplace through the display of unacceptable behaviors. A supervisor can deal with problem employees in two primary ways. The first is to address issues during the performance appraisal or on a daily basis. This second way is a continual process whereby the employee receives immediate feedback instead of a delayed confrontation, which would be the case in a formal quarterly or annual review process (Balser and Stern 1999). In short, dealing with performance problems is a formal and informal negotiation process and can be ongoing.

One subject of debate is the extent of supervisory involvement in intervening with troubled workers. One perspective is that the supervisor's role should be limited to detecting and documenting inadequate job performance—a proxy measure that the employee is having problems. Another point of view, based on the assumption that supervisors are in positions of leadership because of their positions or jobs, is that workers look at supervisors as a helping resource. According to this perspective, supervisors are more social service than control agents and should have some degree of involvement in assisting troubled workers. At a minimum, for example, the supervisor should encourage such workers to use company resources such as the Employee Assistance Program (EAP) or an appropriate community resource (Hopkins 1997).

Informal discussions between supervisors and employees are critical to remedying poor performance. This informal exchange is the area for negotiating and defining expectations, evaluations, and remedies of employee job performance. It is also a way for supervisors and employees to resist or conform to prescribed organizational roles. Balser and Stern (1999) developed a classification model from their research on how supervisors respond to conflict and interact in performance issues. This classification scheme is shown in Figure 3–2.

Supervisors in the conformist category are willing to engage in direct conflict with employees. Conformist employees, by contrast, are more cooperative and are not willing to engage in conflict over the issue. In these types of interactions, supervisors take the lead about the issue and believe that the employee conforms to the supervisor's position on the issue. In confrontational dyads, both parties are willing to engage in conflict over desired behaviors. In this category, employees are willing to engage in and show resistance over the issue at hand. Characteristics of this dyad are expressed conflict, employee resistance, tolerance, and, ultimately, cooperation and issue resolution. In both the conformist and confrontational dyads, supervisors

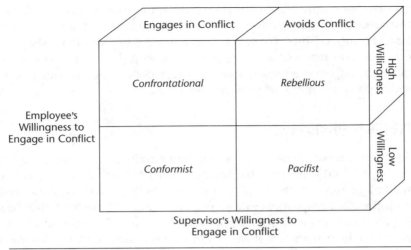

Adapted from Balser and Stern (1999).

FIGURE 3–2 ■ Classification of Supervisor/Employee Conflict Interactions

and employees participate in the account exchange. Account exchange occurs when the supervisor and the employee exchange their own accounts of the situation. When the two accounts are similar, cooperation occurs. When the two accounts differ, resistance occurs (Balser and Stern 1999).

In rebellious dyads, supervisors fail to recognize employee behaviors as signs of poor performance. Such supervisors also tolerated or excused employee behavior without setting effective limits on the poor performance. Supervisors in this category also deferred confrontation over the issue. In the pacifist category, supervisors do not exert their authority, and employees do not attempt to redefine their performance (Balser and Stern 1999).

One of the most important elements of this model is the speed at which supervisors should address problem behaviors. An effective supervisor needs to address issues immediately. In the rebellious dyad, for example, supervisors eventually did express conflict but perceived that the employees resisted supervisory efforts to address the issue(s). This perception could be attributed to the fact that the employees took their behaviors for granted and regarded them as acceptable because they became ingrained or habitual. When ultimately confronted about their behaviors, however, the employees displayed the highest levels of resistance of the four dyads, based on the perceived "correctness" of their behavior, as they were habituated and not immediately addressed as a concern when they occurred (Balser and Stern 1999).

Regardless of the confrontational style, perhaps one of the greatest errors a supervisor can make when dealing with a problem employee is to become emotionally involved in the issue. Regardless of the situation, supervisors must remain objective and unemotional. When a supervisor becomes angry, the employee and other employees could interpret the supervisor's behavior as having lost control of the situation. Having lost complete control of the situation, the only "tool" the supervisor has left to use is a primitive emotional response: anger or rage.

Supervisors are often the only people employees trust in the organization and to whom they turn when they have personal problems. Although some organizations have Employee Assistance Programs that the supervisor can refer employees to, the supervisor must still deal with the immediate and pressing problem, regardless of whether expert assistance is available somewhere in the company. If the company does not have an EAP, a supervisor is not exempt from attempting to provide assistance to employees.

Although the level and degree of assistance may vary from company to company, supervisors must, at a minimum, be trained as referral agents. A referral agent is not a counselor. Supervisors are not generally trained in counseling skills but can receive training on where to refer employees who have personal problems. If and when these employees do have personal problems, the supervisor can readily send them to professional-based programs that have the expertise and time to effectively deal with the employees' needs and concerns.

When an employee approaches a supervisor about a personal issue, one key consideration is confidentiality. The employee has placed a great deal of trust in approaching the supervisor with a personal issue, and confidentiality must be maintained. In short, a supervisor who is told personal information that does not impact the organization should keep it confidential. Although some supervisors may think it appropriate to talk with other supervisors and managers about the issue, the motto maintained by the Hell's Angels motorcycle gang comes into play: "Three can keep a secret when two are dead."

One exception, however, is when a personal issue may have an impact on the organization. Suppose that an employee is receiving threats from a coworker. This issue is both personal and organizational. In these situations, supervisors must clearly notify the employee that because it can directly impact the organization, the issue cannot remain completely confidential.

Employees may resist the supervisor's legitimate requests. Explanations could range from difficulty with authority to low self-esteem to personal insecurities. Other explanations may be related to the employee's unmet expectations at the workplace, problems with a previous supervisor, responsibilities, and degree of autonomy and authority.

Although the explanations may be numerous, Anshel (1992) suggests that resistance to supervision can be reduced by considering the following points.

1. Supervisors need to communicate the need for a certain degree of worker independence.
2. Employees should be given a sense of freedom to make mistakes and take risks without painful repercussion.
3. Supervisors need to reinforce the employee's responsibility to set and meet performance goals.
4. In praising employees for their performance, supervisors need to explain the reasons behind the praise.

■ CONCLUSION

One of a supervisor's primary responsibilities is to supervise a specific number or group of employees to ensure that they are successful in carrying out the organization's goals or objectives. An effective supervisory relationship is one in which the supervisor can train, guide, and encourage subordinates' development. One of the most critical elements is to develop an effective supervisory relationship built on trust and respect.

Taking a supervisory role requires one to assume significant types of responsibilities and decision-making authority. A primary responsibility is establishing a degree of control over production processes and employees. Although the level of control varies among organizations, owing in part to their underlying philosophies, supervisors need to establish and regulate the degree of autonomy that is given to employees. Supervisors also need to define the subordinates' responsibilities while monitoring their performance. Effective delegation is also a key determinant of supervisory success. The successful supervisor must delegate whole, meaningful tasks to employees and must also deal with problem employees in a timely and professional manner.

Effective communication is the key to successful supervision. Engaging in active listening will ensure that all the subordinates understand the supervisor's directions.

The communication process includes using one's upward, downward, and horizontal influence to achieve organizational objectives. Effective supervisors maintain an ethical climate in the organization. Supervisors should serve as role models for ethical behaviors in the workplace. All these traits will require the organization to recognize that supervisors are not created overnight, calling for effective supervisory development programs in the company. If not, the result may be abusive supervisors, an outcome that will have serious, detrimental effects on employees and the success of the organization.

■ KEY TERMS

Active listening	Leader-member exchange (LMX)
Affective commitment	Leadership
Autonomy	Monitoring
Benevolence	Noise
Body language	Normative commitment
Continuance commitment	Objective credibility
Control	Oversight
Delegation	Petty tyranny
Global self-esteem	Self-respect
Identification	Span of control
Influence	Span of support
Internalization	Supervision
Job breadth	Trust

■ DISCUSSION QUESTIONS

1. Define the leader-member exchange theory. What are some types of leader-member relationships? Which of the dyads are the most effective, and why?
2. What are the three bases of commitment? Based on your employment experiences, which type of commitment have you displayed?
3. At what two levels does commitment occur?
4. What are some characteristics a supervisor should have in order to build trust?
5. What is the difference between span of control and span of support? What three factors impact one's span of control?
6. What is the OSTTI? What are the key components of this model?
7. What are some ways to ensure the successful delegation of tasks?
8. What are some delegation failures? How will delegation failure impact the supervisor and the organization?
9. Explain the communication process. What are some barriers to effective communication? How can supervisors prevent communication problems?
10. What are some influence tactics a supervisor can use? Which are the most effective, and why? Provide an example of a positive influence tactic.
11. What are some traits of an abusive supervisor?
12. What are some ways a supervisor can deal with a problem employee? Which method has been found to be the most effective?

■ REFERENCES

AFHOLDERBACH, S. E. 1998. Supervisory techniques: A supervisor's perspective. *Supervision* 59 (6): 11–13.

ANSHEL, M. H. 1992. Cognitive-behavioral strategies: Effective staff supervisory meetings and performance evaluation. *Journal of Managerial Psychology* 7 (6): 11–16.

ASHFORTH, B. 1994. Petty tyranny in organizations. *Human Relations* 47 (7): 755–778.

BALSER, D. B. and R. N. STERN. 1999. Resistance and cooperation: A response to conflict over job performance. *Human Relations* 52 (8): 1029–1053.

BAUER, T. N., and S. G. GREEN. 1996. Development of leader-member exchange: A longitudinal test. *Academy of Management Journal* 39 (6): 1538–1567.

BECKER, T. E. 1992. Foci and bases of commitment: Are they distinctions worth making? *Academy of Management Journal* 35 (91): 232–244.

BECKER, T. E. and R. S. BILLINGS. 1993. Profiles of commitment: An empirical test. *Journal of Organizational Behavior* 14 (2): 177–191.

BIRDWHISTELL, R. 1970. *Kinesics and context: Essays on body motion communication:* Philadelphia: University of Pennsylvania Press.

BLAIR, E. H. 1999. Which competencies are most important for safety managers? *Professional Safety* 44 (1): 28–32.

BUHLER, P. 1995. Leaders vs. managers. *Supervision* 56 (5): 24–25.

CHAMBERS, D. 1996. Police-defendants: Surviving a civil suit. *FBI Law Enforcement Bulletin* 65: 34–39.

CHEN, Z. X., A. S. TSUI, and J. L. FARH. 2002. Loyalty to supervisor vs. organizational commitment: Relationship to employee performance in China. *Journal of Occupational and Organizational Psychology* 75 (3): 339–356.

CLUGSTON, M., J. P. HOWELL, and P. W. DORFMAN. 2000. Does cultural socialization predict multiple bases and foci of commitment? *Journal of Management* 26 (1): 5–30.

COUSINS, R. B. 1996. Active listening is more than hearing. *Supervision* 57 (12): 14–15.

DONEY, P. M. and J. P. CANNON. 1997. An examination of the nature of trust in buyer-seller relationships. *Journal of Marketing* 61 (2): 35–51.

ELLEMERS, N., D. DEGUILDER, and H. VAN DEN HEUVEL. 1998. Career-oriented versus team-oriented commitment and behavior at work. *Journal of Applied Psychology* 83 (5): 717–730.

ENGLE, E. M., and R. G. LORD. 1997. Implicit theories, self-schemas, and leader-member exchange. *Academy of Management Journal* 40 (4): 988–1010.

EVANS, T. J. 2003. Transitioning from superstar to superteam. *Supervision,* 64 (9) 12–13.

FULK, J., and E. R. WENDLER. 1982. Dimensionality of leader-subordinate interactions: A path-goal investigation. *Organizational Behavior and Human Performance* 30: 241–264.

GARDNER, D. G., and J. L. PÍERCE. 1998. Self-esteem and self-efficacy within the organizational context: An empirical examination. *Group organizational management* 23 (1) 48–70.

GERSTNER, C. R., and D. V. DAY. 1997. Meta-analytic review of leader-member exchange theory: Correlates and construct issues. *Journal of Applied Psychology* 82 (6): 827–844.

GITTELL, J. H. 2000. Paradox of coordination and control. *California Management Review* 42 (3): 101–117.

GLENDINNING, P. M. 2002. Performance management: Pariah or messiah. *Public Personnel Management* 31 (2): 161–178.

GRAEN, G. B., and T. A. SCANDURA. 1987. Toward a psychology of dyadic organizing. In Staw, B. and L. L. Cummings, eds. *Research in Organizational Behavior* 9: 175–208. Greenwich, CT: JAI Press.

GREGERSEN, H. B. 1993. Multiple commitments to work and extra role behavior during three stages of organizational tenure. *Journal of Business Research* 26 (1): 31–48.

HERSCOVITCH, L., and J. P. MEYER. 2002. Commitment to organizational change: Extension of a three-component model. *Journal of Applied Psychology* 87 (3): 474–487.

HIGHTOWER, R. T. 2000. Manufacturing supervisors and conflicting demands: Determining supervisor behaviors that meet the expectations of the plant manager and employees. *Production and Inventory Management Journal* 41 (3): 24–30.

HOPKINS, K. M. 1997. Supervisor intervention with troubled workers: A social identity perspective. *Human Relations* 50 (10): 1215-1238.

KLIEMAN, R. S., J. A. QUINN, and K. L. HARRIS. 2000. The influence of employee-supervisor interactions upon job breadth. *Journal of Managerial Psychology* 15 (6): 587-605.

KO, J. W., J. L. PRICE, and C. W. MUELLER. 1997. Assessment of Meyer and Allen's three-component model of organizational commitment in South Korea. *Journal of Applied Psychology* 82 (6): 961-973.

KOMAKI, J. L. 1994. Emergence of the operant model of effective supervision or how an operant conditioner got hooked on leadership. *Leadership and Organizational Development Journal* 15 (5): 27-32.

KOMAKI, J. L., M. L. DESSELLES, and E. D. BOWMAN. 1989. Definitely not a breeze. Extending an operant model of effective supervision to teams. *Journal of Applied Psychology* 74 (3): 522-529.

LEANA, C. R. 1987. Power relinquishment versus power sharing: Theoretical clarification and empirical comparison of delegation and participation. *Journal of Applied Psychology* 72: 228-233.

LEE, D. S., and N. J. CAYER. 1994. *Supervision for success in government.* San Francisco: Jossey-Bass.

MASTERSON, S. S., B. M. LEWIS, and M. S. TAYLOR 2000. Integrating justice and social exchange: The differing effects of fair procedures and treatment on work relationships. *Academy of Management Journal* 43 (4): 738-748.

MCCONNELL, C. R. 1995. Delegation versus empowerment: What, how, and is there a difference? *Health Care Supervisor* 14 (1): 69-79.

MCGRATH, R. G. 2001. Exploratory learning, innovative capacity, and managerial oversight. *Academy of Management Journal* 44 (1): 118-131.

MCMANUS, K. 1995. Acquiring knowledge and skills for twenty-first century supervision. *Management Development Review* 8 (5): 18-22.

MEIER, K. M., and J. BOHTE. 2003. Span of control and public organizations: Implementing Gulick's research design. *Public Administration Review* 63 (1): 61-79.

MEYER, J. P., and N. J. ALLEN. 1991. A three-component conceptualization of organizational commitment. *Human Resources Management Review* 1: 61-89.

NEWSTROM, J., D. GARDNER, and J. PEIRCE. 1999. A neglected supervisory role: building self-esteem at work. *SuperVision* 60 (2): 9-12.

PAINTER, C. 1995. Effective supervision for the new supervisor. *SuperVision* 56 (8): 3-5.

PARKER, S. K., C. M. TURNER, and N. TURNER. 2000. Designing a safer workplace: Importance of job autonomy, communication quality, and supportive supervisors. *Journal of Occupational Health Psychology* 6 (3): 211-228.

RAM, M. 1999. Managing autonomy: Employment relations in small professional service firms. *International Small Business Journal* 17 (2): 13-30.

RAMSEY, R. D. 1999. The "snoopervision" debate: Employer interests vs. employee privacy. *SuperVision* 60 (8): 3-5.

ROTHSTEIN, D. S. 2001. Supervisory status and upper-level supervisory responsibilities: Evidence from NLSY79. *Industrial and Labor Relations Review* 54 (3): 663–680.

SETTOON, R. P., N. BENNETT, and R. C. LIDEN. 1996. Social exchange in organizations: The differential effects of perceived organizational support and leader-member exchange. *Journal of Applied Psychology* 82 (3): 219–227.

SHEEHAN R., and G. W. CORDNER. 1989. Introduction to police administration. Cincinnati: Anderson.

SHERONY, K. M., and S. G. GREEN. 2002. Coworker exchange relationships between coworkers, leader-member exchange, and work attitudes. *Journal of Applied Psychology* 87 (3): 542–548.

SPARROWE, R. T., and R. C. LIDEN. 1997. Process structure in leader-member exchange. *Academy of Management Review* 22 (2): 522–552.

TEPPER, B. J. 2000. Consequences of abusive supervision. *Academy of Management Journal* 43 (2): 178–190.

TEPPER, B. J., M. K. DUFFY, and J. D. SHAW. 2001. Personality moderators of the relationship between abusive supervision and subordinate's resistance. *Journal of Applied Psychology* 86 (5): 974–983.

TOWNSEND, J., J. S. PHILLIPS and T. J. ELKINS. 2000. Employee retaliation: The neglected consequence of poor leader-member exchange relations. *Journal of Occupational Health Psychology* 5 (4): 457–463.

TRACEY, T. J., and P. SHERRY. 1993. Complementary interaction over time in successful and less successful supervision. *Professional Psychology: Research and Practice* 24 (3): 304–311.

UMIKER, W. 1993. Powerful communication skills: The key to prevention and resolution of personnel problems. *Health Care Supervisor* 11 (3): 30.

VANAUKEN, P. M. 1992. Being an ethical supervisor. *Supervisory Management* 37 (10): 3–4.

WEICK, K. E. and K. H. ROBERTS. 1993. Collective mind in organizations: Heedful interrelating on flight decks. *Administrative Science Quarterly* 38: 357–381.

WIMBUSH, J. C., and J. M. SHEPARD. 1994. Toward an understanding of ethical climate: Its relationship to ethical behavior and supervisory influence. *Journal of Business Ethics* 13 (8): 637–647.

WIMBUSH, J. C., J. M. SHEPARD, and S. E. MARKHAM. 1997. An empirical examination of the relationship between ethical climate and ethical behavior from multiple levels of analysis. *Journal of Business Ethics* 16 (16): 1705–1716.

YUKL, G. 1998. Leadership in organizations. 4th ed. Englewood Cliffs, NJ: Prentice Hall.

YUKL, G., and J. B. TRACEY. 1992. Consequences of influence tactics used with subordinates, peers, and the boss. *Journal of Applied Psychology* 77 (4): 525–535.

YRIE, A. C., S. HARTMAN, and W. P. GALLE. 2002. An investigation of relationships between communication style and leader-member exchange. *Journal of Communication Management* 6 (3): 257–268.

ZELLARS, K. L., B. J. TEPPER, and M. K. DUFFY. 2002. Abusive supervision and subordinates' organizational citizenship behavior. *Journal of Applied Psychology* 87 (6): 1068–1076.

chapter four

Planning and Decision Making

A plan is like a road map. It tells us where we are and provides us with a direction for where we want to go. We can reach our destination in a variety of ways. This requires the navigator to decide which route would be the best to reach the objective. We need both the road map and good decisions in order to reach our goals in the workplace. We need effective planning and decision making.

In the business world, we can see the outcomes of effective planning and decision making. Crainer (1999) identifies some of the best and worst managerial decisions ever made. Following are some of the best decisions.

- Henry Ford's decision in 1903 to produce vehicles created a mass market for automobiles, started a new industry, and revolutionized industrial production.
- Michael Dell decided to sell built-to-order PCs directly to customers, making his company one of the largest online computer sellers in the world.
- Richard Sears' decision to start a mail-order catalog opened up a new market—rural America—for his products.
- A kitchen equipment salesman was impressed by a fast-food chain owned by Dick and Maurice McDonald. In 1954, Ray Kroc purchased the rights to the brothers' franchise for $2.7 million. In 2003, McDonald's Corporation generated more than $3 billion from its operations.

Following are some of the worst decisions ever made.

- Apple Computers' decision not to license its Mac operating system, and subsequently not allowing its products to be cloned, resulted in IBM clones' domination of the PC market.
- Charles Goodyear, who developed the process of vulcanization for rubber, did not register patents and was generally considered a poor businessman. He made little money off his inventions, lived in poverty, and at his death, was $200,000 in debt.
- In 1899, the bottling rights for Coca-Cola were sold for $1. It was assumed that the drink would be sold only at soda fountains. Today it is one of the world's leading beverage manufacturers.

As in the preceding examples, new opportunities in the security industry share the common feature of uncertainty. In this fast-moving world of uncertainty, managers need to be effective planners and decision makers. For without the ability to effectively plan and act on those plans through effective decision processes, organizations could lose potential market share and their ability to meet the needs of their constituents, becoming an example of poor decision making.

■ OVERVIEW OF PLANNING

Planning bridges the gap between where we are now and where we want to be. As pointed out by Korey (1995, 46), "planning includes identifying and solving problems, exploring and determining the best ways and means of attaining established objectives; arranging in sequence and scheduling all significant activities that have to be carried out by the institutions; providing adequate resources, personnel and facilities; maintaining effective coordination, and establishing necessary controls." Planning also means assessing our desired objectives, anticipating problems, and developing solutions. It requires practical thinking in order to "isolate, determine and schedule the actions and achievements required to attain our objectives. It is the formulation and development of the blueprints we expect to follow" (Korey 1995, 44).

Hudzik and Cordner (1983) state that planning is a fundamental managerial activity to the point that the terms "management" and "planning" should be considered simultaneously. They assert that planning should be the first step in the managerial process, preceding such other managerial activities as organizing, staffing, directing, coordinating, reporting, and budgeting. Planning also involves designing a work plan that "specifies (1) what events and actions are necessary, (2) when they must take place, (3) who is to be involved in each action and for how long, and (4) how the various actions will interlock with one another" (p. 24).

The need for planning emanates from discovery of an existing or anticipated problem. Planning takes place in advance of an action and is used as a tool for predicting the future while at the same time attempting to control and influence future events in an organization. For example, an article about the increase in the theft of trade secrets may inspire a manager to review existing security measures. Based on the review of the company's existing practices, new policies are written and key employees trained on ways to prevent the theft of trade secrets. Because planning discovers problems and proposes ways to deal with them, it can also be considered a problem-solving tool for managers and organizations.

The functions of planning are broad, can be general or specific, and can be short- or long-term. Regardless of their functions, any realistic planning process includes four requirements. Planners must know what resources are at their disposal, understand the organization's past performance, have an accurate analysis of the present situation, and know the future goals of the organization (Korey 1995).

Any planning process entails four steps (Stoner and Freeman 1989):

1. *Establishing a goal or set of goals*—The first step in any planning process is to establish goals. In a broad sense, goals are what the organization needs or wants. Goals are necessary in order to ensure that the organization uses and commits its limited resources effectively.

2. *Defining the present situation*—Organizations need to understand their current situations before they can draw up plans for the future. In some situations, defining the present situation can be quite easy. For example, a company may want to return to profitability in the next fiscal year. In other cases, the present situation could be more complex or obscure, as would be the case in companies operating in highly competitive and rapidly changing markets.

3. *Determining or identifying aids and barriers*—Because planning is future oriented, organizations need to determine what factors can help them reach their goal(s) and what factors will cause problems.

4. *Developing a set of actions*—The final stage in the planning process involves developing alternative courses of action to achieve the goals, evaluating those courses of action, and choosing the most suitable alternative.

■ TYPES OF PLANNING

Strategic Planning

Strategic planning is the process for managing the future direction of the company "in relation to its environment and the demands of external stakeholders, including strategy formulation, analysis of agency strengths and weaknesses, identification of agency stakeholders, implementation of strategic actions and issue management" (Soonhee 2002, 237). An agency's strategy can be considered its direction to reach long-term objectives.

Strategic planning is a heavily used productivity-improvement tool that addresses issues or concerns that are fundamental to the nature of the organization. These long-range plans are concerned with innovation and organizational change (Hudzik and Cordner 1983). Strategic planning provides a direction for the company in the context of what it wants to do in the future. For example, one company in the business of private investigations decided to expand its operations into contractual security operations. This change would be considered strategic, as the fundamental nature of the organization changed from an investigative function to a contractual security provider, with investigations as a secondary service it could provide to clients.

Usually, strategic planning was reserved for top-level managers and executives in the organization. These types of plans are important to the company because of the scope of their impact or because of the long-term implications they have for the success of the organization. However, some feel that strategic planning is an oxymoron because of inherent problems in long-term planning (changes in the economy, market share, and so on). Many strategic plans are modified or completely changed soon after their implementation.

The basic model for any strategic plan involves five components, as shown in Figure 4–1 (Steiss 1985). The first component, basic research and

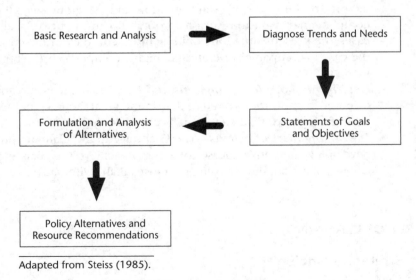

Adapted from Steiss (1985).

FIGURE 4–1　■　Components of the Strategic Management Process

analysis, involves a broad needs assessment and collection of data: an analysis of the internal and external environment and client groups and a determination of the planning horizon. In the next component, planners analyze micro- and macrolevel trends, facilities, and specific needs. In the third component, planners determine the desired state of the organization, based on the identified outcomes as established through research and analysis and identified trends and needs. Next, during formulation and analysis of alternatives, planners identify potential areas of conflicts and agreement, based on the identified objectives. This process serves as both an educational and a planning tool, as it increases the participants' level of awareness about changes that may take place in the organization. The final component of strategic planning involves translating the identified goals and objectives into general policies that the organization will follow. The explicit policies focus on the objectives (what is to be accomplished), priorities (when they are to be accomplished), where they are to be accomplished (the locus), means (how they will be accomplished), and standards for evaluating, or measuring, the goals and objectives.

Scenario-Based Planning

One specific planning tool a manager can use in strategic planning is scenario-based planning. Scenario planning is a futures-based planning tool designed to simplify a large amount of information into a series of possibilities, or alternatives, for consideration. This information is constructed into scenarios, or stories that will assist individuals in making effective decisions. These scenarios attempt to "capture the richness and range of possibilities, stimulating decision makers to consider changes they would otherwise ignore. At the same time it organizes those possibilities into narratives that are easier to grasp and use than great volumes of data . . . scenarios are aimed at challenging the prevailing mindset" (Shoemaker 1995, 27).

Scenario planning is designed to correct two common errors in decision making: underprediction and overprediction of issues. Scenario planning is accomplished by dividing one's knowledge into things that are known (the past) and things that uncertain and unknowable (the future). Although it encompasses an objective analysis of key issues, scenario planning, by its very nature, also includes subjective interpretations of future events.

An effective scenario-planning session involves a 10-step process, as listed in Box 4–1. Although scenario planning provides possible futures, not strategies, perhaps one of its greatest strengths is that it encourages diverse thinking. At the same time, it also provides for and builds a shared framework for strategic thinking in the organization (Shoemaker 1995).

BOX 4–1 ■ Steps in Scenario-Based Planning

1. **Identify the relevant issues by studying the past**, especially its sources of turmoil and change. In this stage, decision makers need to identify the time frame—for example, 10 years—and scope of analysis such as products and technologies.

2. **Identify the major stakeholders who have an interest or could influence or have an interest in the issues.** Stakeholders can include employees, customers, the government, and so forth.

3. **Identify the basic trends that will affect the issues identified in step 1.** Issues include but are not limited to social, technological, legal, and industry trends.

4. **Identify key uncertainties,** including events whose outcomes are uncertain but will significantly affect the issues that the organization is concerned with. With each uncertainty, the group should develop possible outcomes, such as, for example, increased security legislation passed or not passed at the federal level.

5. **Construct initial scenario themes.** After identifying the trends and uncertainties, planners can group initial scenario themes into extremes on a continuum from positive to negative "worlds" the organization may face.

6. **Check for consistency and plausibility.** In this stage, individuals need to check whether the trends in their "draft" scenarios are compatible with the time frame they chose and whether the scenarios combine outcomes of uncertainties that go together.

7. **Develop learning scenarios.** After the "draft" scenarios are checked for consistency and plausibility, general themes are identified, and then possible outcomes and trends are organized around them.

8. **Identify research needs.** At this stage, the planners may need to do further research to gain a better understanding of the trends and uncertainties that were identified.

9. **Develop quantitative models.** The development of formalized numerical-based models will help the organization quantify the consequences of the scenarios, such as determining the future compensation of employees by considering changes in inflation rates, GNP, and the size of the labor force—while assisting them from straying into unlikely scenarios.

10. **Evolve toward decision scenarios.** Now, the company needs to decide which learning scenarios, if any, are most appropriate, based on the issues that the company will face. These scenarios will then be used to generate new ideas and test company strategies. If no scenarios are found to be appropriate, planners should repeat the preceding steps.

Adapted from Shoemaker (1995).

Tactical Planning

Whereas a strategic plan tells individuals what to do, a tactical plan explains how individuals and the organization will achieve the strategic plan(s). Tactical plans translate the strategic objectives of the company into specific action plans and ensure that the various activities are aligned with the strategic goals of the company (Harbone 1999). Tactical plans have a shorter time horizon than do strategic plans and are concerned with the distribution of resources in the company to make sure that the organization's mission, as set forth in the strategic plan, is accomplished. Tactical planning is similar to operational planning, in which agency-wide operational plans are developed in a short-term context, such as one budget cycle. Tactical plans also include more detailed operating plans for specific units in the organization, one-shot plans designed to deal with a given situation, and standard operating procedures (Hudzik and Cordner 1983).

Contingency-Based Planning

A contingency plan is what an organization will follow in the event of a crisis. Contingency planning deals with the what-if issues the company may face in response to the issues, as well as unanticipated situations that may arise (Digman 1999). Contingency plans deal with disasters and isolated disruptions, such as power outages, in the organization.

Contingency plans are not limited to physical damage. Rather, they should look beyond the emergency and consider incidental damage. For example, United Airlines constructed a $3 million disaster-recovery site for its operations control center in 1999. Even before the complex was completed, a fire in its main operations center required United to use its new recovery site. It was estimated that without this recovery site, United would have been shut down for 2 to 3 weeks, with an operating loss of approximately $60 million per day (Steel 2000).

The preceding example shows how a contingency plan is beneficial for an organization. Creating contingency plans forces planners to think in terms of many possible outcomes rather than the most likely outcome and to prepare for the worst-case scenario, thereby improving the organization's ability to cope with and to eliminate complete surprises with unexpected developments. Contingency plans also reduce uncertainty, indecision, and delays when a situation occurs. At the same time, these plans allow individuals in the organization to respond rationally to unplanned events, playing through their reactions, which will subsequently reduce levels of panic and fear if or when a crisis situation does occur (Digman 1999).

The creation of strategic plans increases individual and organizational adaptiveness. Developing scenarios enables individuals to identify and to better understand the critical components of the business (Jordan 1999). However, contingency-based planning is not the same as scenario-based planning, which explores many uncertainties at a time instead of only one (Shoemaker 1995).

Many organizations do not have contingency plans. One study on contingency planning for IT functions concluded that attitudes toward risks were complacent. The primary reasons for not having plans were insufficient resources and low priority (Jordan 1999). Organizations need to establish these plans. These plans should be creative; planners should "think outside the box" when anticipating unexpected situations. At the same time, however, a contingency plan should not become a "fantasy document." According to Clarke (1999), some organizations become overconfident and presumptuous in their contingency planning. As a consequence, the plans become unrealistic in addressing the identified emergency situation. Therefore, planning simply becomes rhetoric that is directed toward outside audiences that need to be reassured about safety concerns.

■ MODELS OF PLANNING

Rational/Comprehensive Planning

This theory of planning is the traditional approach. Under this model, problem solvers consider all alternatives and outcomes to an issue. Following the identification of goals and objectives, the planners explore all options, choosing the best alternative identified. Although the most commonly used planning process, this approach is considered by some to be unrealistic and an oversimplified process for solving issues, as individuals cannot possibly know all the alternatives to a problem (Ross and Leigh 2000). This type of planning was traditionally a top-down centralized approach, with analysis limited to technical considerations, including economic forecasting, budgetary planning, and personnel allocation.

Transactive Planning   Transactive planning is a situation-specific technique that draws together through face-to-face interactions those who will be directly affected by the plan(s). This participatory process involves mutual learning; the transactive planners, who can be best thought of as small-group facilitators, meet with usually no more than 20 people to explore and discuss issues related to a plan. This type of planning is desirable when experiential-based knowledge is more important than technical knowledge, but it is not recommended when the stakeholders or beneficiaries are difficult to define or are inaccessible to the planners (Alexander 1994).

In redesigning a security program for a local school system, the planners used transactive planning. Key individuals who would be affected by the proposed transition from a contractual to a proprietary security department were included in the planning meetings. Among these individuals were the facilities director, the head of the school system's budget and finance department, principals from the affected schools, the director of school safety, and representatives from the school board. Based on open and candid discussions, members of this group shared their concerns and views of the future of the security program in their school district. This process provided a solid foundation and ideas on which to base the new security program.

Advocacy Planning   Advocacy planning is seen in planning activities for social policy. It takes the position that some groups that may be affected by the outcomes of planning have been traditionally excluded or underrepresented in the planning process and argues that the planning process should be more democratic. The key to advocacy planning is the concept of pluralism, which recommends that the plans be created by community organizations and individuals who have multiple concerns and viewpoints, rather than by a technical or centralized staff of planners. This type of planning generates a greater range of alternatives, and the process may also generate higher-quality plans than a traditional, centralized planning process (Ross and Leigh 2000).

■ DECISION MAKING

Decision making is an important aspect of the planning process. A decision is a choice that a person or a group makes when faced with a set of alternatives. Decision making is that process of identifying, evaluating, and selecting alternatives to solve a specific issue.

Decision making can be a complex activity for many organizations. Downs (1967) reveals that the more often a bureau encounters the same circumstances, the more likely it is to have developed rules that govern the behaviors of the employees, as it has precedents on which to base rules. This bureaucratic phenomenon subsequently limits the nature and the extent of the worker's ability to make decisions, reserving the true decisions for high-level executives. At the same time, the more an organization faces unpredictable situations, the less likely it is to have formalized rules governing what should be done.

As a consequence of these unpredictable situations, with no guidelines on how to act, an individual's capacity to make decisions may be impaired because of the lack of experience in making decisions in stable bureaucratic environments. Many security organizations may be encountering this situation in contemporary society. Encountering these unpredictable situations is a challenge facing security organizations. To properly address them, all individuals in the organization—from top management to line-level employees—must have a comprehensive understanding of the decision-making process.

Simon (1960), suggests that decision making encompass three principal phases: finding occasions for making a decision, finding possible courses of action, and choosing among those courses of action. Decisions can also exist on a continuum. At one end are programmed decisions, which can be considered repetitive, or routine. A definite procedure has been worked out so that when a manager encounters these types of situations, they are not treated as a new problem. For example, employees and managers who need to order replacement parts and supplies have done this habitual and repetitive activity many times before, so the issue and solutions to the issue are not new or novel.

At the other end of the continuum are the nonprogrammed decisions. These problems are new, unstructured, and consequential. There is no standardized method or procedure for handling these types of problems, because they have not happened before or because the problem is complex. The 9/11 attacks on the World Trade Center led to nonprogrammed decisions. Emergency service personnel had never had to respond to a terrorist attack involving airplanes striking large structures and then cope with and then address the collapse of the buildings.

The Rational Decision-Making Model

The classical approach to decision theory, this model "attempts to prescribe, on the basis of some rather precise assumptions, the conditions under which managers should make decisions in formal organizations" (Harrison 1993, 29). This model has a clearly defined process that consists of four sequential steps: defining the problem, diagnosing the causes, designing possible solutions, and deciding which solution to the problem is best. This process can best be understood as a "thinking-first" model of decision making (Mintzberg and Westley 2001).

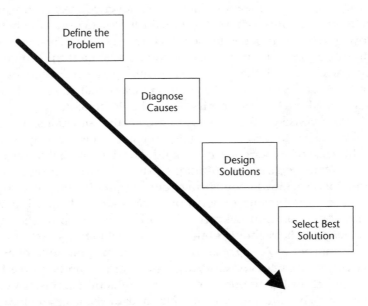

FIGURE 4–2 ▪ The Rational Decision-Making Model

This traditional decision-making model assumes that the decision maker is aware of all the available options, or courses of action. Based on a comprehensive and exhaustive understanding of the issue and alternatives, the decision maker can choose the option that maximizes the value of that decision (Vecchio 1988).

The rational model also assumes that the decision maker must meet two principal requirements, or axioms.

1. Based on the available options, the decision maker is able to select the best plan available that will provide the highest positive utility, or payout, for the organization. This is known as the closure axiom.
2. The rational decision-making model assumes that decisions are transactive in nature. This transactive axiom means that the decision maker is able to rank-order preferences among the plans, choosing the best alternative first, then the second, and so forth (Harrison 1993).

This model has several weaknesses, however. First, many organizational decisions are based on uncertain situations and are not unidimensional. A decision is neither right nor wrong. Instead, numerous decisions could be correct, and it may be impossible to know all courses of action when making the decision. This makes it difficult to ascertain whether corporate actions were truly rational in nature (Peng 1992). At the same time, decision makers often assume that their decisions are truly rational, which could lead to what is known as hyperrationality. Hyperrationality occurs when decision makers do not admit that they have incomplete information on which to base their decisions. They deny their ignorance—a natural byproduct of one's limited cognitive abilities—and act as though that factor is unimportant in the decision-making process (Shulman 1997).

Simon (1957) examined this idea and asserted that true rational decision making does not occur. Instead, one's decisions are influenced, or affected, by bounded rationality. Bounded rationality does not imply that individuals are irrational when making decisions but rather suggests that any rational behavior is limited, or "bound," by certain constraints. For example, decision makers may have imperfect or limited knowledge of their decision environment, meaning that people have only a fraction of the information they need to know to make a decision (Forest and Mehier 2001). Other specific constraints may include one's education or lack thereof, age, and life experiences.

Because individuals lack complete information, the decision maker adopts what is known as a "satisfycing" strategy. Rather than finding the optimal solution, which would be difficult or impossible because of the constraints associated with bounded rationality, the decision maker finds a solution that is good enough, or satisfactory, for that particular issue or issues (Simon 1957). As a consequence, the decision maker simply uses guesses, hunches, or estimates to simplify decision making, evaluating a small number of alternatives while focusing on a few key aspects of the problem (Busenitz 1999).

Disjointed Incrementalism

Another explanation of how decision makers deal with incomplete information is called disjointed incrementalism, which too is a weakness. Disjointed incrementalism, as does bounded rationality, assumes that problem solvers do not have complete knowledge of a situation, based on the complexity of an issue. Therefore, the classical, rational-deductive model of decision making will not work. Instead, decision makers adopt a coping strategy, comparing and evaluating options, incrementally moving toward a solution. They do not jump to a conclusion. Rather, they often slowly, or incrementally, move toward their desired end state.

While moving incrementally toward a solution, decision makers also engage in reconstructive analysis, which involves redefining problems to simplify them and to make them more manageable. This means that decision makers make reconstructive responses to the problem, based on data they receive. As a result of more information, they may change both their means and end states of the problem.

Suppose, for example, that a complaint is lodged against an employee. The immediate problem may be identified as the named employee, and a manager may be predisposed to sanction—the end state—that employee. However, careful investigation revealed the additional information that the employee did nothing wrong. The problem was with the "system," not the employee against whom the complaint was lodged. Now, a new problem exists: how to address the complainant's misperceptions.

Under disjointed incrementalism, decision makers engage in serial analysis and evaluation. Instead of resolving the issue completely they have only accomplished a serial step in attacking the problem. In the previous example, a new problem was discovered. Talking to the affected employee to solve the issue is one step in the larger problem of improving employee/security relations.

Finally, decision makers may not be concerned with well-defined future states. Instead of stable long-term solutions, decision makers are generally more concerned about dealing with particular "evils," or imperfections, that arise. In the earlier example, because of the complexity of employee relations, the particular short-term problem involving the incident would be easier to address for the organization (Braybrooke and Lindblom 1963).

The Garbage Can Model of Decision Making

If one does not have complete knowledge of a situation and lacks complete rationality, how does one make decisions? How does one make a satisfactory decision? According to the "garbage can" model of decision making, individuals use standardized methods when responding to issues. In this model, decision makers construct decisions from the raw materials that are provided to them. These raw materials, the "garbage," are the problems, solutions, and energy that are "dumped" into the garbage can as they are produced. This garbage is then collected and a decision made, based on the ready-made, or preprogrammed, standardized responses to the issue (Cohen, March, and Olsen 1972).

This model of decision making exists in "organized anarchies." These types of organizations share three common characteristics.

1. The overall objectives of the organization are unclear.
2. The internal functioning of the organization and the relationship between the organization and the external environment are subject to confusion.
3. Participation is fluid, as individuals participate in decisions on an inconsistent basis, and the effort and time given by the actors change according to the decision being made and the length of time needed to make the decision.

As a consequence of this unstructured anarchy, organizations rely on four interrelated streams of information that empty into the garbage cans that become decisions. These streams flow throughout the organization, and in a haphazard but intentional manner they converge into a garbage can to produce a decision (Newmann 1998). The streams are problems, solutions, choice opportunities, and participants. Figure 4–3 shows these four variables.

This model assumes that the garbage can contains everything needed to solve the problem, including the problem itself. That is, decision makers hav already

FIGURE 4–3 ■ **The Garbage Can Model of Decision Making**

experienced similar situations and can draw from those past problems and experiences to solve the new problem. This model also assumes that the garbage can contains ready-made solutions so that individuals can use a standardized, or programmed, response to solve the problem.

At the same time, decision makers have choice opportunities, or a chance to make a decision. These chances always exist. However, they may be missed because the organization does not recognize an event or passes up the event or opportunity. The last variable in one's garbage can is participants in the process. People may participate in decisions in an inconsistent manner and have varying degrees of involvement, thereby affecting the decision.

The Seeing-First/Doing-First Model of Decision Making

In the rational model, thinking comes first. Mintzberg and Westley (2001) propose that the rational model be supplemented with the seeing-first/doing-first model. They assert that because of the inherent limitations of the rational model, combining facts (the rational model), ideas (seeing first), and experiences (doing first) will lead to better decisions.

The seeing-first decision model focuses on solutions rather than on problems. This type of decision making focuses on ideas instead of facts and relies on visual instead of verbal stimuli, which can be considered a linear problem-solving process, as it relies on composing words in a linear order.

Take, for example, a simulated problem with an alarm system. The seeing-first model would have decision makers look at the problem by touring the facility where the alarms are located rather than simply talking out the problem. Based on their observations, the decision makers could then make appropriate decisions.

In defense of the seeing-first model, Mintzberg and Westley (2001, 91) point out that "many decisions are driven as much as by what is seen than is actually thought." In another example, an individual who has to make decision about a new product will find it quite useful to see the product in action (seeing first) rather than perhaps reading the product manual.

If seeing the problem does not help to make a decision, perhaps just doing something may lead to effective decisions. As Mintzberg and Westley (2001, 89) point out, many successful individuals experiment when they are stuck: "We just don't think in order to act, we act in order to think." For example, when one's car will not start, the individual, even though not a mechanic and lacking a great deal of knowledge about motor vehicles, may nonetheless open the hood to check whether the "basics" of the vehicle are intact and physically inspect the engine compartment to make sure that all the spark plug wires and the distributor cap are connected, hoping that "wiggling" the wires would solve the problem.

The thinking-first, or rational, model may work best when there is structure, clear issues, and reliable information or data. The seeing-first model may be best when a person needs some creative solutions, as is the case in new-product development. The doing-first decision-making approach may work best when the issue is new and confusing and existing methods of solving problems may impede the decision-making process (Mintzberg and Westley 2001).

Improvisational Decision Making

Improvisation is an activity that one undertakes to deal with a problem or to seize an opportunity. Improvisation is not an action but a process that one uses to make decisions (Sharkansky and Zalmanovitch 2000). As pointed out by Weick (1998, 546), improvisation "involves the embellishment of something." Musicians who improvise may enhance an existing melody. In the context of organizational decisions, the improviser uses the same skills as the musician. Both rely on past experiences and knowledge so they can "use their experience of having been there to recognize that one is now somewhere else, and that the somewhere else is novel and may be valuable, notwithstanding the rules which declare that one cannot get there from here" (Weick 1998, 549).

Both doing first and improvising require speed, so the inhibitions that individuals may have when thinking first are eliminated (Weick 1998; Mintzberg and Westley 2001). This type of decision making may be most suitable for organizations facing difficult situations or seeing a sudden opportunity. For example, some researchers have determined that Israeli policymakers engage in improvisational behaviors when making decisions. In an environment filled with uncertainty and risk—terrorism, external threats, prior wars, and so on—Israeli policymakers have been found to use improvisation to respond quickly and ingeniously to the various threats, as no plans exist to deal with these issues, or the plans that do exist prove inadequate when problems arise.

The preceding example shows that improvisation is appropriate when given pressure to make a decision in a short period of time and little evaluation of alternatives to the situation is made. As a consequence, improvisation prevents paralysis in decision making, enabling the decision maker to act in real time.

Improvisation has some dangers, however. It is an art, not a science, and could lead to poor decisions and irresponsibility by decisionmakers. Making poor decisions could also lead to a waste of organizational resources (Sharkansky and Zalmanovitch 2000).

Crisis Decision Making

In many decision-making settings, individuals do not have the luxury of engaging in the linear-based decision making associated with the rational model. Rather, decisionmakers are often confronted with crisis situations, which can be described as an "unpleasantness in unexpected circumstances, representing unscheduled events, unprecedented in their implications and, by normal routine standards, almost unmanageable" (Rosenthal and Kouzmin 1997, 277). The characteristics of these crisis situations challenge the traditional rational model and limit it as an effective decision tool.

Crises require a change in the way decisions are made. Crises require one to break away from the regular, formal, time-consuming bureaucratic policies governing the "traditional" decision-making process in the organization ('tHart, Rosenthal, and Kouzmin 1993). Now, decisions must be made as accurately as possible, and critical choices must be made under time pressures and uncertain circumstances that in some manner are threatening to the well-being of the organization (Rosenthal and Kouzmin 1997). The decision-making process is also removed from those traditionally delegated to make decisions, and it often becomes a centralized activity. Called the "mobilization of bias" principle, individuals may confer only with the most powerful, skilled, and trusted individuals. Decision makers also do not consider all alternatives and resources when making decisions under crisis situations (O'Sullivan and Down 2001). In many instances, the decision(s) made are short-term, symbolic "quick fixes" to the crisis for which, time permitting, the decision makers can apply a more rational approach to solving the problem.

Examples of these types of situations abound in organizational settings. They include the 9/11 attacks on the World Trade Center and the 1994 earthquake in California's San Fernando Valley, which was one of the costliest disasters in the United States, estimated at $30 billion (Hooper 1998). Other crisis situations include industrial accidents, as well as serious and unexpected criminal events in the workplace. Although the events may differ, the characteristics of a crisis are the same. They pose a severe threat to the organization, uncertainty is high about knowing all relevant information related to the crisis and whether the decision is accurate, and the decision maker(s) face extreme time pressures to solve the problem ('tHart, Rosenthal, and Kouzmin 1993).

The application of the crisis decision-making model can be seen in the context of a hypothetical incident involving an employee assaulted and subsequently seriously wounded by a coworker. As a result of this event, many coworkers were psychologically traumatized, and the company received a great deal of unwanted media attention. In this situation, company executives would need to address this issue immediately and in doing so, would not have the luxury of following the rational model. Rather, short-term symbolic and immediate decisions to increase the number and visibility of security in and around the company would be decided on. The quick fix of hiring more security personnel would let the employees and media know that the company was concerned about the event and its employees. This decision to hire security would not follow the traditional process. The human resources department would not be involved in the process. Rather, the president and other key officials would authorize the hire. Because of the time constraints, other important, but not as immediate, concerns, such as critical-incident stress debriefing to address issues with posttraumatic stress disorder, and other feasible alternatives to increase security would not initially be considered until the immediate crisis had been addressed.

■ FACTORS AFFECTING DECISION MAKING

As pointed out earlier, all decision makers have some degree of bounded rationality. Individuals simply cannot have complete and perfect knowledge on which to base a decision. One's ability to make decisions can be affected by several variables: individual, cultural, environmental, and organizational.

Individual Attributes

A person's type and extent of education can reduce one's amount of bounded rationality. At the same time, one's education will expand one's level of knowledge in a particular area. This domain knowledge includes both declarative and procedural knowledge that one possesses relative to a particular field of study. Declarative knowledge refers to knowing about things, facts, and concepts that can be verbally communicated or held in mental models. Knowing how, which is procedure knowledge, refers to the skills of knowing how to perform particular activities or tasks.

To be effective decision makers, individuals need to master both components of domain knowledge. In fact, individuals who are considered experts have been found to store a larger body of domain knowledge, which is stored in complex patterns, or hierarchies, that enable them to integrate the existing information with their domain knowledge, increasing their decision-making speed (Chen 2000).

Another attribute that could affect one's capacity for decision making is age. In this context, age refers to the nature and extent of one's education and experience, which will enhance decision-making abilities. Age is also related to generational differences. These generational differences among employees shape the way they view authority and leadership in the workplace, as well as their orientation toward technology and working in groups, to name just a few age-related dynamics that have an impact on an individual's capacity for problem solving and decision making (Zemke, Raines, and Filipzak 2000).

Individualized socialization issues may affect decision making in the context of the amount of risk that one is willing to take. Research has shown that males have a higher rate of drowning than females; males take greater risks in aquatic settings, in part because they are overconfident and subsequently overestimate their swimming abilities (Howland et al. 1996). Research has also found that, compared to females, males exhibit greater levels of financial risk taking when making financial investments (Jianakoplos and Bernasek 1998).

Cultural Attributes

The larger social culture and values in which decision makers live and work influence decisionmaking. Cultures provide different rules and principles that assist individuals in making decisions. For example, people from East Asian cultures have been found to use more compromising activities than do individuals from North American cultures (Briley, Morris, and Simonson 2000). It has also been found that U.S. managers are more prone to take risks and are more oriented toward short-term profits than are Japanese managers, who are more future oriented and interested in long-term market share and building customer relations. In addition, Japanese managers scored higher on uncertainty avoidance than did their U.S. counterparts (Beldona, Inkpen, and Phatak 1998).

Other researchers have suggested that both individual and situational factors that moderate ethical behaviors are influenced by a manager's national culture. For example, managers from collectivist societies tend to follow a utilitarian—the greatest good for the greatest number of people—theory of ethical decision making, whereas managers from individualistic-based cultures, such as the United States, emphasize their own personal good in their decision (Robertson and Fadil 1999).

In another example, researchers found that in unified Germany, East German doctors had higher cautiousness scores and engaged in fewer risk taking activities than did their West German counterparts (Trimpop and Kirkcaldy 1998).

Environmental Attributes

The environment—in the context of stability and change that one operates in—may impact the abilities of a decision maker. As discussed earlier in this chapter, the rational decision-making process may require a great deal of time. Therefore, the rational model may be most appropriate for organizations that operate in very stable and unchanging environments. For those organizations experiencing a declining market share and operating in environments that could be classified as threatening, hostile, or unstable, ecological components dictate the use of other decision-making models, as the rational model may be too slow a process. In uncertain environments, in which the availability of information from the environment may be reduced and the sources of information change dramatically, a comprehensive analysis of all the alternative decisions may be impractical (Koberg, Tegarden, and Wilsted 1993).

The environment in the context of technological complexity is another factor that affects an organization's decision-making abilities. Perrow (1984) asserts that the organizational complexity of some industries will impact the organization's ability to make effective decisions. Perrow states that as industrial complexity increases, as is the case with nuclear power plants, for example, individual and organizational abilities to make appropriate decisions decrease. The reason is that these technologies are so complicated that decision makers cannot fully comprehend the operations or complexity of those facilities, especially when unanticipated accidents occur.

Organizational Attributes

Because it acts as an interpretive frame, organizational culture has a direct influence on the decision-making process. If an organization has a very conservative orientation, a decision maker may be less willing to make innovative decisions and rather follow the prevailing cultural norms on how to address the issue. The way managers make decisions is based on the concept of organization predisposition. This term means that decision making is affected by the organization's past experiences and its rule orientation, which create organizational routines for decision makers. This suggests that one's decisions may not always be based entirely on specific conditions and issues. Rather, the rules, policies, and procedures may limit the way individuals can respond to issues, with previous decisions setting precedents on how the organization will address current issues (Ashmos, Duchon, and McDaniel 1998). A policy or past practice of limiting top managers in making strategic decisions will eliminate lower-level managers from having input into the process. In addition, a manager who tries a novel approach to an issue and fails may not attempt similar actions in the future.

■ COMMON ERRORS IN DECISION MAKING

Groupthink

The term "groupthink" was coined by Janis (1972), who examined group dynamics in decision making. Groupthink is considered a detrimental group process and a decision defect that exists when decision makers are so cohesive or have such a high degree of group solidarity that they fail to explore alternative decisions and courses of actions. Groupthink occurs when group members' motivation to reach unanimity in a decision does not allow them to appraise other alternatives to problems (Choi and Kim 1999).

One example of groupthink occurred when President Lyndon Johnson's cabinet sought concurrence on decisions rather than critically debate issues, which is believed to have led to defective decisions about the Vietnam War. Similarly, the failure to foresee the attack on Pearl Harbor and the Kennedy administration's decisions about the Bay of Pigs invasion are other examples of how individuals' dependence on group affiliation overrode their own identities, which resulted in these decision makers' failure to explore other options in the decision-making process (Kim 2000).

Although groupthink is considered a problem in decision making, one of its positive points is that team performance may improve to a point. The reason is that feelings of unanimity and invulnerability can increase morale and confidence levels, subsequently increasing the motivation levels and group identity of the decision makers. However, when group identity moves from moderate to high, team decision making may also deteriorate. Now that confidence levels have increased, the group considers itself invulnerable and will no longer realistically appraise alternative courses of action (Choi and Kim 1999).

The Abilene Paradox

Another error in decision making is the Abilene Paradox, which was described by Jerry Harvey after he and his family drove 35 miles to eat at a restaurant in

Abilene, Texas. When they arrived, they realized that none of them wanted to go to the restaurant in Abilene, but each assumed that the others did. In this case, the participants may not like the decision but nonetheless "ride along" with it, knowing that it may not work or that it is wrong (Kim 2000).

Although both groupthink and the Abilene Paradox are decision-making errors, they have distinct differences. The Abilene Paradox is an individual-based process, with decision makers' never agreeing with the outcome. Groupthink, by contrast, results when everyone in the group buys into the decision.

In the Abilene Paradox, individuals go along with the consensus in order to avoid being perceived as an obstructionist or a "killjoy" in the process, and they may also have a fear of separation from the group. In groupthink, individuals go along with the decision because they value their membership in the group and value one another's loyalty. In the Abilene Paradox, this lack of membership, esprit de corps, and loyalty then generate conflict after the decision is made with individuals blaming one another for the decision. By contrast, groupthink results in an increased esprit de corps among the decision makers, as they feel that they have made the correct decision. The Abilene Paradox "coerces" individuals in group decision making, whereas groupthink individuals perceive that they made the decision based on their own free will.

The two types of error also differ in their future orientations. Groupthink individuals see the future in a positive frame, whereas the Abilene Paradox suggests that individuals will see the future in a negative manner, as they never agreed with the decision. The differences between the two can also be characterized in terms of energy. The Abilene Paradox results in conflict, hesitation, and passive attitudes among individuals. Individuals in a groupthink mode, however, display high levels of group cohesiveness, energy, and esprit de corps (Kim 2000).

Organizational Paralysis

Langley (1995) writes that a common error in the formal analysis of problems occurs when the level of participation, power, and managerial opinions result in excessive and unproductive use of the organization's formal analysis procedures. Because of the events, individuals are so overwhelmed that they are incapable of taking any action ('tHart, Rosenthal, and Kouzmen 1993). This problem can be referred to as organizational paralysis and can be categorized into three modes of paralysis by analysis. They are: 1) "The Dialogue of the Deaf," 2) The Vicious Cycle, and 3) The Decision Vacuum (Langley 1995).

Mode 1: The Dialogue of the Deaf   The dialogue of the deaf occurs when an organization's hierarchical levels exchange reports and documents that disagree on the issue. In these cases, some individuals conduct analyses to justify their project but cannot force the issue onto the organizational agenda, because individuals involved in the decision-making process at other levels oppose or are indifferent to the project. Although the individuals may suspect that they are being ignored, they may continue to generate reports and documents to support their ideas or positions. Individuals at other levels, meanwhile, may require additional information rather than categorically reject the idea or proposal (Langley 1995).

In one case, for example, line-level security personnel were interested in carrying oleoresin capsicum (OC) spray for their protection. A manager was told to submit a proposal and report to the risk-management unit, which opposed the idea. Perceived as a delaying tactic by the line-level employees, the risk-management unit continually requested additional documentation, arguing it did not have enough information on which to render a decision. Eventually, the line staff gave up its efforts.

Mode 2: The Vicious Cycle   This type of paralysis by analysis can be classified as a "paper fight" between individuals within the same level in the organization. Each side creates large amounts of formal analyses to persuade and convince the other side. One group presents information to perhaps block another group's attempt at change or may generate research to unlock the block that another group created. Regardless of whether a group is blocking or unlocking, the result is a vicious cycle, not change.

This type of conflict can occur in a diffuse power structure characterized by wide participation and an uncommitted top management (Langley 1995). If decision makers have not provided a clear direction, their directions are ambiguous, or the decision makers are passive or divided, this vicious cycle may exist (Langley 1995).

This type of paper fight occurred in an organization in which young security officers wanted to work a 10-hour shift. The day shift, composed of older officers, opposed this proposal and wanted to remain on their 8-hour shifts. A paper fight between the day and night managers ensued, with both trying to justify their positions but without luck, as top-level managers were complacent.

Mode 3: The Decision Vacuum   The decision vacuum occurs when management has no clear vision for the work or project but nevertheless mandates a staff group, consultants, or analysts to conduct a study that lacks immediacy and a firm deadline. Combined with the uncertain direction of the research and the project, the end results may have no application or not correspond to management's interests.

Decision vacuums may occur for various reasons. This type of planning serves a symbolic function that the organization is addressing an issue or a problem. For nonthreatening issues, it ensures that the company is looking at and dealing with long-term problems (Langley 1995).

In order to avoid these problems, Langley (1995) recommends that managers and organizations reexamine where decisions are being made in the organizational hierarchy to determine whether these levels are necessary. In addition, staff groups or consultants should not be isolated or detached from immediate decision making. Finally, Langley recommends that the organization be prepared to make decisions based on all opinions, including dissenting ones.

Cognitive Nearsightedness

Cognitive nearsightedness means that people tend to respond to problems that are visible and immediate and neglect those issues that may be more significant but removed in time and space. Take, for example, a high turnover rate of entry-level security officers. The immediate response to this issue is that the security firm will need to hire new security personnel. A more significant issue, however, is why the turnover rate is high. Further analysis into this issue may reveal that employees are dissatisfied with the work environment or that this firm's compensation levels are not in line with those of other companies in the area.

Situational Dominance

Situational dominance occurs when individuals bypass formal policies and procedures or rules and respond directly to a situation. This often occurs because the organization did not have adequate plans for such events. The lack of plans results in improvisation at lower levels in the organization. This may not always be negative, however. Situational dominance can lead to quick and effective actions, or what is known as situationally driven direct responses to an issue ('tHart, Rosenthal, and Kouzmin 1993).

Emergency situations are perhaps the best examples of situational dominance. The events of September 11, 2001, caught several organizations unprepared to deal with terrorist attacks. In response to the crisis, many line level managers, mid-managers, and leaders empowered themselves to achieve control and solve the task at hand. Another example involves military operations. Soldiers on the front line take advantage of situations and exploit those situations, turning them into opportunities.

Strategic Evasion

Strategic evasion can be best understood as "it's not my problem," with individuals disassociating themselves from the decision-making process. This situation may occur when decision makers feel that their chances for solving the problem are slight and the consequences of making a poor decision are high or might reflect poorly on them at a later time ('tHart, Rosenthal, and Kouzmin 1993).

■ ATTRIBUTES OF EFFECTIVE DECISION MAKERS

So what makes an effective decision maker? Why do some individuals excel in decisions and others fail? Murnighan and Mowen (2002) assert that when looking at the characteristics of "master" decision makers, one must look at both the process and the outcome. For example, master decision makers ensure that the process is structured and thorough. They also possess ingrained structured processes for making decisions. Master decision makers have a vast repertoire of experience, both good and bad, which can be considered a proving ground for future decisions they will make. Effective decision makers have fun at work, and the work environment encourages and allows for experimentation. At the same time, master decision makers also recognize their own strengths and limitations and are willing to ask for help and to seek the expertise of other people. Last, master decision makers implement decisions with force and precision. When the decision is made, they act.

Frisch and Clemen (1994) suggest that individuals need three basic and interrelated features to make a good decision. First, individuals use consequentialist decision strategies, making decisions on the desirability and likelihood of various outcomes. Second, individuals need to thoroughly anticipate and identify the possible consequences of their decision. Here, the decision maker considers options, determines what will or will not happen because of the decision(s), and determines the desirability of the consequences of the various options. Third, individuals need to use compensatory decision rules to assess what they will "trade off" when choosing particular alternatives over others.

Intuition and Decision Making

Intuition involves synthesizing bits of information and experiences into an integrated, holistic perception of the issue(s) at hand. When making decisions, decision makers, without conscious thought, draw from these stored experiences and the answer "flashes" before them. In fact, decision makers may be unable to consciously understand how they arrived at the answer (Khatri and Ng 2000).

Intuition is a sophisticated form of reasoning, based on chunking, that an individual develops, or "hones," over the course of work experiences. Intuition is based on a deep understanding of a situation, whereby an individual subconsciously "digs deep" into subconscious memory, with its store of knowledge and experience, to make a decision. To have "intuition" requires a great deal of experience in problem solving and a complete grasp of details of the business (Khatri and Ng 2000).

Intuition is a subconscious activity, complex, and quick. Intuition should not be confused with emotion. Emotions, such as fear and anger, cloud or block messages that come from the subconscious to the conscious. "Gut feelings" are not based on bias. Intuition is based on those experiences that are stored in the mind (Khatri and Ng 2000).

Intuition is of several types. Illumination occurs when an individual suddenly is aware of information without really knowing how or why. Detection, another form of intuition, occurs when the person's mind is elsewhere and suddenly finds a solution or insight to the problem. Evaluative intuition provides choices or alternatives and occurs when a decision maker has that "sixth sense" that something is wrong with the decision or that it isn't right for some reason but may not know the reason(s) why (Sauter 1999).

Intuitive decision making may be more appropriate in unstable environments in which an individual needs to make a fast and accurate decision, may not have complete information and precedents on which to base the decision, but still needs to collect and synthesize a large amount of data (Khatri and Ng 2000). Intuition can also be dangerous; managers may reach conclusions too quickly. Intuition may contain bias, and relevant facts may be ignored in the decision process. As a consequence, managers should recognize their own personal strengths and weaknesses when using intuitive thought to make decisions (Sauter 1999).

Other researchers feel that intuition is more complex and allows decision makers to overcome linear modes of thinking and to address complex issues. At the same time, intuition can be quick; a person may know instantly what the best decision should be, based on years of experience and learning. These years of experience may make intuitive decision making more of a rational decision-making method than some would accept or believe (Khatri and Ng 2000).

Risk Taking

Although risk is often thought of negatively, the willingness of a person to take risk is a key to creativity in the workplace. Risk provides motivation to deviate from the status quo and to entertain new, novel ideas and solutions to issues in the workplace. This subsequently leads to innovation, which can be considered the implementation of the person's ideas (Amabile 1997).

Because they have an element of potential loss or danger, all good decisions contain a certain degree of risk. Managers and employees may avoid risk by focusing on what they have to lose instead of what they could gain. Of interest is that when the risk is high, individuals may avoid taking risks. However, even when the risk is low, individuals may opt not to take risk. This can best be described in the context of a sporting event. A football team that is ahead in a game plays more conservatively than when it may be behind (Case and Shane 1998). Some of the more common fears related to risk taking are presented in Box 4–2.

BOX 4–2 ▪ **Common Fears of Risk in Decision Making**

Fear of Failure

The fear of failure occurs when risk-taking opportunities are viewed in a negative context instead of as an opportunity. Individuals who have a fear of failure think that they may be punished or terminated for making a decision that may not work out. Employees who fear failure prefer the status quo and keep a low profile in the organization.

Fear of Success

This is the opposite of the fear of failure and is related to concerns that the employee may lose something. Individuals may be apprehensive that their success would isolate them, setting them apart from other individuals, while increasing their visibility in the organization and perhaps subsequently placing them on a pedestal, resulting in more scrutiny of their activities.

Fear of What Others Will Think

When an individual is concerned about others' opinions, he or she will do only things that others are sure to approve of. Creativity is not a part of making decisions. The employee will tell people exactly what they want to hear and suggest obvious solutions to issues.

Fear of Uncertainty

This occurs when a person is comfortable in the existing position or present job. These people avoid additional responsibilities and/or promotions. These people are concerned about the "unknowns" of new tasks, positions, and responsibilities at work because they face the possibility of the loss of control at work.

Adapted from Sisson (1985).

In many situations, avoiding risk is not the best alternative. In fact, the avoidance of risk may in some instances be more detrimental. For example, a contract security firm that does not keep up with technological advances in the field may not be able to keep up with its competition. At the same time, proprietary firms that do not risk the implementation of new technologies may not be as productive and meet the safety and security needs of their constituents. This implies that companies unwilling to take some risk and experiment may not survive.

Not all risk is good. In some situations, excessive risk taking leads to some unnatural activities by decision makers. For example, in some situations, individuals and organizations persist in supporting failing projects that are no longer economically feasible, knowing that those projects are failing but, because of social and psychological pressures, being unwilling to accept defeat. Instead, they prolong the exposure of their failures by persisting with the issue at hand until "ultimate" failure. Although one may consider this an irrational behavior, it is in fact rational. The decision makers know that they are facing failure (a rational thought). However, they are in a predicament and so take more risks to conceal their failures (Drummond 1998).

Creativity

In order to succeed, the organization must address decisions creatively. Creativity is defined as "the degree to which an employee demonstrates new ideas or applications for activities and solutions at work" (Jalan and Kleiner 1995). Creativity is a process whereby one becomes aware of problems and has a response or an idea that is novel and adaptive. A creative person uses intuition, combined with spontaneity and risk taking, to come up with a novel solution to a problem.

Creativity differs from intuition in the sense that one needs intuition to produce creative ideas (Amitabh and Kleiner 1995). Creativity has been found to be most useful in decision making under circumstances that involve little time but great pressure to come up with a decision, little precedent on which to base a decision, limited facts that do not suggest a direction in which to go, and alternative solutions with good arguments for each (Jalan and Kleiner 1995).

Creative persons have been found to share six common characteristics (Perkins 1981).

1. Creative persons are objective and encourage criticism.
2. They have mental mobility, which means that they are open-minded and have the potential to see the issue from various viewpoints.
3. Creative persons have a high tolerance for complex environments.
4. They have a passion for work or enjoy the job for the rewards they get from it.
5. They are effective problem finders, meaning that they have the ability to discover problems, which subsequently leads to solving them.
6. Creative individuals are willing to take risks in the workplace.

Not all creative persons have all six of these characteristics. However, the more characteristics a person has, the greater the potential for creativity in the workplace.

Entrepreneurship

Effective decision makers exhibit the characteristics of entrepreneurship. Entrepreneurs are individuals who are opportunity seekers. They are determined to succeed, creative and innovative, and willing to take risks and look at failures in a positive manner. Entrepreneurs are also self-confident, resilient to setbacks, and live in the future but manage the present.

Alan Pinkerton is good example of an entrepreneur. Pinkerton was a risk taker who found opportunities in the new field of private security. Pinkerton did not wait for opportunities. He created them. As pointed out in Chapter 1, he created the Northwest Police Agency to protect railroads. He also created and provided the first executive-protection services to individuals, such as President Abraham Lincoln, and provided intelligence and counterintelligence services in the Civil War for the North (McCrie 1988).

One assumption about entrepreneurs is that they take excessive risks when venturing into new business opportunities. The current research suggests that entrepreneurs, in comparison to managers, do not differ in their propensity for risk taking. Instead, entrepreneurs differ cognitively in how they think about and perceive risk. In comparison to most managers in large organizations, entrepreneurs use specific biases and heuristics to sift through and filter out large amounts of information. This inquisitive-based thinking allows these individuals to piece together fragments of information, using their own intuitive guidelines or decision rules, resulting in faster decision making. At the same time, the entrepreneur possesses heuristic rules that provide shortcuts that may differ from organizational policies and procedures. These organizational norms guide the decision-making process and in turn may constrict it. Entrepreneurs, in contrast, do not have these policies and procedures but simply use personal heuristics and decision-making rules to guide decisions (Busenitz 1999).

■ THE ROLE OF MANAGEMENT IN FOSTERING EFFECTIVE DECISION MAKING

The models and theories presented in this chapter are useful in understanding the decision-making process. However, what constitutes a good decision, and how can managers create and maintain a climate for effective decision making in the organization? We want all our employees to make effective decisions at the line level. Moreover, as administrators and managers, we need to ensure that we have made good decisions.

Any decision-making process has two primary components: functional/technical considerations and management/leadership factors. Functional design considerations are related to the work or the organization's activity. In the context of a security firm, for example, some functional considerations are the organization's primary line-level operations, customer service activities, marketing, and sales. Most managers concentrate on the functional issues and are educated and trained in these areas. The success of managers is often based on their functional competence in the organization (Rausch 1999).

Perhaps one of the most important aspects of the decision is the leadership and management associated with the implementation of the decision. One management/leadership aspect of the decision-making process is how decision makers achieve cooperation and coordination in implementing their decisions. This component of the decision-making process addresses issues related to setting and communicating direction, establishing norms, and developing strategies for conflict prevention and resolution, rewards, and performance evaluation. These considerations, however, are often overlooked, as managers may concentrate only on functional issues of their decisions (Rausch 1999).

One model that takes into consideration the managerial/leadership aspects of a decision is called the 3 Cs model (Rausch 1999), which asserts that managers often overlook the reactions of people who are somehow involved or affected by the decision. In order to prevent this from happening and to ensure that a good decision was made, the manager should ask three questions before finalizing a plan. These nonprescriptive questions focus on control/coordination, competence, and climate.

1. How can we make sure that we will gain appropriate control over this process? What else do we have to do to make sure that we will reach the outcome we are setting out to achieve? Additional control-related questions may be whether participation in the decision-making process was appropriate and whether the goals were communicated to all stakeholders.

2. Competence is concerned with the knowledge, skills, and abilities for the functions, including management/leadership and other stakeholder

competencies. Questions may also address what the planners have to do to make sure that all stakeholders will have the necessary and/or desirable knowledge and skills needed for competence.

3. Climate is concerned about the environment in which staff members and other stakeholders can find the maximum possible satisfaction from participating or being affected (Rausch et al. 2001). Questions in this category ask how to ensure a climate for success, as well as what else needs to be done so all the stakeholders are satisfied or not so dissatisfied that they will create roadblocks to the decision.

Ethical Considerations

Decision makers need to recognize that decisions have factual and ethical components. Ethical decisions are both morally and legally acceptable to the larger community. Decision makers need to consider this issue and recognize their motives in rendering the decision. Recognizing one's motives and making sure that they are ethical will result in the development and perpetuation of an ethical organization, which in turn will impact the actions of employees and the larger community that the organization serves.

At the same time, decision makers need to recognize that several motives are at work. These motives may include technological, financial, economic, personal, organizational, and social factors. Combined with other variables, such as the size of the organization, the needs of the stakeholders, and the number of individuals involved in the decision process, decision makers often face morally mixed motives. Some of these motives are ethical, some neutral, and others unethical. It is the responsibility of the decision maker to examine the decision not in a traditional ethical/unethical mode but in a mixed-motive format, in which ethics may exist within a graduated and complex perspective (DiNorcia and Tigner 2000).

The issue-contingent model is one of the most comprehensive models of ethical decision making. This model consists of four sequential stages: recognizing the moral issue, making a moral judgment, establishing moral intent, and engaging in moral behavior(s). This model makes the assumption that all decisions contain a level of moral intensity while also containing a moral issue. Following this recognition of an ethical issue, decision makers need to consider and define the moral intensity of the issue by considering six characteristics of the issue (Jones 1991):

1. The magnitude of the consequences, or the total amount of harm or benefit for or against individuals.
2. Social consensus by the public and the organization that the decision is good or bad.
3. The probability of effect. Will the expected outcomes occur, and will the expected harm occur?
4. The temporal immediacy that considers the length of time between the expected event and any consequences that will occur.

5. Proximity issues that consider the "nearness" of the results of the decision. Terminating a contract with a vendor is "farther away" than terminating one's own employees.
6. Concentration of effect: the number of individuals who are affected by the decision.

Support for Risk Taking

Managers need to improve on and expand the problem- and opportunity-finding competencies of their staffs by encouraging risk-taking behaviors. The key for managers is that they must develop a culture and atmosphere that promotes risk taking. Some of the ways managers can increase risk taking is through modeling, encouraging the positive, accepting mistakes and fears, and providing a non-punitive environment (Appelbaum, Bregman, and Moroz 1998). Through managerial modeling, for example, managers can demonstrate risk-taking behaviors and have an attitude of accepting failures. Encouraging the positive requires that managers have employees focus on the positive aspects of risk taking. This could be accomplished by encouraging employees to share their concerns about risk and to engage in behaviors that improve employees' self-confidence, attitudes, and self-esteem. Managers can also be accepting and supportive of mistakes. Being supportive sends a message to employees that, regardless of the outcome, the manager and the organization will not abandon them (Appelbaum, Bregman, and Moroz 1998). It must be remembered that many employees may be novices in taking risks and making decisions. Because of their limited experiences, they may have a greater potential for failure at the onset.

The creation of a nonpunitive environment requires that managers not punish employees. Managers need to accept the fact that some things may not turn out successfully. Once penalties are removed, employees will be more likely to take risks. It does not mean that the mistakes will be ignored. Instead, the manager should concentrate on what was done right in the decision-making process. If employees are punished for their mistakes, it would lower employee risk taking in the organization (Appelbaum, Bregman, and Moroz 1998).

Another factor that has been found to increase the level of risk taking in an organization is the terminal value associated with the risk. Terminal value can be best understood as "the value that survives a project to benefit other (current or future) projects" (Case and Shane 1998, 773). These terminal values could be associated with how much the organization learned from the project, changes in interdepartmental relationships, building the competencies of employees, and whether communication channels opened among employees and perhaps departments as a result of the decision-making process (successful or not). A project perceived by the decision makers to have a high terminal value has been found to enhance a team's propensity to take risks because it now has a "fallback" position that lessens the downside risk if the project and decisions are not successful (Case and Shane 1998). This means that even if the team decision was unsuccessful, other valuable outcomes were accomplished through the process.

Managerial Attitudes and Decision Success

The Harrison and Pelletier (1995) model for decision success takes the position that decision success is a function of managerial attitudes. Specifically, successful decisions are contingent on the manager's attitudes toward the decision-making process and the decision itself. Attitudes toward the decision-making process itself look at the attainability of the objectives and the openness of the process. If an organization has an objective beyond the reach of the organization, such as 100 percent market share in the alarm industry in a certain geographical area, the decision is flawed; it is not attainable and is out of reach by the organization, resulting in managers' not buying into the objectives.

At the same time, the model also indicates that decision makers should be concerned about the openness of the process, which deals with the extent of interaction between decision makers and stakeholder groups in the external environment. In some situations, decision-making processes are considered to be closed to the external environment, with little consideration or weight given to the external environment. An effective decision requires continuous interaction between decision makers and stakeholders in the external environment, as their support is necessary for a positive outcome from the decision.

The next major component of any successful decision is related to managerial attitudes toward the decision. These attitudes are based on two issues: the quality of the strategies used to arrive at the decision and the nature of the outcome that management seeks from the decision.

Managers should not take a judgmental approach to the success of the decisions, based on the fact that all decisions have a degree of uncertainty. Hence, all decisions may be less than perfect, and managers should recognize and accept the fact that choices are uncertain, based on the human constraints in decision making.

The nature of the outcome looks at the consequences of the alternatives that the decision maker chose. Here, managers should not look to see whether they have exceeded their objective, as this was not the goal, anyway. Rather, the decision will be more successful if managers seek satisfactory outcomes, looking to see whether they met the objectives of their decisions realistically in light of the fact that they had to rely on imperfect information to make the decision at the onset (Harrsion and Pelletier 1995).

A Shared Vision

All organizations have a vision of the future. However, not all employees understand the vision of the organization. If they do not understand its vision, however, they cannot make effective decisions. Decisions are not made in a vacuum. They are made in the context of the organization's vision for the future. One of the keys to any decision is its consistency with the organization's vision statement. This future-oriented statement defines what the organization is going to be in the next few years. Vision statements differ from mission statements. Mission statements define what the organization does and keep the organization focused on its services, key customers, and products.

Vision statements provide a structure and a direction for decision makers. Without a clearly defined vision for the organization, decision makers do not have a direction or a means to evaluate new opportunities and problems that they experience. Not having a clear vision for the organization will also result in a workforce that lacks direction, engages in in-fighting, and has apathetic attitudes. Some of the issues to consider when creating or updating the organization's vision statement are the following (Brown 1998).

1. The vision statement should paint a picture in the employee's mind of where the organization wants to be.
2. The vision statement should be brief to the extent that an employee can easily recall it.
3. A vision needs to be verifiable to the point that individuals could agree that the vision has or has not been met.
4. The vision should be focused on one or two aspects of the organization or the major goals that the company is trying to achieve or that are important for future success. It should not concentrate on multiple issues that could make the vision unclear for employees.
5. The purpose of the vision statement is to communicate the direction of the company. Hence, it must be understood by all the employees.
6. The vision should be inspirational so employees are motivated to help the organization achieve it.

A Learning Organization

Throughout the evolutionary process of humans, individuals have learned and evolved from their decisions. As pointed out by Rode and Wang (2000), the evolution of humans is one of learning from their decisions. Irrational choices or decisions may have in fact been functionally adaptive for humans because decision quality was a determinant of survival. They learned from their mistakes and moved on. This same analogy can be taken in the context of the modern organization. Organizations can learn from their mistakes and adapt to their environment in order to evolve, compete with other organizations, and succeed.

The concept of a learning organization is briefly discussed in Chapter 6. Under the concept of a learning organization, the entire organization can learn from its success and perhaps failures in making decisions. In the context of a failure, employees and managers can use those failures to learn what they did right and perhaps what they did wrong. This will ensure that similar errors do not happen in the future, while ensuring success in the future, as individuals will avoid the same or similar errors in future decision-making ventures in the company.

Organizational Redesign

If the decisions faced by organizations require it, managers should make conscious efforts to redesign the organization to ensure that the decision-making process is effective. For example, if line-level employees are not involved in the decision-making processes despite recognition that this is needed, a philosophical change and modified organizational policies and procedures should occur to include the individuals in the decision-making process.

Managers and, of course leaders, can also create conditions that foster an entrepreneurial spirit through redesign. One way is to limit bureaucratic barriers that may stifle creativity because of the hierarchical decision processes that exist in the organization. An entrepreneurial spirit can also be created by including all employees in the decision-making process, regardless of position. Successful entrepreneurs also make mistakes. This means that the organization needs to accept that mistakes are an inevitable component of decisions, making all employees less risk averse when confronted with issues that need to be solved (Osborne 1995).

Empowerment

To be effective leaders may also mean that managers give up some of their decision-making control, empowering employees to use their creativity to solve problems. This also means that managers must build a level of trust and cooperation between themselves and their employees in order to encourage them to take "smart risks" that result in a win-win situation for themselves, their managers, and the organization. Empowerment will lead individuals to believe that they are competent at decision making, which in turn will result in increased levels of competence and self-confidence in the workplace.

Wide participation in problem solving in the organization, regardless of an individual's position or power, is a form of worker empowerment. Involving employees in the decision-making process will reduce what is referred to as the trap of professional arrogance. Professional arrogance occurs when managers assume that they have all the answers or solutions to issues and disregard subordinates, failing to empower or allow them to participate in relevant decision-making activities in the company (Cohen-Rosenthal 1994). Research has also found that increased participation leads to decreased absenteeism and turnover and an increase in job-satisfaction levels (Soonhee 2002).

Allowing everyone in the organization to make "tough calls" can increase the organization's responsiveness to issues. This empowerment, in fact, is one way to improve or speed up organizational decision making. Empowering employees in the decision-making processes can be best described as participative decision making (PDM). PDM exists on a continuum, ranging from low to high, depending on the company's philosophy and attitudes toward empowering employees in the decision-making process.

Research has shown some positive outcomes related to PDM. Increased levels of PDM have been found to reduce role conflict and ambiguity, which are two major stressors in organizations, as individuals now have some degree of control over manipulating their work environment to reduce stress levels. As a result, increased levels of PDM are also beneficial for one's level of job satisfaction (Daniels and Bailey 1999). Increased decision making has also been found to increase organizational citizenship behaviors (OCBs): being conscientious, helping coworkers, being courteous, and willing to take on another task, without complaining, to help out a coworker for the good of the company. OCBs have been found to be reciprocal. Increased decision making leads to employees' perceiving that managers support them, which in turn leads to the employees' reciprocating increased levels of OCBs in the workplace (VanYperen, van den Berg, and Willering 1999).

Managers should consider empowering groups to make decisions. By including multiple individuals who have diverse educational and life experiences, to name only two attributes, the degree of bounded rationality will be expanded, and options not previously considered by only one decision maker will be discovered.

However, group decision making has some drawbacks. As pointed out earlier in this chapter, groups can experience decision defects, including groupthink and the Abilene Paradox. In order to prevent some group-based decision defects, organizations should first recognize potential defects and consider the use of a group facilitator. To be effective, a group facilitator should concentrate on three major areas of the group problem-solving experience: preplanning the group's direction, conducting a group problem-solving session, and producing a postsession report and holding a postsession review.

The preplanning stage involves setting the objectives of the meeting, establishing the meeting agenda, determining what issues will be discussed, selecting team members, and establishing ground rules for the planning process. The next stage is the group session. Here, the facilitator is responsible for guiding and supporting the participants. The key is to manage the internal group relations to make sure that the group makes accurate and effective decisions. The facilitator needs to have knowledge about group dynamics and group problem-solving techniques. The facilitator should also be flexible and encouraging. After the meeting, the facilitator is responsible for writing a report identifying the outcomes of the meeting. This is the postsession review. The primary purpose of this stage is to produce a written document that describes the outcomes and solutions of the meeting(s) and next steps that need to be taken to achieve the desired outcomes (Nelson and McFadzean 1998).

■ CONCLUSION

Effective leaders and managers have the ability to influence the success of decisions and the subsequent success of their organizations through the planning and decision process they choose to use in the course of their daily activities. Proper planning gives purpose and direction to the organization. The functions of planning are broad and include strategic, tactical, and contingency-based planning activities. Within these types of plans, managers have a variety of models—rational/comprehensive, transactive, and advocacy-based planning—they can follow to ensure that the plans they create are successful for advancing the needs and objectives of the organization.

An important aspect of the planning process is making effective decisions. The primary model of decision making is the rational model, which follows a clearly delineated linear-based problem-solving process. Because of the problems associated with this model, such as disjointed incrementalism and bounded rationality, alternative models of decision making have been proposed: the garbage can model of decision making, the comprehensive seeing-first/doing-first model, and the crisis decision-making model.

Several factors affect one's decision-making abilities. These factors can be categorized into individual attributes, including one's knowledge, age, and gender; the culture in which the decision maker lives; and the environment, including its culture, in which the organization operates.

Decision makers also need to recognize common errors in decision making. Two such errors are groupthink, a group-based decision process, and the Abilene Paradox, which is an individual-based defective decision process. Other common decision-making errors are organizational paralysis, cognitive nearsightedness, situational dominance, and strategic evasion.

Effective decision makers possess certain attributes. To look at effective decisions, one needs to look at both the process and the outcomes of the decision. Effective decision makers are intuitive, engage in risk taking, are creative, and possess an entrepreneurial spirit.

This chapter has also provided recommendations to improve the organization's decision-making abilities. Managers need to be effective leaders and understand that decision success is based on their positive attitudes. Managers need to ensure that decisions are ethical and to encourage their employees to take risks. Effective decision making will also require empowering employees and nurturing their intuitive powers. Managers should also consider creating a learning organization while also making sure that those decisions made are consistent with the organization's vision.

■ KEY TERMS

Abilene Paradox	Decision making
Advocacy planning	Disjointed incrementalism
Bounded rationality	Entrepreneurship
Cognitive nearsightedness	Ethical decisions
Contingency-based planning	Garbage can model
Creativity	Groupthink
Crisis decision making	Hyperrationality

Improvisation
Issue-contingent model
Intuition
Organizational paralysis
Participative decision making
Planning
Rational model
Rational/comprehensive planning
Risk taking

Scenario planning
Seeing-first/Doing-first model
Situational dominance
Strategic evasion
Strategic planning
Tactical planning
3 Cs model
Transactive planning

■ DISCUSSION QUESTIONS

1. What are some benefits of group-based problem solving?
2. What are the similarities and differences between strategic and tactical planning? When should scenario-based planning be used?
3. What are the four stages in any planning process?
4. List some of the common decision defects. What are some of the primary differences between groupthink and the Abilene Paradox?
5. What are some of the weaknesses or problems associated with the rational decision-making model?
6. As a manager, what are some ways you can ensure decision success?
7. Explain the garbage can model of decision making.
8. What are some factors that limit an individual's decision-making abilities? As a manager, how would you address these deficiencies?
9. What is the role and impact of intuition in the decision-making process?
10. What are some issues to consider when implementing any decision?

■ REFERENCES

ALEXANDER, E. R. 1994. The non-Euclidean mode of planning. *American Planning Association* 60 (3): 372–376.

AMABILE, T. M. 1997. Monitoring creativity in organizations: On doing what you love and loving what you do. *California Management Review* 40 (1): 39–58.

AMITABH, J. and B. H. KLEINER. 1995. New developments in developing creativity. Journal of Managerial Psychology, 10 (8) 20–23.

APPELBAUM, S. H., M. BREGMAN, and P. MOROZ. 1998. Fear as a strategy: Effects and impact within the organization. *Journal of European Industrial Training* 32 (3): 113–127.

ASHMOS, D. P., D. DUCHON, and R. R. MCDANIEL, JR. 1998. Participation in strategic decision making: The role of organizational predisposition and issue interpretation. *Decision Sciences* 29 (1): 25–51.

BELDONA, S., A. C. INKPEN, and A. PHATAK. 1998. Are Japanese managers more long-term oriented than United States managers? *Management International Review* 38 (3): 239–256.

BRAYBROOKE, D., and C. E. LINDBLOM. 1963. *A strategy of decision*. New York: Free Press.

BRILEY, D. A., M. W. MORRIS, and I. SIMONSON. 2000. Reasons as carriers of culture: Dynamic versus dispositional models of cultural influence on decision-making. *Journal of Consumer Research* 27 (2): 157–178.

BROWN, M. G. 1998. Improving your organization's vision. *Journal for Quality and Participation* 21 (5): 18–21.

BUSENITZ, L. W. 1999. Entrepreneurial risk and strategic decision making: It's a matter of perspective. *Journal of Applied Behavioral Science* 35 (3): 325–340.

CASE, R. H., and S. SHANE. 1998. Fostering risk taking in research and development: The importance of a project's terminal value. *Decision Sciences* 29 (4): 765–783.

CHEN, C. 2000. Using realistic business data in teaching business problem solving. *Information Technology* 18 (2): 41–50.

CHOI, J. N., and M. U. KIM. 1999. The organizational application of groupthink and its limitations in organizations. *Journal of Applied Psychology* 84 (2): 297–306.

CLARKE, L. 1999. Mission improbable: Using fantasy documents to tame disaster. Chicago: University of Chicago Press.

COHEN, M. D., J. G. MARCH, and J. P. OLSEN. 1972. A garbage can model of organizational choice. *Administrative Science Quarterly* 17: 1–25.

COHEN-ROSENTHAL, E. 1994. On arrogance and participation. *Journal for Quality and Participation* 17 (2): 58–64.

CRAINER, S. 1999. *The 75 greatest management decisions ever made, and 21 of the worst*. Chicago: American Management Association.

DANIELS, K., and A. BAILEY. 1999. Strategy development processes and participation in decision making: Predictors of role stressors and job satisfaction. *Journal of Applied Management Studies* 8 (1): 27–42.

DIGMAN, L. A. 1999. *Strategic management: concepts, processes, decisions*. Stanford, CT: Thomson.

DINORCIA, V., and J. TIGNER. 2000. Mixed motives and ethical decisions in business. *Journal of Business Ethics* 25 (1): 1–13.

DOWNS, A. 1967. *Inside bureaucracy*. Boston: Little, Brown.

DRUMMOND, H. 1998. Is escalation always irrational? *Organizational Studies* 19 (6): 911–929.

FOREST, J. and C. MEHIER. 2001. John R. Commons and Herbert A. Simon on the concept of rationality. *Journal of Economic Issues* 35 (3): 591–605.

FRISCH, D., and R. T. CLEMEN. 1994. Beyond expected utility: Rethinking behavioral decision research. *Psychological Bulletin* 116 (1): 46–54.

HARBONE, R. 1999. Power planning! An integrated business planning process. *Strategic Finance Magazine* 81 (4): 47–53.

HARRISON, E. F. 1993. Inter-disciplinary models of decision making. *Management Decision* 31 (8): 27–33.

HARRISON, E. F., and M. A. PELLETIER. 1995. A paradigm for strategic decision success. *Management Decision* 33 (7): 53–59.

HOOPER, M. K. 1998. The day the earth shook. *Security Management* 42 (3): 38–44.

HOWLAND, J., R. T. HINGSON, T. MANGIONE, T. W. BELL, and B. S. NICOLE. 1996. Why are most drowning victims men? Sex differences in aquatic skills and behaviors. *American Journal of Public Health* 86 (1): 93–94.

HUDZIK, J., and G. CORDNER. 1983. *Planning in criminal justice organizations and systems*. New York: Macmillan.

JALAN, A., and B. H. KLEINER. 1995. New developments in developing creativity *Journal of Managerial Psychology* 10 (8): 20–23.

JANIS, I. L. 1972. *Victims of groupthink*. Boston: Houghton Mifflin.

JIANAKOPLOS, N. A., and A. BERNASEK. 1998. Are women more risk averse? *Economic Inquiry* 36 (4): 620–630.

JONES, T. M. 1991. Ethical decision making by individuals in organizations: An issue-contingent model. *Academy of Management Review* 16 (2): 366–395.

JORDAN, E. 1999. IT contingency planning: Management roles. *Information Management and Computer Security* 7 (5): 232–238.

KHATRI, N., and H. A. NG. 2000. The role of intuition in strategic decision making. *Human Relations* 53 (1): 57–86.

KIM, Y. 2000. A comparative study of the "Abilene paradox" and "Groupthink." *Public Administration Quarterly* 25 (2): 168–190.

KOBERG, C. S., L. F. TEGARDEN, and W. D. WILSTED. 1993. Environmental and structural influences on the strategy-making process of banks. *Journal of Applied Business Research* 9 (3): 58–68.

KOREY, G. 1995. TDM Grid: An effective tool for implementing strategic plans. *Management Decision* 33 (2): 40–47.

LANGLEY, A. 1995. Between "paralysis by analysis" and "extinction by instinct". *Sloan Management Review* 36 (3): 63–67.

McCRIE, R. D. 1988. The development of the U.S. guard industry. *Annals of the American Academy of Political Sciences* 498: 23–33.

MINTZBERG, H., and F. WESTLEY. 2001. Decision making: It's not what you think. *MIT Sloan Management Review* 42 (3): 89–93.

MURNIGHAN, K., and J. C. MOWEN. 2002. *The art of high stakes decision making: Tough calls in a speed-driven world*. New York: Wiley.

NELSON, T., and E. McFADZEAN. 1998. Facilitating problem-solving groups: Facilitator competences. *Leadership and Organizational Development Journal* 19 (2): 72–82.

NEWMANN, W. W. 1998. Foreign policy decision making, garbage cans, and policy shifts: The Eisenhower administration and the "chances for peace" speech. *American Review of Public Administration* 28 (2): 187–212.

OSBORNE, R. L. 1995. The essence of entrepreneurial success. *Management Decision* 33 (7): 4–9.

O'SULLIVAN, D., and B. DOWN. 2001. Policy decision making models in practice: A case study of the western Australian sentencing acts. *Policy Studies Journal* 29 (1): 56–70.

PENG, W. 1992. A critique on H. A. Simon's administrative behavior theory. *Public Administration Quarterly* 16 (2): 254–264.

PERKINS, D. 1981. *The mind's best work.* Cambridge, MA: Harvard University Press.

PERROW, C. 1984. *Normal accidents: Living with high-risk technologies.* New York: Basic Books.

RAUSCH, E. 1999. Management/leadership decision guidelines: Critical ingredients for competitiveness. *Competitiveness Review* 9 (2): 19–27.

RAUSCH, E., S. M. HALFHILL, H. SHERMAN, and J. B. WASHBUSH. 2001. Practical leadership in management education for effective strategies in a rapidly changing world. *Journal of Management Development* 20 (3): 245–258.

ROBERTSON, C., and P. A. FADIL. 1999. Ethical decision making in multinational organizations: A culture-based model. *Journal of Business Ethics* 19 (4): 385–392.

RODE, C., and X. WANG. 2000. Risk-sensitive decision making examined within an evolutionary framework. *American Behavioral Scientist* 43 (6): 926–939.

ROSENTHAL, U., and A. KOUZMIN. 1997. Crises and crisis management: Toward comprehensive government decision making. *Journal of Public Administration Research and Theory* (7) 2: 277–304.

ROSS, C. L., and N. G. LEIGH. 2000. Planning, urban revitalization, and the inner city: An exploration of structural racism. *Journal of Planning Literature* 14 (3): 367–380.

SAUTER, V. L. 1999. Intuitive decision-making. *Communications of the ACM* 42 (6): 109–115.

SHARKANSKY, I., and Y. ZALMANOVITCH. 2000. Improvisation in public administration and police making in Israel. *Public Administration Review* 60 (4): 321–329.

SHOEMAKER, P. J. 1995. Scenario Planning: A tool for strategic thinking. *Sloan Management Review* 36 (2): 25–40.

SHULMAN, S. 1997. What's so rational about rational expectations? Hyperrationality and the logical limits to neoclassicalism. *Journal of Post Keynesian Economics* 20 (1): 135–148.

SIMON, H.A. 1957. *Models of man: Social and rational.* New York: Wiley.

SIMON, H.A. 1960. *The new science of management decision.* New York: Harper & Row.

SISSON, S. 1985. Managerial risk taking. *Training and development Journal* 39 (1): 39–42.

SOONHEE, K. 2002. Participative management and job satisfaction: Lessons for management leadership. *Public Administration Review* 62 (2): 231–241.

STEEL, J. 2000. Altitude recovery. *Risk Management* 47 (12): 23–26.

STEISS, A.W. 1985. *Strategic management and organizational decision making.* Lexington, MA: D.C. Heath.

STONER, J.A., and R.A. FREEMAN. 1989. *Management.* 4th ed. Englewood Cliffs, NJ: Prentice Hall.

'THART, P., U. ROSENTHAL, and K.A. KOUZMIN. 1993. Crisis decision making: The centralization thesis revisited. *Administration and Society* 25 (1): 12–45.

TRIMPOP, R., and B. KIRKCALDY. 1998. Stress indicators among medical personnel in Germany: A comparison of the "old" and "new" Länder. *Journal of Managerial Psychology* 13 (1/2): 22–27.

VanYperen, N. W., A. E. Van den Berg, and M. C. Willering. 1999. *Journal of Occupational and Organizational Psychology* 72 (3): 377–392.

Vecchio, R. P. 1988. *Organizational behavior*. Hinsdale, IL: Dryden Press.

Weick, K. E. 1998. Improvisation as a mindset for organizational analysis. *Organizational Science* 9 (5): 543–555.

Zemke, R., C. Raines, and B. Filipzak. 2000. *Generations at work*. Chicago: American Management Association.

chapter five

Recruitment and Selection

One of the many challenges facing the security manger in the twenty-first century is to find highly qualified and motivated individuals to meet the increasing demands and changes in the security industry. In order to find those individuals who have those requisite skills and the potential to grow and excel in the organization, managers will need to have effective recruitment and selection procedures.

Recruitment is the process of finding qualified individuals and encouraging them to apply for employment with the organization. Selection is the process of choosing among those applicants (French 1994). In both of these distinct but interrelated processes, the organization is interested in "screening out" applicants who are not suitable and "screening in" individuals who meet the qualifications established by the organization (Ryan and Lasek 1991).

An underlying theme in this chapter is that organizations need an effective recruitment and selection process if they want high-quality employees. Most, if not all, managers would agree that the quality of their personnel is very important and that they are one of the most important assets the organization possesses. Yet the importance of establishing an effective recruitment and selection process is often disregarded, with the end result that the best or brightest individuals are not recruited and selected. Rather, the organization engages in a form of decision making defined by Simon (1976) as satisfycing. Satisfycing occurs when managers adopt the first decision they reach rather than search for the optimal solution to the issue. Simply stated, managers may use inappropriate recruitment and selection methods that fail to find the most qualified individual for the position. These

126

managers have satisfied and achieved their basic need: an employee. But have they found the best employee, or has the organization just hired a "25-year liability"?

The recruitment and selection process is also important in maintaining a stable and productive workforce. Some sectors of the private security industry, particularly entry-level contract security positions, have a high employee turnover rate. Turnover in the labor market is the rotation of employees from job to job and company to company.

Turnover may produce a phenomenon called churn. Churn occurs when employee turnovers produce no improvement in the match, quality, and contribution of the employee to the new organization. Rather, employees simply move from one company to another, which translates into undue costs to the employer in the context of hidden and direct costs associated with discharging the employee, if necessary; costs associated with recruiting and selecting new employees; and costs related to training the new employee (Verkerke 1998).

To help security managers plan an effective recruitment and selection process, this chapter explores issues related to the recruitment and selection of security employees, focusing on planning and preparing for the recruitment and selection process through job analysis. This chapter also provides an overview of some of the more commonly used recruitment and selection techniques. As these techniques must comply with administrative laws, relevant federal guidelines that govern their use and application are also discussed. In addition, this chapter discusses liability claims in recruitment and selection—specifically, claims related to negligent hiring and defamation.

■ EMPLOYMENT LAWS

Any of the processes used or not used could come under the scrutiny of the courts. Legislation and case law require that employers be able to verify the components of their recruitment and selection procedures to ensure that they are legal and nondiscriminatory. If issues should arise because of a defect in the recruitment and selection process, the organization could be exposed to a myriad of legal challenges that could negatively impact the firm's reputation and future attempts in recruiting and selecting employees. Some of the major pieces of legislation that need to be considered are the Civil Rights Act of 1964, as amended; the Americans with Disabilities Act (ADA) of 1990; and the Age Discrimination in Employment Act (ADEA) of 1967.

Title VII of the Civil Rights Act of 1964

Title VII of the Civil Rights Act of 1964, as amended, prohibits discrimination on the basis of race, color, religion, sex, or national origin in any employment practice that includes hiring, firing, promotions, transfers, and other employer activities throughout the employee's tenure with the organization. An unlawful employment practice is established when the complaining party or group of individuals demonstrate that race, religion, sex, or national origin was a motivating factor in the employer's discriminatory practices. These parties can file a complaint with the Equal Employment Opportunity Commission (EEOC), which is charged with enforcing this act and other employment-related legislation, or file a suit in the federal courts. Title VII violations can be based on the theory of disparate treatment and disparate impact.

Disparate Treatment   Disparate treatment occurs when an employer intentionally discriminates against an individual who belongs to a protected group in some type of employment practice (Johnson 2000). Disparate treatment has two major forms. The first type, known as overt disparate treatment, occurs when an employment practice or policy is, on its face, discriminatory. In order to prove this form of discrimination, the plaintiff simply needs to show membership in a protected group against which the employment policy or practice discriminates (Fielding 1990). As pointed out by Johnson (2000), disparate treatment is what most people think of when they hear the term "discrimination."

An example of overt disparate treatment is an employer that refused to hire a female candidate because she told the interviewers that she planned on having children. Later, the employer told the applicant that she was denied employment because it was felt that her personal goal of having children would interfere with the company's needs. Because of her gender, this applicant was treated differently from other applicants, creating a claim of disparate treatment under Title VII.

Another form of disparate treatment occurs when the plaintiff can establish a prima facie case of discrimination. In order to prove that the evidence is sufficient to support a finding of disparate treatment, the plaintiff must show membership in a protected group, have suffered from an adverse employment action, was qualified for the position, and was treated less favorably than members of other classes (Johnson 2000). The plaintiff must prove that the employer's employment policy contained a hidden intent to discriminate (Fielding 1990; Zuck 1989). That is, the employer had a covert intent to discriminate against an individual belonging to a protected group. If the plaintiff is successful in proving a prima facie case, the burden of proof falls on the employer to prove that it had a legitimate and nondiscriminatory reason for the challenged action (Johnson 2000).

Disparate Impact   Disparate impact occurs when an entire group of claimants protected under Title VII are somehow discriminated against in an employment decision. A claim of disparate impact usually occurs when the employer engages in an activity that may appear to be "neutral" or nondiscriminatory on its face, but somehow adversely affects a protected group to a greater degree than the balance of the population (Johnson 2000). Because they impact an entire group of individuals protected under Title VII, claims involving disparate impact are often easier to prove in court than are cases of disparate treatment.

To successfully prove a claim of disparate impact, a claimant must prove (1) membership in a protected class, (2) that the employer has a "neutral" employment practice, and (3) that this practice has a disproportionate negative effect on that protected class (Johnson 2000). For example, disparate impact may exist when an employer has created a non-job-related physical agility test as a screening tool that fails the majority of female applicants. Although not "intentional," this hiring practice has impacted an entire group of individuals who are protected under Title VII legislation.

The courts can use several techniques to determine whether disparate impact has occurred. One method is to simply let the "statistics speak for themselves" (Canton 1987). For example, if the organization employs very few, if any, individuals from protected groups, compared to the overall number of its employees or the total labor force available, a prima facie case of discrimination could result. One way the courts will determine this is to simply compare the hiring practices of the organization in the context of the people it hires and compare those practices to a proxy or pool. This proxy or pool could consist of the available workforce in the particular area—the Standard Metropolitan Statistical Area (SMSA), or the metropolitan labor market—the general population of the area, applicant figures, or the workforce of the city. Although the choice of proxy is important, no hard-and-fast rules govern which one to use (Canton 1987). In other cases, the courts use measures of statistical significance and standard deviation analysis (Rominger and Sandoval 1998). These types of tests usually compare the percentage of individuals who passed the test rather than selection rates or the percentage of individuals hired (Canton 1987).

Another common method to determine whether an employment practice is discriminatory is to follow the requirement set forth in the *Uniform Guidelines on Employee Selection Procedures* (1978). These requirements stipulate that an employer validate any selection procedure that has an adverse impact on protected groups: members of any sex, race, or ethnic group. If the selection rate for any race, sex, or ethnic group is less than four-fifths of the group with the highest selection rate it will generally be regarded as evidence of adverse impact. In this capacity, the courts compare selection rates, or the percentage of applicants who completed the test and were hired. In a combined method, some courts determine discrimination on the bases of the substantial or significant standard. In applying this standard, the court may analyze cases under the four-fifths rule and then use statistical analysis to determine whether the statistical disparity is substantial or significant (Canton 1987).

Exceptions to Title VII Violations

In some situations, an employer can have discriminatory employment policies that affect individuals who belong to protected groups. These permissible discriminatory practices are allowed if the employer can prove that its employment actions were related to a bona fide occupational qualification or if the discriminatory practice was related to a business necessity.

Bona Fide Occupational Qualifications   When it passed Title VII, Congress also included a defense to some Title VII violations. The bona fide occupational qualification (BFOQ) is a defense for disparate treatment against a person's sex, national origin, or religion (Fielding 1990). When using a BFOQ defense, the organization admits to discriminatory practices but argues that it was necessary or justified, owing to the nature of the employment or the specific job (Johnson

2000). The employer engages in a discriminatory hiring practice because otherwise, its business operation would be adversely affected. That is, discrimination was necessary to ensure the normal operation of a business. Some examples of BFOQs are readily found in the field of law enforcement and may include age, primarily in the federal sector, size and weight, and vision standards. An example of sex-based BFOQ that has held up in the courts is hiring only female nurses to work in hospital labor and delivery units. This gender-based BFOQ is necessary to protect the privacy interests of hospital patients (Berman 2000). BFOQ defenses apply to all protected criteria except race. BFOQs do not apply to racial discrimination (Bryant 1998).

Business Necessity   The business-necessity defense (BND), like the BFOQ, is used to defend the employer's practices in business decisions. The BND applies to situations that involve disparate impact. The BND is less restrictive than a BFOQ, applying to all protected groups, including one's race (Fielding 1990). The key in using the BND is that the practice is essential to the continued success of the business. This defense was first recognized by the U.S. Supreme Court in *Griggs v. Duke Power Company* (1971) (see Box 5–1).

> ### BOX 5–1 ■ Employment Discrimination: *Griggs v. Duke Power Company* (1971)
>
> Griggs, a black employee of the Duke Power Company, filed a Title VII suit alleging that the company's use of aptitude tests and the requirement for applicants to have either a high school diploma or an equivalent score on an aptitude test for promotion to other departments in the organization essentially segregated blacks into lower-paying positions and excluded them from other opportunities in the company. The employer was unable to show any meaningful relationship between the high school education and testing requirements and job performance.
>
> The Supreme Court's decision concluded that the high school diploma and test score requirements were not job related and stated that "employment tests are to be used as a measure for the person for the job, not the person in the abstract."
>
> The Court also determined that an employer using a test having an adverse impact on minorities must prove that the test is a business necessity. The burden of proof in these situations rests on the employer, not the complainant.
>
> To prove that it has a valid testing procedure, the company must be prepared to prove four issues or points.
>
> 1. The tests are job related.
> 2. The tests serve a legitimate business purpose, such as enhancing the efficiency of the selection decision.
> 3. The tests have been developed to meet professional standards.
> 4. The tests measure the professional standards (Rominger and Sandval 1998).

According to Grover (1996), an employer must prove the following elements under the BND.

- The ultimate business goal the employer seeks to achieve through the practice is essential to the business.
- The tasks that the practice measures are essential for achievement of that ultimate business goal.
- Workers selected for the positions in question must be able to perform the tasks.
- The practice selected is necessary to measure the ability to perform those tasks.

The BND can become quite complex. Courts have determined that requiring English-speaking workers, which could be discrimination, based on the person's race, for oil-drilling operations is a justifiable business necessity because of the hazardous nature of the work. With safety as the primary goal of the organization, the organization's English-only BND can be analyzed by using the following four points (Lye 1998).

1. There is an overriding legitimate business purpose such that the practice is necessary for the safe and efficient operation of the business.
2. The business purpose must be sufficiently compelling to override any racial impact.
3. The challenged practice must effectively carry out the business purpose it is alleged to serve.
4. There must be available no acceptable alternative policies or practices that would better accomplish the business purpose or accomplish it equally well with a lesser differential racial impact.

The Impact of Title VII on Recruitment and Selection

All the preceding issues must be considered when designing and implementing the recruitment and selection process. For example, a company's recruitment process may purposefully or inadvertently affect protected groups. The Civil Rights Act (2000) prohibits employers from using advertisements "indicating prohibited preference, limitation, specification, or discrimination based on . . . except when these bases are a bona fide occupational qualification for employment." Hence, certain advertisement techniques, although on their face not discriminatory, may result in disparate treatment of some protected groups. For example, if an organization relies solely on word-of-mouth advertising for positions, the result may be that certain protected groups are excluded in the employment process, exposing the organization to scrutiny and perhaps litigation over its recruitment and selection procedures for security personnel.

Title VII violations can exist with selection tools. The EEOC's *Guide to Pre-Employment Inquiries* indicates that questions that either directly or indirectly require the disclosure of information about protected-class status may constitute evidence of discrimination protected by Title VII. Accordingly, the EEOC *Guide* cautions against the use of questions that directly inquire about protected-class status, such as race, age, and religious beliefs. The interviewer should also always remember that questions that appear to be innocent or neutral may have a disparate impact in screening out individuals who belong to a protected class. For example, asking questions about an individual's height and weight may lead to the disqualification of a disproportionate number of individuals in a protected class, such as females (Befort 1997). Asking about an applicant's arrest record constitutes illegal discrimination, but one can ask whether the applicant has been convicted of any crime or has plead guilty or no contest (Clay and Stephens 1995).

Americans with Disabilities Act

The Americans with Disabilities Act (ADA) of 1990 prohibits organizations with 15 or more employees from engaging in discriminatory activities against disabled persons in any area of the employment relationship, beginning with the recruitment and selection process, and extending also to promotions, training, and other terms and conditions of the job (Goldman 1993). The ADA applies to employees who have or may develop a disability, as well as to individuals seeking employment opportunities with the company. This relatively new and broad piece of legislation will challenge managers in all facets of the employment relationship, including the recruitment and selection process.

The ADA defines a disability as (1) a physical or mental impairment that substantially limits one or more of the major life activities of the individual, (2) a record of such an impairment, or (3) being regarded as having such an impairment. Physical impairments include almost any malady or injury; mental impairments include psychological disorders, such as mental retardation, organic brain syndromes, emotional or mental illness, and specific learning disabilities. Major life activities include caring for one's self, performing manual tasks, walking, seeing, hearing, speaking, breathing, working, and learning. "Being regarded as" occurs when an employer discriminates against an individual perceived to have a disability. An example would be discriminating against a candidate who walks with a limp (from a weekend athletic accident) because the employer thinks he or she may have a crippling and permanent muscular or skeletal disease.

Not all "disabilities" are qualified disabilities. ADA legislation prohibits discrimination only against individuals who have a qualified disability, which is defined in Box 5-2. The key to this definition is that the employee must be able to perform the essential functions of the job. As pointed out by Goldman (1993), these essential job duties embrace the skills, judgments, expertise, and tasks the individual must perform in order to succeed in the position. If an applicant cannot perform these essential functions, the employer can discriminate against the person in the employment decision.

BOX 5–2 ■ Factors to be Considered in Determining Undue Hardship of ADA Accommodation.

(8) Qualified individual with a disability

The term "qualified individual with a disability" means an individual with a disability who, with or without reasonable accommodation, can perform the essential functions of the employment position that such individual holds or desires. For the purposes of this subchapter, consideration shall be given to the employer's judgment as to what functions of a job are essential, and if an employer has prepared a written description before advertising or interviewing applicants for the job, this description shall be considered evidence of the essential functions of the job.

(9) Reasonable accommodation

The term "reasonable accommodation" may include—

(A) making existing facilities used by employees readily accessible to and usable by individuals with disabilities; and

(B) job restructuring, part-time or modified work schedules, reassignment to a vacant position, acquisition or modification of equipment or devices, appropriate adjustment or modifications of examinations, training materials or policies, the provision of qualified readers or interpreters, and other similar accommodations for individuals with disabilities.

(10) Undue hardship

(A) In general

The term "undue hardship" means an action requiring significant difficulty or expense, when considered in light of the factors set forth in subparagraph (B)

(B) Factors to be considered

In determining whether an accommodation would impose an undue hardship on a covered entity, factors to be considered include—

(i) the nature and cost of the accommodation needed under this chapter;

(ii) the overall financial resources of the facility or facilities involved in the provision of the reasonable accommodation;

(iii) the number of persons employed at such facility;

(iv) the effect on expenses and resources, or the impact otherwise of such accommodation upon the operation of the facility;

(v) the overall financial resources of the covered entity; the overall size of the business of a covered entity with respect to the number of its employees; the number, type, and location of its facilities; and

(vi) the type of operation or operations of the covered entity, including the composition, structure, and functions of the workforce of such entity; the geographic separateness, administrative, or fiscal relationship of the facility or facilities in question to the covered entity.

United States Code Annotated Title 42. The Public Health and Welfare Chapter 126—Equal Opportunity for Individuals with Disabilities Subchapter I—Employment

The ADA uses three factors to define the term "essential job functions."

1. The function may be essential because the reason the position exists is to perform the function.
2. The function may be essential because of the limited number of employees available in the organization to which the job function can be distributed.
3. The function may be highly specialized so that the incumbent in the position is hired for expertise or the ability to perform the particular function.

To further clarify what an essential job function is, the EEOC, which administers the ADA, has provided a list of factors for employers to consider when determining whether a job function is essential: (1) the employer's judgments as to which functions are essential; (2) written job descriptions prepared before advertising and interviewing applicants; (3) the amount of time spent on the job performing the function and the consequences of not requiring the incumbent to perform the function; (4) the terms of a collective bargaining agreement, if applicable; (5) the work experience of past incumbents in the job; and/or (6) the current work experience of incumbents in similar jobs ([29 CFR § 1630.2(n)(2) (1994).

The employer must provide an employee having a qualified disability reasonable accommodation for that known disability. Reasonable accommodation can be thought of as the employer's meeting the needs of the disabled worker, balanced against legitimate business needs (Goldman 1993). Examples of a reasonable accommodation include making the workplace physically accessible to a disabled person, modifying existing or providing specialized equipment, and rearranging the workplace to accommodate the needs of a wheelchair-bound employee (Hein and VanZante 1993). In the recruitment and selection process, reasonable accommodation must also be considered. In this context, the employer must provide accommodations to applicants who have qualified disabilities.

The ADA does not require that employers hire all individuals who have a disability. But as with Title VII violations, the company may need to prove that its employment practices did not discriminate against an individual or group of individuals. Similarly, demonstrating that the discrimination was based on a BFOQ or a business necessity is a defense for these discriminatory practices. Unique to the ADA is the undue-hardship defense. The ADA defines an undue hardship as a significant difficulty or expense related to providing the reasonable accommodation. To determine whether an accommodation can be refused, an employer needs to consider the six factors listed in Box 5–2.

The ADA also requires that an employer give candidates a conditional offer of employment prior to asking any medically related questions. This conditional offer of employment is premised on the belief that prior to the ADA, employers were denying employment opportunities to candidates who had some type of disability. This conditional offer does not necessarily mean that the person is qualified. Pending the conditional job offer, the firm can then ask medically related questions or questions related to a disability. On discovery of an applicant's disability during a postconditional-offer medical exam, the employer can withdraw the offer for discriminatory reasons as long as the withdrawal is related to an essential job function.

Impact of the ADA on Recruitment and Selection

As pointed out earlier, the ADA prohibits discrimination in an employment practice and requires the removal of barriers that have historically prevented individuals with disabilities from gaining or maintaining employment. Individuals making a claim under the ADA must demonstrate the following three points to the courts.

1. They have a disability.
2. They are qualified for the job with or without reasonable accommodation.
3. The employer made an adverse employment decision because of the disability.

A consideration of discriminatory practices must begin with an analysis of the existing recruitment and selection practices the employer uses to ensure that no issues related to a candidate's disability are discussed or revealed prior to making a conditional job offer to the applicant. Employers need to make sure that no medical-related question is asked prior to the conditional job offer. Asking questions of this nature could be construed as a medical exam or a disability-related inquiry.

Employers need to review their existing recruiting methods to ensure that they are ADA compliant. Employers should review job advertisements to ensure that they describe essential job functions and do not discourage individuals with disabilities from applying (An ADA checklist . . ., 1994). If a job fair is part of the recruitment process, the employer must also provide reasonable accommodations by ensuring that the location is accessible for individuals with disabilities.

The ADA may also require employers to change the sequence of some of their selection procedures. Background checks that include medical questions may now have to be delayed until after a conditional offer is made. Some psychological tests that the company uses may contain medical-related questions. If such tests are used, the company will need to extend a conditional job offer to the candidate prior to test administration (Rubin 1994). In the context of alcohol testing, however, it is the same as any other medical examination inasmuch as the individual must be given a conditional offer prior to receiving the test. Under the ADA, drug testing is not considered a medical examination and can therefore be used as a screening tool prior to the individual's receiving a conditional offer of employment. This is premised on the ADA's belief that being drug free is inherently job related and consistent with business necessity (Ferraro and Judge 2003).

Besides changing the nature and sequence of selection tools, managers involved in the recruitment and selection process will need to be trained in ADA-related issues. This may be particularly important in interviewing. For instance, the employer would be in violation of the ADA by asking whether the applicant has a disability that would prevent the person from performing the essential functions of the job, with or without accommodations. However, the interviewer can ask whether the applicant can perform the essential functions of the job with or without accommodations. This is not considered a medical question because it did not ask whether the person had a disability (Duston 1994). If an applicant volunteers information related to a disability, the employer cannot follow up on the statement or use that information as a basis for making an employment decision.

Age Discrimination in Employment Act of 1967

The Age Discrimination in Employment Act (ADEA) of 1967 made it illegal for an employer to discriminate against individuals between the ages of 40 and 65 on the basis of age except where age is considered a bona fide occupational qualification, based on reasonable factors other than age (Schiff 1993). To show a prima facie case of age discrimination under the ADEA, the plaintiff must show that the employer uses a mandatory retirement policy or has an age-based hiring policy and that she or he is 40 years or older, was denied employment on the basis of age, and would have met the job qualifications, with the exception of a BFOQ (Schiff 1993). As for Title VII and the ADA, the EEOC is responsible for the administration of the ADEA. In order to prove age as a BFOQ, the employer must prove that an age limit is reasonably necessary to the essence of the business, that all or substantially all individuals excluded from the job are in fact disqualified, or that some of the individuals so excluded possess a disqualifying trait that cannot be ascertained except by reference to age (Schiff 1993).

Two standards related to BFOQs have been applied in age-discrimination cases. The Timiami standard applies a two-prong test to determine whether age is a legitimate BFOQ. The first prong considers safety in determining whether the job qualification is reasonably necessary to the essence of the business. The second prong requires that the employer show that it had either reasonable cause or a factual basis for believing that all or a substantial number of older employees possess traits that preclude safe and efficient job performance. Another defense for the employer is that it would be impractical or impossible to test reliability on an individual basis related to the employee's ability to perform safely and adequately the duties of the position. In essence, this test requires more than reasonableness in establishing age standards, but it does not require a Title VII analysis of the classifications (Schiff 1993).

The second standard, known as the Hodgson standard, simply bases the employer's BFOQ age policy on reasonable belief that increased age increases the risk of harm (Schiff 1993). Both of these standards were based on the premise that overriding safety factors, in the context of bus drivers, minimize the level of proof required to establish a BFOQ. Based on these standards, Schiff (1993) concludes that when the degree of risk to the public or other employees is high, the fixing of an age may be more arbitrary and accepted by the courts.

■ ESTABLISHING A RECRUITMENT AND SELECTION PROGRAM

Delegating Responsibility

Usually, the responsibility for establishing a recruitment program is assigned to the human resources department. In other instances, individuals from the specific organizational unit that has openings serve as recruiters. They may work with or independently of employees in the human resources department. Usually, the recruitment responsibilities are an addition to the daily responsibilities of the assigned individuals. The position of recruiter may also be semipermanent, as many recruitment sources may take a long period of time to nurture and develop.

The selection of a recruitment officer is paramount to a successful hire. One key consideration that a company should have when selecting recruiters is that they should have characteristics that have been identified as the most important attributes a candidate should possess to be employed by the company. Recruiters are diplomats for the company. Their professionalism and demeanor are a direct reflection of the company's organizational culture.

In one company, for example, the selection of the recruiter was taken for granted. The company had a "problem" employee who, for the past 2 years, had not been performing to expectations. This manager was habitually late for work, did not attend all departmental meetings, and did not turn in work on time. As a "punishment," this individual was designated as the recruiter who needed to travel. This individual stated lack of interest in the recruiter position. Nevertheless, this employee did represent the company in its recruitment drives. This action raises several questions and issues about the company's recruitment efforts. One question is how effective the recruitment effort was when the worst employee, who told management that he did not want the position, was sent to recruit new employees.

Job Analysis

Any recruitment and selection process must begin with job analysis, the systematic and thorough study of specific tasks related to one's position. These tasks, when combined, are used to construct job descriptions and to select employees for the firm. According to Coulton and Field (1995, 228), "job analysis provides information . . . and should delineate clusters of activities that, when combined, comprise important aspects of the job being evaluated. These are called dimensions."

These job activities, or clusters, can be divided into three main areas: task, behavioral, and abilities data. Task data reveal the work performed and why it is performed; behavioral data, the behaviors that occur on the job; and abilities data, what underlying skills or knowledge the worker must possess for satisfactory performance on the job (Milkovich and Boudreau 1991). The tasks are then ranked according to their relative importance, and a test is constructed to measure the significant abilities needed for successful job performance (Canton 1987).

Depending on the design and purpose of job analysis, a variety of sources can be used to identify the various work dimensions. These sources may include the use of internal subject-matter experts (SMEs) and focus groups; one-on-one interviews with workers, supervisors, and administrators; training manuals; and closely observing the performance of employees on the job. The firm can also employ outside consultants or SMEs to identify the job dimensions. The means to determine or measure the knowledge, skills, and abilities

(KSAs) of the position can also be accomplished via preconstructed question-naires or inventories that vary in cost, length, and complexity.

■ THE RECRUITMENT PROCESS

As stated earlier in this chapter, recruitment is the process of finding a pool of qualified individuals and encouraging them to apply for positions with the orga-nization. Recruitment is a dynamic process that is influenced by both the organi-zation and the environment. Some of the organizational influences that may affect recruiting are the firm's financial solvency, or health; its overall size, loca-tion, and reputation; and compensation, including pay and benefits (French 1994). Recruitment decisions can also be based on the talent and expertise of the recruiters, based on their educational levels, background, and creativity.

Environmental issues or factors also influence recruiting. These factors in-clude the costs related to recruitment, time constraints, and the available candidate pool in the external and internal labor markets. Other factors are the organization's philosophy about recruiting, past recruitment practices, tradition, and the level of commitment the organization has toward recruiting existing employees (French 1994). The environment also includes social attitudes toward particular segments of the security industry. For example, attitudes toward contract security for some applicants may not be as positive as opportunities in proprietary security opera-tions. As a consequence, the contract security firm may have to engage in more cre-ative and aggressive recruitment programs to attract suitable employees.

Recruitment efforts can be either general or specific. In general recruiting, the organization is looking for employees who possess those general skills need-ed to perform the job effectively. To attract applicants, the company follows sim-ple and standardized procedures (Stoner and Freeman 1989). An example of general recruiting is an organization that needs to fill an entry-level security posi-tion that has no high-tech or specialized skills. To find qualified applicants, the company uses the same recruitment sources used to fill the existing line-level po-sitions: newspapers, schools, and employee referrals.

In specific recruiting, the organization wants a particular type of individual who has special skills and talents. Individuals having these talents receive specialized attention and treatment from company representatives. This specialized attention may be thought of as "courting." This type of recruitment may also extend over a long period of time. Usually, specialized recruiting is reserved for higher-level execu-tives and specialists (Stoner and Freeman 1989). For example, specific recruiting might entail a manager's establishing a professional friendship with a person who has special training and experience in corporate espionage. Throughout this rela-tionship, the manager would be "selling" the company to the prospective applicant.

Recruitment Strategy

Regardless of the recruitment process, the recruitment strategy should be based on the needs of the organization, the position(s) to be filled, and the findings from the job analysis. Although the firm may use a wide variety of recruitment strategies and tools, the key to any plan is that it be simple, workable, logical, practical, cost-effective, ethical, and legal.

An often overlooked component in any recruitment plan is that the information used to recruit prospective employees must accurately reflect the job responsibilities of the position. That is, the organization must ensure that it does not inflate the expectations of the job. In one instance, for example, the recruitment efforts by the owners of a contract security firm included the promise that entry-level contract guards would have the opportunity to be used in private investigations and protection services for sports figures and rock stars. In the short run, this strategy served to fill entry-level guard positions. In the long run, however, the "promised" assignments did not materialize, and some of these new employees quit. Those who stayed had lower levels of trust and morale, and they also warned potential applicants about this particular company's practices.

This example shows that a company needs to be ethically sound in its recruiting. One way to ensure this is to provide applicants with a realistic job preview (RJP). An RJP is any method, written or verbal, that gives recruits a balanced picture of both the negative and positive aspects of the job (Roth and Roth 1995). A properly designed RJP also reduces employee turnover. Research involving salespersons, for example, has found that the accuracy of job information given to candidates prior to hiring is a strong predictor of whether they decide to leave their positions (Pitt and Ramaseshan 1995). Additional research involving 2,500 insurance agents found that those who received accurate and sufficient job descriptions had a 41 percent survival rate for their jobs, compared to a 21 percent rate for those who were given inaccurate and insufficient job descriptions (Duncan 1994).

Recruitment Methods

A variety of recruitment techniques can be used to attract the most qualified and suitable candidates. When determining which recruitment methods to use, the organization should engage in recruitment studies. Recruitment studies follow up, track, and monitor previously used recruitment sources to determine which of the methods provided the company with high-performance employees. Recruitment studies examine what recruitment sources have resulted in success for the organization as measured in attracting, selecting, and retaining employees. This process, however, may be overlooked when planning the recruitment process. Two reasons for not using recruitment studies have been the lack of time to implement them and beliefs related to the overall usefulness of the practice (Terpstra and Rozell 1997).

Even though the organization may have a sound recruitment program, variables not directly related to recruitment may thwart its recruitment attempts and outcomes. For example, hours worked; compensation packages, including health insurance and wages; the location of the firm; the corporate culture; the public's perceptions of the company or entire industry group; and the organization's reputation will also affect recruitment. These and other variables should be considered when designing the recruitment strategy and engaging in postrecruitment studies, discussed later.

Higher-Education Institutions   Career services departments at community colleges and four-year universities can provide security organizations with a large applicant pool. Depending on the size and structure of these departments, recruiters may be allowed to advertise positions, conduct interviews, and access information on students seeking employment. In many instances, career services departments periodically sponsors career fairs so that recruiters can promote their organizations and conduct on-site interviews.

Another recruitment source involves contacts with specific departments or schools at these institutions. Contacting business, criminal justice, and other departments or schools can assist the organization in finding student applicants whose skills may be appropriate for the company's needs. Recruiters might also establish working relationships with faculty members who, for example, could announce positions in classes. These relationships could be reciprocal. For example, faculty members could have the recruiters come into their class to speak on specific topics, and the guest speakers could recruit students from these classes.

Career Fairs   Career fairs can be conducted at a higher-education institution, or an organization may consider conducting its own career fair, sponsored by one or more employers. One of the benefits of industry-based career fairs is that they cater to job seekers interested in that specific field. Besides attracting a large pool of interested job seekers, specialized career fairs may be cost-effective for firms.

On-site career fairs provide a more personalized approach to recruiting. Depending on the format, potential employees can meet with multiple company representatives, including managers and line-level workers, and get a tour of the organization. The employer also receives a greater amount of face-to-face exposure with the candidate, which may result in the candidate's receiving a more comprehensive understanding of the organization. These recruitment strategies may be more cost-effective than others, as the organization's expenses for travel, lodging, and other expenses are eliminated.

Expo\sitions and Conferences   The primary reason for expositions and conferences is to exchange information, exhibit new technologies, and sell products. A secondary outcome of these events is that they offer the security company an opportunity to "sell" itself to a pool of qualified and perhaps interested individuals to apply with the company. This recruitment strategy can be very competitive, as many companies are competing for prospective employees attending these functions.

E-Recruiting   Five million Americans had access to the Internet in 1995; four years later, more than 10 times as many—50 million—were connected. Estimates from the U.S. Census Bureau show that the number of people going online from home rose from 57 million in late 1998 to 94 million in mid-2000. In this same time period, the number of households with one or more computers rose from 42 percent to 51 percent (U.S. Dept of Commerce 1998).

Savvy organizations have recognized this growing trend and have begun Web-based recruiting. Web-based recruiting can be conducted in-house or, if the organization does not have a Web site or lacks expertise, through use of the growing number of job-posting sites, which charge the company a posting fee. According to Cober et al. (2000), some of the advantages of recruiting from Web sites are

- *Cost.*   The average recruiting cost for U.S. companies ranges from $8,000 to $10,000 per applicant, depending on the position. Online recruiting can be as low as $900 per person.
- *Applicant/organizational fit.*   Web sites give applicants more information on the company's culture than do other, traditional, recruitment materials. This increase in information allows the applicant to make a more informed assessment of fit with the organization.
- *Expediting the application process.*   Organizations can instantly screen applications that are filled out on their Web sites. Unqualified candidates can be quickly eliminated and more qualified ones promptly contacted before they are hired by other organizations.
- *Communication of unique organizational qualities.*   E-recruiting allows the organization to distinguish itself from other organizations by providing unique and interesting information.
- *First impressions.*   Web pages influence the formation of impressions, which, if favorable, might encourage the candidate to apply to the company.

Another advantage is that e-recruiting gives individuals immediate access to vacancies and announcements, instead of waiting for printed-media sources, such as professional trade magazines and newspapers. E-recruiting can be delivered to a much wider audience than other recruitment devices, serving to increase the applicant pool (Lavinga 1996). Internet users have been found to be more educated and computer literate (Zall 2000), which may result in the organization's finding a better-quality applicant. E-recruiting could also be a selection tool. If the organization is seeking applicants who have computer-based skills, having applicants apply online could systematically eliminate those who lack those computer skills to access and apply via the Internet. Web pages also provide continual exposure to an organization, whether or not it is hiring.

Setting up Web-based recruiting requires some general procedures. According to a study of 140 companies, some of the best Web site features for users included an easy site layout, attractive graphics, detailed and concise descriptions of career opportunities, résumé builders, and job-search advice. Some e-recruiting strategies that were found to be the most effective included an easy-to-find career section on the corporate Web site, up-to-date and easy-to-read job listings and job descriptions, interactive links to a human resources contact person, and a clear and concise application process (Williams 2000).

Internal Labor Markets   Recruitment does not necessarily always require the organization to look for applicants outside the organization. Rather, the security manager can recruit from the internal labor market (ILM), and hire from within instead of from outside the organization. According to Kotorov (2001), an ILM allows employees to build their careers inside the company rather than looking for opportunities at other companies. ILM also serves as a reward system for an employee's continued commitment and loyalty to the organization. An ILM requires that the organization create an opportunity system that lets employees see what opportunities exist in the company and allows employees to apply for those positions that best fit their career goals.

In ILMs, hiring is concentrated at certain points in the job hierarchy, and for many positions, internal candidates are favored over external ones. Advancement within this ILM consists of movement along more or less clearly defined job ladders, or positions, in a progressively upward movement. For example, in a health care institution, many of the security personnel were hired from such entry-level positions as the guest services department, which served as a "gate," or entry point, of the ILM. In turn, former security officers now hold executive positions in the organization, including the risk-management department, whereas others have become physicians, based in part of the organization's educational reimbursement program. The ILM has been beneficial for the organization, which now has employees who are loyal, committed, and familiar with the entire organization.

ILMs can also be used by security managers as a recruitment tool. Candidates may find it appealing that more opportunities are available within the organization. Besides being a recruitment tool, the internal labor market encourages long-term employment relationships, with seniority and merit playing an important role in determining who gets promoted. ILMs also promote and allow for the development of firm- or industry-specific skills that workers who change employers do not frequently acquire, thereby enhancing workforce productivity (Abraham and McKersie 1990).

The use of internal labor markets may require changes in the recruitment and selection process. With ILMs, the recruiter may take a more global approach to hiring. Instead of looking for an individual who has those requisite skills to perform in security, the recruiter may now be looking for individuals who possess those skills that are best suited for the entire organization, including the security function. This will also require that security managers become less "possessive" of their employees. Managers may need to recognize that they may eventually lose employees to other departments in the organization. However, this should not be considered a loss. The organization has kept an individual who has training and experience in security and who carries these principles to the new position. In effect, the security function has inadvertently spread throughout the organization by way of the ILM.

Employee Referrals   Another intraorganizational recruitment source is the organization's employees. Existing employees recruit new employees into the organization through a process known as employee referrals (ER). Having an ER program decreases the time and costs associated with hiring and recruiting, and hiring an ER shows a level of trust the company has in the referring employee (Lachnit 2001). An ER program can also result in candidates who are prescreened by their sponsors to ensure cultural fit. ER serves as a team-building device between employees and management, and it provides the new hire with a built-in support system. Depending on the design of the ER program, employees may receive cash awards, or a "bounty," for finding the employee (Morehart 2001).

Microsoft Corporation's ER program empowers and makes all employees responsible for recruiting, regardless of their rank or position in the organization. The program is tied to the strong corporate culture that anyone who works at Microsoft has a stake in the ownership and future of the company. Microsoft's recruitment department also extensively trains other employees in recruiting and interviewing. This program has been successful. Microsoft has reported that up to 30 percent of new software developers are found via employee referrals. Of interest is that unlike other organizations that provide employees with cash incentives or other rewards for recruiting employees, Microsoft employees receive no inducements or incentives for their efforts (Taninecz 1995).

Advertisements   Advertisements include written and verbal recruitment mediums. Traditional print formats can include newspapers, trade magazines and journals, posters, billboards and fliers, or handouts. With the advent of the Internet, classified advertisements can be found on the Web in specific employment Web sites that are similar to the traditional classified sections of newspapers. Organizations that have Web pages can create their own classified pages. Verbal mediums include radio and television advertising.

Through the process of recruitment studies, organizations need to determine which form of advertising works best for them. Although classified advertising is still the most widely used recruitment tool for companies (Salopek 1999), it may not prove to be the best source. For example, with the use of classified ads, it may be that the only people who read classifieds are those individuals looking for work because they do not have jobs. Depending on the labor market, this may suggest that they are not the most attractive candidates for the position (Matthews and Redman 2001). Instead, the firm may consider using radio advertising. Studies have found that 95 percent of Americans listen to the radio sometime during the week, with an average listen time of 4 hours. Unlike classified ads, radio advertising can target an audience (such as listeners of classic-rock stations), may appear to be more personable, and goes out to all individuals, regardless of whether they are looking for a job (Joinson 1998).

Internships   In an internship, students are given college credits for receiving practical experience in their chosen fields of study. An internship is a cooperative venture among a student, an educational institution, and an employer. Internships can be paid or unpaid and vary in length, duration, and quality. Usually, the company has no large stake in interns, if they are not paid. On completion of the internship, the relationship is dissolved, and the organization and intern have the option of whether they will create an employment relationship.

Internships can be an effective recruitment tool. First, the internship experience gives a potential employer the opportunity to view the candidate in a work setting and determine whether this intern will be a suitable employee. Because the student has already "worked" in the organization, the internship has served as a means for the employer to attract the employee. Interns already know what is expected of them at the workplace, so internships also help to reduce gaps in expectations that may occur with noninterns who are hired (Big budget 2001).

Shadowing   Some candidates may be interested but lack complete knowledge of a position, regardless of other recruitment tools used. To better inform these individuals, the organization could have them participate to some degree in the position by shadowing, or observing, existing employees (Lozada 2001). Several alternatives to shadowing are available. An organization may simply opt for a quick tour, the candidate could be assigned to another employee for as little as an hour or a complete shift, or the candidate could receive in-depth exposure to the job, depending on the recruitment and selection strategy designed by the organization. Perhaps one of the best examples of job shadowing is the National Groundhog Job Shadow Day. This yearly event encourages youth to shadow a working adult through a typical day on the job.

Shadowing has several benefits. It gives the candidate a realistic job preview. By observing someone at work, the candidate's interest in the position may increase. This recruitment tool also serves as a selection tool, as some individuals may opt out of applying for the position. Hence, the candidate self-screens, saving the organization costs related to the expenses associated with the selection and training process, not to mention costs associated with lost productivity, as the new employee would not be fully effective immediately in the organization.

Staffing Agencies   A wide variety of temporary-employment companies, search firms, placement offices, and professional recruiters, or headhunters, can help organizations recruit employees. Staffing agencies may be a good source for recruiting employed individuals who do not have time to conduct their own in-depth job searches. Staffing agencies may also provide some level of prescreening and reference checking and may be part of a national network that can access additional candidates to meet the organization's needs.

Some staffing agencies also provide temporary employees, allowing an employer to "try" a candidate without being obliged to hire this individual (Baber 1998). Similarly, temporary employees may be suitable for organizations that operate in cycles, with demands for security fluctuating with demands for the firm's services or products. However, staffing agencies may be expensive for the organization to use, and the quality of employee may not be as high as with other recruitment methods available to the organization.

Other Sources   Other recruitment sources are limited only by the creativity of the organization and recruiters. Some other common recruitment sources are the military, unemployment offices, and local organizations that are specific to the needs of the organization. For example, the local chapter of the American Society for Industrial Security could provide an applicant pool ranging from entry- to executive-level positions.

Other recruitment means can be more creative. Recruiters have been known to offer cash incentives or bonuses to applicants and to provide free products for completing a job application. Other organizations have provided some of the intrinsic rewards of the job. One major hotel chain, for example, offers its security personnel heavily discounted rates at any of its hotels throughout the world. This incentive has attracted college students and retired police officers who were attracted to and have remained with this company for long periods of time because of the travel cost savings.

The "Best" Recruitment Source

Although the results of research are mixed as to which procedure works best, some research has shown that college recruiting, employee referrals, and executive-search firms are the top three recruitment techniques (Terpstra 1996). However, there are no set procedures for recruiting, and other types of recruitment methods may be better suited, based on the organization's needs.

Determining which recruitment strategy works the best can be accomplished via postrecruitment studies. Postrecruitment studies, for example, could be conducted on a cost basis to determine how much it cost on average to recruit an applicant or which method had the greatest yield per dollar spent. Postrecruitment studies could also examine the attrition rate and what source provided the greatest yield of qualified employees. Another alternative would be to base the recruitment strategy on the quality of the hire. In this context, the organization may consider examining the knowledge, skills, and abilities that the employee brought into the organization.

■ SELECTION TECHNIQUES

Selection is the process of screening and choosing individuals from an applicant pool that has been constructed from the recruitment effort. As with recruitment techniques, the organization must plan what selection processes it will use to find the most qualified applicants and to filter out those individuals the organization has determined to be unsuitable.

The selection process should be considered a progressive process. That is, the employer can implement various selection or screening devices that gradually eliminate candidates from the pool. Designing appropriate selection methods, however, can be confusing, owing to the wide variety of techniques available to the organization. To compound this issue, no single procedure can determine the right approach in selecting employees. No two organizations have the same organizational cultures and needs. The organization needs to use job analysis to conduct an accurate assessment of the position to be filled. Managers can then use a variety of selection tools or methods, based on the outcomes of job analysis, to find the most qualified employee from the applicant pool. Some of the more commonly used selection devices, used alone or in combination with other instruments, are applications, résumés, interviews, background investigations, and reference checks.

Applications

Findings from the Private Security Task Force (U.S. Department of Justice 1977) indicate that the employment application is the basis for the employee screening process. At a minimum, the employment application reveals some basic information: the candidate's name, current residence and phone number, educational background, previous employment, and military service. Additional specific information, based on the position and the findings from job analysis, can also be included in the application. Usually, the application is one of the first stages of the selection process. The information recorded on the application will screen out individuals who do not meet the minimum qualifications for the position.

The format of the job application varies, depending on the position. If, for example, the employer is interested in seeing whether an applicant has the ability to write and produce a good report, the application could ask the applicant to write a brief biographical sketch or a description of prior life and work experiences. Instead of providing only the basic background information, now the application process has served a secondary role as a test, as it screened out those individuals who did not demonstrate proficiency in writing.

Applications do not have to be the traditional paper- and-pencil format. As previously discussed, e-recruitment and other advancements in computer technologies now allow employers to have applicants apply online. Computers, not human resource professionals, now screen applicants, based on the information provided on the cyberapplication.

How the application is designed and administered may limit the number of applicants. Purposefully limiting the number of applicants into the hiring process is called a candidate reduction strategy (CRS). One CRS might have individuals file applications in person, shortening the length of time for accepting applications, and distributing only a certain number of applications on a first-come first-served basis. Other CRSs might make the candidate complete a willingness questionnaire: one that includes questions related to the less desirable aspects of the job, such as willingness to work third shift, be on call, and work weekends, and require all supporting documentation related to education and other qualifications (Coffee 1998). These candidate reduction strategies may prove useful when a surplus of labor is available. When the labor market is tight or the demand for employees is high, however, the organization should reevaluate its application procedures to make sure that it has an adequate pool of candidates and that it has not inadvertently created a candidate reduction strategy.

Résumés

Résumés are biographical sketches, or outlines of a candidate's educational and employment background, including information about the applicant's professional accomplishments and achievements. Research has found the résumé to be the most important tool used in the initial screening of applicants (Ray, Stallard, and Hunt 1994). The résumé, however, should never be a substitute for the job application but rather should be a supplement that the employer uses to verify the candidate's knowledge, skills, and abilities.

The review of a candidate's résumé may reveal problems with a former employer, as evidenced through short time periods in the employment relationship, multiple previous jobs, and the lack of good reasons for terminating the employment relationship. At the same time, employers should recognize the potential for exaggerations and falsifications on an applicant's résumé. Research has shown that in a significant number of cases, the information contained in résumés is often inaccurate or misleading. One study found that 25 percent of 1,000 resumes were fraudulent in some way (Cole-Gomolski 1999). Therefore, the employer should verify the résumé information through other investigative techniques, including a thorough background investigation.

Computer technology has changed the nature of résumés. Candidates can now electronically submit them to organizations, and traditional printed résumés can be scanned via electronic résumé management systems for keywords matching the applicant's qualifications with the job requirements. A study of Fortune 500 companies revealed that 36 percent now use electronic résumé management (ERM) systems, with more firms expected to implement them in the future (Baker, DeTeinee, and Smart 1998).

Interviews

An interview is a controlled conversation between the applicant and the organization's representative(s). Interviews can be screening or recruitment-oriented in nature. In a screening orientation, the primary goal of the interview is to evaluate the applicant's qualifications for the position. Applicants are screened in or out of the hiring process. Usually, this type of interview occurs when demand for these workers is low, combined with an ample supply of workers. If the interview is recruitment oriented, the goal is not to screen out an applicant but rather to attract an applicant's interest in the company. Usually, this type of interview occurs in situations of high demand and limited supply of these types of workers (Stevens 1998).

Employers may conduct one or several interviews with the applicant, depending on the position that needs to be filled. In the selection of a security manager, for example, the interview process may begin with a representative from human resources. With the successful passing of this interview, the candidate may be invited to a series of more in-depth and directed interviews with other company representatives, including managers from the security function, the vice-president, and perhaps the CEO of the organization: It all depends on the prearranged plans for selecting individuals for the organization. These interviews could also be conducted by one person or a panel of individuals.

Interviews are usually thought of as verbal dialogues between an applicant and an individual or a group of individuals from the company. With the advent of new technologies, interviews can be conducted with the use of computers, eliminating the need for a human to ask questions. Interviews can be either structured or unstructured.

Structured Interviews   In a structured interview, specific questions are created in advance, based on the dimensions gathered through job analysis. Some of these identified dimensions are planning, organizing and prioritizing, relating effectively with others, decision-making abilities, the ability to adapt, the candidate's level of motivation and initiative, physical requirements, integrity, oral communication skills, and having the ability to effectively evaluate information (Pulakos et al. 1996).

A key feature of the structured interview is that the process is consistent from one candidate to another. All the applicants interviewed are also held to the same standards via the questions asked and how they are asked. To ensure consistency, structured interviews are often written out or scripted in advance. Many interviews use behaviorally anchored scales, and the interviewees are ranked according to their behaviors and abilities as outlined through the information contained on interview forms (Lowry 1994a). The use of these forms will also ensure that the applicant is not compared to other applicants, which could lead to bias. Instead, applicants' scores are compared against one another.

The structured interview has some benefits. It provides greater uniformity in the hiring process, as all candidates are asked the same questions. Therefore, structured interviews may be a more legally defensible method of selecting individuals. Intrinsically tied into defensibility, structured interviews have a high degree of validity if administered correctly (Pulakos et al. 1996). Structured interviews may also be cost effective. In comparison to assessment centers, which are discussed later, structured interviews take between 25 percent and 50 percent less time and are less expensive to administer (Lowry 1994b). If the employer states in advance that all candidates will be asked the same number and series of questions, candidates may also perceive the process as fairer than other interview processes.

Unstructured Interviews   The opposite of a structured interview is the unstructured interview, in which the majority of questions are nondirective, or open-ended. The purpose of this type of interview is to let applicants express their own thoughts and opinions. In doing so, the interviewer keeps the questions to a minimum and simply encourages applicants to keep talking, directing the interview through a series of probing questions (French 1994). Examples of unstructured interview questions are: Describe your personality. What was one of the greatest challenges you ever faced? How would you describe your work ethic?

The open-ended nature of these interview questions provides some benefits to an employer. This format may provide richer information about the applicant's experience, personality, and knowledge (Terpstra 1996). Therefore, it is often integrated with a structured interview; standardized areas are covered in the structured portion, and open-ended questions allow applicants to express their opinions.

One drawback is that the unstructured interview requires more time and may fail to touch on important aspects of the applicant's qualifications (French 1994). Unstructured interviews, if not properly administered, may also be lead to a greater number of legal challenges. Some of the probing questions may lead to responses that are protected and in violation of employment laws, including EEO and the ADA.

Effective Interviewers

Regardless of whether the interview is structured or unstructured, the organization must recognize that interviewers will have different competency levels. Therefore, interviewers must be properly trained in the skill of conducting effective interviews. Interviewers need to be trained to concentrate on job-specific questions to prevent themselves from digressing into trivial, non-job-related topics, regardless of whether the interview is structured or unstructured. Interviewers should also be taught the skill of cognitive scripting, which refers to the behaviors, actions, and events that occur in a social exchange. These cognitive scripts are used to control the interactions in interviews (Stevens 1998). An example of cognitive scripting in an interview includes greeting and establishing rapport with the candidate, asking questions, responding to the applicant's questions, and then disengaging, or closing the interview (Tullar 1989).

Interviewers should be trained to properly record the candidate's responses and their own observations during the interview. Some research has concluded that note taking during an interview does not ensure accurate evaluation of the candidate. Some interviewers simply record information, failing to take time to think about what was communicated (Burnett et al. 1998). Instead, interviewers may consider taking notes immediately after the interview is over.

Interviewers should be trained to recognize how their behaviors and attitudes could affect the interview and interview outcome. An interviewer's first impression of the candidate may lead to establishing a preconceived belief, which may subsequently alter the questions asked and lead to behaviors to confirm the initial impressions (Pulakos et al. 1996). Some interviewers may possess ideal-applicant stereotypes, which occurs when the interviewer constructs a mental concept of the ideal candidate. This stereotyping may result in the interviewer's altering or influencing how questions to the applicant are asked (Stevens 1998).

Similarly, the interviewer's actions during the interview could influence applicant attraction to the organization (Stevens 1998). A carefree attitude by the interviewer may be interpreted by the candidate as lack of interest. Interviewers should also recognize how the personality dimensions of the applicant can affect the interview. Research has shown that the candidate's level of extroversion is the single best predictor of whether a job offer is made (Caldwell and Burger 1998).

The introduction of new technologies into the interview process can eliminate some of these problems. For example, an organization could use computer-aided interviewing techniques; the applicant, prior to a face-to-face interview, answers a series of structured questions on a computer. These completed questions are then used in a structured one-on-one interview, with the interviewer asking more in-depth, probing questions, based on the candidate's responses, if necessary. This type of interviewing procedure also eliminates first impressions and adds a great deal of structure to the interview, ensuring that all major points will be covered or completed in the interview process (Computer-aided . . . 1995).

Background Investigations

Regardless of the type(s) of selection procedures used, a preemployment background investigation must be conducted to verify information that the candidate has provided on application materials. The findings from the investigation may also uncover derogatory information that the applicant attempted to conceal or did not provide the employer (Adler 1993/1994). The information collected from official and personal sources during the investigation will help the firm construct a comprehensive personal and career history of the applicant.

How extensive the background investigation is depends on the type of position, industry standards, and any relevant legislation that governs preemployment screening. For example, if the position requires a specific level of education and the handling of money, the organization, should at a minimum, verify the individual's educational records and conduct a criminal-history check and financial-history/credit check. If the position calls for the applicant to operate a motor vehicle, a review of the individual's driving record is necessary. Although no specific guidelines can be established about what comprises an effective background check, the organization should be aware that an ineffective background investigation and a subsequent incident involving that employee could lead to a negligent-hiring claim against the organization.

Some general principles govern background investigations. The organization should establish a written policy on minimum guidelines that must be followed when conducting background investigations. The background investigation must be consistent from one candidate to another, and consistent with the position for which the candidate applied.

Bradford (1998) recommends that companies construct a background-investigation manual and establish procedures to be followed to ensure an objective inquiry into the applicant's background. This manual should target three primary areas:

1. The true identify of the applicant, that is, positive candidate identification
2. Issues related to the candidate's credit history, driving record, interviews with references, educational history, conduct of duties, and ability to work with individuals of color and the opposite sex.
3. The candidate's criminal history

The information collected from these sources should be compiled in the manual and subsequently serve as an effective and comprehensive means of evaluating the candidate (Bradford 1998).

Employment Reference Checks

Another commonly used selection tool is the employment reference check. Here, the employer contacts a candidate's former place(s) of employment to verify dates of employment, duties, and responsibilities. The information collected from these sources is used to gain an understanding of the individual's work habits and performance. Although useful and important in the selection process, former employers may be reluctant to provide specific information about prior employees, fearing litigation. Nonetheless, this should not be overlooked as a primary means of verifying a candidate's work history and any other relevant information that could be obtained from former employers.

■ EMPLOYMENT TESTS

Some of the first standardized employment tests were used by the U.S. military during World War I to match recruits with appropriate jobs or positions (Rominger and Sandoval 1998). Since then, employment tests have become more sophisticated. For example, although some tests are administered through traditional paper-and-pencil formats, others can be adapted for computer use or exist solely online. This relatively new delivery mechanism is quite advantageous, as the computer can control the rate of information presented to the candidate; is cost-effective, as it requires only a limited staff to administer the tests; and can score response sheets automatically. Computer testing can also test other dimensions of the candidate. For example, the time it takes for an individual to answer—response latencies—can be recorded, the tests can be built around the response patterns of the individual, and changes in the subject strategy can be recorded (Landy, Shankster, and Kohler 1994).

Regardless of their design, employment tests are used to draw inferences about candidates, based on objective and measurable criteria about a candidate's suitability for employment (Berger and Ghei 1995a). Regardless of their design, employment tests screen out those applicants who do not meet basic requirements or rank-order candidates based on test performance. Used as a stand-alone tool or with other selection methods, employment tests can be a highly reliable and valid component of the selection and hiring process (Rominger and Sandoval 1998).

Assessment Centers

Assessment centers originated in World War II with the selection of intelligence agents for the Office of Strategic Services (OSS), the predecessor of the Central Intelligence Agency. In selecting operatives or agents, the OSS staff developed a series of complex simulations that focused on dimensions of human behavior to see how prospective agents would perform in real-life tasks or events. In order to measure these behavioral dimensions, the OSS staff created a series of assessment tests. Over a 3-day period, candidates were tested via traditional paper-and-pencil tests, leaderless-group activities, assigned-leadership activities, role-playing exercises, and stress interviews (Fiske et al. 1996).

This concept of using multiple behavioral dimensions to select agents was later researched, modified, and applied to the private industry by Howard Bray in 1956. Bray is considered the modern-day founder of assessment centers. As an employee in the Aviation Psychology Program in the Army Air Forces, he had developed observational measures of performance in training via simulated bombing missions. Later, he introduced the benefits of the assessment center to AT&T to assess entry-level managers in the organization and tested them over a 4-year period to measure their success. In 1958, the assessment center was expanded to select managers from AT&T rank-and-file employees (Bray 1995). By the 1970s, the use of assessment centers had expanded to other organizations and industries, including the public sector. Research has shown that 62 percent of cities of 50,000 or more use assessment centers for police and fire personnel (Lowry 1996).

Description   An assessment center is not a location but rather an evaluation method used for selecting entry-level employees, middle managers, and executives. An assessment center can also be used for promoting employees, identifying employees' training needs, and, evaluating management succession (Spychalski et al. 1997). An assessment center allows the employer to observe and record the actions of candidates in various exercises and work-related simulations instead of relying on other selection techniques, such as the interview, that may not be able to fully measure or assess the applicant's behaviors in work-related situations or practical situations.

An assessment center measures multiple dimensions of the individual being tested. An assessment center usually has three or more simulations or exercises. Simply having one dimension or exercise in a testing procedure does not constitute an assessment center. The dimensions that an organization uses should be based on the findings from job analysis. The organization may want to test for such dimensions as oral communication, sensitivity, time management, persuasion, organization and planning, initiative, and problem solving. If an assessment center is used to promote or select managers, it could also include structuring and staffing tasks, structuring jobs, recruiting and selecting, establishing effective work-group relationships, and handling daily problems and information in the organization (Joyce, Thayer, and Pond 1994).

Depending on the dimensions selected, an assessment center can be classified as task or dimension specific. A task-specific center, for example, may include a role-playing exercise involving a personnel problem, a leaderless-group exercise, and a written/oral analysis of one or more problems. In a dimension-specific center, some of the dimensions may include written and oral communication skills, problem-solving skills, leadership skills and traits, and the ability to effectively plan and organize activities (Lowry 1994b).

These dimensions or traits are observed by an assessment panel: a group of trained assessors. These individuals may be employees of the organization or external consultants. In either case, the assessors should receive formal training in assessment techniques, including how to classify, evaluate, rate, and record applicant behaviors. The assessors should also be trained how to integrate data and provide oral and written evaluative feedback to the applicants (Spychalski et al. 1997).

Prior to testing, candidates must be adequately informed of the assessment center. Some of the areas that the participants should be educated in are the objectives and purpose of the center, the method of participant selection, the voluntary nature of the center, the composition and training of the assessors, material or information that will be collected, and the type of feedback the respondents will receive (Spychalski et al. 1997).

Candidates are rated or evaluated on each procedure or exercise used in the assessment center. When rating the candidate, assessors do not rate the candidates against one another. Instead, all the candidates are compared or ranked against the global standard that was developed prior to the assessment (Lowry 1994b). After recording their observations independently, the assessors have a structured discussion to integrate or pool the results of their evaluations to compile a comprehensive profile of each candidate. The assessors then make a recommendation to the organization (Assessment centers . . . 1998).

Components Depending on the position the organization needs to fill, a variety of assessment procedures can be used. Some of the more common assessment procedures or exercises used to measure the candidate's traits or dimensions are shown in Box 5-3.

BOX 5-3 ■ **Components of Assessment Centers**

- LEADERLESS GROUP

  In a leaderless-group situation or a leaderless-roundtable discussion, applicants engage in a half-hour discussion of a relevant topic. Assessors observe the candidates and note which ones take the initiative, redirect, and contribute to the discussion (Assessment centers 1998).

- SITUATIONAL EXERCISES

  In situational exercises, observational skills are assessed to determine whether the candidate has the ability to draw logical conclusions from the available information (Coulton 1995). In this type of test, a candidate may be asked to examine, within a set amount of time, the office of an employee who has mysteriously left town. Later, the candidate will write a report or complete an open-ended questionnaire and construct an explanation for the employee's disappearance.

- WRITTEN SITUATIONAL TESTS

  These tests can consist of written exercises in which the participants record how they would address or deal with each of the situations presented (Joyce, Thayer, and Pond 1994).

continued

- ROLE PLAYS
  In this exercise, the candidate may be required to role-play with an employee who has a particular problem. The candidates must identify the problem in a timely manner and bring closure to the issue (Michelson 1987).

- VIDEO-TAPED SITUATIONS
  In these exercises, the candidate is asked to evaluate what happened on the tape (Coulton 1995). For example, a candidate may watch two security officers deal with a homeless person. The tape could be stopped at various points to let the candidate explain what he or she would do in the situation and perhaps identify their perception of activities or behaviors of the security officers as incorrect and correct.

- BASKET EXERCISES
  These exercises are designed to measure how an applicant is able to effectively handle typical management issues, prioritize time, and address job-specific problems. This exercise also offers an excellent look at how the candidate assesses emergencies—real and perceived—deadlines, and delegates responsibility and authority for tasks (Assessment centers 1998).

- FORMAL PRESENTATIONS
  Here, the organization can evaluate how well the applicant can think under pressure, as the panel may have the opportunity to ask the applicant questions to clarify or test positions and ideas; act under deadlines, as the candidate is given a short amount of time to prepare for the speech; and speak in public.

Benefits For an organization, the primary benefit of an assessment center is that it provides a great deal of information on how candidates will perform in situations similar to those they may encounter on the job. An assessment center also allows assessors to observe candidate characteristics that are difficult to assess or capture using other selection techniques. Although an assessment center may be more expensive to administer than other selection devices, these initial costs could be offset by a decrease in employee turnover. If designed correctly, an assessment center could screen out liability-prone candidates. In the context of liability reduction, some federal courts have determined that assessment centers are the preferred technique to address gender and/or racial discrimination; other attorneys and judges consider assessment centers to be a fair measure of job-relevant activities (Coulton 1995).

Assessment centers are also beneficial for candidates. Research from the public sector found that respondents felt that assessment centers were one of the most accurate selection tools (Lowry 1996) and were perceived as a fair selection tool by the candidates (Coulton 1995). Assessment center activities will also provide candidates with a realistic job preview. Assessment centers also identify candidate weaknesses. If this individual is hired, the information could then be used at a later time for additional in-service training in that specific area. Over time, the assessment center may identify some patterned deficiencies among employees and the training department or organization, could establish specific in-service training programs to address those deficiencies.

Drawbacks   One of the major drawbacks to assessment centers is their cost. Research has indicated that it costs about $350 per candidate if outside assessors are used; this was reported by individuals in the public sector to be the largest deterrent to using assessment centers (Lowry 1996). This figure, however, does not include the expenses related to training assessors and the start-up costs associated with the center activities (Coulton 1995). The organization may also lose more revenue if the individuals serving as assessors are in-house employees. These individuals cannot contribute to the overall productivity of the agency while conducting assessments.

Personality Tests

A personality test is a psychologically based test used to improve employee selection by determining the candidate's affective, or nonintellectual, behaviors (Black 1994). These tests measure a series of personality dimensions often referred to as the "Big Five": neuroticism, extroversion, openness to experience, agreeableness, and conscientiousness (Landy 1994). Depending on their design, these tests can also identify individuals who are able to work well in teams or who are highly motivated, flexible, and adaptable (Terpstra 1996). The underlying assumption of these tests is that they will identify candidates having personality characteristics that the organization feels are important for success on the job.

Hundreds of personality tests are available for organizations to use. These tests can be categorized into objective- or projective-based tests. An objective-based test is a self-report, paper-and-pencil-based test. Such tests can be administered, if necessary, on a group basis (Black 1994). One of the most common objective-based tests used by employers is the 550-question Minnesota Multiphasic Personality Inventory (MMPI), which measures socially undesirable behaviors (Black 1994; Kelley, Jacobs, and Farr 1994). Other common objective-based tests are the California Psychological Inventory, which measures such socially acceptable behaviors as self-assurance, socialization, maturity, personal orientation and attitudes, and achievement potential, and the Myers-Briggs Type Indicator, which measures the candidate's personality type (Black 1994).

Projective personality tests are individual-based tests that require the candidate to interpret ambiguous stimuli (Black 1994). The rationale underlying projective tests is that, when interpreting the ambiguous stimulus, subjects "project" aspects of their personalities through their answers (Lilienfeld 1999). One of the many projective instruments available is the Rorschach test; here, the psychologist assesses the subject's interpretation of an inkblot. Another projective test is the Thematic Apperception Test, which requires the subject to interpret a picture by writing or telling a story about it. Candidates' responses are then analyzed for any abnormal themes (Black 1994). These types of tests may be more expensive to administer than objective-based, paper-and-pencil tests, as the answers need to be analyzed by trained examiners or psychologists (Berger and Ghei 1995b).

Honesty, or Integrity, Tests

Some organizations have incorporated the use of commercially available psychological-based paper-and-pencil honesty, or integrity, tests as a component of the selection process. Although many such tests are on the market, all are based on the notion that the applicant's personality tendencies and inclinations translate into behaviors reflecting their propensity toward honesty, theft, productivity, and compatibility with other employees in the organization.

Integrity tests have some advantages. They may reduce employee theft, serve as a screening tool to manage large numbers or pools of applicants, and subsequently simplify the hiring process (Faust 1996). Integrity tests are easy to administer, as they do not require any specially trained examiners, many do not require any specialized equipment and/or facilities, and the vendor scores the completed tests (Dalton and Metzger 1993).

Integrity tests also have some negative points, however. One problem is the validity of some integrity tests. Such tests may have a high false-positive rate or erroneously identify individuals who have an integrity/honesty problem. Some research has concluded that the tests are 13.6 percent accurate at their best and only 1.7 percent accurate at their worst and therefore should not be used as a selection tool (Dalton and Metzger 1993). As pointed out in Box 5–4, employers should also be concerned with privacy issues.

> ### BOX 5–4 ■ The Integrity Tests and the Right to Privacy: *Soroka v. Dayton Hudson* (1991)
>
> The plaintiffs in this class action case challenged the use of a psychological integrity test, the Psychscreen, that Target Stores used to select store security officers (SSOs). The plaintiffs, who had been denied employment based on the results of the test, contended that questions related to applicants' religious attitudes and sexual orientation violated California's constitutional right to privacy and California's Labor Code, which guaranteed employees the right to be free from employer coercion and intimidation, based on their political activities. Target Stores conceded that the test did constitute a limited intrusion into the privacy rights of their applicants but also indicated that the Psychscreen was intended to screen out applicants who "may be emotionally unstable, who may put customers or employees in jeopardy, and who will not take directions and follow Target procedures" (p. 81).
>
> Under review, the appellate court remanded to the trial court for further proceedings, concluding that Target's use of a psychological screening test as a

preemployment tool violated both the constitutional right to privacy and statutory provisions against improper preemployment inquiries and discriminatory conduct because the test inquired into the applicant's religious beliefs and sexual orientation. This was based on the court's conclusion that any violation of the right to privacy of job applicants must be justified by a compelling interest. The court concluded:

"While Target unquestionably has an interest in employing emotionally stable persons to be SSOs [store security officers], testing applicants about their religious beliefs and sexual orientation does not further this interest. . . . To justify the invasion of privacy resulting from the use of the Psychscreen, Target must demonstrate a compelling interest and must establish that the test serves a job related purpose. . . . Target made no showing that a person's religious beliefs or sexual orientation have any bearing on the emotional stability or on the ability to perform an SSOs job responsibilities" (p. 86).

Although this case and the subsequent decision did not make integrity tests illegal per se, it did reveal issues to consider when using such tests. Hence, the test and subsequent questions used must be relevant or have a job-related purpose. If not, it is the employer's responsibility to prove that it has a compelling interest to use the particular test.

Physical Ability Testing

A physical agility test measures the applicant's ability to perform various activities related to a specific position in the organization. In implementing a physical ability test, the organization must first consider what it is attempting to measure and why. For example, physical agility differs from physical fitness. Someone who is physically fit is physically healthy, and this health can be measured by a variety of methods, including cardiovascular endurance, strength, muscular endurance, and body composition. Physical agility, by contrast, refers to the candidate's ability to perform a specific motor-related task (Hoover 1992). Physical ability tests are of three general categories: job simulation, physical agility, and physical fitness norms.

Job Simulation　　Job simulation exercises are physical agility or stamina tests that simulate required on-the-job behaviors (Hoover 1992). The justification for this type of test is based on its job relatedness. The key to an effective and legal test is that it must be related to essential tasks of the position. For example, the requirement of a 5-mile run for an entry-level security position may be questionable. However, if the position requires knowledge and use of fire equipment, a simulation exercise requiring the applicant to drag a fire hose a set distance up and down stairs, wearing appropriate fire gear and a self-contained breathing apparatus (SCBA), would be appropriate if this were an essential component of the position. Regardless of the job simulation exercise, Hoover (1992) asserts that the tasks chosen must be safely performed by the applicants; the tests should be designed to be reasonably close to what the applicant would experience in the field; and they must be practical to administer in the context of personnel, time, and equipment necessary.

Physical Agility/Stamina   Physical agility tests measure the applicant's general strength and stamina (Hoover 1992). For example, to measure whether an applicant has upper-body strength, the test may require the individual to do a certain number of push-ups. These tests do not measure direct simulations of those behaviors required on the job. Instead, they measure a construct, which is the individual's general physical condition.

These tests can be administered more economically, safely, and conveniently than job simulation exercises, and there is no blending of job-related skills and physical abilities. However, tests of physical agility and stamina, have fared worse in the courts, as it may be difficult for the employer to determine the exact cutoff value, or score constituting effective performance in the context of physical agility or stamina (Hoover 1992).

Physical Fitness   These types of tests are norm-referenced and do not have adverse impact because performance standards are based on the vast numbers of individuals who have been physically tested previously. This form, or model, of physical agility testing is premised on the belief that individuals, such as security officers, need to be physically fit. This model also requires differentiated standards based on the age and gender of the individual being tested (Cordner 1992).

Drug and Alcohol Tests   With the increased awareness of the effects of drugs and alcohol on productivity and the overall health of an organization, many organizations now require applicants to undergo drug and alcohol tests as a condition of employment. Drug and alcohol testing is a dichotomous screening test; the applicant simply passes or fails. This is different from other testing procedures, perhaps, in which the applicant may be provided some latitude in the selection procedure (Arthur and Doverspike 1997).

Drug testing can incorporate a wide variety of techniques or procedures that vary in cost, intrusiveness, accuracy, and acceptability by the courts. Biochemical tests include urinalysis, blood and saliva analysis, and hair analysis. Observational methods, by contrast, incorporate awareness of physiological traits such as horizontal gaze nystagmus (unnatural eye movement and tracking due to the effects of certain drugs on the visual and central nervous systems) and self-report questionnaires that could serve as indirect measures of drug use. An effective background investigation may also gather information about the applicant's use of drugs and/or alcohol (Arthur and Doverspike 1997).

SELECTING THE EMPLOYEE

Regardless of the test or combination of techniques used in the selection process, the final stage of recruitment and selection is hiring the most qualified candidate(s) from those remaining in the candidate pool. Perhaps one of the easiest ways to do this is to hire the "best" candidate. However, if the pool is large, other methods can be used. One method is to rank-order the candidates, based on their scores on the selection methods. For example, the candidate who scored the highest on the selection techniques will be offered the position.

With banding, another alternative, applicants are grouped into score bands, based on their performance in the selection process. In fixed-band systems, candidates are selected from a particular band until all individuals in that band are depleted. For example, if the band has eight candidates, all individuals are selected from that band until it contains no more names or until all positions in the organization are filled. If the organization needs to fill more positions, a new band is created, and employees are selected from that particular band until all positions or jobs are filled.

In a sliding-band system, a new band is established every time an individual is hired or eliminated from the applicant pool. This is achieved by reconstructing the band. For example, if the original band contained all candidates who scored between 100 and 90 on the tests and an individual with a score of 98 is selected from that band, the new band includes those individuals who scored between 98 and 88. Unlike the fixed-band system, which must be depleted before it can move, this type of banding system provides more opportunities for lower-scoring individuals, as the bands move down through the distribution of applicants.

Another type of banding systems is random within-band selection. In this system, the organization selects candidates from within the band, with or without minority preference (Murphy, Osten, and Myors 1995).

The primary benefit of banding is that it reduces adverse impact. As adverse impact could occur as the result of small differences in test scores, placing candidates into bands treats and considers them as functionally equivalent. A related issue is that banding also eliminates the unreliability of the test as a whole and the adverse impact that the testing instruments may have caused. Because the employer is selecting from within these bands, a higher number of individuals from protected groups will be selected, eliminating some concerns related to adverse impact. Banding also eliminates the problem of having two candidates with the same score, as they are now in the same band. Banding can also minimize the effects of group differences (Murphy, Osten, and Myors 1995).

LEGAL ISSUES IN RECRUITMENT AND SELECTION

As previously discussed, a variety of laws and regulations must be considered when recruiting and selecting employees. However, some liability issues also arise in the context of hiring the "wrong" individual. Primarily, an organization should be concerned about a negligent-hiring claim.

Negligent Hiring

Negligent hiring means that the employee was unfit for hiring or retention or was fit only if properly supervised. Under the theory of negligent hiring, the employer has "the duty to exercise reasonable care in view of all the circumstances in hiring individuals who, because of the employment, may pose a threat of injury to members of the public" (Long 1997, 190).

Negligent hiring is different from the doctrine of respondent superior, whereby an employer can be held liable for its employees' actions when they are operating under the scope of their employment and the employee(s) cause injury to a third party to whom the employer owes a duty of care (Ryan and Lasek 1991). The theory behind negligent hiring is broader: The employer can be held liable through the foreseeable actions of the employee(s), even if these acts exceed the scope of their authority or authorized duties. In the context of foreseeability, however, the employer does not have to foresee the precise injury or harm. Instead, it is incumbent on the employer to reasonably discover the act that led to the injury (Ryan and Lasek 1991).

Research has revealed that negligent-hiring claims generally rest on three types of situations: a lack of a required knowledge, skill, or ability; physical harm or injury; and intentional employee misconduct (Ryan and Lasek 1991). All these areas of liability can be reduced through an effective and thorough recruitment and selection process. As previously discussed in this chapter, what constitutes a preemployment inquiry has no definitive answer, as the breadth and depth of the inquiry will vary, depending on the position to be filled (Ryan and Lasek 1991).

Nevertheless, when one considers that the security field has a higher degree of expectation by the public and clients that the employee has received the appropriate and necessary preemployment inquiry, a greater degree of caution and care should be exercised by the employer. When coupled with the fact that in many security sectors, supervision may be impractical or decreased and contact with third parties is more likely, a thorough preemployment inquiry is even more important (Ryan and Lasek 1991).

Negligent-hiring claims may arise when an organization fails to conduct or gather adequate information during its selection procedures, particularly the background investigation.

Five conditions must be present for an employer to be held liable for negligent hiring (Ryan and Lasek 1991).

1. The employee, acting under the auspices of employment, must have caused some type of injury.
2. The employee must be shown to be unfit.
3. The employer should have known about the unfitness.
4. The injury must be shown to be a foreseeable consequence of hiring the unfit employee.
5. The hiring of the unfit employee must be shown to be the proximate cause of the injury.

In the context of injury or harm, it must be shown that the employee committed the injury on the job or while acting as a representative of the employer. For example, in *Sherill v. Compcare Health Services Insurance Corporation* (1993), the Court of Appeals examined the actions of an individual (Zollicofer) who, while performing his duties as a bouncer, shot someone. In its decision, the Court of Appeals determined that, although the owners of the tavern stated that the bouncer had acted contrary to instruction that he not possess a gun (and he acted out of fear for his own life), "it [was] for the jury to determine if the shooting was so closely connected with Zollicofer's responsibilities and was fairly and reasonable incidental to them or if the act was extraordinary and disconnected from the service contemplated" (p. 8).

The issue of proving that a person is unfit and that the employer should have known about the unfitness and that the act was foreseeable can also be confusing. In *Gregor v. Kleiser* (1982), the defendant (Kleiser) hired an individual (Pape) to be the "bouncer" at a private party of approximately 200 teenagers. Later that evening, Pape physically attacked the plaintiff, causing serious and permanent injuries. In the resulting suit, the plaintiff alleged that the defendant knew of Pape's extraordinary strength and propensity for violence. The Court of Appeals held that the complaint sufficiently stated a cause of action, as the allegations, "taken together with the other allegations of fact well pleaded were legally sufficient to support a course of action against the defendant upon the theory of negligent, reckless or willful and wanton conduct in the hiring of Pape as a bouncer" (p. 1107).

Proximate cause may also be difficult to ascertain. In *Carter v. Skokie Valley Detective Agency* (1993), Harris, a uniformed contract security guard, arrived for work at the gas station he was assigned to. However, he was told that he was rescheduled; when leaving the site, he asked for a ride from a gas station employee, whom he later murdered. It was later discovered that the security company did not conduct a detailed investigation and background check, which would have revealed that Harris had been fired from another security company and had several misdemeanor convictions and an outstanding warrant for carrying a gun off duty. Although the security firm, Skokie Valley, did not contest that it was negligent in hiring Harris, the appellate court determined that the security company was not liable, as "Skokie Valley's negligence in hiring Harris was not a proximate cause of plaintiff's decedent's injuries and death. It was not the fact that Harris [the killer] was a security guard that got him into Emma's car and proximately caused her injuries and death; it was the fact that she trusted him because she knew him from work where he happened to be employed as a security guard. . . . We do not believe that the concept of proximate cause should be extended this far" (p. 83).

Of all the selection processes, one defense against negligent-hiring lawsuits is to have documented reference checks (Adler 1993/1994). According to Faust (1996), in a negligent-hiring claim, courts must determine whether the "former employer conducted a reasonable investigation into the employee's background vis-à-vis the job for which the employee was hired and the possible risk of harm or injury to the co-workers or third parties that could result from the conduct of an unfit employee" (p. 226).

The collection of information from previous employers can be quite limiting. This creates a double-edged sword for employers. They must collect information about the candidate in order to avoid a negligent-hiring claim. In many instances, however, the former employer is reluctant or unwilling to divulge information to the prospective employer out of fear of a civil suit premised on defamation. To avoid this problem, employers should consider using other screening or selection tools.

Another defense is based on negligent referral. This concept implies that an employer can be held liable for the injury or harm resulting from references that misrepresented or omitted facts about an employee's dangerous propensities. This defense, however, could cause problems. For example, an employer that reveals derogatory information may expose itself to defamation claims. An employer that does not provide information may expose itself to negligent-referral claims (Long 1997).

■ CONCLUSION

Recruitment and selection is a dynamic process that may appear to be complicated because of the techniques available, legislation controlling and regulating recruitment and selection processes, and the liability issues for organizations that negligently hire and defame former employees. Nevertheless, the recruitment and selection process is paramount for effective human resource management and is a vital factor in organizational survival, for without effective and efficient employees, the organization will soon fail.

The key to organizational effectiveness is to find and retain employees who best fit the needs of the organization, based on factors identified through job analysis. By skimping on the recruitment and selections process, as often occurs, the end result is incongruence between the individuals eventually selected and what the organization needs. The result may be a lower-quality, less productive workforce, as the organization may not have selected the "best" employees for the positions. Poor recruitment and selection could also lead to increased turnover or attrition rates in the organization. This turnover would lead to increased organizational inefficiency in terms of position vacancies; inefficiency of new or incoming employees, who may need time to adjust and may subsequently not be fully productive; and inefficient colleagues, who may have to help new employees adjust.

Coupled with these issues, various laws and regulations related to the employment and selection process must be followed. If not, the poorly designed and improperly administered programs will also expose the organization to undue claims related to employment legislation and claims related to defamation and negligent hiring.

■ KEY TERMS

ADA
ADEA
Assessment centers
Banding
Bona fide occupational qualification
Disparate impact
Disparate treatment
General recruitment
Internal labor market
Job analysis

Negligent hiring
Negligent retention
Qualified disability
Realistic job preview
Recruitment
Selection
Structured interview
Title VII
Unstructured interview

■ DISCUSSION QUESTIONS

1. What are some strengths and weaknesses associated with assessment centers?
2. What is recruitment? How does it differ from selection?
3. Identify the major issues related to Title VII. What is adverse impact? What is adverse treatment?
4. What is a BFOQ?
5. What is the ADA? Whom does it protect? What are some issues a manager needs to consider in the context of the ADA and recruitment and selection?
6. What are some recruitment sources for private security managers? What are the strengths and weaknesses of these sources?
7. What is negligent hiring? What five points need to be present for a negligent-hiring claim to be successful?
8. What is job analysis? Why is it important?
9. What is employee turnover? How does it differ from employee churn?
10. What are some advantages to using a structured rather than an unstructured interview? Provide an example.

■ REFERENCES

ABRAHAM, K., and R. MCKERSIE. 1990. *New developments in the labor market.* Cambridge, MA: MIT Press.

An ADA checklist for implementation and review. 1994. *HR Focus* 71 (7): 19–21.

ADLER, S. 1993/1994. Verifying a job candidate's background: The state of practice in a vital human resources activity. *Review of Business* 15 (2): 3–9.

ARTHUR, W., and D. DOVERSPIKE, 1997. Employment-related drug testing: Idiosyncratic characteristics and issues. *Public Personnel Management* 26 (1): 77–86.

Assessment centers: An intriguing way to hire. 1998. *South Dakota Employment Law Letter* 3 (9): 15–16.

BABER, B. J. 1998. Creative recruiting strategies. *Legal Assistant Today* 15 (5): 92–93.

BAKER, W. H., K. DeTEINEE, and K. L. SMART. 1998. How Fortune 500 companies are using electronic resume management systems. *Business Communication Quarterly* 61 (3): 8–19.

BARRETT, R. S. 1992. Content validation form. *Public Personnel Management* 21 (1): 41–52.

BEFORT, S. F. 1997. Pre-employment screening and investigation: Navigating between a rock and a hard place. *Hofstra Labor Law Journal* 14: 365–422.

BERGER, F., and A. GHEI. 1995a. Employment tests: A facet of hospitality hiring. *Cornell Hotel and Restaurant Administration Quarterly* 36 (6): 28–32.

———— 1995b. Attributes of tests. *Cornell Hotel and Restaurant Administration Quarterly* 36 (6): 32–34.

BERMAN, J. B. 2000. Defining "the essence of the business": An analysis of Title VII's privacy BFOQ after Johnson Controls. *University of Chicago Law Review* 67: 749–762.

Big budget recruiters should try internships. 2001. *ENR,* 246 (11): 68–69.

BLACK, K. R. 1994. Personality screening in employment. *American Business Law Journal* 32: 69–124.

BRADFORD, D. 1998. Police officer candidate background investigation: Law enforcement management's most effective tool for employing the most qualified candidate. *Public Personnel Management* 27 (4): 423–445.

BRAY, D. W. 1995. Centered on assessment. *Personnel Psychology* 48 (2): 468–470.

BRYANT, W. R. 1998. Justifiable discrimination: The need for a statutory bona fide occupational qualification of race discrimination. *Georgia Law Review* 33: 211–242.

BURNETT, J. R., C. FAM, S. J. MOTOWILDO, and T. DEGROOT. 1998. Interview notes and validity. *Personnel Psychology* 51: 375–396.

CALDWELL, D. F., and J. M. BURGER. 1998. Personality characteristics of job applicants and success in screening interviews. *Personnel Psychology* 51: 119–136.

CANTON, D. 1987. Adverse impact analysis of public sector employment tests: Can a city devise a valid test? *University of Cincinnati Law Review* 56: 683–709.

Carter v. Skokie Valley Detective Agency. 1993. 256 Ill.App. 3d 77.

Civil Rights Act. 2000. *U.S. Code.* Vol. 42, sec. e-3 (b).

CLAY, J. M., and E. C. STEPHENS. 1995. Liability or negligent hiring: The importance of background checks. *Cornell Hotel and Restaurant Administration Quarterly* 36 (5): 74–81.

COBER, R. T., D. J. BROWN, A. J. BLUMENTAL, D. DOVERSPIKE, and P. LEVY. 2000. The quest for the qualified job surfer: It's time the public sector catches the wave. *Public Personnel Management* 29 (4): 479–495.

COFFEE, K. 1998. Candidate reduction strategies. *Public Personnel Management* 27 (4): 459–473.

COLE-GOMOLSKI, B. 1999. Bloated resumes drive up hiring managers' time, costs. *Computerworld* 33 (3): 40–42.

Computer-aided interviewing helps overcome first impressions. 1995. *Personnel Journal* 74 (3): 11–16.

CORDNER, G. W. 1992. Human resource issues. In *Police management: Issues and perspectives,* ed. L. T. Hoover. Washington, DC: Police Executive Research Forum.

COULTON, G. F., 1995. Using assessment centers in selecting entry-level police officers: Extravagance or justified expense? *Public Personnel Management* 24 (2): 223–254.

DALTON, D. R., and M. B. METZGER, 1993. Integrity testing for personnel selection: An unsparing perspective. *Journal of Business Ethics* 12 (2): 147–151.

DUNCAN, S. R. 1994. Be realistic. *Manager's Magazine* 69 (11): 15–17.

DUNN, P. A. 1995. Pre-employment referencing aids your bottom line. *Personnel Journal* 74 (2): 68–72.

DUSTON, R. L. 1994. EEOC issues ADA guidelines on medical exams and testing. *Law and Policy Reporter* 4: 172.

FAUST, Q. C. 1996. Integrity tests: Do they have any integrity? *Cornell Journal of Law and Public Policy* 6: 211–229.

FERRARO, E. and W. J. JUDGE. 2003. Put your drug policy to the test. *Security Management* 47 (5): 94–99.

FIELDING, J. 1990. Discrimination law—impermissible use of the business necessity defense and the bona fide occupational qualification. *Western New England Law Review* 12: 135–165.

FISKE, D. W., E. HANFMANN, D. W. MACKINNON, J. G. MILLER, H. A. MURRAY, and E. HANFMAN (1996). *Selection of personnel for clandestine operations: Assessment of men.* Laguna Hills; CA: Aegean Park Press.

FRENCH, W. 1994. *Human resource management.* 3rd ed. Boston: Houston Mifflin.

GOLDMAN, C. D. 1993. Americans with Disabilities Act: Dispelling the myths. A practical guide to EEOC's voodoo civil rights and wrongs. *University of Richmond Law Review* 27: 73–101.

Gregor v. Kleiser. 1982. 111 Ill. App. 3d 333.

Greggs v. Duke Power Company. 1971. 401 U.S. 424.

GROVER, S. S. 1996. The business necessity defense in disparate impact discriminate cases. *Georgia Law Review* 30: 387–430.

HEIN, C. D., and N. R. VANZANTE. 1993. A manager's guide: Americans with Disabilities Act of 1990. *S.A.M. Advanced Management Journal* 58 (1): 40–43.

HOOVER, L. T. 1992. Trends in police physical ability selection testing. *Public Personnel Management* 21 (1): 29–40.

JOHNSON, B. I. 2000. Six of one, half-dozen of another. *Mullen v. Raytheon Co.,* as a representative of the federal circuit courts erroneously distinguishing the ADEA from Title VII regarding disparate impact liability. *Idaho Law Review* 36: 303–343.

JOINSON, C. 1998. Turn up the radio recruiting. *HR Magazine* 43 (10): 64–70.

JOYCE, L. W., P. W. THAYER, and S. B. POND. 1994. Managerial functions: An alternative to traditional assessment center dimensions? *Personnel Psychology* 47 (1): 109–122.

KELLEY, P. L., R. R. JACOBS, and J. L. FARR. 1994. Effects of multiple administrations of the MMPI for employee screening. *Personnel Psychology* 47 (3): 575–591.

KOTOROV, R. P. 2001. Corporate residency policy: To have or not to have a residency requirement. *Corporate Governance* 1 (2): 13–15.

LACHNIT, C. 2001. Employee referral saves time, saves money, delivers quality. *Workforce* 80 (6): 66–72.

LANDY, F. J., L. SHANKSTER, and S. KOHLER. 1994. Personnel selection and placement. *Annual Review of Psychology* 45: 261–292.

LAVINGA, R. J. 1996. Innovation in recruiting and hiring: Attracting the best and brightest to Wisconsin state government. *Public Personnel Management* 25 (4): 423–437.

LILIENFELD, S. O. 1999. Projective measures of personality and psychopathology: How well do they work? *Skeptical Inquirer* 23 (5): 32–39.

LONG, A. 1997. Addressing the cloud over employment references: A survey of recently enacted state legislation. *William and Mary Law Review* 39 (177): 177–205.

LOWRY, P. E. 1994a. The structured interview: An alternative to the assessment center? *Public Personnel Management* 23 (2): 201–213.

_____ P. E. 1994b. Selection methods: Comparison of assessment centers with personnel records evaluations. *Public Personnel Management* 23 (3): 383–395.

_____ P. E. 1996. A survey of assessment center processes in the public sector. *Public Personnel Management,* 25 (3): 307–318.

LOZADA, M. 2001. Job shadowing: Career exploring at work. *Techniques* 76 (8): 30–33.

LYE, L. 1998. Title VII's tangled tale: The erosion and confusion of disparate impact and the business necessity defense. *Berkeley Journal of Employment and Labor Law* 19.

MATTHEWS, B. P., and T. REDMAN. 2001. Recruiting the wrong salespeople: Are the job ads to blame? *Industrial Marketing Management* 30 (7): 541–550.

MICHELSON, R. S. 1987. A candidate's perspective of assessment centers. *Law and Order* 35: 26–30.

MILKOVICH, G. T. and J. W. BOUDREAU. 1991. *Human resource management.* Boston: Irwin.

MOREHART, K. K. 2001. How to create an employee referral program that really works. *HR Focus* 78 (1): 3–5.

MURPHY, K. R., K. OSTEN, and B. MYORS. 1995. Modeling the effects of banding in personnel selection. *Personnel Psychology* 48 (1): 61–79.

National Advisory Committee on Criminal Justice Standards and Goals.

Office of Strategic Services. 1948.

PITT, L. F. and B. RAMASESHAN. 1995. Realistic job information and saleforce turnover: An investigative study. *Journal of Managerial Psychology* 10 (5): 29–37.

PULAKOS, E. D., N. SCHMITT, D. WHITNEY, and M. SMITH. 1996. Individual differences in interviewer ratings: The impact of standardization, consensus discussion, and sampling error on the validity of a structured interview. *Personnel Psychology* 49 (1): 85–117.

RAY, C. M., J. J. STALLARD, and C. S. HUNT. 1994. Criteria for business graduates' employment: Human resource managers' perceptions. *Journal of Education for Business* 69 (3): 140–144.

ROMINGER, A. S., and P. SANDOVAL. 1998. Employee testing: Reconciling the twin goals of productivity and fairness. *DePaul Business Law Journal* 10: 299–347.

ROTH, P. G., and P. L. ROTH. 1995. Reduce turnover with realistic job previews. *CPA Journal* 65 (9): 68–70.

RUBIN, P. N. 1994. *The Americans with Disabilities Act and criminal justice: Hiring new employees.* Washington, DC: U.S. Department of Justice, National Institute of Justice.

RYAN, A. M., and M. LASEK. 1991. Negligent hiring and defamation: Areas of liability related to pre-employment inquiries. *Personnel Psychology* 44: 293–319.

SALOPEK, J. J. 1999. Low-tech ads, high tech CFO's. *Training and Development* 53 (8): 19–21.

SCHIFF, M. 1993. The Age Discrimination in Employment Act: Whither the bona fide occupational qualification and law enforcement exemptions? *St. John's Law Review* 67 (13): 13–54.

Sherill v. Compcare Health Services Insurance Corporation. 1993. 181 Wis.2d 366.

SIMON, H.A. 1976. *Administrative behavior: A study of decision-making processes in administrative organizations.* New York: Free Press.

Soroka v. Dayton Hudson Corporation. 1991. California Court of Appeal, First District. 235 Cal. App. 3d 654, 1 Cal. Rptr. 2d 77.

SPYCHALSKI, A. C., M.A. QUINONES, B.B. GAUGLER, and K. POHLEY. 1997. A survey of assessment center practices in organizations in the United States. *Personnel Psychology* 50 (1): 71–90.

STEVENS, C. K. 1998. Antecedents of interview interactions: Interviewer's ratings, and applicants' reaction. *Personnel psychology* 51 (4): 55–85.

STONER, J.A., and R. E. FREEMAN, 1989. *Management.* 4th ed. Englewood Cliffs, NJ: Prentice Hall.

TANINECZ, G. 1995. In search of creative sparks. *Industry Week* 244 (22): 43–45.

TERPSTRA, D. E. 1996. The search for effective methods. *HR Focus* 73 (5): 16–19.

TERPSTRA, D. E. and E. J. ROZELL. 1997. Why some potentially effective staffing practices are seldom used. *Public Personnel Management* 26 (4): 483–493.

TULLAR, W. L. 1989. Relational control in the employment interview. *Journal of Applied Psychology* 74: 971–977.

Uniform quaderes on Employee Selection Procedures. 1978. Section 60–3. 43 FR 38295.

U.S. Department of Commerce. 1998. The emerging digital economy. http://www.commerce.gov.

U.S. Department of Justice. *Report of the task force on private security.* 1977.

VERKERKE, J. H. 1998. Legal regulation of employment reference practices, *University of Chicago Law Review* 65: 115–136.

WILLIAMS, K. 2000. Online recruting: A powerful tool. *Strategic Finance* 82 (6): 21–23.

ZALL, M. 2000. Internet recruiting, *Strategic Finance* 81 (12): 66–72.

ZUCK, S. R. 1989. Shifting burdens of proof under disparate impact analysis: Conflict and problems of characterization. *Duquesne Law Review* 27: 535–566.

chapter six

Training

Increased competition, rapid technological changes, an increasingly diverse workforce, organizational restructuring, and economic changes are altering jobs or positions in organizations. In turn, organizations and managers are facing the increased responsibility of having greater workforce skills.

One way to meet these demands is to properly recruit and select incoming employees and at the same time provide them with organization-specific skills. Correspondingly, as Walton (1986) points out, a requisite concern for any manager is to maintain and advance the skill development of the existing workforce. Even with state-of-the-art tools, technology, and equipment, if workers are not competent in using these tools, the efficiency and effectiveness of the organization will be impaired. Hence, managers and organizations must recognize the need and importance of training their employees in order to improve the level and quality of the organization's human capital.

Although many private security agencies may indicate that training is a fundamental concern, their actions and organizational philosophy prove otherwise. Organizations that rely on training as a fundamental practice are, in effect, learning organizations. A learning organization, according to Pont (1995), has the following characteristics:

- The ability of employees to challenge prevailing thinking and the status quo and to learn from that experience

- The ability to use the creative attributes of individuals while building shared visions
- The ability to think systematically
- The creation, design, and facilitation of new learning activities that are diffused throughout the organization
- Support from the chief executive for developing the organization as a learning system
- The ability of subordinates to reorganize their systems of work while being encouraged to deviate from standard norms of practice in the context of a learning opportunity

These principles reflect the notion that training is an essential component of the learning organization. Paradoxically, one area of learning that an organization can control is the training of its people. Yet many organizations fail to recognize the importance of training as encouraging a learning system rather than simply course-building activities.

■ DEFINITION OF TRAINING

Training is both a term and a process. According to Pont (1995, 7), training is "the relatively systematic attempt to transfer knowledge or skills from one who knows or can do to one who does not know or cannot do." Training is an investment in human capital, as it serves to increase the cognitive and psychomotor skill levels of the worker through various educational techniques and delivery mechanisms. As a process, training is a form of organizational development. Training makes workers more productive and increases their levels of empowerment, resulting in greater levels of organizational competence in the context of improved profitability, ability to manage and cope with change, and increased levels of competitiveness in the organization's external task environment.

Although employees can take personal responsibility for their own training and development, this chapter focuses on those efforts by the organization to improve its human capital and on the need for adequate and proper training in the workplace. The chapter also reviews and discusses various training mediums, discusses how to properly design and administer training programs, describes barriers to effective training, and explains how to write a training proposal. Legal issues related to training are also discussed.

The State of Training

Training, or the lack of training, in the security industry is not a new topic of concern. The Private Security Task Force/National Advisory Committee on Criminal Justice Standards and Goals (U.S. Department of Justice 1977) called for the establishment of certification programs, at least 8 hours of preassignment, and

32 hours of basic training, of which 16 could be in-service, or on-the-job training. Other specific recommendations included training in firearms when applicable, the training of supervisors and managers, ongoing training and the involvement of appropriate state agencies to coordinate and approve training curricula, the certification of instructors, and accreditation of training schools. These and other recommendations set forth in the report did not result in any federal legislation but did help security-related organizations compare their existing levels of training to those established by the task force. The recommendations serve as a framework, or guideline, for future training efforts.

The Hallcreast Reports I and II also provide some insight into the state of training in the security industry. Findings from the Hallcreast Report I: Private Security and Police in America (Cunningham and Taylor 1985) determined that clients have few methods for verifying the training of contractual guards, even in those states that have mandated training. This report also found that the misrepresentation of the level of training given to contract security guards was a frequently reported complaint from clients and competing guard firms. On-the-job training was often the only type of training that a security officer received. As reported in the Hallcreast Report II (Cunningham, Strauchs, and VanMeter 1990), the issue of training was still a concern: Training was reported by the interviewees to be the major challenge facing the private security industry.

The extent of training in other industry groups parallels that in the security industry. Salzman (1998) revealed contradictions in the state of training in the United States, where organizations are growing more dependent on a higher skill level for their workers but are not giving their workers significant increases in training or skill development. This controversy can be attributed to three factors.

1. The shift in skills can often be gradual, not dramatic. As a result, the magnitude or the importance of the demand for a new skill is not sudden and is viewed as an episode rather than a large problem or issue for the organization in the context of training.
2. Training may not be a primary concern for some organizations because individuals being hired have more than adequate technical and other skills.
3. Some firms have not recognized the need for increased training, because they have been successful in finding individuals who already possess the required skills.

Training exists in various domains. Local, state, and federal government agencies may set training standards, although no specific federal legislation sets forth industrywide minimum training standards for the private security industry. Depending on the specific industry, however, the federal government may have some established training standards. For example, the U.S. Department of Energy sets training requirements for security guards employed at nuclear power plants. The federal government also indirectly influences the training requirements for security personnel. One example is health and safety standards, which the security function is often responsible for enforcing in the workplace. These standards are enforced by the U.S. Department of Labor's Occupational Safety and Health Administration (OSHA).

Some mandated training does exist at the state level. Some states require an individual to receive a minimum number of hours of in-service training before performing the functions of a security officer. For example, the state of New York requires 8 hours of preassignment training, 8 hours of on-the-job training within 90 days of hire, and 8 hours of annual in-service training in order to be licensed as a contract security guard. In California, the state's Bureau of Security and Investigative Services of the Department of Consumer Affairs sets minimum training standards for a person to be eligible to be licensed and work as a contract security guard.

Private organizations also establish various training standards and programs to increase the level of expertise and professionalism in their particular sector of the private security industry. The International Association for Healthcare Safety and Security (IAHSS) provides a 40-hour training and certification program for healthcare security officers. The American Society for Industrial Security (ASIS), through its Certified Protection Professional (CPP) program, has established educational requirements and the certification of those individuals who successfully pass the CPP exam. ASIS also offers security managers and employees a host of professional development training programs on a continual basis.

Some training programs are organization specific. Many companies have internal training programs whose level, quality, and commitment to training exceed those established by governmental agencies and private organizations. Organizational factors that may affect training are the resources available to the organization, including funding and adequate staffing; the philosophy and attitude the organization has toward training; and the industry group in which the organization operates.

The status of the organization could also affect the nature and degree of training. The Hallcreast I Report (Cunningham and Taylor 1985) found that contract security employees received fewer hours of training than did proprietary employees, which may be attributed to the costs associated with training. Because training is costly, the level of training that contract security firms may be providing to their employees, if it is not state mandated or required by the client, may be minimized and the training function passed on or made the responsibility of the client. This lack of training may also be compounded by the high turnover rate associated with the contract security industry. With high turnover rates, organizations may be hesitant to invest a great deal of money in employees perceived to have a short-term tenure with the company. This, however, could later expose the company to increased liability related to the failure to train.

One of the last domains of training is higher-education institutions. This domain encompasses universities, community colleges, and secondary schools that could provide a host of training programs for organizations (Ferman et al. 1990). The education an individual receives through formal educational institutions, especially universities, may differ from other forms of training. The education an individual receives through a formal educational system is often based on theory and abstract forms of thinking. This difference was best described by Harrison and Hopkins (1967, 433), who indicated that "formal systems of higher education in the United States provide training in the manipulation of symbols rather than of things; reliance on thinking rather than on feeling and intuition; and commitment to understanding rather than to action."

Some of these training programs are the result of state legislation related to the certification and licensing of security-related occupations, with students earning traditional college credits on successful completion. Other training could be more advanced and organization specific, with the course content designed specifically for the needs of the client. The training delivered through these specialized courses may also allow the participants to gain lifelong education credits that could be applied to various degree programs offered by the institution.

Benefits of Training

Effective training of employees is important for several reasons, based on the needs of the organization and satisfying the needs of the employees.

Organizational Benefits According to Ferman et al. (1990), social, technical, economic, and organizational factors have changed the need for and types of training. Some of the social changes that have promoted new forms of training are changes in the labor force. If the existing labor pool lacks those requisite skills that are needed, training is necessary to fill in the "skill gap." The aging of the workforce, combined with increased retirements, may also require changes in training to make up for those years of experience and the subsequent knowledge base that are leaving the organization.

Organizations are becoming more technologically advanced, again requiring the continual training of employees to remain competitive. Economically, many organizations now compete in a global economy and recognize that training is one component of economic development and competition. Last, organizations have undergone tremendous organizational changes over the past decade. New forms of workplace empowerment, management styles, personal career advancement and opportunities, and other workplace issues will require an increase in training programs.

Training may also serve as a recruitment tool. If the organization provides employees with advanced training, it may serve as a means to attract and recruit other individuals to the company (Kanter 1989), appealing to their drive for increased self-empowerment and personal need for achievement and fulfillment. Advanced forms of training may motivate the individual to choose this particular organization over others, as additional training will serve to provide increased opportunities in the organization's internal labor market. In one particular company, for example, the security staff is encouraged to become eligible for other careers or positions in the organization by taking any forms of training the organization provides. The increased level of training in multiple areas in the organization provides employees with opportunities in the internal labor market. This, in turn, may result in greater retention levels of employees, as they may be less inclined to leave the company for other opportunities. This training strategy results in a better-trained security officer who is cross-trained in comprehensive subjects that influence the entire organization. It also increases the level of communication and networking between security employees and other employees through relationships established during the training programs.

Effective training leads to increased productivity, and it is important to ensure that the organization has a skilled and up-to-date workforce. An effective training program also ensures that the organization has, within its internal labor market, a requisite pool of skilled and talented individuals for promotion, thereby reducing the need to recruit from the external labor market or task environment.

Employee Benefits   Both the direct and the indirect training outcomes increase the quality of life in the workplace for employees. Besides increasing the competency levels of workers, training increases the levels of meaningful, positive communication and trust among employees and can increase employee participation in confronting issues and solving problems rather than ignoring them or deferring the responsibility to management. Training programs can also change the structure of authority in the workplace. The changes associated with training may create an environment in which authority is based on expertise instead of traditional forms of delegated authority based on the individual's position.

Productivity and organizational effectiveness can also improve through training. As mentioned earlier, training programs can increase the level of talent in an organization. Through cross-training, the organization will have a pool of individuals with those requisite talents, subsequently increasing productivity and organizational effectiveness. Training related to customer service may improve the profitability and reputation of the organization. Because training increases the productivity level of employees, wages may increase after training to reflect the increased level of output or productivity (Barron, Berger, and Black 1997).

Other benefits related to increased or improved training may be less tangible but equally important. Training programs and their subsequent documentation often serve as a liability-reduction tool or shield for the employer. Effective training programs may also lower insurance premiums and prove that the organization is compliant with applicable regulations. Training may also reduce employee turnover, as employees are given increased opportunities that meet their needs for self-fulfillment. The decrease in turnover will subsequently reduce costs related to recruitment and selection while ensuring that productivity will be maintained.

Drawbacks to Training

Some drawbacks are related to training, however. First, training can be a costly venture for any organization. A properly designed training program requires staffing, and perhaps external trainers, as well as other expenditures associated with training. Training requires employees to attend the programs rather than be "producing" for the organization. Other critics of training point out that employees may leave the organization as a result of the increased training and the subsequent demand from the external labor market for their particular skills (Deierlein 1995).

■ TRAINING MEDIUMS

Training can be divided into two distinct categories: group-based and individual. Some examples of group-based training are lectures, group discussions, role-playing exercises, analysis of case studies, outdoor training programs, management games, and video training. Individual forms of training include on-the-job training, text-based and planned reading, technology- or computer-based training programs, and mentoring or coaching programs. These two categories are not mutually exclusive. Techniques from both the individual and group-based categories can be used to complement each other, depending on the training objectives.

When selecting the proper training method, the trainer or training staff should determine what types of skills to train for. Generally, these skills can be categorized as hard or soft skills. Hard skills can be readily observed or measured and usually require some degree of physical activity. Examples of hard-skills training are learning how to operate a particular machine or training in specific computer programs. Soft skills are difficult to measure and assess. These more cognitive types of skills may include training in teamwork, effective communication, problem solving, dealing with coworkers and the public, and planning.

Seminars and Lectures

The use of seminars is one of the most frequently used training mediums. Seminars traditionally use the lecture-style format, with a single moderator or group of moderators transmitting information to the learner. Usually, the seminar/lecture format dichotomizes the learning environment into the moderator and the audience. This medium is effective for transmitting a great deal of information in a short period of time to large audiences. Seminar and lecture methods, however, can also be incorporated with other training mediums. Seminars can incorporate the training of both hard and soft skills.

One of the drawbacks of this medium, in its traditional format, is the lack of meaningful dialogue between the participants and the moderator(s). The learners are passive recipients of the information in the training process. This subsequently raises the issue of how much information they receive and retain.

On-the-Job Training

According to Lawson (1997), on-the-job training (OJT) is a structured learning or training process conducted at the employee's work area to provide the skills and knowledge required to perform a job. OJT is a task-based learning process focused on the general or specific tasks the employee performs on a daily basis. The goal is to increase the individual's level of productivity. A general task includes those skills that an individual can transfer to another organization. Specific tasks are those skills that are unique to the organization and cannot be transferred to other organizations (Barron, Berger, and Black 1997).

An example of a general task in the area of private security is radio operations or use. This skill is easily transferable to another employer. An example of a specific task is a proprietary software package that gives the security employee knowledge related to a custom computer program that has no relevance to another security organization.

Usually, OJT is achieved by assigning the individual to another employee who has more experience and expertise. This individual is responsible for teaching and often evaluating the performance of the new employee. It is a one-on-one process, with an experienced individual working directly with the trainee. The trainer demonstrates the task or skill, allows the trainee to practice, and guides, checks, and corrects the individual's work through practice.

On-the-job training is not a formalized training program. The information transferred to the worker is usually not standardized. Instead, because each trainer's style for conveying the necessary information is different, the transmission of information and skills is nonuniform or inconsistent. Because each trainer may have unique methods of training, OJT requires the careful planning and supervision of the trainers to ensure that core information is included in the training program.

On-the-job training involves various steps, according to Lawson (1997):

1. Arousing curiosity and prompting speculation
2. Having the employee perform the task silently
3. Describing the task and placing it in context for the employee
4. Performing and explaining the task step by step
5. Exchanging roles with the trainee
6. Observing the trainee's performance and giving feedback
7. Letting the trainee practice independently
8. Conducting periodic checks and monitoring progress

On-the-job training programs may include apprenticeships, mentoring, coaching, and training models.

Apprenticeship Programs In traditional apprenticeship programs, individuals are trained in specific work-related skills through hands-on training combined with vocational-education-based trade programs. Apprenticeship programs blend work experiences in the organization with a sequential course of broad-based skills training related closely to the industry's standards. With these outcome-based forms of training, the student or employee must be able to successfully demonstrate ability to complete the assigned task with a high level of expertise by the end of the program. Usually, an apprentice takes a test administered by external bodies at the end of training to become certified, perhaps receiving a journeyman certificate, in the particular vocation (Moskal 1991). Depending on the trade or craft, apprenticeship programs may take years to complete.

Apprenticeship programs require the support of industries, vocational educational institutions, and governments. Such programs are heavily used in European countries for the metalworking, machining, and printing trades. In the United States, apprenticeship programs are not as widely used and are supervised and accredited by the federal government and cover various craft-related careers. U.S. apprentice programs have relied heavily on trade unions for their organization and administration (Loveman, Piore, and Semgenberger 1990). Although the use of apprenticeship programs is quite old, both businesses and government officials are calling for the resurrection of apprenticeship programs to deal with shortages of skilled workers, rapidly changing technologies, and poorly prepared employee candidates, and to upgrade the skills of current workers. Apprenticeship programs are generally skill based, teaching a specific craft or skill over a long period of time.

Apprenticeship programs have some drawbacks. Apprenticeship programs can be quite long, taking years for a trainee to advance to the top grades and pay levels. Therefore, some individuals may not be interested in participating in these programs. Further, individuals in apprentice programs may become disinterested or disillusioned in the process, increasing the level of attrition in the program. Apprenticeship programs may not receive institutional support or acceptance by some industries, leading to the lack of suitable apprenticeship sites for interested individuals.

Mentoring   Mentoring is usually an informal process whereby an individual is assigned to help the new hire or transferee adjust to the organization. The mentor provides resources, ideas, and information to the mentee(s). As a result of these diverse responsibilities, the mentor serves as a trainer in the organization. Generally, one mentor can handle no more than three individuals, depending on assigned responsibilities and commitment to the mentees (Auer 1995).

An important benefit of mentoring programs is that they provide employees with an opportunity to seek out relevant information from peers in a safe and informal atmosphere. Mentoring programs also serve as an ongoing orientation program for the company. They allow for the transmission of established cultural values from professionals in the organization, reinforcing normative standards of conduct in the workplace. These programs have also been found to improve communication, increase the motivational levels of employees, and assist the organization in succession planning and employee development (Pont 1995).

One of the drawbacks to mentoring is that the mentors may not be able to achieve any personal development on their own while actively mentoring. This problem can be attributed to the amount of time and the level of commitment needed in the mentoring process (Auer 1995).

Coaching   Often, coaching is considered a form of training, but the two have some significant differences. Training is usually group oriented, providing individuals with basic skills to do their jobs; coaching is a one-on-one developmental or ongoing process designed to enhance the competency or performance of the individual. According to Pont (1995, 148), "coaching helps people go beyond the basic requirements to release skills that have not yet been released . . . it enables individuals to develop their potential and often to the full."

Coaching can be considered a win-win training tool. It enhances the performance of an employee and is a strong reward for the coach's performance in the workplace.

Unlike trainers, coaches do not have to be experts in what is being coached; nor do they have to have the same skills as the individuals they are working with. Professional athletic coaches, for example, do not have the same skill levels as their players. Instead, the role of the coach is to provide support, encouragement, and feedback to facilitate continuous improvement. Some of the benefits of this long-term relationship include improving employee performance and opening up or improving lines of communication in the organization (Pont 1995). Coaching is a cost-effective method for improving self-confidence and the skill level of the employee. In order to accomplish an effective coaching program, top management must be committed to it. Individuals selected as coaches should also have some basic skills, including effective verbal and empathic communication skills (Pont 1995).

Training Models   A more formalized process in using existing staff in the training process is through the use of training models. In this type of program, senior employees are assigned to junior employees. This type of training focuses on what the employee is doing right or wrong. Some of the benefits of using senior employees as training models is that trainers may be relieved of some of their field-training burdens, and senior employees may gain some additional insight from the new employees (Keenan 1994). As with any training program, clear objectives and guidelines must be established prior to implementing the program. Senior employees participating in the program must also be trained so they can teach and evaluate the new hires.

Computer-Based Training

Computer-based training ranges from the very simple to the very complex and can be classified as passive or active. In a passive mode, the learner simply scrolls or reads through the information presented on the computer screen. In active techniques, the learner has some type of interaction with the computer and can engage in higher forms of problem solving, alone or perhaps in networked groups.

AN EXAMPLE OF COMPUTER-BASED TRAINING

One example of merging computer and university training is the partnership between the School of Criminal Justice at Michigan State University (MSU) and Target Stores, where loss-prevention personnel can complete, via the Internet, an entire master's degree in criminal justice with an emphasis in private security. Students enroll for courses at MSU and then are given an access code for the server containing the courses. Students are required to complete assignments and papers and submit them to the instructor. Other activities are similar to classroom experiences but without going to class. Open discussions allow the student to talk with instructors and other students and to participate in problem-solving exercises.

In case-based reasoning, an active computer training system, the student must make logical and correct decisions on questions or prompts that appear in the training module or exercise. Some programs have recorded video segments by experts in the field to guide the student in subsequent decisions. If the student should make a wrong decision, for example, a video clip appears, with an expert on the topic explaining why the decision was wrong. In effect, the student must solve the problem through the decisions made. Thus, the student reaches a conclusion based on listening to the series of stories or educational segments that provided guidance in making correct choices in the training program (Garfinkel 1995).

Computer-based training has some advantages. Participants can take classes or training sessions away from the workplace at their own convenience. Such programs not only save the employer money but also may encourage individuals to pursue additional avenues of training in their free time. This type of training allows students to complete the required work at their own pace. Advanced forms of computer training also allow online discussions that promote learning or interaction.

This type of training has some disadvantages, however. Many computer-based training modules may be suited only for "soft" skills, as they may be too general for the specific needs of the organization. Another problem is identifying what programs or training materials are best suited for the organization. Depending on the type of training and the sophistication of the software package, these training mediums can be quite expensive. Combined with the fact that the organization may also have to purchase additional computer equipment, it may not be financially feasible for all organizations. Some individuals may be computer illiterate or hesitant to engage in these new forms of training. As a consequence, the organization may have to train employees in the fundamentals of computer use before implementing the computer training package.

Case Studies

The goal of a case study training program is to have attendees find solutions to real-life workplace incidents, problems, or situations. The case study approach requires individuals to sort through information and develop solutions or decisions that are based on theory, company policy and procedure, feasibility, and various short- and long-term ramifications their actions would create. This allows students to learn on their own while discovering their own solutions, instead of receiving directions or solutions from the instructor. This, in turn, hones the students' critical-thinking skills and increases their confidence and competency in solving issues or problems.

Case study training methods vary considerably. Traditional forms of case studies rely on real-life incidents or fictitious narratives created by trainers to meet their specific objectives. Case studies are usually group-based training projects, as this method stimulates dialogue, group problem solving, and the enhancement of collegial relationships. Using the case study format to review prior security incidents that happened at the organization is one of the easiest and most effective training tools. Case study training can also be designed and used in individual-based training programs or modules. Audiovisual and computers are other delivery techniques for case studies.

The case study usually requires a facilitator who is responsible for guiding the discussion, providing feedback and encouragement, and maintaining a positive learning environment. A properly designed case study also requires the development of questions at the end of the narrative to facilitate and channel the learning objectives of the training session and to provide a framework or foundation on which attendees can base their responses. All these activities occur in a "safe" environment in which employees can learn through their mistakes and subsequently improve their performance in the organization.

Scenario-Based Training

Scenario based training occurs when participants in the training program are "placed" into real-life situations. In these forms of training, the trainee applies the particular skills needed to deal with the situation correctly. The context of these scenarios can be the past, current, and future environments and can be individual- or group-based. Depending on the needs of the training, scenarios vary from simple to complex.

An effectively designed scenario should enable the trainee to demonstrate both hard and soft skills, allowing the participant to practice and think differently in a safe learning environment. For example, a trainer can write scenarios in which participants explain their decisions in writing or verbally. In role-play scenarios, participants must demonstrate effective use of nonverbal and verbal communication skills. If recorded, these scenarios can also be reviewed in an individual or group setting, increasing the impact of the learning process.

One benefit of scenario-based training is that it requires participants to engage in forward- and outward-based thinking while dealing with ambiguity. To ensure its effectiveness, the training scenario must be adequately planned with identifiable training goals present in the scenario. One of the drawbacks associated with scenario-based training is that it may be expensive. It may require a great deal of time in the context of administering the training program (Schriefer 1995).

Video-Based Training

Organizations can purchase, rent, or produce video-based training packages that concentrate on both soft or hard and general or specific skills. Although many video training packages lack interactive capabilities, they can, if properly designed, include such methods. For example, a group of employees could view a video, engage in group discussions and problem-solving exercises, and generate solutions or answers to the issues presented in the video.

Any video-based training must have structure and be relevant to the organization. The videos must also be current and professionally produced. In many situations, organizations may develop a video library for individuals to check out and review training modules in their free time on or off duty. If video training is used, the organization should document the training the individual received. In addition, some form of assessment should be conducted to ensure that the participant has learned the subject matter in the video. This assessment could be as simple as a short multiple-choice exam that the employee completes at the end of the video training segment.

Joint Training Programs

Joint training programs are the combined efforts of unions and management to provide training in areas related to both personal and skill development. Although the employer usually pays for these types of programs, they are participant driven through joint decisions made by union and management membership. The training agenda is often set forth through committees composed of union officials, employees, and management representatives; these committees determine the workers' needs, set training priorities, and organize the training programs, based on skill, personal development, and long-term career planning. Hence, many of these programs are structured or based on the expressed needs of the workers and are more concerned with lifetime employment, education, and training (Ferman et al. 1990). Both union and management members govern the training, and the training program has a high degree of local control. Often, this type of training occurs onsite or at skill centers created by the organization and the union.

AN EXAMPLE OF A SUCCESSFUL LABOR MANAGEMENT TRAINING PROGRAM

The United Steel Workers of America (USWA), in conjunction with union members and employers, established the Institute for Career Development (ICD) in 1989 to improve the skill levels of steelworkers. The ICD contracts with 13 companies; all members of the USWA employed by the participating companies are eligible for enrollment in high school/GED, traditional college courses, and customized classes that are designed by the union membership (Sunoo 1999). The end result of these programs is that participating companies now have a more skilled and educated workforce (Hequet 1994).

Training Manuals

Training manuals may be another training option for the organization. Training manuals can be based on general or specific topics and can be used to supplement existing training programs or as a stand-alone product. The manuals themselves may take the form of bound books or loose-leaf handouts or be designed as self-tutorial programs that can be completed on company time or away from the workplace during the employee's free time. Properly designed training manuals may also provide the framework for an individual to engage in self-training or study of particular concepts or areas of their jobs. Such materials can be very cost-effective compared to other training-delivery mechanisms.

Consortiums

Training consortiums are groups of organizations that join together to achieve mutually beneficial outcomes from human development programs. The consortiums can be quite creative, ranging from the construction and staffing of training centers to the development of electronic libraries to share training information.

One of the primary benefits of training consortiums is that they are often cost-effective, as the organizations share costs associated with training. Instead of one organization's paying for all the expenses related to a training program, the consortium members share these expenses, subsequently reducing the financial costs associated with training. With lower training costs, organizations may offer more training programs.

Consortiums also reduce redundancy in training. Instead of having multiple organizations perform the same training function, organizations can pool their resources, determine the core skill areas for training, proceed with curriculum development, and implement appropriate training programs. Consortiums also establish training standards and enlarge the training possibilities for all the organizations involved. As individuals from various organizations are involved in the planning and administration of the training programs, these joint efforts may ensure a better-quality training product while also ensuring that the training programs are up to date in content and process. Consortiums also allow the members to purchase items, such as expensive computer-based training programs, that may have been cost prohibitive on an individual basis. Consortiums also encourage networking. They open up new avenues of joint projects, while increasing communication, teamwork, and levels of trust among organizations.

Other Training Methods

Training can be combined with real-world or work-related activities. For example, the U. S. Marine Corps assists local and federal law enforcement efforts in drug-interdiction efforts along the southwest border of the United States. Some of the hard skills learned by the Marines during these reconnaissance missions include communications procedures, command and control, and intelligence collection. Soft skills learned include improved leadership, decision making, and confidence building (Lehmann 1998).

A creative security manger could construct similar training activities that combine practical experiences with the training dimension. For example, if a crisis or emergency situation, such as heavy storm damage, should strike a community, the security function could volunteer the services of its staff. Skills related to communication, leadership, and teamwork would be enhanced, and concepts of emergency management would be learned and perhaps applied to the organization's practices.

Another alternative may be adventure training. Here, learners are presented with outdoor challenges requiring teamwork and group decision making to reach the objectives. Although the majority of these training programs concentrate on general skills, such as effective communication, leadership, teamwork, and problem solving, they can also be designed to incorporate specific skills, if necessary.

■ TRAINING PROGRAM DESIGN CONSIDERATIONS

Models of Learning

Before determining the type of delivery mechanism, the trainer should consider the needs, proficiency, and limits of the learners. The organization needs to be aware that the design and implementation of what it chooses as its delivery mechanism will affect the individual in the learning process. The two main models related to learning are pedagogy and andragogy. Pedagogy is the art and science of teaching children. Andragogy is the art and science of helping adults learn. These two models are not antithetical. Both learning models can be used together. For example, a training program could include a pedagogical aspect—a lecture—followed by an andragogical aspect—discussion, group problem solving, and other learner-centered activities.

Pedagogy   This is the "traditional" teaching paradigm, premised on the concept that any training environment has two distinct parties: the teacher and the learner. This dichotomy means that the two parties have little interaction. The model is teacher centered, with students passive participants in the learning process. This model has little, if any, two-way communication, or "connective" feedback in the form of open discussions and questions presented in the class. Pedagogy may also be characterized by strong teacher/student roles in a learning environment in which the emotions of the learners rarely appear in classrooms. Such a learning environment usually fosters little praise, enthusiasm, or intensity.

Nonetheless, many training and educational programs are premised on pedagogical models, which do have some benefits.

- These models are effective in the delivery of a great deal of information in a timely manner.
- Individuals may be comfortable in a pedagogical environment, as that is what they are accustomed to through their prior educational experiences.
- Trainers may also be comfortable with pedagogical models, having complete control of the training environment.
- Trainers may be comfortable with this model because this is what they were trained to do through their education to become a trainer.
- As indicated by Knowles (1984a), pedagogical teaching models may also be appropriate for learners if the content of the training is unfamiliar and exact skills are involved, as for machine operation.

Andragogy   Andragogy focuses on the needs of the adult learner and is based on five assumptions.

1. Adults have a need to be self-directing and oppose situations of dependence.
2. Adults have a vast repertoire of knowledge they can relate to the learning while also using it as a resource for learning.
3. Adults are eager to learn things that they need to know or be able to do in order to succeed.
4. Adults learn through a problem-centered orientation, compared to a subject-centered learning orientation for children.
5. Adults are motivated to learn via internal factors, such as increased self-esteem, over external rewards, such as increased pay or promotions (Knowles 1984b).

The andragogical training process is based on mutual respect and alliance, with the student as the central figure in the learning process. The needs of the student are paramount, and the students are considered to be a community of thinkers whose opinions are central, encouraged, and respected. To be effective using this style, the trainer must value the learner's experience and use it, adopt a learner-centered instructional strategy, and serve as a change agent through individual coaching and facilitating small-group discussions. The trainer must also improve the individual's cognitive, planning, organizing, information seeking, and communication skills.

This mode of training may be more difficult for the trainer. Instead of simply providing information to the students, the trainer must now use and incorporate the student's knowledge and experience as an integral part of the training program.

The andragogical model has several benefits. First, andragogical models of learning allow for greater levels of critical thinking to occur; individuals in this model of learning have the ability to interpret, criticize, and evaluate the information being presented. In addition, learners will be more motivated to learn, improving the output of the training program as reflected in greater productivity, motivation, and self-actualization. The use of andragogical models, however, will require the trainer to be more cognizant of the needs of the learner when planning the training program. The trainer may have to more fully diagnose the needs of learner, while finding the most appropriate adult-centered delivery mechanisms.

Transferability

Another issue to consider when designing a training program is transferability, or how the skills learned in the training process can be fed back into the organization (Bennis, Benne, and Chin 1962). In some situations, the training medium(s) used and the topics learned may not be easily brought back into the organization or applied. Issues related to organizational constraints, including behavioral norms and expectations, defined work rules, and so on, could impair the application of these topics in full or in part.

The issue of transferability is often overlooked. Perhaps one of the most disparaging actions an employer can do is to provide an employee with training that cannot be used or applied in the workplace. It must be remembered that one of the primary outcomes of a training program is to motivate the learner. As discussed earlier, training, when used as a motivational tool, results in greater levels of productivity and personal satisfaction in the workplace. Therefore, the effective training program should have some immediate results for the learner. If, however, an employer provides training that is not transferable, the training could have both long- and short-term ramifications. Training could be considered or labeled by employees as "a waste of time" or "worthless," affecting their own and other employees' attitudes toward existing or future training programs and their level of motivation in the workplace. The impact of the lack of transferability could also affect the company's employee retention and recruitment efforts.

Cost

Cost is a primary concern when designing a training program. The extent and the nature of training, including the methods used to deliver training, can often be quite expensive. Perhaps one of the most difficult issues to consider is the relative gains of the training versus the direct and indirect costs related to the design and implementation of the training program. Management will want to know the value that training adds to the business equation in the context of profitability. In this aspect, it may be difficult to cost out the short- and long-term benefits of some training programs. Through an effective training-needs assessment (TNA) process, discussed later in the chapter, the issues related to cost can be addressed and often mitigated.

Location

The location of the training program is another issue to consider. Depending on the nature of the training and the delivery mechanism, the organization may opt for on- or off-site training locations.

On-Site Training On-site training programs are easily accessible by all individuals attending the training program, and no costs are generally associated with securing training rooms and other resources needed for the training program, as they are readily available. If the organization is using in-house trainers, they are well versed and comfortable in the training environment. The company can easily monitor the progress of the program and may have a greater degree of control on the quality and delivery of the training session.

One primary drawback to on-site training is that it may appear to some participants as routine and subsequently not worthwhile. Depending on the training topics, some participants may also be hesitant to express their opinions and attitudes in on-site training situations. On-site training could also increase levels of distraction, as participants would have access to their offices and coworkers. These distractions could result in individuals trying to carry on their own daily work on breaks and not fully concentrating on the training being provided.

Off-Site Training To address some of the drawbacks associated with on-site training, the organization may consider an off-site location. One of the benefits of off-site training is that the location may be specifically designed for that training in the context of equipment and resources needed. Another benefit involves the perceptions of the learner. An off-site location may appear to be more professional. The learner may also perceive this location to be "safer" for experimenting freely and openly communicating with other attendees, especially if the organization did not use its own training staff at the off-site location.

Off-site training also has some drawbacks. One drawback is related to rental costs of the facility and necessary equipment. Another large expense could result if the company is not providing the trainer at the off-site location. Organizations may also be responsible for per diem expenses, including the employee's food, travel, and lodging expenses. Depending on the length, quality, type of training, and number of employees attending the training, these expenses could easily be more than the direct costs of the training program.

Matching Training to Workers

Another challenge facing organizations and managers is ensuring that the training is an appropriate match with their employees. Organizations that have a diverse workforce in age, education, language, years of experience, and gender, for example, could find it challenging to design and implement a training program. Although some of these issues can be resolved prior to training through a comprehensive review of the attendees, other issues may be more subtle.

For example, an unplanned mismatch between course content and attendees arose at a seminar on computer crimes. Before the seminar began, each participant was issued a laptop computer. The younger attendees immediately demonstrated greater levels of proficiency in general computer skills and readily "played" with their computers before the seminar and during breaks. Some of the older, more experienced attendees, however, did not use their laptop computers at all during the first day of training. Instead, they looked on or worked with other, more proficient computer users. To ensure that the less proficient users would not feel excluded from and lose interest in the 5-day program, the trainer had to modify the course. The trainer provided introductory training in computer use on the second day of the seminar in order to ensure the proper match between training content and users.

■ ADMINISTERING TRAINING

Establishing the Training Program/Department

Usually, the human resource, or personnel, department is responsible for the training function. In other instances, training is assigned to a specific individual in the security department. Regardless, people involved in the training function face several demands. First are demands on resources. In many organizations, training is not a primary issue. As a result, training programs may be one of the first areas that experience budget cuts. If financial issues are not a concern, resources, including a training staff, the training location, and the types of training, may also be limited. Trainers and training departments may also be required to train employees in a relatively short period of time, further increasing the demands placed on them.

The basic role of any trainer is to provide a learning structure for an organization and its members. This means having an entity for developing training programs. Once these training programs are developed, however, a variety of individuals are capable of performing the training function. One of the key requirements for any trainer is to understand the fundamentals of training while recognizing that the trainer is a role model, educator, facilitator, and skill builder.

Because of these diverse trainer roles and responsibilities, training can be placed on a continuum. At one end, training is limited and trains to specific organizational interests or issues. In this capacity, the trainer performs the traditional tasks of establishing, planning, and evaluating training programs. Often, in these instances, the training function is not an integrated component of the organization but performs those tertiary duties only when needed.

Besides the "pure" training function, an expanded role may include working with management on organizational development issues. In this role, the training department, officer, or unit may also serve as a resource tool for employees, providing them with the information they need to engage in self-initiated, self-guided, and self-fulfilling training on their own time.

This expanded role of the training function may result in greater awareness of the needs of the organization's managerial priorities. This increased involvement, for example, may increase the reputation and credibility of the training function in the organization. In this capacity, trainers can expand their roles and responsibilities, serving as internal consultants and becoming involved in strategic planning while helping other decision makers find creative and effective solutions to increase performance and, hence, profitability. In short, trainers become facilitators and catalysts for positive change in the organization. They become an integral component of the organization's change and planning processes.

Developing Training Programs

One of the primary goals in developing any training program is to ensure that the training and the desired results are linked. A training program is a progressive plan that looks at the present state of the organization's training needs and considers where the organization needs to be in the future. To achieve this desired outcome, a well-designed training program should be proactive, continually scanning the organization for its various training needs and adjusting the program as necessary.

Part of any well-designed and implemented training program is the training-needs assessment. This often lengthy process involves creating training objectives and developing both the training program(s) and methods of delivering the training. The TNA process also requires that the organization evaluate the training program(s) at various stages (Taylor and O'Driscoll 1998).

An effective TNA program has several benefits. First, TNA helps other human resource functions in the organization. For example, the results of the TNA process could lead to changes in the recruitment and selection of new employees. The TNA process may also identify new levels of knowledge, skills, and abilities that the organization will need. The TNA process also helps the organization in writing or revising job descriptions, as part of the TNA process outlines or describes the tasks or duties involved in jobs. TNA helps in career development and improves the training function. Through its analysis of training needs, TNA serves as a liability-reduction tool for the organization. Although TNA can be costly to develop and administer, the TNA process also justifies training, as it gives the organization a greater understanding of the cost and benefits related to training (Schneier, Guthrie, and Olian 1988).

The TNA involves three interrelated components as shown in Figure 6-1: a needs analysis, the design and delivery of the training, and evaluating the training

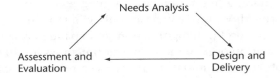

FIGURE 6–1 ■ Components of Training-Needs Assessment

program. This process is ongoing. Once a training program has been completed, an additional needs analysis should be conducted to determine the additional training needs of the organization.

Needs Analysis

Before engaging in any training, the organization should conduct a needs analysis to find discrepancies between the existing level and desired performance levels. The primary purpose of this analysis is to identify training gaps in the organization. This is an important step in designing any type of training. The organization must properly plan, manage, and administer the program while preserving organizational time, resources, and money.

The needs-analysis stage can be quite time consuming, depending on the scope and depth of the issue being examined. Although no true standard exists, the needs-analysis process should use multiple data-collection methods to ensure a comprehensive, valid, and reliable analysis of the training needs.

Zemke (1998) points out that an organization can follow six steps when conducting a needs analysis:

1. Identify the problem.
2. Determine the solution requirements.
3. Identify alternative means to solve the problem.
4. Select the solution, based on costs and consequences, and implement it.
5. Determine the effectiveness and efficiency of the identified solution.
6. Revise as required.

Needs analysis can also be divided into additional areas: organizational, person, task, and demographic. Organizational analysis examines the goals and objectives of the company to determine where appropriate training is needed in the organization. The need for training can be based on what knowledge, skills, or abilities employees need to perform various work-related responsibilities. This is known as task analysis. Person analysis examines which employees need what training, based on performance appraisals or other tests that measure individuals' abilities. Last, demographic analysis identifies the training needs of the employees, based on their age, levels in the organization, and perhaps gender (Taylor and O'Driscoll 1998).

Needs analysis can also be conducted by scanning the external environment. For example, the risk management or legal department could examine existing and future liability issues to determine training needs. Likewise, and consistent with liability reduction, the organization can also compare its existing standards and needs for training to those of similar organizations in its geographical area and region, if necessary. Other methods may include referring to professional associations and organizations affiliated with the security industry to identify additional training needs.

The needs-analysis process can also be quite formal. Depending on the research design, these methods could be laborious and slow for the organization. Some of the methods used in this process could include attitudinal surveys and questionnaires, interviews, focus groups, and behavioral observations. Conversely, the process can also be informal. Alternative methods may include using existing information or data, such as letters, grievances, performance records, and incident reports, and continually "scanning" the organization. The training function can also pay closer attention to those issues, problems, and needs employees have. Another method involves rapid analysis. This method is used when the organization implements a training program and changes or modifies it as the trainer or the organization learns more about the problem (Zemke 1998).

Some researchers call for a departure from the traditional needs-assessment approach and recommend examining factors outside the training domain. Tracey and Tews (1995) call for the examination of individual and work/environmental characteristics that may affect training. The authors state that doing so is important because an individual's ability to learn, personal background, attitude toward work, commitment to the job, and motivation to learn affect training outcomes.

In the context of the work environment, the characteristics of the job may also be important. First, an individual who is performing diverse responsibilities may not have the opportunity to use new skills learned through training. Second, one should also consider the social networks in the organization. If the organization facilitates and encourages the use of the new knowledge and skills, it will have a positive influence on employees' willingness to learn while transferring the learning back to the job. Last, the organization's reward systems should ensure that learners use their new skills by providing raises or promotions based on skill acquisition, when appropriate.

Following the needs analysis, a training proposal should be written. The training proposal documents the need for, and purpose of, the training program. The proposal documents the goals, objectives, and outcomes of the program. At a minimum, the training proposal should list the following:

- A statement of the need for the training
- Who the training is designed for
- The content of the training program, in detail
- The length of the training program
- Trainers used
- Location

- Resources needed for the training
- Outcome measures to assess the training
- Follow-up of the training program

Program Delivery

The implementation and delivery of the training program(s) to the learner follow the needs-analysis stage. The type of training and delivery techniques used should coincide with what was identified through the needs analysis. Needs analysis, however, does not end with the delivery of the training program. During this stage of the TNA process, the trainer needs to "scan" the training audience, monitoring the status of the training program. The trainer should also use those same techniques that exist in the needs-analysis phase. If issues are discovered, the training should be adjusted accordingly.

Training Assessment

In order to measure the impact the training has on the employee, a benchmark measure of the existing worker attributes needs to be obtained. This subsequently requires that the organization conduct a training assessment *prior* to training. This preassessment will enable the organization to measure the workers' existing skill levels. The development of a skills-inventory checklist will later serve as a basis for assessing the effectiveness of the training program.

Multiple methods can be used to assess the effectiveness or impact of a training program. According to Malcolm (1998), these assessment methods exist on a hierarchy of four levels, ranging from the easiest to most difficult for the organization to measure the success or impact of the training program(s). Level 1 measures or surveys the attendees to see how well they liked the training. Level 2 tests the participants' new skills or attributes. Level 3 reviews or checks whether the skills learned are being used on the job or how the training has impacted the individual's job. Level 4 measures the impact the training has had on the organization. Regardless of what level the organization decides to measure, the findings or results of the training program should be able to be easily communicated to management so it can assess the impact of the program.

■ INSTRUCTIONAL STRATEGIES

The Training Environment

The learning environment is anything—social or physical—that has an impact on the learning process. For example, a concrete block training room painted in "institutional" drab colors may impart a negative impression on trainees. Similarly, a room that is too cold or too hot or both during a training session is likely to have a negative impact. Other environmental factors are whether the chairs are comfortable, the availability of refreshments during breaks, and the lighting and acoustical qualities of the room. Although often overlooked, these and other issues can be controlled to a great degree in the proper planning of training sessions.

The Trainer

The selection of a trainer is very important. Whether the trainer is in-house or contracted, some basic requirements must be met. First, the trainer must have the requisite communication skills essential for training, as well as the correct credentials or training in the subject matter. The trainer must be able to speak the language of those being trained and be able to communicate with employees from all levels of the organization. The trainer should also adapt to the trainees' learning styles and organizational beliefs or practices, allow trainees sufficient time to accomplish the objectives, and be genuinely committed to training, respectful, and encouraging.

A great deal of training may be conducted by in-house trainers. One of the first issues to consider is whether an individual who already works for the organization has the requisite skills or level of expertise. How credible is this person with the employees in the organization? An in-house trainer who does not have a good work record or reputation could impact the effectiveness of the training.

Using in-house trainers can result in indirect benefits for the organization, however. Managers may consider sending some of their staff to become trainers in topics that they have an interest in. Doing so would enhance and enrich those employees' positions. Such training could also serve as a motivational tool for other employees, as they recognize the potential to become trainers based on their performance and commitment to the organization. In-house trainers may also be cost-effective. Despite the up-front costs associated with training the employee, the organization will, over time, save money, as it will no longer have to hire outside experts for some types of training.

The organization may opt to use contracted trainers, especially for training that is highly technical. When selecting external subject matter experts (SMEs), the training department must be careful to make sure that they have the requisite background in training and are comfortable with the appropriate instructional strategies and methods that will be used. SMEs should also have the correct attitude, image, and respect for those being trained, to ensure that a positive training environment will occur (Reiss 1991).

Contracted trainers or consultants may be able to provide the training quickly, as they already possess those skills and have established training programs. Other advantages of using outside trainers are that they may provide a higher-quality product, which could be verified by other clients, may possess those requisite skills and knowledge that the organization lacks, and may be more credible in the eyes of the participants. Contracted consultants may also be cost-effective, as their services can be terminated rapidly; with in-house trainers, by contrast, costs are associated with designing the training program and maintaining a training staff. However, contracted trainers' training programs may not be specific enough for the organization, may be costly, and they may not be under the direct control of the organization (Munson 1984).

Room Layout

Room layout is a critical component in an effective training session. Room design should be considered in the context of the physical and psychological needs of the student. The trainer should then balance those needs with materials and learning models that will be used.

Figure 6–2 shows some of the room designs that can be used in training programs. Although some of these layouts are designed for the traditional classroom, other forms allow for the use of andragogical models of learning. For example, a traditional classroom setting is suitable for training a large number of individuals. But this setting is not so conducive for group problem-solving exercises and discussions. A trainer who prefers group problem solving may consider the roundtable design, which allows for ease of communication, or the modified roundtable, which allows the entire training group to interact during the training.

Room design does not have to remain the same during the course of training. In a sequentially developed training program, the trainer may first provide some basic information to the participants through the traditional lecture format. During this phase of the program, the U-shaped, chevron, or V-shaped classroom may be used. During a scheduled break, the trainer could redesign the room for the open discussion and problem-solving portion of the training. Now the roundtable or modified roundtable design would be more appropriate, to facilitate an open discussion among the participants on the issues and topics presented during the lecture.

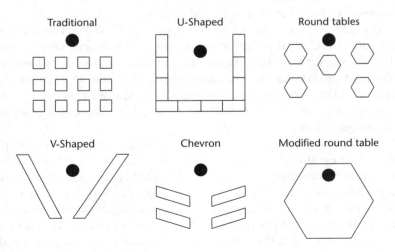

FIGURE 6–2 ■ Options for Room Layout

Spatial Factors

The length, duration, and location of the training program must be considered. The training program should be designed with the realization that many adult learners may not be used to some forms of training, as when the training is different from the work that an employee normally performs or the training session(s) cover a long period of time. A training program with a poor spatial design could affect the satisfaction and motivational levels of workers and negatively affect the organization's future training efforts.

Hours per Day   Long training programs may result in participants' losing interest and "zoning out" of the training experience. One simple and effective way to prevent this from occurring is to schedule an adequate number of breaks during the training program. The training schedule should also be flexible enough to allow unscheduled breaks when needed. Trainers should also consider the sequencing of course materials. Showing a video after the lunch break may not be a good idea. Many participants may be tired after a meal. An alternative could be an interactive group problem-solving exercise that requires some physical activity to energize the trainees.

Days per Program   Training programs that run for several days may result in decreasing levels of employee interest. One way to avoid some of the problems associated with lengthy training programs is to divide the training into modules. Training modules are a clearly defined part, or segment, of the complete training program, incorporating and building on preceding training blocks until the learners complete the modules or become proficient in the skill area(s) (Bland 1995). This compartmentalization of the training may provide a sense of finality to learners. Instead of one large and lengthy program that could be intimidating to some learners, the modular approach allows a sense of completion in one part of the training before moving on to the next training component.

Setting up training in modules is particularly effective for long training sessions. This modular approach was used in a 10-month program that addressed supervisory development. In this particular program, participants met once a week every month for 10 months. Participants were given the complete training schedule the first week of the program. This schedule showed the participants that the 10-month training program consisted of 10 management-related modules. This modular approach made the training program less intimidating and cumbersome to the participants.

Scheduling Programs   Spatial factors also include appropriate scheduling of the days and months of the training program. For example, scheduling training events in December may interfere with some employees' vacation plans. Scheduling training during the opening days of deer hunting and fishing seasons could also lead to some problems. One of the best ways to avoid such time conflicts is to include the employees in the scheduling process.

Multiple Locations   Another spatial issue is whether the organization has multiple locations. A large organization with a national or international training program must carefully administer and plan the delivery of these programs. The organization must also consider whether the training needs to be modified from location to location. In such a case, the training can be modified to the location's specific needs while still maintaining the core training objectives. For example, a large firm may need to train all its security personnel in alarm operations. However, various sites have different alarm systems. To meet the training outcomes, the firm will need to have basic training in alarms that are used companywide. During the same training, the firm will also need to have specific training related to a site's particular alarm system.

Motivating Learners

Throughout this chapter, the motivation level of the employee has been mentioned as an important training component and outcome. In order to maximize the training experience, trainer(s) need to motivate the learner. According to Spitzer (1995), these motivational aids or tools can be divided into three main areas: pretraining, training, and posttraining.

Pretraining   One of the most important aspects of pretraining is to communicate the importance of the training. This is best achieved by including training in the firm's core philosophy. Commitment to training could also be instilled via the participation of all employees in training programs. Although the training program is specifically designed for line-level workers, midlevel managers and the CEO of the company could attend to demonstrate their commitment to the training. Another pretraining motivational tool could simply be to schedule adequate time to show that the organization values training.

Training   The training program itself should motivate workers. A key motivator in any training program is that the organization provides and encourages a safe learning environment by ensuring confidentiality and trust among the participants. Workers' motivation levels may also increase through the use of active training formats that include the employee, such as role-plays, making the training fun through interactive techniques, and using a variety of delivery mechanisms other than traditional pedagogical techniques. Other motivational techniques, as pointed out by Spitzer (1995), that should be used in training include maintaining a high degree of social interaction—problem-solving exercises, small-group discussions—that allow individuals to share their expertise with one another. The training should allow the participants to positively measure their advancement or success and should allow them to practice their new skills in this safe learning environment.

Posttraining   Posttraining issues are concerned with maintaining the employees' motivational level for future training programs by way of the existing training. To achieve this, the employees should be able to use new skills learned immediately on the job, assuring individuals that the training was needed and relevant. In addition, the individuals should also be given some form of performance assistance. In cooperation with other employees through a follow-up meeting, the trainer can clarify some questions the trainees have about the training. Last, the employees should be recognized for their improvement in performance through positive reinforcement and coaching from the supervisory staff in the course of daily activities.

■ LEGAL ISSUES IN TRAINING

Failure to Train

One of the primary liability concerns related to training is the failure to train. The basis for a negligent failure to train action rests on the assumption that the organization had an affirmative duty to train its employees adequately and correctly and failed to do so.

In order to prove the organization negligent in its training, a plaintiff must prove, based on the preponderance of evidence, that the four components of negligence theory were breached or violated. These components are that (1) the organization had some type of duty to train, (2) the organization somehow breached its duty to train, (3) this violation of a need or duty to train led to a proximate cause between the failure to train and the injury or harm that resulted, and (4) damage, injury, or harm to the plaintiff resulted.

What confounds this issue is that the level or standard of the duty to train is often unclear or vague. One of most common, and often easiest, methods to prove that the firm failed to train is to demonstrate that the organization was in violation of existing laws or regulations. If the organization did not comply with existing local, state, and federal regulations or laws, a failure to train suit will be quite difficult to defend. The issue of comparability will also become an issue. Known also as peer review, according to Nichter (1996), this can be used when the adequacy of training in the organization under question is compared or benchmarked to that of similar organizations in the context of size, nature of the business, and location.

Reducing Liability

An organization can reduce its exposure to liability in several ways. In short, train the employee, make sure that the training is effective, and properly document all training activities.

As this chapter has pointed out, organizations should train employees for many reasons. If the organization has not provided any forms of training to its staff, the elements related to negligence can be easily proved, and the organization has a very limited or no basis for a defense in the civil proceedings.

The second component of liability reduction (which should be considered during the TNA process) is to ensure that the content of the training program(s) reduces liability. According to Nichter (1996), five content areas must be considered when designing a training program in security:

1. *General knowledge* in the role of security and the fundamentals of security.
2. *Documentation* of all training activities that occur. Through proper documentation, the organization can defend itself by showing that it has trained to those specific, and perhaps anticipated, incidents that occur on or around the organization.
3. *Laws related to the industry* that encompass the organization. For example, individuals providing security services in a retail establishment must be cognizant of laws related to retail theft, arrest, and search and seizure.
4. *Life safety and building skills* covering all natural and other disasters that impact the organization.
5. *Specialized skills* for tasks require some type of action or activity, such as driving, transporting individuals, and operating specialized types of equipment.

The organization must maintain training records. If the organization should ever encounter a liability situation, the training records will be requested or subpoenaed. If, however, there are no records or if they are incomplete or inaccurate, issues related to the training will arise. As a consequence, the organization should develop a comprehensive record-keeping system for training. At a minimum, the training record or log should include

- A complete and up-to-date file of all training courses or programs the employee has received to date
- The training proposal, to prove the validity of the training
- The length, time, and date of training
- Information related to each specific training program (course outline, content, and so on)
- Scores or other measures related to the individual's performance, if applicable

■ CONCLUSION

Although training or skills development is only one component of success and organizational effectiveness, as well as a liability-reduction tool, it is nevertheless the one component that the organization can control, in comparison to other influences in the firm's internal and external task environment. However, many firms overlook this benefit and take a very limited responsibility for the skills development of their staff. The learning organization recognizes that training is of paramount importance to meet existing challenges and to prepare the organization, its stakeholders, and members for success.

Successful training is not easy and requires a long-term commitment on the part of the organization, and its outcomes may be difficult to assess as a cost-benefit ratio. An effective training program requires support from top management, effective planning and delivery of the training programs, and acceptance from those who receive the training. To achieve these objectives, the training function has several alternatives to achieve these goals, beginning with a comprehensive needs analysis. Following needs analysis, the proper delivery techniques must be implemented in order to maximize the effect of the training on the employee while ensuring that the training meets the needs of the employee both professionally and personally.

■ KEY TERMS

Active training
Andragogy
Apprenticeship
Coaching
Failure to train
General tasks
Joint training programs
Learning organization
Liability-reduction tool

Mentoring
On-the-job training
Passive training
Pedagogy
Specific tasks
Training
Training models
Training-needs assessment
Transferability

■ DISCUSSION QUESTIONS

1. What is a learning organization? What are the major components of a learning organization? How do they relate to training?
2. What is the difference between a hard and a soft skill?
3. What are some organizational benefits of a well-designed training program?
4. What are some pretraining issues an organization needs to consider when designing a training program?
5. Why is it important to conduct a posttraining analysis?
6. How can a well-designed training program serve as a liability-reduction tool for the organization?
7. Describe the TNA process. Why is it important?
8. What are some issues to consider when selecting a trainer?
9. What is transferability? Provide an example.
10. Who establishes training standards for the private security industry?

■ CLASS EXERCISES

You have just been hired as a security supervisor with Car and Earth Moving Parts (CEMP) Products, an international manufacturer of quality components for the automotive and earth-moving industries. Your staff of 16 is quite diverse in terms of years of service and knowledge of security and principles of management and business. Some of the new hires have college degrees ranging from business administration to criminal justice. The older staff members have no advanced degrees but possess a great deal of practical experience.

One of your new responsibilities as the security supervisor is to develop a comprehensive training program for your staff. The old security supervisor discounted the importance of training and subsequently did not pursue any staff development; he did not keep any training records and did not allow or schedule those staff members who wanted training that was offered from the organization in business-related principles. Some of the older members of the security staff supported his decision because earlier training programs had been boring, inappropriate, and conflicted with their days off.

As a consequence, your security department now has a "knowledge gap." Some of your staff members have no understanding of the current production processes and are not familiar with current managerial practices or concepts, making it difficult to effectively communicate with other employees in the factory. To complicate the issue even more, your officers lack some of the requisite knowledge in security principles, specifically, emergency procedures and the operation of the new access card control system installed at CEMP.

The organization has recognized these problems and wants you to develop a comprehensive, long-term commitment to the development of your employees. What are some of your training priorities? What types of delivery techniques should you propose? What are some of the problems you may encounter in the development of the training program? Keep in mind that your training proposal must be cost-effective and meet the needs of the organization.

■ REFERENCES

AUER, K. 1995. Smalltalk training: As innovative as the environment. *Communications of the ACM* 38 (10): 115–117.

BARRON, J. M., M. C. BERGER, and D. A. BLACK. 1997. *On-the-job training*. Kalamazoo, MI: W. E. Upjohn Institute for Employment Research.

BENNIS, W. G., K. D. BENNE, and R. CHIN. 1962. *The planning of change*. New York: Holt, Rinehart and Winston.

BLAND, T. 1995. Developing a successful turnover training program. *Corrections Today* 5 (6): 116–118.

CUNNINGHAM, W. C., J. J. STRAUCHS, and C. W. VANMETER. 1990. *The Hallcreast Report II*. Stoneham, MA: Butterworth-Heinemann.

CUNNINGHAM, W. C., and T. H. TAYLOR. 1985. *Private security and police in America*. Boston: Butterworth-Heinemann.

DEIERLEIN, B. April, 1995. Training: An investment in the future. *Fleet Equipment* 21 (4): 23–25.

FERMAN, L. A., M. HOYMAN, J. CUTCHER-GERSHENFELD, and E. J. SAVOIE. 1990. *New developments in worker training: A legacy for the 1990's*. Madison, WI: Industrial Relations Research Association.

GARFINKEL, S. 1995. AI as a training tool. *Technology Review* 98 (6): 16–20.

HARRISON, R. and R. L. HOPKINS. 1967. The design of cross-cultural training: An alternative to the university model. *Journal of Applied Behavioral Science* 3 (4): 431–460.

HEQUET, M. 1994. The union push for lifelong learning. *Training* 31 (3): 26–32.

KAETER, M. 1995. International development. *Training* 32 (5): 23–25.

KANTER, R. M. 1989. *When giants learn to dance*. New York: Simon and Schuster.

KEENAN, W. 1994. Managers try checklist training. *Sales and Marketing Management* 146 (13): 41–43.

KNOWLES, M. S. 1984a. *The adult learner: A neglected species*. 3rd ed. Houston: Gulf Publishing.

_____1984b. *Andragogy in action: Applying modern principles of adult learning*. San Francisco: Jossey-Bass.

LAWSON, K. 1997. *Improving on-the-job training and coaching*. Alexandria, VA: American Society for Training and Development.

LEHMANN, G. C. 1998. Counterdrug missions: A tactical perspective. *Marine Corps Gazette* 82 (4): 30–31.

LOVEMAN, G. W., M. J. PIORE, and W. SEMGENBERGER. 1990. The evolving role of small business and some implications for employment and training policy. In *New developments in the labor market: Toward a new institutional paradigm*, ed. K. G. ABRAHAM and R. B. MCKERSIE. Cambridge, MA: MIT Press.

MALCOLM, S. E. 1998. The 100 percent solution. *Training* 35 (7): 72–74.

MOSKAL, B. S. 1991. Apprenticeships: Old cure for new labor shortage? *Industry Week* 240 (9): 30–32.

MUNSON, L. S. 1984. *How to conduct training seminars*. New York: McGraw-Hill.

NICHTER, D. A. 1996. Training on trial. *Security Management* 40 (9): 75–78.

PONT, T. 1995. *Investing in training and development: Turning interest into capital*. London: Kogan Page.

REISS, C. J. 1991. Turning technicians into trainers. *Training* 28 (7): 47–49.

SALZMAN, H. 1998. Restructuring and skill needs: Will firms train? *Annals of the American Academy of Political and Social Science* 559: 125–140.

SCHNEIER, C. E., J. P. GUTHRIE, and J. D. OLIAN. 1988. A practical approach to conducting and using the training needs assessment. *Public Personnel Management* 12 (2): 191–205.

SCHRIEFER, A. E. 1995. Getting the most out of scenarios: Some questions and answers. *Planning Review* 23 (6): 37–40.

SPITZER, D. R. 1995. 20 ways to motivate trainees. *Training* 32 (12): 52–54.

SUNOO, B. P. 1999. Labor-management partnerships boost training. *Workforce* 78 (4): 80–85.

TAYLOR, P. J., and M. P. O'DRISCOLL. 1998. A new integrated framework for training needs analysis. *Human Resource Management Journal* 8 (2): 29–50.

TRACEY, J. B., and M. J. TEWS, 1995. Training effectiveness: Accounting for individual characteristics and the work environment. *Cornell Hotel and Restaurant Administration Quarterly* 36 (6): 36–41.

U.S. Department of Justice. National Advisory Committee on Criminal Justice Standards and Goals. 1977. *Report of the task force on private security*.

WALTON, M. 1986. *The Deming management method*. New York: Perigee.

ZEMKE, R. 1998. How to do a needs assessment when you think you don't have time. *Training* 35 (3): 38–44.

chapter seven

Motivation

- Scanlan (1973, 341) quotes Dwight D. Eisenhower defining motivational leadership as "the ability to get a man to do what you want him to do, when you want him to do it, in the way you want it done, *because he wants to do it.*"
- Baron and Greenburg (1993, 11) define motivation more precisely as "the set of processes that arouse, direct, and maintain human behavior attaining a goal. Basic human needs and deprivation of needs provide the drive that arouse workers."
- Hiam (1999) gives us a view of motivation as people rising to the challenge on their own initiative. He instructs us in his work that "however good your people are, they could be a lot better."
- Kotter (1990) suggests that for management, motivation means getting people to comply and to keep employees from deviating from company policies and procedures. Conversely, leadership motivation means "pulling" people by satisfying basic human needs of personal achievement, belonging, recognition, self esteem, a sense of control over one's life and living up to one's ideals.

Basically, one can think of motivation as causing people to act, to move, or to produce. In addition, one can conceptualize motivation as being concerned with causing individuals to act to do basics, such as arrive at work on time, fill out forms, patrol as directed, and so on. One can also think of motivation as getting people to do a lot better: to excel. This chapter attempts to view both managerial and leadership aspects of motivation in application. However, the greater emphasis is on leadership: getting the firm, its executive group, and employees to excel—to continuously improve.

The responsibility for getting people in an agency to excel belongs to the executives who act as managers and leaders. This chapter takes a somewhat different approach to most textbook presentations on motivation and suggests that motivated employees are a product of motivated managers with a commitment to give the best service possible to the organization's customers. This chapter also instructs executives or future executives to consider their own level of motivation before they consider methods or techniques to motivate employees.

When considering levels of motivation, managers should not confuse working long hours with being motivated. All too often, managers work long hours because they are not skilled at motivating employees and coworkers. As a result of their inability to lead, manage, and motivate, managers find themselves performing tasks by default. Motivating employees is a result of skilled management and leadership on the part of company executives. From a *management perspective*, employees must be given clear goals and objectives, trained in the skills and expertise needed to achieve the firm's objectives, given the responsibility and opportunities to perform, and given extrinsic rewards and recognition for successful performance. From a *leadership perspective*, executives must establish a work environment in which employees' basic personal needs can be met. The management focus is on the structural aspect of the firm: budgets, planning, setting objectives, organizing, coordinating, policies and procedures, and so on. Leadership focuses on dealing with people and relies on a good understanding of basic human needs and strong interpersonal skills. A firm balanced with good management and leadership will find its employees working at a high level of productivity.

This chapter covers the more common theories of motivation and applies them to the private security workplace. Direction, ideas, and implications for the executive in the management and leadership process will become apparent throughout the chapter. The chapter summarizes the principles discussed in their application. It is imperative, however, to begin by discussing the need for owners and executives to have a high level of motivation themselves.

■ MOTIVATED MANAGERS AND THE "PROFIT" MOTIVE

Discussion of motivation typically focuses on ways and means for managers to motivate employees. It is a fallacy to assume that managers and bosses are always motivated and that it is subordinates who need a good dose of motivation. Managers and even owners of firms are not always motivated: Just ask customers and employees. The simple truth is that highly successful firms are directed by motivated top managers who are proud of the agency and its work. Motivated executives model the way, creating a work climate that infects all the members of the agency. Conversely, unmotivated managers breed unmotivated employees. It is also logical that an unmotivated cadre of managers will not be motivated to provide the best possible service to their customers.

A commitment by core management to provide top-notch service to clients is the starting point for the success and prosperity of the firm and its entire staff. In the competitive private security business, the relationship between the firm and the customer, through the firm's employees, is fundamental to success or failure. Motivation of core management and employees begins with a *real* commitment to give clients the best possible service.

In his book *The Pursuit of Wow!*, Tom Peters provides some excellent examples of inspired and motivated firms (1994, 100). For example, a medium-size plumbing company (called De-Mar) publicly proclaims its commitment to excellence in customer service through its advertising. De-Mar promises and delivers same day service, flat rate guaranteed prices, and a one-year guarantee on all work. It takes the position that their workers (called Service Advisors) are businessmen whose truck is their franchise. These businessmen also follow a strict grooming and dress code, set annual sales goals, earn a monthly sales commission, and consider their clients as long-term customers and not simply as profits.

The plumbing company, having publicly announced this rather lofty commitment, now has set *expectations* and *clear goals* for its core management and staff. To help implement the commitment, management must *model,* through its interactions with staff, the attitude and behaviors it will take to carry out the commitment. In addition, employees will probably be given *responsibilities* to share in the *challenges* set forth by the company. The firm will give a high level of responsibility to its staff only if it *assumes* that *employees naturally desire responsibility and challenges.* In a very real sense, core management will, through a *socialization process*, be establishing performance and customer relations roles for its employees. If successful, the company will receive *monetary* and status *rewards* from its customers that will need to be redistributed to its employees, whereas the individual plumbers may receive *praise* from clients for excellence in service. Core management must also find a way to share with all employees the *extrinsic and intrinsic benefits* the company will receive from providing such rich service. In a sense, all the major theories of motivation will be used as a result of the commitment to quality service. It all begins with a planned effort to fulfill the *needs* of customers.

A private security firm is obliged to accrue a monetary profit for its goods and services. This is the natural and healthy interest of any private-sector firm functioning in a competitive market. Moreover, to maximize profits in a competitive industry for the long term, it is imperative to get employees to maximize their performance. However, a common approach to maximizing profits, at least in the short run, is to provide low-cost service by using substandard equipment and/or paying employees lower wages than the industry norm. For example, the Substandard Alarm Company (SAC) might decide to install second-rate equipment and hire underqualified employees for low wages to keep costs down and profit margins high. Training of employees in this hypothetical alarm company would be minimal, and, depending on the demand for labor, the turnover rate would likely be high. High turnover would prevent the development of a critical mass of employees with the appropriate skills to install the alarm systems properly. It is also reasonable to argue that SAC employees would have little or no attachment to the company or its customers. Therefore, employees would not have an intrinsic commitment to do a good job. In sum, SAC employees may not have the willingness or ability to perform basic tasks without extensive and constant supervision on the part of SAC managers.

Motivation at SAC will be based primarily on constant monitoring of employees to keep them from dong things incorrectly. Extrinsic sanctions and rewards may be used to motivate employees. Under these conditions, with probably little consideration for employees, managers can opt to be autocratic and punitive and motivate employees by threat of dismissal. Conversely, managers can opt to be employee centered, but their primary source of motivation will be begging and pleading, lacking the structure to apply motivational strategies.

To compensate for turnover and limited skills of staff, core management may find itself working an inordinate number of hours to correct and compensate for the work of the employees. Despite their long working hours, claims of being motivated, and efforts at modeling for their employees, these managers' thinking has a fallacy. First, management's goals may have little or nothing to do with *employees' goals, wants, or needs*. Second, employees and, possible core managers, will receive few, if any, *intrinsic rewards* from highly satisfied customers. Certainly, employees' monetary, or *extrinsic, rewards* are not linked to the firm's success or failure. In fact, employees understanding their status by their low pay, will make no extraordinary efforts to do a worthy job and may even take steps or behave in a manner that negatively affects profit margins.

Additional efforts to control costs may place the imaginary firm in the "low-rent district" while providing staff with poor offices, minimal parking, and subpar breaks and restrooms. SAC may also provide its staff with cheap uniforms, poor equipment, and general policies that make it an unpleasant work experience. Lacking these basic *hygienic* factors will make the application of motivational principles difficult, if not impossible. The goals of the imaginary firm, along with the operating principles it follows, may motivate its employees to expend energies at being unproductive.

To further imprint this argument, one can create a security firm that makes a customer service commitment like the earlier plumbing example above. The FoolProof Alarm Co (FPA), an imaginary but highly motivated company, might put out this advertisement for consumers of alarm services to consider:

> *FPA prides itself on customer service.*
> *We will make every effort to give you the system you need at a price you can afford.*
> *We guarantee all our work in writing; you will know exactly where you stand with us.*
> *Twenty-four-hour service for repairs.*
> *Emergency work and repairs made within 2 hours of calls or sooner, if required.*

> *All our employees are trained in technology, maintenance, and customer relations; we will ask you to rate them.*

FPA has a set of goals that meet customer needs and high expectations for management and employees alike. Again, if the commitment to service is serious, the foundation for highly motivated management and staff has been established. Serious commitments require that an agency express and follow a set of core values and beliefs that support and direct any commitment to excellence in service.

One can again take advantage of Tom Peters' work and examine the core values and beliefs of a small, highly successful firm that he reviewed. According to Peters, this service firm, with annual $10 million revenue, strives to live by the following operating principles (1994, 18–19). Some of the more interesting points include:

1. Attract exciting people—more than a few of whom are a little offbeat.
2. Raise hell, constantly question "the way things are done around here," and never, ever rest on our laurels. (Today's laurels are tomorrow's compost.)
3. Make sure that those who leave us, voluntarily or involuntarily, can testify to having learned a lot, having had a special experience, and having made fast friends while they were here. (You shall be known by your alumni.)
4. Have a collegial, supportive, yeasty, zany, laughter-filled environment where folks support one another, and politics is as absent as it can be in a human (i.e., imperfect) enterprise.

This is a clear description of a firm that intends to put a great deal of enthusiasm, energy, and effort into giving its customers consistently excellent service while providing an exciting environment in which its employees can thrive. This company thrives on motivation. The cornerstones of high-level motivation—*clear goals, opportunities for employee growth, giving staff responsibility, and elbow-room in which to operate*—are spelled out in the company's operating principles.

In summary, executives concerned with motivating staff to achieve higher levels of productivity need to take a few moments and examine their behaviors and beliefs about customers, employees, and the value of their firm's service. Managers are always motivating employees. However, the manner in which they serve clients and customers, treat their staff, and structure their firm may direct the behaviors of the members of their organization in negative as well as positive directions. Executives who come in early, leave late, take home piles of work, and work on weekends may be driven and compulsive. However, executives who work at this pace are probably lacking in both management and leadership skills. Understanding the basic principles of motivating and directing human behavior in the workplace is essential to developing as a skilled manager and leader.

■ THEORIES OF MOTIVATION

So far, this chapter has provided examples of motivational theory in story form, using italicized keywords, such as *clear goals, responsibility, and extrinsic and intrinsic rewards.* These words are descriptors of motivational theories that lay a foundation for a detailed discussion of theories of motivation. The examples have contrasted two firms: one whose executives believe in providing extraordinary service and one interested only in short-term profit margins. Just as executives have theories and assumptions about the limits and possibilities of their organizations, they have assumptions about the individual employees and their potential to contribute to the goals of the company. These assumptions dictate the manner in which employees are treated, which in turn affects the extent to which employees are or can be motivated. In that regard, Douglas McGregor's (1960) classic work on the conflicting intuitive assumptions that executives may hold toward employees is pertinent.

Theory X and Theory Y

McGregor (1960) cautioned that managers' assumptions about people, especially employees, frame both the manner in which work is structured and the relationship between management and employees. McGregor offered two distinct assumptions, *Theory X* and *Theory Y*, that are typically made about employees. Theory X is a negative view of employees; Theory Y represents a positive view.

THEORY X

1. The average person has an inherent dislike for work and will avoid it if he or she can.
2. Because of this dislike for work, most people must be coerced, controlled, directed, threatened, and punished to get them to put forth adequate effort toward achievement of organizational objectives; even promise of reward is not enough. Only threat will do the trick.
3. The average person prefers to be directed, wishes to avoid responsibility, has little ambition, and wants security above all—mediocrity of the masses.

Theory Y

1. Expenditure of physical and mental effort in work is as natural as play or rest; depending on controllable conditions, work may be a source of either satisfaction or dissatisfaction.
2. External control and the threat of punishment are not the only means for bringing about effort toward objectives. Individuals will exercise self-direction and self-control in the service of objectives to which they are committed.
3. Commitment is a function of the rewards associated with the achievement of objectives.

4. Under proper conditions, people will not only accept but also seek responsibility. Avoidance of responsibility, lack of ambition, and emphasis on security are not human characteristics.

5. The capacity to exercise imagination, ingenuity, and creativity is widely, not narrowly, distributed.

6. The intellectual potential of the average person is being only partially utilized.

McGregor 1960, as cited in Scanlan 1973, 362–363.

The implications underpinning these assumptions are crucial to creating strategies to motivate employees. To begin with, firms or managers will invariably think about their customers, clients, and suppliers with the same assumptions they apply to their employees. Initially, this proposition may not appear logical. After all, one might reason, clients and customers would normally be treated well by a private-sector for-profit firm. However, individuals who accept Theory X as a premise for human behavior tend to hold negative and cynical views toward almost everyone. Theory X managers, for example, consider negative feedback from customers as disingenuous or habitual and ignore important information. Theory X firm owners and managers may not see the value of pursuing excellence in service and generally may not find value in intrinsic rewards for delivering a quality product or service.

In the earlier examples of motivated firms, it is not likely that managers who are pessimistic and negative about people will strive to provide customers with an excellent product. Their pessimism will lead these managers to conclude that quality service will not really be appreciated and hence has no value. Managers with a more positive view are more likely to be motivated to provide excellent service and create an efficient and effective organization. It is in firms driven by motivated managers—that is, individuals who constantly try to improve and provide better services—that employees are more likely to be motivated.

Scanlan (1973) suggests that managers who subscribe to Theory X find fault with employees and blame them for shortcomings in results. Conversely, managers who subscribe to Theory Y take responsibility for shortfalls in productivity and results and attempt to create changes in the structure or system to facilitate the natural tendency of employees to do a worthy job. Theory X managers go to motivational seminars to learn "tricks," or methods to manipulate employees. Theory Y managers, on the other hand, seek better ways to organize tasks, give recognition and rewards, and work to upgrade the skill levels of their employees. Theory X managers emphasize detection of errors, mistakes, and noncompliance and cure problems with threats or punishment to employees. Theory Y managers like to discover people doing things well and give out recognition. Theory X managers keep tight control over workers, provide them with narrowly defined tasks, and allow them little discretion and responsibility. Theory Y managers give employees responsibility, an appropriate latitude of discretion, and tap into their ingenuity and creativity. In effect, Theory Y managers motivate individuals by meeting their basic psychological job-related needs, such as the following (Emery and Emery 1974, 47):

1. Adequate elbow room. Workers need a sense that they are their own boss and (except in unusual circumstances) they will not have a boss breathing down their necks.
2. Chance to learn on the job and go on learning.
3. An optimal level of variety.
4. Help and respect from work mates.
5. A sense that one's work is meaningful to social welfare.
6. A desirable future.

It is important to understand that Theory X and Theory Y are not specifically theories of employee motivation. Rather, the application to motivation is indirect: The activity of work is no different from the activity of play, and most individuals seek responsibility and want to do a worthwhile job. Deming (1986) supports this proposition, suggesting that doing quality work engenders pride, and pride in one's work makes it fun. Therefore, individuals are naturally motivated. Hence, it is management's job to create a work environment in which this natural motivation can be actualized. Conversely, creating a system and work environment based on Theory X will reduce employees' natural motivational level.

This concept is easy to apply to private security firms. To allow their natural motivation to develop, employees must be given a level of responsibility that they can manage, appropriate freedom from supervision, a chance to develop and improve their skills, and recognition and rewards for work well done. Poor performance and mistakes need to be dealt with by supervisors, but negative reinforcement should not be the primary tool to direct employees. Excessive reliance on negative reinforcement, punishment, verbal admonishments, and so on, will *motivate* employees to duck responsibility, become skilled at covering their backsides, and pass blame up the chain of command. In effect, excessive reliance on negative reinforcement—paying attention only to what people do wrong—will create a negative work environment in which employees will expend their ingenuity and creativity on minimizing rather than maximizing their contributions to the agency's objectives. Staff should be reminded frequently that their work is important and why it is important. In the process, management may remind itself of the value of the firm's service. If management does not understand the social importance of the firm's service, the firm will not be motivated, will deliver mediocre services, and will experience reduced profit margins or eventually go out of business.

Most individuals who join a workforce fit Theory Y assumptions. However, it could be proposed that all persons fit the Theory X stereotypes some of the time, and some individuals may fall into the Theory X pattern of behavior most of the time. A properly managed private security agency should have an adequate personnel recruiting process to screen out potential employees to whom the assumptions of Theory X apply. However, a firm with a solid recruiting process but managed with Theory X assumptions can turn potentially good employees into marginal employees simply by treating responsible and competent individuals as if they were irresponsible and incompetent. In addition, if firms recruit competent people but fail to provide adequate training, employees may begin to behave like Theory X people simply because they may not know what their tasks are and how to perform them.

Private security firms that are in business for a quick profit and that cut costs by paying the lowest possible wages may end up recruiting personnel who fit the Theory X assumptions. In this case, management needs to give employees narrowly defined tasks with clear short-term goals and limited responsibility, coupled with constant and direct supervision. Agencies with Theory X employees may, for example, require security officers to walk a perimeter area and punch a time clock at the end of each trip to make sure that they have made rounds. Punching a time clock, coupled with frequent visits by a supervisor, can help ensure that the officer has completed the most basic task of being in approximately the right place at the right time. However, the security purpose—patrolling a perimeter and being alert for security breaches—may be lost if the expectation of the officer is reduced to simply walking around a designated area in a particular time frame. In this scenario, Theory Y–thinking managers will give the officer more responsibility than simply going through the motion of making rounds. That is, the officer will be told the purpose and value of making rounds, trained on recognizing and dealing with perimeter security problems, and, after acquiring some level of experience, be allowed to use his or her judgment on frequency of perimeter patrols.

Needs Theory

This theory assumes that individuals naturally strive to fulfill their basic needs. Moreover, individuals instinctively seek opportunities to fulfill these needs. Employers can, therefore, motivate employees by giving them opportunities to meet their basic needs in the workplace. Maslow's (1943) theory of motivation is based on a hierarchy of five types of human needs: physiological, security, social, psychological, and self-fulfillment. The significance of the hierarchy is that lower-order needs must be fulfilled before an individual will strive for higher-order needs.

Physiological Needs   In the hierarchy of needs, individuals first seek employment to satisfy their most basic, physiological needs: a paycheck to obtain clothing, shelter, and food. A paying job satisfies an individual's need for basic survival. Once the physiological needs have been met, individuals strive for the next-higher need in the hierarchy: security.

Security Needs   Individuals' security needs are both physical and economic. Individuals strive to protect their physical selves and to establish economic security and certainty. To fulfill their need for security, individuals seek employment at a pay level they feel will buy groceries and pay bills. At this need level, employees are motivated to do what is required to ensure that they have a secure future with the firm but little else. A private security firm that chooses to function at this level of needs satisfaction and ignore higher-order needs of employees runs the risk that they will not have any identification with the agency's mission and will do as little as possible without getting fired or disciplined. Moreover, if employees earn a relatively low income and their higher-order needs are not met, employee turnover will be higher than necessary.

Employees' need for security, coupled with their social needs, can be a powerful management tool to motivate individuals to meet basic agency expectations. This is true, however, only if the agency's expectations are made clear to the employees and they feel certain that conforming to agency expectations will provide a reasonable chance for job security. Conversely, employees need to believe that not meeting expectations may threaten their job security.

One of the reasons for poorly motivated employees at this level is the result of subjecting them to inconsistent expectations. Management may be unclear or inconsistent in communicating or enforcing basic task expectations. In a security agency, for example, staff may be given an area to patrol or secure but not be told what is expected in nonroutine situations. In the context of shopping mall security, for example, staff may not know what to do if a fight breaks out or if a fire alarm is set off. In these situations, the officer may choose to report the incidents but little else. Also, security supervisors may give inconsistent or contradictory instructions, leaving security staff doubtful about basic job tasks.

Expectations may be stated clearly but enforced inconsistently. For example, security officers with seniority or who are part of a well-established friendship clique may be able to come in late and/or leave early and do substandard paperwork, whereas other staff may be held to higher standards. In agencies managed with inconsistent expectations or an inconsistent application of expectations, it will be difficult for staff to achieve their basic security needs. This will cause turnover, stress, conflict, and motivate employees to do a poor day's work.

Social Needs Individuals can be motivated by security needs to meet basic job expectations. However, employees may be motivated to move beyond basic work expectations when striving to fulfill higher-order needs. It is common for employees for fulfill a great part of their *social needs* in the workplace. This makes sense when one considers that most of employees' waking hours are spent on the job. For some, work may be the most significant opportunity to meet their social needs. An employee can achieve social needs in the workplace only if accepted as a part of the work group's *social system*. In brief, a social system is a group of individuals sharing basic assumptions about its purpose, values, and goals.

A social system also possesses rules, etiquette, and symbols that distinguish the group from others. The individual becoming a part of the group—being accepted—will take on the assumptions, beliefs, and goals of the group (Schein 1992). In the security agency workplace, the basic assumptions of an employee group can range from high belief in its members as professionals serving the public to underpaid, second-rate, and unappreciated "rent-a-cops." The work group may share a higher purpose—to service—or a purpose dedicated to self— to get a paycheck and to get by with the least effort. The pivotal issue motivating staff is the extent to which the rules and assumptions of the employee social system dictate a high, modest, or poor work ethic and belief in service.

Management will always impact the workplace social system. Private security agencies managed by individuals who are excited about their profession, motivated to provide quality service to customers, and openly express and model these values will positively impact the employees' social systems. This is the first and most important step in using employees' social needs to motivate high levels of performance. In this regard, managers are impacting the informal, or unplanned, socialization process of staff.

New employees can also be brought into the firm through a formal socialization process developed and implemented by managers. Formal socialization is done through employee orientation and training. It is important for managers to take the entry process seriously and to indoctrinate new staff with the agency's values and beliefs, as well as its rules and expectations. If this is done poorly, new employees will be motivated to conform to the rules and expectations of their fellow employees rather than those of management. In private security firms that place little emphasis on the initial orientation process and provide minimal training, employees may by default conform to the rules and expectations of informal work groups. To the extent that informal work groups and management share differing work rules and expectations, conflict will exist in the agency, and managers will have difficulty in controlling and motivating staff.

In other words, management has an important opportunity through the formal socialization process—recruiting, training, and coaching—to actualize the *social needs* of new employees as a motivator to ensure their understanding and conformity to the agency's mission, beliefs in customer service, and practices (Stojkovic, Kalinich, and Klofas 2002). On the other hand, a private security agency that minimizes expenditures on training and other formal socialization methods is missing opportunities to *socialize* staff into the company group. Moreover, a firm that does not rely heavily on a formal socialization process for its employees is more than likely to see employees as units of production and not members of the company's community.

Ignoring the need to formally socialize employees is symptomatic of firms in which management does not think of the workplace as a community. This may not be a significant problem in small firms, where managers or owners are an active and visible part of the workforce. In this situation, management has the authority and social influence to socialize its staff on an ongoing basis, as well as to play the key role in accepting new members. Moreover, in small firms in which owners or managers are highly visible, their own motivational levels tend to rub off on their employees.

Psychological Needs Once individuals satisfy their social need to be accepted as a member of a group, they are then motivated to achieve *psychological*, or *ego*, needs. These needs are satisfied through receiving status, recognition, and personal prestige within that group. Managers can tap into this level of motivation by giving employees increasing levels of discretion, responsibility, and trust. This can be done formally by giving employees promotions or a wider latitude of authority in their work. Employees can also be given formal recognition through awards and letters of commendation for jobs well done.

Power to satisfy these needs abounds at the informal level. In addition, managers can seek *and use* employees' input and advice. Suggestion boxes are always empty because the process is impersonal. If they are asked in person by managers about problems, conditions, and solutions, employees may feel a sense of status and recognition and may offer valuable suggestions.

It is important for security managers to "get out from behind the desk" and seek out opportunities to interact with their staff. Some supervisors and executives may feel safe sitting behind their desks. However, to get in touch with employees' psychological needs, managers need to meet with them face to face, frequently, and for the purpose of recognizing and praising their good work. If managers follow this human procedure, employees will see to it that they can be found doing good work. Also, employees can be brought into the decision-making process as a manifestation of their worth. Mechanical methods, such as the old "suggestion box," give managers a false sense that they are including employees in the decision-making process. To give employees status and recognition, managers need to meet with people face to face in almost an ad hoc manner, listen to them, and develop the art of arguing and losing (Kouzes and Posner 1995). Finally, good interpersonal skills on the part of managers is important for developing genuine connectedness with employees. Treating employees with simple courtesy and politeness also goes a long way to making them feel that they are valued, a significant level of status in itself.

Needs theory also provides insights into managers who demoralize employees. Managers with insatiable psychological, or ego, needs will never satisfy employees' ego needs in a positive manner. Egotistical individuals need excessive recognition. Egotistical managers give responsibility to their employees and hold them accountable for failure and mistakes but take all the credit for successes and keep recognition and rewards for themselves. Egotistical managers may also have a hard time seeing the value of satisfying employees' psychological needs. Moreover, egotistical managers may even "motivate" staff to perform poorly or even to sabotage their own efforts to achieve agency expectations.

Self-Fulfillment Needs   Once individuals satisfy their psychological needs, they seek self-fulfillment. That is, people seek to grow in skills and abilities and their capacity to contribute to their fullest extent. This is a more difficult human potential to actualize in agencies, especially in security agencies that ostensibly require "semiskilled" work. After some degree of experience, employees may have fully acquired the skill level to perform their duties well and have little opportunity to gain additional skills and abilities. At this point, staff may get into a rut, perform duties mechanically, and not pay attention to job tasks.

A good example is posting a security officer to watch a number of video monitors. Initially, the officer may take the challenge to heart and watch the monitors intently. However, owing to the simplicity of the task, the work will become boring for the officer in a short period of time, causing the officer to watch the monitors less intently. Eventually, the officer may pay little attention to the monitors, thereby creating a potential security breach.

In other words, allowing an individual to work at tasks that are simple and predictable reduces the level of motivation the employee brings to the job. What is required of management is to create opportunities and challenges for employees to increase their skill and knowledge. In duties similar to the example used here, it may be advisable to rotate assignments and keep the time at each task short.

Hygienic Factors and Motivational Factors

Frederick Herzberg (1964) developed the important concepts of hygienic and motivational factors. Herzberg considered the two factors as two distinct dimensions of employee motivational problems in organizations. *Hygienic factors*, according to Herzberg, are on one end of a continuum of concerns and *motivational factors* at the opposite end. Hygienic factors are those conditions that can lead to some basic level of job satisfaction or dissatisfaction; motivational factors are those conditions that will lead to positive attitudes and individual incentives toward better workmanship. Hygienic factors include wages, fringe benefits, the physical working environment, and management's attitude and philosophy toward employees. According to Herzberg, having positive hygienic factors in place will eliminate job dissatisfaction but will not, on their own, result in motivated employees with positive attitudes toward productivity.

Motivational factors include recognition, feelings of accomplishment, opportunities for growth and advancement, being valued and having a sense of importance, and having challenging opportunities. The importance of understanding this distinction is that employees will not be motivated simply by being provided with good hygienic conditions in the workplace. Good hygienic conditions will lead to job satisfaction, which in turn will facilitate the application of motivational efforts on the part of managers and supervisors. Conversely, having poor hygienic factors in place will create job dissatisfaction on the part of employees and make motivating employees a difficult or even impossible task.

The lesson from Herzberg for private security executives is rather straightforward. First, it is important to provide employees with good hygienic conditions. Firms that offer basic and unsophisticated security services and are functioning in a highly competitive market will often be tempted to minimize on hygienic factors. Firms may opt to pay employees low wages, not provide fringe benefits, and have old offices, equipment, and second-rate uniforms. Under these conditions, it is not likely that employees will be readily subject to motivational efforts on the part of management. It is easy to understand how employees who are dissatisfied with their jobs and the workplace will reject as insincere any rewards or indicators of recognition from management.

Firms that operate at this level are functioning in a "cash-flow trap" from which there may be no escape. Employees may give less than minimum effort in return for minimum wages, eventually forcing the firm out of business. The best motivational strategy for security firms that need to keep wages low and other hygienic factors at a minimum to obtain contracts is to commit to improving hygienic factors as future revenues increase. Such a commitment made to employees may make them feel as though they are part of the initial struggle—creating a sense of belonging and responsibility on the employees' part—and allow them to help work their way out of the existing conditions.

Many private security firms have the funds and understand the importance of providing good working conditions to attract and keep qualified staff. This is especially important for firms providing sophisticated levels of security, such as information systems security, which require employees to possess highly marketable skills or credentials. The pivotal issue here is that good hygienic factors alone will not act to motivate employees. High wages, excellent fringe benefits, new offices and computers, and even clean restrooms are important to promote employee satisfaction levels in the workplace.

In addition, treating employees with respect and basic dignity is a significant factor in promoting satisfaction in the workplace. Firms that rely exclusively on hygienic factors to motivate employees may find that they have a costly but unproductive workforce. Good hygienic conditions lay the groundwork for higher-level motivational forces. Looking at this phenomenon through needs theory, employees may reach a certain level of satisfaction in having their basic needs met. However, to encourage them to achieve higher levels of productivity, employees must be motivated, based on their higher-order needs, such as the need for recognition, status, growth, and being challenged.

Equity Theory of Motivation

Equity theory is based on the assumption that employees are sensitive to differential or equitable treatment. That is, employees compare their wages and other work-related conditions to those of other employees in their firm. Moreover, the comparisons impact individual performance. Employees prefer equitable or fair treatment for themselves, based on the treatment of other employees.

Equity theory focuses on the employee's response to inequitable treatment. Individual employees will adjust their productivity upward or downward, based on the extent to which they perceive that they are being treated inequitably. The theory includes employee comparisons of wages, as well as such other conditions as quality of office space and furnishing or other artifacts that carry status. For example, security officers earning similar wages may feel a sense of underpayment inequity if they are assigned old vehicles for patrol purposes and other security staff are allocated new vehicles. This comparison could include quality and condition of uniforms, decor, and such environmental conditions as heating and air conditioning in work areas, parking assignments, locker space, assignments, and computers. The comparisons fall into three states (Baron and Greenburg 1993):

1. *Overpayment inequity* occurs when employees believe that they are receiving higher wages or better conditions than others who are performing comparable tasks. People who are overpaid respond with feelings of guilt.
2. *Underpayment inequity* occurs when workers feel that they are receiving lower pay or lower-level working conditions than others who are performing comparable tasks. People who are underpaid respond with feelings of anger.
3. *Equitable payment* occurs when employees feel that they are receiving similar pay and are working under similar conditions as other employees performing comparable tasks.

The significance of equity theory depends on how employees act or perform under conditions of overpayment, underpayment, or equitable payment. Essentially, employees will be motivated to remove their sense of inequity by varying their performance levels or work activities. Security employees who are angry owing to a sense of underpayment can reduce their vigilance, overlook situations that would require their initiative or personal risk, come to work late and leave early, or help themselves to company property, such as pens, paper, ashtrays, or even computers, viewing such behavior as a justifiable method to correct *underpayment inequity*.

Routine customer service may also suffer. Mall security officers, for example, who are angry about low pay may reduce the effort and quality of their work by ignoring customer service. Specifically, an officer who feels underpaid may ignore a customer whose car has a flat tire in the mall parking lot. That officer may see this situation as an opportunity to force one of the higher-paid officers to "get his nice new uniform dirty." If the customer complains about not getting help, "even better," the underpaid officer might reason. The officer would feel a sense of vindication by creating a customer complaint. When encountering a merchant or a customer with a complaint or a request, the officer may be gruff, uncivil, or refer the complaint to officers considered to be overpaid. Security staff who have a sense of underpayment inequity may also adjust the amount of time spent on the job, coming in late, leaving early, and taking longer lunch and break periods. In other words, employees who feel a sense of *underpayment inequity* will adjust their work habits and production downward to a point at which they feel they are in an equitable payment state with higher-paid employees. If all else fails to alleviate the anger, employees who feel underpaid may terminate their employment.

Workers in a state of *overpayment inequity* will typically feel a sense of guilt. To ameliorate their feelings, they will attempt to increase their productivity and dedication to a level at which they feel their payment is equitable. In other words, employees suffering from overpayment guilt can feel justified in receiving overpayment by producing more than other employees performing similar tasks. In contrast to underpaid security officers, employees suffering from the guilt of overpayment will come in early, stay late, and assume extra responsibilities and tasks to appease their conscience.

Research has borne out the behavioral consequences of over- and underpayment inequities. One can rest assured that employees suffering from *underpayment inequity* will suffer from low morale, will be motivated to perform poorly, and will have little or no loyalty to the company. Such employees who do put in a good day's work may ultimately find ways to create negative productivity, or sabotage.

Managers can also be assured that employees who suffer from overpayment inequity will be high-level producers. One may incorrectly conclude, therefore, that creating a group of overpaid employees is an asset. However, creating a cadre of employees who suffer from overpayment inequity requires that a number of individuals within the firm will suffer from underpayment inequity, with all the resulting consequences to productivity. In short, this inequity could create a deadly cycle of events that results in no positive outcomes for managers or the company.

A single firm in an industry, however, can create a condition of *overpayment inequity* for all its employees. To create this state, all employees of the firm must be paid higher wages and work under better conditions than their counterparts in similar firms. Second, employees must have a clear understanding that their wages and conditions far exceed comparable industry wages and conditions. That is, employees need to sense that they are in a fortunate and unique situation. Third, employees must be concerned that their failure to increase their levels of productivity will threaten the profitability of the firm and their futures. This state is difficult to achieve and maintain in a competitive private security service market. Also, employees may become accustomed to the high wages and superior working conditions, diminishing their sense of overpayment inequity.

A state of *underpayment inequity* is most likely to occur in firms that cut costs by reducing wages, benefits, or the quality of work conditions. This state can be worsened when a segment of a firm's workforce faces reductions in wages. This can happen most readily in security firms that pay new hires dramatically lower wages than other employees. For example, it has been the practice of firms to pay new hires minimum wages without fringe benefits while other employees enjoy higher wages and benefits. To the extent that the new employees believe that their contributions and assignments are similar to those of other employees, they may become angry and reduce their level of productivity.

A good example of structured inequity payment can be found in private prisons and correctional institutions, especially in states with strong correctional officer unions. Private prisons save money primarily through savings on personnel expenditures. Savings are made through reduced staffing, having fewer officers per inmate than state institutions, and/or paying their officers lower wages (Mays and Gray 1996). Prison work can be dangerous and difficult. Officers in private institutions who learn that they are performing typical correctional officer duties but at lower wages than officers in public prisons are likely to develop a sense of *underpayment inequity* and may become more concerned with their personal safety and security than in performing their duties. To protect their safety, they may avoid supervising inmates, be reluctant to use force to restore order, and pass most problems they cannot avoid up to management.

Giving noticeable pay increases to select employees can also create a state of inequity payment. Select increases in wages can be a result of dramatically increasing the wages of managers and supervisors while wages for all other employees remain the same. In addition, mergers of private security firms may create pay disparity and inequity. In general, when private security firms enter a long-run plan to cut personnel costs through mergers or paying new employees substantially less than regular employees, a state of inequity payment will exist among a number of employees, who will, in turn, be motivated to do less.

The optimal state for a firm to achieve is *equitable payment.* This state does not require that all employees receive the same economic rewards and enjoy similar working conditions. Rather, it requires pay differentials that are considered reasonable or justifiable on the part of most employees. Reasonable pay differentials are established through past industry practices, whereby employees who perform similar tasks but have higher levels of seniority receive higher wages. This recognized past practice is justified by considering experience as important in developing skills. Also, grading pay upward with experience is a common mechanism to retain employees. In addition, it is expected that members of management will receive somewhat higher wages, better offices, and other fringe benefits than line personnel. Finally, employees who are assigned greater responsibilities or tasks that require higher levels of skill will be expected to receive higher wages than others.

Nevertheless, a sense of payment equity on the part of employees is not in and of itself a mechanism that will motivate employees to higher levels of productivity and achievement. What is significant is that a sense of payment inequity will motivate employees to produce less and to work hard at underachieving. Moreover, in a firm in which a number of employees are working harder and longer to alleviate the guilt resulting from a sense of overpayment inequity, the remaining employees will feel that they are relatively underpaid and will respond accordingly. In a state of overpayment or underpayment inequity, morale will suffer, the level of stress on managers and staff will increase, and legitimate efforts to motivate employees will fail.

It is possible to pay employees doing similar tasks differential wages without creating payment inequity. Specifically, differential pay increments, such as bonuses and merit pay increases, based on differential quantity and quality of work produced, can be given to employees without creating a sense of payment inequity. Such methods can also motivate employees by linking monetary rewards to productivity. However, such systems, although relatively easy to implement in production-oriented industries, where goals and tasks are clearly linked, may be difficult to implement in service-oriented industries, such as private security firms.

Theory of Expectancy and Path/Goal Relationships

Expectancy theory and path/goal relationships suggest that individuals can be motivated by the promise of an incentive, or reward, for accomplishing particular tasks, on the premise that individuals must believe that they have the competence or skills necessary to complete the assigned task for which a reward is being offered (Vroom 1964). To motivate a worker through the use of incentives, therefore, the following conditions must be met.

First, the individuals being motivated by the promise of an incentive must value the incentive (Lock 1976). Money, for example, may be considered a universal incentive. However, when money is scarce in organizations, other rewards must be devised to act as employee incentives. At the same time, it may be difficult for managers to develop incentives that employees value. For example, an incentive of a golf outing or a free lunch with the boss may have little value to many employees. To establish incentives that employees value, supervisors must know their employees. One method to determine what employees would value as an incentive is to simply ask them (Nelson 1994).

Second, employees must believe that they have a legitimate opportunity to perform the tasks required to be granted the incentive. Implicit in this second condition is that the employees must have the skills required to perform the task, be given the same opportunity as other employees to perform the task, and believe that their accomplishment of the task will be visible and recognized. In other words, employees must have a clear goal to work toward or must understand what must be accomplished or achieved to receive rewards. Employees must also value the reward and must believe that they have a reasonable opportunity to perform the activity(s) required to be granted the reward.

Although this concept is easy to understand, it can be difficult to apply. Managers must have a reasonable understanding of what incentives employees will value. In addition, managers need to structure the incentive system such that employees understand how different levels of performance link to different levels of rewards. Finally, managers must be reasonably sure that workers have the opportunities and abilities to perform tasks required to earn incentives.

These operational contingencies can be best explained by example. A common incentive is the employee-of-the-month award. A security firm may plan to motivate employees toward higher levels of customer courtesy by giving this award to those identified as being exceptionally courteous to customers. Before putting this approach into practice, management must consider the extent to which security staff would place positive value on this award. If, for example, management is perceived as not caring a great deal about customer service and/or lacks credibility with staff, employees may not value this award. In addition, staff may assume that officers who are "in" with management will be given the award as a stroke for "sucking up" to management. Staff may also feel that such an award is too abstract and symbolic and may lack value for them. If, however, management is correct in assuming that employees will value being selected as the employee of the month, the award can be a strong incentive.

Developing rewards takes creativity and knowledge of staff preferences (Nelson 1994). One security firm, for example, often couples a preferred parking spot for the employee along with the symbolic award. One security sergeant in the firm created an informal employee-of-the-week award. Although no official company fanfare was attached to the award, the sergeant gave his personal parking spot to the employee he selected as employee of the week. In this situation, the award was highly valued, as it had material substance—a reserved parking spot—and showed sincere appreciation, as it required a recognizable sacrifice on the part of the sergeant.

In addition to identifying an incentive that staff would value, management must establish clear criteria that identify the winner or winners of the award and that make sense to employees. That is, employees must view the criteria as having relevance to job performance. The criteria must be published and communicated to the staff. The employees must have faith that the criteria will be followed in selecting the employee who will receive the award. Finally, almost all employees must believe that they have the skills and opportunity to live up to the criteria that spell out or define the employee of the month.

For example, if management is attempting to motivate security staff to treat shopping mall customers with higher levels of courtesy, some definition of "higher levels of courtesy" needs to be given as a basis for behavioral expectations. Such a definition could be stated as a customer service policy:

- Greet shoppers when they enter the mall.
- Offer to help customers who look lost or confused rather than have them ask for help.
- When possible, open doors for senior citizens and parents with children, handicapped individuals, or other customers needing assistance.
- Always use common courtesy with customers: Use "please" and "thank you" abundantly, refer to customers as "sir" or "ma'am," and always be gracious and pleasant under the worst of circumstances.
- Present yourself with an upbeat and positive demeanor.

Once some general criteria for good customer service are established, management must publish and communicate the criteria to employees. In addition, a fair and equitable method must be established to identify the employee who provides outstanding customer service. In application, this aspect is perhaps the most difficult. In the mall security example, management is usually left to rely on unsolicited reports from customers to evaluate staff/customer interactions. Moreover, opportunities to provide exceptional service to customers may not be equally available to all staff. Therefore, officers who have less frequent contact with customers may feel that they have little opportunity to receive this award and will not be strongly motivated to alter their behavior toward customers by such an incentive.

Interpersonal Skills, Leadership, and Motivation

A reoccurring theme throughout this chapter has been the need for managers to interact directly with staff. Methods to recognize and reward employees, however well thought out and planned, will fail if managers and supervisors have poor interpersonal skills. Employees may consider supervisory staff with poor interpersonal skills as insincere, unfriendly, and even condescending. Supervisors with poor interpersonal skills may therefore erode planned efforts to recognize and reward employees by virtue of their attempts to directly interact with employees. Conversely, outstanding leaders and motivators have well-honed interpersonal skills (Fritz et al. 1999). It is a mistake for individuals to assume, by virtue of having been promoted to supervisory positions, that they have good "people skills" and fail to further develop in this area. People's common assumptions about their abilities in this area may be inaccurate. As a consequence, both employees and supervisory personnel need to improve in this area. Good interpersonal skills, like any other set of skills, can be honed by study and practice.

Interpersonal skills that allow leaders to genuinely influence others are based on a number of factors, but the most significant is to be genuinely interested in fellow employees and staff. In addition, good listening skills, being aware of the interest of others, and being able to make people feel appreciated are important attributes of individuals with truly good people skills. Learning interesting things about coworkers and remembering employees' names are important skills that can be developed. It is also important to let others do most of the talking and to respect opinions of others. Successful leaders like to argue and lose. They understand that in the long run, it is more important to gain the respect of others than to win an argument. Moreover, individuals with good people skills know the importance of trying to understand the point of view of other people.

Good interpersonal skills are also important in the art of delivering critical feedback in a positive manner. Giving praise is relatively easy and obviously important. Praise encourages people to higher levels of accomplishment. This chapter has argued that a key to motivating employees is to recognize them for doing their jobs properly. However, supervisors sometimes must give employees critical feedback, advising them of what they are doing wrong and what they need to do to make corrections. If done poorly, the event is painful and counterproductive for the subordinate. It is also a common belief that criticism will discourage and negatively motivate employees. Hence, supervisors often find ways to avoid being critical.

Giving critical feedback can be done in a positive manner by beginning with praise and honest appreciation for the employee's past efforts. A supervisor can also talk about the value of mistakes as a learning experience. Often, the feedback can be framed in a series of questions addressed to the employee about the situation. Typically, the employee will take ownership of a mistake. Finally, allowing an employee to "save face" during a critical feedback session is the hallmark of good interpersonal skills on the part of a supervisor. In effect, critical feedback can be given in a way in which the employee feels valued, respected, and ultimately encouraged to do better.

Contrary to popular belief, good interpersonal skills do not depend on the degree of charm, humor, or charisma a person possesses. Such characteristics may advance one's ability to get along with people, at least in the short run. Possessing charm and charisma will help attract people, but the basis for good interpersonal relationships is to have a sincere interest in the needs and well-being of others (Covey 1992).

Good interpersonal relationships are built on mutual respect, trust, and the ability to disagree and share differences. Building respect begins by respecting the needs and concerns of others. Implicit in this requisite is the willingness and ability to understand the other person's needs, feelings, and point of view.

Some individuals are concerned solely with their own needs and interests and what they can get out of a relationship. In this regard, supervisors often enter into instrumental relationships with employees with the goal of controlling and using them as a means to an end. Instrumental relationships are short lived, and the credibility of individuals who are being instrumental erodes rather quickly. Leadership grounded in sound traditional principles, such as honesty, fairness, trust, and justice, is more effective in motivating people than instrumental leadership (Covey 1992). However, managers and leaders who are natural motivators value people and their potential as well as their ability to contribute to the goals of the organization. Therefore, building good interpersonal relationships begins with sincere interest in and respect for other individuals. Sincere interest in others is shown by having a stronger need to understand than to be understood.

A great deal more can be said about building positive interpersonal relationships and developing good interpersonal skills. The purpose of this chapter is simply to make clear that most of what one does in service organizations is based on linking people together into a system. Supervision, management, leadership, and motivation are often spontaneous, based on face-to-face relationships. Hence, managers concerned with motivating employees to higher levels of productivity need to develop good interpersonal skills.

■ CONCLUSION

Owners, managers, and supervisors in security firms need to take a look at the extent to which they are excited about providing top-quality service to their clients. To provide top-quality service, management needs to value the firm's customers or clients. This is a key consideration, as people in management set the tone for the organization (Steers 1977) and model the way for employees for better or for worse. Managers and supervisors who complain about poorly motivated employees may be projecting their own lack of enthusiasm onto others in the organization rather than facing their management responsibility. Hiam (1999) suggests that under conditions of low motivational levels, managers have to look in the mirror and ask whether it is "us" or "them." He argues that the answer to this question is "us," management. Supervisors in the private security industry should assume that it is "us" when motivational levels are low. Thus, the first step in changing the motivational levels of employees is for managers to improve their own. To do this, managers need to find ways to keep themselves excited and motivated.

The second fundamental consideration is the extent to which managers and security firms value their employees. Agencies that value employees and believe that employees thrive on responsibility and challenges invariably create a work environment in which motivational levels will generally be high (Schein 1997).

Southwest Airlines is a classic management and leadership example in how to build a successful business through motivating and inspiring employees. Southwest takes great pride in its workforce and as a main human relations component obliges employees to make work fun. A core value of Southwest Airlines is that employees come first and that customers come second (Freiberg and Freiberg 1998). Making employees come first is achieved in a number of ways. For example, Southwest staff members are encouraged to have fun at work, and part of their personnel evaluation is based on employees' ability to bring excitement, energy, and a positive attitude into the workplace. As a result of the spirit and enthusiasm employees have for Southwest Airlines, employee productivity is almost twice as high as in the rest of the industry, and its customers get great service. Southwest has also experienced consistent growth and strong annual profits, whereas many other airlines have failed and filed for bankruptcy.

On the other hand, a firm that does not value its employees and/or treats them as if they were Theory X people will generally not be able to motivate individuals by meeting their intrinsic needs. That is, supervisors who do not value employees' contributions will similarly not recognize them for their accomplishments. Employees working under such conditions are unlikely to find status and prestige as a result of doing their jobs. Managers who hold Theory X beliefs about workers will be limited to using extrinsic rewards, such as monetary incentives, as motivators.

An organizational system that facilitates the motivation of employees to perform basic duties requires, therefore, that management establish clear goals, assign employees tasks they can perform, and provide employees with good feedback about goal attainment through supervision. To the extent that employees expect to be rewarded for attaining goals, management is responsible for creating a clear path for employees to follow to achieve their assigned goals.

Management is also responsible for considering the hygienic factors in the workplace. If hygienic factors are poor, it may be difficult to motivate employees to conform to basic agency rules, meet basic task goals, or achieve higher levels of productivity. Management is also responsible for creating programs of job enrichment and enlargement for employees who find their tasks becoming redundant and unchallenging.

Throughout this chapter, some of the more common theories of motivation have been reviewed and applied to the business of private security. Wading through all the theories will be helpful, but going back to the basics can be quite beneficial. First, managers need to routinely assess their own sense of enthusiasm about the mission and service of the agency. Second, the people hired should be reliable and relied on. Third, expectations of employees should be clear. Fourth, employees need to be given responsibilities and challenges. Fifth, everyone in the firm should feel valued and included. Finally, success should be celebrated, mistakes regarded as opportunities to learn, and recognition given often for good work.

■ KEY TERMS

Equitable payment	Overpayment inequity
Equity theory	Path/goal relationships
Expectancy theory	Physiological needs
Formal socialization	Psychological needs
Hierarchy of needs	Security needs
Hygienic factors	Self-fulfillment
Interpersonal skills	Social needs
Motivation	Theory X
Motivational factors	Theory Y
Needs theory	Underpayment inequity

■ DISCUSSION QUESTIONS

1. Define motivation. Why is motivation so important for organizational success?
2. Explain Theory X and Theory Y. What are the main assumptions of these two approaches about people? Which theory is better suited for security organizations, and why?
3. What is needs theory? What need hierarchy can an effective security manager help fulfill for an employee?
4. What are hygienic and motivational factors, according to Herzberg?
5. What are some of the various forms of inequity that could exist in organizations? As a security manager, how can you prevent or improve these issues?
6. Explain expectancy theory. What conditions must be met to motivate workers through the use of incentives?
7. What is the importance of having interpersonal skills in the context of motivation?
8. What are some of the cornerstones of a high-motivation company? Which ones does your company possess?
9. What are some of the challenges in motivating line-level employees in the field of private security?
10. Why is formal socialization an important issue in motivating employees?

■ REFERENCES

BARON, R.A., and J. GREENBERG 1993. *Behavior in organizations: Understanding and managing the human side of work*. Boston: Allyn & Bacon.

BLANCHARD, K.H., and S. JOHNSON 1982. *The one minute manager*. New York: Penguin Putnam.

COVEY, S. R. 1992. *Principle-centered leadership*. New York: Simon and Schuster.

DEMING, W. E. 1986. *Out of the crisis*. Cambridge, MA: MIT Press.

EMERY, F. and M. EMERY 1974. Participative design: Work and community life. Center for Continuing Education, Australian National University.

FRIEBERG, K., and J. FREIBERG. 1998. *Nuts*. New York: Broadway Books.

FRITZ, S., W. BROWN, L. POVLACS, and E. BANSET. 1999. *Interpersonal skills for leadership*. Englewood Cliffs, NJ: Prentice Hall.

HERZBERG, F. 1964. The motivation-hygiene concept of and problems of manpower. *Personnel Administration* 27 (January/February) 3–7.

HIAM, E. 1999. *Motivating and rewarding employees*. Holbrook, MA: Adams Media.

KOTTER, J. 1990. *Force for change*. New York: Free Press.

KOUZES, J. M. and B. Z. POSNER 1995. *Leadership challenge: How to keep getting extraordinary things done in organizations*. San Francisco: Jossey-Bass.

KOUZES, J. M. and B. Z. POSNER 2000. *The five principles of exemplary leadership*. London: Routledge.

LOCK, E. A. 1976. The nature and causes of job satisfaction. In *Handbook of industrial and organizational psychology*, ed. M. Dunette. 2nd ed. Palto Alto, CA: Consulting Psychologist Press.

MASLOW, A. 1943. A theory of human motivation. *Psychological Review* 50: 370–396.

MAYS, G. L. and T. GRAY 1996. *Privatization and the provision of correctional services: Context and consequences*. Cincinnati, OH: Anderson.

McGREGOR, D. 1960. *The human side of enterprise*. New York: McGraw-Hill.

NELSON, R. 1994. *1001 ways to reward employees*. New York: Workman.

PETERS, T. 1994. *The Pursuit of Wow!*. New York: Vintage Books.

SCANLAN, B. 1973. *Principles of management and organizational behavior*. New York: Wiley.

SCHEIN, E. 1997. *Organizational culture and leadership*. 2nd ed. San Francisco: Jossey-Bass.

STEERS, R. 1977. *Organizational effectiveness: A behavioral view*. Santa Monica, CA: Goodyear.

STOJKOVIC, S., D. KALINICH, and J. KLOFAS. 2002. *Criminal justice organizations: Administration and management*. New York: Wadsworth.

VROOM, V. H. 1964. *Work and motivation*. New York: Wiley.

chapter eight

Performance Appraisal

The following scenario provides an example of how a great deal of controversy and conflict can be generated within an organization because of how employees are formally evaluated. Performance appraisal has been one of the most hotly debated topics for managers. In many situations, managers do not want to do them, and employees feel threatened and intimidated during and after the appraisal process. You will see how it might have happened at one company.

THE POWDER KEG AT RBS

It was time for annual performance reviews at RBS Security Consulting. Because of the number of employees and the limited time the supervisor had to conduct the appraisals, each security officer was allowed 15 minutes for the review meeting. Officers were e-mailed the date and time for their appraisal and told to wait outside the supervisor's office with their coworkers. At the assigned time, each officer was called into the office to review information related to reports, quality, response times to events, attendance records, and customer reviews, a new component of the appraisal process.

Each of these components of the evaluation was numerically rank-ordered, with a score of 0 being the lowest and 5 being the highest the employee could achieve for each performance category. The standards for these criteria were not known. In fact,

continued

many employees were surprised when the supervisor told them that he had just created his own quantitative system for scoring the employees. In one instance, an employee had published an article in a leading security journal. Instead of praising the employee's success, the supervisor stated that he still had more publications, diminishing this potential life event for the employee. This contradicted the organization's motto of being an employee-driven company.

Perhaps the most controversial component was the anonymous customer reviews. Based on the information on these comment cards, the supervisor determined whether the comments were positive or negative, a highly subjective method that was based on the supervisor's opinion and attitude. When sharing these comments with the staff, the supervisor did not allow the employees to explain the good or poor comments they had received or attempt to place them in the context of the events that had occurred. Rather, the supervisor determined the context and numerical score of customer service, which was "nonnegotiable." The supervisor also told the employees where he would like to see improvements and why, with no input from the employees. In fact, there was little, if any, employee input into the evaluation process. Each employee was ranked against others in the company. Salary increases were also based on this ranking system.

Some employees were bold enough to question their subsequent ratings and rankings during the evaluation. These concerns and needs were immediately dismissed, with the supervisor stating, "I am in control of this company." The supervisor stated that as he was once a line-level employee, he knew all the employees' needs and concerns. He also stated to some officers that he knew best how he could develop their skills and make them successful in the company. Employees were then required to sign the evaluation, acknowledging that the annual review meeting had been conducted. It was a very humiliating and demeaning process.

Some of the long-term ramifications of this meeting were competition instead of cooperation among employees; fear of evaluations, as they offered little, if any, input and growth potential; and a general distrust and, in some cases, hatred of the manager, which ultimately led to increased organizational conflicts and divisiveness among the employees. Top management soon recognized a need for a change in management.

The following year, the new manager conducted another performance evaluation. Existing fears and concerns related to the previous year's evaluation immediately emerged and became the topic of discussion among the officers. Things were different, however. Well in advance of the meetings, the new supervisor personally told all the employees how they would be evaluated, allowing them to prepare for the meeting. He also gave each employee a written copy of the performance evaluation.

The evaluation meeting was completely different from the one the prior year. Instead of telling employees where they needed to improve and controlling the evaluation, the supervisor asked them: What are your strengths? What can I do to help you succeed in your work? What additional resources can I provide you? How can I change your work environment to best suit your professional needs?

No longer were the employees compared against one another. They were evaluated on their own merit. Instead of assuming that the employees needed improvement, the new manager took a progressive approach, assuming that all the employees were already good and wanted to excel, with the organization's assistance and support. This was a radical departure from the previous supervisor, whose approach to the performance appraisal had been pathological.

After their meetings, many employees walked out of the manager's office in surprise. Instead of a demeaning and threatening environment that pitted employees against one another for pay and recognition, they had been treated with respect and given the motivation to succeed. As the new supervisor said, "We are all good. My job is to make sure that you excel in your positions. If you do not excel, it is my fault for failing to provide you with the resources and coaching to help you to reach your personal and professional goals in the workplace."

The design and implementation of an appropriate performance appraisal system for security personnel is essential, especially because many individuals working in the private security industry have considerable freedom in how they perform their jobs. While engaged in work-related activities, employees often operate without direct supervision and have direct contact with customers and the citizenry. In all practical terms these employees are serving as the de facto representatives of the firm and therefore affecting its public image and reputation. For some organizations, whose line-level employees are the major revenue generators for the firm, an effective performance evaluation system is crucial for organizational survival and competition.

This chapter describes several types of performance appraisals and discusses their benefits and drawbacks. The chapter also highlights some issues, including relevant legal issues, to consider when designing and implementing the appraisal process and provides some tips on how to conduct meaningful performance appraisals.

■ DEFINITION OF PERFORMANCE APPRAISAL

Performance appraisals (PAs), regardless of whether they are called reviews, assessments, or evaluations, are systematic assessments of how well employees are performing in the organization. PA encompasses a variety of activities "through which organizations seek to assess employees and develop their competence, enhance performance and distribute rewards" (Fletcher 2001, 473). According to Taylor, Pettijohn, and Pettijohn (1999), PA is the process of assessing information based on the performance of an employee so evaluations can be made on that employee's activities. PAs are also a form of organizational recognition that motivates employees and increases their performance and their satisfaction levels in the workplace. All these activities can be summarized under two main topics: an information source for management and a feedback instrument for employees in the organization.

PA is an essential managerial activity that has been regarded as the most complex activity in human resource management (Roberts 1998) and the most important of the four components of effective human resource management, as it is a prerequisite for the selection, training, and motivation of employees (Latham and Wexley 1994). Although often viewed as a static activity that occurs perhaps quarterly or once a year, PA, in a broader perspective, is a dynamic and continual process intrinsically linked to the philosophy and the mission of the organization. Without following the philosophy and the mission of the organization in the context of performance evaluation, decoupling could occur between organizational goals and practices, and chaos could result.

PA also serves as a form of individual and corporate accountability. In the individual context, the employee's performance is assessed in comparison to organizational goals and perhaps other employees in the company. Measuring the performance of employees also serves as justification to stockholders that employees are productive and are generating profits for the company. PA can protect a company from legal issues and can be used for workforce reductions and discipline-related issues.

Benefits of Performance Appraisal

PA has four primary benefits. PA provides the employee with feedback about performance and is a socialization tool and means of controlling employees. PA is also used to assign compensation and is part of the organizational development process.

Periodic Feedback on Performance   Appraisals provide formal and periodic feedback and role clarification to employees on how well they are performing in the company (Gabris and Ihrke 2001). This periodic and timely feedback ensures consistency between an individual's behaviors and the organization's mission, goals, and objectives. This may be particularly important for new employees, who need feedback related to performance and normative expectations in the workplace. In particular, Morrison (1993, 560) indicates that "newcomers seek both performance feedback, or information about how others are perceiving and evaluating their job performance and social feedback or information about the acceptability of their non-task behavior."

PA will help employees learn about their current levels of performance and what the employer expects from them. In their simplest form, PAs allow the organization to distinguish between good and bad performance. In some situations, "they [the employees] are often not provided with the information that they need to master their jobs" (Morrison 1993, 560). This feedback, either positive or negative, is information that serves to reduce uncertainty, define individuals' roles, and clarify their responsibilities and expectations in the workplace. Through the information from PA, employees could develop more effective work habits. The outcomes of the PA process will also serve to motivate employees, resulting in an increase in productivity and quality while reducing employee turnover.

Organizational Socialization and Control   PAs are means for employees to assess goal accomplishment, focus on specific organizational goals, and link the outcomes of their activities to organizational performance. Through formal and informal PA processes, employees are socialized on organizational expectations, culture, and workplace norms. As a consequence, if they want to receive favorable PA scores, employees must behave within certain parameters as set by management (Gabris and Ihrke 2001).

The PA process is part of the organization's control system. Control systems provide information and administer rewards and punishments (Challagalla 1996). Appraisal systems are designed around organizational objectives and those behaviors that management prefers to see in its employees. In short, control is achieved through effective organizational socialization. The outcome from the PA process can also be used for disciplinary actions against the employees, based on their performance, if necessary. Documentation of employee performance is an integral component of the disciplinary process. This issue, however, is one of the more controversial uses of a PA.

Compensation and Merit Awards   PA is often tied to the organization's compensation system. If it has a policy of linking pay to performance, the organization will need to establish criteria to justify pay raises, based on employee performance. PA can also be used for merit increases in organizations that offer bonuses in excess of normal pay raises. The information collected through the PA process can also help the organization in promoting individuals and transferring top-performing employees to specialized positions in the company.

Organizational Development   PA is part of the organizational development process. The findings from PAs help the human resource function in training and developing employees (Taylor 1999). If properly administered, a PA program can strengthen those employees who already possess the traits necessary to excel in the organization. Through the PA process, employees learn what activities are important, relevant, and peripheral (Miller 1996) and to adjust their actions as necessary. In some applications, the PA process also results in employees' and managers' setting goals for future appraisals. The appraisal process also helps employees refine their skills, leading to increased motivation, personal fulfillment, and increased levels of satisfaction and productivity in the workplace.

PA can also serve as a motivational tool for average employees and push them to greater levels of success and personal satisfaction in the workplace. As pointed out by Scott and Einstein (2001, 108), PA influences motivation by "identifying and specifying mutually agreed on outcomes, directing attention to specific tasks, objectives and assignments and specifying the behaviors that are needed to accomplish them, recognizing skill acquisition and identifying deficits for further training and development . . . and providing the rationale for distributing rewards."

■ DRAWBACKS OF PERFORMANCE APPRAISAL

One of the primary concerns about PAs is their legitimacy and applicability in the workplace. One of the biggest opponents of PA was W. Edwards Deming, the founder of the principle of Total Quality Management (TQM). Deming felt that problems related to performance are not related to the employee but rather to a dysfunctional system that does not allow employees to reach their full potential, based on the design of the job and the system (Walton 1986).

Deming considered PA one of the seven deadly management diseases or sins that can have devastating results on the organization. According to Deming, PAs often encourage short-term performance, "discourage risk taking, build fear, undermine teamwork and pit people against each other for the same rewards. On a team it is difficult to tell who did what. The result is a company composed of prima donnas, of sparring fiefdoms. People work for themselves and not for the company" (Walton 1986, 91). Deming concluded that appraisals (1) result in an increased reliance on numbers, (2) measure only short-term results, (3) tend to consider only evidence that can be counted, and (4) depend on the subjective judgments of the supervisor (Walton 1986).

Other critics have attacked the designs of some PA programs. In some situations, PAs incorporate factors that are not directly related to the individual's performance. Bolman and Deal (1997) discuss how the PA process is often ambiguous, with criteria based on the manager's subjective assessments of social and politically correct behaviors in the workplace. In some cases, individual performance may be difficult to assess separately from group performance, especially if the company uses a team-based approach for service delivery.

The negative issues associated with PA suggest that companies should not consider using them. These points may also imply that organizations should eliminate their existing PA programs. Although these negative points are valid, the total elimination of the PA system raises the question of how else to measure how employees are performing. As Kennedy (1999, 51) points out, "only an appraisal can officially deliver the word that an employee hasn't evolved in sync with the department or organization. A message that serious requires the formality that a PA provides."

■ DESIGNING THE APPRAISAL SYSTEM

To avoid some of the negative aspects of PA, a comprehensive model of the PA process must be constructed. Some of the issues or factors to consider in designing the process, as well as desired outcomes, are the following:

- Organizational goals and objectives
- The responsibilities of the worker in the context of the organization's mission and goals
- The individual's social needs in the workplace and how they combine with performance
- The psychological needs of the worker
- Skills needed in the performance of the job
- Other needs of the employee
- Individual versus team performance evaluations
- Organizational culture and/or philosophy

The underlying goals of any PA system are that it be reliable (accurately measure and assess), valid (use criteria known to the raters and ratees), and be standardized. Although these issues are straightforward, they are often inadvertently overlooked when designing and implementing the PA process.

An often neglected and overlooked issue is that the PA process will impact other components of the organization both directly and indirectly. The program must be designed so that all the organizational procedures and practices, including the PA processes, work in harmony.

Purpose

PAs will be much more effective if the procedures used are matched with the nature of the tasks that are being performed by the workers (Orpen 1997). One of the first things the organization needs to consider is the true purpose behind the PA process.

An organization may use PAs for evaluative or development purposes or a combination of the two. Evaluative purposes are related to administrative activities, including promotion, salary decisions, and the individual's performance in comparison to that of other employees in the organization. The PA can also be used for developmental purposes, in which case it is used to provide performance feedback and to identify the person's strengths and weaknesses. Through this process, the organization can then identify the individual's needs for appropriate training (Boswell and Boudreau 2000; Smith, Hornsby, and Shirmeyer 1996).

Evaluative models are not well received by employees, because their perception of the process in the context of fairness is tied to the outcome. For example, an employee who receives a good review will have a more positive attitude toward the process. Developmental PA, however, has been shown to have a consistent positive attitude by employees because the purpose of the review is to improve the person's performance and subsequent job and career development in the company.

In many situations, performance is tied to compensation. Part of setting up the program is that employees and management should determine in advance the extent to which the PA will be used in the compensation process. In some settings, such as unions, the use of the PA will have limited relevance to compensation. In other situations, however, the PA may have a great impact on compensation. This is important to consider because if it is used strictly for compensation or promotional reasons, the PA may generate a greater degree of concern and stress than if it is used for developmental purposes. The frequency of appraisals is also important. If it is used on a continual instead of an annual basis, the PA may cause the employee less stress and apprehension.

Fairness

The key to any PA system is that it must be regarded as fair to the employees who are evaluated under the system (Gabris and Ihrke 2001). This requires that the organization consider the concepts of procedural and distributive justice.

Procedural Justice　Procedural justice refers to the degree to which the individuals perceive the process to be fair. Employees want to feel that their supervisors will rate them objectively and without bias. When considering procedural justice, the employer needs to critically look at the evaluation process, regardless of the outcome of the process, to ensure that it is fair. Research has found that even if employees do not receive a favorable evaluation but perceive that the process was fair, they will have higher levels of job satisfaction (Blau 1999). The degree to which employees have a voice in both the design of the system and the PA process may also increase levels of procedural justice (deLeon 1997).

Two psychological processes underlie procedural justice: instrumental control and relational concerns. In any situation in which a person may be affected by the decision rendered by the organization, the employee will want to have some degree of control over the process, which may be instrumental in improving the person's outcome and relationship with the other party. This is known as instrumental control (Taylor et al. 1995). Another critical component of instrumental control is the concept of voice, the practice of allowing individuals who are being appraised to present information that is relevant to the evaluator's decision. Also known as process control, voice gives the individual the perception of indirect control over decisions by having a chance to indirectly influence the decision. The individual's comments, meanwhile, are intrinsically valued regardless of whether the input influenced the decision (Korsgaard and Roberson 1995).

Individuals also care about their long-term social relationships with their managers and the organization. Procedures that are positive in nature and treat the person as having full status in the employer/employee relation are perceived as fair. In performance evaluations in which the employee is treated rudely or disrespectfully, the employee will feel that the treatment was unfair. These are known as relational concerns (Taylor et al. 1995).

Due Process and Procedural Justice The concept of procedural justice calls for the application of the judicial due-process model. Due process, as the name implies, provides for a degree of perceived fairness in the process. Research has found that when a due-process model is used, employees rate their supervisors as more competent, regardless of whether the evaluation produced positive or negative outcomes for the employee (Taylor et al. 1995).

The due-process model of PA includes three components: adequate notice, a fair hearing, and a judgment based on evidence. For adequate notification, employers need to explain performance standards to employees, explain how and why they need to be met, and provide for regular and timely feedback on performance. The fair-hearing component requires a formal review meeting at which the employee should be allowed to challenge assessments felt to be unfair. Last, judgment based on evidence requires that employers consistently apply the PA criteria across all employees while ensuring that the appraisal is conducted in an honest and fair manner (Taylor et al. 1995).

Six rules need to be followed in a due-process appraisal system (Taylor et al. 1995).

1. Consistency in standards over time and among employees
2. Bias suppression, including limiting one's self-interest by discussing expectations and discrepancies
3. Accuracy in reviews by training managers and employees to properly record performance information and to prepare accurate reports
4. Correctability, which requires managers to listen to the employee under review and, if appropriate, change the evaluation
5. Representativeness, which addresses the needs and concerns of the employee and manager throughout the evaluation process
6. Ethicality, which deals with ensuring that those procedures used are compatible with existing ethical and moral standards

Distributive Justice The concept of distributive justice refers to how rewards are allocated among employees (deLeon 1997). Some research has found that negative perceptions of distributive justice lead to greater levels of burnout among employees. To avoid burnout and other issues that an unfair reward system could lead to, rewards related to the outcomes of the PA process must be allocated in accordance with the findings from the appraisal. The link between performance and rewards must be clear and understandable to the employee.

Employee Involvement

Procedural justice implies that employees be involved in the design and implementation of the PA process (Taylor, Pettijohn, and Pettijohn 1999). Involvement should be at all levels of the organization: executives, managers, and line-level employees. This will ensure that all interested parties have had the opportunity to be involved in the process.

One way to involve employees in the development and implementation of a PA system is called action research (AR). The AR process involves three stages: assessing, focusing, and implementing the program. The assessment stage involves data collection to survey and interview all parties that have an interest in or will be affected by the performance evaluation. Following the collection of information, organizational members meet to discuss the appropriate changes and focus on both long-and short-term implications, threats, opportunities, beliefs, and values the participants hold. Through the implementation stage, these values, beliefs, and ideas are incorporated into the program. Plans and procedures are then developed to carry out the project.

Employees can also be involved in the appraisal process. Management can look at employees in the PA as active or passive. If looked at passively, the PA would be one-directional, with the manager imposing on them the findings and expectations for improvement. If active, it would be a two-way exchange of information giving the employee some degree of input into the performance evaluation process.

Establishing Criteria

The selection of the criteria by which employees will be evaluated is another critical factor. Employees who feel that they have been evaluated on inappropriate criteria are less likely to be satisfied with their jobs (Pettijohn, Pettijohn, and d'Amico 2001). This suggests that managers and employees should be in agreement on how employees are going to be evaluated.

Depending on the supervisory philosophy, nature of work, and organizational culture in the context of empowering workers, a PA system may be based on the behavioral dimensions of activity or capability control. Activity control, for example, relies on the specification of routine work activities, more frequent monitoring of behaviors the employee is expected to perform on a regular basis, and administering rewards and punishments, based on the individual's performance. Capability control, on the other hand, emphasizes the development of individual skills and abilities over employee monitoring. The function of capability control is to positively influence performance by ensuring that employees possess the set of skills and abilities that ensure good performance.

These differences affect employee satisfaction and performance. For example, capability control "is likely to satisfy a person's innate psychological need for competence and increase his or her intrinsic motivation. . . . Activity evaluation requires the frequent evaluation and top-down determination of routine activities, people are more likely to experience a loss of self-determination, which gives rise to negative feelings" (Challagalla 1996, 98). Research related to activity versus capability control determined that activity control is not as effective as capability control. Instead, the two should be balanced. In the context of performance evaluation, a balance should be established between improving skills and monitoring the employee's day-to-day activities.

In addition to behavioral dimensions, the organization needs to consider what types of criteria it will use in the PA. Input-behavioral criteria are related to the person's background. Input-based appraisals provide insight into the person's behaviors and level of knowledge. They assume that the inputs, or characteristics the individual possesses, will influence workplace performance or outcomes. Performance is defined based on the person's observable actions and specific activities. The results of these types of appraisals can lead to increased motivation, commitment, and satisfaction levels in the company (Orpen 1997).

Output-based appraisals are usually quantitative, or number-driven, evaluations that focus on the person's productivity in the organization (Pettijohn, Pettijohn, and d'Amico 2001). They define performance in terms of whether the person has met certain goals or targets (Barney and Griffin 1992). Through this process, specific and quantifiable results gained from the employee's efforts on a regular basis can be measured. These measures may include such factors as the number of calls for service, the number of self-initiated activities the employee performed, or the employee's response time. In the context of a security salesperson, these measures may include sales volumes and sales volumes compared to those of the previous year. A security hardware salesperson may be evaluated on the number of products sold over a certain period of time or the number of dollars in profit generated. If this is the appraisal method chosen, it measures only output.

Outcome- or output-based criteria are the most frequently used types of appraisals. They are simple and objective, requiring little monitoring by management of the employees' activities on a regular basis. These evaluations concentrate on past activities for which rewards and sanctions are imposed on the employee. If observed solely within this framework, the organization has failed to discover the real value of the program, which is the improvement of the individual's performance. Outcome-based appraisals are usually most successful when they are part of a comprehensive program in which the manager and the employee set clear, challenging, and defined goals prior to the evaluation (Scott and Einstein 2001).

However, output is not fully controlled by the employee. Rather, output may be affected by environmental factors, such as the size of the area and the economic health and level of competition in the area. For example, a line-level security guard can be evaluated on the number of self-initiated activities with clients. But an employee who works the third shift will have very few opportunities for contact with clients. If the company uses input criteria, however, this person would be appraised on level of motivation, training, and commitment to the company—specific attributes over which the person has control (Pettijohn, Pettijohn, and d'Amico 2001).

Individual Characteristics and Performance Appraisal

An organization must consider several characteristics of individuals when design-ing and conducting performance evaluations. One is the employee's personality. Herold, Parsons, and Rensvold (1996) suggested that employees can be shapers and manipulators of the feedback environment and that by knowing these per-sonality differences, managers could gain a better understanding of how feed-back, motivation, learning, and performance in the workplace will be affected. For example, employees can be classified as passive or active recipients of feedback. Passive employees simply receive feedback and act on it. Active employees, by contrast, actively seek out feedback sources and generate feedback cues.

The researchers also studied individuals' propensities to like, seek, and use feedback from various sources. The researchers found that employees could be categorized as External Propensity, Internal Ability, and Internal Propensity. Exter-nal Propensity employees show a preference for externally mediated feedback sources, such as supervisors and coworkers, and prefer having the organizational structure and other people available to help the individual in learning, perfor-mance, and motivation. Internal Ability employees seek out more feedback from their jobs than from other people and prefer jobs that provide more indepen-dence from the scrutiny of others. Internal Propensity individuals prefer internal feedback but use external feedback to reconcile any differences.

Fedor, Rensvold, and Adams (1992) found that employees with a low toler-ance for ambiguity need higher levels of external feedback than do other em-ployees. Employees with a high level of self-esteem are more reluctant to ask for feedback. This finding suggests that supervisors should recognize employees' per-sonalities and try to modify the PA process to meet these individual personalities and needs. This may ensure that the PA process is more readily accepted and rec-ognized as a tool for self-actualization or personal achievement and improvement in the workplace.

The status of the employee in the organization will also affect the PA process. New employees have been found to seek three types of appraisal: refer-ent information about job instructions, appraisal feedback about their perfor-mance, and relational information on how others feel about them (Miller 1996). Thus, new employees may need more attention than employees who have been with the organization for a longer period of time.

Frequency of Appraisals

Formal PAs generally occur only once or twice per year. However, some re-searchers recommend that PAs occur as often as every eight weeks (Taylor, Petti-john, and Pettijohn 1999) or at least three times a year (Hitchcock 1996). This increase in appraisals could result in less role ambiguity and an increase in the perceived fairness of the process, as it is no longer an annual event. Problems as-sociated with evaluations, such as central-tendency bias (i.e., an inclination to rate all performances as average), could be reduced. Having more evaluations would also give an employee who is having problems a better chance of improving, on account of the increased frequency and amount of feedback from the appraisals (Lee 1996).

Informally, PAs can take place on a daily basis, as employees may engage in feedback-seeking behaviors that include eliciting and monitoring. Eliciting behaviors occur when employees ask their supervisors or fellow employees directly for feedback. Monitoring behaviors occur when individuals use indirect feedback techniques, such as observing the actions and nonverbal behaviors of other employees, to determine whether their performance is appropriate in the given situation (Fedor, Rensvold, and Adams 1992). The behaviors chosen for feedback depend on the situation. For example, individuals asking for direct assistance may expose their weaknesses in a particular area, whereas monitoring may lead to misinterpretation when interpreting social cues (Morrison 1993).

■ TYPES OF APPRAISALS

The primary goal of any appraisal system is to be reliable and valid. Reliability means that if the appraisal were administered again at a different time, the conclusion would be the same. Validity refers to whether the appraisal system accurately measures performance issues. The evaluation criteria must also be known to both the raters and the ratees (Cheung 1999). In addition, the appraisal process must be appropriate for the employee. For example, having employees with limited literacy skills complete an essay-based performance evaluation would not be a good "fit." Such a format would deter those employees from participating in the PA, making them fear the very process.

Depending on the needs of the organization and the employee, several types of appraisals can be used: downward or upward; horizontal, or peer-based; and self-evaluative. Some PAs may be hybrids, or mixtures of these forms. The dominant, or traditional, form of PA is the downward method, whereby the supervisor evaluates the performance of subordinates. This one-way form of communication monopolizes communication structure: The supervisor tells the subordinates how they are doing and receives or asks for little upward feedback. Depending on the organization, multiple methods can be used at one time. This section discusses some of the more common appraisal tools.

Subjective methods, based on feelings and emotions, are the most common type of employee appraisal. Under subjective methods, the employee's performance is assessed through the eyes of someone else. Some subjective methods are performance ranking, behaviorally anchored rating scales (BARS), and performance rating (Barney and Griffin 1992).

Appraisals can also be standardized or unstandardized. Research has shown that the majority of organizations use a standardized form when appraising employees (Hitchcock 1996). These standardized forms can be obtained or purchased from resource consultants and organizations, or the organization itself can create standardized employee appraisals. Organizations may also use unstandardized forms when appraising employees. Doing so, however, may expose the organization to unnecessary legal challenges.

Rating and Ranking Methods

Some of the more common appraisal methods are rating scales and employee rankings. Rating scales are a list of behaviors, traits, or activities with values from poor to outstanding. The manager simply rates the worker's productivity, knowledge of the job, quality of work, or some other characteristic determined to be important. One of the criticisms of rating scales is that they are subjective and generally are not defined in terms of the jobs performed (Daley 1993). Others have determined that the acceptability of a rating system is a function of organizational and individual characteristics and the perceived accuracy and quality of the rating forms (Hedge and Teachout 2000). An example of a graphic rating scale is given in Box 8-1.

BOX 8–1   ■   Graphic Rating Scales

Outstanding __; __; __; __; __; __; __; __; __; __ Poor

ABILITY TO LEARN: Consider how quickly
the employee learns (is able to retain
instruction and information)

Outstanding __; __; __; __; __; __; __; __; __; __ Poor

QUALITY OF WORK: Consider accuracy of work
regardless of volume

Outstanding __; __; __; __; __; __; __; __; __; __ Poor

APPEARANCE: Consider neatness,
personal dress, and personal habits

Ranking methods are used to compare employees to one another, based on their job performance. A modified version of employee ranking is called forced distribution; here, the manager is required— "forced"— to evaluate employees in proportion to the normal distribution, or bell-shaped curve, with a certain percentage of employees ranked high, low, or average. This method may not accurately reflect the true distribution of employee performance, as many top or bottom performers would be categorized as average. Because it appraises individual performance, this type of tool may lead to increased competition among employees for higher ratings. This individual-based competition could also affect and decrease the amount and quality of teamwork (Murphy 1993).

Performance Management

Performance management, a radical departure from the standard annual PA, is a system that includes reviews, coaching sessions, goal setting, and tracking one's performance in the organization. Unlike traditional performance evaluations, performance management is a comprehensive program that attempts to help people manage their actions to meet the organization's goals (Lee 1996).

The key to performance management is that it is an ongoing process in the organization. Unlike traditional PAs, which may be conducted only on an annual basis, performance management involves having managers and employees meet several times a year to make sure that they are on track and that their goals are consistent with those of the company. These periodic meetings give the employee the opportunity to improve over the time period and the manager to provide assistance to help the employee reach goals. Now the employee and the manager share the responsibility for reaching organizational goals.

A performance management system requires organization development activities for both managers and employees. Managers may need to be trained in coaching techniques while creating an atmosphere that encourages individual initiative. At the same time, employees may need to be trained and encouraged to actively ask their managers how they are meeting the organization's goals and to take a more active responsibility for their own performance (Lee 1996).

Performance management has several benefits. This system "creates" better managers because they are now actively involved with employees. Managers must coach, provide regular feedback on the individual's performance, and offer rewards and reinforcement for the individual's actions. PAs still occur, but these evaluations will be less adversarial. Feedback is ongoing rather than yearly, employees are active participants in their performance evaluation, and the process is focused on performance feedback instead of pay raises, which disconnects developmental issues from compensation issues (Lee 1996).

Performance management systems are also appropriate for companies that operate in rapidly changing environments. In organizations that conduct annual appraisals, needed changes related to employees' activities may not occur in a timely manner to meet external changes, as performance meetings occur only on a yearly basis, for example. In those companies that use performance management, the company can realign its goals and objectives more quickly, as performance can be readjusted as needed through the frequent performance-based meetings between managers and employees (Lee 1996).

Peer Evaluations

Peer evaluation is an intergroup, or team, appraisal approach in which other employees at the same occupational level critique one another. This method does not rely on supervisors or managers. Depending on the design, this approach can be based on a rating or a nomination method. Under the rating method, all members of the specific group evaluate other members from worst to best. Under the nomination method, employees compare members of their group in the context of the worst and best and are forced to categorize a certain number in the "worst" and "best" categories.

Some of the benefits of peer evaluation are that it increases levels of participation and that colleagues should have good knowledge of one another's abilities because of the extent and nature of their interactions (deLeon 1997; Schwartzwald, Koslowsky, and Mager-Bibi 1999). Peers may also have a greater frequency of contact with those being appraised and may be able to assess a wider range of dimensions. The information peers possess may be more accurate than that of supervisors. In some organizations, peer evaluations may be necessary because supervisors lack knowledge about an individual's specialty area (Barclay and Harland 1995). As some organizations may emphasize a team approach to the job, this may also encourage teamwork and a greater emphasis on group problem solving. Because of the large amount of input from many evaluators, this method has also proved to be a reliable measurement of one's performance on the job (Schwartzwald, Koslowsky, and Mager-Bibi 1999); research has also found that employees have accepted this practice (Hitchcock 1996).

Peer evaluations have some disadvantages. One of the primary concerns is bias. Bias may be caused by interpersonal relationships between the rater and ratees; raters may lack knowledge and competence in conducting reviews, and the individuals being evaluated may view their peers as less competent raters than their supervisors. This bias may be intentional or unintentional, perhaps because the rater misinterprets the performance-related information (Barclay and Harland 1995). Competition, real or perceived, and friendships could affect one's rating of another (deLeon 1997). If the group is too large under the nomination technique, individuals may lack information on other group members, raising issues related to the validity of the process. In the rating method, peers may assign high scores to all members in the group, also raising issues related to validity (Schwartzwald, Koslowsky, and Mager-Bibi 1999).

Several issues need to be considered when developing a peer appraisal system. First, the organization needs to pay particular attention to who is selected to be peer reviewers. When selecting these reviewers, the organization needs to solicit input from those employees on what constitutes a competent rater. After gathering this information, the organization needs to develop a pool of raters who possess the characteristics identified by each group of employees to be rated. Next, the organization needs to consider the design of the evaluation process (Barclay and Harland 1995).

One of the key issues in this evaluation method is peer approval and the notion of procedural justice. The organization should also consider the following issues: (1) whether peers have a good opportunity to observe the dimensions they are evaluating; (2) the experience levels of the raters; (3) the number of raters used, with more being better than fewer raters; and (4) the validity of the ratings (Barclay and Harland 1995).

Self-Evaluations

Self-appraisal performance evaluations, as the name suggests, are conducted by the individuals themselves. This type of system allows employees to participate in the process; they may be the most suitable to evaluate their performance, as they are the best informed about their performance (deLeon 1997). This factor may be particularly important in "flat" organizations that do not have multiple layers of supervision and that encourage autonomy and self-development (Baruch 1996).

Self-appraisals can be used to supplement traditional PAs. Self-appraisals may make individuals more acceptive of feedback, more self-aware of their actions, and more committed to the PA process (Kolb 1995). Self-appraisal techniques also transform the role of the manager. Because the manager did not evaluate the employee, the employee may be less hostile toward the manager during the appraisal. The role of the manager has subsequently changed from the disciplinarian to one of a coach or career mentor, eliminating the confrontational atmosphere that exists with some evaluations (Falcone 1999).

Research has found that self-ratings of performance are more biased and that less variability is reported in performance compared to peer or subordinate evaluations. Self-raters also report more desirable behaviors and inflate their performance compared to others who assessed their behavior (Kolb 1995).

Upward Feedback

Upward feedback is an appraisal process that is often used to evaluate the performance of managers, with the manager's subordinates doing the evaluation. Some companies use the upward performance appraisal (UPA) system, with subordinates evaluating their supervisors on how well they provide feedback, set performance plans, deal with disciplinary issues, and allocate workloads. Although UPA is not heavily used in corporations, two of its primary benefits are that it leads to improved levels of worker satisfaction and that, through the communication process that occurs in this type of evaluation, the organization has improved supervision. It has also been determined that UPAs foster greater attention to the needs of the subordinate (Hall, Leidecker, and Dimarco 1996).

These types of appraisal can be anonymous or accountability based. In anonymity-based systems, subordinates evaluate the performance of the manager but do not have to put their names on the evaluation, or their comments are presented in a redacted format before the information is presented to the manager. Anonymity is thought to allow employees to be more candid about their manager's performance and could also protect employees from retaliatory acts by managers for negative comments on the evaluation. One of the complaints about this procedure is that management may perceive that anonymity could result in unfair evaluations because the employee cannot be identified and is not accountable for the evaluation (Antonioni 1994).

In accountability-based systems, raters must identify themselves on the evaluations they complete. Research on the two different methods has found that under accountability methods, raters inflated their manager's performance compared to subordinates who gave anonymous responses. At the same time, subordinates indicated that they preferred to provide anonymous responses. Managers also viewed accountability-based evaluations more positively than anonymous-based appraisal procedures because raters could be identified, leading to a degree of responsibility in their ratings (Antonioni 1994).

Upward appraisals may provide some benefits for an organization. These appraisals may detect problems or concerns from employees that may not have been detected via other appraisal techniques. Employees may also have the best understanding of the manager's strengths and abilities. This appraisal procedure may encourage teamwork, as supervisors under this system may have to interact more with employees (deLeon 1997). Additional research, by Kolb (1995), found that subordinates' feedback combined with self-assessment decreased the gap between desired and actual performance, as the individual now had two different performance evaluations: their own perceived performance and their performance rating appraisals from their subordinates.

UPAs have some drawbacks. Besides the concerns related to anonymous appraisals, subordinates may not be qualified to accurately rate their managers, lacking appropriate and complete information on the manager's performance. In addition, employees' personal biases, either positive or negative, could affect the outcomes of the appraisal. Supervisors may also perceive that their authority is being undermined via the evaluation process. Through proper design, administration, and training of all employees in the organization, some of these obstacles can be overcome (Hall, Leidecker, and Dimarco 1996).

Multisource Feedback

Multisource feedback methods are a relatively new tool for assessing employee performance. Also known as 360-degree, or multirater, appraisals, this approach relies on multiple individuals to evaluate employee performance. These individuals may be peers, managers, and the individuals themselves. For example, both peers and the supervisor might evaluate a security officer on predetermined performance criteria.

This comprehensive employee appraisal is achieved by including feedback from all individuals over whom the employee has influence (Ramsey 1998). These types of evaluations are nearly universal among Fortune 500 corporations (London 1995).

The primary organizational benefit of multisource feedback appraisals is that the observations from multiple sources will yield more meaningful and useful information that can be used to more accurately assess employee performance (Church and Bracken 1997). This appraisal method also includes information that simply does not exist from other evaluation methods. This additional information makes the supervisor's job easier, as it provides more information on which to base the evaluation outcomes (Ramsey 1998).

Another benefit is that it is a personal development tool for managers; the feedback received from all levels in the company translates into a greater amount of information on which managers can base decisions, subsequently improving their managerial skills (Wells 1999). In addition, the information helps the company in designing training programs, in leadership and managerial development activities, and in succession planning (Church and Bracken 1997).

Compared to other types of appraisals, multisource evaluation methods will also provide employees with a more global or comprehensive understanding of how they are performing or contributing to organizational success. Employees will receive more information about their performance in comparison to methods that rely solely on supervisory feedback. This could lead to employees' improving their self-understanding and avenues for self-improvement and development (London 1995). These multiple sources will also identify employees' strengths, weaknesses, or areas for skill development and increase their motivation levels in the organization (Kolb 1995). Multisource feedback will help employees better understand how they are viewed by others, which in turn will help them develop a more accurate sense of goal accomplishment and self-competence (London 1995).

Research on 360-degree systems has found that they increase levels of procedural fairness as all individuals are held accountable to the same standards and are rated on the same behavioral competencies. These systems have also been found to provide more useful information to employees, to increase the levels of trust and cooperation with coworkers, and to increase the levels of communication with supervisors (deLeon 1997).

Multisource appraisals may have some disadvantages. If the peer evaluations are not anonymous, there may be some issues related to low employee participation rates, which could be attributed to confidentiality, the purposes behind the ratings, and the rater's beliefs about the appropriateness of upward feedback (Westerman and Rosse 1997). Multiple sources of information may lead to conflicting information about the employee's performance. Issues related to the truthfulness of responses could also arise (Vinson 1996), raising questions about the validity and the reliability of the information that has been collected.

Customer feedback may also be used in multirater techniques. Although customers may provide additional feedback, some issues need to be considered before incorporating customers into the feedback process. Customers may feel uncomfortable evaluating a person and may see only the final product or service and not know whether the employee has any performance problems. Simply asking a customer for feedback could also imply that the employee is having problems that could negatively impact the customer's perception of that employee. Including customer feedback in the evaluation process will also require the development of separate questionnaires and lead to more administrative work by managers as well as to concerns about the reliability and the validity of the information collected (Pollack and Pollack 1996).

Team-Based Appraisal Systems

Organizations may want to consider evaluating and rewarding teamwork as part of their PA program to realign their appraisal system with what occurs in the workplace. To some extent, individual performance is intrinsically linked to the collective performance of many employees who can directly affect the success of the company. In the majority of organizations today, employees' responsibilities extend well beyond their individual tasks. This implies that organizations rely heavily on teamwork for their success. This concept of teamwork, however, is often overlooked in the PA process. A team appraisal occurs when the performance of a group of individuals is used as a basis for determining the individual's success, or performance, in the organization.

The concepts of individual and team are not mutually exclusive but rather are interdependent variables that have a profound impact on the organization's productivity. For example, an appraisal system can easily be designed to evaluate the performance of security officers in their individual responsibilities. Hourly rounds or periodic safety inspections would be considered an individual-based activity. At the same time, however, this security officer does not operate in a vacuum but works with and interacts with a larger group of individuals known as the team. In this capacity, the manager may want to consider how the team members engage in problem-solving activities and work with one another to solve organizational problems and issues.

The appraisal of a team can be more challenging than the evaluation of a single person. Therefore, one of the first things a manager needs to do is find out exactly what the team is supposed to do, determining where the team is operating in the organization. If the team is composed of midlevel managers, for instance, their major responsibilities would be related to financial and market-related measures and issues. When evaluating this team, the manager may be concerned about how the team increased the number of contracts and billable hours over the past quarter. When evaluating a line-level team, issues related to customer satisfaction and the delivery of security services would be key. The task of defining team responsibilities should be conducted by the teams themselves, managers, or both.

All team members need to have a complete understanding of what they need to do to support the team's common objectives. Team members need to be fully aware of their duties and responsibilities. One way to accomplish that is to create a matrix that lists the key tasks the team must accomplish and the valuable accomplishments each member needs to contribute to the team to ensure its success (Zigon 1994). Box 8-2 shows a matrix format of how security officers can contribute to team success, based on their individual accomplishments. The top row lists the key tasks, and the left column lists the "players" on the team. Each cell in the matrix lists valuable accomplishments of each team member.

BOX 8–2 ■ Loss-Prevention Team Evaluation Matrix

Employees	Team Tasks			
	Inventory Control	Surveillance	Apprehensions Loss/Theft	Internal
Brian				
Shannon				
Phil				
Jim				
John				

In many instances, the team can evaluate its own performance and report its findings to management. As suggested by Rees (1999), teams should evaluate their own performance, as self-evaluation will motivate the team. Actions that need to be taken to achieve positive changes will occur because they are self-initiated rather than imposed. However, this self-evaluation session should be conducted by an outside facilitator, such as a manager, to ensure that the evaluation was procedurally fair to all members of the team. Some of the components of an effective team evaluation session are shown in Box 8–3.

BOX 8–3 ■ Components of Effective Team Evaluation

Following are some factors to consider to achieve an effective team evaluation.

- Establish that the discussion is confidential.
- Create a nonthreatening and positive atmosphere.
- Encourage objectivity and honesty.
- Ensure that everyone is treated with respect.
- Look at the entire team.
- Avoid embarrassing team members by singling anyone out or rating individuals.
- Emphasize that responsibility for improvement rests with each team member.
- Foster open dialog and probing.
- Acknowledge the team's strengths, as well as needs for improvement.
- Encourage the team to set specific goals and strategies for itself.
- Focus on one or two areas for improvement and try to energize the team around making changes.
- Allow time for meaningful discussions and planning.

Adapted from Rees 1999, 39.

These team appraisals can be used as a stand-alone evaluation or be incorporated into individual-level PAs. Under these appraisal designs, team members can still be appraised in the context of their individual performance and their contribution to the team.

As with the other evaluation methods discussed, team evaluations are another way for organizations to increase their knowledge of employee performance. One of the concerns with team-based evaluations is "social loafing," or the fact that some individuals may begin to shirk their responsibilities to the group when they know that their individual contributions will not be recognized or evaluated. In order to prevent social loafing, an organization may want to conduct a two-tier evaluation of the employee (Scott and Einstein 2001): a team appraisal, followed by an individual performance evaluation.

Behaviorally Anchored Rating Scales (BARS)

Behaviorally anchored rating scales (BARS) are one of the more frequently used PA processes. These subjective evaluations link individual performance with organizational goals. This type of appraisal assumes that managers can systematically assess the competency level of the employee. Specific tasks are assessed against standards, or benchmarks, that are created from defined job performance standards (Daley 1993). These effective criteria to perform the job are placed on scales ranging from least to most effective. Each scale or cell contains a brief description of the behavior that fits each scale level. The manager is responsible for identifying the behavioral anchor that best reflects the activities of the employee, based on that specific dimension. Box 8–4 gives an example of a BARS related to effective communication skills.

BOX 8–4 ■ Behaviorally Anchored Rating Scale: Report Writing and Verbal Communication Skills

Category	Poor (1)	Fair (2)	Good (3)	Very Good (4)
Verbal Communication Skills	Experiences a great deal of difficulty in communication	Often uses language that is unclear and lacks specificity	Communicates satisfactorily with clients and coworkers	Communicates effectively with clients and coworkers
Sentence Structure and Grammar	Commits many errors in sentence structure and grammar	Commits frequent errors in sentence structure and grammar	Makes infrequent errors in sentence structure and grammar	Uses proper sentence structure and grammar in reports

Quality of Reports	Presents ideas and information in confusing and disorganized manner	Presents ideas and information in an unclear, rambling, and contradictory manner	Presents ideas and information in a well-organized and understandable manner	Presents information in a comprehensive and well-organized manner

BARS do not concentrate on outcomes or personality traits of the employee but instead address the key aspects of job performance. The use of BARS requires that the company create a list of critical incidents, or behaviors, that result in good or bad performance. They then need to be sorted into categories ranging from extremely good to extremely bad. Behavioral statements also need to be created for each cell or category to represent ineffective, average, and effective performance levels for the particular job behavior. Careful attention should also be given to make sure that the incidents and categories do not overlap.

Management by Objectives

Management by objectives (MBO) is another popular PA technique (Smith, Hornsby, and Shirmeyer 1996). MBO is a managerial philosophy, with managers and employees establishing and defining quantifiable objectives that will be used in the employees' performance evaluation. The key to MBO is participatory management and goal setting (Romani 1997). Employees are directly involved in planning, directing, and controlling their jobs; employees help determine measurement for their performance and receive continual feedback on their progress toward their goals. Through this direct involvement, it is felt that employees become more motivated and committed to the organization's mission and goals, which leads to improved performance in the workplace (Marlow and Schilhavy 1991).

One of the primary advantages of MBO is that it increases the employees' perception that the process is fair—and hence their level of acceptance—as they have been allowed to determine what criteria will be used in their forthcoming evaluation. A well-designed MBO program also results in a greater awareness of organizational goals, forces planning for both managers and employees, and provides specific performance criteria for employees so they know what is expected of them. The MBO program measures performance in an objective manner that links the evaluation process directly to the employee's performance (Marlow and Schilhavy 1991).

One weakness of MBO is that it is often tied to individual performance. In many companies, jobs are interrelated, which limits the employee's control of the job and freedom of action. Because it is individual based, MBO may also lead to increased competition and avoidance of teamwork, with individuals beginning to work for themselves and not with others in the company. MBO may also result in the company's measuring only short-term, quantifiable results that occurred during that evaluation period instead of looking at long-term quality-related issues (Walton 1986). Because MBO programs are objectively based and focus on specific goals, weight or recognition may be given to the discretionary activity of employees. MBO programs may also limit the personal objectives and needs of the individual (Marlow and Schilhavy 1991).

■ ADMINISTERING PERFORMANCE APPRAISAL PROGRAMS

The success or failure of any performance evaluation program hinges on the level of support and commitment the program receives. Resistance to the appraisal process can exist on two levels: management and line.

One of the first issues is to ensure managerial acceptance of the appraisal program. Three primary issues affect the degree of commitment by managers: the manager's superior, peers, and subordinates. Superiors, or top management in the organization, may not be committed to and support the appraisal system or methods; raters may inflate their performance ratings because they may think that their peers are also inflating evaluations (Robinson, Fink, and Allen 1996). Other managers may foresee potential conflict with employees they are evaluating. Some managers may also have personal difficulties in evaluating employees and may have a fear of legal challenges associated with the appraisal (Taylor, Pettijohn, and Pettijohn 1999). Of these three factors, superiors have the greatest impact in determining the rater's level of commitment to the appraisal process (Robinson, Fink, and Allen 1996).

Another explanation for managerial resistance to the appraisal process is the rationalization that the time and effort expended on the appraisal process are not worth the returns. With competing issues, managers may avoid appraisals because they take up too much time that could have been devoted to some other, more meaningful managerial activity (Taylor, Pettijohn, and Pettijohn 1999).

One of the primary ways to reduce these levels of apprehension and resistance is to properly train all individuals involved in the appraisal process. Wells (1999) indicates that, in order to be effective, raters should be trained in advance in order to avoid issues related to inexperience. Individuals should also be trained in providing feedback to those being appraised and use the feedback for job-related and behavior changes.

The training of managers is also needed to alleviate a condition known as performance appraiser discomfort (PAD), or apprehension toward the administration of a performance appraisal process. Three factors contribute to PAD. The first is related to the beliefs the rater has toward the importance of the PA. If the organization is diligent and conducts frequent appraisals and holds raters accountable while involved in decisions related to pay increases and promotions, the rater's PAD may be higher on account of increased concern or discomfort when conducting the appraisal. PAD is also influenced by communication reticence, which occurs when individuals perceive themselves to be ineffective communicators, and is affected by the manager's degree of experience. As effective communication is a key in the appraisal process, raters who perceive themselves to be ineffective communicators and also lack experience in appraisals will have higher levels of PAD. Last, PAD can be influenced by the length of a rater's relationship with the ratee. Raters who have had short-term relationships with the worker may feel less comfortable evaluating an employee because they have not had the opportunity to develop effective communication patterns with these individuals. Research on PAD has found that the importance the organization places on the appraisal significantly increases the rater's PAD level (Smith, Harrington, and Houghton 2000).

Employees too may resist the appraisal process. To overcome employee resistance, management needs to educate employees on the importance of the feedback generated from the PA and how it will contribute to their continued success in the company. Of course, educating employees should have been done well in advance of the appraisal meeting.

Management also needs to educate employees on the process itself. By this stage, employees should already know what the information from the appraisal will be used for. These purposes, however, should be reiterated at this stage to clarify any misperceptions the employees may have. Employees should be informed about the appraisal process to reduce any feelings of anxiety that could negatively impact the meeting. Furthermore, the content of meeting should not be a surprise. If managers are doing their jobs correctly and providing feedback to their employees on a continual or daily basis, employees should have a relatively complete understanding of any positive or negative performance-based issue that will be brought up at the meeting.

Ethical Considerations

The proper treatment of people is a fundamental ethical issue and concern for managers. One of the key considerations in any PA is that it is ethically sound. Managers should provide an honest and accurate assessment of the individual's performance. This requires that managers be straightforward and tell employees exactly where they stand in the context of their performance in the organization. At the same time, managers must ensure that employees' self-esteem or self-worth is not threatened.

At times, this may be difficult to do because managers may want to avoid confrontation. However, if managers fail to address problems immediately, the result will be a long-term problem that will affect the manager/employee relationship, eventually leading to larger issues for employees, managers, and the organization.

The Politics of Performance Appraisal   One component of the appraisal process that is often not acknowledged and that has ethical implications is its political side. In some situations, accuracy in performance evaluations may not be the primary objective. Managers may recognize other variables as being more important. For example, a manager may be more interested in avoiding conflict and promoting group harmony. But if a manager's assessment of certain employees is not accurate, conflict and competition could increase—the opposite effect of what the manager wanted to achieve. In other instances, managers may purposefully inflate reviews to move poor performers out of their department or as a means to manipulate the employee's salary. In other situations, managers may use the PA as a shock effect; in this situation, a lower than deserved rating is given to make the employee improve performance. The PA could also be used to generate more documentation in order to have the chain of evidence necessary to discharge the employee (Thomas 1997). In other situations, the manager may perceive pressure from superiors to alter evaluations or assessments out of fear that they may be looked on with skepticism. For example, if an employee is performing poorly, is it because of the employee or the actions or inactions of the manager?

The politicization of the PA process can be avoided only by recognizing that it can be and often is a political process. Then the organization and the manager can take measures to avoid the politicization process. One of the best ways to do so is to have a properly designed system that takes into account this dilemma and eliminates some of the more politically "hot" issues. For example, if the appraisal is used solely for employee development and not for compensation, promotion, or tenure, the major political issues related to money could be avoided entirely. If the politics of PA do surface, managers must take a strong stance and do what is ethically right.

Common Mistakes in Performance Appraisal   In some instances, raters make mistakes that could lead to the employee's perceiving that the process is biased or unethical. One of the major concerns in PA is related to rater bias that can occur unintentionally or, in some cases, deliberately. Some of the more common rater mistakes are shown in Box 8–5.

BOX 8–5 ■ Common Errors in Rater Evaluations

Type of Error	Description
Halo effect	Occurs when the appraiser assigns positive attributes to a person, based on extraneous factors, such as age and gender (McBey 1994). The rater's entire evaluation is based on this one positive characteristic, even though this person may have some negative performance attributes.
Horn effect	The opposite of the halo effect. Occurs when one's negative attribute(s) cloud the judgment of the evaluator to the point that the individual is regarded as a poor performer, despite positive performance attributes.
Recency effect	Remembering and using only recent performance-related activities as a basis for the appraisal; failing to recall earlier activities, regardless of whether they were positive or negative.
Latency effect	Remembering and using only earlier performance-related activities as a basis for the appraisal; failing to recall current

activities in the appraisal process, regardless of whether they were positive or negative.

Spillover effect   Occurs when information for a previous performance appraisal biases the rater's assessment of the employee's current performance (McBey 1994).

Central tendency   Occurs when the manager rates a large number of employees as "average," although they may be performing above or below performance expectations. Raters who are unable or unwilling to remember poor performance or are concerned about conflict and offending employees who are performing poorly may give them higher ratings on the evaluations. Similarly, high-performance workers may receive satisfactory or average ratings (Burns 1996).

Rater bias and characteristics   Occurs when raters unconsciously give higher ratings to employees who are demographically similar to them (Burns 1996). Raters need to consider that bias related to physical appearance, gender, race, and age may affect their performance appraisals (Cook 1995). Other research has found that even after controlling for age, gender, and race, smokers were rated lower than nonsmokers, based on the social stigmas attached to smoking (Gilbert, Hannan, and Lowe 1998).

Ingratiating behaviors   Behaviors that are widely recognized but not widely popular. Managers need to consider three forms of ingratiating behaviors that influence performance appraisals (Cook 1995):

1. Job focused: Arriving for work early, staying late, taking inappropriate credit for things
2. Supervisor focused: Praising the supervisor, taking interest in his or her private life, doing favors for the supervisor, complimenting the supervisor, and supporting the supervisor's ideas
3. Self-focused: Impressing management by working harder when the supervisor will notice, letting the supervisor know that one is trying to do a good job and is a polite and friendly person

Favoritism   Occurs when a supervisor favors some individuals over others, giving them better and more recognized tasks, for example. These individuals enjoy the manager's confidence and receive higher ratings on their evaluations.

Rater mistakes may vary according to the type of appraisal being performed. One study analyzed more than 57,000 employees evaluations, finding that employee PAs used for administrative purposes were ranked higher than those used for employee development purposes (Jawahar and Williams 1997). The authors concluded that managers intentionally biased their ratings to avoid providing negative feedback to motivate poor performers to be better, and to obtain pay increases for the employee. However, evaluations used for employee development purposes were found to be more accurate; managers wanted to help their employees by being accurate in their appraisal and identifying and correcting their performance deficiencies.

Recognition of these issues is one of the simplest ways to eliminate their impact on the appraisal outcome. Another way to control for some of these common errors is to "design out" the problems. For instance, the halo and the horn effects are caused by interpersonal affect, a cognitive process whereby the rater simply likes or dislikes the individual under review. One way to control this problem is to eliminate subjective performance measures and replace them with more objective measures. Now, ratings would be based on information that have clear and observable performance standards—task-related activities that require raters to make fewer inferences about performance—making them less vulnerable to interpersonal affect (Varma, Denisi, and Peters 1996).

In addition to bias mistakes, environmental issues may affect PA outcomes. Physical distance from the evaluator, for instance, may impact the PA process. Individuals who work in remote locations and have little contact with supervisory personnel may be less satisfied with existing PA methods (Thomas 1999). These employees may perceive the process to be biased and unfair, as managers rarely see them. This may require a different PA process or at least a greater effort by managers to have a greater degree of contact with employees located in remote locations. For example, a security manager may make regular visits to third-shift employees working in remote locations to mitigate this issue.

Conducting Performance Appraisal Meetings

Regardless of which appraisal method is used, some basic issues should be considered. First, employees must be given feedback on their performance through some type of meeting. Although the feedback session may do little to affect the employee's performance per se, one of the major reasons this meeting is important is related to fairness of the process. Although employees should have already been informed of the appraisal process, managers will need to cultivate acceptance of the appraisal system by giving them an understanding of the true goals of PA. Managers also need to review the evaluation criteria prior to reviewing employees' performance. Doing so will decrease levels of conceptual disagreement over the criteria and the definitions of performance being used in the evaluation as well as reduce the anxiety and potential fears employees may have.

One of the keys to PA is to recognize individual differences when conducting PAs. Research has found that individuals who are performing poorly are generally more reluctant to ask for feedback (Northcraft and Ashford 1990). This suggests that when dealing with poor performers, managers will have to go the extra mile to get the individual involved.

Another key to conducting a PA meeting is effective communication between the manager and the individual being evaluated. London, Larsen, and Thisted (1999) write that for performance evaluation to be successful, managers must create an environment in which employees engage in feedback-seeking and self-management activities. An effective manager should begin the meeting in a positive manner and clearly state its purpose. Throughout the meeting, the manager should remain objective and honest and discuss how to improve without blaming the employee for performance. Further, the manager should listen more than talk. The manager should allow the employee to talk candidly, telling the manager what he or she needs to work on.

Effective communication is paramount to an effective appraisal meeting. Kikoski (1999) recommends a multistep microskill approach to conducting PA sessions. These steps are shown in Box 8.6.

BOX 8–6 ■ Effective Communication Microskills

- *Nonverbally attend to the individual through effective body language to encourage open and two-way communication.* Individuals may be fearful of the evaluation process. Managers should recognize how their nonverbal cues, or body language, will affect the appraisal process in both positive and negative ways. A manager may nonverbally attend to the employee by leaning slightly forward, speaking calmly, and maintaining eye contact.

- *Use open and closed questions.* Use nonjudgmental, open-ended questions by beginning with such words as "could," "how" or "what." These words will stimulate discussion: "Could you tell me how you feel about your new responsibilities?" is an open-ended question. Use close-ended questions as a follow-up to clarify, focus, or narrow discussion areas. Close-ended questions usually evoke simple yes/no responses. "Would you be willing to try out this new CCTV system?" is a close-ended question.

- *Paraphrase.* Restate the individual's response in your own words. Paraphrasing lets the person know that you are listening and that you understand the responses. Paraphrasing should be nonjudgmental and factual. "So you're saying that this new equipment has some problems" is an example.

- *Reflect feeling.* Restate in your own words how you perceive someone to be feeling. Use the subordinate's name, an initial stem, a label of the emotion, and a final checking stem. "David, it appears that you are very frustrated with your report writing. Is this correct?" is an example of reflection of feeling.

continued

- *Feedback*. Use this four-step process to convey present-tense statements. Feed-back should always be nonjudgmental and presented in a matter-of-fact for-mat. Feedback should also include a present-tense statement and deal with a correctable issue: "You seem to be too eager when responding to calls for ser-vice. This might be interpreted as aggressive by some people. How can you be more professional when responding to these calls?"

Because one of the primary goals of the PA is to change or improve one's performance, the issues discussed at the meeting need to be transformed into ac-tion. The rater and the ratee must form plans and goals for improving future per-formance. This requires some type of commitment and closure to the meeting to ensure improved performance and personal development.

Following the meeting, some other procedural issues should be consid-ered. Employees should be required to sign the appraisal form(s) to acknowl-edge that an appraisal was conducted and that the information in the appraisal was accurate. The manager should always remember that written performance appraisals are lasting documents that become part of the employee's history with the organization. These documents may be subsequently used for important events in the individual's career. Therefore, the manager must exercise great care and be conscientious when conducting PAs. Organizations may also consider an appeals process for employees. An appeals process will provide a safeguard for employers to prevent unintentional or intentional inaccuracies with the ap-praisal process (Davidson 1995) while ensuring a greater degree of procedural justice for the employee.

■ LEGAL ISSUES IN PERFORMANCE APPRAISAL

One of the key liability issues with PAs is the simple fact that they can be used for or against an employer in a lawsuit. Therefore, managers should be aware that they will need to defend their appraisals and what they wrote in the PA in court. This may mean that, in some cases, appraisals can be a double-edged sword. They can serve as a devastating weapon for the employee who may have been some-how wronged by the employer. They may also serve as an impenetrable shield for the employer (Davidson 1995).

Plaintiffs can seek recovery in the state courts for damages related to PAs. Under a wrongful-discharge suit, a plaintiff can claim that an inaccurate or incom-plete appraisal led to termination with the company. If not a wrongful-discharge claim, a poorly administered or designed appraisal could result in a defamation suit whereby the plaintiff's reputation was somehow damaged as the result of the ap-praisal outcome. A plaintiff who can prove being forced to resign as the result of the performance evaluation can also seek recovery under a claim of constructive discharge, as the evaluation was a pretext for being forced to quit (Davidson 1995).

In the federal courts, a plaintiff can seek damages under Title VII, the ADA, and the ADEA for discrimination in the workplace, whether for a termination, failure to be promoted, or any other employment action that relied on information from the PA. If a plaintiff can successfully demonstrate a prima facie case of discrimination in any facet of the employment relationship as a result of the PA(s), it is the responsibility of the employer to prove a nondiscriminatory reason for the employment decision (Davidson 1995). The standard of proof is often not difficult to attain. In the Supreme Court decision in *Bazemore v. Friday* (1986), Justice Brennan stated that a plaintiff does not need to prove discrimination with scientific certainty but instead only on the "preponderance of evidence."

Research on cases brought before the Federal Court of Appeals has found some common criteria that influence judges' opinions. Judges place emphasis on agreement among the raters when rendering a decision on whether the appraisal process was fair or unfair. Judges also consider whether the employee had the opportunity to review the results and whether the appraisal was based on job analysis. Another key finding was that judges consider due-process issues in the context of the procedural fairness of the PA process or systems they are reviewing. Judges were more concerned about whether the appraisal process was applied fairly rather than about the method used in the appraisal process and were less concerned with issues related to the reliability and the validity of the instruments (Werner and Bolino 1997).

In many situations, claims against existing PA systems have been found to be discriminatory when they were affected by sexual or racial bias, based on subjective and poorly defined criteria. Other claims were based on the fact that information used in the PA was not standardized across individuals, subsequently affecting the reliability and the validity of the process (Clifford 1999). In other cases, plaintiffs have been able to prove that employers intentionally altered PAs as a pretext to terminate the employee. In one case, for example, a company was found to have used white-out correctional fluid to change an employee's evaluations. These negative evaluations were then used as a pretext to terminate this person (Davidson 1995).

Employers can do a number of things to reduce their exposure to claims involving their PA processes. First, supervisors should be trained in all aspects of the PA to ensure that the process is procedurally the same across all employees (Bisom-Rapp 1999). All activities should be described in an objective manner, as the courts examine facts, not opinions. Appraisals should be written in nonambiguous language, and expectations of the employee's performance should be clearly stated (Falcone 1999). As pointed out earlier in this chapter, some managers may not be completely honest and accurate in their employee appraisals and, for a variety of reasons, overrate the employee's performance. If this employee is later terminated or denied a promotion, for example, the appraisal may undercut the legitimacy of the employer's decision in court. The court would question why this high-performing employee was terminated over other, lower performers.

Employers should require that employees sign and receive a copy of their evaluations. This may later serve as a liability shield, as it could be used as evidence that the appraisal was accurate and that the employee was forewarned of poor performance (Davidson 1995). It also demonstrates that the appraisal was not a sword but a supportive "good faith" tool to assist the employee in improving performance. Last, employers must use the process in an ethical manner. If employers view the appraisal as a means to terminate employees instead of helping them, this practice will soon become well-known, defeating all attempts to improve performance through an effective manager/employee exchange of information.

■ CONCLUSION

The PA process should be a partnership, not an adversarial process. The primary objective of a PA is to improve employee performance. It is a process by which the organization collects and processes information related to the performance of its employees. This information can be used as an organizational socialization and control method; it can be used for compensation and promotional decisions; and it can be used as an organizational development tool. Although PAs have several advantages, managers should also be aware of some of the negative aspects, particularly that appraisals might cause increased conflict and competition in the company.

Appraisals must be properly designed. One of the key considerations is the purpose of the appraisal. Whether they are used for evaluative or for developmental purposes, appraisals must be procedurally fair and follow the due-process model. Rewards should also be distributed fairly, based on the information from the appraisal. Besides the concept of justice, employees should be involved in the design of the appraisal process. Other issues to consider in the design stage include the criteria that will be used, employee needs, personalities, and the frequency of appraisals.

This chapter also reviewed and discussed some of the more common types of PAs. Two common appraisal formats are rating and ranking systems. Another appraisal tool is performance management, which is a global approach to PAs. Managers may conduct appraisals; other forms are peer based, team, and self-evaluations. Other appraisals are upward based and may include employees evaluating managers or customers evaluating employees. Appraisals may also use multiple sources in order to properly assess the performance of employees. Two of the most common methods discussed in this chapter are behaviorally anchored rating scales (BARS) and management by objectives (MBO).

The administration of the appraisal is as important as the design. Organizations need to recognize those factors that affect managerial resistance to the program, or performance appraisal discomfort (PAD). Line-level employees may also show signs of resistance, which can be overcome through various managerial activities. Managers need to recognize the ethical treatment of employees during the process, understand that politics may be an issue, and recognize some of the more common mistakes when conducting evaluations. This chapter also provided guidelines for conducting an effective appraisal meeting and the importance of linking the outcomes of the meeting to changes in employee performance.

PAs may be scrutinized by the courts. Employees can file claims in both the federal and state courts under allegations that the performance appraisals were used in an inappropriate manner that negatively impacted an employment decision, including terminations and promotions. One way to prevent these claims is to have a properly designed objective-based program that has clearly defined criteria. The legally sound appraisal is also ethically sound.

■ KEY TERMS

Action research
Activity control
Behaviorally anchored rating scales
 (BARS)
Capability control
Developmental appraisals
Distributive justice
Due-process model
Evaluative appraisals
External Propensity employees
Halo effect
Horn effect
Input-versus output-based appraisals
Instrumental control

Internal Propensity employees
Management by objectives
Multisource feedback
Peer evaluations
Performance appraisal
Performance appraisal discomfort
 (PAD)
Performance management
Procedural justice
Process control
Self-evaluations
Team-based appraisals
Upward feedback

■ DISCUSSION QUESTIONS

1. What are the differences between evaluative and developmental purposes in the performance appraisal process?
2. Review the case study at the beginning of this chapter. What were some of the primary issues that led to the failure of the appraisal process?
3. What is process control? Why is it important?
4. What are the components of the due-process model? Explain the six rules that should be followed.
5. What types of criteria are used in performance appraisals?
6. What are some advantages and disadvantages of peer evaluations?
7. What is the difference between multisource and team-based appraisals?
8. What are the differences between MBO and BARS?
9. What are some primary issues to consider when designing the appraisal program?
10. What is performance appraisal discomfort? How can a manager decrease PAD?

■ REFERENCES

ANTONIONI, D. 1994. The effects of feedback accountability on upward appraisal ratings. *Personnel Psychology* 47 (2): 349-359.

BARCLAY, J. H., and L. K. HARLAND. 1995. Peer performance appraisals: The impact of rater competence, rater location, and rating correctability on fairness perceptions. *Group and Organization Management* 20 (1): 39-61.

BARNEY, J. B., and R. W. GRIFFIN. 1992. *The management of organizations.* Boston: Houghton Mifflin.

BARUCH, Y. 1996. Self-performance appraisal vs. direct manager appraisal: A case of congruence. *Journal of Managerial Psychology* 11 (6): 50-66.

Bazemore v. Friday. 1986. 478 U.S. 385.

BISOM-RAPP, S. 1999. Bulletproofing the workplace: Symbol and substance in employment discrimination law practice. *Florida State University Law Review* 26: 959-1038.

BLAU, G. 1999. Testing the longitudinal impact of work variables and performance appraisal satisfaction on subsequent overall job satisfaction. *Human Relations* 52 (8): 1099-1113.

BOLMAN, L. G., and T. E. DEAL. 1997. *Reframing organizations: Artistry, choice, and leadership.* 2nd ed. San Francisco: Jossey-Bass.

BOSWELL, W. R., and J. W. BOUDREAU. 2000. Employee satisfaction with performance appraisals and appraisers: The role of perceived appraisal use. *Human Resource Development Quarterly* 11 (3): 283-299.

BURNS, J. A. 1996. Use and abuse of performance appraisals. *Employee Relations Law Journal* 22 (2): 165-170.

CHALLAGALLA, G. N. 1996. Dimensions and types of supervisory control: Effects on salesperson performance and satisfaction. *Journal of Marketing* 60 (1): 89-115.

CHEUNG, G. W. 1999. Multifaceted conceptions of self-other ratings disagreement. *Personnel Psychology* 52 (1): 1-30.

CHURCH, A. H., and D. W. BRACKEN. 1997. Advancing the state of the art 360-degree feedback: Guest editors' comments on the research and practice of multirater assessment methods. *Group and Organization Management* 22 (2): 149-162.

CLIFFORD, J. P. 1999. The collective wisdom of the workforce: Conversations with employees regarding performance evaluation. *Public Personnel Management* 28 (1): 119-155.

COOK, M. 1995. Performance appraisal and true performance. *Journal of Managerial Psychology* 10 (7): 3-8.

DALEY, D. M. 1993. Performance appraisal as an aid in personnel decisions: Linkages between techniques and purposes in North Carolina municipalities. *American Review of Public Administration* 23 (3): 201-212.

DAVIDSON, J. E. 1995. The temptation of performance appraisal abuse in employment litigation. *Virginia Law Review Association* 81: 1605-1629.

DELEON, L. 1997. Multi-source performance appraisals. *Review of Public Personnel Administration* 17 (1): 22-36.

FALCONE, P. 1999. Rejuvenate your performance evaluation writing skills. *HRM Magazine* 44 (10): 126-136.

FEDOR, D. B., R. B. RENSVOLD, and S. M. ADAMS. 1992. An investigation of factors expected to affect feedback setting: A longitudinal field study. *Personnel Psychology* 45 (4): 779-805.

FLETCHER, C. 2001. Performance appraisal and management: The developing research agenda. *Journal of Occupational and Organizational Psychology* 74 (4): 473-488.

GABRIS, G. T., and D. M. IHRKE. 2001. Does performance appraisal contribute to heightened levels of employee burnout? The results of one study. *Public Personnel Management* 30 (2): 157-168.

GILBERT, G. R., E. L. HANNAN, and K. B. LOWE. 1998. Is smoking stigma clouding the objectivity of employee performance appraisal? *Public Personnel Management* 27 (3): 285-301.

HALL, J. L., J. K. LEIDECKER, and C. DIMARCO. 1996. What do we know about upward appraisals of management: Facilitating the future use of UPA's. *Human Resource Development Quarterly* 7 (3): 209-226.

HEDGE, J. W., and M. S. TEACHOUT. 2000. Exploring the concept of acceptability as a criterion for evaluating performance measures. *Group and Organization Management* 25 (1): 22-44.

HEROLD, D. M., C. K. PARSONS, and R. B. RENSVOLD. 1996. Individual differences in the generation and processing of performance feedback. *Educational and Psychological Measurement* 56 (1): 5-22.

HITCHCOCK, D. 1996. What are people doing around peer review? *Journal for Quality and Participation* 19 (7): 52-55.

JAWAHAR, I. M., and C. R. WILLIAMS. 1997. Where all the children are above average: The performance appraisal purpose effect. *Personnel Psychology* 50 (4): 905-926.

KENNEDY, M. M. 1999. The case for performance appraisals. *Across the Board* 36 (2): 51-52.

KIKOSKI, J. F. 1999. Effective communication in the performance appraisal interview: Face to face communication for public managers in the culturally diverse workplace. *Public Personnel Management* 28 (2): 301-322.

KOLB, J. A. 1995. Leader behaviors affecting team performance: Similarities and differences between leader/member assessments. *Journal of Business Communication* 32 (3): 233-251.

KORSGAARD, M. A., and L. ROBERSON. 1995. Procedural justice in performance evaluation: The role of instrumental and non-instrumental voice in performance appraisal discussions. *Journal of Management* 21 (4): 657-670.

LATHAM, G. P., and K. N. WEXLEY. 1994. *Increasing productivity through performance appraisal.* 2nd ed. Reading, MA: Addison-Wesley.

LIND E. A., and T. TAYLOR. 1988. *The social psychology of procedural justice.* New York: Plenum.

LEE, C. 1996. Performance appraisal: Can we "manage" away the curse? *Training* 33 (44): 10.

LONDON, M. 1995. Can multi-source feedback change perceptions of goal accomplishment, self-evaluations, and performance-related outcomes? Theory-based applications and directions for research. *Personnel Psychology* 48 (4): 803–832.

LONDON, M., H. H. LARSEN, and L. H. THISTED. 1999. Relationships between feedback and self-development. *Group and Organization Management* 24 (1): 5–27.

MARLOW, E., and R. SCHILHAVY. Expectation issues in management by objectives programs. *Industrial management* 33 (1): 29–32.

MCBEY, K. 1994. Performing performance appraisals. *Security Management* 38 (11): 23–26.

MILLER, V. D. 1996. An experimental study of newcomers' information seeking behaviors during organizational entry. *Communication Studies* 47 (1–2): 1–33.

MORRISON, E. W. 1993. Newcomer information seeking: Exploring types, modes, source. *Academy of Management Journal* 36 (3): 557–589.

MURPHY, K. J. 1993. Performance measurement and appraisal: Merck tries to motivate managers to do it right. *Employment Relations Today* 20 (1): 47–63.

NORTHCRAFT, G. B., and S. ASHFORD. 1990. The preservation of self in everyday life: The effects of performance expectations and feedback context on feedback inquiry. *Organizational Behavior and Human Decision Processes* 47: 42–64.

ORPEN, C. 1997. Performance appraisal techniques, task types and effectiveness: A contingency approach. *Journal of Applied Management Studies* 6 (2): 139–148.

PETTIJOHN, C. E., L. S. PETTIJOHN, and M. D'AMICO. 2001. Characteristics of performance appraisals and their impact on sales force satisfaction. *Human Resource Development Quarterly* 12 (2): 127–146.

POLLACK, D. M., and L. J. POLLACK. 1996. Using 360-degree feedback in performance appraisal. *Public Personnel Management* 25 (4): 507–529.

RAMSEY, R. D. 1998. How to write better employee evaluations. *Supervision* 59 (6): 5–7.

REES, F. 1999. Reaching high levels of performance through team self-evaluation. *Journal for Quality and Participation* 22 (4): 37–39.

ROBERTS, G. E. 1998. Perspective on enduring and emerging issues in performance appraisal. *Public Personnel Management* 27 (3): 301–321.

ROBINSON, R. K., R. L. FINK, and B. M. ALLEN. 1996. The influence of constituent groups on rater attitudes toward performance appraisal compliance. *Public Personnel Management* 25 (2): 141–151.

ROMANI, P. N. 1997. MBO by another name is still MBO. *Supervision* 58 (12): 6–8.

SCHWARTZWALD, J., M. KOSLOWSKY, and T. MAGER-BIBI. 1999. Peer ratings versus peer nominations during training as predictors of actual performance criteria. *Journal of Applied Behavioral Science* 35 (3): 360–372.

SCOTT, S. G., and W. O. EINSTEIN. 2001. Strategic performance appraisal in team-based organizations: One size does not fit all. *Academy of Management Executive* 15 (2): 107–116.

SMITH, B. N., J. S. HORNSBY, and R. SHIRMEYER. 1996. Current trends in performance appraisal: An examination of managerial practice. *SAM Advanced Management Journal* 61 (3): 10–16.

SMITH, K., V. HARRINGTON, and J. D. HOUGHTON. 2000. Predictors of performance appraisal discomfort: A preliminary examination. *Public Personnel Management* 29 (1): 21–31.

TAYLOR, A. J., L. S. PETTIJOHN, and C. E. PETTIJOHN. 1999. Salespersons and sales managers: A descriptive study of topics and perceptions of retail sale performance appraisals. *Human Resource Development Quarterly* 10 (3): 271–291.

TAYLOR, M. S., K. B. TRACY, M. K. RENARD, J. K. HARRISON, and S. J. CARROLL. 1995. Due process in performance appraisal: A quasi-experiment in procedural justice. *Administrative Science Quarterly* 40 (3): 495–424.

THOMAS, G. E. 1999. Leaderless supervision and performance appraisal: A proposed research agenda. *Human Resource Development Quarterly* 10 (1): 91–94.

THOMAS, S. L. 1997. Performance appraisals: Any use for training? *Business Forum* 22 (1): 29–32.

VARMA, A., A. S. DENISI, and L. H. PETERS. 1996. Interpersonal affect and performance appraisal: A field study. *Personnel Psychology* 49 (2): 341–361.

VINSON, M. N. 1996. The pros and cons of 360-degree feedback: Making it work. *Training and Development* 50 (4): 11–13.

WALTON, M. 1986. *The Deming management method*. New York: Perigee.

WELLS, S. J. 1999. A new road: Travelling beyond 360-degree evaluation. *HRM Magazine* 44 (9): 82–91.

WERNER, J. M., and M. C. BOLINO. 1997. Explaining U.S. court of appeals decisions involving performance appraisal: Accuracy, fairness and validation. *Personnel Psychology* 50 (1): 1–24.

WESTERMAN, J. W., and J. G. ROSSE. 1997. Reducing the threat of rater nonparticipation in 360-degree feedback systems: An exploratory examination of antecedents to participation in upward ratings. *Group and Organizational Management* 22 (2): 288–310.

ZIGON, J. 1994. Making the performance appraisal work for teams. *Training* 31 (6): 58–64.

chapter nine

Discipline and Discharge

In any organization, employees engage in deviant or unacceptable activities that may violate formal and informal organizational norms, policies and procedures, and relevant legislation, such as OSHA regulations, governing the organization. These activities can be categorized as "employee deviance." According to Kaplan (1975, 62), employee deviance is "behavior that violates significant organizational norms and in so doing threatens the well being of an organization, its members or both. Employee deviance is voluntary in that employees either lack the motivation to normative expectations of the social context or become motivated to violate expectations."

Some research has attempted to ascertain the extent and degree of workplace deviance. One study revealed that between 35 percent and 75 percent of the employees studied had engaged in theft, computer fraud, embezzlement, vandalism, sabotage, and absenteeism (Harper 1990). Other researchers have examined the extensive use of alcohol, controlled substances, and other counterproductive behaviors against the organization, including not working while "on the clock" and producing low-quality, low-output products (Hamper 1991). The literature and research on violence in the workplace—see, for instance, Lord 1998; Lucerno and Allen 1998—further illustrates the scope and severity of workplace deviance in organizations. These and other counterproductive behaviors threaten both the company and its employees.

Although deviant behaviors are broad in range, they generally vary along the dimensions of minor versus serious, and interpersonal versus organizational.

Robinson and Bennett (1995) have further divided deviant behaviors into four distinct categories:

1. *Production deviance*: Behaviors that violate the formally proscribed norms delineating the minimal quality and quantity of work to be accomplished
2. *Property deviance*: Unauthorized employee acquisition or damage of the tangible property or assets of the work organization
3. *Political deviance*: Minor and interpersonally harmful deviant behavior; social interactions that put other individuals at a personal or political disadvantage
4. *Personal aggression*: Serious and interpersonally harmful deviant behavior; behaving in an aggressive or hostile manner toward other individuals.

One of the keys to controlling deviant workplace behaviors while improving the quality of life of the worker and organizational health is to have a properly designed and administered disciplinary program. Such a program will reduce deviant behaviors, subsequently increasing the quality of work life for the employee and enhancing the profitability of the organization.

Perhaps one of the most difficult responsibilities of the security manager is to enforce work rules and the policies and procedures established by the organization in a fair and equitable manner to control organizational deviance. The way the security manager addresses the disciplinary process could greatly enhance this person's effectiveness as a supervisor, for discipline is an important component of an effective and positive employee/management relations program. Conversely, if discipline is not handled effectively, organizational effectiveness and the supervisor's reputation and authority could be undermined.

This chapter focuses on the principles and philosophy of the disciplinary process, as well as guidelines for developing, administering, and maintaining a disciplinary program. Issues related to the discharge process are also analyzed. Legal issues involving discipline and discharge are presented in the context of reducing the organization's exposure to liability when terminating an employment relationship.

■ DEFINING DISCIPLINE

All definitions related to the concept and the practice of discipline share the common theme that, regardless of its type, discipline is a corrective action designed to bring about a change in an individual's behavior (Bielous 1993). Besides developing positive changes in an individual's behavior, effective discipline increases and builds personal commitment to achieving and maintaining organizational procedures, rules, and objectives. An effective disciplinary program sets and controls standards of behavior in the organization to ensure conformity, as well as to build group cohesiveness through the establishment of normative structures of conduct in the workplace.

An employer can impose two types of discipline on an employee. With the use of summary actions, the employer focuses on punishing or correcting past behavior by using corrective strategies, such as warnings and suspensions (Employee Discipline . . . 1987). The employer may also use forms of corrective actions that attempt to alter future behaviors through the application of various remedial sanctions, including employee counseling.

Discipline exists in both negative and positive paradigms. Most organizations rely on the punitive model, whereby the corrective actions taken by management are negative and are meant to correct a problem or a deficiency. Instead of correcting the problem, however, this form of discipline may have unintentional effects against the organization. For example, the corrective action against the individual may be perceived only as punishment, with no beneficial outcome. Hence, this paradigm often results in antagonizing and instilling fear in employees instead of motivating them and changing work practices and behaviors in a positive fashion.

Disciplinary issues are often considered only "problems," not opportunities, for organizations. This belief, however, limits some of the positive attributes that disciplinary problems bring to the firm. A learning organization can look at disciplinary problems in the context that they will educate the organization on the particular needs or issues it must address. Other positive aspects are that employee deviance may provide a safety valve for the employees, and it may serve to enhance teamwork and esprit de corps, alerting group members to recognize their common interests. Disciplinary problems also provide a warning sign to the organization of particular problems, or "hot spots," that must be addressed (Robinson and Bennett 1995).

Discipline must be consistent with the underlying philosophy of the organization. With the introduction and increase of employee empowerment, combined with progressive management principles and practices and subsequent organizational changes, the role of the employee and the manager and the philosophy of discipline will change. Now, nonpunitive forms of discipline lead and encourage workers to be more committed to the organization. Instead of coercive techniques, these nonpunitive forms of discipline will correct employees' deficiencies while improving their work ethic, self-esteem, and commitment to the organization.

Effective discipline is both formal and informal, existing on both organizational and personal levels. In its formal capacity, discipline exists in written policies and procedures, collective bargaining agreements, and relevant legislation. In its informal context, discipline occurs through the establishment of normative behaviors by employees and groups of employees. These informal workplace codes of conduct, work rules, and production norms reinforce the official disciplinary programs. Organizationally, the company sets forth those expected actions and standards it expects of its employees. On a personal level, however, discipline is a self-initiated process that originates with the employee and is positively reinforced through the actions of the organization and management.

The establishment of an effective disciplinary program is of paramount importance for the organization and management. Without a disciplinary program that is aligned with the core philosophy of the organization, a discipline program could impair productivity and decrease morale in the workforce. For example, an organization may have rigid policies and procedures that clearly dictate what corrective actions or penalties will be applied for failing to adhere to established standards. Yet this same organization may call for creativity and experimentation in the workplace. With creativity and experimentation, however, workers may make mistakes. Hence, the disciplinary program is inconsistent with the organization's philosophy, and creativity and experimentation will be limited or not occur, out of fear of punishment.

Conversely, a team-based, or employee-empowered, organization will need a different disciplinary program, one that meets the open management style and organizational philosophy. This is the difficult responsibility of the organization: to establish and maintain a disciplinary program that balances the needs of the organization with the needs of the workforce.

Progressive Discipline

Progressive discipline means that the organization and management address disciplinary problems or concerns through a fair and equitable approach. Usually, the organization responds to the first offense with a minimal form of discipline, dealing with subsequent offenses with more serious corrective actions, up to and including dismissal, if necessary. Progressive discipline does not mean that all offenses are dealt with in the same manner. In some situations, an offense may be so serious that the disciplinary measure entails no progression. For example, an employee who commits a serious violent crime against a coworker while on duty would most likely be terminated. In other, less serious situations, such as a person who is late for work, the progression of disciplinary measures would likely start with a verbal warning. The fundamental goal of progressive discipline is to detect and correct problems early to avoid more serious or pressing employee problems later on.

According to Falcone (1997), the process of progressive discipline begins with the recruitment process and continues throughout the employee's orientation process, training, performance evaluations, and day-to-day activities. An effective program will also ensure that disciplinary actions are conducted in a timely manner and that employees are given a reasonable period of time in which to improve their performance (Falcone 1997).

A progressive discipline program, if properly designed and applied, serves many functions for both the employee and the organization. Besides helping to correct employee behavior, the progressive disciplinary program or system, according to Bernardi (1996), keeps employees' conduct within acceptable standards, deters other employees from engaging in similar behaviors, and maintains control in the workplace. Discipline, in effect, becomes a positive means to meet organizational objectives, educate the employee, and provide a source of guidance for employee actions and conduct in the workplace (Falcone 1997). Progressive discipline is not the responsibility of one individual or department in the organization but rather the responsibility of the entire organization.

A properly designed progressive disciplinary program will also ensure a degree of industrial due process for the employee. Many of the rights that individuals enjoy as citizens do not carry over into the workplace. Free speech or expression, a First Amendment right that individuals enjoy outside the workplace, and in public-sector employment, to a degree, is not a right that an individual can freely exercise in the workplace. Instead, codes of conduct and policies and procedures dictate what an employee can do.

In order for the disciplinary program to be effective in the context of due process, employees must have a clear understanding of the employer's expectations and the consequences of not following established policies and procedures. The employer must also show consistency in the application of discipline. Workers have the right to consistent and predictable employer actions when a rule is violated. Arbitrary, unreasonable, and discriminatory practices by the employer will decrease morale, increase employee turnover, expose the organization to lawsuits, and reduce the credibility of the supervisor, employer, or organization (Falcone 1997).

Depending on the needs of the organization, a progressive disciplinary process may include several stages, progressing from less to more serious threats to the employment relationship. These stages are shown in Figure 9–1.

Counseling   Employee counseling occurs on a daily basis and is designed to identify and solve employee performance issues, weaknesses, and behavioral problems. Counseling also helps the employee overcome differences with other employees and the organization, ranging from individual or personal problems to social relationships in and outside the workplace. The goal of counseling is to address issues before they grow more complicated (see McConnell 1997).

Unlike other forms of discipline, counseling can be positive, as the manager helps the employee reveal hidden strengths and attributes. Counseling therefore serves as a means of personal growth and fulfillment in the workplace. Depending on the organization, a host of counseling alternatives may be available to the employee.

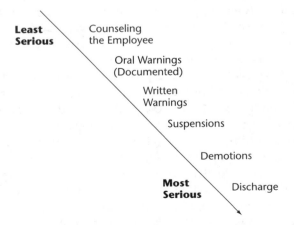

FIGURE 9–1 ■ The Progressive Discipline Process

Oral Reprimands   Oral reprimands are verbal forms of discipline used to address minor infractions in the workplace. Although it is an informal disciplinary procedure, an oral reprimand should clearly explain the nature of the deficiency, include clear standards for acceptable performance and expectations, request cooperation from the employee, and delineate further consequences if the problem persists. An oral warning should always be documented with an informal note summarizing the reprimand (Ramsey 1998).

Written Warnings   The next stage in the progressive disciplinary process is a written warning, which is used for more severe or repetitive problems. This written warning should include the following elements:

- A description of the events/problem: a statement about the basis of the reprimand, such as complaints or observations
- An explanation of the negative results of the problem
- A statement of what is expected of the employee and what the supervisor is willing to do to help the employee correct the behavior
- A future date for reviewing the employee's behaviors

Unlike the oral warning or reprimand, the warning should be written on the organization's letterhead, and a copy should be given to the employee (Ramsey 1998). This letter should be kept in the employee's personnel file in order to maintain an accurate disciplinary record and to serve as a link in the progressive disciplinary process, if needed at a later time.

Suspensions   A suspension is the temporary removal of an individual from the organization. This serious message tells the employee that continued employment with the organization is in jeopardy. Depending on established policies and procedures, existing union contracts, and other forms of documentation that delineate the employment relationship, suspensions may be with or without pay. Organizational policies or collective bargaining agreements may specify a set time period for a suspension. In other cases, the length of a suspension may vary, pending the timely outcome of an investigation.

Demotions   A demotion is the temporary or permanent move of an individual to a lower position within the organization. Demotions occur when other forms of progressive discipline have not produced successful changes in the behavior or attitude of the employee. Demotions take several forms, depending on the existing organizational policies: a reduction in the degree of responsibility, a stripping of the individual's title and/or formal status, or a reassignment to a position requiring less skill or responsibilities.

Transfers   A transfer occurs when an individual is moved from one location to another in the organization. Transfers can be forced or voluntary. In lateral transfers, the individual does not lose any pay, status, or benefits. Other types of transfers, however, involve a loss of status, pay, and/or other benefits.

The transfer serves several purposes. One is to move the individual to a more controlling environment in which behaviors can be observed more closely. Another reason is to remove the employee from issues or factors that were determined to impede or negatively affect performance. An individual may also be transferred because of problems with other employees in a particular environment.

One of the problems with transfers, however, is that it may appear to be a "secret process," as other employees may not understand the actions of the employer. At the same time, some employees may perceive that the individual is being rewarded rather than punished and is being transferred to a better position or location in the organization. Another problem is that the organization may simply transfer the employee and not investigate the underlying causes that led to the corrective action. In such a case, the problem employee may continue to engage in the same or similar derogatory behaviors and actions that led to the disciplinary transfer.

Terminations/Dismissals A termination is the permanent removal of the individual from employment with the organization. Terminations are the most severe of disciplinary measures and are used as a last resort when all other forms of progressive discipline have been exhausted or have proved not to change the behaviors or attitudes of the employee. Termination guidelines are discussed in detail later in this chapter.

Positive Discipline

Unlike normal disciplinary procedures that rely on coercive methods, or penalties, the goal of positive discipline is to correct future behavior rather than punish previous behaviors, to educate employees, and make individuals accountable for their actions. Under a positive disciplinary program, the employee may be reminded of existing company policies or work standards while being asked by management for "assistance" in solving the disciplinary problem.

Under positive forms of discipline, the employee "learns" from the experience and changes the behavior in a positive manner. These changes could have a large impact on the organization. For example, General Electric's Meter Business Department's program of positive discipline has resulted in increases in employee morale and the amount of positive contact with workers. The program has also improved supervisors' levels of self-confidence and problem solving and has reduced the number of employee terminations and disciplinary problems (Bryant 1984).

An organization can use two types of positive discipline: decision days and decisional leaves (see Sunco 1996).

Decision Days Decision days occur when an employee with a disciplinary problem is given a day off by the employer. During this time off, the employee is instructed to reflect on and decide whether to solve and correct the problem(s) immediately and return to work with a commitment to perform up to the standards established by the organization. Although one may conclude that this is a suspension, the underlying intentions between the two differ. Decision days are based on correcting a problem. Suspensions are based on punishing the individual for a particular infraction.

Decisional Leave   This is similar to decision days in that employees are given a day off to reflect on their commitment to the organization. Unlike decision days, however, decisional leave days also require the employee to come back to work with a written plan for changing the behavior. The employee may be required to address such questions as the importance of the job for the employee, the impact on the employee of losing the job and what the employee is willing to do to keep the job. The written plan should also include a statement on how the employee will ensure that the disciplinary problem will not occur again.

Depending on the policies of the organization, decision days or decisional leaves can be time off with or without pay. One problem with paid days is that some employees may resent that the organization is allowing an employee with disciplinary problems to have a day off with pay. The organization should also consider that the employee facing positive forms of discipline may be exploiting the organization. An employee who wants to take a day off but does not want to use vacation time could cause a disciplinary problem that would result in the employer's granting a decision day or a decisional leave.

Positive discipline could also include problems about the competence of the supervisor and the employee. The organization will have to change the philosophy behind "discipline," which will require supervisors to be trained in the principles of positive discipline and counseling techniques. Positive discipline could also have negative effects on employees. Employees who lack effective writing skills may not be able to write letters of commitment. Instead of a "positive" form of discipline, this employee may perceive it to be humiliating and punitive, leading to an increased level of frustration with the organization. If the organization operates in a union environment, the union may assert that positive discipline programs limit or eliminate the union's role in assisting the employee in disciplinary actions (Sunco 1996).

The use of positive discipline will require employers to develop and educate their managerial staff on coaching and counseling techniques. No longer will employers be responsible simply for punishing the employee for their infractions. Instead, employers will have to use counseling techniques, including meeting with the employee, to determine the root cause of the disciplinary problem.

■ CREATING AND DESIGNING THE DISCIPLINARY PROGRAM

Several issues must be considered in developing, redesigning, or modifying an organization's disciplinary program. Does the program coincide with the existing organizational culture? Is the disciplinary program legal? Are the components of the program enforceable?

At the same time, as it is designed to assist the employee's performance and level of satisfaction in the organization, the disciplinary program should be created or established with employee input. Having employees involved in the design and implementation of the disciplinary program makes them interested stakeholders in the implementation and enforcement of the company's policies and regulations. Employee involvement in the design of the disciplinary program will also increase the level of commitment to the rules. If they were involved in the design of the rules, employees will most likely be more committed to upholding them.

Organizational Culture and Philosophy   The organization must consider matching the disciplinary program with its existing culture to ensure a proper "fit" between the two. For example, if the organization expounds that it is a learning organization that values risk taking and experimentation, the disciplinary program should not punish individuals for making some work-related errors. Many organizations also support and promote a teamwork orientation in the workplace. These self-managed teams may have several responsibilities, including scheduling assignments, quality control, and training. Included in establishing a teamwork philosophy is the subsequent empowerment of employees to assume some of the supervisory responsibilities, including discipline, that were once relegated to middle management. Now employees will take over the traditional responsibilities of management, including discipline.

Legal Considerations   The disciplinary program must be consistent with relevant legislation and case law, existing collective-bargaining agreements, and any other contracts between the employer and employee. Title VII of the Civil Rights Act of 1964 prohibits discriminatory actions by an employer in any employment practice. Disciplinary activities are employment practices in that the outcomes could raise a claim of disparate treatment against an employee or of disparate impact against a group of employees affected by the outcomes of the disciplinary process. If it operates in a union setting, the organization must ensure that disciplinary activities also follow the collective-bargaining agreement and do not cause any unfair labor practices against employees.

Enforceability   The employer should realize that parts of the disciplinary program may contain unenforceable policies or rules. The inability to enforce work rules can be attributed to the fact that they are outdated and have not been modified to meet current organizational needs. In other instances, the rules may be difficult to interpret because they are too vague.

One example is a company's blanket policy that "hearing and eye protection shall be worn on the shop floor." Although safety is a fundamental concern for the employee and the organization, a vague work rule such as this one may be difficult to enforce. First, does the policy apply to all employees or only those line-level employees on the shop floor? What about visitors? Second, how does the organization designate "shop floor": Is it the entire organization or limited areas? Third, what constitutes appropriate ear and eye protection?

These unenforceable policies or rules will lead to confusion and conflict over their interpretation, as well as to apathetic attitudes toward discipline by managers and employees alike. A simple rule to avoid this problem is the following: If the policy cannot be enforced on a consistent and fair basis, management should reevaluate and subsequently eliminate or redesign the policy to ensure enforceability. Without such modifications, particular policies in the disciplinary program could be detrimental, devaluate the entire disciplinary program in the process, and expose the organization to unnecessary liability.

■ ADMINISTERING THE DISCIPLINARY PROGRAM

The underlying objective in designing a disciplinary program is to create and maintain a motivated and productive workforce; protect organizational assets, including employees, and ensure steady and quality production levels in the firm. The administration of the program must ensure that these program goals are achieved. To accomplish this, the organization must address some fundamental issues in administering the disciplinary program.

Responsibility for Discipline

Responsibility for discipline varies according to organizational culture and philosophy, management styles, and existing policies and procedures. The traditional paradigm of discipline typically dictated that the first-line, or direct, supervisor was responsible for the application and enforcement of the organization's disciplinary program. As an outgrowth of this paradigm, discipline and disciplinary programs have been considered to be an operational—related to the production needs of the facility—rather than a strategic function (Raper and Myaya 1993). This limited operational approach to discipline has made some organizations fail to realize the intrinsic and indirect values of a properly designed and administered disciplinary program.

Another paradigm related to the administration and enforcement of disciplinary procedures is that everyone in the organization is responsible for discipline. This strategic paradigm shifts the concept of discipline from a truly operational function to one that incorporates discipline into the overall strategy and, hence, effectiveness of the organization. For example, some individuals call for the use of concertive control methods to increase organizational discipline. Concertive control, unlike the traditional operational paradigms, calls for work teams to set normative standards of conduct. Using the existing core values of the organization, these employees set normative standards by negotiating and reaching consensus on how to shape their behaviors to meet organizational goals. As indicated by Sewell (1998, 408), this results in employees' changing their attitude from "we do it because the rules say so"— an operational paradigm—to "we do it because it is right/good/proper"— a strategic paradigm.

The Manager's Role in the Disciplinary Program

Regardless of whether an organization views discipline from an operational or a strategic perspective, responsibility for the administration of discipline ultimately falls on the manager. Management is responsible for accepting the disciplinarian role, counseling employees on issues associated with discipline, and clearly communicating the disciplinary program and goals of the organization. Managers are also responsible for ensuring fairness in the disciplinary program.

Accepting Supervisory Responsibility   In many organizations, individuals assigned or promoted to management positions may lack those requisite management and leadership skills needed to excel in their positions. Therefore, new managers may be unsure of how to act in some situations, out of the fear or apprehension of making a mistake. This may be particularly apparent in administering the disciplinary program, which is an often overlooked but greatly needed skill for managers.

Managers need to accept their particular role and responsibility in enforcing and maintaining discipline. In many cases, however, this does not happen, and managers engage in "discipline apprehension," failing to act in an appropriate manner when needed. The failure to take appropriate actions can be attributed to the fact that discipline is associated only with rule violations; confronting those who violated the rules and imposing sanctions may be an uncomfortable experience. Another reason for discipline apprehension may be that more senior individuals in the organization are responsible for discipline-related tasks. Through proper organizational development strategies—training—however, the degree of disciplinary apprehension can be reduced, making the manager an effective component of the disciplinary process.

Coaching and Counseling   Coaching and counseling are important for not only training but also the disciplinary process. Coaching involves helping employees grow in their competence on the job on a daily basis. As a coach, the manager uses positive reinforcement and feedback to set challenging goals and educate employees on organizational expectations. The coach also evaluates employees' progress toward meeting the organizational goals (French 1994).

Coaching is different from counseling. Coaching concentrates on job performance, whereas counseling focuses on potential or existing problems. A security manager who trains a new officer in community and customer relations is performing a coaching function. If this same officer has received some complaints from customers about attitude or demeanor, the manager is performing a counseling function when addressing this disciplinary issue.

Individual- and organizational-based impediments related to coaching and counseling exist. On an individual basis, personal issues may impair the manager's coaching and counseling abilities. First, the manager may lack training in coaching and counseling. Second, the manager may be sympathetic to the employee's problems. Third, friendship with coworkers and the fear of, or intimidation by, employees may also mitigate the manager's coaching and counseling activities (McConnell 1997).

Organizational barriers may exacerbate other problems associated with coaching and counseling. One common organizational barrier may be time pressures that limit the quality and degree of coaching and counseling a manager can provide. Just as managers may be discipline averse, so too may the culture of the organization.

To counteract both individual and organizationally based impediments to the discipline process, training is essential. Any basic training program related to counseling and coaching should include a review of all policies and procedures in the organization and appropriate disciplinary measures that can be used in various circumstances. Managers should also be trained on the positive aspects of discipline. Basic communication skills, including empathetic and active listening skills, should be stressed in the training program to ensure the positive interchange of information between managers and employees.

Communication and Consistency   The managers of the organization must clearly transmit work rules and standards before employees can be expected to meet them. The work rules, policies and procedures, OSHA requirements, and other governmental and regulatory codes that affect the employee's job performance need to be written and published in employee handbooks and periodically reviewed at briefings, training sessions, and other times as established by managers or the company. Components of the disciplinary program can also be "taught" by managers on a daily basis. Managers should serve as role models, "acting by example," to their employees by following and adhering to their organization's rules. If managers violated rules or established their own de facto policies that conflicted with organizational rules, the legitimacy of the disciplinary program would decrease in the eyes of the employees.

Management must also apply work rules and disciplinary measures consistently to all employees. For rules to be considered fair and equitable by employees, similar behaviors should be rewarded and disciplined on an equal basis. Without the consistent application of rules and performance standards, the organization may face a costly and embarrassing lawsuit, as discussed in detail later in this chapter.

Guiding Principles

Fairness   The workplace disciplinary program must be firm but fair, striking a balance between the needs of the organization and those of the employee. In order to achieve this balance, the program should ensure that the rules are non-confrontational and written with the employee's welfare in mind.

The organization should inform employees of the reasons for limiting some activities and explain that, as members of a group, the employees must act according to group norms or standards (Levine 1998). The ramifications and sanctions for violating rules should be consistent for all employees and not harsh.

Related to the concept of progressive discipline, Levine (1998) recommends that offenses be graded according to their degree of seriousness and that employees be penalized for accumulated rule infractions rather than for single acts.

Procedural Guidelines Managers must follow existing procedures established by the organization for handling disciplinary cases. Coupled with procedural compliance, managers should ensure that due-process issues were adhered to by guaranteeing that all applicable policies in the organization's procedures that deal with discipline and discharge were properly followed. According to Ramsey 1998), other due-process considerations for the employee may include the following:

- The right to notice
- The right to a hearing
- The right to representation
- The right to review evidence
- The right to call witnesses
- The right to cross-examine
- The right to a written response to the allegation(s)

Appropriate Level of Discipline As previously discussed, the underlying philosophy of the progressive disciplinary program is that violations perceived as minor should not be sanctioned as harshly as violations considered serious. Although there are no hard-and-fast rules for determining what the appropriate disciplinary measure should be, consideration needs to be given to the seriousness of the offense, existing personnel policies, and past disciplinary or corrective measures for similar past offenses. Guidelines set forth in collective-bargaining agreements, prior arbitration, and court decisions may also serve as guidelines. Of paramount importance, however, is that corrective actions taken by management must be tied to the offense and not to the employee. Individuals are disciplined for job-related activities, not for personal differences or biases a manager may have.

Documentation All employee disciplinary issues must be thoroughly and properly documented to establish a clear and concise chain of evidence, proving that the employee did violate employment rules and regulations. A general rule of thumb is that if the activity was never documented, it never happened. It is also important to document management actions to correct the problem(s) that were discovered.

■ CONDUCTING DISCIPLINARY INVESTIGATIONS

The purpose of a disciplinary investigation is to collect evidence to substantiate, verify, or invalidate disciplinary issues. In order to accomplish this objective, the investigator must first adequately plan the investigation. By creating a proper foundation for the disciplinary investigation, the investigator has a rudimentary road map to follow through the course of the investigation. Some of the basic issues the investigator must consider are the who, what, when, where, and why of the investigation.

The importance of an investigation can be seen in the case of Lois, a problem employee who, over the past few months, has been displaying aggressive behaviors toward her coworkers. She has verbally intimidated junior associates, slammed doors, refused to help coworkers, and spread false rumors about the performance and attitudes of other employees.

On the surface, Lois appears to have a "bad attitude," which perhaps justifies her termination. However, a thorough investigation of the reported incidents, including an interview with Lois, revealed that she has a severe alcohol-dependency problem coupled with chronic depression. Based on company policy, Lois was sent to the organization's Employee Assistance Program (EAP), which offered a number of services. The agreed on 60-day review of her progress showed that Lois was again meeting and exceeding her expected performance levels in the organization. No new complaints have been lodged against Lois by her coworkers or managers.

This example provides insight into the importance of conducting a thorough disciplinary investigation. First, if a thorough investigation had not been conducted in this example, Lois probably would have been fired. Second, when investigating disciplinary issues, the organization should keep in mind that the violation of a company rule or policy can be a symptom of another, deeper problem. As a consequence, mere punishment for the infraction may not result in corrective behaviors by the violator. Instead, a progressive manager should look for symptoms or causes of the violation and then take corrective actions to eliminate the cause of the problem.

Regardless of the violation that is being investigated, some basic rules should be followed. Of primary importance is that the investigation is objective and conducted in a fair manner. An objective investigation will ensure that the information collected is factual and supports or refutes the disciplinary issue. This factor is concerned primarily with procedural aspects and the collection of information. The second point, fairness, is concerned with the subjective interpretation of the individual(s) under investigation and the coworkers. In the majority of disciplinary investigations, employees are not terminated, so the manager and the employee will still have a relationship "after the fact." An investigation perceived to be biased and unfair could have some serious long- and short-term ramifications for the disciplinary program, managers, and the organization as a whole.

The issue of objectivity and fairness will also require consistency across investigations. By following the same procedures in every investigation, the organization will show that it takes all complaints and issues seriously and prove that it did not engage in any unethical practices while maintaining the integrity of the disciplinary program. The concept of fairness may also require that the employee be included in the investigation by being given an opportunity to explain the facts and present other relevant information.

Basic Issues

Who Is Responsible for Investigations?   The answer to this question varies by organization and is contingent on existing policies it has established for conducting investigations. Regardless of who conducts the investigations, the organization needs to designate the investigator(s) in advance. Investigations may be carried out by direct supervisors, representatives from the human resource department, impartial committees, and individuals who have some degree of personal, and perhaps professional, separation from the individual under investigation.

In order to assess who the most appropriate individual is to conduct the investigation, several factors should be considered. To ensure that the investigation is objective and free from all personal bias and prejudice against the person being investigated, the investigator or team of investigators needs to be impartial. Therefore, the organization must be aware that other individuals may be aggravating factors in the employee's behavior. For example, the individual's direct supervisor may be a factor in the disciplinary problem. Hence, the organization may determine that it would be improper to have the investigation carried out by that individual directly associated with the employee in question.

What Should Be Investigated?   The next consideration is what disciplinary problems should be investigated and to what extent. A general principle is that every disciplinary issue should be properly investigated and documented, with those disciplinary actions determined to be serious receiving a more in-depth investigation than disciplinary issues determined to be minor.

Two points should be considered. First, investigations should be based on the type of infraction that occurred. This means that the scope and the depth of the investigation of a particular offense, such as alcohol consumption on the job, must be equal in the context of the investigation's scope and depth from one case to another. If not, issues related to objectivity and fairness could arise. Second, because the courts could scrutinize the investigatory process and subsequent disciplinary action(s), the depth of investigation should, at a minimum, ensure that the civil law's standard of the preponderance of evidence was achieved. This standard requires that the evidence collected must have greater weight or be more convincing or credible than evidence that is offered in opposition to the evidence collected.

To ensure a greater degree of objectivity and fairness, the depth of investigation may also coincide with the criminal court's standard of beyond a reasonable doubt, especially if the organization is investigating a case that could result in criminal charges against the employee(s). This criterion is much more stringent than that of preponderance of evidence. According to this criterion, a prudent person who analyzed the facts of the case would have no doubt that the facts did prove that the individual was guilty of the issue(s).

When Should the Investigation Be Conducted?   Disciplinary problems, regardless of whether they are minor, should be investigated as soon as reasonably possible and practical. A prompt investigation will ensure that the organization will be able to collect and preserve evidence necessary to render a decision. If the investigation is delayed, some physical evidence could be lost, tampered with, or destroyed. For example, the area could be cleaned and evidence mistakenly thrown away, or the employee and friends of the employee may dispose of some evidence. Eyewitnesses may forget important facts or be reluctant to help management. Other witnesses, such as customers and clients, may not be willing to come back at a later date to give a statement.

Investigatory Interviews and Weingarten Rights

Weingarten rights are standards an employer must follow when conducting an investigatory interview that may result in the discipline or discharge of an employee. These rights are based on the U.S. Supreme Court's decision in *National Labor Relations Board v. J. Weingarten, Inc.* (1975) and originally applied only to employees in a union environment. In 2000, the National Labor Relations Board extended this right to the nonunion environment in a case involving the Epilepsy Foundation of Northeast Ohio.

Weingarten rights are based on the U.S. Supreme Court 's interpretation of section 7 of the National Labor Relations Act (NLRA), which states that employees have the right to engage in concerted activities for mutual aid and protection. The Court determined that employees have the right to representation in investigations, for without such protection, "a single employee confronted by an employer investigating whether certain conduct deserves discipline may be too fearful or inarticulate to relate accurately the incident being investigated, or too ignorant to raise extenuating factors." That is, requiring a lone employee to attend an interview might perpetuate inequality.

Regardless of whether working in a union or a nonunion setting, an employee can request that a representative be present at an investigatory interview at which the employee has reasonable belief that the results of the interview may result in disciplinary action. Following are the guidelines for conducting an investigatory hearing based on the *Weingarten* decision.

- The right arises only if the employee requests representation. The employee may choose to forgo or waive this guaranteed right.
- The right to request representation is limited to situations in which the employee reasonably believes that the investigation will result in disciplinary action. The rule is not applied to run-of-the-mill shop floor conversations, training, instructions, and correcting work techniques.
- The right may not interfere with legitimate employer prerogatives. This means that the employer can give the employee a choice between having an interview without representation and/or having no interview at all. The employer can also conduct an investigation independent of the employee in question, acting on information derived or collected from other sources.

- In a union setting, the employer has no duty to bargain with any union representative who is permitted to attend the investigatory interview. The role of the representative, in a union or a nonunion setting, is to clarify the facts of the case and to provide or suggest other employees who may have additional knowledge of the situation. In a union setting, this role also ensures that other employees in the bargaining unit can obtain the union's aid and protection, if requested.

Once an employee requests representation, the employer has four options:

1. Granting the request and continuing with the interview
2. Terminating the interview and assessing discipline
3. Terminating the interview and conducting an investigation without the benefit of the interview
4. Offering the employee a choice of continuing with the interview without a coworker or having no interview at all

Weingarten rights do not extend to all employees but cover only those employees protected under the NLRA and exclude salaried personnel, such as managers and supervisors (Bland and Knox 2001).

In many situations, interviews will also need to be conducted with individuals or witnesses who have some information that will assist in the investigation. Managers must always consider the degree of credibility of this information. One method of doing so is to compare statements made by the individual under investigation to evidence provided by other individuals, checking for consistency and any contradictions.

Maintaining the Chain of Custody   To protect the integrity, or the value, of the evidence and the privacy rights of the individual(s) under investigation, the collected evidence must be maintained by as few individuals as possible and be kept secure and confidential. Evidence can be maintained by creating a "chain of custody" policy and procedure that designates and limits who controls and has access to evidence collected in investigations. The creation of the chain of custody requires that the organization assign one individual as the primary investigator responsible for the security of the evidence in order to prevent the evidence from becoming "contaminated." This policy should also contain procedures for the inventory and security of the evidence, including access-control measures.

If evidence is misplaced, lost, or contaminated or if multiple individuals are allowed access to where the evidence is secured, the issue that the evidence was corrupted or the chain of custody was not maintained may become an issue. As a result, labor arbitrators and courts may question the validity or the strength of the evidence, possibly making the disciplinary action against the individual(s) invalid.

Assessing Evidence   The policy and the procedure violated help to determine what forms of evidence will be useful in proving a disciplinary violation.

Nevertheless, anything that might lead to the factual conclusion that the individual(s) violated a disciplinary policy or procedure is important as evidence. Evidence can be classified as real or circumstantial. Real evidence is perceptible to the senses: It can be presented and can be seen or touched. An employee injured as the result of a fight, a videotape of an individual pilfering supplies, and a damaged piece of machinery as a result of employee sabotage are examples of real evidence. Circumstantial evidence, by contrast, does not directly prove a fact but instead provides a logical inference or reasoning that leads one to incriminate a person or to conclude that an event or activity did occur. For example, in the investigation of a missing laptop computer from a secure area, an individual who has keys to a restricted area, who was seen carrying a large box in the vicinity of the incident, and who later sold a laptop computer to a friend could lead an investigator to conclude that this individual was responsible for the theft of the company's computer.

Pending the investigation, it is the responsibility of the investigator to determine what evidence is factual and what evidence is the "best" evidence in the investigation. Determining the reliability of the collected evidence is at times difficult, requiring the assessment of evidence based on the criterion of "factual" evidence and the relevant value this factual evidence has in the investigation. According to Bennett and Hess (1998, 11), a fact is "an action performed, an event, a circumstance, an actual thing done or an occurrence that has taken place, as opposed to what might have taken place." This is the opposite of an opinion, which is one's personal belief.

Along with establishing fact, the investigator should also assess the value of the collected evidence. One method of establishing the value of the evidence is to apply the courts' "best-evidence" rule, which requires that the highest degree of proof—best evidence—be used, produced, or applied to prove the case. This means that no evidence can be used when "there is an apparent possibility that the party who offers it can obtain better evidence" (Klein 1997, 175). This is a paramount issue, for if an arbitrator or the courts should ever review a disciplinary action, this rule of evidence may be applied.

Although usually limited to situations involving documentary evidence, the best-evidence concept can be applied when the investigator must use the best original evidence in proving the disciplinary case. In a situation involving two employees fighting in the workplace, for example, the "best" evidence would be a videotape of the actions of the employees in question, rather than eyewitness testimony of the incident.

The Final Report   The final report should be based solely on fact, comprehensive, and "readable." This final report, like the evidence collected for it, should be confidential. At a minimum, documentation of the infraction should include vital statistics about the employee, including the employee's social security number, name, age, date of birth, employee identification number, current position, and the date of hire. The final report should also include a summary of all previous disciplinary measures taken against the employee, a detailed report of the event that resulted in disciplinary measures, and a copy of the company rules or policies and procedures that the employee violated (Lisoski 1998). Usually, these reports remain internal to the organization. In some cases, however, they could be used in external proceedings: civil, criminal, and arbitration.

Disciplinary Sessions

After conducting the investigation and writing the incident report, the employer needs to hold a disciplinary session to correct and modify the employee's behaviors. These sessions should not be used to humiliate or embarrass the individual. As the purpose of discipline is to correct a problem, the manager must ensure that the employee does not view the disciplinary session as a punitive measure, for the employee may then become upset, defensive, and resentful (Raper and Myaya 1993).

This task may be difficult to achieve, but some methods can alleviate this perception that the individual is being punished. According to Day (1993), an effective disciplinary session requires 10 steps, as follows.

1. Determine whether discipline is needed.
2. Have clear goals for the meeting/discussion.
3. Hold the discussion in private.
4. Be calm and control all emotions.
5. Time the discussion carefully. (For example, do not have the disciplinary meeting on a significant day, such as the employee's birthday.)
6. Prepare opening remarks in advance.
7. Get directly to the point of the meeting.
8. Plan on two-way communication, but do not allow the session to turn into a bargaining session.
9. With the employee, establish a follow-up plan to ensure that the goals of the disciplinary meeting are achieved.
10. End the session on a positive note.

As in earlier steps in the disciplinary process, the events and the discussion at the disciplinary meeting must be documented by careful notes taken during or immediately after the session. The organization, depending on the existing policies and procedures, contractual agreements, and the situation, may also consider having an impartial third party attend the meeting. If necessary this individual could, at a later time, verify the events and discussions that took place during the corrective session.

The needs of the employee should also be considered. The employee should be given specific examples of the unacceptable behavior(s) that led to the disciplinary meeting. The meeting should also provide direction to the employee on how to correct the behavior in order to prevent similar or future incidents. The employee and the employer should also establish a reasonable time frame for the employee to improve on the behavioral or performance issue (Flynn 1998).

■ DISCIPLINE AND DISCHARGE IN A UNION SETTING

Although the general steps and issues involved in the creation and administration of a disciplinary program are the same in union and nonunion environments, in a union environment, the disciplinary process must also conform to the collective-bargaining agreement. This agreement specifies the due-process rights employees have in the organization, including the employee's rights in investigations and disciplinary procedures.

All collective-bargaining agreements contain discipline and discharge provisions. These provisions will not prevent employees from being discharged; they do however, clearly delineate the discipline and discharge program, the procedures and steps that must be followed in investigations and disciplinary proceedings, and procedures for appealing the corrective actions by the organization.

One of the most important sections of the collective-bargaining agreement addresses the employee's right to appeal disciplinary actions by the employer. This grievance-arbitration clause of the contract specifies what issues can be brought up by the claimant, procedures for filing a grievance with the employer, issues about union representation, and particular stages that must be followed in the grievance process. Without such a grievance clause in the contract, employees would be unable to appeal the corrective actions taken against them by management. Employees would also not be able to resolve disputes about the interpretation of other issues in the employment contract.

The grievance process, like the organization's disciplinary program, is progressive, advancing from informal to more formal and legalistic stages. The grievance clause regularly begins with the aggrieved employee's discussing the dispute with the direct supervisor, with the assistance of a union representative or steward. If the dispute is not resolved at this stage, the next stage may include the employee's filing a formal grievance against the employer. This formal grievance may then involve union officials and upper-level company representatives. If not resolved at this stage, the aggrieved party may then request an arbitration hearing, which is usually the terminal stage in the grievance-arbitration process, unless challenged in the courts.

At the arbitration hearing, representatives from the union and management, along with a neutral third party, determine the validity of the grievance filed by the union on behalf of the aggrieved individual. This arbitrator conducts the quasi-judicial hearing, allowing the submission of evidence and testimony from all parties to the dispute. The subsequent decision rendered by the arbitrator is considered final and binding on the parties involved in the dispute.

■ FUNDAMENTALS OF DISCHARGE

Discharge is the permanent dismissal of an employee from the organization. The employer terminates the employment relationship between the employee and the organization. Discharge usually occurs because the employee's actions have been determined to be harmful to the organization or it is based on organizational decisions about corporate downsizing, or "rightsizing." Discharge can also be referred to as organizational capital punishment or change by decree.

Employment at Will versus Just Cause

The concept of at-will employment can be traced to English common law. A contemporary interpretation of the doctrine is that an employer may, for any reason or no reason, terminate an employee. Employees too can terminate their employment at any time with their employer. Under the at-will doctrine, employers have the authority to regulate, or control, all terms and conditions of employment.

Although the at-will employment doctrine still exists, it has been modified through court decisions, labor laws, collective-bargaining agreements, and civil service systems. Employers themselves have modified at-will employment through the development of policies and procedures related to discipline and discharge.

Many employers have created forms of industrial due process related to the discipline of employees. Just-cause doctrines require that the employer have a fair and honest "cause," or reason, to dismiss the employee. This reason could be based on legitimate business needs, progressive disciplinary issues that have not been corrected, and criminal activities that have occurred in the workplace.

Appropriateness of Discharge

One of the primary issues an employer should consider before terminating an employee is whether the discharge is appropriate. One of the best measures of that is whether the employee was given advance warning, that is, whether the employer has a progressive disciplinary program that clearly explains the ramifications of violating particular policies and procedures. As with disciplinary problems that do not warrant discharges, the employer must also follow all administrative guidelines and conduct an in-depth investigation to determine whether the employee violated the rule (Lisoski 1998), as well as document all the employee's actions.

The employer should also determine whether the policies and procedures that were violated were related to the safe and efficient running of the organization (Lisoski 1998). If the employer can verify that they were and if the termination is consistent with relevant employment laws, personnel policies, and any applicable collective-bargaining agreements, the decision to discharge is legal.

Guidelines for Terminating Employees

The termination of an employee is a serious action and must be properly planned and executed. Existing organizational practices and policies and procedures may provide guidelines for terminating employees, but the manager should recognize that the dynamics of each termination meeting will differ, contingent on the actions of the individual being terminated.

Preplanning   Discharge meetings must be thoroughly planned in advance to ensure professional and fair treatment of the employee. Determining who will be present and creating an agenda for the meeting must also be done in advance. This will allow the meeting to progress in a timely manner. The organization should also consider scripting the discussion of meeting. Scripting does not mean that the manager must read verbatim from a document that is prepared in advance. Rather, the script should be thought of as a presentation outline for the manager. The scripting process ensures that all individuals are prepared and know exactly what will need to be said at the meeting. A review of the script will also ensure that the discussion will be factual, professional, and legal.

As part of preplanning, the organization needs to conduct a threat assessment to determine whether and what types of aggressive behaviors the employee may display or undertake at the meeting (Caudron 1998). This threat assessment should also review prior disciplinary actions and activities that occurred, interviews with coworkers and supervisors about the employee's behaviors that could be expected, and consultation with experts in workplace violence on how to reduce the threat of such disorders.

Attendees at the Termination Meeting   To respect the rights and dignity of the employee, the meeting should be kept as confidential and as private as possible, and the number of individuals attending should be minimized. Lisoski (1998) recommends that the individual conducting the termination; another management witness, preferably someone from the human resource department; the individual being terminated; and a union representative, if applicable, be present at the termination meeting. If the potential for violence exists, a representative from the security department should also be present.

Location   The location of the dismissal meeting should maximize the employee's privacy and be conducted in a neutral location either on or off property. An on-site meeting could take place in a conference room instead of the manager's office, because the employee may find the office environment too intimidating, raising the potential for violence. In the context of safety and security, the location of the meeting should be held near an exit to ensure the safety of other employees in the organization and to expedite the departure of the employee. A meeting room with multiple exits should also be considered. Rooms with multiple exits will allow the safe and quick exit of individuals attending the meeting if a violent episode should occur.

Timing   In the majority of situations, the individual to be terminated knows that the serious charges/accusations being levied will lead to discharge. In order to prevent undue stress on the employee, the meeting should be as timely as possible and be held immediately at the beginning of the shift or workday.

Another concern is what day to carry out the termination. One recommendation is to terminate an employee on a workday other than Friday. The rationale for not terminating an employee on the last day of the workweek is that the employee can begin to look for new work immediately rather than wait two days and reflect on the job loss (Lisoski 1998). Keeping the former employee busy—looking for a new position—may reduce any propensity for workplace violence.

Content of the Meeting   The purpose of the termination meeting is to present factual information in a prompt and professional manner. For this reason, a termination meeting should not turn into a debate. Although the employee should be allowed to state why the termination may be inappropriate, the content or course of the meeting must result in the firm statement that the employee is terminated.

Howard (1988) presents some guidelines for conducting the termination meeting.

- Come to the point at the termination hearing. Make the reasons for the termination as clear as possible, and come to the point of the meeting within the first 2 or 3 minutes.
- Do not accuse the individual; present the facts to the individual in a logical and factual manner.
- Do not allow yourself to change your mind. Remain firm in your decision, and do not allow yourself to become involved in a negotiation situation.
- Keep the meeting as short as possible.
- Do not interject any personal opinions or beliefs at this meeting.

Posttermination Planning   The organization should also have some posttermination procedures that address what the organization should do immediately after the employee is terminated. One issue to consider involves notifying all departments in the organization that the employee has been terminated (Howard 1988). In order to prevent a possible defamation lawsuit, the organization should not allow the release of information about reasons for the termination or any facts found from its investigation. Experts in workplace violence, such as Caudron (1998), suggest that the organization conduct surveillance activities on individuals who may be prone to violence, based on the initial threat assessment. These surveillance activities could warn the organization of retaliatory efforts by the terminated employee.

Other posttermination issues that the organization should consider are

- Escorting the employee off the property.
- Having the employee return all company property immediately, especially keys, access devices, and identification cards.
- Denying access to information systems, computers, and so on. Passwords and access codes to computers, other electronic data, and sensitive areas of the building should be immediately revoked.

Treatment of the Employee   Throughout the termination hearing, the employee should be treated with dignity and respect. If professional levels of conduct are maintained, the employee may not perceive the meeting as vindictive or vengeful, diffusing hostile intentions or motives and reducing the risk of workplace violence and the potential for a vindictive and unsubstantiated civil suit against the organization.

Resignation versus Discharge

In some instances, an employee may be given the option to voluntarily agree to terminate the employment relationship instead of being fired. The resignation, instead of an outright termination, will allow the employee to move on to a another career without the stigma of a firing on an application or résumé. If the individual has a propensity for violence, the voluntary separation or resignation may also mitigate these violent propensities, protecting organizational members from violent and vindictive actions.

Resignations could also shield the employer from some, but not all, lawsuits involving the employer's action. The organization, however, should also ensure that it did not coerce the employee into resigning. If this was the case, an employee could have legal standing to challenge the "resignation."

Allowing an employee to resign may have some negative aspects. Resignations may result in rouge employees, a pool or class of individuals who may move from job to job and who may be hired if new employers do not conduct thorough background investigations on these individuals. Because many of these individuals may not move to a different industry group, the new organization has hired an employee who may display the same or similar negative behaviors in the new organization. As a consequence, the de facto policy of allowing individuals to resign may have created individuals in the labor pool who wander from employer to employer, possibly displaying the same or similar poor actions at their new place of employment.

■ LEGAL ISSUES IN DISCIPLINE AND DISCHARGE

Employees have several defenses to get their jobs back or to receive damages for being disciplined and discharged. Some of the most common defenses may include harassment, discrimination, misrepresentation of the facts, lack of due process, an isolated incident, lack of proper warning, lack of adequate time to correct the problem, and lack of proper notice.

In all these incidents, a properly defined and administered progressive disciplinary program can alleviate some of these problems. Research by Bohlander (1994) found five factors that lead arbitrators to reverse or overturn disciplinary actions by managers: lack of evidence, mitigating circumstances, procedural errors in handling the case, management itself being partly at fault for the disciplinary problem, and overly harsh discipline imposed on the employee for the infraction committed.

In order to avoid lawsuits related to the termination of an employee, managers must be trained in relevant employment law and also understand the basic fundamentals of discipline and discharge. Some of the most common lawsuits related to discipline and discharge, particularly discharge, include defamation, constructive, and wrongful discharge.

Defamation Lawsuits

Defamation is oral (slander) or written (libel) communication about a prior employee who harms an individual's reputation (Ryan and Lasek 1991). Defamation can take many forms, ranging from remarks made by a previous employer to a prospective employer to discussing employee matters with nonauthorized individuals (Jacobson 1998). Defamation does not always occur when the individual is dismissed from the organization. Defamation also exists if the individual has left the organization on good terms but the reference given by the employer is defamatory (Ryan and Lasek 1991).

Courts have imposed defamation awards to deter employers from unjustly harming an individual's chances for reemployment. This so-called scarring occurs when a future employer denies a job to someone on the basis of information, or lack thereof, from a former employer (Verkerke 1998).

In order to demonstrate defamation, the following elements must be present.

- The defamatory statement must have been communicated to another party. In this context, the plaintiff must show that the former employer communicated false information to the prospective employer. Known as the element of publication, the defamatory information must be proved to have been communicated to someone other than the employee or the plaintiff. Traditional forms of publication include verbal and written mediums. With the advent of new technologies, such as the Internet, this is another source of potentially defamatory information (Jacobson 1996).
- The statement must be a false statement of fact. In this context, the defendant, not the plaintiff, must show that the statement was true and based on fact. If the defamatory remark or comments are based on opinion, they are not actionable (Jacobson 1996).
- Injury to the plaintiff's reputation must have occurred. Such injury is often inferred, based on the nature of the statements made (Ryan and Lasek 1991).
- The employer must not be protected under absolute or qualified immunity. Under absolute privilege, an employer is protected from making a defamatory statement as long as it is made in a judicial or quasi-judicial proceeding. Under qualified privilege, an employer is immune from defamatory statements by showing that the statement was made with a good-faith belief that it was truthful, served a business interest or purpose, was published or communicated to proper parties only, and was made on a proper occasion (Ryan and Lasek 1991). The employer may lose this privilege if the evidence shows that the information was given with malicious intent, the employer did not have reasonable grounds for believing the truth of the statement, and it was published or communicated with reckless disregard for its veracity (Ryan and Lasek 1991).

An employer that has been truthful in communicating with the new employer generally cannot be held liable under defamation. The difficulty, however, is proving that the communication in essence was "truthful." In order to prove that it was truthful, an employer can maintain effective employment records. In addition to having documented performance records, the employee should be made aware of these records and sign to their truthfulness.

One of the simplest ways a firm can protect itself from a defamation is to simply not provide references on former employees. This policy or practice could have an impact on the individuals, as future employers calling for a reference may infer from the employer's "no-comment" policy that the employee was a problem, when in fact that was not so (Long 1997). Although this may appear to be a proper response to the fear of a defamation suit, the organization should also consider societal interests. One belief is that it is in society's best interest to have organizations exchange information or references because the information obtained from such interchanges will result in the employer's making an informed decision when filling vacancies (Long 1997). However, such actions tend to "chill" this socially beneficial activity, which may result in the new employer's not having a good fit with the new employee or, even worse, bringing a potentially violent employee into the workplace.

The effectiveness of the "no-comment" policy however, can be lessened through compelled self-publication. In this emerging doctrine, the candidate or applicant publishes the defamatory statement instead of the employer. This occurs when the individual states at an interview or explains on an application the reason for leaving the previous employer (Ryan and Lasek 1991). To demonstrate self-compelled publication, it must be shown that the employer could foresee that the plaintiff would be compelled or have a strong compulsion to explain or reveal the reason(s) for leaving the previous employer, as the individual had no reasonable means of avoiding the publication or would be under a strong compulsion to publish the statement(s) (Jacobson 1996).

To date, courts have adopted three approaches to dealing with the concept of self-publication. The first category includes those states that simply have rejected the doctrine of defamation based on self-publication. The second category allows the concept of self-publication when it is reasonably foreseeable that the defamatory matter would come to the knowledge of a third person in the ordinary course of events. The third category allows a self-publication defamation suit when it is considered to be reasonable for the originator of the defamatory matter to believe that the defamed party would be under a strong compulsion to disclose the contents of the defamatory statements to a third party (Siegel 1994).

One defense to a defamation suit is the common-law application of the common-interest privilege. This concept is based on the premise that because former and prospective employers have a common interest about their candidates or applicants, employees who provide references are immune from defamation claims unless the plaintiff can prove that the employer violated this privilege in some way. For example, the employer may publish the information for a purpose other than a reference, or the information provided is not necessary to accomplish "the purpose for which the occasion is privileged" (Verkerke 1998).

The majority of states give organizations some degree of protection from defamation suits. Research has shown that the majority of legislative endeavors taken by states that have passed employer reference statutes have a good-faith presumption. Good-faith presumptions indicate that employers are immune from liability unless the plaintiff/employee is able to show, based on the preponderance of evidence or clear and convincing proof, that the employer, depending on the state, acted with malice, disclosed false information, or disclosed the information with reckless disregard for the truth (Long 1997). Other states, such as Pennsylvania, have absolute privilege; even if the employer's motive was hostile, the employer cannot be found liable for defaming an employee (Siegel 1994).

Constructive Discharge

A constructive discharge may occur when an employer takes deliberate actions to force the employee to leave or resign from the organization (Perry 1997). An employer's actions may make the employee so miserable as to resign to escape the unpleasant circumstances the employer has imposed. Continually scheduling an employee to work third shift on weekends and assigning that person the worst job activities over a period of time could lead to a constructive-discharge suit. The plaintiff would only have to prove having been somehow treated differently from the other employees when the employer assigned these shifts and duties as way to force resignation.

Wrongful Discharge

Wrongful discharge occurs when an employer promised an employee job security but then terminates the employee without cause. According to Andreason (1993), a wrongful-discharge claim has merit under three conditions. First, under the public policy violation, if an employee is fired for "whistle blowing," or reporting unlawful acts, or refuses to commit another type of wrong, the employer may be liable. Second, an employer may be found liable under not discharging for "good cause." That is, an employee who is not dismissed for the failure to perform job duties or another legitimate business need may have standing in court. Third, employers who violate their own personnel policy in terms of content and procedure may also create a wrongful-discharge situation.

Another issue that may expose a company to a wrongful-discharge lawsuit is creating unintentional contracts with the employee. An example of an implied contract may occur when individuals are repeatedly told that they have a long-term future with the company or are told they would never be dismissed. This verbal or written promise is an implied contract, which in turn alters the at-will employment status of the employee, if applicable.

Although little consistency exists in the doctrine or application of at-will employment across states, several actions or activities by employers may result in some courts' interpreting that an implied contract existed between the employer and the employee. Applying a totality of circumstances approach, some evidence courts may consider in determining whether a wrongful discharge occurred includes (McGowan 1998):

- The employee's length of service
- Any promotions, awards, or other forms of recognition the employee received
- The lack of criticism, documented, over the course of the individual's employment
- Any assurances of continued employment by the employer, either written or verbal
- Existing employer policies, such as job-security provisions or the provision of just-cause terminations
- If the employee and employer engaged in preemployment negotiations related to job security
- If the terms of employment were specifically negotiated
- If the employee has a contract with the employer
- Just-cause provisions in the employer's personnel policies, handbook, or policy and procedure manual that require due process in discipline and discharge cases
- Collective-bargaining agreements or civil service regulations

Other circumstances may lead to a wrongful-discharge case. The courts may look at how other employees who have received similar guarantees or promises were subsequently treated (Perry 1997). Another exception, depending on the state, is the public policy exception, under which an employer can be held liable if an employee is discharged for refusing to perform an illegal act, is exercising a statutory right or obligation, or reports an employer's statutory violation of laws and regulations—whistleblowing— (Munson 1997).

One of the best ways for an organization to prevent a wrongful-discharge lawsuit is to properly document all disciplinary actions against employees and clearly communicate their disapproval to the employee in question. The organization must also make sure that no promises or guarantees of lifetime or continued employment are promised or implied to the employee. Another way to preempt and prevent a wrongful-discharge suit is to thoroughly educate staff on employment law and personnel policies, while treating employee problems in a consistent and fair manner.

■ CONCLUSION

Discipline is any corrective action designed to bring about positive changes in a person. Discharge is the removal of the employee from the organization. Organizations, regardless of their size and structure, require well-designed disciplinary programs to set normative standards of conduct for workers and to achieve the organization's objectives. Regardless of whether an organization has a punitive or a corrective philosophy toward discipline, these programs should be progressive in nature.

Some of the implementation issues that must be considered when designing a disciplinary program are how it will complement the existing organizational culture and philosophy. Issues related to legal issues, enforceability, and whether the program will help employees should also be considered. Following implementation issues, an organization also needs to consider the administration of the disciplinary program. The organization should delegate in advance who is responsible for employee discipline and ensure that these individuals accept their disciplinary responsibilities. Managers also need to be able to effectively communicate work rules, follow existing guidelines, and properly assess what levels of discipline are necessary to correct employee problems.

The administration of the disciplinary program requires that the organization conduct a thorough investigation of an incident before imposing any corrective actions. Issues to consider when conducting investigations are delegating who is responsible for the investigation, determining the breadth and depth of investigations, and deciding how soon investigations should be conducted. Other issues include preserving the chain of custody, assessing the value of evidence, writing the final report, and conducting disciplinary sessions. When conducting investigative interviews, managers should be aware that employees can invoke their Weingarten rights.

The discharge of an employee is a very serious employer action. Regardless of whether employees are terminated at will or for cause, some procedures need to be followed. Termination should be a preplanned event about issues related to the treatment of the employee, attendance, location, and timing, and the content of the meeting. Posttermination should also be considered. In some situations, an employer may give the employee the option of resigning instead of being fired. Finally, organizations should be aware of legal issues in discipline and discharge, particularly with issues related to defamation and constructive and wrongful discharge.

■ KEY TERMS

Best-evidence rule

Chain of custody

Circumstantial evidence

Constructive discharge

Corrective actions

Defamation

Discharge

Disciplinary session

Discipline

Employee deviance

Employment at will

Grievance arbitration clause

Just cause

Personal aggression

Political deviance

Positive discipline

Production deviance

Progressive discipline

Property deviance

Real evidence

Summary actions

Wrongful discharge

Weingarten rights

■ DISCUSSION QUESTIONS

1. What is discipline? Why is it important for an organization?
2. What are the two major types of discipline? What are the major differences between the two?
3. What is progressive discipline?
4. What are the three main issues to consider when designing a disciplinary program?
5. What is the role of the manager in the disciplinary process?
6. What are the key issues to consider when conducting a disciplinary investigation?
7. What are Weingarten rights? To whom do they apply?
8. What are the steps needed for an effective disciplinary session?
9. What types of deviance does an effective disciplinary program address?
10. What is the difference between at-will and just-cause discharge?

■ REFERENCES

ANDREASON, A. A. 1993. Avoiding wrongful discharge law suits in Montana. *Montana Business Quarterly* 31 (2): 22–25.

BENNETT, W. W., and K. M. HESS. 1998. *Criminal investigation*. 5th ed. New York: Wadsworth.

BERNARDI, L. M. 1996. Progressive discipline: Effective management tool or legal trap? *Canadian Manager* 21 (4): 9–10.

BIELOUS, G.A. 1993. How to discipline effectively. *Supervision* 54 (4): 17–19.

BLAND, T. S. and D. P. KNOX. 2001. Investigatory interviews: The non-union employee's right to a representative. *Federal Lawyer* 48: 34–38.

BOHLANDER, G. W. 1994. Why arbitrators overturn managers in employee suspension and discharge cases. *Journal of Collective Negotiations in the Public Sector* 23 (1): 73–89.

BRYANT, A. W. 1984. Replacing punitive discipline with a positive approach. *Personnel Administrator* 29 (2): 79–85.

CAUDRON, S. 1998. How to terminate potentially violent employees—and live. *Workforce* 77 (8): 50–52.

DAY, D. 1993. Training 101: Help for the discipline dodgers. *Training and Development* 47 (5): 19–22.

Employee discipline: Written guidelines protect employees and employers. *Small Business Report* 12 (10): 37–42.

FALCONE, P. 1997. The fundamentals of progressive discipline. *HR Magazine* 42 (2): 90–94.

FLYNN, G. 1998. You can say good riddance to bad attitudes. *Workforce* 77 (7): 82–84.

FRENCH, W. L. 1994. *Human resource management*. 3rd. ed. Boston: Houghton Mifflin.

HAMPER, B. 1991. *Rivethead: Tales from the assembly line*. New York: Warner.

HARPER, D. 1990. Spotlight abuse—save profits. *Industrial Distribution* 79: 47–51.

HOWARD, C. G. 1988. Strategic guidelines for terminating employees. *Personnel Administrator* 33 (4): 106–109.

JACOBSON, T. A. 1996. Avoiding claims of defamation in the workplace. North Dakota Law Review, 72: 247–266.

KAPLAN, H. B. 1975. Self-attitudes and deviant behavior. Pacific Palisades, CA: Goodyear.

KLEIN, I. J. 1997. *Law of evidence for criminal justice professionals*. 4th ed. New York: West/Wadsworth.

LEVINE, G. 1998. Firm-but-fair approach key in workplace discipline. *Bobbin* 39 (5): 69–70.

LISOSKI, E. 1998. How to terminate an employee with their dignity intact and you out of the courts. *Supervision* 59 (5): 7–9.

LONG, A. B. 1997. Addressing the cloud over employee references: A survey of recently enacted state legislation. *William and Mary Law Review* 39: 177–222.

LORD, V. B. 1998. Characteristics of violence in state government. *Journal of Interpersonal Violence* 13 (4): 489–503.

LUCERNO, M. A. and R. E. ALLEN. 1998. Fighting on the job: Analysis of recent arbitration decisions. *Dispute Resolution Journal* 53 (3): 51–57.

MCCONNELL, C. R. 1997. Effective employee counseling for the first-line supervisor. *Health Care Supervisor* 16 (1): 77–86.

MCGOWAN, K. C. 1998. Unequal opportunity in at-will employment: The search for a remedy. *St John's Law Review* 72 (1): 141–183.

MUNSON, G. M. 1997. A straightjacket for employment at will: Recognizing breach of implied contract actions for wrongful demotion. *Vanderbilt Law Review* 50 (6): 1578–1617.

National Labor Relations Board v. J. Weingarten, Inc. 1975. 420 U.S. 251.

PERRY, P. M. 1997. Think before you fire: Avoid these nine costly errors when terminating employees. *Rural Telecommunications* 16 (5): 48–54.

RAMSEY, R. D. 1998. Guidelines for the progressive discipline of employees. *Supervision* 59 (2): 10–12.

RAPER, J. L., and S. N. MYAYA. 1993. Employee discipline: A changing paradigm. Health Care Supervisor 12 (2): 67–78.

ROBINSON, S. L., and R. J. BENNETT. 1995. A typology of deviant workplace behaviors: A multidimensional approach. *Academy of Management Journal* 38 (2): 555–569.

RYAN, A. M. and M. LASEK. 1991. Negligent hiring and defamation: Areas of liability related to pre-employment inquiries. *Personnel Psychology* 44: 293–319.

SEWELL, G. 1998. The discipline of teams: the control of team-based industrial work through electronic and peer surveillance. *Administrative Science Quarterly* 43 (2): 397–428.

SIEGEL, H. J. 1994. Self-publication: Defamation within the employment context. *Saint Mary's Law Journal* 26: 1–29.

SUNCO, B. P. 1996. Positive discipline—sending the right or wrong message? *Personnel Journal* 75 (8): 109–112.

VERKERKE, J. H. 1998. Legal regulation of employment reference practices. *University of Chicago Law Review* 65 (1): 115–178.

chapter ten

Labor Relations

Because the roles of a security firm or unit within an organization are quite diverse, security managers and officers are often exposed to issues that encompass the field of labor relations, especially in a union environment. Without a fundamental understanding of labor relations, the security function could inadvertently cause labor unrest or dissension in the organization.

This chapter provides a basic overview of labor relations in organizations that operate in a union setting or are experiencing an organizational drive. A review of the history of the labor movement and security role in that movement is provided, along with a discussion of the complexities involved in union organizing, the various roles and functions a union performs in the workplace, and collective-bargaining and grievance processes. Issues related to the roles and responsibilities of the security function operating in a union environment are discussed, with particular attention to avoiding and preventing unfair labor practices that may occur through the activities and functions of security in the company.

▇ THE LABOR MOVEMENT IN THE UNITED STATES: A BRIEF HISTORY

In comparison to organized labor in European countries, the U.S. labor movement has taken a narrower approach in improving the working conditions of its membership. In many European nations, labor became more involved in politics by forming broad, class-based political parties that sought broad changes on national levels. Labor in the United States, although involved in politics, sought changes in the workplace through membership in trade unions instead of political parties. The U.S. labor movement relied on collective-bargaining agreements instead of the larger social-reform movements, based on legislative changes, that were characteristics of European labor organizations. U.S. unions were also more narrowly based and in some cases excluded certain industries or trades in their efforts. Many trade unions also excluded members on the basis of gender, race, and national origin (Forbath 1989).

Private-Sector Unionization

The U.S. labor movement began in the late eighteenth century. During this period, labor was characterized by master craftsmen aided by journeymen apprentices in crafts production. Work was done in small shops that made products primarily for sale at the local level. The seeds of capitalism were born with the growth of markets and transportation and the masters' tendency to bring in inferior workers and to increase production. Workers formed trade societies to protect their wages, hours, conditions of work, and positions. Some of the first craft-based societies were the Philadelphia Carpenters in 1791, the Typographical Society of New York in 1794, and the Baltimore Tailors in 1795 (Hoxie 1966).

During the first half of the nineteenth century, internal improvements in transportation and communications laid the groundwork for the creation of a national market. Later in the nineteenth century, some of these early trade societies formed unions of trade associations, such as the Mechanics' Union of Trade Associations in Philadelphia in 1827. This was the first time in history that trade organizations from one city had united for a common cause. During the early to mid-nineteenth century, other trade societies grew and became powerful in many cities in the eastern United States, engaging in both economic and political activities. This growth of unions continued after the Civil War, and labor organizations in many states were successful in getting legislation passed that supported organized labor (Perlman 1950).

The labor movement grew in popularity and strength in the latter half of the nineteenth century. One of the larger U.S. labor organizations in the late 1800s was the Knights of Labor, which was founded in 1869 and grew to approximately one million members in the 1880s (Forbath 1989). The Knights of Labor included both skilled and unskilled workers in its membership and was critical of the social inequalities that existed in the United States in the 1800s. The Knights believed in a worker's republic, criticizing U.S. capitalism for the inequalities it created in society. By 1895, the Knights of Labor was no longer a viable labor organization, due to its perceived radical positions (Crain and Matheny 2001).

The 1880s also saw the emergence of the American Federation of Labor (AFL), led by Samuel Gompers. Unlike the Knights of Labor, the AFL organized craft-based, or skilled, workers and sought to create disciplined unions and a nationally coordinated system of craft unions. The AFL largely ignored industrial workers (Forbath 1989). Unlike the Knights of Labor, which wanted to change the social structure of U.S. industrialism—socialist consciousness—the AFL sought job consciousness unionism, or business unionism, a protectionist ideology that did not seek to change the basic structure of production but wanted instead to make sure that union members would receive their fair share of the wealth that they created for their employers. Later, in 1937, the Congress of Industrial Organization (CIO) was created. This splinter group from the AFL identified itself as an industrial rather than a craft union. The CIO, unlike the AFL, concentrated its organizing efforts on industrial workers. By the late 1930s the CIO had successfully organized mass-production workers in entire industry groups (Gifford 1997). In 1955, the AFL and CIO merged, forming the AFL-CIO (Crain and Matheny 2001).

Although they used the political process to achieve their goals, the Knights of Labor and the AFL relied more heavily on strikes and collective bargaining to change their members' working conditions. To counteract the use of the strike, employers relied on the courts to issue injunctions against the strikers. (In fact, unions were considered to be semioutlaws by industrialists and the courts, which sympathized mainly with the industrialists.) Some of the first injunctions were used in the railway strikes in 1877. Injunctions soon became used extensively, with more than 4,300 issued against collective actions between 1880 and 1930. The 1920s, however, had the greatest number of court-imposed injunctions. Approximately 25 percent of all strikes—or a total of 2,100 strikes—had injunctions against them during this period.

The increase in court-imposed injunctions is attributed to a large increase in the number of strikes called by unions, a shift from small local strikes to larger strikes that were called by national or regional unions, and an increase in boycotts, sympathy strikes, and recognition strikes. The use of these injunctions, or decrees, was based on the premise that collective actions were conspiracies against the property rights of businesses. As union actions injured an employer's profit-making abilities, such actions encroached on the employer's property rights (Forbath 1989). Federal courts granted most of these injunctions, as locally elected individuals were more sympathetic to union activities (Forbath 1989).

In several collective actions, the unions ignored these injunctions. Because local law enforcement was sometimes sympathetic to the strikers, in some cases even deputizing strikers to police their own ranks, the federal courts also empowered, or deputized, strikebreakers and private security guards to enforce the injunctions. This often resulted in violence between strikers and the strikebreakers and private security guards employed on behalf of the company. With the growing power and influence that labor developed in the late nineteenth and early twentieth centuries, labor sought anti-injunction bills. According to some labor historians, the injunction was one of the primary problems for industrial unrest in the United States. Eventually, in 1932, Congress passed the Norris-LaGuardia Act, which severely limited the use of the labor injunction in industrial disputes (Forbath 1989).

Attempts to maintain labor peace were also made through legislation. In the last half of the nineteenth century, railroads became important in the growth and expansion of the United States. At the same time, several railroad strikes occurred.

As a consequence of the importance of railroads in U.S. commerce, this industry segment was one of the first to be affected by federal legislation. The Arbitration Act of 1888 called for a panel of three arbitrators—one chosen by each side and a neutral—to prevent the strikes of railroad workers over the negotiation for a new contract (Nolan and Abrams 1983). In 1898, the Erdman Act replaced the 1888 Arbitration Act, establishing permanent machinery for mediation and arbitration (LaRue 1987). In 1926, the Railway Labor Act was created. This act and its amendments called for a National Mediation Board to mediate labor disputes and provided for voluntary arbitration of disputes between employers and unions. If necessary, the act also allowed for the president of the United States to establish an ad hoc Emergency Board to investigate and publish its findings on labor disputes that had the potential to interrupt interstate commerce or threaten the nation of essential transportation services. In 1936, the airline industry was incorporated under the act. This act, with its subsequent amendments, still governs labor activities in the airline and railroad sectors (Northrup 1990).

Strikes nevertheless continued but did not go unnoticed by lawmakers. In 1935, the National Labor Relations Act (NLRA), also known as the Wagner Act, was passed, in part to preserve industrial peace and to maintain uninterrupted production for U.S. industries while reducing the disruption to commerce that labor unrest caused. The lawmakers also recognized inequalities in bargaining powers between unions and employers, with employers often holding the advantage (Crain and Matheny 2001). Others also felt that collective-bargaining legislation would increase workers' wages, which in turn would improve the economy (Hansen 2000). The Wagner Act also gave employees and their unions the right to strike, safeguarding this right from intrusion by the federal courts, which had been characteristic of their earlier involvement in strikes (LeRoy 1996b).

However, many employers ignored this legislation, feeling that the U.S. Supreme Court would find the Wagner Act unconstitutional. This belief was based on the notion that laws dealing with labor were outside the powers of Congress under the Interstate Commerce Clause of the Constitution. Hearing a series of cases related to the Wagner Act in 1937, the Supreme Court upheld the constitutionality of the NLRA (Hansen 2000).

The 1930s and 1940s saw a large increase in union membership and favorable public sentiment toward unions. A wave of strikes followed World War II, and some people felt that unions had been granted so much power from the NLRA that the monopolistic powers of some unions now disenfranchised companies. Some members of Congress also perceived that unions were sometimes oppressive and violated the rights of workers. As a result of these sentiments, Taft-Hartley—amendments to the NLRA—passed in 1947 (LeRoy 1996b). These amendments added a list of unfair union labor practices, changed the composition of the NLRB from three to five members, increased the number of staff attorneys, and made other structural changes to the NLRB, including broadening the review of board decisions by the judiciary. These and other changes were reported to have changed the role of the government in union matters from one of a protector of unions to that of an umpire in labor issues (Oberer et al. 1986).

Other changes that occurred with the NLRA as a result of the Taft-Hartley amendments included the right of workers to free speech in union matters. One of the largest changes that occurred was the right to decertify unions as the employees' bargaining representative. Lawmakers felt that union abuses were the result of the fact that unions had the potential to abuse a member's rights, as they were their dedicated union. The power of decertification of that union would keep the union in check to ensure that the union as the representative of its members was meeting their needs. If not, employees now had recourse to find another union that would be more receptive to the employees' needs (LeRoy 1996b).

In 1947, the Federal Mediation and Conciliation Service (FMCS) was founded as part of the amendments to the NLRA to prevent strikes and labor unrest by providing conciliation and mediation services to parties in dispute. This nonadjudicative agency has jurisdiction in the public sector and in any dispute that is remotely involved in interstate commerce. The FMCS has a staff of 200 mediators and handles approximately 30,000 cases in a typical year (Newman 1990).

Another major piece of legislation that amended the NLRA was Landrum-Griffen, also known as the Labor-Management Reporting and Disclosure Act of 1959. Based on concerns over highly publicized investigations of union racketeering and corruption, combined with the fact some labor unions were dishonest, members of Congress felt that legislation was needed to make sure that labor unions were run honestly. Some of the major components of this act were aimed at improving union democracy; it also required management consultants to report their activities to the federal government, to control corruption. Components of the act were also designed to ensure that unions would not be infiltrated by Communists (LeRoy 1996b).

The Labor Movement in the Public Sector

In the private sector, all collective-bargaining activities are governed by the NLRA and related legislation, but no single labor policy governs the public sector. The NLRA does not apply to individuals employed in the public sector. Instead, each state has its own collective-bargaining legislation, establishing what, if any, employee groups have collective-bargaining rights. Some states, for example, prohibit all public-sector collective bargaining. Others have meet-and-confer rights: An employer must meet with unions to hear their concerns or demands, but they have no bargaining responsibilities. Others states have full-fledged bargaining rights quite similar to those provided in the private sector under the NLRA.

Because the public sector is not covered by the NLRA, collective bargaining for public-sector employees had to be granted on a state-by-state basis. The main impetus for states to adopt collective-bargaining rights for public employees was in response to the federal government. In the late 1950s and early 1960s, federal employees began to demand to be allowed to bargain over the terms and conditions of their employment. Eventually, in 1962, with the origination of Executive Order 10988 by President Kennedy, federal employees were granted the right to collectively bargain (Lowenberg 1982). At about the same time, states began experimenting with public-sector bargaining; Wisconsin in 1959 was the first state to grant bargaining rights to public-sector employees (Chvala and Fox 1979). The majority of these public-sector bargaining statutes were passed between 1968 and 1975 (Petro 1992). These statutes were met with little resistance, because of union pressures and the premise that "workers without strong unions are bound to be abused by employers, and that such abuse is likely to occur in the public as in the private sector" (Petro 1992, 17).

With the granting of collective-bargaining rights, states also had to address the issues and controversies related to the strike. In the private sector, if a union and an employer cannot agree on a new contract, the economic weapons of the strike and the lockout can achieve a final resolution of the dispute. In the public sector, in certain states, individuals employed in essential services, such as law enforcing, fire fighting, and related services are not permitted to strike, out of fear that public services may be disrupted and the safety of the public put at risk (DiLauro 1989; McGinnis 1989). The "products" in the public sector, unlike those in the private sector, make it difficult to inventory products, as governments provide nontangible products, or services, that are performed in a monopolistic setting, with no competitors to compensate for the loss of the production of such services (Chelius and Extejt 1983). Other public-sector employees, including teachers, may also be banned from striking. To offset the absence of the strike, some states have legislated a variety of alternative dispute-resolution techniques (ADRs). ADRs are established mechanisms, or procedures, that encourage an early settlement of a dispute by methods other than litigation (Coulson 1985). ADR techniques are generally of three types: mediation, fact finding, and arbitration. These techniques are discussed in detail later in the chapter.

The Labor Movement and Security: A Sordid Past

Unfortunately, security companies, both contractual and proprietary, have often had a contentious relationship with organized labor, with violence often the outcome of their relationship. The security forces' employers often used them in antiunion activities, including various strike-breaking activities, enforcing court-imposed injunctions, and serving as deputies for the local police, who carried out the employers' antiunion policies.

Violence was often an outcome when security and union members encountered one another. This was the case with the Homestead, Pennsylvania, strikes in 1892. Steelworkers organized under the Almagamated Association of Iron, Steel and Tin Workers at the Homestead Works, owned by Carnegie Steel, were locked out of the factory, and others eventually went on strike. To make sure that Carnegie could not bring in strikebreakers, the workers formed a militia of approximately 4,000 members to watch for the arrival of the strikebreakers and to prevent them from entering the Homestead Works. To protect company property and to provide protection for the strikebreakers the company planned on using, the company sent 300 armed Pinkertons by barge down the Monongahela River to occupy the plant in advance of the strikebreakers. The militia was alerted to the Pinkertons' coming down the river. Workers and family members alike armed themselves and stormed the Homestead Works. A 12-hour battle ensued, and five strikers and three Pinkertons were killed. The Pinkertons eventually surrendered and were "escorted" by the strikers out of town and their barges burned. In response to the violence, the governor of Pennsylvania mobilized more than 8,000 state militia to protect the Homestead Works and the strikebreakers. Carnegie eventually was successful in breaking the union (Serrin 1992). Because of the negative publicity of the Homestead strike, Pinkerton stated that it would no longer use its employees as strikebreakers (Lipson 1988).

In the early twentieth century, the coal industry too was experiencing labor unrest. In 1913 and 1914 in Colorado, a series of coal mine strikes—the Colorado Coal Wars—occurred in part because the coal companies would not abolish the use of armed mine guards. In one instance, approximately 1,000 strikers armed themselves and engaged in open warfare against company mine guards and the state militia after their demands were not met. Contract guards who had a previous record of ruthless and brutal treatment of strikers were hired. By the end of the incident, armed strikers controlled a large amount of Colorado, and more than 50 people had been killed, including 9 guards, some of whom were ambushed by United Mine Workers members or outright assassinated by union members (Husband 1997).

Another example of labor violence and the use of security forces for antiunion activities occurred in the automotive industry. Between 1934 and 1936, General Motors spent more than $1 million on labor espionage activities, making it the Pinkerton Agency's biggest client at that time. Perhaps one of the best examples of the role of security in antiunion activities was with the Ford Motor Company. In an ongoing effort to prevent his plants from being unionized, Henry Ford in 1921 created a security organization known as the Ford Service Department. To run this department, Ford hired Harry Bennett, who was described as a "thug" with connections to organized crime figures throughout the United States. Hiring criminals, ex-convicts, and professional athletes, the Service Department was described as the largest and most formidable private army in the world, numbering between 3,500 and 6,000 men, reaching a ratio of 1 Serviceman to every 25 Ford employees at one time. Although their primary responsibility was "to let workers know that they were being watched" (Norwood 1996, 372), Service Department employees had the authority to fire at will, engage in espionage activities, harass union organizers, and intimidate family members, to name just a few of their antiunion activities.

Violence was often a key component of their antiunion efforts. In 1932, members of the Service Department, led by Bennett, were responsible for the deaths of 4 workers and the wounding of another 28 when he and his fellow Servicemen fired into the crowd of protesters at the Rouge Plant in Dearborn, Michigan. In another incident at the Rouge Plant, in 1937, known as the "Battle of the Overpass," Bennett's Servicemen attacked United Auto Worker organizers while the Dearborn Police looked on; the chief of Dearborn's police department was on Bennett's payroll. In 1938, Bennett failed in his attempted kidnapping of Walter Reuther, Detroit's local UAW organizer. Although the NLRB issued cease-and-desist orders against Ford, many of them were ignored. Eventually, Ford capitulated to the UAW; one of the union's conditions was that Ford put his Servicemen in uniform in order to make spying on employees more difficult. After the death of Henry Ford in 1945, Henry Ford II fired Bennett and dismantled the Service Department. Discussing Ford's Service Department, one author said, "His [Bennett's] methods differed only in degree from those of other auto manufacturers who also engaged in widespread labor espionage, relying upon municipal police, rather than private armies, to physically intimidate workers" (Norwood 1996, 391).

The U.S. Labor Movement Today

Union membership has been on the decline since 1954, when the membership of nonagricultural labor unions was at a high of 34.7 percent, or approximately one-third of the nation's workforce. According to Bureau of Labor Statistics data, approximately 16.3 million workers were union members in 2001, comprising 13.5 percent of all wage and salary workers in the United States (U.S. Department of Labor 2002). When controlled for sectors of the economy, the data show that approximately 40 percent of the public-sector, or government, workers are unionized, compared to less than 10 percent of the private workforce. Those private-sector occupational groups that have above-average unionization rates include the construction and manufacturing sectors of the economy (U.S. Department of Labor 2002). Unionization rates also vary by region and state. For example, half of the 16.3 million union members in the United States lived in six states: California, New York, Illinois, Michigan, Ohio, and Pennsylvania.

The decrease in union membership over the past 50 years has several explanations. After World War II, the United States was virtually the only economic power left intact in the world, leading to the growth of union members. This left the United States as one of the sole powerhouses in such industries as steel and automobile manufacturing. With the emergence of other economic powerhouses in the 1970s—Japan and Germany—these traditional union strongholds in the heavy-manufacturing sector were severely downsized, leading to a reduction in union memberships in their traditional strongholds. Other reasons for the decline in union membership over the past 50 years are more relaxed trade policies with the world—for example, NAFTA—and the emergence of a global labor market that unions have little or no control over. At the same time, the United States has shifted from an industrial to a service-based economy. The traditional stronghold of labor unions has been in the industrial sector, and labor organizations have been slow to enter into the service side of the economy.

Public sentiment toward unions has also changed. Individuals may no longer honor the picket line, which was a mainstay of the union's power at one time (LeRoy 1996a). Legislation at the federal level may also explain the decline in union membership. In fact, some say that unions have done such a good job that they have legislated themselves out of business. For example, a traditional goal for unions has been to seek better wages and conditions of employment for its members. Historically, when unions sought these and other improvements in the workplace, no federal legislation granted these rights to workers. Now legislation prohibits child labor, and the Fair Labor Standards Act restricts the number of hours that can be worked. Other job-protection provisions that were the traditional domain of the union are now also seen in antidiscrimination legislation, such as Title VII of the Civil Rights Act of 1964, as amended.

■ UNIONS

The National Labor Relations Act 29 USC (1935), also known as the Wagner Act, defines a labor organization as "any organization of any kind where employees participate, which exists for whole or in part in dealing with employers involving grievances, labor disputes, pay, hours of employment and working conditions." Since World War II, U.S. unions can be best described as business unionism. When the AFL and the CIO merged in 1955, the new AFL-CIO committed itself to a mixture of job and class consciousness that came to be called business unionism. Unlike earlier unions, such as the Knights of Labor, business unionism does not challenge the fundamentals of capitalism. Business unionism accepts capitalism and takes the position that its primary goal is to ensure that union members receive a fair share of the wealth they create (Crain and Matheny 2001). The underlying tenets of business unionism can be seen in the following quote (Crain and Matheny 2001, 1780):

> Unions exist in order to address the immediate and practical concerns of unionized workers. The objective of unions is to protect their members economically, primarily by negotiating and enforcing the union contract. Unions are seen essentially as service organizations, whose task is to insure fair wages, increase job security, protect against victimization, improve the conditions of work, and provide additional economic benefits. In the arena of politics, unions are concerned with only those issues that have a direct or indirect impact on unions, their members, and the industries in which they function.

Modern-day unions can also be understood as organizations that protect the collective rights and not the individual rights of an employee (Crain and Matheny 2001). A union can also be considered a guardian of an employee's rights, as prescribed in the collective-bargaining agreement, as well as an organization that exists to limit the power of an employer. Others posit that unions can be considered interest groups, as a union "promotes a shared interest different from, and possibly in conflict with the interests of the public" (Gifford 1997, 106).

Another way of understanding the functions of a union is to examine it in the context of the model of collective goods. This model explains that unions improve the well-being the workers in four ways. First, a union can secure a collective good by exercising monopolistic power. An example of monopolistic power is the use of the strike against the employer. Second, unions achieve collective good through their collective voice; union representatives bring forth the needs of the employees, informing the employer of the workers' needs. Third, unions secure collective goods in exchange for ensuring the cooperation and productivity of the employees. Last, a union can purchase collective goods for its members by trading off benefits of a lesser value, such as a wage increase, over a no-layoff clause in the collective-bargaining agreement (Leslie 1984).

Union Structure

Unions are usually organized at three levels: the local, the national, and in affiliation with the AFL-CIO. The local union—often referred to, for example, as the Acme Union, with a number designation for that particular local union—is the most important of the three levels. The local is responsible for the day-to-day operations of servicing the union and the collective-bargaining agreement. The local union is financed through the collection of union dues that are spent on administrative costs associated with activities the local unions perform. If affiliated with a national union, the local union is also responsible for paying a per capita tax to the national. Depending on the union, union members may in some cases pay their dues directly to the national union. The national union, in turn, then reimburses the local.

The national union charters locals and oversees their activities and makes sure that the locals are in compliance with national requirements. Some of the activities of the national union include establishing union policy, assisting the locals in collective-bargaining activities, grievance administration, and any legal issues that should arise. These national unions are operated by full-time employees and officers who are elected by members of the local or by union delegates sent to national conventions. Depending on the union, nationals may be considered "internationals" if they have locals in foreign countries, such as Canada or Mexico.

The AFL-CIO is not a union but rather a confederation of unions. The AFL-CIO does not engage in collective bargaining or other "traditional" union activities. The role of the AFL-CIO is primarily political. The AFL-CIO promotes its national labor policy established through its Executive Council, proposes and lobbies for legislation that favors unions, and develops international and national positions on various labor-related issues. At the state level, the AFL-CIO has 51 federations—one for each state and one for Puerto Rico—that coordinate with local unions and engage in political and legislative activities. The AFL-CIO is also active on the local level, with approximately 570 central labor councils that engage in local political and legislative activities, while promoting unionization efforts. Funding for these and other activities comes from those unions that are affiliated with the AFL-CIO. Not all national unions belong to the AFL-CIO; affiliation is voluntary.

Successful Unions

For a union to be successful, it needs to have network embeddedness and political vitality. Network embeddedness refers to the nature and extent of its ties or relationships to external organizations. It includes vertical relationships with a labor federation—the AFL-CIO—for sharing information and improving problem-solving skills. Network embeddedness also exists on a horizontal archetype, that is, relationships with community groups and other unions in the area. Through effective horizontal embeddedness, a union can turn to other unions for mutual aid and support. Political vitality, by contrast, is measured in the context of how responsive the local union leaders are to their membership. It includes issues related to the union's internal political practices on how responsive the union is to its membership. Political vitality is also measured in relation to how effective the union is in maintaining and nurturing a relationship with its shop-floor union stewards (Frost 2000).

　　Unions also need additional traits to be successful. Four capabilities that any union needs in order to have influence and success with employers are listed in Box 10–1.

BOX 10–1　■　Four Components of Effective Unions

1. **Ability to access information** Unions need to be able to access information internally from their membership and from external sources to be effective problem solvers. Union accomplishments require active collection of information from those who will be affected through the proposed changes sought in the collective-bargaining process.

2. **Ability to educate and mobilize the membership** Unions need to have the ability to educate and mobilize their membership. Union members need to be actively involved in proposed changes and have a shared vision with the union. This is achieved by educating members on that vision. A successful union will be able to mobilize its membership to support that vision.

3. **Ability to access decision making at multiple points** Successful unions need to access the organization's decision-making process at multiple points to get their points or needs across to management. By having union members serving on labor-management committees, for example, a union can apply pressure at several levels to ensure that its interests are addressed. Informal pressure from workers on their supervisors can be combined with pressure from shop stewards through the grievance process. This will ensure that management at multiple levels gets more information of greater accuracy than it could have if the union gained access to management only at a single point or had no access at all.

4. **Ability to balance cooperation and conflict** Successful unions need to maintain their independence from the employer to avoid claims of co-optation while also engaging in cooperative efforts with the employer. A union cannot be overly cooperative but also cannot maintain a conflict-ridden relationship with the employer at the same time. Successful unions need to establish an environment of mutual respect. Through this mutual respect, beneficial changes for both the union member and employer will result.

Adapted from Frost 2000.

Organizing Strategies

A primary goal for any union is to attract and retain members. Obtaining new members and bargaining units for unions is accomplished through organizing activities. Three environmental characteristics influence union organizing: (1) the latent demand for union services, (2) the nature or degree of employer opposition to unions, and (3) factors related to employment growth. Latent demand is associated with the nature and extent of job dissatisfaction and how instrumental a union could be in improving wages, benefits, and conditions of work. The more the latent demand, the greater the potential for union organizing efforts.

Employer opposition can affect organizing in two ways. Employers could reduce dissatisfaction levels of their employees, thereby decreasing their interest in unionization. Employers can also engage in suppression activities, such as legal maneuvering and campaigning against unions. In the context of employment growth, if certain industry sectors are experiencing growth, new bargaining units for unions could be created (Fiorito, Jarley, and Delaney 1995).

Historically, unions had exclusive jurisdiction of a particular trade or industry, thereby limiting organizing efforts by other unions. Many unions practiced representational specialization, focusing on particular types of employees or representing workers in a particular industry or craft-based position (Fiorito, Jarley, and Delaney 1995). For example, the United Auto Workers had exclusive jurisdiction over assembly-line workers in the automotive industry, and the Teamsters had exclusive jurisdiction over the transportation, or trucking, industry.

With the decline of unionization in the private sector, the notion of exclusive jurisdiction has eroded in the public sector, where some unions are seeking opportunities outside their traditional zones of specialty or control. For example, with the growth of the unionization and opportunities in the public sector, the UAW has organized secretaries, and the Teamsters have organized police officers. Although exclusive jurisdiction still exists in principle, organizing efforts have changed in practice such that employees have the option to select several unions for possible representation.

An employee or group of employees can approach a union and seek its assistance in organizing, and a representative of the union will work with these individuals in their organizing efforts. At the same time, unions may seek out employees to organize. Regardless of whether an organizing effort is employee or union initiated, organizing requires financial, human, and technical resources and can consume a lot of a union's time and effort.

Unions will consider a variety of issues in a cost-benefit perspective before organizing an employee group. Some issues that unions may consider are the probability of success in organizing, based on the degree of interest in unionizing; the number of employees having the potential to become union members; and the employer's attitude toward unionization and the degree of resistance it may have toward organizing. Unions may also consider the future benefits in the context of how much money they will generate from union dues and whether organizing at this particular location could lead to further success in organizing attempts with other employers. Organizing may also protect the union's interest in firms it has already organized, by preventing the spread or increase of nonunion industries in that sector or area.

Unions can use a variety of strategies to organize in a cost-effective and timely manner. They may include traditional organizational efforts that use media sources, such as the newspapers and television. Unions may also use grassroots campaigning, with union members soliciting employees outside the workplace by handing out brochures and other information on the benefits of organizing under their particular union. At the same time, employees may be campaigning for unionization inside the workplace. Unions may also engage in raiding, or campaigning to convince workers to switch from one union to another. This interunion rivalry is heavily discouraged in those unions that are affiliated with the AFL-CIO, whose Internal Dispute Plan sets forth jurisdictional and representational rights, including a dispute-resolution process if a dispute should arise between members (Bohlander 2002).

Another organizing strategy is called "salting," which occurs when a full-time union organizer applies for a position in a nonunion company. Once hired and entrenched in the workforce, this union organizer begins an organizing campaign to unionize from within the company. Similar to the mythical Trojan horse, the union organizer, still employed by and being paid by the union and unbeknownst to the employer, "emerges" from within the company to organize workers (Fine 2002). In *NLRB v. Town and Country Electric* (1995), the U.S. Supreme Court found that salting is an appropriate union strategy but that the refusal to hire union organizers because of their union affiliation or the discharge of individuals who work for unions and the employer at the same time constitutes an unfair labor practice under the NLRA.

Salting is not a new strategy. Its origins date back to organizing Welsh miners in the 1800s. Salting was widely used in the early 1900s by labor organizations, such as the International Brotherhood of Electrical Workers (IBEW) and the garment workers. Salting is still a widely used organizing tactic in the construction trades (VanBourg and Moscowitz 1998).

During an organizational drive, unions may also engage in organizational picketing to convince an employer to recognize and bargain with a union. It is also used to convince or force employees to select the union as their bargaining representative. However, a union cannot engage in organizational picketing when the employer has lawfully recognized another union or when an NLRB election has been conducted within the preceding 12 months. Organizational picketing is not allowed for more than 30 days unless the union has submitted a petition for election with the NLRB. Union picketing for more than 30 days is considered an unfair labor practice.

The NLRA does not differentiate among organizational, publicity, and area-standards picketing. Conceptually, organizational picketing is done to induce an employer to recognize a union as the bargaining representative of employees. Publicity picketing involves advising the public that an employer does not hire union members or have a contract with a union. Area-standards picketing involves a union demand that the employer pay union wages. Confusingly, area-standards picketing can have a recognitional purpose because the union may also be demanding that the employer recognize it as the legitimate bargaining representative of employees.

The NLRA grants employees the right to self-organization, stating that it is an unfair labor practice for employers to interfere with that right. However, unions are limited in their campaigning activities. Employers can set rules about the solicitation and distribution of union materials during work hours. During scheduled breaks and lunch periods, employees can discuss or participate in union organizing activities. But at other times, employers can prohibit such activities, as they could distract, disrupt, or interfere with production activities.

Employers can also restrict union solicitation and distribution activities on their property by nonemployees. If union organizers can reasonably access employees off company property, employers do not have to allow them on their property. Companies can also prohibit the distribution of union literature on their property. This distribution of written materials carries the potential for littering and is a potential hazard, as debris could affect production and employee safety. Employers can also prohibit union solicitation via e-mail through its computer system—the computer system is private property—if employees can be reached in another manner for organizing purposes (Macik 2001). If employees cannot be accessed by union organizers and the employer does not allow organizers on its property, the NLRB can issue an access order that requires the employer to allow organizers onto company property (Hartwell 1985).

■ THE BARGAINING RELATIONSHIP

The NLRA requires that an employer bargain with employee representatives who have shown convincing evidence that they have the majority support of the employees. A union can become a representative of a bargaining unit in three ways. The first way is through voluntary recognition, which occurs when an employer recognizes a union as the employees' representative without using the NLRB election process. The union shows the employer that the majority of union representation cards that are signed by employees designate that particular union as their bargaining representative. The employer then acknowledges the union, and they engage in the collective-bargaining process. Although the union does not have NLRB certification, the employer and the union must abide by the NLRA.

In other cases, employers will not recognize a union and will insist on an NLRB-conducted election. This secret-ballot election conducted by the NLRB is the most common way a union is certified as the employees' bargaining representative. In a union-certification election, the goal of the union is to become the certified representative of a bargaining unit. A bargaining unit is simply a group of jobs or positions that share some common interests in a firm. Winning an NLRB-certified election certifies a union. In order to have an election, the union must demonstrate that it has the support of at least 30 percent of the members of the bargaining unit. Members of the bargaining unit are required to submit authorization cards stating that they wish to have that particular union represent them. On receipt of the authorization cards, the board determines whether the cards are valid and if they are, notifies the employer of the union's request for a certification election and then schedules a representation election.

The NLRB must first determine the appropriate bargaining unit for collective bargaining after the union submits the election petition to the board. This process is important because the definition of an appropriate bargaining unit determines the number of workers eligible to vote in the election (Chiaravalli and Lardaro 1985). The "community of interest" standard is used for establishing a bargaining unit. Under this standard, employees who have similar jobs or responsibilities or could be reasonably grouped together form a bargaining unit (National Labor Relations Board). Some of the issues that the NLRB may consider when investigating the proposed bargaining unit are similarity of pay, benefits, and hours of work, as well as similarity in the employees' qualifications, skills, training, and work performed. Depending on its size and the work performed, a company could have several bargaining units and unions to deal with. Truckers may be one bargaining unit organized by the Teamsters, whereas line workers may make up another bargaining unit organized by the UAW (Leslie 1984).

The NLRB is not responsible for finding the most appropriate bargaining unit but simply decides whether the proposed unit is appropriate (Leslie 1984). In a factory, for example, production employees share similar job responsibilities. Supervisors, however, have different responsibilities that would make it inappropriate to include them in the same bargaining unit. Individuals with specialized crafts, skills, or responsibilities, such as tool-and-die workers, would also be more suitable for membership in another bargaining unit. The community-of-interest standard may also apply to multiple locations. If a company has several retail stores, the NLRB may determine that all cashiers can belong to the same bargaining unit, as they all perform the same type of work, regardless of location (National Labor Relations Board).

The employer may contest the composition of the bargaining unit. If this occurs, the NLRB is responsible for conducting an investigation and holding a hearing about the issues raised by the employer. The NLRB itself may initiate an investigation and subsequent hearing leading to what is known as a Regional Director Directed Election (RDDE) (Chiaravalli and Lardaro 1985). If the employer and the union are in agreement with the composition of the bargaining unit and other specifics of the election, it is known as a consent election (Flanagan, Waller, and Deshpande 1995).

Following the determination of an appropriate bargaining unit, the board can conduct an election to decide which union, if any, will represent the workers. The certification election is conducted by secret ballot. If a union receives the majority of the votes from the bargaining unit (50 percent plus 1), that union becomes the employees' exclusive bargaining representative. The NLRB then "certifies" the union and informs the employer that it has a duty to bargain in good faith with that particular union (Grewach 1985). Representation elections can have more than one union on the ballot. If multiple unions are on the ballot and if no union has received a majority of votes, a runoff election is conducted between the voters' top two choices. The outcome of this election then determines what union, if any—as workers could have voted for no union—will represent the bargaining unit (Flanagan, Waller, and Deshpande 1995).

A third way for a union to become the representative of a bargaining unit is when the NLRB recognizes a particular union as the bargaining agent without an election. This occurs when a union can prove to the NLRB that the employer has committed unfair labor practices that would make a fair election unlikely or has somehow undermined the union's majority, causing an election to be set aside. Because of these activities, there is no feasible way the union could be certified as the bargaining representative, and the NLRB then makes the de facto union the legitimate union for employees (Oberer et al. 1986).

Successorship and Representation Rights

Under the doctrine of successorship, union status or certification can exist even if a company is sold. In the case of *NLRB v. Burns International Securities Services* (1972), the U.S. Supreme Court determined that a successor employer has the obligation to recognize and bargain with the union certified as the bargaining representative of the predecessor's employees. However, the successor company is not obligated to adopt or follow the terms of the collective-bargaining agreement or adhere to the former owner's agreement with the union. The new owner can set its own initial terms and conditions of employment before engaging in collective-bargaining activities with the union.

The NLRB considers a new employer a successor if (1) it has acquired the assets of the company—not the stock—or has taken over a service-providing business as a leasee or licensee of the former employer; (2) the majority of employees were also employees of the predecessor employer; and (3) the new employer's business is basically the same as the former business. Usually, the two main factors considered are whether the new employer's workforce consists of employees of the former employer and whether employees have "substantial continuity," or sameness, in the work they perform (Sturner 2001).

Under successorship rules, new owners can maintain preexisting terms of employment; if they don't, they must issue a "Spruce Up Announcement" notifying the union and employees that their terms and conditions of employment will be different from those under the prior collective-bargaining agreement. In essence, what a new employer does is fire all the existing employees and then notify them that they are now new job applicants, that their employment will be different from before, and that the application for employment will be used if they understand and accept the new conditions and terms of employment prior to the invitation to accept employment (Sturner 2001). Of interest is the fact that a new employer's refusal to hire members of the former employer's unionized workforce is unlawful discrimination based on union affiliation, as it could be construed as a union-busting activity.

Representation Rights of Security Guards Under the NLRA

Unlike other industry groups that organize under the NLRA, security guards have some specific restrictions on their rights when joining a union. Under Section 9(b)(3) of the NLRA's 1947 Taft-Hartley amendments, the NLRB is prohibited from certifying any bargaining unit or union that has both guard and nonguard employees in its membership (Rattay 1983/1984). This section also prohibits the certification of unions that admit nonguard members or when a union is directly or indirectly affiliated with a union whose members are nonguards (Grewach 1985; McCabe 1985). This means that guards can belong only to unions that represent only security guards.

This restriction is premised on the historical and philosophical grounds that existed in the mid-1940s. During World War II, plant guards who worked for companies that had military contracts became civilian auxiliaries of the military police (Jensen 1985/1986).

Many of these guards then sought unionization under the NLRA. Employers, however, subsequently argued that the guards were not employees under the NLRA but were now part of the military (Grewach 1985). Another argument was based on the premise that if guards belonged to the same union as nonguards and a strike occurred, the guards would have conflicting, or divided, loyalties and would be responsible for protecting the assets of the company while enforcing rules against their fellow union members (McCabe 1985).

Although Section 9(b)(3) of the NLRA prohibits the NLRB from certifying guard/nonguard unions, employers can still voluntarily recognize such mixed unions. When employers do recognize these unions, the union does not enjoy many of the benefits of NLRB protections, such as election and certification procedures or unit clarification processes. Because these voluntarily recognized unions do not have NLRB certification, employers can also withdraw their voluntary recognition during a bargaining stalemate, such as a strike (Grewach 1985).

Withdrawing Union Recognition

Unions can also become decertified because of economic, employer, and union activities. An increase in decertification elections has resulted from increased foreign competition and effective employers' human resource programs that make employees question the usefulness of their unions (Biogness and Pierce 1988). In other situations, union members may become dissatisfied with the delivery of union services, feedback, degree of democracy and negotiation of collective-bargaining agreements (Jarley, Sarosh, and Casteel 1990). Management campaigns in promoting a nonunion environment also explain why employees may seek decertification of their union (Jelf and Dworkin 1997).

Once a union is certified, the NLRB assumes that this union has the majority of support for one year. After this first year, the presumption of majority support does not exist. Members of a bargaining unit can decertify their existing union and petition the NLRB for a new election. Employers can also withdraw their recognition of a union as a representative of the bargaining unit when they can affirmatively prove that the union no longer enjoys the majority support of the bargaining unit or that their refusal to bargain is based on a good-faith or reasonably grounded doubt that the union had a continued majority support of its members. One way this can be accomplished is by polling employees on their union sentiments (Silbergeld 1990).

The first step in union decertification requires an employee, a group of employees, or the employer to petition the NLRB for a decertification election. As with the certification election, if the petition is filed by a group of employees, the petition must show that at least 30 percent of the employees are seeking decertification of their union. Following the petition for decertification, the NLRB conducts an investigation. Once a finding about the question of representation is made, an election by secret ballot is conducted. Any decertification election has three possible outcomes. If 50 percent (plus 1) of the voters vote against the union, the union is decertified as the exclusive bargaining representative in the bargaining unit. Union members can also vote to return to nonunion status. The outcomes of the vote may also result in the union members' retaining their existing union as their bargaining representative (Biogness and Pierce 1988).

■ COLLECTIVE BARGAINING

One of the most visible and well-known union activities is negotiating the collective-bargaining agreement. Collective bargaining is both an event and a process. It is an event in that representatives from the union and the employer meet and negotiate a new collective-bargaining agreement. The parties to the process engage in bargaining activities that lead to the collective-bargaining agreement that they will work under for a specified period of time, which is on average 3 years. The enforcement and administration of the contract is also an ongoing process for both the employer and the union. Once the contract is agreed on, it must be administered, which requires a great deal of time. The negotiation process can often be considered to be continual. Once a contract is agreed on, the parties often begin preparing for the next round of bargaining.

A collective-bargaining agreement is the constitution of the workplace. Many workers may inadvertently assume that they have full constitutional protections in the workplace. But that it is not the case. In the context of some constitutional provisions, such as freedom of speech, employees can be terminated for expressing ideas and posting various printed media that an employer may deem to be inappropriate. The Fourth Amendment, which protects citizens from unlawful search and seizures by the state, is also limited in the workplace. Employers can request that employees be searched on arrival and departure from the workplace, search lockers and other areas that one may consider to be "private," and monitor the activities of employees over the course of the workday. All these activities can be legally conducted because employers are not state agents and subsequently do not need probable cause to engage in such activities. Through the collective-bargaining agreement, some of these rights are restored or exist in the workplace. Without an agreement, employees are left to the whim of employers and relevant labor legislation that offers them some protections if they do not have some type of an employment contract.

Collective-bargaining agreements can be quite long and detailed, running to more than 100 pages. These contracts cover all aspects of the employment relationship and clearly define the rights of the employer and employee in the workplace. The collective-bargaining agreement also specifies the due-process rights that an employee has about any issues or disputes that may arise in the employment relationship. These due-process rights are expressed via the contract's grievance arbitration clause, which spells out the procedural rights employees have when they feel that their "rights" as prescribed in the collective-bargaining agreement have been violated.

The Wagner Act requires unions and employers to bargain in good faith with respect to wages, hours, and other terms and conditions of employment. Subjects of bargaining can be either mandatory or nonmandatory. A mandatory subject of bargaining means that the employer and the union must negotiate the subject. Mandatory issues generally impact the financial well-being of employees, such as wages and benefits. A mandatory subject of bargaining does not mean that either party is obligated to make a concession about the issue. It simply means that the parties must discuss the issues in good faith, meaning that they meet and engage in a purposeful and meaningful dialogue related to the negotiation of a new collective-bargaining agreement. If either party refuses to discuss or negotiate the issue in "good faith," an unfair labor practice has occurred.

An employer has no legal duty to bargain over managerial decisions that lie at the core of managerial control, regardless of whether these decisions impact union members. These types of decisions are referred to as managerial prerogatives, or management rights. They are permissive subjects of bargaining and may include activities related to production and the introduction of new products or other activities that are essential to the running of the business (Summers 1995). Although they are not mandatory subjects of bargaining, they may be included by the employer as a concession or trade-off in the negotiation process. An example is the creation of a joint labor-management committee to improve production in the workplace.

The parties can take two basic models, or negotiating techniques, during contract negotiations: distributive or integrative. According to Lewicki et al. (1993), distributive bargaining adopts a win-lose style. This type of bargaining can be compared to two professional football teams competing for the Super Bowl title. Each party's goals are in direct conflict with the goals of the other (Lewicki and Litterer 1985). This adversarial-based model was the traditional paradigm in union-management relations in the nineteenth and twentieth centuries, when antagonism existed between the parties before, during, and after the negotiation process.

By contrast, parties operating under the cooperative-based model of union-management negotiations, known as an integrative, or win-win approach to collective bargaining, define or determine a common problem and use various strategies, such as compromise, collaboration, and accommodation, to achieve those goals. This cooperative-based approach subsequently generates trust among the parties, as well as a motivation to work together, subsequently reducing the time required to reach a decision (Lewicki and Litterer 1985). This approach has been found to serve the long-range plans of both the employer and the union by promoting production and profitability and increasing the degree of industrial democracy in the workplace (Summers 1995).

One cooperative-based model that has been used successfully in contract negotiations is the PAST model (Brommer, Buckingham, and Loeffler 2002). PAST stands for: principles, assumptions, steps, and techniques.

Effective *principles* include focusing on issues and interests instead of personalities and positions while seeking mutual gain for the parties involved. *Assumptions*, meanwhile, deal with believing that a win-win outcome is possible going into the bargaining process. Parties should adopt the perspective that they can help one another "win" and succeed through open dialogue that expands the options and opportunities available to each party. *Steps* deal with procedural issues. Successful bargaining requires that the parties expect to follow a progression in their activities: preparation; opening statements; issue identification; assessing interests, options, and standards for one issue; and then testing the options against the standards to try to achieve a settlement. *Techniques* refers to specific strategies that the parties might use during negotiations, such as brainstorming, consensus decision making, and idea charting.

Just as negotiating styles vary, so too do bargaining strategies. One bargaining strategy is pattern bargaining, which occurs when a union requests the same provisions as those negotiated with a different employer. The end result of using comparisons is that the unions have the same or similar outcomes in their negotiations of new collective-bargaining agreements. This type of bargaining is often intraindustrial in nature and has been found to occur in the automotive and steel industries, which have similar wages and benefits across employers (Erickson 1996). As a basis for their positions on issues, unions and employers often use comparables, or what other employers or unions are providing in wages and benefits in their area or region for similar or like activities in the workplace.

If an employer or a union does not bargain in good faith, either party—usually the union—can file a complaint with the National Labor Relations Board for an unfair labor practice. It is then the responsibility of the NLRB to investigate these complaints. If an unfair labor practice is found to exist, the NLRB can enjoin the union or the employer from engaging in these activities. The decisions by the NLRB are enforceable through the courts, and either party can appeal the board's decisions in the federal courts.

Union Security Agreements

Besides the "bread and butter" issues, the union can negotiate a union security agreement into the collective-bargaining agreement. As the name suggests, a union security arrangement secures the well-being of the union in the workplace. It is an agreement between the employer and the union that the employer will require of all employees in that particular bargaining unit some level of union support as a condition of employment (Dau-Schmidt 1990). One traditional union security agreement was the closed-shop agreement, which under the collective-bargaining agreement required employers to hire only union members. Another union security agreement was the union shop clause, which required that all employees join the union after they were hired. Both the closed- and union-shop agreements have been determined to be unlawful by the Supreme Court because employees have the right not to join unions (Levine 2001).

The union can also negotiate an agency-shop clause into the collective-bargaining agreement in those states where they are legal. This clause is an agreement between the employer and the union that all employees must pay union dues and work under the negotiated union contract. Under the agency-shop clause, employees do not have to belong to the union and can quit their membership at any time. Regardless of their affiliation with the union, they must still pay their equal share of union membership dues (Levine 2001). By requiring all employees to pay union dues, the union can remain financially solvent and can afford to administer the collective-bargaining agreement.

Union Dues

Union fees or dues are also part of the collective-bargaining agreement, and the union dues check-off system is a mandatory subject of bargaining. On average, a union member pays an equivalent of 2 hours wages per month as dues, which are used to defray the costs of contract administration and negotiations. The dues are also used for political expenses the union incurs. Unions must keep these political funds separate from their operating funds. By law, union members can request a refund from their union for that portion of their dues used for political purposes. Union members are required to contribute only their "fair share" of union expenses related to contract administration and negotiation but do not have to contribute to any political-related activities and subsequent expenses (Wright 1982).

The Grievance Clause

Disagreements in the workplace can be a daily occurrence. When they happen, an employee has three options. One is to simply ignore the issue, anticipating that it will go away or not occur again. A second option is to resolve the issue without the assistance of the union. The third, most formal option is to invoke the grievance process.

As discussed earlier, a collective-bargaining agreement gives workers rights that they may not have without such an agreement. The formal process for resolving workplace disputes is found in the grievance clause of the collective-bargaining agreement. This clause makes the collective-bargaining agreement a "living contract" by allowing the grieving party or parties a "voice" in the workplace. The grievance clause also allows for the agreement or a specific clause in it to be interpreted by the third-party neutral. Both of these components ensure industrial democracy in the workplace. Rights arbitration is widely accepted and used in the United States, with approximately 95 percent of the public- and private-sector contracts having some type of rights provision (McGinnis 1989).

At the heart of any grievance is a real or perceived wrong. An issue that is not covered in the collective-bargaining agreement may indicate that a new issue has arisen or that the employer and the union cannot agree on a reasonable course of action. In essence, the contract remains "silent" on an issue. The more common situation is disagreement on a managerial practice, with the union feeling that the employer has violated the conditions of the collective-bargaining agreement.

One behavioral model of grievance initiation posits that any grievance process has three actors: the supervisor, the employee, and the union, with the supervisor being the primary agent or the initiator of grievances (Bemmels 1994). Issues that can either aggravate or mitigate grievance initiation include the degree to which a supervisor emphasizes productivity over friendly relations with employees and the degree to which union stewards attempt to persuade employees to file grievances (Bemmels 1994). It should be recognized, however, that unions, as well as employees, are also responsible for grievances. An employer can file a grievance against the actions or inactions of the union for violating the terms and conditions set forth in the collective-bargaining agreement.

The grievance process in any organization is progressive. It begins with the least-complicated method of resolving a dispute and often ends with a neutral third-party arbitrator settling the disagreement between the parties. The grievance process follows the organizational hierarchy, beginning with the immediate supervisor, progresses to the departmental supervisor, and then moves onto the higher levels in the organization. A great majority of disputes are settled on the shop floor and can be considered "simple" issues. As it moves up the hierarchy, the grievance process becomes more formal and complex, involving many actors.

One of the first steps in the grievance process is to notify the shop or union steward of the perceived wrong. The steward, depending on the behaviors of the supervisor and aggrieved employee, has two options: (1) resolve the issue informally by discussing the issue with a supervisor or (2) help the employee file a formal written grievance if the issue is not resolved on the shop floor. Stewards themselves can file grievances in the name of the union on behalf of an employee or convince other union members to file a grievance if they perceive a violation in the collective-bargaining agreement. In the case of one contract that covers nurses, the grievance process begins with an oral discussion with the immediate supervisor. If not resolved at this stage, it is forwarded to the associate director for nursing services and then to the labor relations department. The grievance procedure can stop at any stage in the process if satisfactory agreements are made; employees have the option of union representation, and both parties have established time limitations for the filing and responses to grievances.

Grievance Arbitration

Most grievance clauses call for mandatory arbitration as the terminal stage in the grievance process. Rights, or grievance, arbitration occurs when a mutually selected impartial arbitrator must settle a dispute, violation, or perceived violation on the application or interpretation of an existing collective-bargaining agreement, law, policy, or customary practice (Elkouri and Elkouri 1985; DiLauro 1989; McGinnis 1989). External law, however, does not mandate this right's provision. Instead, a grievance-arbitration clause must be negotiated into the collective-bargaining agreement; the clause specifies what, if any, issues are considered to be arbitrable or heard in the workplace. As with the grievance procedure, arbitration hearings require deadlines for submission and the selection of an arbitrator, who is usually jointly selected or appointed by the parties, pursuant to the agreed on method of selection that was predetermined in the collective-bargaining agreement.

Rights arbitrators are usually selected jointly by the parties in dispute. Arbitrators can be selected from rosters held by the FMCS, state agencies, and the American Arbitration Association (AAA). The parties can also mutually select an arbitrator; in some instances, the parties may have a permanent arbitrator or an arbitration panel that is used by some large U.S. corporations (Elkouri and Elkouri 1985). Both parties must share the cost of arbitration, and the final decision or award is final and binding.

Some agreements, however, have expedited or additional stages before arbitration. A teachers' collective-bargaining agreement has an expedited method whereby a grievance can be immediately sent to the board of education. In the case of a nursing contract, nurses engage in a prearbitration hearing with the labor relations department. If, however, the disposition of the grievances is not satisfactory, the final recourse is arbitration.

According to Nolan (1979), arbitration is a process whereby the parties in a dispute voluntarily agree to follow the decision of an impartial person who, outside of a judicial process, bases the decision on the facts, evidence, and arguments presented in the form of a less formal setting that resembles a judicial proceeding. *Black's Law Dictionary* (1979, 96) defines arbitration as "the reference of a dispute to an impartial (third) person chosen by the parties . . . instead of carrying it to established tribunals of justice . . . intended to avoid the formalities, the delay, the expense and vexation of ordinary litigation." Coulson (1985) indicates that arbitration involves giving a third party, a neutral individual, or a panel the power to make a decision. Feuille, Delaney, and Hendricks (1985) consider arbitration to be a dispute-resolution tool that results in the arbitrator's version of a fair settlement, because at the foundation of any dispute between the parties is the issue of perception of fairness. If the parties cannot agree on a fair settlement because of their disagreement over what a fair settlement would be, the arbitrator must subsequently render the award.

The role of the arbitrator in the arbitration hearing is quite diverse. The arbitrator is responsible for scheduling the hearing, conducting all aspects of the hearing, and writing the arbitration award. More specifically, the role of the arbitrator in rights arbitration is to interpret what the parties intended in the contract (Balfour 1987). In doing so, the arbitrator must base the decision on the "four corners of the contract," or the content of the existing negotiated contract. In determining those situations in which the contract is silent or vague on the issue(s) in dispute, the arbitrator must render a decision, based on the past practices of the parties involved. This decision is then final and binding on the parties.

Rights arbitration has also been accepted and reinforced through Supreme Court decisions that have indicated deference to rights arbitration over the parties seeking judicial relief. One of the most famous series of decisions, known as the Steelworker's Trilogy, examined the role of arbitration in terms of its finality and preference over judicial decisions.

The preference for arbitration over court proceedings was indicated in *United Steelworkers of America v. Warrior and Gulf Navigation Co.* (1960), in which the U.S. Supreme Court declared:

> The collective bargaining agreement is part of an attempt to establish a system of industrial self-government, the gaps in which may be left out to be filled in by reference to the practices of the particular industry and of the various shops covered by the agreement. The labor arbitrator is selected for his knowledge of the common law of the shop and for his ability to bring to bear considerations which may indeed be foreign to the competence of the courts. . . . The ablest judge cannot be expected to bring the same experience and competence to bear upon the determination of a grievance, because he cannot be similarly informed. (pp. 1351–1353)

Besides deferral to the arbitrator, the Court, in *United Steelworkers of America v. American Manufacturing Co.* (1960) examined the issue of arbitrability. In this decision, the Court determined that its responsibility in grievance arbitration was to simply determine whether the type of dispute could be arbitrated under the collective-bargaining agreement. This decision was based on the contention that national labor policy favors arbitration and the "processing of even frivolous claims may have therapeutic values of which those who are not part of the plant environment may be quite unaware" (p. 1346). Consequently, the Court would not determine the merits or claim of the grievance, as "whether the moving party is right or wrong is a question of contract interpretation for the arbitrator" (p. 1346).

In *United Steelworkers of America v. Enterprise Wheel and Car Corp.* (1960), the Court examined the enforcement of arbitration awards and the role of the courts in reviewing and overturning arbitration awards. Adopting a substantive-based position, the Court determined that if courts have the final say or decision on the merits of the arbitration award, the role of the arbitrator and rights arbitration would be undermined. Thus, arbitration awards cannot be overturned "as long as it [the arbitration award] draws its essence from the collective bargaining agreement" (p. 1361). However, the Court also determined that "where it is clear that the arbitrator's words manifest an infidelity to this obligation" (p. 1362), the courts can refuse to enforce the award.

Although rights arbitration is the preferred terminal procedure, a party or parties could possibly seek relief from the courts, based on the type of grievance. If the employer has violated an individual's constitutional or statutory right, such as Title VII of the 1964 Civil Rights Act, as amended, after the arbitration proceeding, the individual has the right to seek judicial relief through the courts (Malin and Ladenson 1993). This was decided in the case *Alexander v. Gardner-Denver Co.* (1974), in which the Supreme Court determined that "there is no suggestion in the statutory scheme [of Title VII] that a prior arbitral decision either forecloses an individual's right to sue or divests federal courts of jurisdiction" (p. 47).

■ STRIKES

The Union's Role

One of the most powerful tools that a union possesses is the power of the strike, a collective action in which employees refuse to continue to provide their labor to the employer. In fact, some authors feel that "the strike plays the same role in labor negotiations that warfare plays in diplomatic negotiations. It facilitates agreement precisely because the consequences of failure are serious, unpleasant and costly" (Getman and Marshall 2001, 703).

Under the NLRA, employees have the right to strike for the purpose of mutual aid and protection. The right to strike is not absolute, however. In some cases, the parties may have negotiated a no-strike clause in the bargaining agreement, and if the union called a strike, it would be breaching the agreement and constitute an unfair labor practice under the NLRA. In other instances, when a strike can be found to be abnormally destructive or threatens the health or safety of the citizenry, the government can use a court-imposed injunction to force employees back to work.

Strikes occur for various reasons. One is incomplete information. Management and union representatives have complete information about the bargaining process, but union members may have unrealistic expectations, which subsequently force the union to seek the strike, even though it may perceive the needs of the employees to be unrealistic. As a strike continues, however, members may become more receptive to realistic terms. This protects the union from a politically damaging situation of accepting terms that were lower than what was initially accepted by the union members (Nieswiadomy, Raj, and Slottja 1995). In other situations, the strike can be a sign of solidarity and power for the union and its membership. Strikes also occur simply because the union has no other means to force the employer to meet its demands.

In a strike situation, union members engage in picketing activities. Picketing does not have a precise definition but is usually defined as an activity that induces action and inaction. Usually, picketing is associated with union members' patrolling an area with signs. Picketing also includes having signs posted, passing out leaflets, or simply patrolling without signs. Organizational picketing must have the purpose of informing the public that the employer does not hire or have a contract with the labor organization. Organizational picketing cannot interfere with deliveries or other services from employees of other employers (Modjeska 1983).

The use of the strike is not immediate. In the contract negotiation, it is a terminal procedure that is preceded by good-faith bargaining by the parties. During the negotiation process, the parties in some instances reach disagreement on certain issues. When these disagreements cannot be overcome or negotiated, the parties are said to be at impasse, or deadlocked, in the negotiation process. In several instances, time and further negotiations may resolve the issues at impasse. In other situations, however, it may require the intervention of a neutral third party to resolve the issues or to simply get the parties back to the bargaining table to discuss the issues at impasse.

In an effort to preserve labor peace and avoid strikes, the NLRA requires that, if the parties have not created a new contract within 30 days of the expiration of a contract, they must submit a legally required notice of intent to open a collective-bargaining agreement with the Federal Mediation and Conciliation Service (FMCS). The parties must also notify their appropriate state agencies. The role of the FMCS mediator is simply to provide neutral advice and direction to help parties resolve the conflict(s) they have over the negotiation of the new collective-bargaining agreement (Newman 1990).

If conciliation and mediation should fail, the union can then call for a strike vote. If the members vote yes, a strike is called for on a particular date. The employer is then warned of the impending strike. In order to garner support for the strike, unions often issue press releases announcing their proposed strike date and time to enlist the public's support for their cause and to invoke and encourage economic action against the employer. The announcement and publicity surrounding the strike may also persuade the employer to reevaluate its positions on the issues in dispute.

■ THE EMPLOYER'S RESPONSE

There are some traditional ways for an employer to respond to the strike. In the manufacturing sector these have included stockpiling inventory in advance of the strike, staffing struck positions with managers and other nonunion employees who work for the firm, subcontracting the work, and hiring temporary replacement workers, commonly termed "scab" workers (LeRoy 1996a). These workers are then terminated once the strike is over.

As long as they have not engaged in an unfair practice, employers can hire permanent replacement workers. In *NLRB v. McKay Radio & Telegraph Co.* (1938), the Supreme Court concluded that an employer can hire permanent replacements for economic strikers and that it is not an unfair labor practice to replace strikers, as the company is simply trying to continue with its business. Using replacement workers is known as the McKay doctrine (LeRoy 1995). Under the Laidlaw doctrine, by contrast, employers are required to reinstate a replaced striker once a suitable vacancy exists in the company (LeRoy 1996). This practice of hiring replacement workers has always occurred in strike situations (LeRoy

1995a) but has been increasing since the 1970s. In 1981, President Reagan fired 11,000 air traffic controllers who belonged to the Professional Air Traffic Controllers Organization (PATCO) (Northrup 1984).

Employers can use the lockout as a response to the strike. A lockout occurs when an employer prevents employees from entering the workplace, based on the premise that if a union can withhold labor through the strike and cause economic hardship to the company, the company can withhold work and wages from employees, causing economic hardship, too. Under a lockout, an employer can hire temporary employees but not permanent replacement workers. Lockouts were widely used in the 1990s. Lockouts can be both defensive and offensive. Defensive lockouts can be used in response to a union's use of the economic weapon. Offensive lockouts can be used to force a settlement (LeRoy 1996b).

A replaced worker differs from a locked-out worker. LeRoy (1996b, 1024) explains the difference this way: "The key difference between replaced workers and locked out and replaced strikers is that the former did not use its economic weapon, while the latter did, thereby assuming the risk of replacement. In other words, the former group was put out of work, not as a result of their miscalculated aggression, but because of an aggressive action initiated by an employer."

An effective lockout occurred when owners of National Basketball Association teams locked out their players at the beginning of the season. Because of the lockout, players did not receive their paychecks, but fans were not as disappointed as they would have been if players had gone out on strike during the season. The lockout gave the owners a more advantageous bargaining position than if the players had gone on strike. Research on lockouts has shown that the duration of most lockouts is less than 4 months or greater than 1 year (LeRoy 1996b).

■ DISPUTE-RESOLUTION TECHNIQUES

Dispute-resolution procedures are the formal and informal rules that individuals and groups use to resolve problems in the workplace. These rules function "as a system of private law, . . . with its own interpretations, practices, and customs built up over time" (Thomson 1974, 1). Some of these procedures are also designed to protect employees against arbitrary authority and unjust punitive action while providing a systematic review of complaints and grievances (Scott 1965). As pointed out earlier in this chapter, employers and unions have a variety of dispute-resolution procedures available to them to ensure that productivity will not be impacted. Generally, three types of dispute-resolution procedures are found in the private and public sectors: mediation, fact finding, and contract arbitration.

Mediation

In mediation, a third-party neutral, or go-between, helps the parties reach an agreement (Somers 1977). It is anticipated that both parties are willing to accept some compromises in their positions (Fossum 1979). Mediation serves a series of purposes, including educating and helping the parties gain a better understanding of the opposing positions, reducing hostility, providing a problem-solving agenda, and presenting alternatives in a context that allows all the parties to save face.

According to Balfour (1987), the mediator has procedural, definitional, and substantive functions. In these roles, the mediator is responsible for scheduling meetings and determining negotiation sites; meeting with the parties jointly and separately; assisting in determining, explaining, and presenting the positions of the parties; identifying issues; and engaging in substantive issues related to assisting parties in structuring proposals and counterproposals. In short, the mediator changes the dynamics of the collective-bargaining experience while identifying those issues or positions that may have contributed to the impasse. The mediator, however, does not render a decision. The ultimate goal is to get the parties to voluntarily agree to a settlement through persuasion (Elkouri and Elkouri 1985) by increasing or facilitating communication between the parties, while getting the parties to move toward settlement, if possible.

According to Lewis (1981), mediation is the most-used and least-studied alternative dispute-resolution technique, as it is the least visible of alternative dispute-resolution techniques. Because of the "behind-the-scene" nature of mediation and the fact that some feel that it is more of an art than a science, mediation is difficult to generalize and investigate scientifically. One example of the use of mediation is the FMCS, which intervenes during impasse to prevent strikes.

Fact Finding

Fact finding is primarily a public-sector impasse-resolution process initiated between the stages of mediation and arbitration. Fact finding can, however, be invoked in the private sector under the Taft-Hartley Act or the Railway Labor Act if the potential for a national emergency would result if the parties were permitted to strike (Kochan and Katz 1988). According to Balfour (1987), fact finding may also be referred to as a board of inquiry, advisory arbitration, or a special-master process. The primary goal of fact finding is to settle disputes and to make public the positions of the parties by the publication of the issues in dispute by a third-party neutral individual or panel (Hirlinger and Sylvia 1988).

As in mediation, the fact finder does not render a decision but instead investigates or assembles all facts in the labor dispute by conducting a fact-finding hearing. In this capacity, some theorists suggest that fact finding is similar to arbitration because both procedures include a hearing, testimony, and findings (Lewis 1981). More specifically, the role of the fact finder is to hear the parties' arguments, make public the findings of the hearing regarding each party's position, and then make some nonbinding recommendations (Helsby et al. 1988). In doing so, the fact finder or third-party neutral serves a quasi-judicial role in which the findings and recommendations are made public (Somers 1977).

Although the hearing process and the public presentation of each party's positions is a primary role of fact finding, the process also serves other functions. Fact finding may make the parties rethink or clarify their positions, as they will be presented to the public (Gilbert 1987; Ries 1992). Public pressure may also make the parties accept the fact finder's recommendations (Lewis 1981). According to Gallagher and Pegnetter (1979), fact finding may also have a "sobering effect" as the parties respond to the fact finder's report about the negative and positive aspects of each party's position. This factor results in fewer cases and issues proceeding to the arbitration stage. The potential threat of, or invoking of the fact-finding process may also motivate the parties to a negotiated settlement.

Fact finding also has some drawbacks. Fact finding may not be a viable solution to an impasse when severe financial conditions exist, as the distance between the parties' needs or wants cannot be reconciled or compromised to the degree necessary to reach a decision (Lewis 1981). Gilbert (1987) indicates that parties in fact finding may not present realistic final offers but instead rely on the fact finder to dictate the terms of agreement in anticipation that it will be more favorable. Likewise, those states that have fact finding followed by arbitration may have duplicative effects, as both procedures are very similar in terms of the hearing and the presentation of issues by the parties. Parties may also become dependent on fact finding (McKelvey 1969). Further, the availability of fact finding may extend the negotiations to the fact-finding stage, so good-faith bargaining occurs at this stage instead of at collective-bargaining sessions (Zack 1979). According to research by Kochan and Katz (1988), fact finding has a low rate of settlement and does not avoid strikes for those parties legally allowed to strike.

Contract Arbitration

Contract arbitration is used primarily in the public sector. Unlike rights arbitration, which deals with the interpretation of an existing collective-bargaining agreement, contract arbitration deals with the creation of a new collective-bargaining agreement. Contract arbitration is often used as a substitute for the strike, which is often banned for some public-sector employees. For example, contract arbitration would be used with essential-service employees, such as police, firefighters, and 911 dispatchers, who are not allowed to strike. Therefore, several states mandate that their disputes over the creation of a new collective-bargaining agreement be ultimately determined by a neutral third-party arbitrator whose decision is final and binding on the parties.

■ THE ROLE OF SECURITY IN AN ORGANIZED LABOR SETTING

As discussed earlier in this chapter, the actions of supervisors can result in an increase in the number of grievances filed by union members. This same issue applies to security personnel, as security can often be considered an extension of supervisors and the company. This fact requires that the security function, whether it be contractual or proprietary or at the line or supervisory level, understand that its actions can lead to labor problems.

First, security personnel need to be trained and understand the collective-bargaining agreement. In some organizational settings, security personnel may be unaccustomed to operating with unionized employees. This can be attributed to the fact that in some situations, security personnel may not be unionized. However, they may be working with unionized employees in either proprietary or contractual settings. In one case, for example, a nonunion contract security officer working in a union environment helped clerical staff answer a telephone that was at his workstation. Although this officer's actions were innocuous and simply a gesture of goodwill to help out the staff, with the permission of some staff members, a union staff member complained to the shop steward that this officer had infringed on a union position, raising an issue that the union could lose a position to a nonunion contract employee if it continued. The shop steward resolved the issue with management without having to file a formal grievance.

At the same time, the security function also needs to realize that its activities could lead to the union's filing a complaint with the NLRB. For example, some activities may not be considered to be violations but simply aggressive or perhaps good security work. A deeper understanding of the collective-bargaining agreement and labor law may prove otherwise. One NLRB case, for example, found that an employer committed an unfair labor practice by "threatening" a employee for her handbilling activities—a protected union activity. A security guard asked an employee her name during handbilling, followed her in when she started her shift, asked the employee's manager for her name, and after the employee refused to reveal her name, immediately asked to speak with the director after learning the employee's name. Although the previous incident may have been purposeful, other violations may be accidental in nature because of value-added security activities. In another NLRB case, the employer committed an unfair labor practice when security guards asked a union handbiller her name and engaged in a pleasant discussion with her for 15 minutes while offering an umbrella to protect her from a light rain. The NLRB concluded that the guard's activities amounted to illegal coercion (*Pikeville United Methodist Hospital of Kentucky, Inc. v. United Steelworkers of America* 1997).

Surveillance Issues

Security managers need to be aware of surveillance issues. An employer can engage in surveillance activities to document union trespass or issues related to union violence, however it needs to be quite careful. In one NLRB case, for example, the employer was found to be in violation of the NLRA when security officers videotaped union members congregating and participating in organizing activities while on their lunch hour. The NLRB has held that an activity of this nature "chills" union activities and intimidates union members (*California Acrylic Industries Inc. v. NLRB* 1998).

The key to unlawful surveillance is related to the degree of intrusiveness in union activities. A review of NLRB decisions shows that employees have a limited expectation of privacy when engaging in union activities on or near the employer's property. Thus, if the activity occurs on the employer's property and if the employer does not do anything out of the ordinary or create an impression of surveillance, the employer has a right to observe union activities and is not in violation of Section 8 (a) (1) of the National Labor Relations Act. In Roadway Package System, Inc. (1991), for example, the NLRB determined that employees conducting their activities openly or near company premises have no reasonable expectation of privacy from the employer. As a result, employers can observe union-related activities as long as they do not interfere with those activities. The administrative law judge concluded that the open observation by the respondent's manager standing near a guardhouse was permitted.

Surveillance on company property by company officials, however, does have its limitations. In Impact Industries Inc. (1987), the NLRB determined that engaging in conduct by assuming positions closer to union activities constitutes a violation of Section 8 (a) (1), as it tends to discourage employees from participating in union activities. This issue of interference was further exemplified in Hoschton Garment Company (1986), in which the Board determined that conduct having a clear and obvious tendency to interfere with an employee's receipt of literature constitutes a violation of Section 8 (a) (1).

The NLRB has established criteria for what constitutes unlawful surveillance of union activities. In Metal Industries (1980), the Board determined that Section 8 (a) (1) of the NLRA is not violated unless such officials do something out of the ordinary. An example of an unordinary activity occurred in the case of Advance Transport (1990). Here, it was determined that an employer unlawfully interfered when it created the impression that it was watching the employees to see which ones opposed its mandatory profit-sharing plan.

Besides the simple actions of an employer or representative of the employer engaging in acts that are considered unordinary or intrusive, photographing union activities may constitute an unordinary and intrusive activity and a violation of the NLRA. In proving unlawful photographing of employees, the burden of proof is on the employer. The employer must provide a justification for photographing union activities. If the employer cannot provide adequate justifications for its actions, the activity is unlawful and in violation of Section 8 (a) (1). In United States Steel Corporation (1981), for example, the employer failed to establish any legitimate reason for its actions. The NLRB concluded that "purely 'anticipatory' photographing of peaceful picketing in the event something 'might' happen does not justify [an employer's] conduct when balanced against the tendency of that conduct to interfere with the employees' right to engage in concerted activity" (p. 1338).

Some exceptions to photographing employees apply, however. Photographing union activities to establish that individuals were trespassing or demonstrating on the employer's property is not a violation of the NLRA, because the employer has an interest in protecting its rights as property owner. The videotaping of pickets is also lawful if the employer can prove that previous union activities involved violence directed at the employer's property and working employees. Another exception to the rules established for photographing to be in violation of the NLRA is that employers can videotape nonemployees to secure evidence of trespassing activities.

The Role of Security in Strikes

Under the Norris-Laguardia Act of 1932, unions cannot be held liable for the actions of their membership unless there is clear and convincing proof that the labor organization had ratified, participated in, or authorized the violent activity. In order for a union to be held liable, it must have some level of active involvement in the situation (Carlson 1990). This is not to say that unions and union leaders are immune from legal penalties. They can be found guilty of unfair labor practices and criminally and civilly liable under other federal and state criminal statutes (Getman and Marshall 2001).

Perhaps the security function is most likely to clash with unions during strike situations. A primary concern for an employer during the strike is the protection of assets and ensuring continued production capabilities. The use of security in these situations can lead to complaints of unfair labor practices and decisions against the company if the security function, either contract or proprietary, is not used in a lawful manner.

One issue that security managers need to consider is the deployment of security forces during strike situations. Employers also maintain the right to maintain a security force at levels that are "necessary for the furtherance of a legitimate business interest" (The Broadway 1983). This level may even include bringing in additional security during a strike situation to protect the health and well-being of customers or guests (*Parsippany Hotel Management Co. v. NLRB* 1996). Conversely, security officers' observation of strike activities that is not necessary to protect the employer's property creates an impression of surveillance and may violate some parts of the NLRA. NLRB decisions that have examined surveillance cases have found it unlawful when employers engage in intensive repeated observations of strikers, take notes, and photograph employee activities (Silbergeld 1990).

■ CONCLUSION

The labor movement in the United States dates back to the late 1700s, when craftsmen banded together for mutual aid and protection against their employers for job security and to maintain and improve their economic well-being. This growth of unions continued well into the nineteenth and twentieth centuries, when the courts, legal ideology, and violence were the three primary factors that shaped the U.S. labor movement. Private security forces participated in enforcing court-ordered injunctions and often participated in antiunion activities, which often led to violence between union members and security officers.

The National Labor Relations Act, passed in 1935, the subsequent Taft-Hartley amendments in 1947, and the Labor-Management Reporting and Disclosure Act (LMRDA) of 1959 have shaped the nature of organized labor in the United States. The public sector, which now has a greater proportion of unionized employees than the private sector, is not covered under these laws. Instead, each state has its own forms of legislation.

Unions are structured at the local and national levels and can be affiliated with the AFL-CIO. Since World War II, unions can be best described as practicing business unionism. To be successful, unions need network embeddedness and political vitality. One of the primary goals of any union is to attract and retain new members through organizational efforts. These organizational efforts lead to establishing a bargaining relationship with the employer that can be achieved through voluntary recognition, an NLRB-certified election, or recognition of the union as the bargaining agent by the NLRB. Security guards, however, follow different requirements when forming a bargaining unit and joining a union.

One of the primary responsibilities of a union is to negotiate a collective-bargaining agreement where the parties can engage in distributive or integrative forms of bargaining. The NLRA requires the employer and the union to bargain in good faith about wages, hours, and other terms of employment. Other issues that are negotiated include union security agreements and union dues check-off provisions. If good-faith bargaining does not occur, an unfair labor practice has occurred. These agreements can be quite long and complex. An important part of the collective-bargaining agreement is known as the grievance clause, which sets forth grievance procedures to be followed when the employer or the union perceives that the collective-bargaining agreement has not been followed. The last stage in the grievance clause is known as arbitration.

Security organizations have an integral role in labor relations. Security officers and managers need to have a comprehensive understanding of unions and collective-bargaining agreements in order to operate effectively and to prevent their activities from causing unfair labor practices. Some of the primary concerns facing the security function are its day-to-day activities with union members and responding to strike situations, in which they need to balance protecting the assets of the employer and avoiding unfair labor practices with unions.

■ KEY TERMS

AFL-CIO
Arbitration
Business unionism
Collective bargaining
Community-of-interest standard
Contract arbitration
Distributive bargaining
Exclusive jurisdiction
Fact finding
Federal Mediation and Conciliation Service
Grievance
Grievance administration

Labor-Management Reporting and Disclosure Act (LMRDA) of 1959
Lockout
Mediation
McKay doctrine
National Labor Relations Act
Norris-Laguardia Act
Organizational picketing
Raiding
Railway Labor Act
Salting
Successorship
Taft-Hartley amendments

■ DISCUSSION QUESTIONS

1. What was the historical role of security in labor unrest in the late nineteenth and early twentieth centuries?
2. What are the three ways a union can establish a bargaining relationship?
3. What are the major pieces of legislation that affected the growth and development of unions in the private sector?
4. How are unions structured? What contributes to a union's success?
5. What are some common union organizing strategies?
6. What are the representation rights of security guards under the NLRA?
7. What is collective bargaining?
8. What are union security agreements? What are three types of union-security agreements?
9. What is a grievance? Explain the grievance process and its importance in a collective-bargaining agreement.
10. What is the role of security in strike situations?
11. What are some issues to consider regarding the surveillance of union activities?
12. How do mediation, fact finding, and arbitration differ?

■ REFERENCES

Advance Transport. 1990. 299 NLRB 140.

AFL-CIO. *Alexander v. Gardner-Denver Co.* 1974. 415 U.S. 36. How the AFL-CIO works. http://www.afl-cio.org/index2.cfm.

BALFOUR, A. 1987. *Union-management relations in a changing economy*. Englewood Cliffs, NJ: Prentice Hall.

BEMMELS, B. 1994. The determinants of grievance initiation. *Industrial and Labor Relations Review* 47: 285–290.

BIOGNESS, W. J., and E. R. PIERCE. 1988. Responding to union decertification elections. *Personnel Administrator* 33 (8): 49–53.

BOHLANDER, G. W. 2002. AFL-CIO's internal dispute plan. *Dispute Resolution Journal* 57: 21–27.

The Broadway. 1983. 267 NLRB 385, 405.

BROMMER, C., G. BUCKINGHAM, and S. LOEFFLER. 2002. Cooperative bargaining styles at FMCS: A movement toward choices. *Pepperdine Dispute Resolution Law Journal* 2: 465–490.

California Acrylic Industries Inc. v. NLRB. 1998. 150 F. 3d 1095, 1100 (9th Cir.).

CARLSON, C. T. 1990. Reducing strike violence by expanding union liability. *Capital University Law Review* 19: 211–231.

CHELIUS, J. R. and M. M. EXTEJT. 1983. The impact of arbitration on the process of collective bargaining. *Journal of Collective Negotiations in the Public Sector* 2 (4): 327–336.

CHIARAVALLI, R. L. and L. LARDARO. 1985. The impact of representation case hearings on certification election outcomes. *Industrial Relations Law Journal* 7: 232–244.

CHVALA, C. J. and M. FOX. 1979. Final offer mediation-arbitration and the limited right to strike. *Wisconsin Law Review* (1): 167–189.

COULSON, R. 1985. Alternative dispute resolution—threat or invitation? *Trial* 21 (10): 20–32.

CRAIN, M., and K. MATHENY. 2001. Labor's identity crisis. *California Law Review* 89: 1767–1846.

DAU-SCHMIDT, K. G. 1990. Union security agreements under the National Labor Relations Act: The statute, the constitution, and the court's opinion in *Beck*. *Harvard Journal on Legislation* 27: 51–141.

DILAURO, T. J. 1989. Interest arbitration: The best alternative for resolving public sector impasses. *Employee Relations Law Journal* 14: 549–568.

ELKOURI, F. and E. A. ELKOURI. 1985. *How arbitration works*. Washington, DC: Bureau of National Affairs.

ERICKSON, C. L. 1996. A re-interpretation of pattern bargaining. *Industrial and Labor Relations Review* 49: 615–633.

FEUILLE, P., J. T. DELANEY, and W. HENDRICKS. 1985. The impact of interest arbitration on police contracts. *Industrial Relations* 24 (2): 161–181.

FINE, C. R. 2002. Union salting: reactions and rulings since *Town and Country Journal of Labor Research* 23 (3): 474–485.

FIORITO, J., P. JARLEY, and J. T. DELANEY. 1995. National union effectiveness in organizing: Measures and influences. *Industrial and Labor Relations Review* 48 (4): 613–635.

FLANAGAN, D. J., M. A. WALLER, and S. P. DESHPANDE. 1995. An empirical study of union elections in motor carriage. *Logistics and Transportation Review* 31 (4): 341–347.

FORBATH, W. E. 1989. The shaping of the American labor movement. *Harvard Law Review* 102: 1109–1197.

FOSSUM, J. A. 1979. *Labor relations: Development, structure, process*. Dallas, TX: Business Publications.

FROST, A. C. 2000. Explaining variation in workplace restructuring: The role of local union capabilities. *Industrial and Labor Relations Review* 53: 559–576.

GALLAGHER, D. G. and R. PEGNETTER. April, 1979. Impasse resolution under the Iowa multistep procedure. *Industrial and Labor Relations Review* 32 (3): 327–338.

GARNER, B. A. (Ed.). 1979. *Black's Law Dictionary*. St. Paul, MN: West Group.

GETMAN, J. G., and F. R. MARSHALL. 2001. The continuing assault on the right to strike. *Texas Law Review* 79: 703–735.

GIFFORD, D. J. 1997. Labor policy in late twentieth century capitalism: New paradoxes for the democratic state. *Hofstra Law Review* 26: 85–160.

GILBERT, G. 1987. Dispute resolution techniques and public sector collective bargaining. *Ohio State Journal on Dispute Resolution* 2 (2): 287–309.

GREWACH, L. D. 1985. The guards trilogy: The NLRB lowers the guard on employee rights. *American University Law Review* 35: 175–219.

HANSEN, D. D. 2000. The sit-down strikes and the switch in time. *Wayne Law Review* 46: 49–133.

HARTWELL, T. M. 1985. Access as a remedial device: The National Labor Relations Board and the valid use of access orders. *Journal of Corporation Law* 10: 1075–1093.

HELSBY, R., K. JENNINGS, D. MOORE, S. PAULSON, and S. WILLIAMSON. 1988. Union-management negotiators' views of fact-finding in Florida. *Journal of Collective Negotiations* 17 (1): 63–74.

HIRLINGER, M. W., and R. D. SYLVIA. 1988. Public sector impasse procedures revisited. *Journal of Collective Negotiations* 17 (4): 267–277.

Hoschton Garment Company. 1986. 279 NLRB 565.

HOXIE, R. H. 1966. *Trade unionism in the United States*. New York: Russell & Russell.

HUSBAND, J. M. 1997. The Colorado coal wars of 1913 and 1914: Some issues still debated today. *Colorado Lawyer* 26: 147–152.

Impact Industries, Inc. 1987. 285 NLRB 5.

JARLEY, P., K. SAROSH, and D. CASTEEL. 1990. Member-union relations and union satisfaction. *Industrial Relations* 29 (1): 128–135.

JELF, G. S., and J. B. DWORKIN. 1997. Union decertification research: Review and theoretical integration. *International Journal of Conflict Management* 8 (4): 306–337.

JENSEN, E. M. 1985/1986. The NLRA's "guard exclusion": An analysis of section 9(b)(3)'s legislative intent and modern-day applicability. *Indiana Law Journal* 61: 457–493.

KOCHAN, T. A., and H. C. KATZ. 1988. *Collective bargaining and industrial relations*. Homewood, IL: Irwin.

LARUE, H. 1987. An historical overview of interest arbitration in the United States. *Arbitration Journal*: 13–22.

LEROY, M. H. 1995. Regulating employer use of permanent striker replacements: Empirical analysis of the NLRA and RLA strikes, 1935–1991. *Berkeley Journal of Employment and Labor Law* 16: 169–208.

———. 1996a. Severance of bargaining relationships during permanent replacement strikes and union decertifications: An empirical analysis and proposal to amend section 9(C)(3) of the NLRA. *U.C. Davis Law Review* 29: 1019–1086.

———. 1996b. Lockouts involving replacement workers: An empirical public policy analysis and proposal to balance economic weapons under the NLRA. *Washington University Law Quarterly* 74: 981–1058.

LESLIE, D. L. 1984. Labor bargaining units. *Virginia Law Review* 70: 353–418.

———. 1992. *Labor law, in a nutshell*. 3d ed. St. Paul, MN: West Group.

LEVINE, P. 2001. The legitimacy of labor unions. *Hofstra Labor and Employment Law Journal* 18: 529–573.

LEWICKI, R. J., B. BARRY, D. M. SAUNDERS, and J. W. MINTON. 1993. *Negotiation: Readings, exercises and cases*. New York: McGraw-Hill.

LEWICKI, R. J., and J. A. LITTERER. 1985. *Negotiation*. Burr Ridge, IL: Irwin.

LEWIS, D. V. 1981. *Power negotiating tactics and techniques*. New York: Simon and Schuster.

LIPSON, M. 1988. Private security: A retrospective. *The annals of the American Academy of Political Science* 498: 11–22.

LOWENBERG, J. J. 1982. The U.S. Postal Service. In Ed. G. G. SOMERS. *Collective Bargaining: Contemporary American Experience*. Madison, WI: Industrial Relations Research Association.

MACIK, M. 2001. You've got mail. A look at the application of the solicitation and distribution rules of the National Labor Relations Board to the use of e-mail in union organization drives. *University of Detroit Mercy Law Review* 78: 591–615.

MALIN, M. H. and R. F. LADENSON. 1993. Privatizing justice: A jurisprudential perspective on labor and employment arbitration from the Steelworker's Trilogy to Gilmer, *Hastings Law Journal* 44 (6): 1187–1231.

MCCABE, J. P. 1985. Voluntary recognition of a mixed-guard union under section 9(b)(3) of the National Labor Relations Act—Bargaining at will: *Truck Drivers Local 807 v. NLRB. Saint John's Law Review* 60: 162–176.

MCGINNIS, W. 1989. Interest arbitration in perspective. *Government-Union Review* 10 (36): 36–49.

MCKELVEY, J. T. 1969. Fact-finding in public employment disputes: Promise of illusion. *Industrial and Labor Relations Review* 22 (4): 528–543.

MODJESKA, L. 1983. Recognition picketing under the NLRA. *University of Florida Law Review* 35: 633–655.

National Labor Relations Act. 1935. 29 USC.

National Labor Relations Act. 1935. § 2(2), as amended, 29 U.S.C.A. § 152 (2).

National Labor Relations Board. The NLRB—What it is, what it does. http://www.nlrb.gov/nlrb/shared_files/brochures.

NEWMAN, W. A. 1990. Use of non-adjudicative third party dispute resolution methods by dispute resolution agencies of the United States government. *Ohio Northern University Law Review* 17: 121–144.

NIESWIADOMY, M. L., B. RAJ, and D. J. SLOTTJE. 1995. Modeling aggregate work stoppage trend behavior in the U.S. in an open economy: NAFTA and beyond. NAFTA: *Law and Business Review of the Americas* 1: 16–35.

NLRB v. Burns International Securities Services. 1972. 406. U.S. 272.

NLRB v. California Acrylic Industries Inc. 1998.

NLRB v. McKay Radio & Telegraph Co. 1938. 304 U.S. 333.

NLRB v. Town and Country Electric. 1995. 516 U.S. 85.

NOLAN, D. R. 1979. *Labor arbitration law and practice in a nutshell.* St. Paul, MN: West Group.

NOLAN, D. R. and R. I. ABRAMS. 1983. American labor arbitration: The maturing years. *University of Florida Law Review* 35 (4): 557–632.

NORTHRUP, H. R. 1984. The rise and demise of PATCO. *Industrial and Labor Relations Review* 37 (2): 167–184.

――――1990. The Railway Labor Act—Time for repeal? *Harvard Journal of Law and Public Policy* 13: 441–515.

NORWOOD, S. 1996. Ford's brass knuckles: Harry Bennett, the cult of masculinity, and the anti-labor terror—1920–1945. *Labor History* 37 (3): 365–391.

OBERER, W. E., K. L. HANSLOWE, J. R. ANDERSEN, and T. J. HEINSZ. 1986. *Labor law.* 3rd ed. St. Paul, MN: West Group.

Parsippany Hotel Management Co. v. NLRB. 1996. 99 F.3d 413, 417-18 (DC Cir.).

PERLMAN, S. 1950. *A history of trade unionism in the United States.* New York: A. M. Kelley.

PETRO, S. 1992. Public-sector bargaining: An assessment. *Government-Union Review* 3 (1): 2–35.

Pikeville United Methodist Hospital of Kentucky, Inc. v. United Steelworkers of America. 1997. 95-6467/6644.

RATTAY, V. A. 1983/1984. Representational rights of security guards under the National Labor Relations Act: The need for a balancing of interests. *Fordham Urban Law Journal* 12: 657-701.

RIES, E. D. 1992. The effects of fact-finding and final-offer issue-by-issue compulsory interest arbitration on teachers' wages, fringe benefits, and language provisions: A comparative analysis of New Jersey and Connecticut, 1980-86. *Journal of Collective Negotiations in the Public Sector* 21 (4): 45-67.

Roadway Package System, Inc. 1991. 302 NLRB 159.

SCOTT, W. G. 1965. *The management of conflict: Appeal systems in organizations*. Homewood, IL: Irwin.

SERRIN, W. 1992. *Homestead*. New York: Random House.

SILBERGELD, A. F. 1990. Withdrawing union recognition: Limits on presumptions about strike replacement's sentiments. *Employee Relations Law Journal* 16 (2): 193-203.

SOMERS, P. C. 1977. An evaluation of final offer arbitration in Massachusetts. *Journal of Collective Negotiations in the Public Sector* 6 (3): 193-228.

STURNER, J. W. 2001. Understanding labor law successorship: A new employer's guide to setting initial terms and conditions of employment at a newly acquired business with unionized workforce. *Law Review of Michigan State University–Detroit College of Law* 2001 (4): 1173-1198.

SUMMERS, C. W. 1995. Comparison of collective bargaining systems: The shaping of plant relationships and national economic policy. *Comparative Labor Law Journal* 16: 467-490.

THOMSON, A. W. J. 1974. The grievance procedure in the private sector. Ithaca, NY: Cornell University, School of Industrial and Labor Relations.

United States Steel Corporation. 1981. 255 NLRB 164.

United Steelworkers of America v. American Manufacturing Co. 1960. 363 U.S. 564.

United Steelworkers of America v. Enterprise Wheel and Car Corp. 1960. 363 U.S. 593.

United Steelworkers of America v. Warrior and Gulf Navigation Co. 1960. 363 U.S. 574.

U.S. Department of Labor. Bureau of Labor Statistics. 2002. http://www.bls.gov/cps/. Union members in 2001.

VANBOURG, V. J. and E. MOSCOWITZ. 1998. Salting the mines: The legal and political implications of placing paid union organizers in the employer's workplace. *Hofstra Labor and Employment Law Journal* 16: 1-45.

WRIGHT, S. F. 1982. Clipping the political wings of labor unions: An examination of existing law and proposals for change. *Harvard Journal of Law and Public Policy* 5: 1-33.

ZACK, A. M. 1979. Improving mediation and fact-finding in the public sector. *Labor Law Journal* 21 (3): 271-280.

chapter eleven

Security Surveys

Based on Ernst & Young's *Global Information Security Survey 2002*, which surveyed 459 chief executive officers, information technology directors, and business executives, many U.S. businesses have alarming gaps in their critical systems and data. The survey found that of the companies surveyed:

- 40 percent do not investigate security breaches
- 74 percent have an information security strategy
- 53 percent have business continuity plans in place

The report concluded that many companies discover far too late that significant technical investments are being undermined by inadequate business processes, the lack of information security training, third parties, and the absence of testing and assurance processes related to information security.

This is just one of the several security issues facing many organizations today. The key to the successful implementation of a security program is a well-thought-out security strategy. This strategy is achieved by first conducting a comprehensive and exhaustive analysis of an organization's existing security practices. This process is known as the security survey.

DEFINITION OF A SECURITY SURVEY

Security surveys, by their purpose and design, determine the degree of risk an organization faces. Risk can be defined as any hazardous or dangerous element and/or factor that exposes a person or an organization to loss or injury. Risks, according to Broder (2000), can be divided into three main areas: personal, property, and liability related.

All individuals and organizations experience some degree of risk in the normal course of their daily activities. If you drive a vehicle, you are exposing yourself to the risk of a traffic accident. Organizations, like individuals, are exposed to a myriad of risks on a daily basis in the course of their business. In order to control these risks, they must be managed. This process is known as risk management. One way to manage the risk of a traffic accident, for example, is to drive when less traffic is on the streets. In organizations, risk management can be a very complex and time-consuming process.

Risk management also refers to the analysis and management of dynamic and pure risks. Dynamic risks have both a cost and a benefit, such as simply doing business. Retail establishments experience the risk of theft from internal and external sources. The company accepts this risk of theft as a cost of doing business. The company can still make a profit even though its profit margin is affected from theft. Pure risks have no benefit (National Crime Prevention Institute 1986). Floods and tornadoes are examples of pure risks. The company experiences no benefit from such risks.

Losses to a company can also be categorized into operational, legal, and reputational risks.

- Operational risk is defined as an organization's potential for loss owing to significant deficiencies in system reliability or integrity. Operational risk can include both internal and external attacks on systems or products (Katz and Claypoole 2001). In recent years, the Basel Committee on Banking Supervision (2003) has had a strong focus on operational risk and published a report showing that the 89 banks supplying information had more than 47,000 losses exceeding $10,000 that were related to operational risk in 2001. About 2 percent of these losses exceeded $1,000,000.

- Legal risk arises from violations of or nonconformity with laws, rules, regulations, or prescribed practices (Katz and Claypoole 2001). Legal risks abound. The recent examples of Enron's and WorldCom's fraudulent reporting of assets and profits are unfortunate examples of financial-based legal risks. Companies also face legal challenges related to other regulatory laws and liability-related claims that can be filed against the organization.

- Reputational risk refers to the value of an organization's reputation. Reputational risk is defined as the risk of significant negative public opinion that creates a lasting public negative image to the point that the organization's ability to establish and maintain customer relationships is significantly impacted. Reputational risk can occur when an organization itself causes a loss of public confidence in its ability to perform critical functions. With the growth of the Internet and e-commerce, companies now allow customers 24-hour access for information and placing orders. This access also permits hackers entering companies' information technology (IT) systems and stealing or destroying confidential and critical information. Thefts of this nature, not to mention shutting down a site because of a security breach, could lead to the loss of revenue, a drop in stock prices, and ultimately a loss in a company's reputation. Reputational risk can also arise in actions an organization takes in response to the actions of third parties (Katz and Claypoole 2001).

These three types of risks are not mutually exclusive but rather are interrelated. Take, for example, legal risk in the context of compliance. The failure of a company to follow legal guidelines will result in damage to its reputation. Risk management is about avoiding losses and identifying opportunities. Well-administered and developed risk-management programs provide organizations with a useful tool to improve the bottom line by reducing all forms of risk. When these forms of risk are reduced or perhaps eliminated, the end result will be greater organizational effectiveness.

The key behind risk-management programs is the control of risk. In order to control risk, it first has to be identified as a risk. This can be accomplished only through a systematic investigation of those risks that a company faces. These systematic investigations are achieved through security surveys.

Security surveys are also called security audits, security inventories, risk analyses, loss-control surveys, internal control surveys, asset-protection surveys, and external control surveys, to name just a few of the terms used. Audits can be understood as an official examination or verification. One often thinks of audits in the context of financial records. Surveys, however, are a formal, specific examination, or appraisal, of the particulars of something.

By their very nature, both "security audit" and "survey" boil down to the same activity and goals. They are an objective research-based activity that measures the nature and degree of risk an organization faces and are used to identify deficiencies that affect the quality of security in the organization (Post and Schachtsiek 1986). These detailed and orderly assessments identify risks and perils an organization may face and are a thorough inspection of operational systems and procedures (Green 1987).

For the purpose of this chapter, a security survey can be considered an exhaustive analysis of physical and psychological properties or factors that affect the overall security and safety of the organization. A security audit is a systematic, thorough, and comprehensive analysis of the organization's entire security operation. The primary purpose of a security survey is to identify assets that need to be protected, and the kinds of risks that may affect the assets involved. It identifies the strengths and weaknesses of existing practices and provides information on how various security practices complement one another. The survey determines the probability of the risk and the impact if a loss does occur. The survey is a present- and future-oriented assessment of the state of security in an organization (Broder 2000).

The Onion Model

Just as the multiple layers of an an onion can be peeled away, the multiple layers of threats that an organization is exposed to can be exposed in a security survey.

One of the first layers that an analyst will want to examine is the external environment, which may include the region where the organization is located. The next layer may be the specific city where the organization is located. Then the survey may want to report the specific city area where the organization is located. By providing an analysis, or overview, of the external environment, the survey reader may gain a comprehensive understanding of how the external environment affects the organization. For example, the analysis of the crime rate regionally, citywide, and then by city neighborhood may give the reader a better understanding of whether the crime rate in that locale is lower or higher than in other areas. The survey can also provide information on how crime is different in that specific city sector.

Next, the model looks at the organization. Areas for examination here may begin with external perimeter controls, such as fencing, lighting, and intrusion alarms, followed by specifics related to the external security of buildings. Issues related to access, alarms, and employee and visitor controls may be examined in this layer. Next would be a consideration of access control and fire suppression in specific units of each building, including the control of proprietary information and other vulnerabilities as determined by the auditor(s).

This onion analogy is similar to the U.S. Department of Defense's Defense in Depth model, a "layered security strategy built around the following aspects of an organization: (1) the training, awareness, physical security, personnel security and system security administration of an organization's people; (2) the framework security criteria, acquisition, risk assessment, certification and accreditation of an organization's technology; and, (3) the assessments, monitoring, intrusion detection, warning, response and reconstitution of an organization's operations" (Katz and Claypoole 2001, 218–219). Loosely defined, Defense in Depth is a set of active security measures and equipment, passive facility design, and policies that become increasingly intense as one gets closer to the object that is being protected. Defense in Depth enlarges security in an organization by increasing the cost of an attack by a would-be intruder. Because of the multiple layers between the organization and the threat, the organization's assets are better protected.

Benefits of Security Surveys

One of the primary reasons a security survey is conducted is to assess the current state of safety and security in the organization. Without conducting periodic security surveys, a company has no definitive objective-based knowledge or information of how well its security program is functioning and no concrete understanding of security deficiencies in the organization. The security department and managers may gain some understanding of their state of security through formal and informal channels, such as customer contacts, accidents, and incidents at the workplace and through information collected by their employees. But these sources of information are not comprehensive in nature; they are fragmented pieces of information that provide an inaccurate analysis of the state of security. The only way a company can gain a comprehensive understanding of the current state of security, deficiencies, and where it stands relative to industry standards is through a comprehensive and well-planned security audit.

As pointed out earlier, the security survey identifies and controls risks. This is one of its primary benefits. The National Crime Prevention Institute (1986) has identified five principal methods of risk management, listed in Table 11-1.

Liability Reduction   Security surveys can safeguard companies against legal actions through the early detection and control of security-related issues. The identification of security issues, combined with appropriate security countermeasures, can relieve organizations of some civil-liability issues.

The findings from the security survey also place organizations on notice. *Black's Law Dictionary* (1999) writes that "notice" means that a person has knowledge of the existence of a fact or a state of affairs. Notice implies that an issue or a fact has been brought to the person's attention through various methods, including oral and written forms of communication. It does not mean that a person has complete knowledge of the facts of a situation. A vulnerability disclosed in a security survey places the organization on notice that something needs to be done to correct that security deficiency. For example, a security survey recommended that an apartment complex needed to increase its access-control measures by installing fencing to reduce property crimes. This information puts the apartment managers on notice that they have a security deficiency that needs to be addressed or corrected. Such notice does not disadvantage an organization but rather serves as a change agent. Notice prompts organizations to correct identified deficiencies.

The lack of security surveys can put an organization at a disadvantage in civil suits. In one case, the lack of a security survey or plan to establish a reasonable

TABLE 11-1 ■ **Five Methods of Risk Management**

Method	Description
Avoidance	Deals with removing the target altogether and completely avoiding the risk. This is the first alternative to consider in risk management.
Reduction	If the risk cannot be completely eliminated without creating a problem for the organization, the next step is risk reduction, achieved by reducing the risk to its lowest level. An example is limiting individuals access to certain areas and times.
Spreading	After risk avoidance and reduction, the next option the organization has is to spread its risk, using security procedures and devices to deter, delay, and deny access to assets in the organization.
Transfer	Involves setting the risk on someone else. Examples of risk transfers are purchasing insurance and passing the value of the losses on to consumers or customers.
Acceptance	After applying avoidance, reduction, spreading, and transfer techniques to their greatest extent, the organization simply accepts the probable loss as the cost of doing business.

standard of care, combined with the failure to conduct a periodic review of security with the community and police department, were some of the factors that led the Court of Appeals of Louisiana to affirm a judgment of $4.3 million against the owners of nightclub where a patron was sexually assaulted (*Peterson v. Gibraltar Savings and Loan, Club West, Inc.* 1998). In a case that involved the murder of a visitor to an apartment complex, the Texas Court of Appeals supported the lower court's decision that the crime was foreseeable, based on the large number of crimes in the area. One piece of evidence that resulted in a judgment against the owners was that they had never conducted a security survey of the apartment complex (*Dickinson Arms-REO v. Campbell* 1999).

These cases show that security audits can be subpoenaed and used against organizations if vulnerabilities were identified and not properly addressed. The audits may be sources of information for plaintiffs. For example, in the World Trade Center (WTC) bombing in 1993, one of the pretrial motions by the plaintiffs, both individuals and businesses allegedly injured, was discovery for WTC building-security documents and plans. The Port Authority, which owned the WTC, refused to provide these documents to the plaintiffs, using the public-interest privilege, which protects governmental entities from disclosing confidential communications on the basis of possible harm to the public interest if sensitive information were to lose this shield of confidentiality. The Court of Appeals of New York determined that not all information falls under the public-interest realm and that some, but not all, information about the security of the WTC would have to be turned over to the plaintiffs (*In the matter of World Trade Center Steering Committee . . .* 1999).

Change Agent Combined with the legal issue of notice, the security survey can be an instrument of change for the organization. All individuals, regardless of level of education, are limited in their ability to fully understand all things at all times. A security survey conducted by an external source can highlight security issues that may have been overlooked by administrators. For those individuals who may discount internal experts, a security survey conducted by an objective and unbiased external consultant will also prompt recognition by other individuals in the organization that changes or modifications are needed.

Educational Component Another benefit of a security survey is that it is an educational tool. If the survey is conducted internally, those individuals assigned to conduct the survey will therefore learn from it. Conducting a security survey will require individuals involved with the survey to gain an in-depth understanding of the existing strengths and weaknesses of the security function. This thorough investigation into risks and vulnerabilities will also result in these individuals' gaining a more comprehensive understanding of the organization as a whole and how it and its employees work in concert with the security function.

The security audit will also educate readers and users of the survey. In some situations, key stakeholders in the organization may not have a complete or thorough understanding of the diverse roles of security in their organization. Also, they may not recognize the importance of security or the various functions that security can perform for organizations. However, a security survey can inform and educate individuals on what security does and can do for the organization. In one security survey conducted for a high school, for example, the findings of the survey were presented to members of the school board. The survey findings about this particular school, combined with the current literature and research on the problems of school violence, educated the school board members. It also resulted in the board's approving the proposal for the creation of a proprietary security program and the hiring of a director of security for the school system.

■ CONDUCTING THE SECURITY ANALYSIS

Any security survey has four primary components: the planning stage, the preliminary survey, the administration of the survey, and the creation of the final report.

Planning the Security Survey

The planning stage is one of the most important components of the security survey and is the most time-consuming stage. Unfortunately, it is often an overlooked component of the process. Administrators should not overlook the importance of spending an appropriate amount of time in planning the survey. Without properly thinking about and planning the survey, several issues could be missed during the administration of the survey. At the same time, problems could arise that should have been identified in the planning stage. Examples are arranging interviews and gaining permission to access certain areas and sensitive information in the organization. These missed points will translate into the researcher's spending more time in the administrative portion of the survey and perhaps amending the original security survey proposal. In the context of contracted expertise, it will mean a loss in profit. With in-house staff, it will mean a loss in reputation and confidence by senior employees.

Following are some of the issues in the planning stage:

- Obtaining organizational support
- Verifying the need for the survey
- Determining who will conduct the survey
- Determining the format
- Determining the audience
- Reviewing industry standards
- Determining the depth and breadth of the survey
- Establishing a time frame

Obtaining Organizational Support   The key to success for the security audit is organizational support. A comprehensive security audit will require organizational support from the top down. By its very nature, a security audit will require access to restricted areas and perhaps access to confidential information not readily available to all employees in the organization. This will require permission and acceptance of the survey from top administrators in the company. In order to ensure organizational support, whether it is conducted by an internal or an external consultant, this support should be in writing, clearly delineating the purpose of the survey and the degrees of access and the roles, responsibilities, and authority that the auditor has in conducting the survey.

Organizational support must also be garnered from the lower echelons. Although top administrators may be quite supportive of the survey, line-level employees may display varying degrees of resistance to an employee or outside consultant "probing" into their practices or observing their behaviors. To alleviate any concerns or resistance by employees, managers should consider educating employees on the reasons behind the survey. To further show their support of this project, managers should distribute a memo to all employees to educate them about the security survey. The only exception to this will be if the organization decides, based on the research design and objectives, that the audit and auditor will remain completely anonymous.

Verifying the Need for the Survey   The reason for the security audit is one of the first issues that needs to be addressed. The need for the survey can be based on proactive and/or reactive needs. Proactive needs can be simply the fact that the organization and its security department are quite progressive and realize the benefits of the security audit. The security audit is simply conducted under philosophical and practical grounds that the findings from such audits will improve the organization on a variety of levels.

In other instances, a security survey is conducted after a crisis in the organization, when a major crime has occurred, or on request of the organization (Fennelly 1996). This reactive response may follow a recent criminal event on the property, for example. In one case, a homicide occurred near an organization that then requested an external security audit. This homicide increased the concern among staff that security procedures were not sufficient. These fears then prompted the owners of the company to request a security audit. In another case, a rash of thefts in the company resulted in employees' challenging existing security practices in the organization. This again resulted in the administration's requesting an external audit to investigate existing security practices in the organization.

Some reasons for conducting security surveys may be both proactive and reactive, involving insurance and compliance reasons. Insurance companies may require periodic audits; compliance or regulatory agencies may require the monitoring of security activities. In some cases, companies may conduct such surveys because they are forced to do so. In other instances, companies may proactively conduct periodic audits to ensure that they are in compliance with existing insurance and regulatory requirements.

Determining Who Will Conduct the Survey   Security surveys can be conducted by one or more internal employees, external consultants, or both. Who will conduct the survey is based on a variety of issues and factors, including the organization's in-house levels of expertise to conduct all or part of the survey. In other instances, competency may not be a primary issue. The organization may want to use external consultants to ensure that a truly objective and unbiased evaluation of the existing security program is accomplished through the survey. Time may also be a factor; in some instances, external auditors may be able to complete the survey more quickly because they have the requisite resources and expertise readily available. Financial resources available to the company will also dictate who will conduct the survey. As a rule of thumb, external contractors are more expensive than internal auditors.

In-house expertise does have its benefits. In-house experts already know the physical surroundings and know the existing structure. Because these individuals already possess a great deal of experience, the survey could be conducted in a timely manner. Internal security specialists may also be cost-effective, as the organization will not need to hire an external security specialist to conduct the survey that could be more costly than using internal expertise. Using internal individuals could also be a form of job and personal enrichment for the employee.

Employees who have that requisite knowledge can be given a new challenge. New challenges also equate to increasing the experience and knowledge base of the security staff. If individuals are given the responsibility to complete a security survey for their employer, the ultimate end result will be that they have been educated through the process. A thorough security survey will require the individuals to engage in inquiry. This inquiry, regardless of the depth of the survey, will require them to explore a series of issues and engage in investigative techniques by talking to and learning from others in the organization. At the same time, the recommendations stemming from the survey must be thorough and accurate. This will require the persons conducting the survey to delve into the existing and current security and safety-related literature.

Internally administered security surveys may also ensure a greater degree of confidentiality. Companies may be reluctant to air their "dirty laundry." Although a professionally administered survey by an external source will include a confidentiality agreement, the company may have concerns about who will have access to the findings of the report. If the findings from the report were accidentally or intentionally revealed to the company's competitors, the findings could be used against the organization. Likewise, if the findings were obtained by a person with a criminal or vindictive motive, the information in the survey could provide some useful information that could result in the company's being exploited and subsequently damaged to some degree.

One of the drawbacks of using an internal candidate is bias, which can exist for several reasons. First, some individuals may not readily want to admit or expose their organization's vulnerabilities, which then may not be included in the final security report. An internal employee may not want to disclose weaknesses in the security survey, concerned about embarrassing coworkers and supervisors, and so may "overlook" certain weaknesses that then do not become part of the official security survey. Individuals conducting the survey may also be very reluctant to reveal weaknesses that could be attributed to the management of the company. This could create an ethical dilemma, and the individuals conducting the survey could face the potential of revealing weaknesses that would embarrass or impact their managers. Fears related to retaliation by management could also make individuals reluctant to reveal deficiencies in the safety and security program.

In other instances, the mere thought of bias may make survey readers question the validity of the findings and the recommendations contained in the report. In one instance, a local school system was interested in expanding the security function from the high school to one of its middle schools. A security audit of this particular site was conducted by security staff. When the school board reviewed the recommendations calling for the construction of a new security office and the addition of CCTV and other technologies, some board members raised the issue of bias and called for an independent security survey.

If the organization chooses to use external sources for the security survey, some benefits apply. First, many individuals have expertise in security surveys. Because of their background and existing experience in conducting surveys, these individuals may have developed some savvy in identifying organizational vulnerabilities that may be overlooked by an internal survey.

Surveys conducted by consultants may also be more cost-effective and timely. Because of their expertise in conducting surveys, these individuals may require fewer hours than internal personnel to complete the assignment and may complete the survey in a more timely manner. An internal source may be conducting this project as an addition to existing responsibilities and therefore may not be dedicated solely to the project. An external source, on the other hand, may be fully dedicated to the project and have rigid timelines to get the job done. This same external source may also have the proper support staff to help them get the project edited and completed in a timely manner.

External sources also have some drawbacks. As with internal surveys, one still has to consider bias. If an organization contracts with an external company that also sells security-related services or products and if this company is unscrupulous and unethical, it may "inflate" the problems identified in the company in order to sell its products. In one instance, for example, a security provider recommended that the company install a costly electronic surveillance system that perhaps was unnecessary. This company also failed to give the client other alternatives.

Other drawbacks include issues related to familiarity. An external auditor may not be familiar with the organization, particular leaders, and the physical surroundings. For one to become familiar with the organization requires time. Because external auditors base their fees on the number of hours it will take to complete the audit or, in some cases, billable hours, it will be more expensive to use these outside consultants.

Determining the Format Security surveys can be categorized as checklist and nonchecklist. On a checklist format, the auditor(s) follow a precreated list when conducting the audit. In its most simplistic format, the auditor simply checks off issues. Some checklists provide only dichotomous responses: yes if that security item is adequate or no to indicate a deficiency. The checklist may not allow for any descriptive analysis of the issue(s) that might expose any fundamental weaknesses in the organization's overall security program.

Other checklists are categorical, ranging, for example, from low to high or from 1 to 10. These types of checklists generally provide limited details on security deficiencies or strengths. In some instances, checklists may also have a section where strengths and deficiencies can be described or explained. These types of checklists may be more suitable, depending on the needs of the organization, as they provide additional descriptive information that would be useful in redesigning or updating security operations in the company.

Checklists can be purchased from vendors and various organizations; some insurance companies may provide them to their clients. Checklists can also be constructed internally or by outside consultants. Many checklists are very comprehensive and provide a detailed analysis of the existing safety and security of the firm. In other instances, the checklist may be limited to that specific company, owing to its degree of comprehensiveness and quality, or may not completely "fit" the organization. For example, a checklist designed for healthcare facilities will most likely not be appropriate for universities.

One key consideration when using checklist-style surveys: The outcomes are tied to the quality of the checklist, not the user of the checklist. Although a variety of checklists are available, their quality is only as strong as their creators.

Using a checklist can be beneficial for organizations, identifying existing strengths and weaknesses while providing the organization with specific risks, vulnerabilities, and areas for improvement. Checklists may not be as expensive to administer as other types of security surveys, because a great deal of the expertise lies within the checklist, not with the user. The auditors must simply have enough knowledge to accurately complete the survey. This may transfer to a savings in not hiring someone with expertise to conduct an analysis and may also enrich and enlarge an existing employee's responsibilities in the company.

If not a cost-saving venture because of reduced administration costs, the checklist may be less expensive because less preparatory time and less time to administer the survey are needed. With checklists, the user simply has to fill in the blanks, which could expedite the completion of the survey. In addition, completing the final report may require less time, especially if the checklist also serves as the summary of the findings.

Checklists have some drawbacks, however. One drawback is related to the construction of the checklist in the context of how comprehensive it is. Many checklists are "stock" items that can be obtained by vendors, outside organizations, and security consultants. Therefore, such checklists are not unique to the organization and may miss out on its unique characteristics, which will be subsequently ignored or overlooked, decreasing the value the survey findings have to the organization. Likewise, a safety or security issue that is not on the list may not be included if the auditor lacks knowledge or expertise in that particular area. Hence, checklists are limited in that they may not include all risks or vulnerabilities the company may face. Combined with their degree of comprehensiveness, checklists may be outdated. Changing codes, standards, and new technologies could make many checklist-based surveys readily outdated and inappropriate to use.

These types of surveys may also be less exciting to administer. Simply checking off items on a list could be less challenging and interesting for some employees to complete.

Effective security audits will also collect a vast array of qualitative information: concepts, meanings, characteristics, and descriptions. Quantitative information, such as on checklists, whose responses can be counted or tabulated, refers to counts or measures of things (Berg 1989). This type of information cannot be easily categorized on a security checklist but instead will require the security professional to use other data-collection processes. These techniques do not rely solely on checklists. Instead, the researcher may use an outline or a list of issues as a guide in the collection of information from various users and individuals who rely on the existing security apparatus in that company. This information is then recorded—not simply checked off—and analyzed at a later time for relevant information. From all this information, a comprehensive review can be made of the existing security, and accurate and thorough recommendations can be made, based on the information collected.

In one security survey, for example, a company was concerned about the existing quality of its security. Although a checklist would have confirmed that this company met all existing safety and security standards, a thorough discussion with the people impacted by the existing security program revealed that the program was not meeting the needs of many of the constituents. Perceptions of the role of security varied among the staff, and some staff members did not recognize or know the security services offered, including escorting employees to their vehicles at night, and so on. These qualitative findings exposed serious and potentially dangerous flaws to the security program.

Determining the Audience   The audience for the report is an important consideration. The audience will often dictate the technical sophistication of the survey. If the survey's primary audience is the security department, for example, specific security-related terms or definitions can be used without explanation. In discussing lighting, for example, the terms "lumens" and "foot candles" may be considered common knowledge. In non-security-related areas, however, the terms may require additional clarification and explanation. For broader audiences of individuals who lack technical expertise or sophistication in security principles, the writer(s) of the survey will need to consider rewriting the results of the survey to avoid technical terms or to include definitional footnotes for some items.

Reviewing Industry Standards   Governments, trade associations, and technical societies may have developed programs, methods, and minimum standards for improving security in their particular sectors. The review of industry standards will also provide some trend-based information for the survey readers, as well as useful information on how the organization compares to others. For example, when a local school system was contemplating the creation of a security force, it needed some trend-based information on school violence. Statistical information from the Bureau of Justice Statistics about trends in school violence, combined with an analysis of information from the state and local and regional school systems, provided a comprehensive overview of school violence. Comparing this information to existing information from this particular school system provided information on where it stood in comparison to national, state, and local trends in the context of school violence.

Some other sources of standards are the *Protection of Assets Manual*, information and standards from the Occupational Safety and Health Administration, and several private organizations that can provide the organization with baseline information. In the case of financial institutions, for example, a variety of resources is available. The Office of the Controller of the Currency (OCC) has published guidelines on how to measure risks in the banking industry. The Federal Deposit Insurance Corporation (FDIC) and the Federal Reserve have also published guidelines for risk-based supervision activities that proactively deal with risk-management issues. The National Institute of Standards and Technology (NIST) provides eight general principles and recommendations for developing computer security programs. Some of the standard security audit techniques include finding vulnerabilities and trying to exploit them—active tools—conducting passive tests that examine the system and infer the existence of problems, using such internal controls as security checklists and audits, and conducting penetration tests by attempting to break into computer systems (Katz and Claypoole 2001). By studying these various security recommendations, organizations can learn what is most important in creating a security system and program and can also draw some conclusions about priorities for protecting their assets.

Determining the Depth and Breadth of the Survey   This element addresses the content and scope of the security audit. Depth refers to the thoroughness of the survey; breadth, how wide ranging the survey will be. The survey's depth and breadth need to be defined in advance of conducting the survey. One individual conducting a thorough review of a regional distribution center, for example, will take a great deal of time and effort. Defining the depth and breadth of the survey in advance will determine whether the survey is attainable, based on the time and resources available to the auditor(s). Determining the depth and breadth in advance will also ensure that appropriate resources are available to the auditor in advance of the administration of the survey.

The purpose of the survey often dictates its depth and breadth. Broder (2000), for example, divides the contents of a security survey into organizational, functional, and operational factors. Organizational surveys deal with people-oriented issues. Functional questions deal with workflow issues, and operational issues address hardware-related security procedures. If the survey is being conducted for insurance reasons, for example, it may cover only those issues that the insurance company requests. On the other hand, if it is truly an exploratory analysis of the company's safety and security program, the survey will have a greater depth and breadth, exploring all facets of safety and security in the organization.

Establishing a Time Frame

Administrators should not overlook the importance of spending an adequate amount of time creating a manageable and realistic time frame for the completion of the survey. Several issues affect timelines. External issues may include customers who demand rapid or timely surveys in contractual security settings because they market themselves and compete on the basis of providing clients with timely and comprehensive security surveys. In proprietary settings, external issues or forces include the needs of insurance companies and accrediting agencies that require various compliance standards and evidence of various security measures on an annual or biannual basis.

At the same time, there may be internal issues that affect the timeline independently of the depth and breadth of the survey. Some organizations may have preestablished due dates that coincide with events such as the budget cycle, the beginning of a new academic year, or the opening of a seasonal business. In other cases, the deadline may coincide with the construction of a new building or annex, or even the restructuring of a particular component of the organization. The survey timeline could be based on personnel available to conduct the survey. In resort settings, for example, surveys may be conducted prior to or after peak tourist time, when the organization can dedicate security personnel to the project because of decreased workload.

An accurate and realistic timeline is key to an effectively planned security survey. One of the best ways to complete the project on time is to have several deadlines or milestones during the project rather than one single deadline. Depending on the overall design of the survey, for example, there could be both external and internal milestones. Components of the survey can also have multiple subsections, so realistic deadlines must be established for each subsection. Perhaps the best analogy of creating a timeline is to liken it to completing a large puzzle. All of the pieces must first be identified, laid out, and assembled piece by piece to get the "big picture." The box containing the puzzle gives the number of pieces, but individuals involved in the security survey process must determine how many pieces comprise the security survey and then determine appropriate timelines for their completion.

Compartmentalizing the survey into smaller components serves many functions. It makes the task less overwhelming. Participants in the process will be better able to meet several deadlines for small projects or phases than for one major project. After these deadlines are met, an evaluation of the survey and procedures to date will reveal issues that may have impeded progress. Identifying and addressing these issues early in the process ensures that similar issues or problems can be avoided in the succeeding phases of the security survey. In addition, having multiple deadlines can serve as a motivation tool if participants meet them and learn that the project is not overwhelming and can be completed by the established end date. Having finished a component of the project also instills pride in accomplishment and motivates participants to complete the next stage of the project. Multiple deadlines also serve a monitoring function. Through compartmentalization, managers can more accurately measure how long each component of the survey took (in the context of resources and personnel). If the project to date is behind schedule, for example, managers can allocate more personnel in the next stage(s) to ensure that the survey is finished on time. This information would also be useful for determining issues related to personnel and resource expenditures for the organization's future security surveys.

The Preliminary Survey

The planning stage provides auditor(s) with a vast array of information for collecting and constructing a final security report. What is still lacking is familiarization with the organization, however. Conducting a preliminary survey will serve as a foundation for the final security report (Broder 2000).

The primary purpose of a preliminary survey is to determine the "true objectives of the operation and to locate and evaluate the key control points. . . . one must understand the management concepts being used and the qualifications and abilities of the employees responsible for the operation" (Broder 2000, 57). The preliminary survey is not overly detailed. Its purpose is simply to gain an understanding of the operations and to summarize the organization in a logical and organized manner. The preliminary survey also identifies those major problem areas in the organization. It focuses on the highlights of the survey, not the details (Broder 2000).

Part of the preliminary survey is to interview the key individuals in the organization. Some of the general questions that need to be addressed are what management perceives to be the major problem areas and what the security survey will accomplish in solving these problems (Broder 2000). For example, in one survey, one major concern was the increase in workplace theft. At the preliminary meeting, management wanted two interrelated goals: recommendations on how to reduce theft and employee awareness that it was serious about addressing the problem and was hiring an external consultant.

Another component of the preliminary survey is an exploratory analysis of the organization, conducted with written permission from management. Individuals in the organization should also be notified that a preliminary audit is being conducted and that their cooperation in the audit is requested. The rationale behind this stage in the process is to gain additional information about the issues presented to the auditor(s).

Perhaps one of the simplest ways to conduct this exploratory analysis is to conduct a walk-through of the organization to gain a better insight into the major security issues. The walk-through and informal contacts with employees will also clarify or frame those major issues that were identified. In some instances, the walk-through is critical. For example, one audit dealt with perimeter-control issues of a 400-acre resort. This organization dealt with training high-level executives through adventure-based activities in a remote wilderness location. The interviews with management revealed security issues, but the only way to gain complete insight into these concerns and to identify other security issues in the process was to walk the trails, visit the lodges and training areas, and talk with staff members at each location.

A letter of agreement is a component of the preliminary survey. Regardless of whether the security survey in conducted by in-house or external consultants, the scope of the security survey needs to be documented. Already in the planning stages of the security survey, the auditor(s) should have established the breadth and depth of their survey. Now, this should be documented and presented to the appropriate managers in the organization for their approval.

The written agreement will serve many purposes. First, it will clarify the objectives to both the auditors and management of exactly what the survey will encompass and it will also establish what will and will not be investigated in the security audit. Second, a properly documented security survey plan will prevent any confusion and disputes over the survey's purpose and content at a later stage in the process. The written agreement will also clarify what other activities the auditor(s) are responsible for. Additional responsibilities could include a formal presentation of the findings and other additional documentation as determined by the parties. This written agreement should also include a confidentiality agreement that the party conducting the survey will keep all collected information and the survey findings confidential from third parties unless specified in the agreement.

Administration of the Survey

Following all the preparatory work and the creation of the preliminary security report, the next step is to begin collecting information that will become part of the final report. As in previous stages, several issues need to be considered in the administration of the security survey. These issues are concerned primarily with the collection of information or data that will serve as the basis for the final report. Depending on the scope of the security survey, researchers have a variety of data sources, including the use of secondary data sources, surveys, and observational activities.

Although data sources may vary, a key concern is that the information collected must be valid and reliable. Validity asks the question: Does the survey truly measure what it intended to measure? If, for instance, one of the findings is that a lack of access-control measures is making the perimeter security poor, the findings have what is known as face validity; that is, the findings make sense, or are logically related. The results must also be reliable. Reliability refers to the consistency of the measurement. If the survey were given over a period of time or conducted by different auditors, would the findings be uniform? In our example, the survey would be reliable if the same finding about perimeter control were discovered by another researcher.

Secondary Data Sources Secondary data analysis is taking existing data sources or research originally gathered for other purposes and using it in its original form or in a combined or reorganized manner to answer a research question. Secondary data analyses has been found to be an economizer of researcher time

(Hagen 1982; Neuman 1997). For example, the FBI compiles and maintains the Uniform Crime Reports, which the FBI and the law enforcement community use to determine the crime rate in the United States and to monitor trends or changes in crime over time. Security managers can use also this information to gain an understanding of crime in their particular area.

Perhaps one of the greatest sources of secondary data related to security can be found in U.S. government publications, many of which can be accessed from the Internet. Table 11–2 lists some of the Internet sites where a researcher

TABLE 11–2 ■ **U.S. Government Data Sources**

Agency	Internet Address	Topical Areas
U.S. Department of State	http://www.state.gov	Travel warnings, Overseas Advisory Council
Federal Emergency Management Agency	http://www.fema.gov	Disaster planning and prevention information
U.S. Environmental Protection Agency	http://www.epa.gov	Environmental laws and regulations; publications
National Oceanic and Atmospheric Administration	http://www.noaa.gov	Weather and environmentally related stats
U.S. Census Bureau	http://www.census.gov	Population and economic stats; maps
Federal Bureau of Investigation	http://www.fbi.gov/ucr/ucr.htm	Uniform Crime Reports/security-related publications
Bureau of Justice Statistics	http://www.ojp.usdoj.gov/bjs	Crime stats, research, and publications
National Criminal Justice Reference Service	http://www.ncjrs.org	Criminal-justice publications
National Institute of Justice	http://www.ojp.usdoj.gov/nij	Crime-prevention publications
Centers for Disease Control and Prevention	http://www.cdc.gov/	Health stats, travel warnings
U.S. Geological Survey	http://www.usgs.gov	Natural-disaster stats, maps
National Institute for Occupational Safety and Health	http://www.cdc.gov/niosh /homepage.html	Safety and health stats
Bureau of Labor Statistics	http://www.bls.gov	Safety and health stats
Occupational Safety & Health Administration (OSHA)	http://www.osha.gov	Safety and health stats

may find relevant information. One location, the FBI home page, provides extensive information about crime and crime rates through its annual Uniform Crime Reports and related publications. The U.S. Census Bureau Web site provides population figures and trends that will be useful in providing baseline information in the security survey.

State and local data sources too can be accessed via the Internet for a host of detailed information. For example, information from local chambers of commerce can provide information on income levels, business growth, and trend-related information in particular cities or geographical areas.

Researchers should also access internal data sources and archived information and records. These sources can include financial documents, shareholder-related information, policies and procedures, internal memorandums, and incident reports. The review of prior security surveys may also provide useful information in the construction of the new survey. Other data sources that may prove helpful in the security survey are organizational flowcharts, customer-satisfaction surveys, position descriptions, policies and procedures, schematics, maps, and blueprints of existing and future facilities. In some instances, organizations have published books on their history, growth, and philosophy. The organization's mission and vision statements and strategic plans will also provide information that could be useful in the survey.

Survey Research   One of the most popular and necessary methods of collecting information for the security survey is through survey research, which involves collecting information by asking people questions. These questions can be answered through questionnaires and interviews.

A formal questionnaire is a series of structured questions that can be mailed or delivered to the respondents to help them prepare for the arrival of the researcher. The questionnaires can be self-administered, meaning that the respondent completes them unaided, or administered with the assistance of the researcher(s). The questionnaires can be passed out or administered at any time during the project, usually near the beginning, and they can be used to gather additional information from employees after all other data-collection methods have been completed.

Depending on the nature of the survey, researchers may construct survey questionnaires to gather information. These surveys can be quite extensive and can include open- and close-ended questions. A respondent can give any answer to an open-ended question. The response is an unstructured free response to the question (Neuman 1997). "What do you think of the current security measures at ACME?" is an example of this type of question. The interviewer needs to transcribe or record the statement made by the individual. Such questions are rich in information but require a great deal of time for recording and later interpreting the results. Open-ended questions may be most appropriate when a researcher is interested in how the respondent feels or thinks about an issue. They are useful when a survey is exploratory—when the researcher is interested in finding out what issues or concerns are important for the respondent(s) (Neuman 1997).

A close-ended question has a structured, or fixed, response. "How would you rate the existing alarm system at ACME?" is a closed-ended question. Respondents could then mark a response box as good or bad. By their design, close-ended questions are quicker and easier to complete for respondents, who simply have to check a box. This format also makes it easier for the researchers to interpret and analyze the responses. One of their primary drawbacks is that closed-ended questions may not provide the same "richness" of responses that open-ended questions do.

Another method of collecting information is the interview, which can be individual based or group based, as well as informal or formal. An interview can also be open, semistructured, or structured, as is the case with a questionnaire. It can also be survey based and field based.

A survey-based interview is structured, follows a prearranged protocol, and occurs in a formal setting in a one-directional process in which the interviewer asks the questions and the respondent answers. In structured interviews, the interviewer controls the direction, topic, and pace of the interview, and keeps the interview on track; and ensures that all questions are answered thoroughly and accurately.

The survey-based interview generally has three stages. During the introduction, the interviewer establishes a position of authority and then secures cooperation from the respondent(s). The main part of the interview is the question-and-answer stage, with questions asked and responses recorded. The last stage of the interview process is the exit stage; respondents are thanked for their cooperation, the interview ends, and the auditor edits the questionnaire and records other relevant details about the interview (Neuman 1997).

In field interviews, the researcher is an active participant, and the interview has no clear beginning or end. The researcher and the respondent control the pace and the direction of the interview. The field interview is a two-way communication process that occurs in an informal, relaxed climate. Generally, three types of questions are asked: descriptive, structural, and contrast. Descriptive questions deal with the setting and other members: the who, what, when, where, and why questions. Descriptive questions also deal with hypothetical questions: the what-ifs. Structural questions are used after spending time in the field; the researcher starts to analyze the data and organizes the information into specific categories. For example, if the descriptive questions revealed a problem with access control, the structural question could be posed as, "Would a person who is not employed by ACME be able to enter the building from the north entrance?" Contrast questions then build on the analysis from the structural questions. Contrast questions focus on similarities and differences between the categories created (Neuman 1997). For example, "Who are these unauthorized individuals who use the company's north entrance?"

Observational Research Methods   One of the strongest ways to collect information for the security survey is to observe the practices, events, and activities in the organization under review. Observing the activities of others can be done through complete observation, participant observation, and secret observation.

- Complete observation means that the researcher's intentions are known to those being observed. The researcher attempts to evaluate the actions of subjects without interfering or biasing activities and subsequent outcomes. For example, a researcher might accompany and observe an employee by simply "shadowing" the person. The researcher keeps a distance, does not interfere in the employee's activities, and simply observes the employee's actions.
- When in a participant-as-observer role, the researcher self-identifies as an observer, states the purpose, and participates in the activities of those individuals being observed. The key is that the researcher participates to some degree in various organizational activities (Fitzgerald and Cox 1989). A researcher who is investigating issues related to security officer patrols, for example, may take the role of a security officer, working directly with others to observe and record their behaviors and activities. This direct observation of activities allows the researcher to ask detailed questions while gaining a comprehensive understanding of the operations and activities of employees. One issue involved with this type of data collection is maintaining objectivity (Fitzgerald and Cox 1989).
- Secret observation occurs when the researcher's true motives or intentions are unknown to those being observed. An example of a secret observation is described in Winkler (1997). Winkler writes about gaining access to and trust from employees in organizations through deceptive, or covert, methods. Through these actions and by not revealing his true identity, he accesses and steals company secrets. Winkler then determines the vulnerability of company trade secrets and confidential information. In another example, students involved with a security audit, with the complete authority and permission of the corporation, became covert employees of the company to conduct penetration tests in various sensitive locations, including the information technology/communications area of the company. Based on their activities, the students then wrote up a comprehensive review of existing weaknesses of the security operations in the context of information security and access control.

Prioritizing the Findings and Estimating Vulnerabilities   Once the information has been collected, the next stage in the security survey is to prioritize the findings to scale vulnerability levels. A vulnerability is a weakness, or anything that can be exploited by a threat (Broder 2000). One method of prioritizing vulnerabilities is to create a scale based on the criticality and probability of occurrence of the identified security issue. Table 11–3 shows an example of how to establish security priorities based on vulnerabilities.

TABLE 11–3 ■ Prioritizing Vulnerabilities

	Value	Degree of Seriousness If Something Occurs
Probability		
	4	Almost certain, if uncorrected
	3	Probable (better than 50-50) if uncorrected
	2	Probable (about 50-50) if uncorrected
	1	Possible but unlikely (less than 50–50) if uncorrected

	Value	Degree of Seriousness If Something Occurs
Criticality		
	4	Loss of life, extreme property and/or financial loss that would shut down the organization
	3	Serious disabling injury, financial, and/or property loss that would cause a serious crisis for the organization
	2	Moderate and temporary injury, financial, and/or property loss that would cause a moderate problem for the organization
	1	Slight injury, if at all, minimal financial and/or property loss to the organization

	Vulnerability Ranking (Probability + Criticality)	
	Numerical Score	Description of Issue
Combined Probability and Criticality Score (High to Low)		

During the administration of the survey, the researcher collects a great deal of information. The next step is to prioritize the findings according to criticality and probability of occurrence. Once these issues are numerically scored, they can be rank ordered according to that numerical value. Vulnerability is then established by adding the criticality and probability estimates and then rank ordering the scores from high to low.

These scores can then be used to rank order the relative degree of importance that each identified security concern should be given toward correcting the issue. For example, if an issue has a criticality value of 4 and a probability value of 4, the total vulnerability score is 8. Because this is the highest score an issue can receive, it would be categorized as a high-priority issue that needs to be addressed by the organization. Issues that have been identified with a vulnerability level of 6 or higher are high-level or top-priority concerns and should be immediately addressed by the organization. Issues having a vulnerability score of 5 are of medium priority and should have corrective actions taken as soon as possible after the top-priority issues have been addressed. Low-priority issues have a composite score of 4 or less. These issues should be taken in order of the numerical rankings and addressed only after the high- and medium-priority issues have been taken care of.

Following the establishment of vulnerability, the security audit should present a continuum of recommendations to remedy the situation. These recommendations can be ranked from maximum to minimum to countermeasure the issue. For example, the most-preferred recommendation would reflect the maximum recommendation. Lesser recommendations would fall into the medium and minimum recommendations. For example, one "maximum," or preferred, way to control access would be through biometric readers. Although effective, these security measures may be quite expensive to install and operate. A less expensive, and perhaps less secure, recommendation could include card-access devices.

Based on these recommendations and justified through factual information, the survey will direct the organization on what issues should be addressed and why. If several security concerns or issues have the same vulnerability level, the decision about which one to address first is based on the expertise of the individuals conducting the survey and the priorities established by leaders in the organization.

The Final Report

Organization   No standard procedure exists for writing the security survey report. The key to any report is that it be organized in a manner that enables the reader to access information easily. The report must be logical, clear, and consistent, as well as comprehensive. Broder (2000) provides a general structure that should be followed when writing the security report. At a minimum, it should consist of the following sections: purpose, scope, findings, conclusion, and recommendations. Other common components of security surveys are an executive summary, a table of contents, and appendixes.

Format   Format will vary, depending on the demands of the client, the writer's personal preference, and the content. If the security survey is simply a checklist, the completed checklist may serve as the final report. In other instances, the report will be very detailed and well organized. Generally, reports are formatted according to the security threats identified. One technique is to prioritize the findings according their level of criticality, with the most critical issues presented first. In other instances, the format of the report will be based on topical sections. For example, one section may be based on perimeter security, another on internal security measures, one on personnel security, and another on information security.

In some situations, the writer may determine that writing the document in paragraph form would be too cumbersome and instead write the report in a bulleted format to highlight critical findings. The report may also contain a combination of traditional paragraphs and bulleted statements to make the report more "readable." An example follows.

ALARM SYSTEMS

To protect the perimeter during and after business hours, the organization may consider contracting with a central alarm system provider. To adequately protect the premises, the following electronic protective measures should be considered:

- Glass breakage sensors on all glass surfaces, including windows and doors
- Contact switches on all perimeter doors
- Internal intrusion alarm systems that include
  - Point or object protection for specific sensitive locations
  - Area protection concentrating on such areas as the main corridor
  - Motion detectors that cover personal offices and the administrative area

As pointed out earlier in this chapter, the degree of technical sophistication may also be an issue in the final report. In some instances, it may be advisable to use footnotes when explaining highly technical issues. The use of footnotes will allow the writer to accomplish two goals of the survey. Technical based findings will be reported, and the report will be easier to read, as the additional technical information and explanations are separated from the findings. The report should also contain diagrams and charts, an economical and practical way of explaining a great deal of information. In many situations, a graphic display of a security issue is far more effective than trying to fully explain it, as "a picture is worth a thousand words" at times.

The report might contain an executive summary, or a brief overview of the report's contents. An executive summary appears first in the report and consolidates the principal points of the document, condensing the entire work or explaining how the results were obtained or why the recommendations were made. The executive summary simply states the results and recommendations, providing only enough information for a reader to decide whether to read the entire work. It is a comprehensive restatement of the document's purpose, scope, methods, results, conclusions, findings, and recommendations. Accuracy is essential because decisions may be made based on the summary by people who have not read the entire document.

The report may contain detailed appendixes. The purpose of an appendix is to provide the report readers with detailed information. However, this information, if included in the body of the report, would "clutter" it and subsequently distract them. An appendix generally contains tables, additional reference materials, illustrations, survey results, and detailed descriptions of buildings and equipment. Appendixes are placed at the end of the document.

Presentation   In some cases, clients or the organization will require that the survey findings be formally presented to interested or affected parties for their review. The purpose behind this presentation is to ensure that the readers understand the findings and for the auditors to clarify any issues or questions that have arisen from the findings. The presentation will also bring closure to the security survey.

■ CONCLUSION

Unfortunately, no accessible assets are totally secure. Security managers and their teams plan a defense for the protection of assets, install technologies to repel intrusions and avoid accidents, and train people to protect the assets of the organization. Creating and following a well-defined security plan eases the process of asset protection. One of the most important parts of the security plan is knowing the present state of security in the organization. This is achieved by conducting a thorough and comprehensive security survey that plans out the security program.

The security-survey process can be divided into four stages: planning, the preliminary survey, administration, and the final report. One of the most important stages is the planning stage. Issues that need to be considered include its purpose and audience. Next, the preliminary report frames the issues and establishes the breadth and depth; the administration of the survey begins by collecting data in various ways. Some of the common techniques are surveys, questionnaires, secondary data analysis, and observational research methods. Once this information is collected, it must be prioritized, based on criticality and probability of occurrence. By mapping the vulnerabilities of the organization, issues can be prioritized and strategies for reducing these vulnerabilities can be achieved. Last, the final report is written. The key to the final report is that it must be comprehensive, logical, clear, and consistent.

■ KEY TERMS

Audit	Risk
Defense in depth	Risk acceptance
Dynamic risk	Risk avoidance
Field interviews	Risk reduction
Legal risk	Risk spreading
Notice	Risk transfer
Observational methods	Risk management
Operational risk	Security surveys
Pure risk	Vulnerability
Reputational risk	

■ DISCUSSION QUESTIONS

1. What are some of the reasons a security survey should be conducted by organizations?
2. What are some ways an organization can control or manage risks?
3. What are the primary benefits of a security audit? What are some secondary benefits?
4. What are the four stages of conducting a security audit?
5. What are some benefits and drawbacks to using in-house staff to conduct a security survey?
6. What are some benefits and drawbacks to using external consultants to conduct a security survey?
7. What do depth and breadth issues address? Is one more important than the other in the security audit?
8. What is the purpose of the preliminary survey?
9. What are two of the most common data-collection methods that can be used in the security survey?
10. What are some observational research methods that can be used in collecting data?
11. How does the researcher determine the degree of vulnerability of assets?

■ REFERENCES

The Basel Committee's work in the field of operational risk. 2003. *Norges Bank Financial Stability* 1 (28): 23.

BERG, B. L. 1989. *Qualitative research methods*. 2nd ed. Boston: Allyn & Bacon.

BRODER, J. F. 2000. *Risk analysis and the security survey*. 2nd ed. Boston: Butterworth-Heinemann.

Dickinson Arms-REO v. Campbell. 1999. 4 S.W. 3d 333.

Ernst and Young (2002) Second annual global information security survey. http://www.ey.com/global/content.nsf/UK/Issues_and_perspectives_-_Library/ (21 June 2002).

FENNELLY, L. J. 1996. *Handbook of loss prevention and crime prevention*. Boston: Butterworth-Heinemann.

FITZGERALD, J. D., and S. M. COX, 1989. *Research methods in criminal justice: An introduction*. Chicago: Nelson-Hall.

GARNER, B.A. (Ed.) 1999. *Black's Law Dictionary*, 7th ed. St Paul, MN: West Group.

GREEN, G. 1987. *Introduction to security*, 4th ed. Boston: Butterworth-Heinemann.

HAGEN, F. E. 1982. *Research methods in criminal justice and criminology*. New York: Macmillan.

In the matter of World Trade Center Bombing Litigation Steering Committee v. Port Authority of New York and New Jersey, Appellant, 1999. 686 N.Y.S.2d 743.

KUTZ, E. M. and T. F. CLAYPOOLE 2001. Willie Sutton is on the Internet: Bank security strategy in a shared risk environment. *North Carolina Banking Institute* 5: 168–227.

National Crime Prevention Institute. 1986. *Understanding crime prevention.* Boston: Butterworth.

NEUMAN, W. L. 1997. *Social research methods.* 3rd ed. Boston: Allyn & Bacon.

Peterson v. Gibraltar Savings and Loan, Club West, Inc. 1998. 711 So.2d 703.

POST, R. S., and D. A. SCHACHTSIEK, 1986. *Security manager's desk reference.* Boston: Butterworth.

Protection of Assets Manual. 2002. New Orleans, LA: EXAMEO, Inc.

WINKLER, I. 1997. *Corporate espionage.* Rocklin, CA: Prima Publishing.

chapter twelve
Budgeting

All individuals have a budget. A budget in its simplest sense is a systematic plan for using scarce resources, such as time. Usually, budgeting is placed in the context of money. When considered in these two perspectives, budgeting can be thought of as an exercise in planning that allows a person or an organization to think through all the events or possibilities that one expects to occur. Budgets may also include planning for the unexpected. Once these events are figured out, the person or the organization needs a plan of action. As such, the budget is the foundation for planning activities in an organization.

In an organizational perspective, budgeting is central to the management of resources. Through the budgeting process, priorities are established. Budgeting is also essential to the financial management and planning processes. The importance of fiscal management is self-evident. Reckless fiscal policies, imprudent investments, and sometimes a blatant disregard for accepted financial practices lead to the demise of an organization. Unfortunately, examples abound.

The process of budgeting can be stressful and confusing for managers. Overman (1996, 489) describes the budgeting process as follows:

> The typical budgeting process is not dissimilar to a chaotic parking lot. Every year budget analysts prepare to repeat the budget process that has not yet even ended for the year before. The budget system moves from near to far-from-equilibrium as more and more energy and involvement from outside the agency is focused on budget priorities and specific expenditure plans. Draft after draft and revision after revision of budget structures emerge and dissipate,

while order emerges out of the chaos and some semblance of the final draft becomes clear. Along the way to formulating a final budget even the smallest incident—like a citizen complaint of a negative personnel action—can redouble in effect many times over, creating new chaos and new order in the budget process and outcome.

Perhaps one of the primary reasons for these fears associated with budgeting is that the process and techniques are not understood. In fact, one study concluded that the number-one area in which financial executives lacked knowledge skills and abilities was budgeting (Crawford and Henry 2000).

This chapter provides a basic understanding of the importance of budgeting in organizations. Budgeting is a process that comprises various steps and distinct purposes. The budgeting process is not simply a financial issue. Instead, the ramifications of the budgeting process impact all facets and operations of the organization, including employees, to one degree or another. This chapter covers not only the importance of budgeting but also types of budgets, process, approaches and techniques of budgeters, as well as budget strategies.

■ OVERVIEW OF BUDGETING

Definition

A budget is the product of a long process. A budget is a tangible, meaningful, and important document that highlights important aspects of organizational behavior, provides information, and directs organizational activities.

According to Lee and Johnson (1998), budgets can be thought of as descriptions, explanations, and statements of preferences, or values. Budgets describe what the organization does, what it accomplishes, and what it purchases. The budget paints a picture of what the organization is doing now, what it did in the past, and what it plans on doing in the future. Budgets also explain relationships, or "a causal process in which work activities consume resources to achieve goals" (p. 15). Third, as statements of preference, budgets show what the organization values in the context of individual and collective preferences in its activities and use of organizational resources.

Origins and History

Budgets have long been used as a means of controlling expenditures and planning for future activities. In the modern era of business and government activity, financial management and budgeting are newer concerns to students of budgeting and financial planning (Welsch 1971). Therefore, most advances in budgeting, financial controls, and management theory have occurred since the turn of the twentieth century. The precursors of modern budgeting can be traced to several sources: the government, the private sector, and research bureaus.

One of the origins of budgeting can be traced to the public sector. With the growth of cities, the concept of using budgets for financial control began in the 1830s and gained momentum after the Civil War, when there was an increase in the growth and demand for municipal services. Later, in the 1880s, with the emergence of the Progressive Era, the public-administration movement was born, as well as the concept of budgeting as it is currently known (Tyer and Willand 1997). Many cities, such as Chicago, experimented with financial reforms that were encouraged by business leaders who also funded various research bureaus to improve public budgeting in the early 1900s (Rubin 1993).

Another source of budgeting and corporate financial management can be traced to early federal legislation and other activities. In the late nineteenth and early twentieth centuries there were concerns about the financial stability of railroads that were heavily financed by the government. When these railroads went under, the public paid a heavy financial toll. In an effort to improve accounting, the Interstate Commerce Commission was created in 1887 to set forth accounting procedures for the railroads. After imposing them on the private-sector organizations, the federal government in turn was pressured to develop and use similar accounting procedures. Other early reforms by the federal government included actions by the Institute for Government Research (forerunner of the Brookings Institute), which lobbied for the adoption of federal budget reforms (Rubin 1993).

As was the case in Chicago, budget reforms originated with the staff members of municipal research bureaus (Rubin 1993). One research bureau that had a great deal of influence on budgets and municipal reform was the New York Bureau of Municipal Research, founded in 1907. The bureau, using corporate models, promoted scientific-management concepts to improve government efficiency in planning and budgeting. This bureau, as well as others, planted the seeds for modern public administrative practices (Tyer and Willand 1997). Rubin (1993) writes that although these bureaus did contribute to the growth of modern budgeting, their importance is often overemphasized or exaggerated in the budgeting literature, whereas the role of government has been underemphasized in budgeting reforms in the United States.

Early budgeting focused on providing the resources needed to maintain the operations of the organization. Achieving goals was a secondary concern of early budgeting. These budgets were crude, basic, and lacked detailed information about activities, objectives, and other financial information. As such, these budgets were not useful for maintaining accountability, managing assets, or planning for growth or expansion. Therefore, later budget techniques necessarily incorporated within their systems the ability to provide detailed information, while maintaining their ability to control costs, direct resources, and adequately plan for future activities.

Beginning with World War II, an effort began to coordinate all the programs needed to provide support for the war. Thus, a major budget reform led to the control and use of materials rather than monetary resources (Novick 1968). After World War II, business and government activity turned toward a postwar expansion and the growing needs and demands of a rapidly changing society. Government was called on again to deal with these diverse issues; at the same time, the need to measure the outputs of government programs and expenditures became evident. This demand led to the adoption of the planned programming-budgeting (PPB) system. The principal aim of PPB was to improve efficiency in government operations (Lee and Johnson 1998).

About the time the government adopted the PPB system, movement was under way to adapt a private-sector approach to budgeting developed by Texas Instruments: zero-base budgeting (Phyrr 1973). As with other budget reforms, government adoption would lag behind business use of the zero-base technique. President Jimmy Carter, who used zero-base budgeting when he was governor of Georgia, tried to control expenses and make government more responsive to critical needs. His program to accomplish these goals included a version of zero-base budgeting. Zero-based budgeting represented a major reform and symbolized two things: (1) government adapts business techniques when appropriate and useful and (2) the pressures of reform and efficiency through prudent budgeting and planning are pervasive.

Overall, history implies and suggests that necessity has been the impetus for budget reforms over the centuries. Both government and business were required to respond to the reforms demanded by the Progressive movement. The Progressive Era ushered in a demand for accountability, professionalism, and fairness, particularly in the practice of government. The corresponding element of importance for business is that it too would have to meet the strong demands for corporate accountability, transparency, and honesty. Central to both government and business improvement in these areas was budgeting and control of scarce resources.

Objectives

"Objectives" are those goals or objects that an organization strives to attain. It is important to understand that the overall nature of budgeting involves a nebulous set of implications. What is inevitable is that poor performance by any organization will be blamed on management and its inability to understand the unknown. For the manager of any organization, bureau, or agency, effective management of financial resources is paramount.

Budgeting is about expecting the unexpected. It is about accurately gauging what will happen in the future and adapting the organization's goals—plans—to the resources—inputs—it can expect during a specific time period (Finney 2000). Understanding what is likely to happen in the future is shaped largely by experience, trends, forecasts, and comparing past expectations with reality. Experiences that help budgeters negotiate uncertainty yield to the primary needs of budget improvement and effectiveness.

Finney (1993) writes that budgets have some composite objectives. Budgets must also satisfy some requirements. These objectives and requirements are shown in Box 12–1.

BOX 12–1 ■ **Budget Objectives and Requirements**

Objectives

- Must be realistic, accurate, and consistent

- Contains information most useful to managers so they can make effective decisions

- Is consistent with the organization's goals and strategies

- Facilitates goal setting and measurement at all levels of the organization

- Communicates strategy, plans, and required outputs to the organization (i.e., what are we going to do; what are our goals?)

- Communicates operating plans across all functions of the organization

- Will be approved by top administrators

- Provides every department with the resources it needs to meet its goals based on the budget

- Shares budgeting objectives with those who will be affected by it

Requirements

- Must be prepared in the proper strategic context within the framework of the strategies, goals, and plans of the company

- Must identify and deal realistically with uncertainty and uncontrollability (i.e., the "what ifs" and unknowns)

- Should provide the most useful and important information for managers (e.g., cash flow, profit, seria) and the best possible numerical predictions for the next year

- Must emphasize excellence in the context of efficiency and effectiveness throughout the organization

- Engages the organization in a coherent and efficient process that ties everything together, including budget requirements, obstacles, and objectives

Adapted from Finney (1993).

As management moves through the budget process, it must accurately gauge resources and allocate them wisely. Therefore, budgeting is focused on efficiency, proper planning, and stringent accountability. The process, nature, and cycle of budgeting address most of these elements. The budget process is meant to ensure that expectations of an uncertain future are within the realistic limits of experience. The nature of budgeting, with its attendant political pressures, produces a plan that is somewhat amendable to all stakeholders. The budget cycle is structured in such a way as to ensure accountability—audit and review stage—and allow for each stage in the cycle to influence and inform the next stage.

Budgeting also has some unintended outcomes. For example, the control of the budgeting system can also be considered a mechanism to maintain or increase one's power. For example, two managers may have different visions for the company, but one of the managers has control of the budget. The person who has a degree of influence over the budgeting process, either directly or indirectly, will succeed. Those individuals responsible for the creation and disbursement of funds have a great deal of power over others. Thus, budget authority tends to be concentrated in organizations.

The Purpose of Budgeting

Why do organizations have budgets? Budgets serve many ends. They range from a simple operating budget to investing in fixed assets (Matthews 1977). Most organizations plan to exist as long as possible, or until their role in society is no longer needed. At this point, organizations change or cease to operate, as was the case with many companies that failed to apply technologies. Organizations have several management imperatives if they are to survive. Properly managed resources give any organization a better chance of prolonged life than their mismanaged counterparts. For example, employees must be kept happy in order to maintain a stable workforce. Tangible assets, such as buildings, equipment, and supplies, are protected and enhanced so that employees can efficiently discharge their duties.

Budgeting has several purposes. The six traditional functions of budgeting are authorization, forecasting, planning, communication, motivation, and evaluation (Otley 1977). Others suggest that budgeting's primary purpose is financial control and a "launch pad" for: priority setting and planning, forecasting, performance measurement, cost management, and a competitive organization (Metzgar and Miranda 2001).

Financial Issues   Financial resources are perhaps the most important to manage. Those who specialize in budgeting and finance contend that financial resources are indeed the most important management function of any organization, public or private. Without properly managed finances, organizations can easily lose the ability to function. The best personnel system a company may develop is useless if it cannot hire, train, or compensate their employees. Future obligations to retired employees, such as pensions, are hollow promises if pension funds are not invested properly. Problems also arise if not enough is invested to cover future pension obligations. At a more basic level, the proper equipment, tools, and resources cannot be ordered without proper financial planning.

As already mentioned, budgeting is one of the essential functions of managing any organization. Governments, businesses, families, and civic groups seek to estimate revenue, or income, and to plan expenditures. Without budgets, fiscal control, accountability, and management are haphazard and circumspect. Therefore, engaging in budgeting and producing a budget are fundamental managerial tasks. Very little is accomplished in any organization without financial resources and planning. The essence of budgeting establishes constraint on behavior and guidelines that members of the organization must follow.

Planning Budgets are plans of action and should be the company's most useful planning document (Finney 1993). Programs and services are not created or implemented without planning. Most organizations plan to exist beyond a year and seek to grow. Growth can include increases in membership, the number of employees, profits, resources, and market share. Budgets help organizations achieve growth goals in long-range, or strategic, planning and short-term planning activities (Ramsey and Ramsey 1985). Budgets, through planning, make sure that programs have the necessary level of funds needed to carry out their missions.

Providing Activities require resources in order to be accomplished. Budgeting allocates and provides resources for activities (Wildavsky 1979). In addition, budgeting for a particular activity or event conveys legitimacy. Budgeted activities then become accepted, funded, and part of future budget struggles.

Budgets are required by law—statutes, codes, constitutions—company rules, policy; or leadership. Budgets provide a mechanism for ensuring that resources are directed where originally intended. In this sense, budgets ensure that money is allocated properly. Additionally, budgets provide a baseline for measuring whether an activity directed by the budget was carried out and to what degree of efficiency.

Prioritizing Priorities are preferences. Budgets read like a book; they reveal priorities. After analyzing a budget, one can quickly learn the priorities and preferences of the organization (Wildavsky 1979). Budgets explicitly state an organization's values and goals. For example, security company A spends 5 percent of its budget on employee training; company B, 2 percent. Assuming that both companies have similarly sized budgets and missions, training appears to be more of a priority to company A.

Explanations Budgets also describe and explain. As descriptors, budgets show what the organization consumes, those activities they perform, and the profits they make. At the same time, budgets explain to the readers what the organization does. Budgets describe organizations in the context of what they spend, purchase, and produce. Budgets also describe the size of the organization, based on the number of personnel on the payroll and types of equipment that are purchased. The review of income and expenditures describes the organization in a historical perspective, giving the readers an understanding of the organization's growth and changes in market share and products and services provided to clients. Budgets also explain causal relationships. As pointed out by Lee and Johnson (1998, 15), "budgetary decisions also imply a causal process in which work activities consume resources to achieve goals." An effective budget will be able to determine the costs of various activities, as well as projected income levels.

Management   Budgets are also tools that help manage an organization. Most organizations do not have an overabundance of resources, so budgets and information systems help managers oversee the implementation of activities, as well as direct resources. During the course of a fiscal year, a new activity may develop. Budgets provide information about available resources and how a change in one activity changes the amount of resources available for the newer program. Budgets can also be linked to performance management. In this context, employees may receive part of their compensation or bonuses based on the performance of their units, which is measured through the budget in the context of money saved or profits.

As can be seen, budgets perform an important role for an organization. Their most important role is fiscal controls, or financial management. Establishing organizational priorities is a necessary function carried out by management during the process. At the end of the process, the budget stands as the source of financial information. The level of information depends on the format or type of budget. Some budget formats provide information easily; others are more vague.

Tools for Budget Preparation

Without any doubt, personal computers have made the tedious work of financial management both easier and more difficult. Software designed to manage large amounts of financial data permits budget officers to run numbers and answer specific questions with relative ease. Spending proposals can be evaluated for their costs and effects on the organization's bottom line quickly and accurately.

The ease with which computers yield information also renders everyone equal in the budget-preparation process. With minor efforts, for example, anyone who is included in the budget process can produce reports and revenue forecasts. This can lead to problems; as the number of budget players increases, so too do the transaction costs associated with managing their suggestions.

Budgeting technology serves several goals. First, it provides for automated financial control, which allows users to monitor and analyze costs and the execution of the budget. Technology also provides for better planning and forecasting and facilitates better reporting procedures, data analysis, and accessing and using this information for planning. Last, technology promotes collaboration and harmonization among all individuals in the budget process (Metzgar and Miranda 2001).

However, too much information can be created. Financial reports, scenarios, and forecasts can be generated beyond a meaningful contribution; financial reports that have little merit are a waste of time and resources. Budget officers are usually paid very well. If part of their time is spent creating useless reports and prodding others to consider them, the real work of managing the organization's financial resources is neglected. High technology can be both positive and negative.

■ TYPES OF BUDGETS

Organizations have various types of budget-based needs. Some of the more common types are capital, operating, nonoperating, and project budgets (Ramsey and Ramsey 1985). Capital budgeting deals with estimating the costs and savings when introducing, for example, new pieces of equipment. Part of the capital budgeting process is determining how the investment in equipment will lead to greater productivity and profits for the organization. Operating budgets look at the costs for goods or services produced on a departmental or product basis.

Non-production-operating budgets, by contrast, are departmental budgets for nonproduction units, such as sales, purchasing, and human resource departments. These units do not directly "produce" a product, but nevertheless consume financial resources to pay employee salaries and expenses related to their specific operations. The use of these limited resources requires careful planning through budgeting. Project budgets are the one-time projects or programs that involve long-term expenditures. They extend over a series of budgets and are used for research-and-development projects and creating and developing major capital assets. An example is the building of a new office complex. In the first year, land must be purchased. In the following budget year, plans would be drawn up; in the third year, construction would begin on the complex.

Budget formats are a matter of organizational preference. The form and substance depend on such factors as organization size, use of technology, and management requirements. The type of budgeting system used may be based simply on custom or tradition. Generally, budget types are consistent from year to year. The fiscal budget year may traditionally go from July to June, for example. Tracking down past budgets will give budgeters a rough idea of the form. What is to be included in the budget is spelled out by those calling for it, discussed later in budgeting process. Some of the typical categories of expenditures in budgets are capital outlays, which are such major expenditures as buildings, equipment (high-value items); personal services, or salaries; travel; commodities, or low-value items; and contractual, or leased, services. Regardless, the various types of budgets have common aspects and differences, of course.

Budget formats are designed to yield more or less information. They regularly include details about sources of income, expenditures, and narratives about what activities are to be undertaken. Some budget formats—program and performance budgets—provide vast amounts of information. Others—line item and lump-sum budgets—are geared toward simply tracking expenditures and providing monetary resources. The key to choosing a format is first deciding what information you want the budget to show.

For most organizations, a format that yields more information is preferable, for several reasons. First, keeping track of activities by type is easier if they are separated by primary function. Second, distinguishing expenditures by revenue type is easier if each activity is clearly linked to its revenue source. Third, having all program activities contained in one budget allows for easier discussions about effectiveness and efficiency. Such formats also clearly reveal how much output one gets for the amount of resources dedicated to an activity.

The various budget types represent the standard formats that are used in various levels of organizational complexity. As technological advances are made in the delivery of information, budget formats can be adapted to provide almost any level of information desired. Some of the most common types of budgets are the line item, performance, program, lump-sum, and zero base.

Line-Item Budgets

Also known as the line object, traditional, or incremental budget, the line-item budget is the most familiar format to those without extensive budgeting experience and is one of the most popular budgeting formats. Its origins date back to the late nineteenth century. In this format, information about spending is spelled out for each item, or expenditure. This type of budgeting works from a base: the prior year's budget. That is, the planners have a general understanding of how much money they will have to budget on a yearly basis, and they can incrementally work with that figure, adding or subtracting monies from that base on a yearly basis, if necessary (Anderson 1998).

Line-item budgets provide detail about what is to be purchased or what activity is to be pursued and are highly usable for fiscal control. Details of expenditures are readily available in line-item budgets. Box 12–2 illustrates a simple line-item budget.

BOX 12–2 ■ Line-Item Budgeting Approach

Labor and Benefits		Amount
	Salaries	$250,000
	Overtime	32,000
	Pension	25,000
	Medical/Dental	82,500
	Contract Labor	47,000
	Total Labor & Benefits	**$436,500**
Equipment		
	Flashlights	$ 500
	Radios	4,500
	CCTV	12,000
	Total Equipment	**$ 17,000**
Supplies		
	Videotapes	$ 1,500
	Batteries	700
	Total Supplies	**$ 2,200**

Strengths   The primary strength of line-item budgets is that they explicitly detail what is to be purchased or spent. Additionally, most employees and managers have experience with this type of budget, and it fits well with most accounting systems. It is also relatively simple to understand and requires little training to use. This type of budget allows for the central control over financial resources; it is uniform and comprehensive in nature, allowing routines in the organization to be established. As each item is on a separate line, cutting certain items is easier to do than in other budget formats (Tyer and Willand 1997). Metzgar and Miranda (2001, 10) point out other benefits of the line-item budget: "Traditional [line item] budgeting makes calculations easy precisely because it is not comprehensive. History provides a strong base on which to rest a case. The present is appropriated to the past, which may be known, instead of the future, which cannot be comprehended."

Thus, the line-item budget enables planners to compare the prior year's budget to those for the current and next years. By examining these budgets in an incremental approach over time, planners can gain an understanding of changes in the organization and new directions that the organization is moving toward.

Weaknesses   However, line-item budgets suffer from the fact that they focus solely on what is to be purchased. They do not look at a desired goal or outcome of the activity to be performed. Combined with the fact that managers can incrementally work through the budget, it may not be the most rational form of budgeting. An item may be included in the budget simply because it was funded the previous year (Anderson 1998). Consider, for example capital equipment that was needed and acquired the previous year. Most likely, the organization does not need to purchase this same equipment again. Nevertheless, it still remains part of the budget. From a managerial perspective, line-item budgets restrict mangers by locking them into specific accounts and line items. This can result in mismanagement through charging expenditures to incorrect accounts in order to circumvent limitations. Finally, informational reports can be generated beyond a meaningful use.

The line-item budget is also considered to be incremental, not comprehensive. It is based on inputs—money coming in—not outputs, or what is "produced" per dollar spent. By its very nature, this type of budget limits managerial flexibility and emphasizes control; only a certain amount can be spent for each "line." Because such budgets are usually prepared annually, at best they provide for only short-term planning, which leads to opportunistic spending (Metzgar and Miranda 2001). For example, if money is left in the budget and the budget cycle is ending, managers are likely to authorize purchases of equipment and other "wish list" items to ensure that the budget is exhausted, out of fear that top managers would cut their budgets in the next year because they did not need all the money allocated to them.

Performance-Based Budgeting

Performance-based budgeting (PBB) describes a variety of budget formats that have the same goal of showing the benefits of public expenditures and that monies are used wisely. PBBs are traditionally associated with the public sector. They are not budgets per se and are not new concepts. The federal government, for example, has been experimenting with various PBB formats for approximately 50 years. The concept of PBB in the federal government began in 1949. It evolved into President Johnson's Planning Programming Budgeting System (PPBS), then to management by objectives (MBO), which was encouraged by President Nixon, and finally to President Carter's zero-base budgeting (ZBB). Their designs differ, but their concepts, or goals, remain the same: to link and align spending decisions with expected performance. These benefits are justified around the impact of the expenditure, the outputs to achieve that impact, and the processes that were used to achieve the output. The goal is to ensure that outcomes, or the results of the agency's work, have been met in a financially prudent manner, or to trace the causal connection between agency outputs and its impact on the public being served (McGill 2001).

Performance budgeting is more complex than line-item budgeting, requiring that planners specify tasks that have an identifiable beginning and end. Following the identification of these tasks, and depending on the task, a standard time for each task can be calculated and standardized. PBB also requires the development of activity levels in the context of how many tasks will be performed each day, month, and year, as well as price and quantity variances related to each activity, that is, the differences between the performance and the plan for a specific item. Box 12–3 provides a simplified example of how outputs are related to inputs in performance budgeting.

BOX 12–3 ■ Planning Programming Budgeting System

Alarm Testing		Amount
	Total Tests	27
	Cost per Test	$ 75
	Total Budgeted	**$ 2,025**
Plant Security (Internal Site 1)		
	Cost per Day (365 days)	$ 1,224
	Total Cost	**$ 446,760**
Perimeter Security (External Site 1)		
	Cost per Day (365 days)	$ 612
	Total Cost	**$ 223,380**

Strengths Line items break down activities in easy-to-understand "bang-for-the-buck" format. Performance budgets increase the level of detail and information about activities and programs (Schick 1966). These budgets also enhance efficiency by relating costs of input to output, focusing on outputs. As a result, this budget format allows for a better determination of costs per service units rendered while giving managers an understanding of where costs are exceeding budgeted costs in certain areas or programs. As such, this format provides managers with a better understanding of the consequences of approving or disapproving budget requests.

Weaknesses Performance budgets are often difficult to administer, however. They contain more extensive information on unit costs than do other formats. As such, they are more time consuming, requiring more accounting efforts to track inputs and outputs. In addition, many functions of an organization, such as those in a proprietary security firm, are not truly measurable using work-cost measurements. In trying to measure deterrence, for example, one would first have to define or operationalize "deterrence" and then devise some crude measurements. Some measurable activities may be diminished loss of property from year to year. Employee satisfaction may improve. Clients may enjoy well-planned and maintained grounds. Sales can increase. These examples reveal that at times, what the manager chooses to measure is arbitrary. Meanwhile, the money spent on activities is easy to calculate. Settling on a definition of success for that expenditure, however, is a matter of perspective. Performance budgets do not shed light on whether a function or a program is worthwhile. Evaluation of the quality of performance is untouched. Finally, output costs are commonly seen as linear. For example, cutting a service in half reduces the cost of the program by half (Wood 1993). This common mistake ignores the fixed costs of providing a service.

Program Budgets

Program budgets are often confused with performance budgets but are more progressive and forward looking. Program budgeting often involves conducting cost-benefit analyses of items, long-range planning, program identification, and goal-setting activities (Tyer and Willand 1997). Program budgets give a total cost for the particular program or function identified and link objectives and performance measurement. Program budgets necessarily reflect and incorporate department objectives.

Strengths The program budget addresses some of the weaknesses of the line-item budget, focusing more on the activity to be performed than on delineating costs (Mosher 1954). Primarily, program budgets seek to integrate all the aspects of a particular program into one budget. These costs include personnel, operating, and capital costs. The major strength of the program budget is that it focuses on what is to be accomplished, which is one of the major weaknesses of the line-item budget. Box 12–4 shows an example of a program budget.

BOX 12–4 ■ Program Budgeting

Program: Building Security		Amount
	Personnel	$ 436,500
	Fire Prevention	87,540
	Alarms	63,000
	Total	**$ 587,040**

Weaknesses   Program budgets can suffer from too much detail and complexity at times. This is especially true when there are too many programs of varying levels of service, such as low, medium, or high security (Wood 1993).

As a double-edged proposition, program budgets without varying levels of service may be rejected if they are viewed as an all-or-nothing proposition. This makes it more difficult to make cuts and increases burdens on record keeping and accounting. It is important to approach program budgets with a willingness to scale back if needed. Most successful programs began as modest spending proposals.

Lump-Sum Budgeting

Lump-sum budgets focus more on providing resources than on providing financial details. Lump-sum budgets, like line-item budgets, are easy to understand. Managers allocate resources to departments or agencies at a specified level. It is then up to the agency, department, or project manger to provide services.

Strengths   The overall advantage of lump-sum budgeting is that it allows managers to manage. It also places a spotlight on managers for their accountability of funds and services. Box 12–5 illustrates a simple lump-sum budget.

BOX 12–5 ▪ Lump-Sum Budgeting

Safety and Security		Amount
	Department	$76,489
	Executive Protection	23,453
	Physical Plant Protection	62,349
	Technology Protection	89,765
	Public Safety Liaison Division	34,987
	Total Safety and Security	**$ 287,043**

Using lump-sum budgets places trust and confidence in division leaders, managers, or department heads. Spending is at the discretion of managers, and they are not bound by line items. The managers' only boundary is providing services at expected levels and fiscal accountability.

Weaknesses   The lack of information is the primary weakness of lump-sum budgets. For those who desire budget details, narratives, hints of efficiency, or other data from the budget, lump-sum formats are probably not ideal. Lump-sum budgeting is not devoid of details, but the minimalist approach to budgeting is usually not sufficient for most organizations.

Zero-Base Budgeting (ZBB)

Zero-base budgeting originated with the U.S. Department of Agriculture in 1962. However, it did not reach popularity in both the private and public sectors until Texas Instruments used it in the late 1960s. Later, Georgia Governor Jimmy Carter adopted it in 1972 to be used in the state government. When Carter became president of the United States in 1976, he introduced it to the federal government (Tyer and Willand 1997).

Zero-base budgeting is a form of "what if" budgeting (Lee and Johnson 1998). It requires the examination of current activities and new activities. Unlike line-item budgeting, which gives managers a base to operate from, ZBB provides no annual base. Rather, managers are required to justify why they need the money they do. ZBB requires managers to prioritize, or rank, their budgetary needs (Anderson 1998). It focuses on what should be done and the best methods of doing it. It requires managers to set goals and objectives and to find alternatives to achieve their accomplishments and funding levels. It also requires managers to set priorities for various activities or programs and then find the best alternative through a cost-benefit analysis. By its very essence, ZBB looks at how effective and efficient various activities or programs are in the organization.

Planners go through a series of steps when using the ZBB method. This process is shown in Figure 12–1. The primary aspects of zero-base budgets are

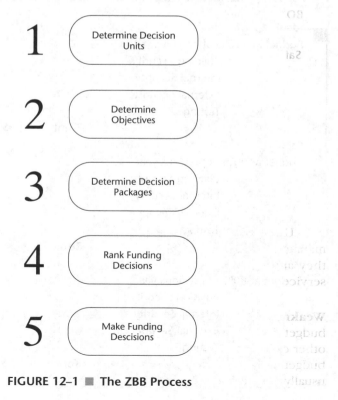

FIGURE 12–1 ■ **The ZBB Process**

decision units and decision packages (Anderson 1998). The process first requires managers to break the organization into decision units, or the activities to be analyzed. These units can be based on existing departments or programs. A security department, for instance, could be further divided into two decision units; physical security and fire protection. Next, managers would be required to determine the objectives related to these decision units and then create decision packages. Decision packages, an extension of decision units, determine the activities and levels of activities to be performed or conducted by that particular unit. Decision packages reflect funding priorities within the decision unit and ask basic questions related to whether the particular program should exist at all or whether an alternative program could achieve the same outcomes with less money allocated to it. Conducting these analyses eliminates the issue with the line item.

For example, if the number of background checks performed last year is a baseline, a security company may want to increase or decrease the number of background checks completed in the upcoming year. The level of background checks to be performed is the overall decision package. These various levels are usually an arbitrary percentage of previous activity. Box 12–6 gives an example, providing 80 percent, 90 percent, or 110 percent of current activity.

BOX 12–6 ■ Zero-Base Budgeting

Ideal		Amount
Budget at 110% of previous year		
Building Security		$ 5,500
Internal Security		143,000
External Security		401,500
Testing		3,300
	Total	$ 553,300
Bad		
Budget at 90% of previous year		
Building Security		$ 4,500
Internal Security		117,000
External Security		328,500
Testing		2,700
	Total	$ 452,700
Worse		
Budget at 80% of previous year		
Building Security		$ 4,000
Internal Security		104,000
External Security		292,000
Testing		2,400
	Total	$ 402,400

The decision units are all the activities of the organization. This type of budget may be produced for a division or an entire company, a town, or any other unit. Each of the activities listed is a decision unit—in this case, the unit is all facets of the organization. The packages are the levels of funding. Rarely will an organization or department lose 20 percent of its budget from the previous year. On the contrary, increasing budgets by 10 percent may be common depending on demand. No manager or director enjoys looking at a budget reduction of 20 percent from the previous year. This anxiety is derived from continually justifying and examining present activities, as well as future ones.

Strengths The major strength of zero-base budgeting is that it requires attention to past practices and the activity to be added and identifies the priority of the program. Organizations and managers who favor cutting budgets may like this format. Managers are required to think in terms of budget consequences. As a result, ZBB requires that planning and the budget be done at the same time. It also requires organizations to set priorities based on program results that can be achieved at different spending levels (McGill 2001). According to Tyer and Willand (1997, 201), "the uniqueness of ZBB was in the formatting of information and redefinition of budget bases to include decrements and not just increases in funding." By its very nature, it is also a bottom-up approach to budgeting. Instead of having a budget imposed on a department and perhaps engaging in activities that are unnecessary, the ZBB process requires analysis and feedback from those individuals who have direct experience with the particular activities to be budgeted.

Weaknesses One drawback to ZBB is that it was designed to replace incremental line-item budgeting, which traditionally fit well with organizational norms and behaviors. Because of the nature of ZBB, many habits or customs were challenged, particularly those related to eliminating customary or habitualized activities that could no longer be funded under ZBB because they could not be defended (Anderson 1997). For example, many line items allow for managers' discretionary spending. Although a tradition in some organizations, these line items could not be well defended under the ZBB concept.

Another problem with ZBB is that it may be impossible to realistically begin with a zero base every year and eliminate politics from the budgeting process. The process is time consuming and inefficient (Anderson 1998). These budgets increase the number of budget games played. For example, important programs may not always be ranked ahead of lesser ones (Schick 1978). Some activities may be preferred by employees but disliked by managers.

■ NEW BUDGETING PARADIGMS

Some issues are associated with traditional budgeting formats and the processes used to create them. One criticism associated with traditional methods is that they focus only on a single year, making them a short-term planning tool, if that.

Traditional budgets, such as the line item, use incremental forms of decision making. Often, budgets preserve past decisions and do not examine them before incorporating them into the next year's budget (Tyer and Willand 1997).

Of particular concern with some of these methods, such as the line item, is that they emphasize control over money without really determining how effectively these monies are being spent in the context of returns on investments or monies spent (Hope and Fraser 2000). In other instances, budgets are used as an oppressive tool with managers focused on mistakes. In other situations, the managerial perspective is too narrow, with managers focused on their own departments instead of the entire organization when preparing their budgets. Further, managers focus on outputs, not processes (Reid 2002).

Hope and Fraser (2000) call for a performance management system that gives budgeting decisions to those who are most impacted by budgets: line-level managers. Hope and Fraser point out that the traditional underlying theme of financial planning is control, with a centralized force emphasizing coercion rather than coordination, focusing on cost controls rather than on creating value, which in turn stifles initiative and keeps the planning and execution processes separate. The visions of chief executives translate into strategic plans, which are then handed down to operational managers, who prepare budgets to meet their vision.

Although these traditional methods provided stability and continuity, this model no longer fits the fast-changing business world and organizational structures that take a decentralized approach to decision making and give great authority to line-level managers. Organizational structures have changed in the context of layers and decision making, whereas budgetary issues have not changed, creating problems.

In an attempt to better link budgeting with planning processes and the long-term mission of the organizations, other, more appropriate, budgeting techniques could be used. These include beyond-budgeting models, rolling budgets, and multiyear budgets (MYB).

Beyond Budgeting

Hope and Fraser (2000) point out that firms need to be innovative and responsive to their environment in order to be successful. However, "the gravitational force of the budgeting system makes it extremely difficult for firms to escape the world of compliance and control. Only by overcoming the constraints of the traditional budgeting approach can managers build a business model that operates at high speed; is self-questioning, self-renewing, and self-controlling; and rewards innovation and learning" (p. 35). One way to accomplish this is called the beyond-budgeting model, which includes the following points.

- Eliminate the annual budget cycle, which is highly deterministic, locking the planning process into only 1 year, limiting long-term planning in the process.
- The performance-management model should be aimed at supporting self-governing business units.

- More responsibility and accountability should be given to a greater number of business units for value creation. This is called "devolution," or moving the decision-making processes down to where there is more expertise and personal investment in the outcomes.
- Autonomous profit centers should be created, so that units in the organization can run their own businesses. By bringing budgetary issues down to those who impacted by it, they will be able to continuously adjust their strategies and encourage team performance at various levels in the organization, as more people now have a stake in impacting the performance of the organization.

All these recommendations will require that organizations properly train managers and give them the freedom to act and the responsibility to deliver results. This means that managers should have a great deal of control over their budgets. With this model, people in the company will beat the competition rather than some negotiated budget. On its face, this budgeting technique makes sense. In some settings, managers may be more concerned with how well they are meeting the budgetary constraints imposed on them instead of comparing their performance to that of the competition. In contractual security firms, for example, they will need to look both internally and externally to be cost-effective, examining their expenditures and how well they are competing with other firms.

Rolling Budgets

Instead of reviewing a budget on a yearly basis, some organizations review their budgets on a quarterly basis. This is known as the rolling budget, with a new budget created every 3 months or, depending on the needs of the company, on a monthly basis (Myers 2001).

The rolling budget has many benefits. First, rolling budgets are a useful tool in planning. By its very nature, the information in the budget is only a few months old, providing "real-time" information. Traditional budgets, by contrast, may be a year old and may be useless, as the information in them may be out of date soon after they are created. By reviewing the budget on a quarterly basis, managers can respond more quickly to changing economic and business issues, improving their forecasting abilities in the process. These issues could result in managers' adjusting staffing levels to control for personnel costs: in the case of profit-oriented security companies, such as the alarm industry, managers could adjust accordingly. For instance, if the organization is producing or selling alarms or security software and if its sales are "soft" for that quarter, the company can discount its products for the next quarter and not have to deal with last-minute discounts to show greater profits at the end of the fiscal year. Because the rolling budget requires a greater degree of monitoring, managerial responsibilities are increased. Hence, managers will become more heavily involved in monitoring the budget. This will subsequently increase their level of decision-making empowerment in the organization (Myers 2001).

Multiyear Budgeting

In some instances, organizations engage in multiyear budgeting (MYB). With MYB, an organization creates a 2-year or more budget. MYB can exist in many formats and includes a 2-year, a 3-year, and a 5-year budget. An organization may have a biennial, or 2-year, financial plan, which is an annual appropriation linked to a spending plan for the following year. With rolling biennial budgets, or 2-year spending plans, the two 1-year appropriations can be adjusted on an annual basis. With a traditional biennial budget, 2 years' worth of expenditures are approved all at once (Jackson 2002).

MYB will improve the organization's long-term planning and priority-setting process. Because individuals have to allocate financial resources and perhaps profits for a longer period of time—more than 1 year— the planning efforts in the organization will improve. At the same time, MYBs allow departments to link their long-term plans and priorities with their budget and decision-making processes. MYBs have also reduced staff hours dedicated to the budgeting process. Instead of tying up staff on a yearly basis to work on budgets, staff work on MYB plans at a minimum of every other year. MYBs also strengthen performance evaluation. Employees can reallocate their time and efforts to monitoring program goals and objectives (Blom 2000).

MYBs also have some drawbacks. Because of their time span, MYBs lack the flexibility associated with annual budgets (Blom 2000). MYB also makes budget forecasting difficult and less accurate, as the time line is extended from 1 year to 2 years (Jackson 2002). For example, MYB is less responsive to rapid economic changes, such as a drop in revenue leading to the security department's receiving less money in its operating budget. Thus, MYBs involve increased uncertainty. When the market sector and/or the economy is unstable, it may be more difficult to determine MYBs. The first time an organization changes from annual budgeting to MYB, there may also be an increased workload, leading to increased stress among those responsible for preparing the budget (Blom and Guajardo 2000).

Balanced Scorecard

The balanced scorecard merges traditional accounting methods with nonfinancial measures of the organization's success in the context of both the short and long term. This approach looks at organizational performance from four perspectives (Crawford and Henry 2000):

1. Financial factors, such as income, return on investment, and cash flow
2. The customer, in the context of product image and service quality as well as cost
3. Internal factors, including employee skills, productivity, and quality
4. A learning and growth perspective, which looks at the organization's ability to be innovative in opening new markets and products, new processes, and improving and creating value in its existing products

All companies are concerned about their financial outcomes and profits. The organization wants to make sure that it is spending its resources in an efficient manner, with the ratio of inputs in the context of money producing those outcomes it prefers. Issues that are considered include sales growth and the return on capital, which serve as targets for the other three categories of the balanced scorecard. In the context of the second category—the customer—the company could evaluate its performance by looking at current levels of customer satisfaction. Issues that could be explored here include reviewing customer and client complaints or issues that were raised. The organization could even survey clients and customers to get even more information on its performance. The company could also identify what are known as performance drivers, which identify and measure factors that affect future customer satisfaction, such as the price and quality of services, response times, and the organization's image and reputation in the field (Ellingson and Wambsganss 2001).

The security firm also needs to be concerned with internal factors and its ability for learning and growth. The internal business category deals with innovation, operations, and service. Innovation refers to research and development activities to create new products to meet customer demands; operations, to the delivery of products and services; service, with such issues as how long it takes to follow up on complaints, return calls, and meet other customer needs, all of which has an impact on customer satisfaction and retention. The category of learning and growth deals with employee satisfaction. Employees are a customer's gateway to the company and are important for customer satisfaction. Factors the security company will want to consider here are its long-term investment in employees, focusing on employee retention, empowerment, training, and productivity (Ellingson and Wambsganss 2001).

When using these four criteria in measuring the organization's performance, planning and performance are shifted from measuring performance based on budget compliance or financial measures to a combination of factors, including financial issues. The balanced scorecard links the performance to the overall mission of the company in a cause-effect relationship. The balanced scorecard makes sure that those resources and efforts are effective in meeting the organization's mission (Ellingson and Wambsganss 2001).

■ THE BUDGET CYCLE

The budgeting process is as important as the budget format. As useful as budgets are, they are not able to overcome the shortcomings of the process used to produce them. Therefore, understanding the budgeting process contributes to a broader understanding of budgets and budgeting.

Budgeting is traditionally delegated to senior-level managers in the organization or particular department. In these situations, the budgeting process is the responsibility of one individual or a small group of individuals called together to create the budget. In other situations, multiple individuals are involved in the process. This participation could be vertical, involving supervisors and managers. It could also be horizontal, involving individuals with the same level of responsibilities and authority. Regardless of who is involved in the process, they should have full participation, not pseudoparticipation, or giving them the false impression they have input (Reid 2002).

The budget in any organization goes through a well-defined cycle, or process, that varies from organization to organization. For some employees and managers, budgeting is an intense process during a specific time of the year. Finance, personnel, and budget officers refer to this time as "budget season." Usually, the budget cycle coincides with the fiscal year. Some organizations' calendar and fiscal years occur simultaneously. Other organizations prefer to stagger the start of their fiscal year to allow time for preparing financial reports and complying with tax laws. Fiscal years will vary from organization to organization. It is very important to know when the fiscal year starts, for the sake of planning and organizing information.

The budget cycle is composed of three budgets: the prior year, the current year, and the budget year. Budgeters often rely on the prior year's budget to design their current budgets, the one the organization is operating under. The budget year is the budget that planners are creating and preparing to use the following year.

The budget cycle consists of five distinct stages, or phases.

Stage 1: The Beginning

Stage 1—the beginning—is usually announced by a call letter from the executive (Reed and Swain 1997). The letter may contain information about the financial outlook for the upcoming year, the usefulness of past activities, and a review of future goals of the organization. This call letter guides the process in terms of both objectives and timetables for completion.

Executives may also take the opportunity to recognize departments, agencies, or programs that appear to be doing excellent work. The call letter becomes a mechanism for lavishing praise, as well as bringing to light important challenges facing the organization.

Stage 2: Preparation and Submission

In stage 2, work begins on preparing the budget. The most essential ingredient for preparing a budget is information. Depending on the budget format, the cost of performing programs and activities must be determined. Increases in the budget must be justified in terms of their overall benefit to the organization and constituents that are served. Both of these require information about effectiveness, need, and potential success.

One way to maintain information is to create and maintain a file. Keeping a budget file helps organize information and lessen frustrations during budget season. Budget files will vary from department to division to organization, but all include the following essential elements (adapted from Wood 1993):

- Feedback, including complaints, about service
- A list of current activities
- Information about overlapping departmental activities
- Media coverage of department or organizational activities
- Evaluations, data, and information related to demand, workload, and employee satisfaction
- Program audits and reviews
- Any new technologies that will help the organization do the job
- Letters or memos that provide evidence or documentation that the organization is performing well

For most organizations, the information in a typical budget file is not readily available. Unless the organization is committed to evaluations, research, and measurement, this information is unlikely to be lying around waiting to be used. What may occur is that organizations will use proxy indicators instead of reliable data. For example, employee turnover rates may be used as a proxy measure of employee satisfaction levels. Measures of client satisfaction could include complaints, anecdotal feedback from clients, and satisfaction surveys.

In addition to preparing a budget file, it is also important to avoid the following common mistakes:

- Not following instructions
- Mathematical errors
- Not requesting sufficient money
- Asking for too much without justification
- Not recognizing routine and controversial expenditures
- Not meeting deadlines
- Not asking questions when uncertain
- Not recognizing where the money comes from, who pays, and where it goes

The mistakes seem trivial, and they are. Meeting the deadline set out in the call letter and avoiding mathematical errors are easily avoided with attention to detail. The fundamental problem related to budget errors is related to inattention to detail. Budgets, regardless of attention, are rarely error-free. Attention to detail will reduce the number of errors and generate credibility for those creating the budget.

Stage 3: Adoption

Adoption of the budget includes its formal incorporation by an organization. Once the budget is at this stage, very few of those who crunched the numbers and gathered the information are involved (Thurmaier 1992). Most budget adoption occurs by management, boards, and other key officials in the organization, such as chief financial or executive officers. The exception to this norm may occur in small employee-owned organizations in which everyone participates in all decisions. Budgets are more likely to be accepted if they conform to the preferences of those who will ultimately adopt them.

Adopting a budget is a highly competitive political process. As in a competition, the budget game has winners and losers. It is at the adoption stage where success is decided. When needs outpace resources, choices have to be made. Priorities must be established. As a consequence, the budget will reflect many competing and conflicting values.

Stage 4: Implementation

Once budgets are adopted, they must be put into action. Implementing the budget requires carrying out the directed activities by the budget at the assigned levels of service. Circumstances regularly dictate a diversion from the budget. As a result, implementation incorporates values and preferences, just as the budget does when it undergoes revisions during adoption (Reed and Swain 1997).

Organizations are continually under pressure to perform, cut costs, and maintain a prominent stature within their communities. These pressures are often competing. Those who have budget authority—the ability to make spending decisions after the budget is approved—must balance the competing interests. Their challenge is balancing prudent spending decisions with providing adequate service to the organization's constituents.

The implementation phase requires routine monitoring. However, this often does not occur, because of time constraints that some managers may face or because some managers are not sure of the budgeting process and are reluctant to ask for help or to expose their weaknesses. This will ultimately lead to problems, because small issues that could easily be detected and readily apparent could evolve into a major crisis for the manager and the organization.

In the implementation phase, it is easy to deviate from the adopted budget. This deviation is sometimes intentional and sometimes unavoidable. Changes in anticipated revenue can squeeze a budget until new sources of income are found. Managers may intentionally withhold spending in order to strictly control subordinates. Regardless of the source leading to deviation from an adopted budget, it does happen. The extent and the acceptability of the changes are determined in the final stage: auditing and review.

Stage 5: Review and Audit

Review and audits of the budget are needed at the end of the fiscal year and sometimes during it. In the case of governmental budgeting, this stage is required by law. With private business, this stage may be done to satisfy shareholders, management, or laws that govern the corporation. Reviews and audits accomplish the same goal. They ensure that expenditures were made in a proper manner. Reviews and audits do not speak to notions of efficiency or complete or total compliance with directives or law. They judge only according to standard methods of accounting.

Trained professionals in the fields of accounting or budget analysis conduct reviews and audits. Budget reviews are conducted internally. An organization fundamentally seeks to "keep up" with where it is spending money. By doing so, the organization can make changes to spending. In a competitive economic climate, reviews are the primary internal method of financial management. Audits are an external review of an organization's books. Audits are required to ensure financial integrity. Auditing roots out spending and accounting that do not comply with the spirit of prevailing ethics, laws, and other regulations. Audits can be detailed or vague, and the level of service rendered by auditing firms will depend on the organization contracting for their services.

Besides periodic reviews and audits, effective accounting procedures must be used throughout the budget cycle. Accounting is a system of tracking receipts and expenditures. As a profession, accounting adheres to a code of ethics and established financial practices. Most organizations employ a staff accountant or budget analyst or someone to keep the books. Auditing, an external function, is a contracted service provided by a firm or an individual.

Tracking expenditures and receipts throughout the year makes a final year-end audit and review simpler. Simpler audits and reviews translate into lower costs to perform them. Clean audits enhance the image of any organization and give it the opportunity to brag about its financial management practices.

■ THE BUDGET GAME

Budgeting is a competition among values. Scarcity of resources necessitates that some values are validated and others not. Learning to "play the game" is the first step to developing budget savvy and seeing that a particular set of values and preferences "wins out." Because budgeting deals with competition over limited financial resources, competition will ensue regardless of whether it is a proprietary or contract forum. In a proprietary setting, for example, the director of security may need to side with another department to build an alliance so they can get their budget approved. In a contract setting, managers or supervisors may compete for an increase in equipment among locations or for "pet projects."

Budget gamesmanship exists to some degree in any organization. Research in police agencies on gamesmanship and budgetary success measured success in two ways: in the context of whether they kept a harmonious relationship with those involved in the budget process and in the context of whether they successfully expanded or defended their existing budgets (Coe and Wiesel 2001). Their analysis of successful police budgeting provides some successful strategies used by police departments to defend and increase their budgets. With minor adaptations, these same points can be applied to the security industry, as presented in Table 12–1.

Issues

In his analysis of public budgeting, Thurmaier (2000) suggests that, in any budget proposal or recommendation, there are three primary issues to consider: social, legal, and political.

TABLE 12–1 ■ Successful Budget Strategies

Method	Description
Use data judiciously	Use requests for service, increased demands for services, workload, and so on, to convince policymakers to spend more money on security.
Get your message out effectively	This deals with image. Security organizations that have a good "public image" may view budget proposals more favorably.
Capitalize on sensational incidents	Provide factual evidence of incidents, preferably from outside your organization, to convince individuals making budget decisions to recognize the need (and perhaps increased need) for security-related services. Workplace violence issues, the attack on the World Trade Center, and other high-profile crimes and security breaches could influence funding decisions.
Mobilize interest groups	This involves mobilizing those groups outside your specific unit to leverage support for your budget proposal. Establishing permanent and positive relationships with users of your services will lead to those individuals' fighting for and defending your services in times of budget cuts. These individuals, of course, can also be advocates for new programs and subsequent increases in security budgets.
Plan strategically	Long-range goals allow decision makers to make better policy decisions. The presence of a strategic plan may also indirectly show that security is using its resources effectively.
Work closely with key decision makers	Creating and sustaining a close working relationship with key decision makers, such as CEOs, directors, and presidents in the organization and responding to their needs and concerns could lead to more favorable budgetary decisions.

Social Issues   Individuals need to consider the social facets of budgeting. If the budget is a reflection of the top decision maker's policies, the financial issues may not drive the budget but rather an individual's or group of individuals' perceptions of what the organization or department should do or look like. Therefore, those who are in charge of creating the budget need to gain an understanding of the social factors involved. As indicated in Table 12-1, maintaining good social relationships with constituents and decision makers is important.

In order to gain an understanding of these social factors, one could analyze old budgets to see what earlier budget priorities were. It is also important to establish personal relationships with those individuals who are involved in the process. In a large organization, these individuals could include agency heads, supervisors, and other personnel who will be directly impacted by the budget. In some cases, it may be a good idea to visit various locations that the organization serves. Suppose, for example, that a large site needs an additional vehicle for patrol or has requested new access-control software. To place the budget request in a proper perspective, it may be prudent to see the site and gain an understanding of how the proposed items would address these needs.

Legal Considerations   Managers also need to consider legal issues when budgeting. In general, the private sector has fewer legal considerations than the public sector does. Nevertheless, those who are responsible for the preparation of the budget need to recognize what legal restrictions they do face. These legal restrictions could include administrative laws related to OSHA (Occupational Safety and Health Administration); government regulations about various levels, types, or forms of security hardware for some industries; and mandatory training issues that may exist for certain organizations.

Political Considerations   The third component consists of the politics associated with budgeting. To the extent that politics involves influencing and strategizing, all budgets and budgeting processes are to some extent political. The political process often requires the building of coalitions or alliances with people and other departments and may also involve compromising when all parties are striving to get what they want. However, only a few of the participants may be satisfied. If this is the case, the once civil process of budgeting may become filled with conflict. One of the most recognized authorities on budgetary politics is Aaron Wildavsky (1979), whose suggestions for engaging in the politics of budgetary process were originally applied to budgets at the federal level. However, his suggestions are also applicable to the private sector to a degree, as politics pervades all organizations to some extent.

The key to budget success is to develop a demand for your service or product. Wildavksy described this as developing clientele. Clientele are important, especially active clientele. Executives and others who adopt budgets respond to the demands of those who use or benefit from their product. Companies must placate not only shareholders but also customers. Governments seek to serve the needs of an electorate. Companies seek to make money and to provide services where needed. In either type of organization, the goals are similar.

Another suggestion for playing the budget game involves developing relationships with decision makers. Budgeters should seek out the favor of those above them who are responsible for deciding the fate of their programs and activities. When requests for justification and accountability occur, the exchange need not be adversarial. If proper relationships have been developed, the chances of success are increased, and conflict is minimized.

The final suggestion is playing the game. In politics, this involves organizing clientele to exert pressures, controlling the language used to discuss the budget, and framing issues favorable to your position. "Playing the game," of course, varies with those issues that managers encounter when engaged in budgeting. Some of the more common issues managers face include dealing with proposed budget cuts and the impact of those cuts on operations, advocating for an increase in their budgets because of the expansion of programs and services, and budgets for new programs.

The main idea surrounding these suggestions is that budgeting is laden with competing priorities. The tactics suggested by Wildavsky (1979) pertain to varying aspects of program development. Conflict, winning, and losing are rarely eliminated from the task of budgeting. Individuals will frequently disagree on the acquisition and allocation of company assets. Becoming a seasoned veteran in the budget game takes experience and time. Choosing the appropriate tactic depends on context; it is not a prescriptive choice. Tactics that work in one context may not work in a similar one. Of course, over time these budget strategies will become salient and easier to use.

Ethics in Budgeting

Budgeting involves expertise and judgment. It also requires that managers act in an ethical manner. In many cases, behavioral and organizational aspects, social pressures, risk aversion, and attitudes toward getting as much of the pie as possible lead to issues of ethics in budgeting. This is sometimes called gamesmanship. Budgeting gamesmanship is when lower-levels managers "play games," or falsify and manipulate their budgets, to somehow benefit them. Terms used include cushioning the budget, hedging, the "kitty," secret reserve, or the cookie jar. Regardless of what it is called, such dysfunctional behavior impairs the budgeting and planning processes in the organization and affects the accuracy of forecasting and the performance evaluations of employees. In short, gamesmanship is an unethical behavior.

One major issue with gamesmanship is budget slack, which is defined as "the discrepancy between a subordinate's best estimate of performance based on his private information and the budgeted level of performance" (Fisher et al. 2002, 850). Budget slack can also be defined as "the difference between the stated budget and an honest budget prediction" (Busch 2002, 156), or the difference between planned and real performance targets or capabilities. It is also referred to as budgetary bias (Douglas and Wier 2000). This "slack" is a problem for organizations. It causes organizational resources to be misallocated, which ultimately results in a poor return on investment and a loss of profits for the firm (Fisher et al. 2002). It is an indicator of the poor use of organizational resources (Busch 2002).

Slack can occur unintentionally or on purpose (Busch 2002). It also exists in two shapes: slack created for personal gain or inducements for the stakeholders or for a reserve managers accumulate so they can "weather" financially difficult times. Accidental slack occurs when the planner overestimates the costs associated with, for example, personnel expenditures. For example, a manager might overestimate the personnel overtime budget where there is a surplus at the end of the budget cycle.

Purposeful slack occurs when planners consciously overestimate costs in the budget in order to maximize the resources for their units (Busch 2002). For example, a manager may overestimate the number of personnel hours, based on an inflated needs analysis. This "increased" demand for personnel could lead to this manager's unnecessarily expanding his or her workforce. In other situations, managers may overemphasize their discretionary expenses to create a "buffer" to ensure that their other line items will have the proper funding if they exceed their allocated budgets for the year.

In other cases, the motive underlying purposeful slack is based on pure personal gain. In some instances, budgets are used for performance evaluation, with an employee's pay somehow related to the budget. In a participatory budgeting situation, the subordinate and the superior may negotiate the budget. This final budget then serves as a benchmark for compensating and evaluating the subordinate's performance. In these situations, subordinates may understate their productivity to get a greater share of the organization's resources or money. In these types of cases, subordinates may understate their true production capabilities, knowing that they will exceed their production norms and subsequently receive bonuses for their "increased" productivity (Fisher et al. 2002). Nevertheless, it is still an unethical behavior.

Some organizations, unfortunately, tolerate and accept these behaviors, with managers admitting to planning slack in their budgets and arguing why they are justified in doing so. Simply put, top managers, regardless of whether slack is accidental or purposeful, accept it as the status quo when budgeting. However, budgetary slack can be easily controlled. Douglas and Wier (2000) recommend that the issue of budget slack be made more morally intense instead of a behavioral and organizational artifact. By creating social consciousness about the fact that slack is detrimental to the goals of the organization and linking this with a strong ethical culture that is demonstrated through practices and exposed values, budgetary slack can be better controlled.

■ CONCLUSION

Budgets are tangible plans for using agency resources. Budgets are required because they provide the basis for fiscal control and managing objectives. The budget is the company's statement of expected financial results for the year and should be thought of as a numerical expression of the new manager's plans for the organization's work for the next year (Finney 1993). As this chapter has shown, budgets are used for a variety of purposes, including setting and monitoring performance goals and considering program performance as part of the budget process. Budgets also describe what the organization does, explain how expenditures are used and allocated, and are statements of preference showing the priorities and mission of the organization. Budgets give meaning to the company's objectives and priorities by planning the following year's work in detail and coordinating and communicating those plans throughout the company.

Budget formats are determined according to agency preferences and needs. Some of the more common formats are the traditional line item, performance, program, lump sum, and zero base. Each has its strengths and weaknesses. Some new budgeting paradigms are rolling budgets, multiyear budgeting formats, and the balanced scorecard, which takes into consideration multiple inputs into the budgeting process. Regardless of the design, budgets go through a series of stages, beginning with the call for a budget, preparation, adoption, implementation, and audit.

This chapter has shown that the budgeting process is laden with preferences, conflict, and struggle. Managers need to recognize the social, legal, and political issues involved in the budgeting process and play the budgeting game in an ethical manner. One of the primary ethical failures is when managers create budgetary slack, which may be committed for personal and unit gains. It can also occur accidentally and on purpose.

■ KEY TERMS

Audit	Incremental budgets
Balanced scorecard	Multiyear budgeting
Beyond-budgeting model	Line-item budgeting
Budget cycle	Lump-sum budgeting
Budget format	Operating budget
Budget game	Performance budget
Budget objective	Politics
Budgeting	Program budgeting
Capital budgets	Rolling budget
Decision package	Slack
Decision unit	Zero-base budgeting

■ DISCUSSION QUESTIONS

1. What is budgeting? What are some of its uses?
2. Why is budgeting important to the success of an organization?
3. What are some effective strategies for playing the budget game?
4. How has public budgeting influenced budgeting in the private sector?
5. How can zero-base budgeting be adapted to any organization?
6. Of the newer budget paradigms, which seems likeliest to become widely used?
7. Is budgeting a rational process?
8. Can politics be eliminated from budgeting?
9. Does the budget cycle yield all the purposes and objectives of budgeting?
10. Do budgets reflect true priorities, or are they reflections of who has power to influence the process?

■ REFERENCES

ANDERSON, J. L. 1998. Techniques for governance. *The Social Science Journal* 35 (4): 493–508.

BLOM, B. 2000. Multi-year budgeting: A primer for finance officers. *Government Finance Review* 16 (1): 39–43.

BUSCH, T. 2002. Slack in public administration: Conceptual and methodological issues. *Managerial Accounting Journal* 17 (3): 153–159.

COE, C. K., and D. L. WIESEL. 2001. Police budgeting: Winning strategies. *Public Administration Review* 61 (6): 718–727.

CRAWFORD, D., and E. G. HENRY. 2000. Budgeting and performance evaluation at the Berkshire Toy Company. *Issues in Accounting Education* 15 (2): 283–319.

DOUGLAS, P. C., and B. WIER. 2000. Integrating ethical dimensions into a model of budgetary slack creation. *Journal of Business Ethics* 28 (3): 267–277.

ELLINGSON, D. A., and J. R. WAMBSGANSS. 2001. Modifying the approach to planning and evaluation in governmental entities. A "balanced scorecard" approach. *Journal of Public Budgeting, Accounting and Financial Management* 13 (1): 103–120.

FINNEY, R. G. 1993. *Powerful budgeting for better planning and management.* New York: AMACOM.

———. 2000. *Office finances made easy.* New York: American Management Association.

FISHER, J. G., L. A. MAINES, S. A. PEFFER, and G. A. SPRINKLE. 2002. Using budgets for performance evaluation: Effects of resource allocation and horizontal information asymmetry on budget proposals, budget slack, and performance. *Accounting Review* 77 (4): 847–865.

HOPE, J., and R. FRASER. 2000. Beyond budgeting. *Strategic Finance* 82 (4): 30–35.

JACKSON, A. 2002. Taking the plunge: The conversion to multi-year budgeting. *Government Finance Review* 18 (4): 24–27.

LEE, R. D. and R. W. JOHNSON. 1998. *Public budgeting systems.* 6th ed. Gaithersburg, MD: Aspen.

MATTHEWS, L. 1977. *Practical operating budget.* New York: McGraw-Hill.

MCGILL, R. 2001. Performance budgeting. *International Journal of Public Sector Management* 14 (1): 376–390.

METZGAR, J., and R. MIRANDA. 2001. Bringing out the dead: Can information technology resurrect budget reform? *Government Finance Review* 17 (2): 9–13.

MIKESELL, J. L. 2003. *Fiscal administration: Analysis and applications for the public sector.* Belmont, CA: Wadsworth.

MOSHER, F. C. 1954. *Program budgeting: Theory and practice with particular reference to the U. S. Department of Army.* Chicago: Public Administration Service.

MYERS, R. 2001. Budgets on a roll. *Journal of Accountancy* 192 (6): 41–46.

NOVICK, D. 1968. The origin and history of program budgeting. *California Management Review* 11 (1): 1–12.

OTLEY, D. T. 1978. Budget use and managerial behavior. *Journal of Accounting Research* 16: 122–149.

OVERMAN, E. S. 1996. The new sciences of administration: Chaos and quantum theory. *Public Administration Review* 56 (5): 487–492.

PHYRR, P. 1973. *Zero-base budgeting: A practical management tool for evaluating expenses.* New York: Wiley.

RAMSEY J. E. and I. L. RAMSEY. 1985. *Budgeting basics.* New York: Watts.

REED, B. J. and J. W. SWAIN. 1997. *Public finance administration.* 2nd ed. Thousand Oaks, CA: Sage Publications.

REID, P. 2002. A critical evaluation of the effect of participation in budget target setting on motivation. *Managerial Auditing Journal* 17 (3): 122–129.

RUBIN, I. S. 1993. Who invented budgeting in the United States? *Public Administration Review* 53 (5): 438–444.

SCHICK, A. 1966. The road to PBB: The stages of budget reform. *Public Administration Review* 26: 243–258

THURMAIER, K. 1992. Budgetary decision-making in central budget bureaus: An experiment. *Journal of Public Administration Research and Theory* 2 (4): 463–487.

———. 2000. The anatomy of a budget recommendation. *Journal of Public Budgeting, Accounting and Financial Management* 12 (4): 569–597.

TYER, C., and J. WILLAND. 1997. Public budgeting in America: A twentieth century perspective. *Journal of Public Budgeting, Accounting and Financial Management* 9 (2): 189–219.

WILDAVKSY, A. 1979. *The politics of the budgetary process*. 3rd ed. Boston: Little, Brown.

WELSCH, G. A. 1971. *Budgeting: profit planning and control*. 3rd ed. Englewood Cliffs, NJ: Prentice Hall.

WOOD, L. 1993. *Little budget book*. Palos Verdes, CA: Training Shoppe.

chapter thirteen

Scheduling

Scheduling is the efficient and balanced use of the human resource to meet the needs of the organization. The purpose of scheduling is to match workload requirements, or the demands placed on the organization, with available resources, including employees.

Scheduling also refers to establishing the employee's starting and stopping times, number of days worked, and length of the workweek. This effort requires blending the number of positions required for the organization to operate with the appropriate number of officers to achieve an efficient and effective organizational operation. Scheduling also requires the manager to comply with all state and federal legislation related to hours and conditions of work.

Scheduling can be very complex and confusing and is considered an "art" by some managers. Some sectors of the security field are particularly confusing, as a manager must schedule on the basis of sector needs, as well as the needs of the organization being secured. If done correctly, scheduling can improve the effectiveness and the efficiency of the security department, as well as worker commitment and morale. Improperly conducted scheduling can result in the reverse, with hostile, aggravated employees and an organization that is not receiving effective, efficient security services.

■ THE IMPORTANCE OF SCHEDULING

One of any organization's greatest assets is its human resources. Balancing the goals and objectives of the organization with its human resources will enhance organizational effectiveness. The development of an effective scheduling plan, or system, is one component of organizational effectiveness. With many industries facing worker shortages and competing for workers within their particular labor markets or regions, scheduling becomes of paramount importance.

The fundamentals of a schedule are easy. But the changing needs of the workforce, employee needs, and organizational factors may make the scheduling process more complex.

A Changing Workforce

The U.S. workforce became increasingly diverse in the last half of the twentieth century and beyond. Changing demographics in age, family composition, and gender are a few of the changes in the workforce population. Individuals born between 1946 and 1964—the baby boomers—are the main labor force, whereas younger and older workers now represent a declining share of employment (U.S. Department of Labor 1997). But as the baby boomers age, organizations will be facing new employees—younger and older.

The composition of the family has also changed. More single parents are in the workforce. Organizations will require creative means to schedule, retain, and attract this employee group. Furthermore, of married couples with children under 18 years of age, more than 50 percent of both parents held jobs in 2002 (U.S. Department of Labor 2003). Often, this dual-income couple becomes the split-shift couple, balancing a daunting work schedule and childcare with efforts to maintain a certain quality of family life.

The number of employees working fewer than 40 hours per week has also increased. More than 24 million U.S. workers in 2003 were classified as part-time employees. The primary reasons why people work part time are non-economic and include issues related to educational, familial, and personal obligations (U.S. Department of Labor 2004). Much of the increase in part-time work has been in fast growing U.S. industries such as the retail trades and service industries (Fallick 1999).

Changing Needs of the Employee

The changes in the workforce translate to changes in workers' needs. In a study of 800 organizations (Narasimhan 1997), more than 75 percent of the managers indicated that flexible work scheduling was an issue they must address. Other research (see Hung 1994, for instance) has reported that workers want more flexibility and control over their schedules in order to spend more time with their families and friends. Childcare was also reported as a problem for 62 percent of the parents.

Budgeting and Fiscal Responsibility

Scheduling is also important in the context of budgeting and fiscal responsibility. An improperly designed schedule that does not combine the needs or demands of the organization with a properly balanced schedule can lead to unnecessary personnel expenditures, including overtime wages and increased administrative costs. An improperly designed schedule can also lead to increased costs associated with the administration of the schedule.

Other Considerations

An effective scheduling process can enhance the quality of work life for the employee. Employees dissatisfied with work schedules may leave the organization, resulting in increased employee turnover and recruitment-related costs. Meanwhile, the remaining employees may have decreased morale and motivation and a poor attitude toward work, ultimately impacting their production of goods or services. A poorly designed schedule will also result in increased absenteeism and sick days. Other research has determined that effective scheduling has a direct effect on the employees' perceptions of control over work and family matters, resulting in lower levels of conflict between the work and family, depression, somatic complaints, job dissatisfaction, and blood cholesterol (Thomas 1995).

■ FACTORS TO CONSIDER IN SCHEDULING

Many factors need to be considered when determining or designing a schedule for the security organization. At a minimum, schedules must be

- Accurate
- Comprehensive
- Readable
- Understood by management and the employees

The art of the scheduling process centers on organizational, employee, and legal considerations.

Organizational Considerations

The Number of Positions or Assignments Needed   The security manager must know how many positions or assignments need to be filled on a daily basis. For a small organization, this demand profile of the organization may be easy, as a shift may have only one or two positions. In large organizations, however, the demand profile may change according to the day, time of day, time of month, and season. This demand profile will also change according to the nature of the organization. Organizations engaged in manufacturing may have more personnel, vendors, and clients on property than do office or service organizations, which tend to have fewer personnel, vendors, and clients on property.

The organization's demand profile must be consistent with the coverage profile, or the number of employees assigned to a shift. Without an effective balance of the two profiles, slack scheduling, or having too many employees working a particular shift, may occur.

As a consequence, the security manager must analyze projected needs on a daily basis to properly allocate, or distribute, personnel by shift and day of week. For example, more personnel may be allocated to normal business hours, when more employees, vendors, and clients are in the organization. Meanwhile, fewer security personnel may be allocated on the off-times—during weekends, for instance—or when the organization is closed.

When determining the demand profile, the manager should determine the number of hours needed, not the number of days. By determining the number of hours needed, the manager can design a schedule that is the most appropriate for the organization.

Compatibility with Schedules of Other Units　When designing the schedule, the manager should also consider the schedules of other employees in the organization and whether any conflict in scheduling exists. In one proprietary security organization, the security staff was on the same schedule as the employees. With no security coverage during shift changes, both personnel and the organization were exposed to a myriad of internal and external threats. For those organizations that contract to other agencies, the security manager should make sure that their schedules complement the needs of their clients.

Ease of Administration and Design　An effective schedule must be easy to administer and use. Software applications have made the scheduling process much easier for the administrator. However, many organizations still rely on the manual calculation of schedules.

The Number of Officers　The demand for employees may fluctuate according to the hour of the day, week, and year. The security manager should also determine whether the positions will be staffed by full-time, part-time, or on-call personnel. Other issues the manager should consider are the average workload, personnel variations, and team versus individual activities.

Health and Safety Issues　Although a schedule may prove to be cost-effective and easy to administer, the manager should also be aware that some work schedules may lead to short-and long-term health-related implications for the employee. These implications could be related directly or indirectly to the work schedule. For example, a 10-hour shift may prove advantageous for the employer, but an employee working in a high-risk area may experience fatigue because of the long hours and the nature of the task.

Unions and Collective Bargaining Agreements   In a union environment, the collective-bargaining agreement or employment contract may specify scheduling issues that the organization must follow. The collective-bargaining agreement could define the workweek, the number of hours and days worked in a workweek, overtime allocation, shift preference, shift bidding, and shift-rotation policies.

Existing Policies and Procedures   Existing organizational policies and procedures may limit the security manager's discretion in designing a schedule. The security manager should work closely with the human resources function of the organization to create a scheduling system that follows all existing policies and procedures.

Training Needs   The schedule must be compatible with the training needs of the organization and employee. If the organization has a commitment to in-service training, the work schedule should be designed to properly accommodate training time during the work schedule. Other organizations, meanwhile, provide training programs outside the work schedule. Hence, management may schedule accordingly to give employees the opportunity to attend these programs.

Equipment and Other Resources   The manager should know what equipment is available to the employee and ensure that those tools and equipment needed for the employees are available. If equipment is lacking and too many officers are scheduled, the organization is ineffective.

A Tool for Recruitment and Retention   A well-designed and innovative schedule that meets the needs of existing employees can serve as an effective recruitment tool for prospective employees. A properly designed schedule that meets the needs of the employee will result in decreased attrition and turnover.

Employee Considerations

In scheduling, managers need to be sensitive to the health of the employee and perceived fairness. According to Coleman (1996), employees have three desires: more days off, better health, not feeling tired and fatigued, and more predictability in their schedules. In addition, managers should also consider several other issues.

The Psychological Contract   Every organization generally has two types of contracts: the written contract—be it a policy and procedure manual or the collective-bargaining agreement—and the psychological contract. The psychological contract deals with expectations that the employee has of the organization and the extent to which these expectations are being met. The employee will contribute loyalty, professionalism, time, and expertise to the organization and in return will expect some inducements. These tangible and intangible inducements may include respect and dignity, fairness, pay, job security, benefits, career opportunities, status, and promotions. The scheduling process should consider these intrinsic and extrinsic factors in order to be successful.

Personal Needs   All employees have personal lives and responsibilities outside the organization. Therefore, the manager must be cognizant of employees' personal needs when designing and implementing the schedule. Employers should respect employees' personal lives and accommodate commitments such as volunteer work, caring for an elderly relative, educational pursuits, and childcare needs.

Job Monotony   The manager should consider job or task monotony in scheduling. McBride (1997) writes that the lack of a challenging work environment, late-night shifts, and repetitious tasks lead to increased boredom and monotony. This monotony, in turn, could lead to an increased risk of injury or accident to the employees and the organization.

Professional Needs   Employees require a work schedule that fits their professional needs. Some shifts or job assignments will provide those employees with additional experience and training that will prepare them for advancement or promotion within the organization. Other employees may require flexible schedules if they are attending professional development educational programs outside the organization.

Maintenance of Esprit de Corps and Team Integrity   In many organizations, work teams have a strong self-initiated esprit de corps and pride. Many of these teams took months or even years to develop. The security manager, however, may affect the organization's esprit de corps and team integrity by inadvertently misscheduling or moving employees in the organization to different positions or schedules.

Biological/Health-Related Concerns   Another issue to consider when planning or developing a shift schedule is worker health. Research by O'Neill and Cushing (1991) reported that sleep alteration, persistent fatigue, behavioral changes, and digestive disorders have been associated with shift work. Research by Violanti and Aron (1995) reported that shift work was ranked sixth of 60 stress-related activities in law enforcement.

Additional research has discussed the impact of shift work, particularly in the context of circadian rhythms, or the body's "natural clock." These circadian rhythms manage the physiological variables. When analyzed over a period of time, these variables—blood pressure, body fluids, and gases—are rhythmic, cycling approximately every 24 hours. In short, each individual has a unique biological time system; some individuals classify themselves as "day" people and others as "night" people. Although this system can adapt and change, it is not instantaneous but rather may take several days to readjust.

Shift work conflicts with this biological clock system and can even reverse the body's circadian rhythms; when the human body expects sleep, it is working. Some short-term effects may include decreased work motivation and performance, mood swings, and increased accidents (Folkard and Monk 1992). Long-term effects could include chronic fatigue, insomnia, and cardiovascular disease (O'Neill and Cushing 1991).

Safety Issues   Related to safety and health concerns, managers must also be cognizant of how the work schedule could affect the safety of the employee, other workers, and the organization's clients. Depending on the nature of the work and type of shift, managers may be needlessly increasing the probability of accidents. For example, the National Transportation Safety Board determined that the third contributing factor of the 1989 Exxon-Valdez oil spill, which sent 11 million gallons of crude oil into Alaska's Prince William Sound, was the third mate's lack of sleep. His fatigue impeded his response to the warnings from the lookout that the ship was in shallow water (Oexman, Knotts, and Koch 2002). Research on the scheduling practices in trucking firms has also concluded that scheduling practices such as nighttime driving requirements contribute to driver fatigue and an increased accident rate (Crum and Morrow 2002). Some organizations have been found liable when their employees had vehicular accidents on the way home after being required to work overtime (Atkinson 1999).

Legal Considerations: Legislation and Employment Law

The Fair Labor Standards Act   The Fair Labor Standards Act (FLSA), as amended, sets minimum wage, child labor standards, overtime pay, and record-keeping practices for organizations. Although the workweek is defined by the organization, those standards set forth in the FLSA must be followed in order to avoid costly overtime and possible litigation.

Other Regulations   The Civil Rights Act of 1964, as amended, may impact scheduling. Title VII indicates that it is unlawful for an employer to give employees a disproportionately large share of less desirable assignments or less favorable hours on the basis of race, color, sex, national origin, or religion. Claims of disparate impact, or treatment, could occur if an employer's scheduling practice intentionally or inadvertently violated the employee's rights under Title VII.

The manager may also have to consider the Americans with Disability Act (ADA) when scheduling. The ADA requires that individuals with a recognized disability be given reasonable accommodation in the workplace. This also applies to employees and how they are scheduled. This may mean that management must design and adjust schedules accordingly for disabled employees. For example, suppose that, to get to work, a disabled security guard requires specialized transportation that operates only during normal business hours. In this case, the employer could easily schedule work hours to normal business hours.

■ THE SCHEDULING PROCESS

The scheduling process must rely on the three fundamental categories discussed: organizational, employee, and legal issues. But the manager must also consider other, more specific issues when designing the appropriate work schedule. These issues address the procedural and mechanical aspects of the scheduling process.

Hours of Employment

The typical employee works a 40-hour workweek five days per week, working a total of 2,080 hours per year, not including overtime, if applicable. The needs of the organization, however, often conflict with the 40-hour workweek. An organization that operates 7 days a week 24 hours per day, for instance, requires 168 hours per week of employee coverage, for a total of 6,760 hours per year.

Determining the Hours in a Workweek

The determination of a workweek is an important component to scheduling, as it will help in reducing and/or eliminating overtime demands. Following is one method to determine the number of hours per week the employee will work in the organization:

$$\text{Average Workweek} = \frac{7 \text{ days} \times \text{Shift Length (in hours)} \times \text{Number of Days}}{\text{Number of Days On} + \text{Number of Days Off}}$$

For example, the ACME Security Corporation uses the traditional 8-hour shift. Recently, however, it has decided to change the schedule from 5 days on/2 days off to 6 days on/3 days off. How will this affect the number of hours worked per week and per year?

$$5 \text{ on/2 off} = \frac{7 \times 8 \times 5}{7} = 40 \text{ hours per week}$$

$$6 \text{ on/3 off} = \frac{7 \times 8 \times 6}{9} = 37.33 \text{ hours per week}$$

Common Steps in the Scheduling Process

Four primary steps are involved in the scheduling process:

1. First, the security manager must determine how many positions need to be filled in the organization.
2. After determining the number of positions needed, the security manager must make sure that enough employees are available to fill the positions. The manager must have adequate staffing levels to avoid overtime compensation.
3. Third, the manager must allocate, or distribute, the employees according the shift on which they are needed and the day of week.
4. Fourth, the manager must construct the schedule.

Other Scheduling Considerations

The Workweek   The workweek is defined as the number of days and hours the employee will work. The workweek consists of the starting and ending days of the week and what days will be worked in that period. Generally, the workweek begins on Sunday and ends on Saturday.

Overtime   Overtime allocation can result in unnecessary overtime compensation, affecting the overall operations budget of the department and organization. According to § 207 of the FLSA, any non-exempt (an hourly, rather than salaried, employee) employee who works more than 40 hours in a workweek receives a minimum rate of one and one-half times the regular wage rate. Although overtime may be unavoidable in some situations, a properly designed schedule can control this to a great degree.

Length of the Schedule   The length of the schedule is generally up to the organization, with the exception of the presence of a collective-bargaining agreement. The schedule length can be weekly, biweekly, monthly, quarterly, or yearly. Longer schedules may be difficult to arrange for management, especially if the needs or demands on the organization fluctuate. Longer schedules, however, may be beneficial for the employees, as they have an increased ability to plan personal events and activities.

Individual-Based or Team-Based Schedules   Depending on the organization's structure and design, the scheduling process may require the teams or groups of individuals to be scheduled together.

Break Periods and Vacations   The manager must consider breaks and lunch periods in the schedule. These requirements should conform to all appropriate legislation, collective-bargaining agreements, and the organization's policies and procedures. Vacations, leaves of absences, and other personal-leave options must be factored into the scheduling process. Usually, employees are required to file in advance for these types of leave to give management adequate notice for scheduling. Many of these personal-leave options are seasonal—more vacation days in summer—which requires advanced planning and forecasting by the manager to ensure adequate staffing.

■ SHIFT SCHEDULES

Many organizations operate and subsequently require personnel beyond the normal working hours or day. This is known as shift work. Shift work has several benefits for the organization:

- Increased use of equipment and machinery, if applicable. If the organization is open only 8 hours a day 5 days a week, the organization may not be using its capital effectively; the majority of the time, it is sitting idle.

- Increased profitability, as the organization can avoid costly start-ups and shut-downs on Friday nights and Sunday evenings, for instance, as productivity is lost when employees are starting up or shutting down instead of producing.
- Organizational necessity, especially for service-driven organizations that serve clientele with diverse needs and demands. For example, an organization that operates 24 hours a day 7 days a week may require around-the-clock security services.
- Increased employment opportunities, as the organization must increase the number of employees together with the increase in working hours.
- If the 5-day 40-hour workers are continually working more days and hours, organizational capital could be saved by scheduling additional employees to cover the extra hours or days required.

Coleman (1989) discusses several organizational problems associated with shift work:

- Lack of alertness
- Reduced safety
- Poor-quality products
- Poor morale
- Higher turnover and the costs of replacing the employee
- Excessive overtime
- Reduced productivity
- Operator error(s)
- Decreased motivation and vigilance

Other problems that have been reported with shift work include psychological fatigue, loss of work enjoyment, and hardening attitudes toward work, the workplace, and fellow workers (Kandolin 1993).

An effective and efficient, or properly designed, shift schedule can alleviate some, if not all, of these problems while at the same time creating a balance between the needs of the organization and those of the employee. Although the type or form of shift schedule must be consistent with the needs of the organization and the employee, some common rules or procedures need to be followed when creating a shift schedule.

Format

Schedules are usually on a grid format, with coverage and the employee's name and position/responsibility on the vertical grid and the days worked on the horizontal grid. Generally, employees are concerned with days off; management, with coverage. As a result, the grid can be read in two ways. A manager will examine the schedule vertically; the employee, horizontally.

Scheduling

The sequence of the shifts may vary. With a rotating shift schedule, an individual scheduled to work days should be rotated next to afternoons. Research on the effect of shift work has indicated that moving the individual forward in time makes adjustment to that shift easier, based on the individual's circadian rhythms (Knauth 1993).

Shift-Rotation Length

A shift schedule can vary from 1 day to more than 1 month. Generally, the shift rotation should not be less than 3 weeks in length. This varies, however, according to the organization's needs and demands, as well as differing management philosophies and techniques.

Times

The starting times for shifts may also vary, requiring the manager to adjust other shifts accordingly. This may require overlapping periods; break shifts to relieve other individuals, teams, and crews; and variable stop and start times, based on the demands on the organization.

■ SHIFT MODELS

Several models exist for designing appropriate schedules. All these models can be applied to the organization's needs independently or, in some situations, combined. One of the most common shift models is the 8-hour three-shift model. Alternative models include the 10- and 12-hour shifts, which have many derivations, depending on the organization's needs.

The 8-Hour Fixed Shift

The 8-hour schedule is the traditional-style schedule, which originated at the beginning of the twentieth century, when labor organizations called for changes in hours and conditions of employment. This shift was quite popular, as it relied on three full shifts and conformed easily to the 24-hour day.

Employees on a fixed shift work days, afternoons, or nights (Figure 13-1). Although starting times can vary, generally 8 hours are worked. This type of schedule does not necessarily allow employees to have weekends off. Their days off may be locked, meaning that employees have the same days off every week.

This shift model can be modified from the three-group operations shown in Figure 13-1 to a four-group operation if the organization operates a 7-day workweek. This will require a "break shift" to cover particular hours, such as weekends.

Person	Mon.	Tues.	Wed.	Thurs.	Fri.	Sat.	Sun.
X	N	N	N	N	N		
Y	D	D	D	D	D		
Z	A	A	A	A	A		

N (nights)　　　= 11 p.m. to 7 a.m.

D (days)　　　= 7 a.m. to 3 p.m.

A (afternoons)　= 3 p.m. to 11 p.m.

= Days Off

FIGURE 13–1　■　The 8-Hour Fixed-Shift Schedule

Figure 13–2 is an example of an organization that operates 24 hours 7 days a week.

With a fixed schedule, employees know exactly what days on and off they will have, allowing them an advanced work schedule so they can plan their personal lives accordingly. But if the organization operates a 7-day workweek and the schedule is fixed, an employee may never have a weekend off. This type of schedule requires careful administration and planning by the manager to ensure that issues of employee equity are met.

The 8-Hour Rotating Shift

Organizations that operate 7 days a week 24 hours a day may require a different form of the traditional 8-hour shift schedule. One form of this type of schedule is

Working Hours	Mon.	Tues.	Wed.	Thurs.	Fri.	Sat.	Sun.
7 a.m. to 3 p.m.	A	A	A	A	A	D	D
3 p.m. to 11 p.m.	B	B	B	B	B	D	D
11 p.m. to 7 a.m.	C	C	C	C	C	D	D

A, B, and C = fixed, full-time shift crews
D = part-time break shift crew

FIGURE 13–2　■　Fixed-Shift Pattern with Part-Time Break Shift for Weekends

to have two consecutive days off per week. In order to determine this type of shift schedule, Tibrewala, Philipps, and Browne (1972) recommend a three-step procedure:

1. Determine personnel demands or needs. To do so, the manager should determine what days have the highest demand for employees and then list in descending order those days with less demand to determine what two consecutive days have lower staffing required. One of the best techniques for doing this is to list the number of employees needed each day for the work schedule and "pair" up those days on which the demand is the lowest.
2. Pair up those days with less demand for personnel. If some days have an equal demand, the manager should calculate pairs of days and take the minimum-sum days for those days that will be determined as "off" days.
3. If a tie exists between two pairs of days, the first of the pairs of days should be assigned as days off.

The 8-hour rotating schedule—5 days on/2 days off) over a 4-week period is designed for an organization that operates 7 days a week 24 hours a day. An example is shown in Figure 13-3; depending on the needs of the organization, employees are rotated through all three shifts. Although it ensures that each employee has 2 days off per week, this schedule may be an unstructured and/or unlocked schedule, meaning that the employee will not have the same days off in the next week.

In this format, the security manager should make a needs determination about what days have increased demand for services. This shift schedule can also allow the manager to provide the employee 4 days off in a row, depending on staffing requirements.

The 8-hour rotating unlocked schedule—5 days on/2 days off—repeated seven times over a 6-week cycle length is shown in Figure 13-4. This schedule is designed for an organization that operates 7 days a week 8 hours a day. This schedule ensures that the employee has 2 days off a week.

In this type of schedule, the manager may assign one employee—or groups or teams of employees—to each bracket or workdays. At the end of each week, the employee or group of employees is rotated to the next workweek.

If used monthly, this type of schedule could help employees plan events and activities in their personal lives, as they have a complete understanding of the shift schedule. Properly designed, this type of schedule ensures equity in the number of weekends off. It also assures management that the correct skills are available across all shifts and that full capital utilization of the workplace is achieved.

This shift model does have some drawbacks, however. The rotating-shift schedule may affect the employees' health in the context of circadian rhythms and sleep deprivation, resulting in lower productivity and a higher attrition rate. If improperly designed, this shift model may also result in increased overtime and may make communication between shifts difficult, shifting or eroding a team-based objective in the organization to a crew-based work concept.

Week	Person	Mon.	Tues.	Wed.	Thurs.	Fri.	Sat.	Sun.
1	X	N	N	N	N	N		
	Y	D	D	D	D	D		
	Z	A	A	A	A	A		
2	X			N	N	N	N	N
	Y			D	D	D	D	D
	Z			A	A	A	A	A
3	X	N	N			N	N	N
	Y	D	D			D	D	D
	Z	A	A			A	A	A
4	X	N	N	N	N			N
	Y	D	D	D	D			D
	Z	A	A	A	A			A

N (nights)   = 11 p.m. to 7 a.m.

D (days)   = 7 a.m. to 3 p.m.

A (afternoons) = 3 p.m. to 11 p.m.

[ ] = Days Off

FIGURE 13–3 ■ The 8-Hour Shift Schedule Rotating over a 4-Week Cycle

The 10-Hour Shift

An alternative to the 8-hour shift is the 10 hour-shift. Although this shift schedule is not as common or as popular as the 8-hour shift schedule, it may be suitable for some organizations. The implementation of a 10-hour shift schedule is contingent on the needs of the organization and the employees.

As with all shift schedules, the 10-hour shift schedule has some benefits and drawbacks. Benefits include the following:

- Three days off per week
- Maintenance of a regular schedule

Week	Mon.	Tues.	Wed.	Thurs.	Fri.	Sat.	Sun.
1	D	D	D	D	(off)	(off)	A
2	A	A	A	(off)	(off)	A	N
3	N	N	(off)	(off)	N	N	D
4	D	(off)	(off)	D	D	D	A
5	(off)	(off)	A	A	A	A	(off)
6	(off)	N	N	N	N	(off)	(off)

N (nights)   = 11 p.m. to 7 a.m.

D (days)   = 7 a.m. to 3 p.m.

A (afternoons) = 3 p.m. to 11 p.m.

[shaded box] = Days Off

FIGURE 13–4 ■ The 8-Hour Rotating Shift Schedule over a 6-Week Period

- Reduced overtime pay
- Fewer hours taken for sick leave
- Reduction of employee turnover

Moore (1995) has indicated the following additional benefits:

- Maximum use of the workforce during critical service-demand hours
- Equal distribution of the workload
- Efficient shift changes
- Balanced use of equipment
- Less overtime pay

Drawbacks of the 10-hour shift schedule include the following:

- Resistance to change by individuals accustomed to other, shorter schedules
- Fatigue of security officers
- Avoidance of overtime
- Problems in maintaining communications
- Does not fit neatly into the 24-hour day

The 10-Hour Fixed Shift

The 10-hour fixed-shift schedule permits an overlapping day, which can be used for training programs and other administrative and managerial activities. This day can also be designed or adjusted according to workload demands and concerns. An example of using the overlapping day for workload demand is to have it on weekends, when there is a greater demand for security services in the organization. An example is given in Figure 13–5.

The 12-Hour Shift

The 12-hour shift is approximately 40 years old and has been gaining some popularity in the law enforcement and security industry. As for other shift schedules, the 12-hour shift may be suitable for some organizations.

Figure 13–6 is an example of a 12-hour fixed schedule on a 4-week cycle for two shifts covering 24 hours.

The 12-hour fixed-shift schedule has some alternatives. The Concord, North Carolina, Police Department, for instance, uses a 12-hour shift schedule based on a 28-day cycle, with each squad working 7 day and 7 night shifts, with 14 days off per month. The schedule consists of 4 night shifts, 3 days off; 3 day shifts; 3 days off; 4 day shifts and 7 days off, with this schedule recycling for the next 28-day period (12 hour shifts . . . 1995).

The 12-hour model can also be used to augment traditional 8-hour shift models. For instance, organizations that rely on the 24-hour 5-day 8-hour fixed-shift schedule—Monday through Friday—may need additional shifts on the weekends. Using the 12-hour model, the manager can schedule two shifts per day instead of three. This "weekend warrior" model may prove advantageous for both the employer and the employee in some situations (Coleman 1995).

The 12-hour shift schedule has the following organizational benefits:

- The reduction from three to two shifts for the 24-hour organization, making scheduling an easier task for the manager. This subsequently results in less administrative work for the manager, as the shift schedule is simplified.
- Increased customer satisfaction, as the new schedule may better meet the needs of the internal and external customers of the organization.
- Better coverage, when needed, if designed properly.
- Can increase organizational effectiveness through teamwork. If properly designed, the individuals in the shift will work together all the time and have the same time or days off (12 hour shifts . . . 1995).
- Workers spend less time getting into the "work groove," subsequently increasing organizational performance and output.

Employee benefits of this model are as follows:

- Increased days off. Employees have 14 days off per month, compared to 8 days for a typical 8-hour shift.

Time	Sun. to Wed. Day Shift	Sun. to Wed. Afternoon Shift	Sun. to Wed. Night Shift	Wed. to Sat. Day Shift	Wed. to Sat. Afternoon Shift	Wed. to Sat. Night Shift
7 a.m.	■			■		
8 a.m.	■			■		
9 a.m.	■			■		
10 a.m.	■			■		
11 a.m.	■			■		
12 p.m.	■			■		
1 p.m.	■			■		
2 p.m.	■			■		
3 p.m.	■	■		■	■	
4 p.m.	■	■		■	■	
5 p.m.		■			■	
6 p.m.		■			■	
7 p.m.		■			■	
8 p.m.		■			■	
9 p.m.		■			■	■
10 p.m.		■			■	■
11 p.m.		■			■	■
12 a.m.		■			■	■
1 a.m.			■			■
2 a.m.			■			■
3 a.m.			■			■
4 a.m.			■			■
5 a.m.			■			■
6 a.m.			■			■

■ = Hours and Days On

FIGURE 13–5 ■ **The 10-Hour Fixed Schedule**

Week	Mon.	Tues.	Wed.	Thurs.	Fri.	Sat.	Sun.
1	Work	Work			Work	Work	Work
2			Work	Work			
3	Work	Work			Work	Work	Work
4			Work	Work			

▨ = Days Off

(a)

Week	Mon.	Tues.	Wed.	Thurs.	Fri.	Sat.	Sun.
1			Work	Work			
2	Work	Work			Work	Work	Work
3			Work	Work			
4	Work	Work			Work	Work	Work

(b)

FIGURE 13–6 ■ The 12-Hour Fixed Schedule: (a) Day Shift (7 a.m. to 7 p.m.); (b) Night Shift (7 p.m. to 7 a.m.)

- If properly designed, the rotating schedule will result in the employees having every other weekend off.
- Improved communications. Instead of having three shifts that are responsible for communicating with one another, only two shifts need to share information.
- Increased levels of employee satisfaction. Employees will have larger blocks of time off for personal business and leisure, as well as more flexibility (Maiwald et al. 1997). This may also lead to reduced job stress and increased morale and productivity.

- Less sick leave and absenteeism, as the employee has less job stress and more leisure time.
- Increased family time for the employee.
- Fewer third, or "graveyard," shifts.
- Opportunity for in-service training and special projects. The 12-hour shift schedule will provide time for training and special projects because of the time overlap in shifts.

But in addition to the problems or drawbacks associated with the 10-hour schedule, some drawbacks may be associated with the 12-hour schedule. For the organization, these drawbacks are as follows:

- Resistance by managers who are accustomed to scheduling with other models
- Union resistance to new schedule models, as a change in schedule models could mean fewer employees in the organization
- Problems in maintaining communications between shifts and among employees, as there will be less contact between employees in different work days/off days, and so on
- Overtime pay, if the 84-hour pay period is not corrected through scheduling a short, 8-hour shift
- Avoidance of overtime, as employees who have already worked a 12-hour day may not want to work any additional hours

The drawbacks for the employee are

- Resistance to change by individuals accustomed to other schedules
- Fatigue of security officers

Findings on fatigue in 12-hour shifts are mixed. As a result, the manager should consider the type of work performed and consult with the employees to determine whether fatigue is an issue.

Some of the research in the field of law enforcement (see Metzger 1995) found no indications of fatigue in the context of officer accidents or a decrease in the number of job-related activities. Other authors suggest that there will be less fatigue, as workers know in advance that they will be working 12 hours, in comparison to employees asked to work overtime. The employees may also pace themselves to be effective throughout the shift.

■ EDUCATING THE EMPLOYEE ON THE EFFECTS OF SHIFT WORK

The organization should consider educating employees on the effects of shift work. At a minimum, management should educate the employee in the aspects of

- *Quality sleep time.* Will help the employee adjust to rotating shift work, alleviating circadian rhythm adjustments and other stressors associated with shift work.

- *Additional exercise.* Has been found to counteract the effects of shift work, indirectly providing restorative sleep while improving alertness during working hours.
- *Need to reduce alcohol intake on days off.* Affects sleep patterns and quality.
- *Proper nutritional habits.* Effect of work on employee's eating habits, which could have adverse effects.

Management should consider establishing a shift-work committee for the organization to provide additional educational advice to employees about health- and productivity-related issues. This committee could also take suggestions by employees about shift assignments while soliciting their concerns. Management could then used this information to design and create alternative work schedules.

■ ALTERNATIVE WORK SCHEDULES

Alternative work schedules differ from the traditional workweek and the number of hours worked. Several forms of alternative schedules are available for the security manager, depending on the needs of the organization and the employee.

Flexible Work Schedules

Following are several types of flexible work schedules available for the security manager (Bailey 1986).

- **Flextime** scheduling occurs when management determines the number of hours and days worked, with the employee choosing the starting times and the number of hours worked per day.
- With **flextour**, the employee determines the starting time of work, and management determines those days and the number of hours worked per day.
- **Flexshift** scheduling occurs when the employee determines what days and hours to work, and management designs a schedule that meets the needs of the employee.
- **Maxiflex** scheduling occurs when the organization determines the work that needs to be performed, accomplished, and completed. The employee determines how to complete that work in terms of the number of hours, times, and days it will take to complete the assigned work and responsibilities.

Depending on the nature of the work, the relevance of some of these flexible work schedules may be inappropriate for some security organizations. With guard services, for example, guards cannot simply show up when they want to or create their own shifts and schedules. Rather, the guards are bound to the needs of the customer, as well as the needs of the organization. In executive-level positions, however, flexible schedules may be appropriate. Now, security planners or administrators could select what times they would work, based on organizational needs and personal needs and preferences.

Flexible work schedules usually have a core period when all employees must be at work. This may include a day or a particular time of day that is dedicated to administrative and/or training purposes. Although this core time is required, employees are allowed to work at some time before and/or after the core time.

Benefits   Flextime scheduling has several benefits for employees. First, they can select a schedule that meets their personal and professional needs. Flextime schedules give employees more scheduling options that fit their lifestyles. Flextime may also allow employees to plan vacations and appointments, schedule college courses, and vacations, further increasing their level of job satisfaction. Flextime may also be beneficial for part-time employees, who may be balancing their full-time career with part-time employment in the organization. Other benefits include

- Greater employee responsibility
- Happier employees
- Opportunities for second-income people to work
- Improved employee morale
- Ability to avoid traffic on the way to work
- Can arrange for child care
- More leisure time

Flextime also offers some benefits for the organization. The extent of various options may lead to decreased tardiness, increased job satisfaction, and less turnover, subsequently providing the organization with savings in recruitment of personnel (Bailey 1986). Other points are

- Higher productivity.
- Reductions in the absenteeism for service-oriented white-collar professionals (Dalton and Mesch 1990).
- Can be seasonal. For instance, some organizations have "summer hours," allowing employees to engage in flextime to enjoy the summer season (Summer hours 1987).
- Reduced turnover.

There are several more benefits to flexible schedules, including:

- *Protecting the investment in good workers.*   A flexible work schedule will allow employees to balance their employment with other responsibilities and demands placed on them outside of work. This reduces interrule conflicts that are caused by the competing demands of work and personal interests (Rau and Hyland 2002).
- *Giving the organization a recruitment edge.*   Flexible work arrangements may increase the number of interested and qualified applicants to an organization (Rau and Hyland 2002).
- *Improving coverage.*   The combination of flexible schedules may give the manager more staffing options (Kussek, Barber, and Winters 1999).
- *Upgrading and expanding employee skills.*   Job sharing promotes knowledge and skill diffusion. It also enables a more comprehensive understanding of the organization (Vandenberg, Richardson, and Eastman 1999).

- *Retaining older workers' skills and experience.* Many older individuals do not desire full-time employment with the organization. As a result, having flexible work schedules allows the organization to retain these individuals on a part-time basis (Paul and Townsend 1993).
- *Reducing office space and overhead expenses.* Flexible work arrangements may reduce the costs of equipment and office space (Frank and Lowe 2003).
- *Improving the quality of work and/or service.* Employees' productivity and commitment will improve if they know that management will assist them in their needs while allowing them to do their jobs (Kussek, Barber, and Winters 1999).
- *Creating transitional relationships with employees and customers.*
- *Achieving fewer absences, lower turnover, and less stress* (Christensen and Staines 1990).

The drawbacks unique to flexible scheduling for the employee include the following:

- Decreased perceptions of organizational fairness. Management must establish effective policies and procedures in the context of shift bidding for individuals, as there may be increased demand for some particular shifts under flexible arrangements (Bailey 1986).
- Increased accident rates attributed to increased fatigue, and so on.
- Restrictive core periods, limiting the degree of flexibility the employee can have.
- Decreased morale, owing to decreased interactions at the workplace, as friends now work different times.
- Inability of some employees to participate in flexible work schedules because of the nature of the work. This could create conflict between the two groups.

Scheduling may also be more difficult for management. Schedules may be difficult to create and set up and administer. Furthermore, management must make sure that its schedules are consistent with the needs or demands of the organization, as demand may fluctuate according to day, time, and season (Bailey 1986). Other drawbacks include:

- Problems coordinating with other departments
- Difficulty in scheduling meetings
- The potential for employee exploitation
- The possibility that the job will lose importance in the employee's life
- Customer service problems resulting from employees' being on unusual work schedules

Flexible work schedules may also require a new form of management style, with the emphasis on results rather than on oversight. This will require managers to shift their perspective to that of coach rather than supervisor, as flexible schedules will lead to more worker empowerment. In turn, this will result in the employees engaging in more self-management activities that may include greater degrees of decision making, self-initiated activities, and increased problem solving.

Permanent Part-Time

Another popular alternative work schedule is permanent part time. Employees on this type of schedule do not work a full 40-hour workweek. Instead, by choice, they work less than a full workweek. This workweek can vary in terms of the number of hours worked per day, the number of days worked in a week, or the number of months worked in a year.

Permanent part-time work is an effective alternative for recruiting and retaining individuals with childcare responsibilities, students, retired and disabled workers, moonlighters, and children of full-time employees. Permanent part-time employees may also lead to reduced labor costs, as these individuals may not be eligible for the same health and other fringe benefits provided to full-time employees. Permanent part-time employees may also be useful for the manager to fill special demands or needs of the organization, as coverage issues could be reduced or eliminated.

One of the problems with permanent part-time employment occurs when the employee has an expectation that the part-time position will lead to full-time employment. This may increase turnover. Although some positions may lead to full-time employment, effective preemployment communication with potential employees will reduce their expectations prior to employment. This fair, open, and accurate communication with employees could then reduce the turnover that some organizations have experienced.

Depending on the labor market, some employers may have difficulty attracting and recruiting individuals who are willing to work part time. However, with effective recruitment programs and procedures, this problem too can be overcome.

■ REDESIGNING THE WORK SCHEDULE

Many scheduling models are available to the security manager, but to effectively change an existing scheduling system can be a long and complex process. Although the factors involved in work schedule redesign are unique to each organization, the manager should consider some common stages, or steps, when redesigning the work schedule.

Similarly, the manager must research and review all appropriate employment laws and relevant legislation—including state laws, if applicable; and the overtime pay provisions of the Fair Labor Standards Act (FLSA)—and make sure that the alternative schedules are in compliance. If applicable, the manager must also determine whether flexible schedules violate the existing employment contract and should meet with union representatives to discuss the proposed changes.

The manager should consider the impact that new schedules will have on the external labor market. For instance, the manager should conduct an external audit of the labor market to determine whether the new schedule meets the needs of the existing labor market. Through this process, the recruitment of additional employees may increase because of the scheduling program.

Coleman (1989) presents some key concepts in designing and implementing a new shift program.

- Do not underestimate the power of changing shift schedules and their impact on employees.
- Define your scheduling goals before you start.
- Do not expect a schedule from another organization to fit your needs.
- The greater the change, the greater the gains.
- The closer the new schedule is to the current schedule, the more easily employees will accept it.
- Education and communication are vital if you want to overcome the vocal opponents who can block, or resist, the change.
- Aim for success, even if it is small.
- A neutral third party can be valuable in providing a solution that balances the schedule designs.
- Your management team will probably have only one chance to make a major schedule change at your organization.

■ THE CHANGE PROCESS

Implementing and designing a new shift schedule involves full organizational commitment to the change. Regardless of the methods chosen for implementing a new shift schedule, employees who are affected should be included in the process to the fullest extent possible. Their involvement is a powerful tool in the change process, helping to minimize or overcome resistance to change while increasing the levels of employee empowerment in the workplace. Employee involvement will also serve as a catalyst for future activities the organization may implement.

Various steps can be followed when implementing a new shift schedule. Following a rational decision-making paradigm, or model, the manager should consider the following steps in the change process:

1. *Recognize that there is a problem.* One of the first steps in designing a new shift schedule is to acknowledge that the existing scheduling process is inferior. This could be attributed to employee dissatisfaction, increased labor costs, scheduling difficulties, or other organizational problems that can be tied to the schedule.

2. *Gain support.* In order to be accepted, the new shift schedule must be supported by both employees and the organization. One effective method of gaining organizational and employee support is to create a change committee composed of managers, supervisors, and employees who will be

affected by the change. Some activities at this stage include brainstorming sessions, team-building exercises, suggestions for improvement, and an analysis of the current schedule to determine the needs of the parties.

3. *Create a change team.*   At this point, the individuals who will be responsible for the administration of the new work schedule are identified or assigned. In the context of management, those individuals in the organization who will be directly involved in the new schedule should be included. Members of the organization who have specialized knowledge, including labor relations and human resource specialists, should also be included. Other departments in the organization should also be included to ensure that effective organizational communication is achieved, while also ensuring that a schedule redesign for one department has no adverse impact on other units in the organization. Selected employees should be included in the program team to ensure a smooth transition.

4. *Conduct research.*   Pending the formation of the change team, extensive research should be conducted into alternative forms of schedules and their impact on the organization and the employee. The change committee should discuss and analyze a variety of factors, including absenteeism, accident statistics, work overload, health concerns, quality, productivity and pay issues, personal and family concerns of employees, and the impact that the change will have on other components of the organization.

   The committee should also analyze the external environment. The change team can conduct site visits and interviews with other organizations that have changed their work schedules. Included in this external task environment is a review of relevant labor laws and similar legislation.

   This research could also include employee polls and surveys, analyses of case studies from available literature, and interviews with other managers who have changed their scheduling. The committee should also conduct an impact analysis on how proposed changes will impact both their internal and external clients.

5. *Design the program.*   Based on the established criteria and research conducted by the change team, the new scheduling system or program is designed in this stage of the change process.

6. *Announce the program.*   The success of the schedule is contingent on all affected parties. Therefore, it is important to keep all interested parties abreast of the scheduling change process while announcing the plans for the new scheduling system. Open discussion should be encouraged during this stage.

7. *Promote the program.*   All employees and members of management who will be affected by the change process should be responsible for program promotion. Likewise, employees must also be involved. For instance, supervisors, team leaders, union representatives, and informal floor or line-level leaders should be included in the promotion process. By involving as many individuals as possible and manageable, these individuals will serve as management representatives to speak for the program and answer questions about the new change. In addition, the change team should publish the

proposed schedule plan. It could be available for all employees for their review, or it could be mailed to them or posted at strategic workplace locations. A "kick-off" luncheon or similar activity could also be planned to announce the new work schedule.

8. *Evaluate the program.* The success of the new schedule needs to be monitored. It should be evaluated on the criteria discussed earlier, including, but not limited to the primary issues of readability, degree of comprehensiveness, level of comprehension, and accuracy. Furthermore, the organizational, employee, and legal issues should also be measured. For example, management could measure organizational goals by conducting a financial analysis on the savings in payroll, turnover, absenteeism, and sick days taken. Individual or groups of employees could also be polled, interviewed, or surveyed to measure their satisfaction levels with the new scheduling plan.

9. *Fine-tune the program.* Based on the results from the program evaluation, management should reanalyze the new scheduling system and modify it accordingly, if necessary. This should be a continual, ongoing process of the manager.

10. *Continually monitor the success of the program.* Continual monitoring of the program will ensure that the new plan has no long-term ramifications that would affect the organization or the employees. Through this continual monitoring, additional issues and concerns unidentified in the original planning stage will be identified and subsequently incorporated into the new work schedule. This stage of the process too should be ongoing in the organization.

■ CONCLUSION

This chapter discusses what is meant by scheduling and how a properly designed schedule will increase the effectiveness and efficiency of the organization and employee. The security manager faces several decisions when designing and administering an equitable work schedule. These decisions are driven by the three main components of a schedule: the needs and concerns of the organization and the employee, and legal considerations. This effort must be commensurate with the needs of the employee while following and adhering to all relevant labor legislation.

Several scheduling alternatives exist for the security manager. These include a 10- and 12-hour work day. Alternative forms of flexible work arrangements also exist, depending on the needs of the organization and the worker. To achieve the objectives of an effective schedule, it must be properly designed through a comprehensive and rational change process involving a cross-section of the organizational members and external task environment affected by the change.

The decision to establish alternative or new work schedules can be difficult. The sheer number and complexity of some plans may appear overwhelming and confusing at first. As noted, organizational objectives, employee needs and concerns, and legislation serve well to guide and define suitable alternatives. Whatever scheduling plan is used or adopted, the program should be considered within the broader spectrum of changes that could be achieved to affect the employee and organizational effectiveness. A thorough understanding of work schedules combined with correct planning and methods can make a significant contribution and difference in the quality of worklife while improving organizational effectiveness or performance.

■ KEY TERMS

Circadian rhythm	FLSA
Demand profile	Maxiflex
Exempt employee	Non-exempt employee
Fixed shift	Psychological contract
Flexshift	Rotating schedule
Flextime	Workweek
Flextour	

■ DISCUSSION QUESTIONS

1. What three steps should be followed when determining shift schedules?
2. What are some strengths associated with an 8-hour shift? What are some weaknesses?
3. What is a fixed shift? What are some strengths and weakness of a fixed shift?
4. What are some issues associated with rotating shifts?
5. What are some strengths and weaknesses associated with the 10-hour shift?
6. What are some strengths and weaknesses associated with the 12-hour shift?
7. What are some issues a manager should know about in the context of reducing the effects of shift work on employees?
8. Explain some of the types of alternative work schedules. What are some benefits for employees? What are some benefits for employers?
9. What are some of the advantages of having a permanent part-time staff?
10. What are some of the issues to consider when redesigning the work schedule?

■ REFERENCES

12-hour shifts: Comments from the field. 1995. *Police Chief* 62 (2): 30.

ATKINSON, W. 1999. Wake Up? Fighting fatigue in the workplace. *Risk Management* 46 (11): 10–11.

BAILEY, J. E. 1986. Personnel scheduling with flexshift: A win/win scenario. *Personnel* 63 (9): 62–67.

The changing workplace: New directions in staffing and scheduling. 1986. Washington, DC: Bureau of National Affairs.

COLEMAN, R. M. 1989. Shiftwork scheduling for the 1990's. *Personnel* 66 (1): 10-15.

————. 1995. *The 24 hour business*. Chicago: American Management Association.

————. 1996. Shift work: The efficiency is in the schedule. *HR Focus* 73 (10): 17-18.

CHRISTENSEN, K. E., and G. L. STAINES. 1990. Flextime: A viable solution to work-family conflict. *Journal of Family Issues* 11: 455-476.

CRUM, M. R., and P. C. MORROW. 2002. The influence of carrier scheduling practices on truck driver fatigue. *Transportation Journal* 42 (1): 20-41.

DALTON, D. R. and D. J. MESCH. 1980. The impact of flexible scheduling on employee attendance and turnover. *Administrative Science Quarterly* 35: 37-387.

Equiflex Project. 1991. *Flexibility: Compelling strategies for a competitive workplace*. San Francisco, CA: New Ways to Work.

FALLICK, B. C. 1999. Part-time work and industry growth. *Monthly Labor Review*, 22-29.

FOLKARD, T. H. and S. MONK. 1992. *Making shiftwork tolerable*. Washington, DC: Taylor and Francis.

FRANK, K. E., and D. J. LOWE. 2003. An examination of work arrangements in private accounting practice. *Accounting Horizons* 17 (2): 139-146.

HUNG, R. 1994. A multi-shift workforce scheduling model under the 4-day workweek and weekend labor demands. *Journal of the Operational Research Society* 45 (9): 1088-1092.

KANDOLIN, I. 1993. Burnout of female and male nurses in shiftwork. *Ergonomics* 36 (1-3): 141-148.

KNAUTH, P. 1993. The design of shift systems. *Ergonomics* 36: 15-28.

KUSSEK, E. E., A. E. BARBER, and D. WINTERS. 1999. Using flexible schedules in the managerial world. The powers of peers. *Human Resource Management* 38 (1): 33-46.

MAIWALD, C. R., J. L. PIERCE, J. W. NEWSTROM, and B. R. Sunoo. 1997. Workin' 8 p.m. to 8 a.m. and lovin' every minute of it! *Workforce* 76 (7): 30-37.

McBRIDE, G. 1997. Training and employee involvement in shift schedule improvements. *Occupational Safety and Health* 66 (6): 45-47, 77.

METZGER, R. 1995. The switch to a 12-hour shift. *Police Chief* 62 (12): 30-36.

MOORE, M. W. 1995. Patrol shift schedule. *Police Chief* 64 (4): 9-11.

NARASIMHAN, R. 1997. An algorithm for single shift scheduling of hierarchical workforce. *European Journal of Operational Research* 96 (1): 113-121.

OEXMAN, R. D., T. L. KNOTTS, and J. KOCH. 2002. Working while the world sleeps: A consideration of sleep and shift work design. *Employee Responsibilities and Rights Journal* 14 (4): 145-157.

O'NEILL, J. L., and M. A. CUSHING. 1991. *The impact of shift work on police officers*. Washington DC: Police Executive Research Forum.

PAUL, R. J., and J. B. TOWNSEND. 1993. Managing the older worker—Don't just rinse away the gray. *The Academy of Management Executive* 7 (3): 67-74.

RAU, B. L., and A. M. Hyland. 2002. Role conflict and flexible work arrangements: The effect on applicant attraction. *Personnel Psychology* 55 (1): 111-126.

Summer hours and the issue of flextime. 1987. *Personnel Journal* 66 (8): 25-26.

Thomas, L.T. 1995. Impact of family-supportive work variables on work-family conflict and strain: A control perspective. *Journal of Applied Psychology* 80 (1): 6–15.

Tibrewala, K., D. Phillippe, and J. Browne. 1972. Optimal scheduling of two consecutive idle periods. *Management Science* 19 (1): 71–75.

U.S. Department of Labor. Bureau of Labor Statistics 2004. Employment characteristics of families in 2003. *Bureau of Labor Statistics News* April: 1–4.

_____. Bureau of Labor Statistics. Employment characteristics of families summary 2003. http://www.bls.gov/news.release/famee.nr0.htm.

_____. Bureau of Labor Statistics 1997. How long is the workweek? *Issues in Labor Statistics* 97 (2): 1–3.

Vandenberg, R. J., H. A. Richardson, and L. J. Eastman. 1999. The impact of high involvement work processes on organizational effectiveness: A second-order latent variable approach. *Group and Organizational Management* 24 (3): 300–339.

Violanti, J. M., and F. Aron. 1995. Police stressors: Variations in perception among police personnel. *Journal of Criminal Justice* 23 (3): 287–294.

chapter fourteen

Futures

Some of the trends about the future of security are already evident in security literature. Estimated 2000 revenues for the security industry were $540 billion, compared to $350 billion in 1994. Estimates for 2005 revenues are $760 billion (Bailin and Cort 1996). Areas of above-average growth potential include security consulting for small and midsize organizations; the public sector, particularly in corrections and other nontraditional services related to executive protection; data security; and drug and alcohol testing.

As pointed out by Bailin and Cort (1996), the demand for security services is concentrated in metropolitan areas, particularly New York, Chicago, and Los Angeles. This demand for security services is based on three factors: local demographics, socioeconomic conditions, and the existence and maturity of the local private security industry. Based on this information, the growth in security is predicted to decline in the Midwest and the East, whereas the South and the West will see growth in the demand for security, owing to an increase in crime rates because of their projected population growth (Bailin and Cort 1996).

This information gives us a general understanding of future trends but does not tell us what specific events will fuel the demand for security. What does the future hold for security? Where will the private security industry go from here? What will the security industry look like in the future? Will security still be classified into the traditional categories of the alarm, armored car, and guard industries (McCrie 1988)? If so, will the functions within these three groups change and become more specialized in their services?

   This chapter presents and discusses a variety of issues related to the future of security. We already know that private security will have a greater presence in those areas traditionally delegated to the domain of the public. In particular, this chapter presents those primary factors that will lead to an increased presence in the public sector. Second, we live in the information society; computers are everywhere. This proliferation of technology will bring an increase in cybercrimes, cyberterrorism, and superterrorism. Third, changes in the global marketplace will affect and expand the role of security. Changes here will include increased economic espionage activities and an increased need and recognition for executive protection in those emerging economies and countries of the world. These changes will require security managers to reevaluate personnel issues related specifically to selection, education, and retention. This chapter discusses factors that will lead to the professionalization of security and how the changing legal environment will also shape security in this century.

■ THE PUBLIC SECTOR AND PRIVATE SECURITY

   In the last 25 years of the twentieth century, the private security industry moved into sectors traditionally performed by the public sector. The Hallcreast I Report (see Cunningham and Taylor 1985) predicted the expansion into the public sector, concluding that privatization would continually increase from the late twentieth century into the twenty-first. To date, that prediction has been quite accurate. Other research has found that in some Western industrialized societies, private police outnumber public police by a 3-to-1 margin (Bayley and Shearing 1996). Brian Forst poignantly illustrates this growth in his discussion of the shift to the privatization of traditional public services. Forst (2000, 21) states: "It has taken centuries for public policing to establish dominance over privately paid security agents, and less than three decades to reverse that trend."

   This increased presence in the public sector has not gone unnoticed in the academic community. As indicated by Manning (1992), public-sector law enforcement is "no longer a secure monopoly, police do in fact compete with private security firms, community action groups, and the media for the right to provide legitimate application of social control" (p. 253). Others have concluded that the shortcomings associated with traditional forms of policing could result "in the continued shrinkage of public law enforcement as a major player in providing for public security" (Sykes 1992, 172).

   Services that have traditionally been considered the sole responsibility of law enforcement are likely to become increasingly privatized. Some research has already concluded that the distinction between "private" and "public" has become increasingly meaningless. Through their research, Bayley and Shearing (2001) determined that policing services have become combined in new ways, making it difficult to separate the public police from private security providers. Using the term "multilateralization," the "security" function will, in the future, fall into four major groups: commercial security companies; nongovernmental entities acting as their own providers, or proprietary security; individuals, or self-protection; and governments that provide additional protection-related services through officers' moonlighting and fee-for-service activities. As these events continue to occur, the distinction between the private and public sectors will become more "blurred," making it more difficult to separate traditional public police forces from their private counterparts.

Figure 14-1 presents those primary factors that have already and will influence the growth of the private security industry in the public sector. These factors are the public's loss of faith, increased demand for services, financial limitations, criminal justice policy, and bureaucratic barriers.

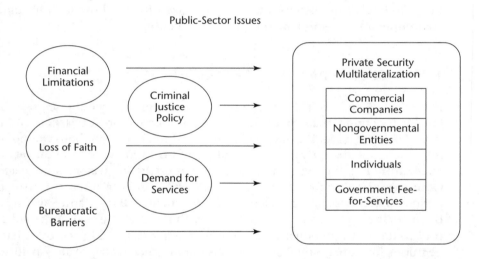

FIGURE 14–1 ▪ Public-Sector Issues Influencing the Growth of Private Security

Loss of Faith

A great deal of the expansion into "traditional" public-service activities can be attributed to the erosion of the public's faith in the criminal justice system. Excessive force was used by the police in the Abner Louima case in New York City in 1997, when police detectives sodomized Louima with a broom handle (Morgan-thau 1999). In a 1999 incident, New York City police officers shot Amadou Diallo, an unarmed West African, 19 times, raising further issues about police misconduct (Toobin 2000). The Los Angeles Police Department's Rampart Division scandal in 1999 resulted in many criminal convictions' being overturned because of perjured testimonies from police officers. Subsequent investigations also revealed that officers had planted evidence and routinely used excessive force against citizens (Skolnick 2000).

This issue is apparent in other nations as well. In South Africa, 14 percent of the national police force was recently charged with corruption. Coupled with a skyrocketing crime rate and a very low conviction and apprehension rate by the police, civilians have opted for private security (Peron 1999).

To control some of the complaints related to abuses in law enforcement, police agencies have introduced civilian oversight committees. The purpose of these committees is to have the citizen members review police complaints, programs, and activities to reestablish a sense of legitimacy in the police department's personnel and policies (see Walker and Bumphus 1992, for example). These committees, many of them established after serious allegations of police misconduct, have done little to impact the delivery and quality of police services. Instead, they have served their political objectives of involving the public.

In the future, citizens may opt to use private security because they may have a greater degree of control over their operations and potential abuses. As these security forces will be contractual, the public may have the power to eliminate their services if abuses of power occur—a privilege that it does not have with the public services. These powers will force private security agencies performing traditional police activities to have a greater degree of accountability to their clients than what traditional law enforcement has provided.

Increased Demand for Services

If the erosion of confidence in law enforcement does not increase the presence of the private security industry in the public domain, the sheer demand for services may be a determining factor. This has always been an issue for the public sector. In his review of the early development of policing in the United States, Johnson (1979) concluded that the demand for localized protection, coupled with the inability of the public police to meet constituent needs, presented many entrepreneurs with the opportunity to offer specialized security. In 1880, for example, the Merchant's Police was founded in Chicago. Subscribing merchants paid $.50 a week for private security patrols and hourly checks of their doors. This same problem exists today with police services. In many instances, state and local governments lack resources—money, personnel, expertise, and equipment—to meet the growing demands for crime control and prevention.

One example is the increased use of special police. In Michigan, on-duty proprietary security personnel in some organizations have been granted full arrest powers. By demonstrating a need to the state for powers of arrest, usually based on demand for such services, approval from the local law enforcement agency and subsequent mandatory training and yearly recertification, security personnel in these private organizations have peace officer status. These private security police can then arrest individuals for felony and misdemeanor crimes that occur on their property. Although this peace officer status is limited to those organizations that fall within the private/public nexus—shopping malls and hospitals—in the future, an increase of this practice is likely in other industry groups.

Some communities have contracted with security companies to address specific concerns. In Atlanta, Georgia, commercial-property owners created their own private police force for $1.2 million, financed through "private" taxes from businesses in that area (Campbell 2000). In 1994, Stamford, Connecticut, used Federal Housing and Urban Development funds totaling $300,000 to establish a private security force to patrol a high-crime public-housing complex (Cavanaugh 1995). With shrinking public services and an increased demand from the citizenry, these services will continue to be subcontracted. This trend will also lead to a reduction in the demand for public police services, as clients may find that private contractors are more cost-effective and reliable than traditional services.

Examples of this trend are also evident in other nations. In Vancouver, British Columbia, the Chinatown Merchants Association contracted with a private security company to patrol on a 24-hour basis, and another business association contracted with private security to supplement existing evening patrols by the police. Vancouver is not alone. The number of licensed firms in British Columbia reflects the demand for services increasing from only 188 in 1992 to 1,250 in 1998 (Hunter 1998). In the turbulent Balkans region, Slovenia has experienced the rapid growth of private security firms. Former police officers, recognizing that the citizenry needs security-related services that cannot be fully provided by the government, have created private security firms to meet the growing demand.

These examples are place-based strategies, using private security in specific hot spots of the community, but in the future, private security will take over the entire law enforcement function in a community. Already in rare instances, municipalities have eliminated their police departments and contracted with private security to perform various order-maintenance activities. This occurred in 1993 in Sussex, New Jersey, which disbanded its four-person police department after a drug scandal and contracted with a private security company to patrol the community (Sullivan 1993a). This contract, however, lasted only 2 months. The Superior Court of New Jersey concluded that the contract violated the general regulatory scheme for the training, qualification, and accountability of police officers (Sullivan 1993b).

Financial Limitations

Another explanation for the increased growth of private security into the public sector is financial. Sapp (1992) writes that many public-sector agencies are ill-equipped to deal with these demands, owing to budgetary constraints. Wealthy communities are already contracting with private security agencies that augment the existing police services. But doing so could be a double-edged sword for the public sector. People who spend more money on private security may wish to spend less for public safety. Hence, the already strained public budgets may see further reductions, as the public will be more reluctant to support tax increases to improve public services. To the extent that private policing takes on the role of supplementing the crime-control function, poor communities will suffer relatively lower services. If private policing is viewed as a crucial adjunct to traditional police services, a voucher system, supported by public funds, may be granted to low-income neighborhoods to allow the community to contract with private firms (Bayley and Shearing 1996).

Criminal Justice Policy

Criminal justice policy will indirectly increase the presence of private security in the public sector. Perhaps one of the best policy examples is the "get tough" sentencing policies related to the nation's war on drugs. These policies have increased the number of prisoners and their length of incarceration, fueling the demand for more prisons and personnel to staff these facilities. An indirect result has been that the public sector has not been able to keep up with the demand for prison beds and the personnel to staff those institutions. The financial resources needed to build more prisons have also been impaired.

In several states, private security corporations, such as Wackenhut and the Corrections Corporation of America (CCA), now operate correctional facilities that were previously operated exclusively by the state. In other instances, these private organizations have also built correctional facilities.

There is some philosophical and ideological resistance to having private firms punishing criminals who are sentenced by the state. There are also concerns about the quality of services and abuse of powers by private vendors (see Benson 1996). Nevertheless, without a major policy change in the area of corrections, there may be no other alternative to what is sometimes called the U.S. imprisonment binge. With no major policy changes in sight, business-savvy private security firms will seek out opportunities in the correctional field. We will continue to see the growth of security in the operations of state-level corrections.

Similarly, there will be a market for security vendors to provide cost-effective and secure facilities for local correctional operations, which also have felt the impact of strict sentencing policies. Many local jails are chronically underfunded and have already privatized a large portion of their staff, including food, janitorial, and medical services. The next logical cost-cutting move would be to contract out their guard services to private security. For local facilities that are chronically overcrowded, the private sector will also offer the solution of housing and controlling the inmate populations for the municipality or county.

There will also be opportunities in alternative-sanction programs: electronic monitoring, house arrest, community service, and intensive probation services. Some alarm companies have already taken advantage of these new opportunities. Security firms have contracted with probation agencies to monitor individuals who have been sentenced to electronic monitoring. Individuals sentenced to house arrest are fitted with an electronic tether that alerts the alarm company that they have violated their conditions of home confinement. The alarm company would then notify the probation officer that a particular individual's "alarm" was activated.

The future will see the increase of the private sector in these areas and other areas of community supervision. In addition, private security firms could easily conduct pre-sentence investigations (PSIs). As they possess investigative and sur-veillance-related technologies, many security firms already possess the resources and expertise to conduct thorough and in-depth investigations for the courts.

Bureaucratic Barriers

Because of the bureaucratic structures that public-sector agencies operate with-in, the private sector will make inroads into those services traditionally provided by the public sector. These large and often impersonal agencies are characterized by a hierarchical structure of formal authority and communication networks, spe-cialization, and extensive systems of formal rules (Downs 1967). In many large po-lice agencies, "layers" of supervision control and manage those employees below them. Each layer of the organization may also contain specialized operations, such as detectives, that follow and abide by in-depth policies and procedures that guide their work and conduct. The result may be police departments that are interested in creativity only within certain boundaries (Cordner 1992).

These and other characteristics may eventually shape the public's perception that these organizations are too rigid and inflexible to meet the needs of the citizenry. For example, Kearney and Hays (1998, 39) point out in their discussion of bureaucracies that "insularity, insensitivity to the wishes of the public, inefficiency, and self-serving motives are traits that are commonly attributed to bureaucracies in both developed and underdeveloped nations throughout the world." As a conse-quence, bureaucracies are unable to rapidly adapt to the needs of their con-stituents, leaving them vulnerable to entrepreneurial private security companies.

If no changes occur, the future will provide the public alternatives to large, unresponsive bureaucratic entities. Private security organizations that are flexible and responsible to their external task environments will find new markets, in-creasing their presence and profitability. Those security firms that follow or re-main under the bureaucratic model will be the losers, following the same fate as their public-sector counterparts.

■ INFLUENCES IN THE PRIVATE SECTOR

The Impact of Globalization

No area of private security, regardless of its size or industry affiliation, will be in-sulated from the effects of globalization. Globalization is both a term and an event used to describe how once-independent markets in the world are now becoming interdependent and interrelated. Globalization will have far-reaching implications for the security industry.

Globalization can be thought of as the shrinkage of economic distances be-tween countries, encompassing trade, finance, and capital (Rajan 2001). Global-ization is not limited to the manufacturing sector but includes banking, software development, data entry, and accounting services (Kierzkowski 2000). Globaliza-tion will affect all organizations: Changes in adjustment are required "not only among the newest, and perhaps the weakest, . . . but also among the oldest and strongest. . . . Globalization implies that the national economies are integrated not only through trade; they are also becoming tightly integrated at the production level. . . . globalization gives rise to an organic and spontaneous integration that escapes the power of national governments" (Kierzkowski 2000, 10).

Globalization events in the late twentieth century provide some insight for future growth trends. In 1994, the North American Free Trade Agreement (NAFTA) came into effect, opening up trade among the United States, Canada, and Mexico, making Mexico the third-largest trading partner with the United States (Gilmore 2000). Proposals are under way to create a larger free-trade zone for the entire hemisphere. Called the Free Trade Agreement of the Americas (FTAA), all 34 countries in the Western Hemisphere could be members (NAFTA for . . . 2001). The FTAA would impact approximately 776 million consumers, or 22 percent of the world's trade. If the current trends continue, the Western Hemisphere will be the largest market in the world (Gilmore 2000) and a new opportunity for the security industry.

Other regions of the world too experienced tremendous change in the last quarter of the twentieth century. The East Asian "tiger" economies—South Korea, Taiwan, Singapore, and Hong Kong—are projected to see continual growth. China and Malaysia are predicted to be the new economic tigers of the twenty-first century (Osman and Toh 1999). Emerging European nations will also have an increased presence in the global marketplace. Making up approximately 24 countries, some of the "transitional economies" of central and eastern Europe already export more goods than China does (Kierzkowski 2000).

Globalization may lead to issues and problems for many of these regions and countries. As the preceding information points out, many of the emerging and existing trade partners of the United States are from emerging third-world nations or transitional economies that previously operated under nonmarket conditions. In many instances, these countries are located in politically unstable regions and may have ineffective or unstable governments. Although this type of environment may prove to be unsuitable for many companies, the inherent qualities of many these countries present opportunities for contract security firms.

One of the primary issues that these emerging nations may face is the lack of a properly developed governmental infrastructure to address issues related to industrialization, social changes, and crime. The majority of needs will be based on "traditional" services that already exist in developed countries, including loss prevention, guard services, corporate security, and private investigation services. One of the best examples of this has occurred in Russia. In the early 1990s, several of the former KGB—secret police—directorates were placed under presidential, or federal, jurisdiction. This restructuring of state security organizations also included the reduction of personnel. The former KGB alone was reduced to 75,000 employees, a reduction of 46 percent. With many new businesses forming and needing security, combined with organized crime groups' intimidating owners and extorting their businesses for protection, many of these former state employees developed their own security companies. In 1992, federal legislation was passed allowing the creation of proprietary, detective, and contract security firms. The result has been an explosion of this industry. In 1999, there were approximately 11,650 security firms employing an estimated 850,000 personnel (Volkov 2000).

When considered in the context that many of the traditional and established markets in the United States may already be overly competitive, saturated, and lack good profit margins, progressive security companies will compete beyond established markets and look to those emerging nations and regions of the world for increased opportunities, market share, and profit. Some companies and organizations have already entered these markets. Pinkerton, for example, has a growing presence in the former Soviet states in several capacities, including guard and consulting services.

Private Military Companies

Security companies may be able to deliver their services as private military companies (PMCs). These private armies provide their client(s) with a variety of security-related services. PMCs are unlike mercenary groups, which are defined by international law as individuals or armies hired to overthrow a government by force or to undermine the order of a state (see Kassebaum 2000). PMCs, by contrast, are corporations that contract with legitimate governments, serving in some manner to enhance those countries' military capabilities (Spicer 1998). These PMCs have been used by countries that lack the political will to engage in military activities, are susceptible to guerrilla wars, lack a degree of military preparedness, or that cannot maintain public order (Zarate 1998).

The primary reason for the growth of private armies has been changes in the geopolitical climate of the world. With the breakup of the Soviet Union and the end of the cold war, the United States and other military powers are no longer providing the level of military support to which these countries previously were accustomed (Zarate 1998). At the same time, many areas of the world have experienced a flood of military-related equipment and personnel, increasing insurgent capabilities against many governments (Howe 1998). Combined with the reluctance and lack of resources of multinational peacekeeping groups, such as the United Nations (UN) and North Atlantic Treaty Organization (NATO) to intervene in some events, this void has been filled by PMC services.

PMCs provide a variety of services, ranging from training and consultation to directly assisting existing armies in offensive-based activities. According to Spicer (1998), the activities of these PMCs can be divided into passive and active. Passive PMCs engage in consulting, advisory, and training activities and work alongside client personnel. Active PMCs deploy in a combat role alongside their client armed forces, serving as "force multipliers," increasing the number of military personnel in that country's army.

Some companies have already found this market niche. One such company is the British-based Sandline Ltd. (Sheppard 1999). Some PMCs are U.S. based. The Dayton Peace Accords in 1995 allowed military forces in the Federation of Bosnia and Herzegovina to receive weapons, training, and equipment but not directly from the

United States. Instead, the U.S. government donated $100 million to the federation, which in turn contracted with Military Professional Resources, Inc., a U.S.-based PMC composed of high-ranking retired U.S. servicemen (Kassebaum 2000).

In the future, PMCs may not be related solely to military responsibilities. Instead, they may be involved in activities that are closely related to the traditional security function, particularly the protection of assets. PMCs may also be used in the future as a neutral security force to protect natural habitats, such as rainforests, that are placed under international protection (Caldwell 1999).

Economic and Industrial Espionage

The global economy increases companies' vulnerability to economic espionage activities. Economic espionage is the theft of information that will give the opposition a competitive edge and more market share. According to the Federal Bureau of Investigation (FBI), economic espionage is foreign-sponsored or coordinated intelligence activities directed against the U.S. government or U.S. corporations to unlawfully obtain proprietary economic information (Fraumann 1997). Economic espionage is a broad-based concept that includes social engineering of employees; theft of trade secrets, intellectual property, and classified documents; and electronic surveillance against executives (Schweitzer 1993). Aerospace, biotechnology, computer hardware and software, transportation technology, defense and armaments technology, energy research, basic research, and lasers are the most frequently targeted industries (Stutler 2000).

Economic or industrial espionage is not a new issue. In the case of nineteenth-century European businesspeople, it was a common activity aimed at increasing their level of competition among Western nations (Bergier 1975; Davids 1995). During the Cold War, espionage concerns were directed primarily toward industries involved in defense-based products and high-tech corporations that had applications in defense (Tuck 1986). The major targets were classified government documents, proprietary information from computer companies, and unclassified but embargoed computer technological data and hardware (Cunningham and Taylor 1985). The common foe at this time was the former Soviet Union and its Warsaw Pact countries (Tuck 1986).

With the end of the Cold War, some nations downsized and converted their military espionage activities to economic espionage efforts. Former employees sold their espionage expertise on the open market to the highest bidder (Fialka 1997). As Schweitzer (1993) points out, a great deal of economic espionage is not committed by those countries that we readily identify as "the enemy." Instead, our military and economic allies in the world commit it. Foreign intelligence services from France and Japan have directed espionage activities against U.S. corporations, and employees in those corporations do so at the request of their multinational companies. It is also reported that some countries encourage and train visiting college students to collect and steal technology-related information for their countries and companies back home while attending school. Other countries are even bolder in their operations. They simply hire U.S. citizens to collect information for them (Schweitzer 1993). One estimate in 1999 projected the losses related to corporate espionage to be more than $250 billion (Trembly 1999).

To address this threat, Congress passed the Economic Espionage Act (EEA) of 1996 to make the theft or misappropriation of trade secrets a federal crime (see Box 14–1). This was the first time that economic espionage and the theft of trade secrets had been outlawed at the federal level (Tucker 1997).

BOX 14–1 ■ The Economic Espionage Act of 1996: PL 104-294 (HR 3723)

October 11, 1996

§ 1831. Economic espionage

(a) IN GENERAL.—Whoever, intending or knowing that the offense will benefit any foreign government, foreign instrumentality, or foreign agent, knowingly—
   (1) steals, or without authorization appropriates, takes, carries away, or conceals, or by fraud, artifice, or deception obtains a trade secret;
   (2) without authorization copies, duplicates, sketches, draws, photographs, downloads, uploads, alters, destroys, photocopies, replicates, transmits, delivers, sends, mails, communicates, or conveys a trade secret;
   (3) receives, buys, or possesses a trade secret, knowing the same to have been stolen or appropriated, obtained, or converted without authorization;
   (4) attempts to commit any offense described in any of paragraphs (1) through (3); or
   (5) conspires with one or more other persons to commit any offense described in any of paragraphs (1) through (3), and one or more of such persons do any act to effect the object of the conspiracy, shall, except as provided in subsection (b), be fined not more than $500,000 or imprisoned not more than 15 years, or both.
(b) ORGANIZATIONS.—Any organization that commits any offense described in subsection (a) shall be fined not more than $10,000,000.

§ 1832. Theft of trade secrets

(a) Whoever, with intent to convert a trade secret, that is related to or included in a product that is produced for or placed in interstate or foreign commerce, to the economic benefit of anyone other than the owner thereof, and intending or knowing that the offense will, injure any owner of that trade secret, knowingly—
   (1) steals, or without authorization appropriates, takes, carries away, or conceals, or by fraud, artifice, or deception obtains such information;
   (2) without authorization copies, duplicates, sketches, draws, photographs, downloads, uploads, alters, destroys, photocopies, replicates, transmits, delivers, sends, mails, communicates, or conveys such information;
   (3) receives, buys, or possesses such information, knowing the same to have been stolen or appropriated, obtained, or converted without authorization;

(4) attempts to commit any offense described in paragraphs (1) through (3); or

(5) conspires with one or more other persons to commit any offense described in paragraphs (1) through (3), and one or more of such persons do any act to effect the object of the conspiracy, shall, except as provided in subsection (b), be fined under this title or imprisoned not more than 10 years, or both.

(b) Any organization that commits any offense described in subsection (a) shall be fined not more than $5,000,000.

§ 1833. Exceptions to prohibitions

This chapter does not prohibit—

(1) any otherwise lawful activity conducted by a governmental entity of the United States, a State, or a political subdivision of a State; or

(2) the reporting of a suspected violation of law to any governmental entity of the United States, a State, or a political subdivision of a State, if such entity has lawful authority with respect to that violation.

§ 1834. Criminal forfeiture

(a) The court, in imposing sentence on a person for a violation of this chapter, shall order, in addition to any other sentence imposed, that the person forfeit to the United States—

(1) any property constituting, or derived from, any proceeds the person obtained, directly or indirectly, as the result of such violation; and

(2) any of the person's property used, or intended to be used, in any manner or part, to commit or facilitate the commission of such violation, if the court in its discretion so determines, taking into consideration the nature, scope, and proportionality of the use of the property in the offense.

(b) Property subject to forfeiture under this section, any seizure and disposition thereof, and any administrative or judicial proceeding in relation thereto, shall be governed by section 413 of the Comprehensive Drug Abuse Prevention and Control Act of 1970 (21 U.S.C. 853), except for subsections (d) and (j) of such section, which shall not apply to forfeitures under this section.

§ 1835. Orders to preserve confidentiality

In any prosecution or other proceeding under this chapter, the court shall enter such orders and take such other action as may be necessary and appropriate to preserve the confidentiality of trade secrets, consistent with the requirements of the Federal Rules of Criminal and Civil Procedure, the Federal Rules of Evidence, and all other applicable laws. An interlocutory appeal by the United States shall lie from a decision or order of a district court authorizing or directing the disclosure of any trade secret.

§ 1836. Civil proceedings to enjoin violations

(a) The Attorney General may, in a civil action, obtain appropriate injunctive relief against any violation of this section.

Continued

(b) The district courts of the United States shall have exclusive original jurisdiction of civil actions under this subsection.

§ 1837. Applicability to conduct outside the United States

This chapter also applies to conduct occurring outside the United States if—

(1) the offender is a natural person who is a citizen or permanent resident alien of the United States, or an organization organized under the laws of the United States or a State or political subdivision thereof; or
(2) an act in furtherance of the offense was committed in the United States.

§ 1838. Construction with other laws

This chapter shall not be construed to preempt or displace any other remedies, whether civil or criminal, provided by United States Federal, State, commonwealth, possession, or territory law for the misappropriation of a trade secret, or to affect the otherwise lawful disclosure of information by any Government employee under section 552 of title 5 (commonly known as the Freedom of Information Act).

§ 1839. Definitions

As used in this chapter—

(1) the term "foreign instrumentality" means any agency, bureau, ministry, component, institution, association, or any legal, commercial, or business organization, corporation, firm, or entity that is substantially owned, controlled, sponsored, commanded, managed, or dominated by a foreign government;
(2) the term "foreign agent" means any officer, employee, proxy, servant, delegate, or representative of a foreign government;
(3) the term "trade secret" means all forms and types of financial, business, scientific, technical, economic, or engineering information, including patterns, plans, compilations, program devices, formulas, designs, prototypes, methods, techniques, processes, procedures, programs, or codes, whether tangible or intangible, and whether or how stored, compiled, or memorialized physically, electronically, graphically, photographically, or in writing if—
   (A) the owner thereof has taken reasonable measures to keep such information secret; and
   (B) the information derives independent economic value, actual or potential, from not being generally known to, and not being readily ascertainable through proper means by, the public; and
(4) the term "owner," with respect to a trade secret, means the person or entity in whom or in which rightful legal or equitable title to, or license in, the trade secret is reposed.

One of the first cases to be tried under the EEA involved the Avery Dennison Corporation, a world leader in adhesives. The employee, Dr. Ten-Hong "Victor" Lee, was approached by representatives from the Four Pillars Enterprises, Ltd., located in Taipei, Taiwan, to steal trade secrets for them in exchange for cash. Four Pillars and Yang were eventually tried and found guilty under the EEA. Stemming from the criminal trial, Four Pillars was also fined $5 million by the U.S. government. In the subsequent civil suit, the jury awarded $40 million to Avery Dennison for damages (Biddle 2000). The facts of this landmark case are presented in Box 14–2.

BOX 14–2 ■ *U.S. v. Yang:* 74 F. Supp. 2d 724 (N.D.Ohio 1999)

On October 1, 1997, the Government filed a twenty-one count indictment against P. Y. Yang, his daughter Sally Yang, and their company, Four Pillars, charging them with eight counts of mail fraud, five counts of wire fraud, two counts of money laundering, one count of conspiracy to launder money, and three counts of receipt of stolen goods. The Defendants were also charged with one count of conspiracy to steal trade secrets and one count of attempting to steal trade secrets in violation of the Economic Espionage Act (EEA).

The Government's case against the Defendants was essentially focused on the Defendants appropriation of proprietary and confidential information from the Avery Dennison Corporation (Avery). Avery's principal business was the production and sale of self-adhesive materials such as labels and tapes. Defendant Four Pillars, a Taiwanese company, marketed the same products in the Far East. Avery invested substantial sums of money into researching and developing products for sale in various markets worldwide. To protect its investment, Avery undertook substantial security measures to properly preserve the confidentiality of its proprietary information. However, Avery was not able to protect itself from one of its own employees, Dr. Ten-Hong "Victor" Lee ("Dr. Lee") and the Defendants.

Dr. Lee was an employee of Avery beginning in May 1986. From the time Dr. Lee began working at Avery until he was caught passing confidential information to the Defendants, he executed five Conflict of Interest and Legal and Ethical Conduct questionnaires attesting, among other things, that he was not employed by another entity or person, that he did not provide his services to a competitor, and that he did not use or allow others to use Avery's confidential and proprietary information for his personal advantage. Dr. Lee, a research chemist, was privy to Avery's confidential and proprietary information and documents and used his position to surreptitiously provide valuable information regarding Avery adhesives to the Defendants.

In July 1989, Dr. Lee was asked by P. Y. Yang, the President of Four Pillars, to serve as a "consultant" for his company. Lee was paid $25,000 for his services by

Continued

Four Pillars before he left Taiwan. The funds were deposited into a Taiwanese bank account in the name of Lee's mother-in-law. This was the start of a long relationship between Dr. Lee and the Defendants. Over the course of the next eight years, Dr. Lee provided confidential and proprietary information to Four Pillars, via the U.S. Mail, in exchange for money. This relationship lasted until September 4, 1997, when the Government arranged, with Dr. Lee's cooperation, to videotape a meeting between the Defendants and Dr. Lee. At the meeting, Dr. Lee was to provide the Yangs with Avery trade secrets.

For the purpose of giving the Government's sting operation context, a brief summary of the facts leading up to it is necessary. In January 1997, Dr. Lee obtained Avery's confidential business plan regarding activities in the Far East with the intent to disclose its contents to the Defendants. Dr. Lee's activities were subsequently discovered by the Federal Bureau of Investigation (FBI) and Avery.

Dr. Lee then agreed to cooperate in the investigation of the Defendants, which eventually led to the sting operation. On August 3, 1997, Dr. Lee telephoned P. Y. Yang to confirm his plans for a visit to the United States in September 1997. Dr. Lee informed P.Y. Yang that he would be able to obtain detailed information about new emulsion adhesive technology and needed to discuss it personally with P. Y. Yang. P. Y. Yang told Dr. Lee that he was also interested in Avery's business plans for the Far East.

On August 31, 1997, P. Y. Yang telephoned Dr. Lee. Upon returning P. Y. Yang's call, Dr. Lee arranged a meeting with P. Y. Yang and Sally Yang in Westlake, Ohio, where Avery's confidential and proprietary information would be turned over to them. The next day, September 1, 1997, Dr. Lee finalized these plans. On September 4, 1997, Defendants P. Y. and Sally Yang met with Dr. Lee in a hotel room in Westlake, Ohio. The entire meeting between Dr. Lee, P. Y. Yang, and Sally Yang was captured by the FBI on videotape. (Government Exhibit 73.) The videotape clearly showed P. Y. and Sally Yang cutting out the confidential markings on the documents they believed to contain an Avery patent application.

Although such cases have served to warn companies of this threat, many other companies have failed to recognize the severity of the problem and have not taken necessary measures to protect their information (Fraumann 1997). This issue is not going to disappear soon. Just because legislation outlaws economic espionage activities in the United States, competing countries will not necessarily abide by these laws. When compounded with the issue that the major growth of U.S. companies will be outside the United States, recognizing and dealing with this problem at the organizational level, not national level, is crucial.

A paradigm change will be required at the organizational level. The traditional paradigm was that corporate espionage was not occurring, because it was an illegal and unethical activity, based on prevailing U.S. cultural norms and business ethics. The security industry must now realize that corporate espionage is a widely accepted practice for many nations, including our "friends" and allies. At the same time, these activities are not limited solely to foreign companies. U.S. companies have also engaged in espionage activities against their national and international competitors (Winkler 1998).

Executive and Corporate Protection

Examples of risks to executives and corporate assets abound. In the context of kidnapping, the Colombian government has estimated that from 1987 to 1997, 103 Americans were abducted (Carter and Skrlec 1999). Although perhaps this number of kidnappings may be considered insignificant, the total number of kidnappings in 1995 in Latin America was estimated to be 6,500 (Hagedorn-Auerbach 1998). The income generated from kidnappings is quite high. It was estimated that from 1991 to 1994, Colombian rebels acquired approximately $330 million in ransom from kidnapping executives (Carter and Skrlec 1999).

If executives are not the threat, perhaps company assets will be. With approximately 90 percent of world trade moving by sea (Brandon 2000), the age-old problem of piracy is already a concern for organizations. Pirate attacks, which occur most heavily in the South China Sea, followed by attacks off the coast of Brazil, have accounted for losses amounting to approximately $16 billion per year. These attacks include taking the contents of the ship or stealing the ship itself (Howell 1999). Firms may also face attacks on their fixed properties, as in the case of Occidental Petroleum, which operates oil-pumping facilities in Colombia. Because of repeated bombings of its pipeline, which pumps crude oil from Occidental's fields, the company invoked *force majeure*, temporarily suspending contractual obligations with the state-controlled company (Colombia Oil . . . 2000).

Several factors explain this increased threat to executives and corporate assets. First, the competitive global marketplace requires corporations to set up operations in many politically unstable countries. If political instability is not a concern, organizations should also be aware that that the social-control structures in these emerging nations may be undeveloped. Many companies doing business may also fail to recognize that they will need to provide their own protection for their employees and cannot rely on the deficient and often corrupt practices of government officials. Firms need to realize the possibility of contemptuous attitudes toward them and their presence in that particular region or country. This "corporate backlash" could be based on fears that these multinational firms exploit workers or undermine the democratic process in that particular country. This backlash could also be based on concerns over these companies' destroying the environment.

Some options exist to address these issues related to executive and corporate protection. The U.S. State Department's Overseas Advisory Council (OSAC) was founded in 1985 to address security issues abroad. This private/public partnership now has approximately 1,600 affiliate member companies and organizations that rely on OSAC for security-related information in those countries where they do business (Overseas Security Advisory Council 2001). Already, some Western companies are hiring former KGB agents to meet this need. The demand is so great for these individuals that an organization called the Club of State Security Veterans in Moscow serves as a clearinghouse for these individuals (Wallis 1998). Other private-sector consultants also offer threat-assessment services for corporations for a fee. In Mexico, corporate and executive protection services are predicted to become a "booming" industry (Zagaris 1996).

Companies will need to establish in-house expertise related to executive and corporate protection threats. Companies in the future will have to think "outside the box" and perhaps rely on unorthodox means of protection. For example, what will a corporation do if the country it operates in is experiencing a civil war and its corporate assets are at risk? Besides halting production, finding safer and longer delivery routes, or abandoning operations, organizations may contract with security companies that specialize in protection from high-risk threats. In Sierra Leone, for example, the government contracted with Life Guard, a private security company, to protect the diamond-mining areas of the country (Akinrinade 2001). Just as the private police in the late nineteenth and early twentieth centuries in the United States were used as strikebreakers (Serrin 1992), private police may be used again to prevent civil unrest and damage to corporate assets in foreign nations.

Executive-protection activities will also expand beyond protecting employees from human threats. With the expansion of corporations into many emerging or developing nations, the security function will require threat analysis and the protection of employees from infectious diseases, some of which are quite deadly. The fatality rates associated with the major Ebola outbreaks in 1976 and 1995 in Zaire were estimated to be as high as 90 percent, with death occurring within 2 weeks of exposure (Preston 1994; Wickelgren 1998). Thranert (1996) writes that more epidemics may break out in developing countries on account of poor hygienic conditions, more people traveling throughout the world, drug-resistant pathogens, and population expansion. To date, the infectious diseases HIV/AIDS and tuberculosis are considered to be "disease burdens" in developing countries. Unfortunately, the proliferation of the HIV/AIDS infection and malaria are projected to increase in the future (Brundtland 1999). Although sub-Saharan Africa is the hardest-hit region in the world for AIDS, it is estimated that by 2010, Asia and India will surpass this region in the rate of infection (Gellman 2000). Ebola and reemerging viruses, including cholera and yellow fever, are also predicted to increase (Emerging . . . 1998).

Disease will also affect the profitability and stability of companies. The World Health Organization (WHO) concluded that health improvements in East Asian countries accounted for at least one-third to one-half of their economic success. Because of the reduction of infant mortality rates, many Asian countries over time experienced an increase in the working-age population. This surplus of labor then led to economic expansion (Brundtland 1999). If estimates are accurate, disease in some nations could eventually lead to severe economic and social problems, increasing the demand for security-related services in these countries. Such diseases as AIDS can be so pervasive that they destroy the infrastructures of countries, beginning with individuals, their families, communities, economic institutions, and the military and police. This concern is so great that in 1999, President Clinton declared AIDS to be a national security concern, as the United States may need to intervene in countries facing the AIDS pandemic.

The assets of a company, including the human resources—regardless of whether they are U.S. citizens or foreign nationals—need to be protected from these diseases. Security will need to address both the short- and long-term ramifications that these diseases may cause. For example, the potential for economic and social instability in certain countries or regions as the result of these diseases will need to be included as an integral component of risk analysis. Security managers will need to look at existing and projected disease trends for those areas. Because of the resulting economic and social instability these diseases may cause, employees will also be more vulnerable to the more "traditional" security concerns, including crimes against property and criminal attacks. This will require security to reassess these threats against employees and to modify existing policies, procedures, and practices for on- and off-property employee protection. Special attention will also need to be paid to emergency evacuation procedures in times of civil unrest or virus breakouts and containment procedures if an infectious disease should emerge.

The protection of employees in unstable regions of the world may require novel methods. Already, employees who work for Occidental Petroleum in Colombia are flown in helicopters from Bogota, the capital, to the oil fields because the roads are too dangerous to travel. In other areas where governments are weak and unable to control crime, disease, and social disorder, which ultimately affect quality of life for the availability of labor for the company, organizations may become de facto social service agents to ensure that they have enough human capital. One method that may be used is reminiscent of the company towns that existed in the nineteenth and early twentieth centuries in the United States. Using this model, organizations could build large gated communities where employees would be provided with housing, education, food, medical treatment, and protection. In effect, these communities would become twenty-first-century castles, and the security function would be responsible for protecting the citizenry and giving them refuge from the dangers outside their walls.

Competitive Intelligence

Although corporate espionage is illegal, one may argue that it is nevertheless important to collect information on the competition to survive in the global marketplace. One method of legitimately collecting information about the competition is through competitive intelligence (CI). Personnel engaged in CI use legitimate sources of information to build a profile of the competition in order to anticipate and learn their competitors' activities and mistakes. Sources of information for CI professionals are vast. Some may include Freedom of Information (FIO) requests, government reports, and information from patents and mission statements. About 7 percent of U.S. corporations have a CI unit (Kahaner 1996). However, the number of companies using CI has increased dramatically. In 1988, it was estimated that corporations spent $1 billion on CI activities; in 1998, CI activities were estimated to be $100 billion (Vedder et al. 1999).

CI is both a process and a product (see Vedder et al. 1999) that offers new opportunities to the field of security. As a process, CI involves the collection of information to make the organization more competitive in the global marketplace. Security departments may already have those personnel who may prove to be the most suitable candidates for CI responsibilities, based on their experiences and expertise. If not solely tasked with the CI function, security could also contribute its investigative knowledge and expertise to assist those units that are responsible for the CI function.

Competitive intelligence will also be a "product" that contract security companies can sell to clients. Current research on what administrative structures are used by companies in CI revealed that the majority of companies had no formal unit devoted to CI activities. Others reported having only informal units that are assigned CI responsibilities on an ad hoc basis (Vedder et al. 1999). Other studies have shown that approximately 23 percent of the members of the Society for Competitive Intelligence Professionals are independent consultants. This suggests that the private security function is already filling this void. Aggressive security companies with the personnel and expertise to perform CI consulting services could perform these strategic planning services on a contractual basis for those companies that lack the resources and expertise for CI activities.

■ TECHNOLOGY AND SECURITY

For the security industry, the majority of the emerging crimes of primary concern will be based on technology. New technologies will mean new opportunities for firms to use and design advanced technologies. But criminals may exploit and use these technologies against individuals, corporations, and even states. It can easily be assumed that the rate and intensity of high-tech crimes will increase as individuals, corporations, and societies become increasingly dependent on computer systems in the information-oriented, technological world. Box 14-3 lists just some of the new technologies that will change security in the future.

BOX 14–3 ■ New Technologies in Security

Smart watchers—satellite and video-networked electronic surveillance ranging from face recognition to suspicious-activity monitoring stored in supercomputers.

Secure wearables—quite similar to chip technology used in pets, these embedded chips will assist in tracking individuals via global positioning satellites.

Biometrics—facial, eye, fingerprint, and genomic scanning devices, which are becoming increasing popular and cost-effective for security applications.

Robotics—cost-effective and dependable robotics systems with satellite uplinks to replace many existing entry-level guard systems. Many robots are quite small and agile. Some are about the size of a large cockroach and are equipped with cameras and can traverse walls.

Facial recognition—with capabilities to "scan" faces and match them with a "watch list" maintained by the airport and fed by the FBI. When a match is found, an alarm alerts security personnel, and the passenger is subjected to a more detailed level of security.

Technology will be a double-edged sword for the security industry. Although technology will greatly help the security industry, these same technologies can be a threat to the organization. In the future, corporations and individuals will be facing a triumvirate of threats from tech-related criminal activities: the potential of attack from corporations, foreign governments, and individuals and organizations. Some tech-based issues to consider will include cyber-related crimes and the consequences of technology in the context of new and more lethal forms of terrorism that technology will have on the environment, raising concerns about environmental security.

Cybercrimes

Cybercrimes are criminal activities committed against computer systems by states, individuals, or organizations. These activities include sabotage, espionage, vandalism, and theft. In other instances, a disgruntled employee may be seeking to disrupt the firm's operations for personal reasons. A cybercriminal could also be a "hactivist," disrupting a company's operations as a means of political activism. Regardless of the intent and who is responsible, these and other unauthorized activities may not only affect a company's financial status but also damage the firm's reputation.

A great deal of cybercrime is simple and involves the theft of information through traditional means, including obtaining seemingly minor personal information (social engineering) and the stealing of hard drives. In other instances, it can be quite complex. As pointed out by Schwartau (1996), these weapons can be used by "information warriors" to destroy the competition's infrastructure—computers—or steal electronic information. Several of the technologies used by the military, such as HERF (high-energy radio frequency) guns, "shoot" a high-power radio signal at a target, such as a computer, and overload and destroy electronic circuitry. If the threat is not interested in destroying the computer, it engages in electronic eavesdropping by purchasing a Van Eck reader (available from $500 to $2,000) that "reads" what is being typed onto a computer screen.

Already, society has recognized the dangers of cybercrime. Sager (2000, 32) writes: "The dirty little secret is that computer networks offer ready points of access for disgruntled employees, spies, thieves, sociopaths, and bored teens. Once they're in a corporate network, they can lift intellectual property, destroy data, sabotage operations, even subvert a particular deal or career." There are several explanations for the increases in cybercrime. First, the global connectedness of firms via the Internet creates global opportunities for cybercriminals and increases the vulnerability of firms to intrusions and attacks (O'Connell 1999). The growing trend in cybercrime is exacerbated by the lack of any consistent or international laws governing the use of computers for cyberintrusion into corporate property. In some countries, such as Japan, Argentina, and Canada, hacking is not considered criminal. In fact, Canada has been referred to as a "hacker haven" because of its lack of regulations against computer theft (O'Connell 1999).

Although the extent of cybercrime is unknown, in one study of 643 European companies, 90 percent of the firms reported that their computer systems had been breached by outside infiltrators (Banham 2000). In the United States, data collected from 521 security practitioners in universities, corporations, financial institutions, and governmental agencies found the following: 62 percent had reported breaches in computer security; 30 percent, intrusions; 57 percent, intrusion via Internet connections; and 26 percent, theft of proprietary information (Keyes and Rapp 1999). A study released by Pricewaterhouse Coopers in 1998 found that 73 percent of the information technology professionals had reported a breach in security; of those, only 20 percent had comprehensive security policies (Jackson 1998). Other estimates place the financial loss of cybercrimes because of damage or loss at $1 trillion (Neeley 2000).

Unfortunately, many firms may not be prepared to combat issues related to cybercrimes. This lack of preparation may be attributed to failing to recognize the risk of such crimes, as well as to the fact that many of these cyberthreats cannot be reliably tracked or identified before an attack. Hence, traditional security approaches of monitoring the activities of known or potential attackers may not work any more, owing to the complexities and unique ways attackers and intruders can access the firm's computer systems (Keyes and Rapp 1999).

The impact of the loss or theft of information as the result of a cybercrime can have some profound effects on an organization. In 1997, for example, Levi Strauss experienced the theft of a computer hard drive that contained the names and social security numbers of about 22,000 employees (Minton 1997). This theft was not high-tech but rather involved the physical theft of a hard drive that was not properly secured. When considering the long- and short-term impact this crime may have had on employees and Levi-Strauss, the company was lucky, as it appeared that the thief took the hard drive not for the information but for the drive itself.

To effectively deal with this issue in the future, security departments will have to recognize the cybercrime threat and become technologically proficient at the same time. This increase in computer-related crimes and the recognition of the sensitivity of information has already created a new profession for security personnel. OpSec, as it is known, looks at vulnerabilities related to open sources of information and industrial espionage. OpSec also focuses on internal concerns. Its primary mission is to protect information about capabilities and intentions of the organization by controlling and protecting evidence of the planning and executing of sensitive activities (Pagell 1998). The creation of departments and computer security specialties, such as OpSec, will also require organizational restructuring. For example, in many organizations, the responsibility for computer issues was delegated to the information technology (IT) department. Cybercrime issues will require that security take an increased responsibility in the IT function, working jointly with these individuals to address these issues.

The future will also see the pooling of resources to combat this issue, as organizations may lack resources to detect and counteract attacks. As described by Stoll (1989), a cybercriminal attacked multiple firms from a location thousands of miles away; security firms will need to develop security networks so that they can work together in a mutually beneficial noncompetitive environment. Already, a National Information Assurance Institute (NIAI) has been proposed to address this issue. This organization would serve as a neutral third-party nonprofit entity composed of government representatives, academia, and private companies that would conduct a variety of security-related services, including threat assessment, research, and assistance related to cybercrime (Carter, Deutch, and Zlikow 1998). The security industry will also see this as an opportunity for consulting and contractual opportunities.

The Changing Nature of Terrorism

The goal of terrorism is to inflict fear on society, with the primary threat usually being the government or symbols of the government, including human beings. The attacks against the American Embassy in Nairobi in 1998, the USS *Cole* in Yemen in 2000, and the World Trade Center in 2001 (see Beeston 2001) are just some of the many terrorist incidents the United States and world have recently experienced. The World Trade Center attack in 2001 changed many opinions that "it can't happen to us," making firms reevaluate their vulnerabilities as primary targets and secondary victims of the cross fire. The New York Stock Exchange was one of the organizations in New York City that was affected; it closed for four days after the attacks, and many others shut down for much longer. Terrorist attacks have resulted in the U.S. government's aggressively dealing with the threat and developing more effective security measures to prevent future attacks. Although this is necessary, the end result of target hardening the United States against attacks will mean that U.S. companies operating in foreign countries and citizens living in these countries will become prime "proxy" symbols and subsequent targets of terrorist organizations.

Although the lethality of terrorism increased in the 1990s on account of religious extremism, the use and availability of technology makes terrorism an increasingly viable threat to companies. The proliferation of high-tech weapons of mass destruction from former Soviet-bloc countries, combined with corrupt officials eager for hard currency, has resulted in these products' falling into the hands of terrorist organizations. For example, Bukharin (1997) writes that the security of weapons-grade plutonium and highly enriched uranium remains a grave security concern and that stolen nuclear material is relatively easy to smuggle to other nations. At the same time, terrorist groups can communicate and recruit members via the Internet and commit cyberterrorist activities.

To date, the United States and companies have been fortunate that they have not had to directly address a chemical, biological, radiological, or nuclear (CBRN) attack by terrorist organizations. Nevertheless, the threat related to a CBRN-related attack is a concern. Although such weapons were historically limited to the military, a potential now exists that other groups can acquire weapons of mass destruction. If they do not have the ability to acquire such weapons or have the capability to manufacture them, as has been the case for many years regarding chemical and biological weapons, what is new is that "there is a new type of terrorist who for the first time really wants to do so" (Thranert 1996, 28). That is, the new threat comes from motivated individuals willing to use CBRN weapons against their perceived enemy. Since 1996, the U.S. government has spent approximately $10 billion on CBRN programs involving at least 20 organizations and federal agencies (Stanton 2001).

What compounds this threat is the ease of application. In the case of chemical and biological agents, the method of delivery may be as simple as contaminating food and water supplies; the impact could be as intense as if they had been delivered from a military warhead. This impact could be measured in the number of fatalities. However, as pointed out by Garrett (2001, 79), "the true costs of a bioterrorist attack might be the consequences of panic, such as the stock market collapse in New York or a commodities market crash in Chicago."

The security function will also need to be aware of chemical and nuclear attacks. Chemical agents are synthetic compounds that vary in intensity and duration. Some of these agents are classified as persistent and can last for days, whereas others are nonpersistent, and their impact or effects disperse quickly. The intensity of these chemicals varies. For example, nerve agents are extremely lethal. Other chemical weapons, such as sarin gas, are less lethal. The March 1995 sarin gas attack on the Tokyo subway system by a Japanese cult group killed 12 people and injured more than 500. The chemical used in this attack was manufactured by the cult and was dispersed from five devices that looked like lunch boxes and soft drink containers (Schofield 1999).

The use of advanced technology in terrorist acts suggests a new form of terrorism, known as superterrorism. Schweitzer and Dorsch (1999, 42) define superterrorism as "committing violent acts using advanced technological tools to cause massive damage to populations and/or to public and private support networks. It includes all forms of nuclear, chemical, and biological attacks except small chemical poisonings."

Of the many forms of emerging superterrorism, perhaps the most serious will be cyberterrorism, which involves the use of computers and computer systems to inflict fear and violence on a society. The effects on a society could be greater than those of a chemical or biological attack. It has been estimated that 20 hackers backed with $1 billion could effectively shut down the entire United States (Chalk 2000). As the role of security is to know these possibilities or potential threats, these new forms of terrorism need to be recognized as a serious concern, and appropriate measures must be designed and taken.

Some initiatives have already been taken. The President's Commission on Critical Infrastructure Protection (Executive Order 13010) was created in 1996 to examine physical threats to tangible properties—gas and oil storage, water supplies, and electrical power systems—and computer-based cyberattacks. In 1997, the commission issued a report revealing that the federal government and companies were not adequately prepared to deal with these threats. To combat cyberterrorism, the committee recommended the creation of information-exchange centers where companies could share information about cyberattacks. Other recommendations by the panel included increased federal research into computer security and the development of an information security curriculum from grade to graduate schools (Machlis 1997). This increased concern for cyberterrorism is also apparent in other governmental activities. In 1999, the U.S. Congress allocated $1.4 billion to combat information terrorism (Maglitta 1999).

The U.S. government cannot handle the threat of cyberterrorism alone. The President's Commission on Critical Infrastructure Protection revealed that the private sector was reluctant to work with the government on this issue because of cost, risk, and interference by the government. Instead, a collaboration composed of the government, military, business, academia, and security groups must band together to ensure that an "electronic Pearl Harbor" does not occur (Maglitta 1999, 35).

Organizations may also be at risk from environmental terrorism, which involves the manipulation of natural environmental forces to be used as a weapon. This broad definition includes using the environment as a conduit for releasing, as an example, chemical, biological, or nuclear threats, as well as targeting the earth by purposely contaminating water supplies (Schofield 1999). The effects of a terrorist attack on the government could include economic decline, reduced agricultural production, and the displacement of populations. These effects could then lead to "subnational" violence in that country and a delegitimation of the state (Litfin 1999).

A direct consequence of the direct and indirect impact of these new terrorist threats is that the security function will become more readily involved in responding to terrorism threats. Currently, responses to this threat are limited and include the military, hazardous materials teams, and high-technology sensors (Garrett 2001). Governmental agencies will not have the capacity to address a bioterrorism threat alone. In the future, private industries that have levels of expertise and necessary resources will become involved with the initial response. Crimes of this nature will require the government, scientists, and trained emergency response workers. These response teams could include contract guards to supplement existing police and, perhaps, military personnel to quarantine areas to proprietary firms, using their knowledge and specialized equipment to contain and clean up such attacks. The future will also see the private security function involved in disaster planning.

As already mentioned, one idea to control some threats is a greater degree of cooperation between governments and industries. Another is to have a Combined Terrorism Reduction Initiative (CTRI) that concentrates on economic development and eliminating social problems in those countries where terrorism originates (Schweitzer and Dorsch 1999). With globalization, this may be a good alternative. To be successful, however, the key is economic development, which by its very nature will require a greater degree of involvement of companies that operate in those areas. This in turn will require a greater level and degree of cooperation among all the parties involved.

Environmental Security

Issues related to the environment will continue to be a pressing concern for security. This will open up environmental security as a new area of specialization and market niche. Environmental security is the prevention of political and social instability as the result of human activities that reduce the environment's capacity to support life (Burkle 2000).

To date, the concept of protecting the environment has been the responsibility primarily of the world's governments. This has been accomplished through agreements and treaties to limit, for example, the production of carbon dioxide emissions. Although this will remain a concern for governments in the future, issues related to the environment will become a concern for private security. One way to destroy the image of an industry group and company is to blame them for some type of environmental abuse. Radical environmentalists may sabotage a company by creating a chemical spill and leaving other biohazards on its property to implicate the company in an environmental issue.

The impact of environmental issues on the private security industry will take two forms. First, corporations may be the direct targets of environmental activists who are protesting corporate policy that impacts the environment. The demand for natural resources, especially oil, will lead to more conflict between environmentalists and oil companies. Already, big business, the government, and environmentalists have been in conflict over drilling in Alaska's Arctic National Wildlife Refuge for oil and natural gas. Although the existing oil fields in Alaska have not been attacked, Lovins and Lovins (2001) point out that one attack on the

Alaskan oil line will raise havoc with the nation's oil supply. With energy demands increasing, oil exploration and drilling activities will likely occur with greater intensity and frequency in these remote, ecologically fragile environments throughout the world.

As a consequence of this perceived or actual corporate insensitivity or abuse of the environment, it will be security's new role to conduct a risk analysis and to identify perceived and actual threats to the corporation. Security in the future will be involved in what is coined the minimum quality of environment (MQE), or the amount and type of environmental management that must be maintained for a community to maintain its identity (Weintraub 1995).

If direct conflict with environmentalists is not considered a serious risk, some firms may also become inadvertently involved in environmental issues. Ecotourism companies, which provide trips to remote areas of the world, will need to recognize that tourists may be at risk from protestors and criminals and design appropriate security programs to address these identified threats. Other companies may be third-party victims. This occurred in 1999 during the World Trade Organization (WTO) conference in Seattle, Washington, where protestors rioted in opposition to the environmental abuses by WTO members. Over the course of the riots, millions of dollars were lost in sales and property damage to those business that were located where the rioting occurred (Flores 1999).

Environmental security will also be an issue with some countries. Nongovernmental organizations (NGOs) that have large land holdings in Africa or the Amazon rainforest may need to protect their resources by contracting with private security organizations. Last, the nature and extent of some of these threats may exceed the capabilities of many countries to monitor and protect these areas. For example, security may need to protect an endangered area from the slash-and-burn tactics of natives in the Amazon region. Moreover, security companies may supplement existing proprietary and governmental services in other areas.

■ "TRADITIONAL" CRIME ISSUES

Although the future will present the private security industry with a host of new challenges, it will still be concerned with preventing normal, or "traditional," crime by applying those principles that have made it successful in the past: concentrating less on rendering justice and concentrating more on deterrence by regulating those behaviors and actions of individuals in an attempt to limit their opportunities to commit crime. At the same time, the security industry will become more associated with crime fighters when tasked with confronting some of the traditional street crimes.

Trends in the Crime Rate

The last quarter of the twentieth century saw an overall decline in violent and property-related crimes. Official statistics have clearly shown an increase in the homicide rate from the years 1950 to 1999. Crime rates are back to their 1960s levels in major cities, and the rates have remained stable in suburbs and rural areas (Fox and Zawitz 2000). According to the Bureau of Justice Statistics (2002), other violent crimes, such as robbery, rape, assault, and violent crimes committed by juveniles, have all decreased since 1994. Property-related crimes, such as burglary, theft, and motor vehicle theft, also continued their decline over a 26-year period.

Several explanations can be given for this overall decrease in crime: a population that is "aging out" of crime, a strong economy, better crime-control activities, and the growth of private security. The public's fear of crime will continue to fuel the demand for traditional services. Although low, crime rates are still high enough to make traditional crimes a concern for many Americans. Low-cost effective alarm systems in homes resulted in the alarm industry's being quite prosperous and competitive in the late twentieth century. Likewise, the rapid growth of gated residential communities has fueled the demand for more contractual guard services.

Although the crime rate may be decreasing in the United States, it is rising in emerging nations. Dramatic social changes have resulted in increasing crime. Because some people in these nations may harbor a degree of resentment against Americans, Americans are being victimized at higher than average rates for both property- and personal-related crimes.

These traditional concerns will also provide new market niches for security firms in the future. One particular area that will be in high demand is specialized security services for our aging populations. U.S. Census projections for the aging baby boomers are that approximately one-third of the U.S. population will be older than 65 in the next 20 years.

This opens up an entirely new niche for companies that will recognize the opportunity today to provide security services to retirement villages, nursing homes, and assisted living centers. For the aged population still living in their homes, alarm systems can offer specialized services that include both traditional and medical-related services. For example, medic alert and other "alarm" systems provide the elderly with immediate medical assistance when requested.

Security Redefined

Historically, the services of private security and public security were clearly delineated. However, the late twentieth century saw a closer working relationship between the two, creating a public/private nexus in some areas, such as shopping malls, universities, stadiums, religious institutions, and other "private" institutions that are easily accessible by the public. Further, in many instances, police departments now patrol some of these private facilities on a contractual basis. Perhaps the best example is shopping malls, which the police often patrol and, in some instances, have set up "storefront" ministations.

One of the issues that will confront the security industry is how society will react to this relationship. Instead of private security having a "second-class" status in social control, the preceding factors will result in private security's achieving an equal status with the police in social control, or peace keeping. As a result, the security industry, particularly as it serves the public, will achieve a greater level of recognition and respect among the general citizenry. The consequence of these changes is that security will have a more clearly mandated cause of action that will align it more with the profession of law enforcement. This may result in the recognition of security by the public and customers as a legitimate and necessary social-control agent and will also increase the expectations that the public has toward security officers and companies.

This redefinition of security will result in a paradigm shift in the philosophy and mission for security officers. The paradigm change in some sectors of the security industry will also result in a redefinition of security's social obligation. In the public sector, police are obligated, via their commitment to the oath of office and an institutional duty, to serve the public. The police "must" act on all incidents. Police officers' personal safety is often subordinated to the needs of the public. An assumption related to the security industry is that the degree of commitment to the citizenry is less binding and intense, based primarily on a moral and contractual obligation to the client. Through the contractual relationship, the security officer has a degree of responsibility that does not subordinate safety over the needs of the client. With this continued expansion in the public sector, security officers and companies will have a greater social commitment and obligation to the public. There will be a philosophical shift from the lesser moral obligation to the higher standard of duty to the public.

In the future, private security firms will be involved to a greater extent in social welfare and political issues, regardless of whether a specific client exists. Security firms will therefore become political actors, even if they prefer not to be involved in politics. To understand how private security can become embroiled in political affairs, consider events occurring in Northern Ireland. With the British troops pulling out of Northern Ireland, private security firms are finding an increased demand for services, particularly from Protestant communities. An estimated 40,000, or 10 percent, of Protestant men are now employed in the security field. The Catholic community, meanwhile, is raising the issue that its employment opportunities in security are being affected, as they are subject to religious segregation (Lundy 2001). These same issues can and will arise with the security industry in the United States. Security firms will become more involved in public policy decisions at unprecedented levels and, in some cases, the services they provide could have a profound impact on the health of the municipality, particularly in the context of racial and social-class relations. Involvement in public policy issues also means that the private security industry will become heavily involved in politics.

As pointed out earlier in this chapter, the traditional paradigm of security has been associated with asset protection and crime prevention. The industry has not performed tasks unless activated by specific client demand. Instead of security's performing a variety of activities related specifically to its industry group or particular organization, the industry will experience a greater shift toward crime control. Security officers will more actively pursue and respond to criminal events in this capacity and will have an identifiable activity quite similar to that of the police.

■ THE NEED FOR ORGANIZATIONAL CHANGE

Change-Ready Organizations

The future will be chaotic but filled with opportunities. Public and private agencies that are rigid and slow to change will be left in the wake of firms that are prepared for the future. Bureaucracies and rigid paramilitary organizations are slow to change. In fact, the stability and consistency implied in a rigid organization have value to society's need for certainty and structure. For example, we would not feel good about our political and economic structure if the Federal Reserve and the Department of Treasury changed dramatically in short time periods. The stability of these institutions provides a base of confidence for investors and the market system. Similarly, customers served by private security firms need to feel a sense of certainty and continuity of service. An organization that stresses order and structure provides such certainty and has its place. However, private security firms need to live in a dual state: have a stable structure to serve today's customers but be flexible to take advantage of new opportunities.

In 1994, five firms—Borg-Warner, Pinkerton, Wackenhut, ADT, and Pittston—accounted for one-quarter of the U.S. security market (Bailin and Cort 1996). Although these large corporations have the financial and marketing resources to leverage themselves into dominant positions in the field of security, "the quickest with the mostest" will take advantage of the opportunities that crop up in the marketplace. The successful future leaders in the security industry will need to be change-ready.

Change-ready firms will expend energy watching the external environment for new opportunities. The structure of these firms is likely to be flat, with a minimum allocation of resources in management and a maximum resource allocation in training and learning. Change-ready organizations have a flat chain of command; power and decision making are decentralized, and reliance on policies and procedures is played down in favor of discretion and judgment on the part of employees. Operating principles and goals will substitute for policies, procedures, and rules and regulations. Change-ready organizations will also typically distribute rewards equitably to employees, as opposed to providing high rewards for management and owners but modest rewards for employees (Burns and Stalker 1961).

Changes in Corporate Culture

Change readiness begins with the organization's underlying philosophy, values, and identity. Private security firms that value new challenges and change and that view the blunders that come with new ventures as an opportunity to learn have a strong foundation for challenges and opportunities. The new, and necessary, corporate culture that exists in these types of environments will be termed the learning organization. Managers and line-level employees will be expected to make seat-of-the-pants decisions; as a consequence, some mistakes will be made. Mistakes in the learning organization will occur. These mistakes should be expected, and employees should not be punished for them but rather applauded for such creative ventures; their mistakes will serve as a guidepost and educational experience for future creative and experimental ventures in the company.

Changes in How We Manage

In existing stable markets, managers have been fortunate that they have been able to use mechanistic managerial approaches. In the future, however, new opportunities will exist in the more turbulent and changing market sectors and areas of the world. No longer will mechanistic styles of managerial decision making be appropriate. Instead, managers operating in these environments will need real-time information; this will lead to creativity within certain boundaries.

Some of the skills managers will need in these environments are those in the art of bricolage. Bricoleurs, as discussed by Weick (1993), are those individuals who have the capacity to make sense out of nonsense. These individuals can respond rapidly to an emergency and effectively solve the problem. Weick (1993, 639) states: "Bricoleurs remain creative under pressure, precisely because they routinely act in chaotic conditions and pull order out of them. Thus, when situations unravel, this is simply normal natural trouble for Bricoleurs, and they proceed with whatever materials are at hand."

This type of person will be needed in the future as society becomes more high-tech and security becomes more involved in high-tech industries. As Perrow (1984) points out, the causes of accidents are attributable to the complexity of some modern-day industries. High-tech industries, such as nuclear power plants, are so complex that human beings cannot fully grasp how the system functions. As a consequence, when an incident does occur, it is beyond the normal comprehension levels of individuals to solve the problem before it erupts into a catastrophic accident.

Formal educational programs alone will probably not provide the necessary training and insight to create the bricoleur security professional. It will require the organization to create a culture that promotes learning and a global understanding of the industry. This could be achieved through in-depth training, with security personnel rotated through various departments in the organization. For example, as security personnel may be responsible for responding to power and other maintenance failures, a rotation through the plant facilities is appropriate. Now, in times of emergency, security personnel will have an in-depth understanding of the complexities of the heating and cooling system, perhaps preventing small incidents in the workplace from becoming serious problems that could result in serious financial and human loss.

Personnel Selection

Meeting these future challenges and opportunities head-on requires a cadre of employees capable of taking front-line action in the face of new challenges. Given present trends, security organizations will need to find employees who are goal-oriented independent operators who can perform effectively in new situations. Employees in change-ready firms must be able to operate with minimal supervision and to formulate plans and carry out the tasks necessary to meet customer demands. Employees will be expected to take leadership roles in new circumstances, as management may not have the time to expend on its traditional responsibilities of directing the activities of employees.

Security officers and managers will require advanced technical skills to effectively perform their jobs. This will be necessary for all components of the security industry, whether the position is entry level or managerial. These technical skills will also be necessary for traditional guard positions. (Some may argue this point and state that traditional positions will not require highly educated individuals.) Because of an increased competition and perhaps a more savvy client base, even traditional entry-level positions that did not require a great deal of expertise and education will be affected through increased competition in the global marketplace.

Although the industry will always need individuals to perform security services, another form of personnel will be used: nonhuman crews. Robotics technology will easily replace the human guard in some settings. Unlike earlier robots, which lacked mobility and were quite large, robots the size of large insects can already traverse walls and crawl across ceilings and are immune to environmental factors, such as heat, radiation, and water. In the long term, these robotics will be cheaper, more effective, and more dependable; they will always be on time for work. Issues related to employee turnover could be dramatically reduced, and other employment-related issues for the security manager will be nonexistent. The use of robotics is unlimited. Robots could be used as a stand-alone product, covertly patrolling and transmitting real-time audio and video information to a central control station. They could also be used in high-tech applications that are dangerous for humans; other robots, equipped with highly sensitive "sniffers," could be used to detect hazardous chemicals, explosives, and contraband.

Educational and Training Issues

Undoubtedly, higher-educated and better-trained security personnel will be needed. The questions for the future are how soon it is needed, who will provide this necessary training and education, and how much education is needed. The first question is quite easy. The change-ready security organization will recognize that it needs to begin an aggressive educational program immediately to be well positioned in the global marketplace.

Higher-education institutions will share the responsibility for security training and education. Security education became the domain of criminal justice programs, based partly on the recommendations of the 1976 National Advisory Commission's publication of the *Private Security Task Force Report*, which resulted in the field's being recognized as a component of the formal criminal justice system (Becker 1991). Other predictions, however, suggest that security programs will need to become multidisciplinary. Research on security executives from Fortune 500 firms (Nalla et al. 1995a) found that the companies preferred to hire individuals with a criminal justice education coupled with coursework in business. Additional research showed that employers ranked individuals with majors in computer science with coursework in security higher than they did other academic disciplines (Nalla et al. 1995b).

With these predictions, the nature of security educational programs will change. Instead of being the sole domain of criminal justice departments, future higher-education programs in security will need to become more diverse. Disciplines that will need to be incorporated are business, computer science, criminal justice, and occupational safety and health, to name a few topics. Instead of having rigid degree qualifications, perhaps students will have a menu of courses that they can take to create a comprehensive major based on their career objectives. This will be a difficult venture. It will require bureaucratic flexibility by universities to cross schools and disciplines to develop those necessary programs.

The success of these programs offered through higher-educational institutions will hinge on the degree of support received from the security industry. The history of the development of private security programs reveals that demands and support from the private sector established the basis on which several security programs were based (see Criscuoli 1988, for example). Unfortunately, at the end of the twentieth century, security programs declined because of low demand for such programs from industries and students alike (Bottom 1986). A realignment of the security industry with higher-education institutions will be needed. This could occur in the context of organizations' exposing students to the opportunities and benefits of a career in security.

Training and educational opportunities will not be the sole responsibility of higher-education institutions. They will also become the organization's responsibility. About one-fifth of U.S. youth are "young, poor, and forgotten" (Wagner 1999, 14) and probably will not have the opportunity for immediate formal training or an advanced education beyond high school. Although this may be considered a tragedy for the undereducated one-fifth of this generation, and perhaps the nation, an opportunity exists for security firms to develop a solid workforce from a large number of individuals looking for a decent and somewhat secure career. To take advantage of this opportunity, security firms will have to provide remedial-educational opportunities. Many of these individuals who receive basic work-and life-skills training will be loyal and dependable employees, decreasing the historically high turnover rates experienced by some sectors of the security industry. Successful employees from this pool can become an excellent internal labor pool available for promotion to management positions after attending formal higher-education institutions and earning degrees related to private security.

Making Security a Profession

A "professional" has specialized knowledge stemming from academic preparation for a particular career or calling. Professionals usually have established standards for their field and proscribe to a certain level of conduct in the course of their chosen vocation. When one looks at a security manager and the security industry, this concept of "professional" may not be as obvious. This ongoing issue for the security industry will continue to be a problem in the future unless corrective efforts are taken to change society's view of the security professional.

One reason that security lacks the designation "professional" could be attributed to the uncomplimentary image of the private security industry in the past, when employees were used as spies and strikebreakers for companies (Sklansky 1999). If the past is not an issue, the citizenry may not have a good understanding of the current activities that the security industry is involved in, as these activities are usually not widely publicized. What people then rely on for their understanding of security is what they see. Usually, this is related to uniformed security personnel, which colors their perception and attitude toward the entire security industry. The industry itself may also be guilty. Those who are responsible for hiring security managers may have the same biases and perceptions that the public has toward the industry (Criscuoli 1988).

Some organizational characteristics may impede the understanding that security is a profession. A profession must be visible. However, in some situations and sectors of the industry, security does not want to be the omnipresent department in an organization. Rather, the security function may prefer to have a more obscure existence in the company. This may be attributed to the philosophy of the company, as well as the functions that security performs for the company. The obscurity of the security function may also be attributed to image. Some companies may have a distorted view that the presence of security implies to employees and customers that the company has some particular problems. Or, employees may perceive security to be the company's "big brother" whose sole responsibility is to detect employee misconduct.

Organizational dynamics may affect the designation of the field of security as a profession. In comparison to other professions, the security industry is much broader with regard to the issues and problems that it deals with; its clientele, locations, or settings where people work; and types of security interventions that are used. As a consequence of its "fluidity," the security industry could be conceptualized as a profession, in many ways. One could examine

- The various types of security companies: proprietary versus contractual, service versus industrial
- Functions that are performed: alarm, crime prevention, loss prevention
- Methods used: CCTV, vehicle patrol
- The population served: upper class versus lower class, white collar versus blue collar

- Level of education
- Degree of expertise and proficiency: line-level guard work versus elaborate computer skills

Security will need to identify those common themes that exist in all the variables. Perhaps the common theme in the security industry today is crime prevention and the protection of assets. As pointed out in this chapter, the future presents many new challenges that will require the security industry to redefine its professional boundaries.

The largest issue facing the security field in the future is that it needs to clarify what security is and is not. Once a clear domain is established, it will be much easier for individuals to recognize security as a profession. Next, the security industry will need to establish a clearly defined mission. For example, the mission of a doctor is to prevent disease and cure individuals of medically related issues. Security will need to establish its mission and vision. In addition, this mission will need to be publicized, so that citizens have a clear understanding of the role of security in the twenty-first century.

Already, such organizations as the American Society for Industrial Security (ASIS) have educated practitioners and public alike on security-related issues. Specialized training sponsored by ASIS and its Certified Protection Professional program has also served to build an educational foundation. Besides the initiatives from the private sector, advances toward professionalization have occurred in the field of higher education. Programs such as the Leadership and Management Program in Security (LAMPS) at Michigan State University, for example, have made inroads in bridging the needs of the security practitioner to the academic field. The future will see these and other security-related organizations taking a more active role in promoting and publicizing the domain and the mission of security and the unique contributions this profession will provide to better society.

Legal Considerations

The private security industry has enjoyed relative immunity from some of the legal challenges that its counterparts in the public sector have faced. In the future, this will not be the case. As the private security industry moves into the public sector, the protections it once had from civil liability for U.S. constitution-based violations that were restricted to public-sector agencies (also known as 1983 claims) will be void. Those firms entering into the public sector, replacing traditional public services, will fall squarely under the Public Function Doctrine, as they will be performing services traditionally reserved for government officials. This fact will require that security providers follow a new set of legal standards when selecting, training, and managing the day-to-day activities of their personnel. Instead of negligence-based claims, managers will need to consider that they will be challenged on intentional based tort theory, which means that they will be held accountable for the direct actions of their employees and their purposeful activities, including use of force and related issues.

Although the industry will be facing new forms of civil liability in the public sector, at some point in the process of globalization, nations will have to transcend traditional boundaries and submit to a body of international laws (Caldwell 1999). As nations submit to these new laws, the security industry will be indirectly affected by complying with this new legislation. For example, as industrial firms expand, the market-driven instinct will be to locate plants in countries without environmental or labor-protection laws, but doing so will necessitate the creation of such laws. Furthermore, international laws governing patent rights, patent infringements, and espionage will also expand. These examples will guide and, to a degree, control the actions of private security. At the same time, direct forms of legislation will control the actions of private security operations. A new standard will be imposed on companies that operate worldwide. For example, as security firms engage in activities that could impact world affairs and regional stability, international bodies, such as the United Nations, will be tasked with setting legislative restrictions on their actions, ranging from licensing to operations.

In comparison to their counterparts in the public sector, the private security industry has been fortunate to date that they must follow few regulations. Existing legislation is located primarily at the state level and has established only minimum standards, which usually include rules for licensing, regulation of security companies, and minimum training requirements for secure personnel. Much of this legislation could be considered piecemeal, as it does not thoroughly cover the entire private security industry—in many states proprietary firms are not regulated—whereas in other instances, the legislation is quite dated and is reminiscent of what security was 20 years ago. Legislation at the federal level, although existent in the defense and aviation sectors, has not advanced to the point that any legislation concerns the entire security industry.

Security managers should expect to see dramatic changes related to legislative controls in the future. As it matures, becomes more prominent in the public sector, and becomes more advanced and sophisticated, the industry should expect to see more controls placed on it through legislation at all levels of government. Unfortunately, it is usually the mistakes of the security industry that will lead it to tighter regulation. For example, increased use-of-force complaints will lead state legislatures to scrutinize existing selection and training requirements for security personnel, whereas other activities by proprietary security firms, using high-tech applications, will expose them to privacy issues. In both of these examples, the public and the legislatures will react to what they perceive as abuses of authority. To avoid these reactive and often knee-jerk responses, the private security industry will need to become more self-regulating. Through a strong ethical foundation and the establishment of sound business and managerial practices, a great deal of controversy surrounding security practices can be proactively addressed. If companies do not begin proactively addressing these issues today, the public and legislatures will establish standards that the industry will have to live with in the future.

■ CONCLUSION

Scanning the environment and assessing the future challenges a firm will face is a crucial aspect of leadership and success for security companies looking to the future for success. Firms that prepare for future contingencies created by likely trends will probably be successful, whereas firms that ignore future possibilities are doomed to failure as they watch the rapidly changing world rush past them while their competitors enjoy the benefits of change. Scanning the environment is more art than science. Scanning the environment begins with recognizing environmental forces that affect demand for service and alter the structure of the marketplace. As this chapter has demonstrated, some of the environmental forces that impact any organization—public or private—include technology, law, demographic changes, changes in the local and international political climate, social conditions, and economic conditions.

■ KEY TERMS

Bricolage	Executive protection
Competitive intelligence	Globalization
Corporate protection	Learning organization
Cybercrime	Minimum quality of environment
Cyberterrorism	Multilateralization
Economic espionage	OSAC
Economic Espionage Act of 1996	Private military companies
Environmental security	Superterrorism

■ DISCUSSION QUESTIONS

1. What are place-based strategies in security? What is the future trend for security?
2. What primary factors from the public sector will lead to changes in the security industry?
3. How and to what extent will globalization change the field of security? In what parts of the world will we see most of the growth for security in the future?
4. What are private military companies? Are they part of the field of private security? Why or why not?
5. What are some trends or changes in corporate and executive protection?
6. What is competitive intelligence? How does it differ from corporate espionage?
7. How has terrorism changed? What is the future of terrorism? What is the role of private security in addressing the terrorism threat?

8. What are some organizational issues that will need to be addressed to prepare and change the field of private security so it is prepared for the future?
What factors will lead to security being recognized as a profession?

9. What three major issues will impact the growth of security in the private
sector?

10. What are some legal issues that the security industry will be challenged with
in the future? How should the security industry prepare for these issues today?

■ REFERENCES

AKINRINADE, B. 2001. International law and the conflict in Sierra Leone. *Notre
Dame Journal of Law, Ethics, and Public Policy* 15: 391–425.

BAILIN, P. S., and S. G. CORT. 1996. Industry corner: Private contractual services in
the U.S. market and industry. *Business Economics* 31 (2): 57–62.

BANHAM, R. 2000. Weapons to fight virtual crime. *Reactions* 20 (6): 26–28.

BAYLEY, D. and D. H. SHEARING. 1996. The future of policing. *Law and Society
Review* 30 (3): 586–606.

————. 2001. *The new structure of policing: Description, conceptualization,
and research agenda.* Washington, DC: National Institute of Justice.

BECKER, D. C. 1991. Security administration: Criminal justice with business input.
Journal of Security Administration 14 (2): 69–77.

BEESTON, R. 2001. Bin Laden video brags of attack on U.S. ship. *Times* (London).
June 22.

BENSON, B. L. 1996. Are there any trade offs between costs and quality in the privatization of criminal justice? *Journal of Security Administration* 19 (2): 19–51.

BERGIER, J. 1975. *Secret armies: The growth of corporate and industrial espionage.* New York: Bobbs-Merrill.

BIDDLE, F. M. 2000. Avery Dennison wins $40 million in secrets case. *Wall Street
Journal.* February 7.

BOTTOM, N. R. 1986. About the security degree—are we losing it? *Journal of Security Administration* 9 (1): 7–20.

BRANDON, J. J. 2000. High-seas piracy is booming. It's time to fight harder. *Christian
Science Monitor.* December 27.

BRUNDTLAND, G. H. 1999. *World Health Report 1999: Making a difference.* World
Health Organization. www.whomsa.org.

BUKHARIN, O. 1997. The future of Russia's plutonium cities. *International Security*
21 (4): 126–158.

Bureau of Justice Statistics, U.S. Department of Justice, Office of Justice programs.
www.ncjrs.org.

BURKLE, F. M. 2000. Lessons learned from the future expectations of complex
emergencies. *Western Journal of Medicine* 172 (1): 33–38.

BURNS, T. and G. M. STALKER. 1961. *The management of innovation.* London:
Tavistock.

CALDWELL, L. K. 1999. Environmental law in a transitional world: Issues in modern international environmental law. On-line symposium. *Colorado Journal of International Environmental Law and Policy.*

CAMPBELL, C. 2000. Private police, public dereliction. *Atlanta Constitution, Reader.* October 29.

CARTER, A, J. DEUTCH, and P. ZLIKOW. 1998. Catastrophic terrorism: Tackling the new danger. *Foreign Affairs* 77 (6): 80-94.

CARTER, T., and J. SKRLEC. 1999. Americans easy targets for greedy kidnappers. *Insight on the news* 15 (115): 42.

CAVANAUGH, J. 1995. Private police for public housing. *New York Times.* November 19.

CHALK, P. 2000. Grave new world. *Forum for Applied Research and Public Policy* 15 (1): 13-20.

Colombia Oil Field Halts. 2000. *New York Times.* August 5.

CORDNER, G. W. 1992. Human resource issues. In *Police Management: Issues and Perspectives.* ed. L. T. HOOVER. Washington, DC.: Police Executive Research Forum. pp. 227-250.

CRISCUOLI, E. J. 1988. The time has come to acknowledge security as a profession. *Annals of the American Academy of Political Science* 498: 98-107.

CUNNINGHAM, W. C., and T. H. TAYLOR. 1985. *The Hallcreast report I: Private security and police in America.* Boston: Butterworth-Heinemann.

DAVIDS, K. 1995. Openness or secrecy? Industrial espionage in the Dutch republic. *Journal of European Economic History* 245 (2): 333-348.

DOWNS, A. 1967. *Inside bureaucracy.* Boston: Little, Brown.

Emerging and re-emerging infectious diseases. 1998. *Fact Sheet 97.* World Health Organization. www.whomsa.org.

FIALKA, J. J. 1997. While America sleeps. *Wilson Quarterly* 21 (1): 48-63.

FLORES, M. M. 1999. Bruised and battered Seattle begins long healing process. *Milwaukee Journal Sentinel.* December 10.

FORST, B. 2000. The privatization and civilianization of policing. In Vol. 2 of Criminal Justice 2000. *Boundary changes in criminal justice organizations.* ed. J. E. SAMUELS, E. JEFFERIS, J. MUNSTERMAN, and P. MCDONALD. Washington, DC: National Institute of Justice.

FOX, J. A., and M. W. ZAWITZ. 2000. Homicide trends in the United States: 1998 update. www.ojp.usdoj.gov/bjs/homicide/homtrnd.htm.

FRAUMANN, E. 1997. Economic espionage: Security missions redefined. *Public Administration Review* 57 (30): 303-308.

GARRETT, L. 2001. The nightmare of bioterrorism. *Foreign Affairs* 80 (1): 76-90.

GELLMAN, B. 2000. AIDS is declared threat to security; White House fears epidemic could destabilize world. *Washington Post.* April 30.

GILMORE, D. M. 2000. Free trade area of the Americas: Is it desirable? *University of Miami Inter-American Law Review* 31: 383-404.

HAGEDORN-AUERBACH, A. 1998. *Ransom: The untold story of international kidnapping.* New York: Henry Holt and Company.

HOWE, H. M. 1998. The privatization of international affairs: Global order and the privatization of security. *Fletcher Forum of World Affairs* 22: 1-9.

HOWELL, L. D. 1999. The open seas are becoming no-man's land. *USA Today Magazine* 127 (2648): 35-36.

HUNTER, J. 1998. Protection business in B.C.: Private police even run the jail in Victoria. *MacLean's* 111 (2): 15.

JACKSON, W. 1998. 1999: The year of computer security—maybe. www.gcn.com-/archives/gcn/1998/december14/1c.htm

JOHNSON, D. R. 1979. *Policing the urban underworld.* Philadelphia, PA: Temple.

KAHANER, L. 1996. *Competitive intelligence: from black ops to boardrooms—how businesses gather, analyze, and use information to succeed in the global marketplace.* New York: Simon and Schuster.

KASSEBAUM, D. 2000. A question of facts—the legal use of private security firms in Bosnia. *Columbia Journal of Transnational Law* 38: 581-592.

KEARNEY, R. C., and S. W. HAYS. 1998. Reinventing government, the new public management and civil service systems in an international perspective: The danger of throwing the baby out with the bathwater. *Review of Public Personnel Administration* 8 (4):38-54.

KEYES, D. and M. RAPP. 1999. Cyber attack. *Electric Perspectives* 24 (5): 60-62.

KIERZKOWSKI, H. 2000. Challenges of globalization: The foreign trade restructuring of transition economies. *Russian and East European Finance and Trade* 36 (2): 8-41.

LITFIN, K. T. 1999. Constructing environmental security and ecological interdependence. *Global Governance* 5 (3): 359-368.

LOVINS, A. B. and L. H. LOVINS. 2001. Fool's gold in Alaska, *Foreign Affairs* 80 (4): 72-85.

LUNDY, K. P. 2001. Lasting peace in Northern Ireland: An economic resolution to a political and religious conflict. *Notre Dame Journal of Law, Ethics, and Public Policy* 15: 699-719.

MACHLIS, S. 1997. U.S. unprepared for cyberterrorism. *Computerworld* 31 (41): 14.

MAGLITTA, J. E. (1999). Cyberterrorism is a serious threat. *Computerworld* 33 (16): 35.

MANNING, P. K. 1992. Technological and material resource issues. In *Police Management: Issues and Perspectives.* ed. L. T. HOOVER. Washington, DC.: Police Executive Research Forum. pp. 251-280.

McCRIE, R. D. 1988. The development of the U.S. security industry. *Annals of the American Academy of Political Science* 498: 23-33.

MINTON, T. 1997. Sensitive files missing from Levi Strauss. *San Francisco Chronicle.* April 29.

MORGENTHAU, T. 1999. Justice for Louima. *Newsweek* 133 (23): 42-43.

NAFTA for the Americas: Q & A on the FTAA. 2001. *Multinational Monitor* 22 (4):17-21.

NALLA, M. K., K. E. CHRISTAIN, M. A. MORASH, and P. J. SCHRAM. 1995a. Hiring preferences of security professionals: A national survey. *Journal of Security Administration* 18 (2): 29-38.

_____1995b. Executive training needs:A national survey of security profession-als. *Journal of Security Administration* 18 (2): 18–28.

NEELEY, D. 2000. Underground web sites. *Security Management* 44 (1): 34–35.

O'CONNELL, T. 1999. Cyber soldiers. *Security* 36 (3): 14–17.

OSMAN, A. M., and T. S. TOH. 1999. International business competitiveness of Asia-Pacific countries:A Singapore perspective. *Competitiveness Review* 9 (1): 1–8.

Overseas Security Advisory Council. 2001. www.ds-osac.org.

PAGELL, R. 1999. Economic espionage and strategic intelligence. *Journal of AGSI* 8: 36–43.

PERON, J. 1999. Crime stoppers: Frustrated by incompetent policing, South Africans are turning to private alternatives. *Reason* 31 (2): 56–57.

PERROW, C. 1984. *Normal accidents. Living with high-risk technologies*. New York: Basic Books.

PRESTON, R. 1994. *The hot zone*. New York: Random House.

RAJAN, R. S. 2001. Economic globalization and Asia: Trade, finance and taxation, *ASEAN Economic Bulletin* 18 (1): 1–11.

SAGER, I. 2000. Cyber crime. *Business Week* 3639: 36.

SAPP, A. 1992. Alternative futures. In *Police management: Issues and perspectives*. ed. L. T. HOOVER. Washington, DC: Police Executive Research Forum. 175–202.

SCHOFIELD, T. 1999. The environment as an ideological weapon: A proposal to criminalize environmental terrorism. *Boston College Environmental Affairs Law Review* 26: 619–647.

SCHWEITZER, G. E., and C. C. DORSCH. 1999. Superterrorism: Searching for long-term solutions. *Futurist* 33 (6): 40–45.

SCHWEITZER, P. 1993. *Friendly spies*. New York: Atlantic Monthly Press.

SCHWORTAU, W. 1996. *Information Warfare*. 2nd ed. New York, NY: Thunder's Mouth.

SERRIN, W. 1992. *Homestead: The glory and tragedy of an American steel town*. New York: Random House.

SHEPPARD, S. 1999. Soldiers for hire. *Contemporary Review* 275 (1603): 66–69.

SKLANSKY, D. A. 1999. The private police. *UCLA Law Review* 46: 1165–1180.

SKOLNICK, J. H. 2000. Code blue: Prosecuting police brutality requires penetrating the blue wall of silence. *American Prospect.* 11(10): 49–53.

SPICER, T. 1998. *An unorthodox soldier*. Pomfret, VT: Trafalgar Square Books.

STANTON, J. 2001. Should approach to bioterrorism change? *Security Management Online* www.securitymanagement.com/library/view_june01.html.

STOLL, C. 1989. *The Cookoo's egg: Tracking a spy through the maze of computer espionage*. New York: Doubleday.

STUTLER, T. R. 2000. Stealing secrets solved. *FBI Law Enforcement Bulletin* 69 (11): 11–16.

SULLIVAN, J. F. 1993a. State is seeking to disband town's private police force. *New York Times*, June 22.

_____1993b. New Jersey bans the use of guards as police. *New York Times*, July 31.

SYKES, G. W. 1992. Stability amid change. In *Police Management. Issues and Perspectives*. ed. HOOVER, L. T. Washington, DC: Police Executive Research Forum 6: 159–174.

THRANERT, O. 1996. Preemption, civil defense, and psychological analysis: Three necessary tools in responding to irrational terrorism. *Politics and the Life Sciences* 15: 228–230.

TOOBIN, J. 2000. The unasked question: Why the Diallo case missed the point. *New Yorker* 76 (2): 38–41.

TREMBLY, A. C. 1999. Cyber crime means billions in losses. *National Underwriter* 103 (26): 19.

TUCK, J. 1986. *High tech espionage*. New York: St. Martin's Press.

TUCKER, D. S. 1997. The federal government's war on economic espionage. *Journal of International Economic Law* 18:1109–1152.

VEDDER, R. G., M. T. VANECEK, C. S. GUYNES, and J. J. CAPPEL. 1999. CEO and CIO perspectives on competitive intelligence. *Communications of the ACM* 42 (8):108–112.

VOLKOV, V. 2000. Between economy and the state: Private security and rule enforcement in Russia. *Politics and Society* 28 (4): 483–501.

WAGNER, C. G. 1999. Young, poor, and forgotten. *The Futurist* 33 (4): 14–15.

WALKER, S., and V. W. BUMPHUS, 1992. The effectiveness of civilian review: Observations on recent trends and new issues regarding the civilian review of the police. *American Journal of Police* 11 (4): 1–26.

WALLIS, D. 1998. The old-spies network. *Success* 47 (7): 24–25.

WEICK, K. E. 1993. The collapse of sense making in organizations: The Mann Gulch disaster. *Administrative Science Quarterly* 38: 628–652.

WEINTRAUB, B. A. 1995. Environmental security, environmental management, and environmental justice. *Pace Environmental Law Review* 12: 533–623.

WICKELGREN, I. 1998. A method in Ebola's madness. *Science* 279 (5353): 983–984.

WINKLER, I. 1997. *Corporate espionage*. Rocklin, CA: Prima Publishing.

ZAGARIS, B. 1996. International criminal and enforcement cooperation in the Americas in the wake of integration: A post-NAFTA transition period analysis with special attention to investing in Mexico. *Southwestern Journal of Law and Trade in the Americas* 3: 1–69.

ZARATE, J. C. 1998. The emergence of a new dog of war: Private international security companies, international law, and the new world disorder. *Stanford Journal of International Law* 34: 75–128.

Index